KEY INDICATORS
FOR ASIA AND THE PACIFIC
2018
49TH EDITION

ASIAN DEVELOPMENT BANK

ADB

© 2018 Asian Development Bank
6 ADB Avenue, Mandaluyong City, 1550 Metro Manila, Philippines
Tel +63 2 632 4444; Fax +63 2 636 2444
www.adb.org

Some rights reserved. Published in 2018.

ISBN 978-92-9261-252-8 (print), 978-92-9261-253-5 (electronic)
ISSN 0116-3000
Publication Stock No. FLS189512-3
DOI: http://dx.doi.org/10.22617/FLS189512-3

Notes:
In this publication, "$" refers to US dollars.
Corrigenda to ADB publications may be found at http://www.adb.org/publications/corrigenda

Cover photo:
Top, left to right
Pavitra works as a cook for the SHG – Gita Swasthya Samooh – that runs a kitchen that supplies midday meals to the government primary, secondary and high schools in Muhali (photo by Ariel Javellana, ADB); Dusk falls over Jakarta's heavily urbanized skyline. Jakarta's economy depends heavily on financial service, trade, and manufacturing (photo by Lester Ledesma, ADB); Children attending school in Barangay Katipunan. Many families from the barangay are recipients of the Conditional Cash Transfer (4Ps) program of the Philippines (photo by Ariel Javellana, ADB).

Bottom, left to right
Built in 1874, the port of Hai Phong is the most important port serving the north of Viet Nam. The port connects to the 244-kilometer Noi Bai-Lao Cai Highway that starts at Noi Bai in a suburb of Hanoi and ends at Lao Cai, on the border with the People's Republic of China (PRC) in northwest Viet Nam (photo by Ariel Javellana, ADB); NPTC engineers and staff monitor the operation of the 1070 MW Nam Theun 2 hydropower plant in Laos PDR. 95% of the power produced by the plant is exported to Thailand and the rest are consumed locally (photo by Ariel Javellana, ADB); A windmill along the new highway from Almaty to Bishkek in Kazakhstan (photo by Andrey Terekhov, ADB); Svaneti, Mestia. A high mountainous area in Georgia. ADB financed the rehabilitation of the main access road to Mestia. The road facilitated faster, more comfortable, and safer transport both for local communities and for the tourists vacationing in Mestia (photo by Daro Sulakauri, ADB).

Printed on recycled paper

Foreword

Key Indicators for Asia and the Pacific 2018, the 49th edition in an annual series, provides statistics on a comprehensive set of economic, financial, social, and environmental indicators for the 48 regional members of the Asian Development Bank (ADB). Importantly, it also covers statistical indicators for the Sustainable Development Goals (SDGs).

The statistical tables and analyses presented as part of *Key Indicators for Asia and the Pacific 2018* confirm that the development of Asia and the Pacific continues to be impressive on many fronts. The region's share of global gross domestic product (at purchasing power parity) rose from 30.1% in 2000 to 42.6% in 2017, and around 780 million people moved out of extreme poverty from 2002 to 2013. Gains have also been made towards achieving gender parity in a number of important areas, including education and employment, alongside improvements in outcomes for women's health issues. Meanwhile, there has been a marked shift in employment away from agriculture toward industry and services. Quality of life, as indicated by the Human Development Index, continues to improve.

The economies of Asia and the Pacific saw a return to robust export growth in 2017, reflecting the recovery of global output and investment, and the region now contributes more than a third of the world's exports. As global value chain statistics show, the region's economies continue to strengthen, broaden, and diversify their participation in global production networks.

The Asia and Pacific region, however, still faces important challenges. The SDG indicators presented in this publication show that poverty and its associated issues need to be addressed as a priority. The indicators highlight the need to improve access to, and quality of, education and health services; expand access to affordable and clean energy sources and safe water and sanitation facilities; and ensure more sustainable patterns of production and consumption. They also emphasize the need to tackle climate change and maintain the growth momentum required to achieve the SDGs.

Timely, reliable, and more granular data are crucial for designing and monitoring policies to meet the sustainable development agenda for Asia and the Pacific. This, in turn, requires appropriate investments in strengthening the statistical capacity of developing economies. In close partnership with the region's national statistics offices and the global statistics community, ADB has been providing technical assistance to its developing member economies to strengthen their capacity in a range of areas. These include national accounts statistics, piloting new methodologies for measuring asset ownership and entrepreneurship from a gender perspective, and fostering the adoption of technological solutions for improving official statistics. We are also working to advance data and statistical standards through international partnerships, such as the estimation of purchasing power parities through the International Comparison Program, the world's largest statistical initiative.

Results from one of ADB's recent technical assistance projects—on the use of satellite data and remote-sensing technology to enhance the quality of agricultural statistics, including estimates of paddy rice area, yield, and production—are presented in a special supplement to *Key Indicators for Asia and the Pacific 2018*.

ADB appreciates the continued cooperation of our statistical partners in regional member economies, who have provided the most recent data from their official sources. We are also indebted to those international agencies from which the data in many of this publication's tables are sourced. We hope that *Key Indicators for Asia and the Pacific* will remain a valuable resource for information on key development issues across the region. It is intended as a universal reference for a wide audience including policymakers, development practitioners, government officials, researchers, students, and the general public. As always, we welcome feedback from our users on both the content and structure of the publication.

Takehiko Nakao
President
Asian Development Bank

Acknowledgments

Key Indicators for Asia and the Pacific 2018 was prepared by the Development Economics and Indicators Division (ERDI) of the Economic Research and Regional Cooperation Department (ERCD) at the Asian Development Bank (ADB). The publication team was led by Stefan Schipper, under the overall direction of Rana Hasan. Pamela Lapitan, Melissa Pascua, and Eric Suan provided technical and coordination support in preparing the data and tables. Kaushal Joshi provided valuable advice at all stages of the production.

The statistical tables that present development indicators for ADB's regional member economies in parts I and II of the printed publication, as well as the 48 tables for individual economies available online, were prepared by ERDI staff and consultants, under the supervision of Kaushal Joshi, Mahinthan Joseph Mariasingham, Arturo Martinez Jr., Lakshman Nagraj Rao, and Stefan Schipper. The research team included Raymond Adofina, Glenita Amoranto, Nalwino Billones, Ulritz Uzein Corcuera, Ephraim Cuya, Criselda De Dios, Madeline Dumaua-Cabauatan, Josephine Ferre, Karen Firshan, Geraldine Guarin, Pamela Lapitan, Melissa Pascua, Lea Rotairo, Iva Sebastian, Christian Flora Mae Soco, Eric Suan, and Orlee Velarde. Proofreading of statistical tables was done by Ma. Roselia Babalo, Aileen Gatson, Oth Marulou Gagni, and Maria Elizabeth Pascual. The analysis of Sustainable Development Goal indicators was prepared by Jose Ramon Albert and Stefan Schipper. The analysis of regional trends was done by Kevin Donahue and Stefan Schipper. The statistical tables and analytical reports for parts I and II were reviewed by Kaushal Joshi, Mahinthan Joseph Mariasingham, Arturo Martinez Jr., Lakshman Nagraj Rao, and Stefan Schipper. Abdul D. Abiad and Mahinthan Joseph Mariasingham led the team comprising Kristina Baris, John Arvin Bernabe, Donald Jay Bertulfo, Nina Ashley Dela Cruz, Paul Neilmer Feliciano, Janine Elora Lazatin, Julieta Magallanes, Dianne Lara Monis, and Resi Olivares, which prepared the statistical tables and analysis for Part III. Valerie A. Mercer-Blackman provided valuable comments on Part III.

We greatly appreciate the contributions from ERCD's statistical partners—regional members and international organizations—who shared their data for the statistical tables on the Sustainable Development Goals indicators (Part I), regional tables (Part II), global value chains (Part III), and individual economy tables. ADB resident missions in Afghanistan, Armenia, Azerbaijan, Bangladesh, Cambodia, Georgia, India, Indonesia, Kazakhstan, the Kyrgyz Republic, the Lao People's Democratic Republic, Mongolia, Nepal, Pakistan, Papua New Guinea, the People's Republic of China, Sri Lanka, Tajikistan, Thailand, Turkmenistan, Uzbekistan, and Viet Nam provided support in compiling the data from their respective economies. ADB's Japanese Representative Office, Pacific Liaison and Coordination Office, Philippines Country Office, Pacific Subregional Office, and Timor-Leste Resident Mission also provided help in data compilation. We also appreciate the continuing cooperation of the governments of ADB member economies and of relevant international agencies.

Paul Dent edited the publication, with the assistance of Lawrence Casiraya as proofreader. Rhommell Rico designed the cover and graphics for the publication, led the typesetting process, and provided technical support for the preparation of all promotional and awareness materials. Edith Creus and Joseph Manglicmot assisted in typesetting. The Office of Information Systems and Technology staff provided database management and technology support, while the Logistics Management Unit of the Office of Administrative Services facilitated the timely and smooth production of *Key Indicators for Asia and the Pacific 2018*. The publishing team in ADB's Department of Communications provided general guidance on production issues and organized promotional and awareness activities.

Yasuyuki Sawada
Chief Economist and Director General
Asian Development Bank

Contents

Tables

PART II: Regional Trends and Tables

PART III: Global Value Chains

Boxes and Figures

Tables

Statistical Partners

The preparation and publication of *Key Indicators for Asia and the Pacific 2018* would not have been possible without the support, assistance, and cooperation of partners in the regional members of the Asian Development Bank and the invaluable contributions of international, private, and nongovernment organizations. These partners—who shared their data, knowledge, expertise, and other information—help provide the Asian Development Bank, policymakers, and other data users with a better understanding of the performance of economies across Asia and the Pacific, so that better policies can be formulated to improve the quality of life for people in this part of the world.

REGIONAL MEMBERS

Afghanistan	Central Statistics Organization (http://www.cso.gov.af/en)
	Da Afghanistan Bank (http://dab.gov.af/en)
	Ministry of Finance (http://mof.gov.af/en)
Armenia	Central Bank of Armenia (http://www.cba.am/en)
	National Statistical Service of the Republic of Armenia (http://www.armstat.am/en)
Australia	Australian Bureau of Statistics (http://www.abs.gov.au)
	Department of Environment and Energy (http://www.environment.gov.au/)
	Reserve Bank of Australia (http://www.rba.gov.au)
Azerbaijan	Central Bank of the Republic of Azerbaijan (http://en.cbar.az/)
	State Statistical Committee of the Republic of Azerbaijan (http://www.stat.gov.az/?lang=en)
Bangladesh	Bangladesh Bank (http://www.bb.org.bd)
	Bangladesh Bureau of Statistics (http://www.bbs.gov.bd)
	Ministry of Finance (http://www.mof.gov.bd/en)
Bhutan	Ministry of Finance (http://www.mof.gov.bt)
	Ministry of Labour and Human Resources (http://www.molhr.gov.bt)
	National Statistics Bureau (http://www.nsb.gov.bt)
	Royal Monetary Authority of Bhutan (http://www.rma.org.bt)
Brunei Darussalam	Autoriti Monetari Brunei Darussalam (http://www.ambd.gov.bn)
	Department of Economic Planning and Development (http://www.depd.gov.bn)
	Ministry of Finance (http://www.mof.gov.bn/)
Cambodia	Ministry of Economy and Finance (http://www.mef.gov.kh)
	National Bank of Cambodia (http://www.nbc.org.kh)
	National Institute of Statistics (http://www.nis.gov.kh)

China, People's Republic of   National Bureau of Statistics of China (http://www.stats.gov.cn/english)
The People's Bank of China (http://www.pbc.gov.cn)
State Administration of Foreign Exchange (http://www.safe.gov.cn)

Cook Islands   Cook Islands Statistics Office (http://www.mfem.gov.ck/statistics)
Ministry of Finance and Economic Management (http://www.mfem.gov.ck)

Fiji   Bureau of Statistics (http://www.statsfiji.gov.fj)
Reserve Bank of Fiji (http://www.rbf.gov.fj/)

Georgia   Ministry of Finance of Georgia (http://mof.ge/en/)
National Bank of Georgia (http://www.nbg.gov.ge)
National Statistics Office of Georgia (http://www.geostat.ge)

Hong Kong, China   Census and Statistics Department (http://www.censtatd.gov.hk)
Hong Kong Monetary Authority (http://www.hkma.gov.hk)

India   Central Statistics Office (http://mospi.nic.in)
Ministry of Finance (http://finmin.nic.in)
Reserve Bank of India (http://www.rbi.org.in)

Indonesia   Bank Indonesia (http://www.bi.go.id/web)
Badan Pusat Statistik-Statistics Indonesia (http://www.bps.go.id)
Ministry of Energy and Mineral Resources (http://www.esdm.go.id)
PT Pertamina (Persero) (http://barata.com/en/)

Japan   Bank of Japan (http://www.boj.or.jp/en)
Economic and Social Research Institute (http://www.esri.go.jp)
Japan Customs (http://www.customs.go.jp/english/)
Japan Statistics Bureau (http://www.stat.go.jp/english)
Ministry of Economy, Trade and Industry (http://www.meti.go.jp)
Ministry of Finance (http://www.mof.go.jp)
The Institute of Energy Economics, Japan (http://oil-info.ieej.or.jp/)

Kazakhstan   Committee on Statistics, Ministry of National Economy of the Republic of
Kazakhstan (http://www.stat.gov.kz)
National Bank of Kazakhstan (http://www.nationalbank.kz)

Kiribati   Kiribati National Statistics Office

Korea, Republic of   Bank of Korea (http://bok.or.kr/eng/engMain.action)
Ministry of Economy and Finance (formerly Ministry of Strategy and Finance)
(http://english.mosf.go.kr)
Statistics Korea (http://kostat.go.kr)

Kyrgyz Republic	National Bank of the Kyrgyz Republic (http://www.nbkr.kg) National Statistical Committee of the Kyrgyz Republic (http://www.stat.kg)
Lao People's Democratic Republic	Bank of the Lao PDR (http://www.bol.gov.la) Lao Statistics Bureau (http://www.lsb.gov.la) Ministry of Finance (http://www.mof.gov.la)
Malaysia	Bank Negara Malaysia (http://www.bnm.gov.my) Department of Statistics Malaysia (http://www.dosm.gov.my) Ministry of Finance Malaysia (http://www.treasury.gov.my)
Maldives	National Bureau of Statistics (http://statisticsmaldives.gov.mv/) Maldives Monetary Authority (http://www.mma.gov.mv)
Marshall Islands	Economic Policy, Planning and Statistics Office (https://www.rmieppso.org/)
Micronesia, Federated States of	Division of Statistics (http://www.fsmstatistics.fm) Department of Resources and Development (http://www.fsmrd.fm/)
Mongolia	Bank of Mongolia (http://www.mongolbank.mn/eng) National Statistics Office of Mongolia (http://en.nso.mn)
Myanmar	Central Bank of Myanmar (http://www.cbm.gov.mm/) Central Statistical Organization (https://www.csostat.gov.mm) Ministry of National Planning and Economic Development (https://www.mnped.gov.mm)
Nauru	Ministry of Finance and Economic Planning (http://www.naurugov.nr) Nauru Bureau of Statistics (http://nauru.prism.spc.int)
Nepal	Central Bureau of Statistics (http://cbs.gov.np) Ministry of Finance (http://www.mof.gov.np) Nepal Rastra Bank (http://www.nrb.org.np)
New Zealand	Ministry of Business, Innovation and Employment (www.mbie.govt.nz) Reserve Bank of New Zealand (https://www.rbnz.govt.nz/) Statistics New Zealand (https://www.stats.govt.nz/)
Pakistan	Ministry of Finance (http://www.finance.gov.pk) Pakistan Bureau of Statistics (http://www.pbs.gov.pk) State Bank of Pakistan (http://www.sbp.org.pk)

Palau	Bureau of Budget and Planning, Ministry of Finance (http://palaugov.pw/budgetandplanning/)
Papua New Guinea	Bank of Papua New Guinea (http://www.bankpng.gov.pg)
	Department of Treasury (http://www.treasury.gov.pg)
	National Statistical Office (http://www.nso.gov.pg)
Philippines	Bangko Sentral ng Pilipinas (http://www.bsp.gov.ph)
	Bureau of Local Government Finance (http://www.blgf.gov.ph)
	Bureau of the Treasury (http://www.treasury.gov.ph)
	Department of Budget and Management (http://www.dbm.gov.ph)
	Department of Energy (http://www.doe.gov.ph)
	Philippine Statistics Authority (http://www.psa.gov.ph)
Samoa	Samoa Bureau of Statistics (http://www.sbs.gov.ws)
	Central Bank of Samoa (http://www.cbs.gov.ws)
Singapore	Department of Statistics (http://www.singstat.gov.sg)
	Enterprise Singapore (formerly International Enterprise Singapore) (http://www.iesingapore.gov.sg)
	Ministry of Finance (http://www.mof.gov.sg)
	Ministry of Manpower (http://www.mom.gov.sg)
	Ministry of Trade and Industry (http://www.mti.gov.sg)
	Monetary Authority of Singapore (http://www.mas.gov.sg)
Solomon Islands	Central Bank of Solomon Islands (http://www.cbsi.com.sb)
	Solomon Islands National Statistics Office (http://www.statistics.gov.sb)
Sri Lanka	Central Bank of Sri Lanka (http://www.cbsl.gov.lk)
	Department of Census and Statistics (http://www.statistics.gov.lk)
Taipei,China	Central bank of Taipei,China (http://www.cbc.gov.tw)
	Directorate-General of Budget, Accounting and Statistics (http://eng.dgbas.gov.tw)
	Ministry of Finance (http://www.mof.gov.tw)
Tajikistan	National Bank of Tajikistan (http://www.nbt.tj)
	Agency on Statistics under President of the Republic of Tajikistan (http://www.stat.tj)
Thailand	Bank of Thailand (http://www.bot.or.th)
	Ministry of Finance (http://www2.mof.go.th)
	National Economic and Social Development Board (http://www.nesdb.go.th/nesdb_en)
	National Statistical Office (http://web.nso.go.th)

Timor-Leste	Central Bank of Timor-Leste (http://www.bancocentral.tl)
	Ministry of Finance (http://www.mof.gov.tl)
	General Directorate of Statistics (http://www.statistics.gov.tl)
Tonga	Ministry of Finance and National Planning (http://www.finance.gov.to)
	National Reserve Bank of Tonga (http://www.reservebank.to)
	Department of Statistics (http://www.spc.int/prism/tonga)
Turkmenistan	Central Bank of Turkmenistan (http://www.cbt.tm/en/)
	Ministry of Finance and Economy of Turkmenistan (http://www.minfin.gov.tm/)
	State Committee of Turkmenistan on Statistics (formerly the National Institute of State Statistics and Information of Turkmenistan) (http://www.stat.gov.tm)
Tuvalu	Central Statistics Division (http://www.spc.int/prism/tuvalu)
Uzbekistan	Cabinet of Ministers (http://www.gov.uz/en/government)
	Central Bank of Uzbekistan (http://www.cbu.uz)
	Ministry of Finance of the Republic of Uzbekistan (http://www.mf.gov.uz)
	State Committee of the Republic of Uzbekistan on Statistics (http://www.stat.uz)
Vanuatu	Department of Finance and Treasury (https://doft.gov.vu)
	Reserve Bank of Vanuatu (http://www.rbv.gov.vu)
	Vanuatu National Statistics Office (http://www.vnso.gov.vu)
Viet Nam	General Statistics Office (http://www.gso.gov.vn)
	Ministry of Finance (http://www.mof.gov.vn)
	State Bank of Viet Nam (http://www.sbv.gov.vn)

INTERNATIONAL, PRIVATE, AND NONGOVERNMENT ORGANIZATIONS

Association of Southeast Asian Nations
Food and Agriculture Organization of the United Nations
International Labour Organization
International Monetary Fund
International Telecommunication Union
Interstate Statistical Committee of the Commonwealth of Independent States
Joint United Nations Programme on HIV/AIDS
Organisation for Economic Co-operation and Development
Secretariat of the Pacific Community
Transparency International
UNESCO Institute for Statistics
United Nations Children's Fund
United Nations Conference on Trade and Development
United Nations Department of Economic and Social Affairs
United Nations Development Programme
United Nations Economic Commission for Europe
United Nations Economic and Social Commission for Asia and the Pacific
United Nations Educational, Scientific and Cultural Organization
United Nations Environment Programme
United Nations Human Settlements Programme
United Nations Office on Drugs and Crime
United Nations Population Division
United Nations Statistics Division
United Nations World Tourism Organization
United States Census Bureau
United States Bureau of Economic Analysis
World Bank
World Health Organization
WHO/UNICEF Joint Monitoring Programme for Water Supply, Sanitation and Hygiene
World Trade Organization

Guide for Users

Key Indicators for Asia and the Pacific 2018 begins with a Highlights section that presents key messages from various parts of the publication.

Part I comprises the data tables and brief analyses of trends of select indicators for the Sustainable Development Goals (SDGs) for which data are available. The indicators are presented according to the United Nations SDG global indicator framework.

Part II explores trends in social, economic, and environmental developments in member economies of the Asian Development Bank (ADB) across Asia and the Pacific. These assessments are grouped into eight themes: People; Economy and Output; Money, Finance, and Prices; Globalization; Transport and Communications; Energy and Electricity; Environment; and Government and Governance. Each theme is further analyzed by specific indicators, which are presented in the 101 regional tables that are incorporated into Part II of the publication.

The SDGs in Part I and the themes in Part II start with a short commentary, complemented by figures and charts describing the status of economies with respect to key trends of selected targets and indicators of the 17 SDGs. The scales used in some figures and charts are adjusted to show very small numbers. In addition, figures and charts appearing in this publication are also provided with a digital object identifier to facilitate easier access to data. Both Part I and Part II also present discussion boxes on how to approach important measurement issues for select indicators.

The SDGs and regional tables presented in Part I and II cover 48 economies across Asia and the Pacific, all of which are members of ADB. The term "country," used interchangeably with economy, is not intended to make any judgment as to the legal or other status of any territory or area. The 48 economies have been broadly grouped into developing ADB member economies and developed ADB member economies. The term "developing Asia" refers to the 45 developing member economies of the ADB. The developed economies refer to the three economies of Australia, Japan, and New Zealand. Based on ADB's geographic operations, the 45 developing ADB member economies are subdivided into five regional groupings: Central and West Asia, East Asia, South Asia, Southeast Asia, and the Pacific. Economies are listed alphabetically within each regional grouping. The term "regional members" often used interchangeably with Asia and the Pacific, refer to all 48 ADB members, both developing and developed. Indicators are shown for the most recent year (usually 2017) or period for which data are available and, in most tables, for a starting year or period (usually 2000). Depending on available data, the starting point may be a year from 2000 to 2008 (usually the year closest to 2000), and the most recent year may be a year from 2009 to 2017 (usually the year closest to 2017). There may, however, be some exceptions to these general principles. In the tables, aggregates for regions include economies with available data and are shown if the indicator is available for more than half of the economies and if more than two-thirds of the reference population is represented.

Part III contains select indicators for depicting participation by economies of Asia and the Pacific in global value chains (GVCs), and the sector-specific comparative advantage of each economy in terms of exports. Typical indicators of international trade, which mainly refer to the value of exports and imports of goods and services, can be traced back to the traditional trading of final goods across borders. Today's globalization has made many economies more open to trade, providing opportunities for firms to scale up production and allocate their resources more efficiently by moving production chains across borders where there is comparative advantage. GVC analysis provides detailed cross-border trading transactions of inputs used in different stages of production—from raw materials, to intermediate inputs, to the final products purchased by the end consumers.

This publication is also available on ADB's website at www.adb.org/ki-2018, along with individual statistical tables for each of the 48 ADB regional members. Data for the SDG indicators, regional tables, and individual member tables are mainly obtained from two sources: (i) ADB's statistical partners linked to regional member economies, and (ii) international statistical agencies, particularly from the United Nations SDG Indicators Global Database, a master set of data prepared by the Department of Economic and Social Affairs of the United Nations Secretariat. The term "economy source", cited as a source in some tables, refers to data provided by the statistical partners linked to the ADB regional member economies.

The data presented for indicators in Part I are from either official country sources, the SDG Indicators Global Database, or databases maintained by international agencies that, based on their areas of expertise, prepared one or more of the series of statistical indicators included in the SDG Indicators Global Database. The data presented in Part III are mainly drawn from the ADB Multiregion Input–Output Tables Database.

Data produced and disseminated by international agencies are generally based on data produced and disseminated by an individual economy (including data adjusted by the economy to meet international standards). However, it should be noted that national data may be compiled using national standards and practices and, as such, international agencies often adjust the data for international comparability. In such cases, data disseminated by the international agencies may differ from data available from national sources. In other cases, when data for a specific year, or set of years, are not available; or they are available from multiple national sources (surveys, administrative data sources, and other sources); or when there are data quality issues; the relevant international agency may estimate the data. Some indicators are regularly produced for the purpose of global monitoring by the designated agency and there are no corresponding data at the national level (e.g., population living on less than $1.90 at 2011 purchasing power parity). In other cases, the differences between data from national and international agencies may be because the most recent and/or revised data available at the national level are not yet available with the relevant international agency. Some data gaps are filled by supplementing or deriving data collected through sample surveys financed and carried out by international agencies. For example, many of the health indicators are estimated using data from the Multiple Indicator Cluster Surveys and Demographic and Health Surveys.

ADB exercises due care and caution in collecting data before publication. Nevertheless, data from international sources presented in this publication may differ from those available within individual member economies. Thus, for a detailed description of how the indicators are compiled by the international agencies, readers may refer to the metadata available from databases of the individual international agencies, or the SDG Indicators Global Database website for metadata of SDG indicators. Comparable and standardized national data gathered through a robust data-reporting mechanism of the international agencies should be the basis for all data in the global monitoring databases, and global indicators should be produced in full consultation with national statistical agencies.

Data obtained from ADB member economies are comparable to the extent that the ADB members follow standard statistical concepts, definitions, and estimation methods recommended by the United Nations and other applicable international agencies. Nevertheless, member economies invariably develop and use their own concepts, definitions, and estimation methodologies to suit their individual circumstances, and these may not necessarily comply with recommended international standards. Therefore, even though attempts are made to present the data in a comparable and uniform format, the data are subject to variations in the statistical methods used by individual economies, so full comparability may not be possible. These variations are reflected in the footnotes of the statistical tables, or noted in the Data Issues and Comparability sections. Moreover, the aggregates shown in some tables for the developing ADB member economies and ADB regional members are treated as approximations of the actual total or average, or growth rates, due to missing data from the primary source. No attempt has been made to impute the missing data.

The data published by ADB do not constitute any form of advice or recommendation. For answers to any questions on the data, users of this publication are requested to seek advice from the relevant data source or organization.

Fiscal Year

There are 24 regional members of the Asian Development Bank with fiscal years that do not coincide with the calendar year. Whenever statistical series (for example, national accounts or government finance) are compiled on the basis of a fiscal year, these series are presented in the column for the single-year during which most of the fiscal year occurred. The 24 fiscal year definitions for 2017 are outlined below.

Regional Member	Fiscal Year	Year Caption
Afghanistan (fiscal year since 2011)	21 December 2016 to 20 December 2017	2017
Brunei Darussalam (fiscal year since 2002) Hong Kong, China India Japan Myanmar New Zealand Singapore	1 April 2017 to 31 March 2018	2017
Fiji	1 August 2016 to 31 July 2017	2017
Australia Bangladesh Bhutan Cook Islands Kiribati Nauru Pakistan Samoa Tonga	1 July 2016 to 30 June 2017	2017
Nepal	16 July 2016 to 15 July 2017	2017
Lao People's Democratic Republic Marshall Islands Micronesia, Federated States of Palau Thailand	1 October 2016 to 30 September 2017	2017

Key Symbols

...	data not available
–	magnitude equals zero
(-/+) 0 or 0.0	magnitude is less than half of unit employed

*	provisional/preliminary/estimate/budget figure
|	marks break in series
>	greater than
<	less than
$\geq$	greater than or equal to
$\leq$	less than or equal to
n.a.	not applicable
%	percentage

Units of Measurement

kg	kilogram
kl	kiloliter
km	kilometer
km²	square kilometer
kWh	kilowatt-hour
kt	kiloton
ktoe	kiloton of oil equivalent
L	liter
m³	cubic meter
mj	megajoule
PM	particulate matter
teu	twenty-foot equivalent unit
t	metric ton
µg/m³	micrograms per cubic meter

Abbreviations

ADB	Asian Development Bank
BPM5	Balance of Payments Manual (Fifth Edition)
BPM6	Balance of Payments and International Investment Position Manual (Sixth Edition)
CIF	cost, insurance, and freight
CO_2	carbon dioxide
CPI	consumer price index
DHS	Demographic and Health Survey
ESCAP	Economic and Social Commission for Asia and the Pacific
FAO	Food and Agriculture Organization of the United Nations
FDI	foreign direct investment
FOB	free on board
FSM	Federated States of Micronesia
FVA	foreign value added
GDP	gross domestic product
GNI	gross national income
GVC	Global Value Chain

HIV	human immunodeficiency virus
IDA	International Development Association
ILO	International Labour Organization
IMF	International Monetary Fund
ISIC	International Standard Industrial Classification
MICS	Multiple Indicator Cluster Surveys
MMR	maternal mortality ratio
MOF	Ministry of Finance
NPL	nonperforming loan
NSO	National Statistics Office; National Statistical Office
NSS	National Statistical Service
ODA	Official Development Assistance
OECD	Organisation for Economic Co-operation and Development
PLI	price level index
PPP	purchasing power parity
PRC	People's Republic of China
UN	United Nations
UNDESA	United Nations Department of Economic and Social Affairs
UNICEF	United Nations Children's Fund
UNSD	United Nations Statistics Division

Unless otherwise indicated, "$" refers to United States dollars.

HIGHLIGHTS

Part I. Sustainable Development Goals

The 17 Sustainable Development Goals (SDGs) to be achieved by 2030, along with their 232 related indicators, provide a global policy framework towards ending all forms of poverty, fighting inequality, and tackling climate change, while ensuring that no person is left behind as economies of the world grow and prosper. Given the breadth and scope of the SDGs, a summary of trends for selected SDG indicators is presented here.

- In developing Asia, the proportion of people living on less than $1.90 a day (at 2011 purchasing power parity) declined from 33.7% in 2002 to 8.9% in 2013. Notwithstanding this reduction, over 330 million people across the region still live in extreme poverty.

- The prevalence of stunting in children below the age of 5 fell or remained the same in 26 of the 30 developing member economies with available data for two data points in time, but the more recent data also showed that at least two-fifths of children younger than 5 had stunted growth in Afghanistan, the Lao People's Democratic Republic, Pakistan, Papua New Guinea, and Timor-Leste.

- Across Asia and the Pacific, the number of women dying during pregnancy, childbirth, and soon after fell from 264 deaths per 100,000 live births in 2000 to 123 per 100,000 in 2015. Mortality of children under the age of 5 similarly declined from 69 deaths per 1,000 live births in 2000 to 33 per 1,000 in 2016.

- In Asia and the Pacific, significant gaps persist when it comes to the representation of women in national parliaments. While 10 of the 43 reporting economies with available data had greater than 25% representation of women in parliaments, in 11 other economies of Asia and the Pacific, this representation was lower than 10%.

- Drinking water is essential to life. From 2000 to 2015, Armenia, Azerbaijan, and New Zealand increased by more than 20 percentage points the proportion of their respective populations using safely managed drinking water services. Despite an increase in the proportion of people in the region with access to safely managed drinking water services, urban-rural disparities still existed in seven of eight economies with available rural data in 2015.

- From 2000 to 2015, the number of people with access to safely managed sanitation services increased in eight of the nine economies with available data, led by the People's Republic of China (PRC). The only exception was Singapore, which already had 100% coverage in 2000 and maintained this to 2015.

- Throughout Asia and the Pacific from 2000 to 2016, economies generally increased or maintained their levels of access to electricity. As of 2016, at least 95% of residents had access to electricity in 31 of the 47 reporting economies.

- In 11 of the 46 economies with available data for 2016, more than 95% of the population had access to clean fuels and technology for cooking, heating, and lighting. This compares with seven economies in 2000.

- Across economies, the PRC registered the highest total domestic material consumption by volume in 2017 (over 35 billion metric tons). However, in per capita terms, Australia, Mongolia, and Singapore had the highest consumption in per capita terms in 2015.

- In terms of disaster risk reduction and management, 28 of the 48 regional ADB member economies had, by at least 2015, formulated strategies and regulatory mechanisms in line with the Sendai Framework.

- In developing Asia, manufacturing value added per person was over $5,000 per person (at constant 2010 prices) in the Republic of Korea, and Singapore in 2017. Since 2000, 14 of the 43 reporting developing economies have doubled their manufacturing value added per capita, with increases of over $1,500 per person in the PRC, the Republic of Korea, Singapore, and Turkmenistan.

- Inequality, measured by the growth rate of household expenditure or income per capita of the poorest 40% of people relative to the overall population, was reduced in 11 of the 16 economies with recent available data.

- While the proportion of firms receiving at least one request for a bribe was as high as 25% or more in 15 of the 28 reporting economies, the prevalence of bribery is 5% or less in Bhutan and Georgia.

- Intentional homicide rates ranged from 0 to 1 per 100,000 people (in the three developed ADB member economies and 11 of the developing member economies) to as high as 10 or more per 100,000 people in two of the developing economies.

- Official development assistance for technical cooperation (including through North-South, South-South, and triangular cooperation) increased in 31 of the 40 developing economies with available data for the period spanning 2000–2008 and 2009–2016.

- Resources made available to strengthen statistical capacity increased from $31.6 million in 2006 to $52.9 million in 2015.

Part II. Region at a Glance

The statistical indicators featured in Part II are grouped into eight themes—People; Economy and Output; Money, Finance, and Prices; Globalization; Transport and Communications; Energy and Electricity; Environment; and Government and Governance. Each of these themes has a brief analysis of key trends of selected indicators, highlighting important recent developments in Asia and the Pacific.

People

- The combined population of Asia and the Pacific, comprising the 45 developing member economies of ADB as well as its three regional developed (nonborrowing) economies, reached 4,141 million in 2017, or almost 55% of the world's total population. In 2017, 5 of the 10 most populous economies in the world were located in Asia and the Pacific, including the two most populous, the People's Republic of China (PRC), with 1,390 million people, and India, with 1,316 million people.

- The region's population is gradually aging amid increasing life expectancy and decreasing fertility rates. In 2050, the number of people in Asia and the Pacific over the age of 65 is expected to exceed the number under the age of 15. Population aging will continue to place fiscal pressures on the governments of Asia and the Pacific, as they address the increasing costs of health care, old-age pensions, and social protection systems.

- Within Asia and the Pacific, there has been a shift in employment away from agriculture toward industry and services. From 2000 to 2017, industry's share of total employment increased in 24 of 36 ADB member economies and services' share increased in 28 of 36 economies, while agriculture's share of total employment declined in 34 of 36 economies.

- Asia and the Pacific has made great strides in education, particularly on improving access to primary education. In the 1970s, the region was home to two-thirds of the world's out-of-school children. In 2017, 9 out of 10 children in the region were enrolled in primary school. However, primary educational attainment was still below 100% for both males and females in most of the region's economies, based on the latest data.

Economy and Output

- Asia and the Pacific, which accounts for a growing share of global gross domestic product (GDP) at purchasing power parity, saw its share of this measure rise from 30.1% in 2000 to 42.6% in 2017. Three economies—the PRC, India, and Japan—accounted for more than 70% of the region's total output in 2017, compared with about 63% in 2000.

- Of 38 ADB member economies in Asia and the Pacific, 36 experienced real GDP growth from 2016 to 2017. The most rapid average annual growth rates were in Armenia and Nepal (7.5% each).

- From 2000 to 2017, gross capital formation as a share of GDP increased in 25 of the 37 regional economies for which data were available. Capital formation comprises fixed investment in the form of buildings, civil engineering, machinery, and equipment.

Money, Finance, and Prices

- In 13 of 47 regional economies, the annual inflation rate exceeded 5% in 2017. The highest consumer price increases were observed in Central and West Asia.

- In 2017, the money supply expanded on an annual basis in 38 of 41 economies in Asia and the Pacific.

The money supply comprises the total currency in circulation and the value of deposits held in banks, including transferable funds, current accounts, and term deposits.

- From 2016 to 2017, the ratio of nonperforming loans to total gross loans decreased in 16 of 29 regional economies.

Globalization

- Foreign direct investment flows to developing Asia were mostly stable in 2017, following a 17% decline in the previous year. The PRC ($168.2 billion); Hong Kong, China ($122.4 billion); and Singapore ($63.6 billion) were among the world's top 10 recipients of foreign direct investment.

- As global trade grew in 2017 at its most rapid expansion in 6 years, Asia and the Pacific accounted for more than one-third of global exports.

- The aggregate level of remittances to developing member economies increased significantly from $35.3 billion in 2000 to $266.8 billion in 2017. On a global basis, remittance flows to low- and middle-income countries increased by 8.5% in 2017, following 2 consecutive years of decline. The top three recipient economies in the world—in dollar terms—were all in Asia: India ($69.0 billion), the PRC ($63.9 billion), and the Philippines ($32.8 billion).

Transport and Communications

- From 2000 to 2017, air carrier departures and the total number of passengers carried across Asia and the Pacific grew faster than the global averages for these two measures.

- In 2016, three of the world's top five developing economies in terms of mobile phone subscriptions were located in Asia and the Pacific—the PRC (first), India (second), and Indonesia (fourth), together accounting for 38% of the total global subscriptions.

Energy and Electricity

- In 2015, Asia and the Pacific led the world by a wide margin in energy use, comprising 42.2% of the global total, compared to 29.4% in 2000.

- Energy production in Asia and the Pacific comprised 34.4% of the global total in 2015, up from 23.9% in 2000. The region's growing share of global energy production since 2000 is due almost entirely to expanded production in the PRC, whose share of global energy production increased from 10.0% in 2000 to 17.6% in 2015.

- As a share of domestic energy use, Timor-Leste (1,737.5%), Brunei Darussalam (490.4%), and Azerbaijan (310.0%) led all economies in energy exports in 2015. A number of Pacific island economies (the Cook Islands, the Federated States of Micronesia, Kiribati, the Marshall Islands, Nauru, and Tonga) and Maldives were almost entirely dependent upon energy imports.

- From 2000 to 2015, energy efficiency gains were realized in 35 of 44 regional ADB member economies, while 9 economies experienced a decline. Most economies with declining energy efficiency during the review period were in the Pacific, where 5 out of 11 economies recorded lower GDP per unit use of energy in 2015 than in 2000.

Environment

- As Asia and the Pacific's share of global GDP expands, so too does its contribution to carbon dioxide emissions. In 2014, the region was responsible for nearly half of total global carbon dioxide emissions, with the top five emitters—the PRC, India, Japan, the Republic of Korea, and Indonesia, respectively—contributing more than 85% of the region's total emissions.

- More than a third of the ADB member economies in Asia and the Pacific increased their total amount of forested land in 2015. The most significant gains in reforestation in 2015 were observed in Taipei,China; the Philippines; and Azerbaijan. Since 2000, the total forested area in developing member economies has increased by 4.8%.

Government and Governance

- 28 of 36 economies in Asia and the Pacific with available data for 2017 incurred a fiscal deficit. As a percentage of GDP, the largest deficits were in Brunei Darussalam (9.9%), Mongolia (6.2%), Pakistan (5.8%), and Myanmar (5.7%). Deficits were present in all economies in South Asia and Southeast Asia, six of seven economies in Central and West Asia, five of nine economies in the Pacific, and two out of four economies in East Asia.

- From 2000 to 2017, government expenditure as a share of GDP rose in 27 of 48 economies in the region. In 2017, the highest shares of government expenditure as a percentage of GDP were observed in Nauru (99.9%), the Marshall Islands (65.1%), Tonga (50.4%), and Solomon Islands (49.9%).

- Since 2005, starting a business has become much easier—as measured by the number of days required to do so—in most developing member economies. From 2016 to 2017, reforms that lowered regulatory costs and simplified compliance procedures had the most impact on reducing the time needed to start a business.

Part III. Global Value Chains

Thanks to continual advances in technology and the progressive lowering of policy barriers to trade since the 1990s, economies across Asia and the Pacific have increasingly been integrating into various global production networks (GPNs). The type and extent of the participation, and the resulting benefits, vary across economies, across sectors, and over time. The Asian Development Bank (ADB) produces statistics and analyses related to global value chain (GVC) participation, using multiregional input-output tables and cutting-edge methods to discern the state, nature, and evolution of involvement by regional member economies in GPNs at the sector level. These statistics and analyses can inform policies that could help economies benefit more from increased participation in cross-border production-sharing arrangements. The following key points summarize ADB's assessment of GVC participation by economies across Asia and the Pacific through to 2017.

- GVC participation varied widely across the economies of Asia and the Pacific. Singapore led in terms of its use of foreign-made goods and services in the production of its exports. Economies such as Viet Nam; Taipei,China; the Republic of Korea; and Malaysia, which were the other leading exporters of electrical and optical equipment in the region, also showed high levels of backward-linked GVC participation through increasing the import content of their high-technology exports.

- Pakistan lagged behind other economies of Asia and the Pacific in terms of its use of foreign inputs in local production processes. This is largely because Pakistan's leading exports were textiles and textile products, whose intermediate goods and services were mainly sourced domestically.

Kazakhstan exhibited similar trends. The country's main exports were either primary goods or processed primary goods that are produced at the upstream segments of value chains.

- Brunei Darussalam, Kazakhstan, and Mongolia are three economies whose exports were dominated by natural resource-based products. All three were highly forward-linked in GVCs through their supply of intermediates to downstream processes in various GPNs, with a large portion of their exports going into the production of other economies. Bangladesh and Cambodia were the least forward-linked economies in Asia and the Pacific. Although Bangladesh's predominant export sector of textiles was well-integrated into global garment supply chains, the economy showed low forward participation since it produced largely final or near-end products. Likewise, Cambodia also displayed low participation due to the large contribution of textile products for final consumption to its exports.

- Given the frequent characterization of the People's Republic of China (PRC) as "the factory of the world," the economy's GVC participation was lower than might be expected. In many sectors and products, the PRC's economy had well-developed local supply chains and, hence, much of the value-added in its exports originated domestically. It is also noteworthy that most of the domestic value-added exported by the PRC was through products for final consumption.

- The exports of Hong Kong, China were dominated by service industries with low dependence on foreign inputs. Such service industries included wholesale trade and commission trade, financial intermediation, retail trade, air transport, and inland transport. This led to a modest backward participation in GVCs for the aggregate economy. At the same time, the economy was also engaged in sectors with high backward participation. Products produced in these sectors included chemicals and chemical products, transport equipment, electrical and optical equipment, rubber and plastics, and general machinery. The result was that the economy showed a wide variation in GVC participation across sectors.

• Over time, GVC participation has changed dramatically in the economies of Asia and the Pacific. Backward participation in Viet Nam increased by over 10 percentage points from 2000 to 2017, while the forward participation of the economy fell notably. The opposite was true for Mongolia, Malaysia, and Indonesia, where backward participation fell, while forward participation increased. Analysis of the data showed that the changes in the backward and forward participation indices for the regional economies generally tended to have a negative relationship.

• The greatest decrease in backward participation was seen in Malaysia, which also experienced the second-highest increase in forward participation among the economies studied. The trend was partly driven by the increase in the domestic value-added in the intermediates used in the economy's high-technology industries. While Malaysia's exports were still led by firms producing electrical and optical equipment, the high-technology sector's backward participation ratio went down by nearly 30 percentage points from 2000 to 2017. On the other hand, forward participation increased by 16 percentage points or by over 80 percent during the same period. This sector of the economy has tended not only to progressively localize upstream segments of the relevant GVCs, but also to expand its intermediate supplies to the global market.

PART I
Sustainable Development Goals Trends and Tables

Introduction

Across the world, individual economies are working towards achieving the 17 goals and 169 targets set within the framework of the Sustainable Development Goals (SDGs). Progress towards meeting the SDGs by 2030 is being monitored through a global indicator framework, currently consisting of 232 statistical indicators.[1] The SDGs were developed through a participatory process[2] and are more ambitious than the Millennium Development Goals (MDGs), with double the goals, triple the targets, and four times the number of indicators.

A key feature of the SDGs when compared with the MDGs is their increased emphasis on level of disaggregation by income, sex, age, race, ethnicity, migratory status, and disability status. In 2017, the Asian Development Bank (ADB) and the United Nations Economic and Social Commission for Asia and the Pacific (UNESCAP) undertook a survey of selected national statistics offices from 22 ADB and UNESCAP member economies on their experience with SDG data compilation. Responses from 16 national statistics offices suggested that, while disaggregation by location was available for several SDG indicators, disaggregation was less common by sex and was far less common, if not absent, for disabled persons and indigenous peoples.

The SDG indicator framework classifies 232 indicators following a three-tier classification of the indicators based on availability of data in the economies and whether the methodology is well established. Tier I indicators are those with a clearly established methodology, where data are being regularly collected by many economies. Tier II indicators are those with an established methodology, but where data are not regularly collected by many economies. Tier III indicators do not have established standards and estimation methodologies. Of the 232 SDG indicators, 82 belong to Tier I, 61 belong to Tier II, and 84 belong to Tier III. The remaining five indicators fall under multiple tiers. In Asia and the Pacific, only 89% of Tier I indicators have some data, while trend analysis can be conducted for only 25% of SDG indicators (UNESCAP 2017).

The challenges associated with data availability are further amplified by a lack of resources devoted to the development of statistics. This problem is pervasive not just for the SDGs but also for national statistical development plans of economies (PARIS21 2017). The Cape Town Global Action Plan for Sustainable Development Data appeals for a commitment from governments and other stakeholders to undertake key actions, such as using a combination of traditional and innovative data sources, increasing the resources made available to statistical infrastructure, and harnessing strategic partnerships for statistics development.

Part I of *Key Indicators for Asia and the Pacific 2018* presents a statistical narrative on the status of economies in Asia and the Pacific towards the Sustainable Development Agenda. The discussion for selected SDG indicators is accompanied by supporting information presented in figures, boxes, and tables. Most of the statistics presented in the tables and charts are presented for two data points from 2000 to 2017. Data gaps and other data-related issues are also discussed to guide actions aimed at meeting the SDGs effectively.

---

1   In March 2016, the United Nations Statistical Commission (UNSC) approved a list of 230 indicators for global monitoring of the SDGs. In May 2018, the UNSC approved a revised list of 232 indicators. Given the differences in circumstances and priorities across economies, and a wide and emerging array of analytical tools and innovative data sources, refinements to SDG indicators are expected.

2   The SDGs resulted from a consultation process across 11 thematic groups and 83 national consultations as well as door-to-door surveys by the UN Working Group on Sustainable Development. The UN also conducted an online My World survey, which asked citizens of the world to identify areas that they would like to see addressed in the SDGs.

Snapshot

- In developing Asia, the proportion of people living on less than $1.90 a day at 2011 purchasing power parity (PPP) declined from 33.7% in 2002 to 8.9% in 2013. This indicates that nearly 779 million people were lifted out of extreme poverty, largely due to achievements of two populous economies—the People's Republic of China (PRC) and India.

- The prevalence of stunting in children below the age of 5 years fell or remained the same in 26 of the 30 developing member economies with available data for two points, but the more recent data also showed that at least two-fifths of children below the age of 5 have stunted growth in Afghanistan, the Lao People's Democratic Republic (Lao PDR), Pakistan, Papua New Guinea, and Timor-Leste.

- Across Asia and the Pacific, the number of women dying during pregnancy, childbirth, or soon after fell from 264 deaths per 100,000 live births in 2000 to 123 per 100,000 live births in 2015.

- In Asia and the Pacific, significant gaps persist, when it comes to the representation of women in national parliaments. While 10 of the 43 reporting economies in Asia and the Pacific had from 25% to 40% representation of women in parliaments, in 11 economies of Asia and the Pacific this representation was lower than 10%.

- Drinking water is essential to life. From 2000 to 2015, Armenia, Azerbaijan, and New Zealand increased by more than 20 percentage points the proportion of their respective populations using safely managed drinking water services.

- In 11 of the 46 economies with available data for 2016, more than 95% of the population had access to clean fuels and technology for cooking, heating, and lighting. This compares with seven economies in 2000.

- Across economies, the PRC registered the highest total domestic material consumption by volume in 2017 (over 35 billion metric tons). However, Australia, Mongolia, and Singapore had the highest consumption in per capita terms in 2015.

- In developing Asia, manufacturing value added per person was over $5,000 per person (at constant 2010 prices) in the Republic of Korea, and Singapore in 2017. Since 2000, 14 of the 43 reporting developing economies have doubled their manufacturing value added per capita, with increases of over $1,500 per person in the PRC, the Republic of Korea, Singapore, and Turkmenistan.

- Inequality, measured by the growth rate of household expenditure or income per capita of the poorest 40% of people relative to the overall population, was reduced in 11 of the 16 economies with recent available data.

- Of the 48 regional ADB member economies, 28 had formulated, by at least 2015, strategies and regulatory mechanisms for disaster risk reduction and management in line with the Sendai Framework.

- Resources made available to strengthen statistical capacity increased from $31.6 million in 2006 to $52.9 million in 2015.

SDG 1. End Poverty in All its Forms Everywhere

Eliminating extreme poverty is the first objective of the SDGs. To achieve this goal, economies must generate gainful employment opportunities for the poor and vulnerable and provide requisite social protection benefits to them.

In 2013, extreme poverty, measured by the threshold of $1.90 a day at 2011 PPP, affected nearly 8.9% of the population in developing Asia, declining from 33.7% in 2002. This indicates that nearly 779 million people were lifted out of extreme poverty, largely due to the achievements of two populous economies—the PRC and India. Notwithstanding this reduction, over 330 million people across the region still live in extreme poverty.

Although rates of extreme poverty fell in developing Asia from 2002 to 2013, considerable variation was observed across the regions. In 2013, the proportion of the population living in extreme poverty ranged from 1.8% in East Asia to 30.3% in the Pacific (Figure 1.1.1). However, South Asia with 16.1% population under $1.90 a day at 2011 PPP continues to have the largest number of people living in extreme poverty (240 million), followed by Southeast Asia (43 million).

In 2017, the proportion of the employed population living in extreme poverty or the working poor was less than 1% in 4 of the 28 reporting economies—Azerbaijan (0.2%), Malaysia (0.1%), Mongolia (0.2%), and Turkmenistan (0.8%)—but was greater than 40% in three economies—Afghanistan (83.4%), the Lao PDR (47.7%), and Bangladesh (41.5%). In 11

Figure 1.1.1: Proportion and Number of People Living in Extreme Poverty, 2002 and 2013

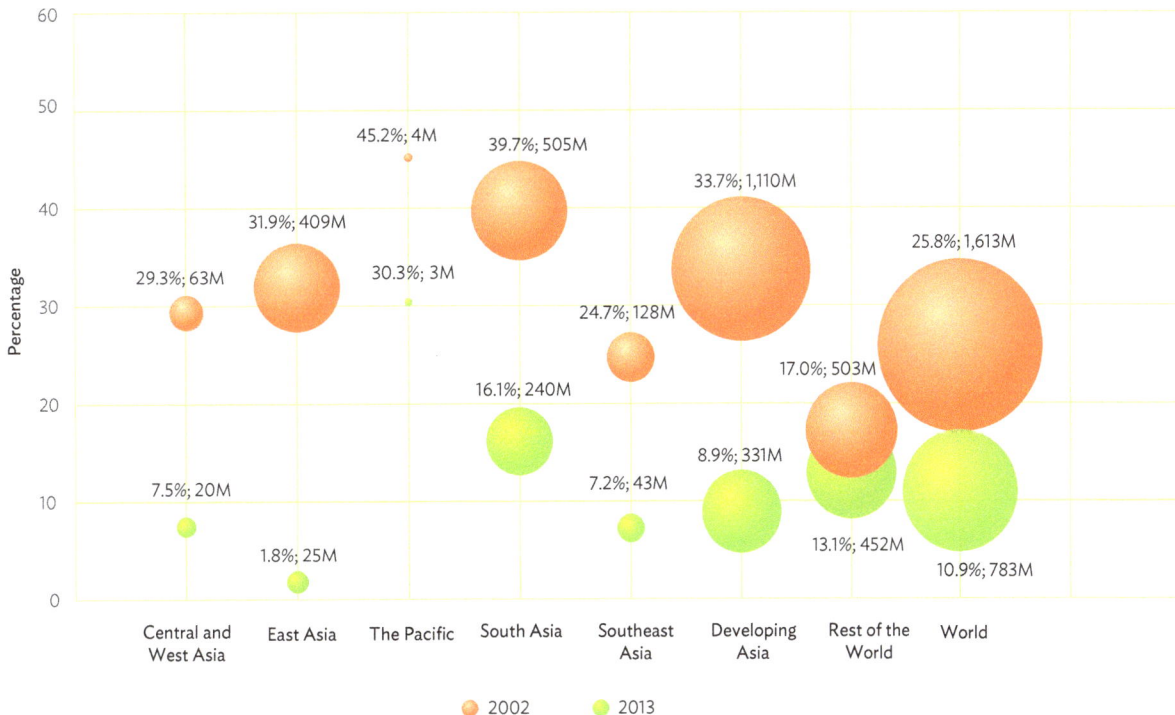

M= million.
Note: The numbers next to the bubbles represent the proportion of population in extreme poverty and the number of extreme poor in millions.
Source: Asian Development Bank estimates using World Bank. PovcalNet Database: http://iresearch.worldbank.org/PovcalNet/home.aspx (accessed 18 May 2018).

of the 28 economies with available data, the rates of working poor are higher among females than among males (Table 1.1.1). In 22 of 28 reporting economies, the proportion of working poor was higher for youths between the ages of 15 and 24 than it was for adults aged 25 years and older.

In 28 of 33 regional economies with available data, poverty rates using national poverty lines fell from 2000 to 2015. Methodologies and definitions of national poverty lines vary across economies. Hence poverty rates based on national definitions are not comparable. Figure 1.1.2 plots the rural poverty rate against the urban poverty rate, using national-level poverty data. The red line is indicative of equal rural and urban poverty rates. Points above this line represent economies in which rural poverty rates are greater than urban poverty rates, while the opposite applies for points falling below the red line. In all reporting economies, poverty rates for the rural population were persistently higher than those of the urban population.

SDG 2. End Hunger, Achieve Food Security and Improved Nutrition, and Promote Sustainable Agriculture

Although significant progress has been made towards meeting food security and nutritional needs in Asia and the Pacific, hunger and malnutrition persist. Children below the age of 5 years are especially vulnerable to food insecurity and malnutrition. Solutions for ending hunger, reducing food insecurity, and eliminating malnutrition require widespread promotion of sustainable agriculture, increased investment in agriculture, and better access to food.

In 2015, the prevalence of undernourishment was below 5.0% in 10 of the 35 economies of developing Asia with available data. As early as 2000, in seven economies in developing Asia

Figure 1.1.2: Proportion of Population below the National Poverty Line in Urban and Rural Areas, Latest Year

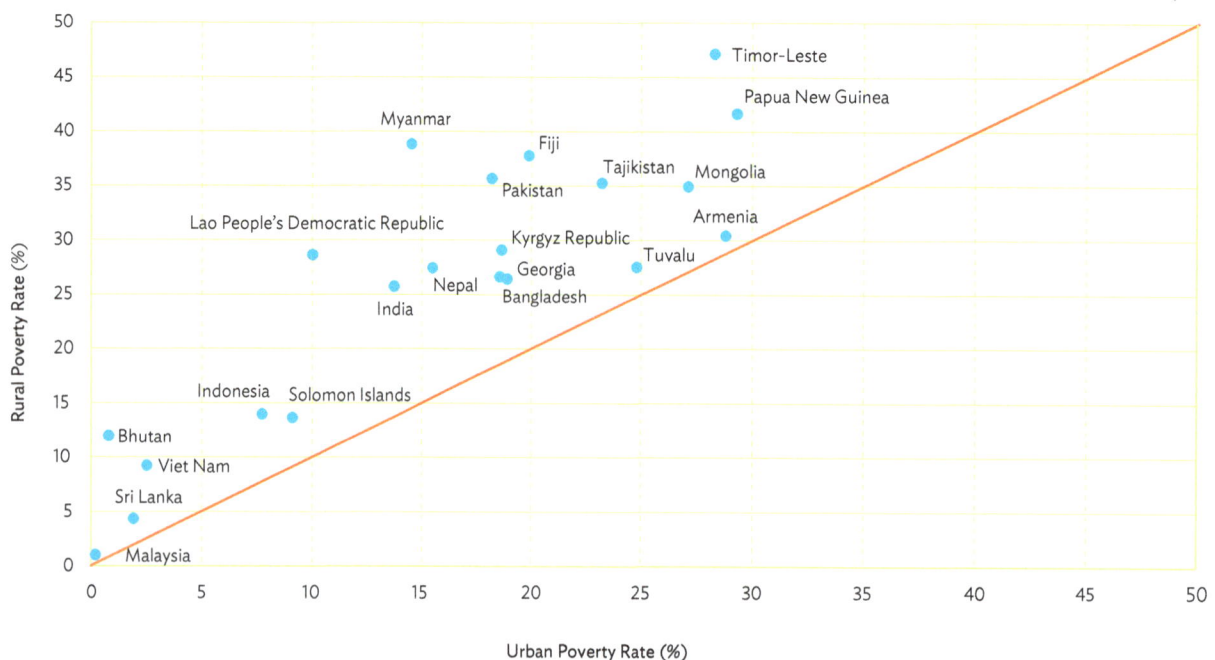

Note: The chart covers the period from 2009 to 2017.
Source: Table 1.1.1, Key Indicators for Asia and the Pacific 2018.

prevalence of undernourishment was less than 5% (Figure 1.2.1). In all the remaining 28 economies in developing Asia, the prevalence of undernourishment decreased from 2000 to 2015. Despite this progress in reducing undernourishment, the prevalence is greater than one-fifth of the population in Tajikistan (30.1%), Timor-Leste (26.9%), Afghanistan (23.0%), and Sri Lanka (22.1%).

Figure 1.2.1: Prevalence of Undernourishment (%)

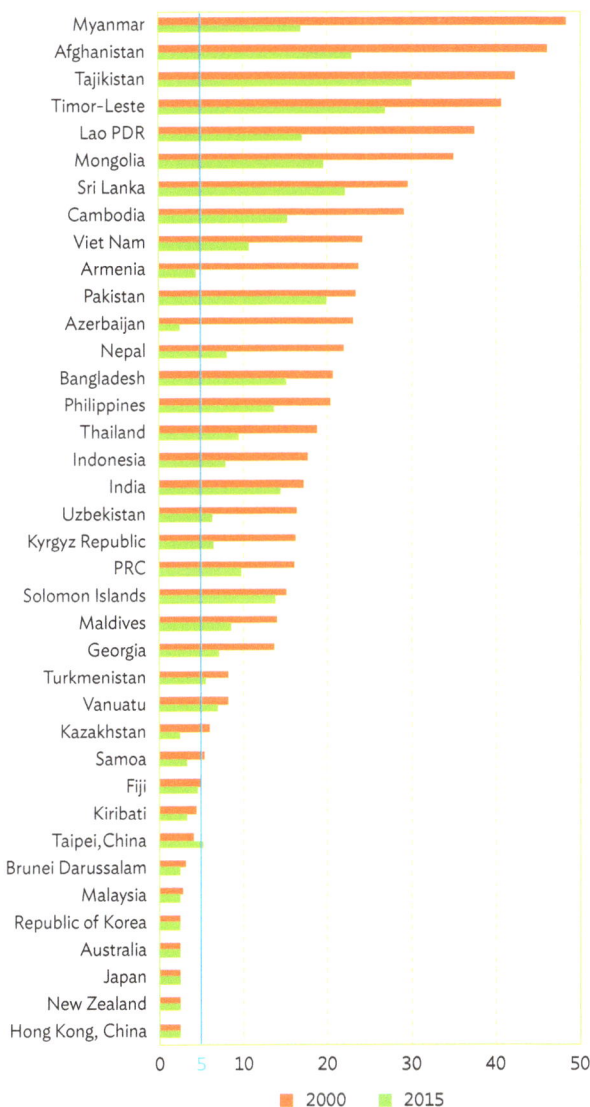

Lao PDR = Lao People's Democratic Republic, PRC = People's Republic of China
Note: 2000 values refer to 3-year average for 1999–2001; and 2015 values refer to 3-year average for 2014–2016.
Source: Table 1.2.1, Key Indicators for Asia and the Pacific 2018.

Stunted growth among children under the age of 5 is declining in developing Asia. The prevalence of stunting in children below the age of 5 years fell or remained the same in 26 of the 30 developing member economies that had two data points available for comparison. However, using the more recent data point (ranging from 2009 to 2016), it was evident that at least two in every five children below the age of 5 had stunted growth in Timor-Leste (50.2%), Papua New Guinea (49.5%), Pakistan (45.0%), the Lao People's Democratic Republic (43.8%), and Afghanistan (40.9%).

SDG 3. Ensure Healthy Lives and Promote Well-Being for All at All Ages

While everyone has the right to live healthily throughout their lifetime, providing adequate health care is a significant challenge. Monitoring SDG 3 will require high-quality, timely, and more disaggregated data on health indicators related to reproductive, maternal, and child health; HIV/AIDS; malaria; tuberculosis; and tropical, noncommunicable, and environmental diseases. Ensuring universal health coverage and access to safe, affordable, and effective medicines and vaccines would be a step forward in achieving the targets set for this goal.

In developing Asia, the number of women dying during pregnancy, childbirth, or soon after fell from 269 deaths per 100,000 live births in 2000 to 126 per 100,000 in 2015. All developing regions of Asia and the Pacific experienced a reduction in maternal mortality ratios (MMRs) from 2000 to 2015, with South Asia reporting the largest drop at 203 fewer maternal deaths per 100,000 live births. East Asia reported the lowest reduction in maternal deaths per 100,000 live births, but East Asia already had the lowest ratio among regions of developing Asia in 2000.

From 2000 to 2015, the MMR decreased in 39 of 43 reporting economies across Asia and the Pacific (Table 1.3.1). The exceptions were the Kyrgyz Republic (from 74 to 76 per 100,000 live births); Taipei,China (from 8 to 12 per 100,000 live births); Tonga (from 97 to 124 per 100,000 live births); and Uzbekistan (from 34 to 36 per 100,000 live births). Afghanistan experienced the largest decline in its MMR, with 704 fewer maternal deaths per 100,000 live births in 2015 than in 2000. Aside from Afghanistan, developing economies with a decline in MMR of at least 250 deaths per 100,000 live births from 2000 to 2015 included Timor-Leste (479), the Lao PDR (349), Cambodia (323), Nepal (290) and Bhutan (275). Economies with fewer than 25 maternal deaths per 100,000 live births in 2015 included Brunei Darussalam (23); Thailand (20); Kazakhstan (12); Taipei,China (12); the Republic of Korea (11); Singapore (10); and Hong Kong, China (2) as well as the developed economies of New Zealand (11), Australia (6), and Japan (5). Economies in which maternal deaths were low also had a high proportion of births attended by skilled health personnel, while those where maternal deaths were high had a low proportion of births attended by medical professionals (Figure 1.3.1).

Child deaths dropped significantly in Asia and the Pacific, with the under-5 mortality rate declining from 69 deaths per 1,000 live births in 2000 to 33 deaths per 1,000 live births in 2016. As with MMRs, under-5 mortality rates were reduced across all regions of Asia and the Pacific from 2000 to 2016. South Asia led the way, with a reduction of 48 deaths per 1,000 live births, followed by Central and West Asia, with 38 fewer deaths per 1,000 live births (Figure 1.3.2). By economy, the largest reductions in under-5 mortality rates were seen in Cambodia (76 fewer deaths per 1,000 live births), Afghanistan (59), Timor-Leste (59), Bangladesh (53), and the Lao PDR (53). Fiji was the only economy in which the under-5 mortality rate stayed constant from 2000 to 2016, at 22 deaths per 1,000 live births.

Figure 1.3.1: Scatterplot of Maternal Mortality Ratios and Proportion of Births Attended by Skilled Health Personnel

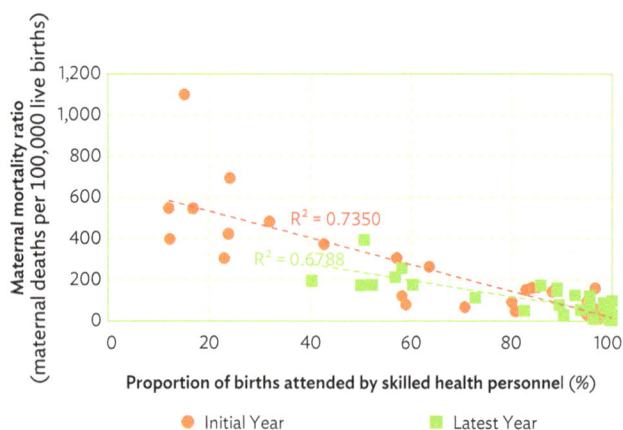

Note: Initial year refers to 2000–2008 and latest year refers to 2009–2016.
Source: Table 1.3.1, Key Indicators for Asia and the Pacific 2018.

Figure 1.3.2: Under-5 Mortality Rate
(per 1,000 live births)

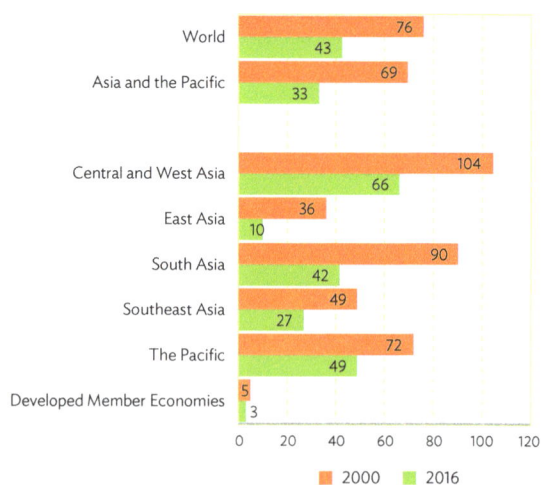

Source: Table 1.3.1, Key Indicators for Asia and the Pacific 2018.

SDG 4. Ensure Inclusive and Equitable Quality Education and Promote Lifelong Learning Opportunities for All

SDG 4 emphasizes that, not only is education a human right, but quality education, relevant training, and opportunities for lifelong learning should be accessible to all. Achieving SDG 4 requires an improvement in the quality of education across the social spectrum, to ensure access to economic opportunities and better income prospects for all.

In developing Asia, based on the most recent data available, 10 of 28 reporting economies had at least 90% of children participating in organized learning 1 year before the official entrance age to primary school. Of these economies, the participation rate for both girls and boys was greater than 95% in the Cook Islands; Hong Kong, China; and the Maldives (Figure 1.4.1). Total participation rates were below 50% in Cambodia (43.0%), Uzbekistan (36.9%), Samoa (31.7%), Azerbaijan (24.9%), and Tajikistan (12.5%) (Table 1.4.1). In Asia and the Pacific, in 16 of the 30 economies that provide sex-disaggregated information, participation rates were higher for females than males.

The proportion of teachers in pre-primary education who had received at least the minimum organized teacher training exceeded 90% in 12 of the 24 member economies with available data. In primary education, the proportion exceeded 90% in 20 of 31 economies, and for lower secondary education, the proportion exceeded 90% in 13 of 22 economies, and for upper secondary education, the proportion exceeded 90% in 10 of 15 regional economies with available data (Table 1.4.2).

Figure 1.4.1: Participation Rate in Organized Learning (1 Year before the Official Primary Entry Age), **by Sex, 2016 or Latest Year** (%)

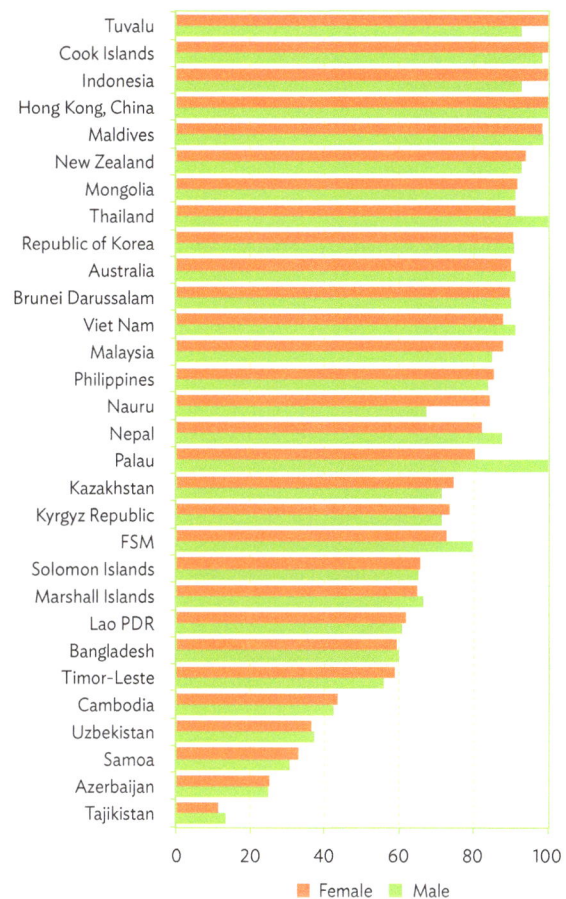

FSM = Federated States of Micronesia, Lao PDR = Lao People's Democratic Republic.
Note: For Kazakhstan, Nepal, Tajikistan, and Uzbekistan, data refer to 2017; for FSM, Republic of Korea, New Zealand, Philippines, Solomon Islands, Thailand, and Tuvalu, data refer to 2015; for Palau, data refer to 2014; for Cambodia, data refer to 2012; and for Bangladesh, data refer to 2011.
Source: Table 1.4.1, Key Indicators for Asia and the Pacific 2018.

SDG 5. Achieve Gender Equality and Empower All Women and Girls

Gender equality is at the core of the SDGs and eliminating discrimination against women due to unfair social norms, general attitudes, and other factors requires women and girls to feel empowered.

This can only be ensured if both sexes are given equal opportunities to education, paid employment, political leadership, and the power to make decisions that affect their lives. SDG 5 has been designed to monitor progress towards the overall objective of gender equality, but its considerations overlap with all other SDGs.

In 11 of 28 economies in Asia and the Pacific with available data, at least one-fifth of women between the ages of 20 and 24 years were married or in a union before the age of 18. Early-age marriage can compromise the education outcomes of a female child; her employment prospects; the type, arrangements, and conditions of her future work; her overall well-being; and the health of her offspring (Nour 2009). At 58.6%, Bangladesh reported the largest proportion of women between the ages of 20 and 24 years being married or in a union before the age of 18 (Figure 1.5.1). Other than

Bangladesh, more than a quarter of women between the ages of 20 and 24 years were married or in a union before the age of 18 in Nepal (39.5%), the Lao People's Democratic Republic (35.4%), Afghanistan (34.8%), India (27.3%), and Bhutan (25.8%). Of these economies, Bangladesh, the Lao People's Democratic Republic, and Afghanistan reported that more than 8% of women between the ages of 20 and 24 years were married or in a union at age 15 years or younger (Table 1.5.1).

In Asia and the Pacific, significant gaps persist when it comes to representation of women in national parliaments. While 8 of 40 reporting economies in developing Asia had greater than 25% representation of women in their parliaments in 2017, less than 10% of legislators were women in another 11 regional economies (Figure 1.5.2). Less than 5%

Figure 1.5.1: Proportion of Women Aged 20–24 Years Who Were Married or in a Union, Latest Year (%)

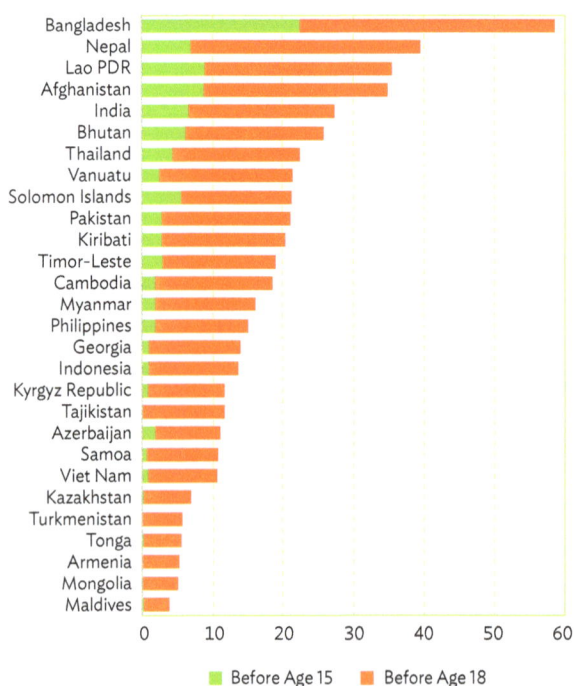

Lao PDR = Lao People's Democratic Republic.
Note: Latest year refers to 2009–2016.
Source: Table 1.5.1, Key Indicators for Asia and the Pacific 2018.

Figure 1.5.2: Proportion of Seats Held by Women in National Parliaments, 2017 (%)

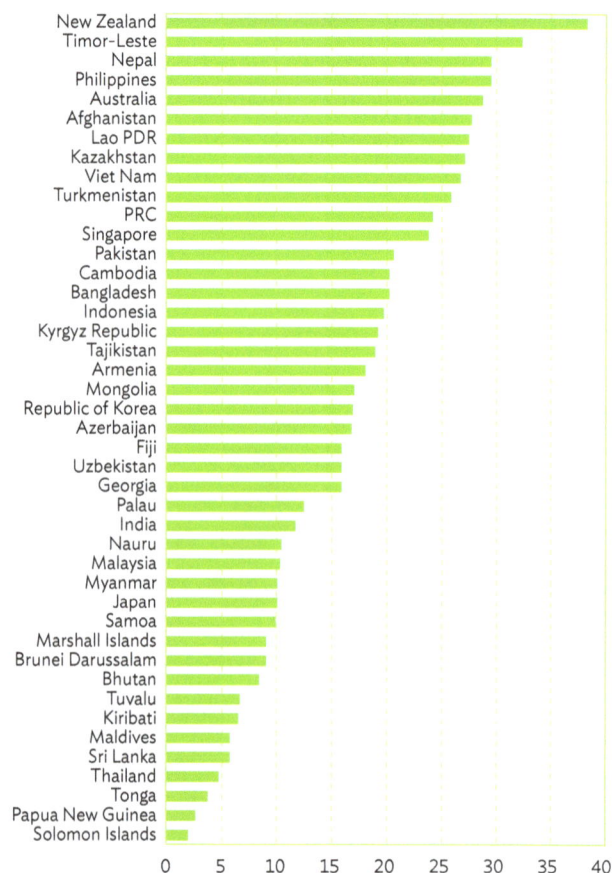

Lao PDR = Lao People's Democratic Republic, PRC= People's Republic of China.
Source: Table 1.5.1, Key Indicators for Asia and the Pacific 2018.

representation of women in parliament was reported in Thailand (4.8%), Tonga (3.8%), Papua New Guinea (2.7%), and Solomon Islands (2.0%). Although the population of Asia and the Pacific has an almost even ratio of women to men, no economy has managed to reach at least 40% representation of women in parliaments (Box 1.5.1).

Box 1.5.1: Lack of Female Representation in National and Local Governments

To ensure that issues relevant to both sexes are given adequate attention, women and men should have equitable representation in leadership positions within the public sphere. Across Asia and the Pacific, men dominate in legislative branches of governments, where important directions are set about laws and policies (Asian Development Bank and United Nations [UN] Women, forthcoming). The pursuit of greater female representation in the realm of governance is key to ensuring developments in the pursuit of gender equality. Women should have a voice in the decision-making process for policies that concern their welfare, such as family leave and recruitment and promotion in the workplace (Piterman 2008).

While necessary, monitoring the number of women in political leadership in national parliaments may not be sufficient. A complementary indicator that keeps track of the proportion of women in local government is also included in the Sustainable Development Goal (SDG) framework. What complicates comparability across countries is the variation in how local governments are defined in each national economy. Despite this lack of comparability, economies are working towards compiling the proportion of women among elected positions of legislative and/or deliberative bodies of local government, to mirror the proportion of national parliamentarians who are women. Economies are also monitoring additional indicators of political engagement, such as the participation of women as voters and candidates in local elections. UN Women is working with individual economies and the UN Regional Commissions to collect and compile the "proportion of positions held by women in local government" following a methodology approved by the Inter Agency Expert Group on SDG Indicators in its November 2017 meeting.[a]

At a UN Women Regional Consultation held in Bangkok on 28 March 2018, some preliminary statistics on female participation in local governance were presented. The results show that, as with national level data, female participation at the local level is far below gender parity levels. A case study in the Philippines suggests that the reason women remain underrepresented in political leadership is that too few women enter electoral politics. Data from the Philippine Commission on Elections suggested that only 17% of the national and local candidates from 2004 to 2016 were women (David et al. 2017).

A shortage of women in elected local leadership posts implies that fewer women will continue into higher elected offices, at both local and national levels. It is necessary to examine the barriers that women face when it comes to electoral politics at both local and national levels. Evidence suggests that the use of gender quotas in political leadership influences policy outcomes and reduces gender discrimination (Pande and Ford 2011).

As positions in national legislature (and local governments) continue to be below gender parity, the region needs to work more on having issues related to protecting women and children better represented in the legislative landscape.

---

a   The methodology is detailed at https://unstats.un.org/sdgs/metadata/files/Metadata-05-05-01b.pdf.

Sources:
ADB and UN Women. Forthcoming. *Gender Equality and the Sustainable Development Goals in Asia and the Pacific: Baseline and Pathways for Transformative Change by 2030*. Bangkok.
C.C. David, J.R.G. Albert, and J.F.V. Vizmanos. 2017. *Filipino Women in Leadership: Government and Industry PIDS*. Policy Notes No. 2017- 22. Quezon City, Philippines: Philippine Institute for Development Studies.
R. Pande and D. Ford. 2011. *Gender Quotas and Female Leadership: Background Paper for the World Development Report on Gender*. World Bank: World Development Report 2014.
H. Piterman. 2008. *The Leadership Challenge: Women in Management*. Greenway, Australia: Government of Australia, Department of Social Services.

SDG 6. Ensure Availability and Sustainable Management of Water and Sanitation for All

Water supply, sanitation, and hygiene are interlinked with poverty, health, gender, environment, and governance. Improper management of water and sanitation services can put people at risk of contracting a wide range of preventable diseases. SDG 6 aims for universal access to safe water and sanitation as well as promoting adequate hygiene services.

Although safe water is essential for daily living, access to safely managed drinking water services was available to at least 95% of the population in only 5 of 18 economies with available data for 2015. These economies include Hong Kong, China (safely managed drinking water services available to 100.0% of the population); New Zealand (100%), Singapore (100%), the Republic of Korea (98.0%), and Japan (97.2%). Meanwhile, less than half of the population in Tajikistan (47.4%), Pakistan (35.6%), Bhutan (34.2%), Nepal (26.8%), and Cambodia (24.1%) had access to safely managed drinking water. From 2000 to 2015, Armenia, Azerbaijan, and New Zealand increased the proportion of their respective populations using safely managed drinking water services by more than 20 percentage points. In the same period, coverage of safely managed drinking water services increased among the rural population in all eight economies of Asia and the Pacific with available data for this measure. This was led by Turkmenistan (36.6 percentage points), followed by the Kyrgyz Republic (23.9 percentage points) and India (20.2 percentage points). From 2000 to 2015, the Kyrgyz Republic improved access to safely managed drinking water in urban areas by 12.3 percentage points. Singapore maintained its coverage at 100% in both 2000 and 2015. Despite an increase in the proportion of

people with access to safely managed drinking water services, urban-rural disparities are exhibited in seven of the eight economies with available urban-rural data (Figure 1.6.1).

Figure 1.6.1: Proportion of Population Using Safely Managed Drinking Water Services, 2015
(%)

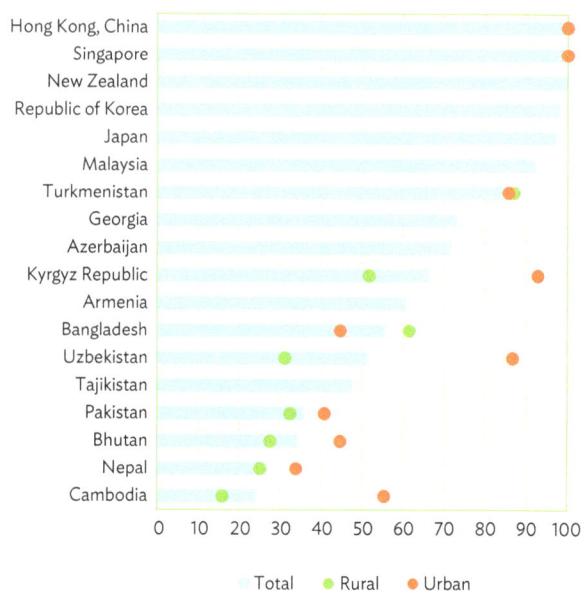

Note: For Uzbekistan, data refer to 2012 (latest available data). This figure excludes economies that provided only urban and/or rural data, with no national totals provided.
Source: Table 1.6.1, Key Indicators for Asia and the Pacific 2018.

From 2000 to 2015, eight of nine economies with available data improved the availability of safely managed sanitations services, led by the PRC. The only exception was Singapore, which already had 100% coverage in 2000 and maintained this to 2015. In the Pacific economies of Palau and Tuvalu, less than 20% of all residents were without access to safely managed sanitation. On the other hand, almost all residents of Japan, the Republic of Korea, and Singapore had access to safely managed sanitation, while four other economies—Australia, Malaysia, New Zealand, and the PRC—reported an access rate greater than 50% (Table 1.6.1). From 2000 to 2015, access to safely managed sanitation services improved in the rural populations of four regional economies, as well as in urban areas of four of the seven economies with available urban data. The scarcity of estimates for safely managed water and sanitation services is discussed in Box 1.6.1.

Box 1.6.1: Lack of Data for Safely Managed Water and Sanitation in Asia and the Pacific

Sustainable Development Goal (SDG) 6 is a commitment to provide universal access to safely managed drinking water and sanitation and the provision of adequate hygiene services. SDG 6 is measured under a more sophisticated monitoring framework than that used for the Millennium Development Goals (MDGs), which had a target calling for "sustainable access" to safe or improved drinking water and basic sanitation.

As there were gaps in nationally representative data in many developing economies, economies traditionally reported on coverage in terms of access to "improved" drinking water and sanitation facilities approximated by basic services. Improved drinking water facilities have the potential to deliver safe water by nature of their design and construction, while improved sanitation facilities are designed to hygienically separate human excreta from human contact. The SDG monitoring introduces a more ambitious indicator of "safely managed" services, which represent a higher level of service than the basic level.[a] Safely managed drinking water services take account of the accessibility, availability, and quality of drinking water. Safely managed sanitation means use of improved facilities that are not shared with other households and where excreta are safely disposed of on site or transported and treated offsite.

The Joint Monitoring Program (JMP) of the World Health Organization (WHO) and United Nations Children's Fund (UNICEF) are publishing regular updates on the progress of the SDGs for water, sanitation, and hygiene (WHO and UNICEF 2017). The JMP has considerably expanded its underlying data sources to cover the additional requirements for SDG monitoring. The updated JPM estimates are based on over 3,400 data sources, for which the administrative data inputs have been increased fivefold. Previously, estimates were based on fewer than 2,000 national data sources, of which two-thirds were household surveys. Despite the expansion of the national data sources, many economies still lack data on one or more criteria for safely managed. For instance, the updated estimates on coverage of safely managed drinking water services are available for only 96 economies around the world and 18 economies in Asia and the Pacific. Similarly, estimates on access to safely managed sanitation services are available for only 96 economies worldwide and 9 economies in the Asia and Pacific region.

The JMP continues to report estimates on lower levels of services, similar to the "improved" categories used in the MDG period. The service level "basic sanitation" for SDG monitoring is equal to "improved sanitation" in the MDG period, while "basic water" is similar to "improved water". Basic water, however, has an additional criterion related to the time required to collect water (not more than 30 minutes for a round trip, including queuing). Universal access to basic services is the target of SDG 1.4. Estimates on the coverage of at least basic drinking water services and at least basic sanitation services are available for 46 economies across Asia and the Pacific.[b] In Asia and the Pacific, 8.6% of the population lacked access to at least basic drinking water in 2015, down from 19.7% in 2000. This, however, means that, as recently as 2015, almost 348 million people across Asia and the Pacific lack access to at least basic drinking water. The proportion of people without access to at least basic sanitation also declined over the same period, from 51.5% to 35.7%. However, this means that, as of 2015, nearly 1.45 billion of over 4 billion people in the region are without access to at least basic sanitation (compared to almost 1.78 billion in 2000).

Wide disparities exist in water and sanitation coverage across regions within Asia and the Pacific as well as between rural and urban areas. Across Asia and the Pacific, 12% of people in rural areas are without access to at least basic water service, compared to 5.1% in urban areas. Further, 50.3% of people are not having access to at least basic sanitation in rural areas, compared to 21.2% in urban areas.

The "universal access" that is incorporated into the SDG 6 targets for 2030 implies a need to expand monitoring efforts beyond households. Monitoring progress towards these targets will be more challenging in some economies and regions than in others, but estimates are expected to improve as more and better data become available.

a   For water, service definitions include safely managed (improved source on premises, available when needed, and free of fecal contaminants); basic (improved source, provided collection time is not more than 30 minutes for a round trip, including queuing); limited (improved source for which collection time exceeds 30 minutes for a round trip, including queuing); unimproved (source is an unprotected dug well or unprotected spring); and surface water (source is a river, dam, lake, pond, stream, canal, or irrigation canal). For sanitation, service definitions include safely managed (not shared with other households, excreta safely disposed of on site or transported and treated offsite); basic (improved facilities that are not shared with other households); limited (improved facilities shared between two or more households); unimproved (pit latrines without a slab or platform, hanging latrines or bucket latrines); and open defecation (disposal of human faces in fields, forests, bushes, open bodies of water, beaches or other open spaces, or with solid waste).
b   For economies with estimates on safely managed services, at least basic includes safely managed services and basic services. For economies without data on safely managed services, the JMP provides estimates for at least basic services.

Source: WHO and UNICEF. 2017. *Progress on Drinking Water, Sanitation and Hygiene: 2017 Update and SDG Baselines*. (Geneva).

SDG 7. Ensure Access to Affordable, Reliable, Sustainable, and Modern Energy for All

The pursuit of SDG 7 is a path toward broader access to affordable and clean energy and improved use of renewable energy by 2030. This requires expanding access to electricity and clean cooking fuels, building sustainable infrastructure, and increasing the financial capacity and willingness of societies to embrace new technologies.

As of 2016, at least 95% of residents in 31 of 47 reporting economies in Asia and the Pacific had access to electricity. Throughout the region, economies generally increased or maintained their levels of electricity access from 2000 to 2016 (Figure 1.7.1). However, less than half of people in Cambodia (49.8%), Solomon Islands (47.9%), and Papua New Guinea (22.9%) had access to this basic service in 2016. The largest disparity in access to electricity between urban and rural areas was observed in Cambodia where the access was 63.5 percentage points higher in urban area, followed by Papua New Guinea (57.2 percentage points), Mongolia (51.6 percentage points), Myanmar (49.7 percentage points), and Vanuatu (45.0 percentage points) (Table 1.7.1). With emerging technologies vastly changing the production and consumption of goods and services, electricity is crucial not only for everyday functions but also to power these technologies.

In 11 of the 46 economies with available data for 2016, at least 95% of the population had access to clean fuels and technology for cooking, heating, and lighting. In 2000, only seven economies, including three developed economies, had achieved this 95% access level (Figure 1.7.2). However, less than one-fifth of the population in 10 economies— Myanmar (18.4%), Bangladesh (17.7%), Cambodia (17.7%), Papua New Guinea (13.4%), Vanuatu (12.6%),

the Federated States of Micronesia (12.0%), Solomon Islands (8.5%), Timor-Leste (6.9%), the Lao PDR (5.6%), and Kiribati (5.5%)—could rely on clean fuels and technology in 2016 (Table 1.7.1). From 2000 to 2016, Maldives reported the largest increase in access to clean fuels and technology at 61.7 percentage points, followed by Indonesia (53.0), Viet Nam (52.5 percentage points), and the Marshall Islands (52.1 percentage points). Lack of access to clean energy puts people at risk of contracting respiratory diseases and other health complications.

Figure 1.7.1: Proportion of Population with Access to Electricity, 2000 and 2016 (%)

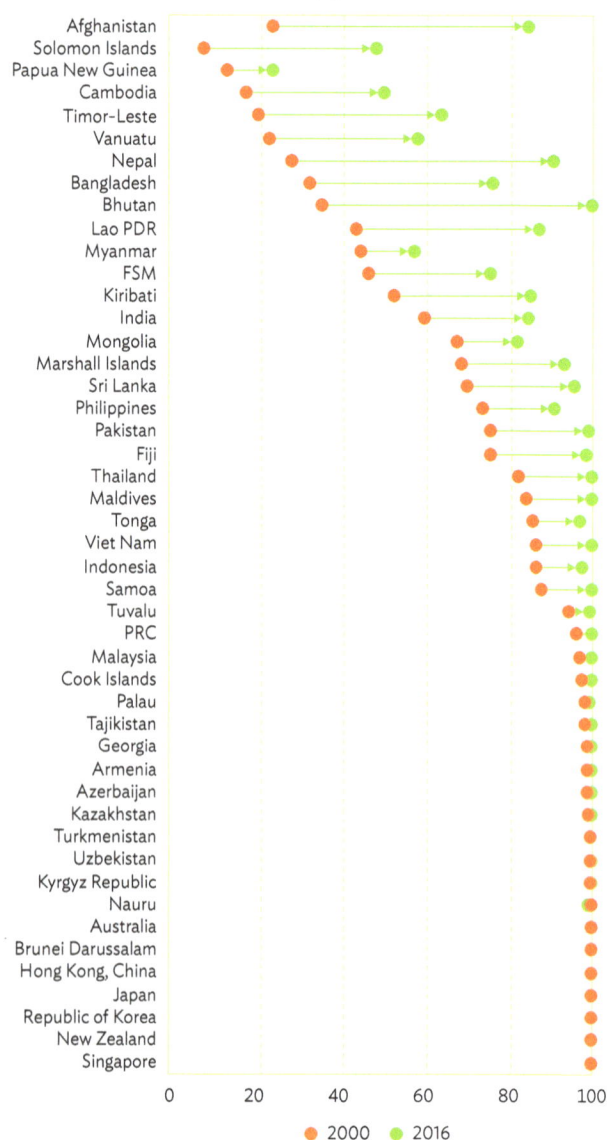

FSM = Federated States of Micronesia, Lao PDR = Lao People's Democratic Republic, PRC = People's Republic of China.
Source: Table 1.7.1, Key Indicators for Asia and the Pacific 2018.

Figure 1.7.2: Proportion of Population with Primary Reliance on Clean Fuels and Technology, 2000 and 2016 (%)

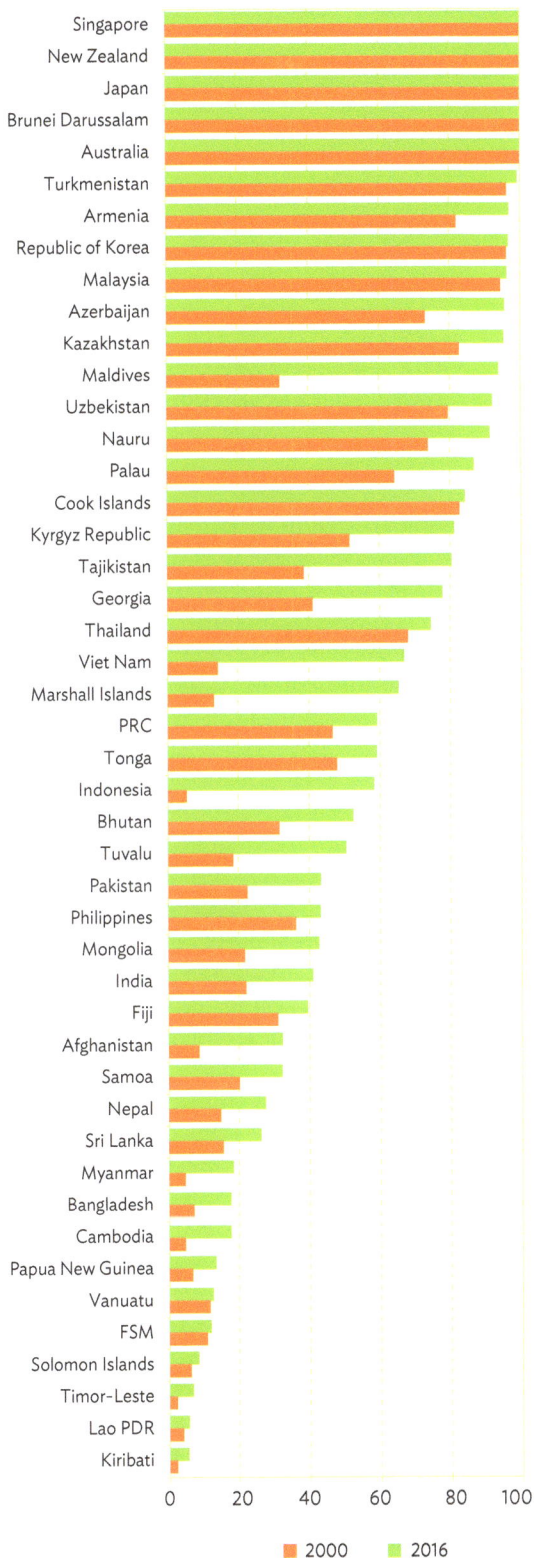

■ 2000   ■ 2016

FSM = Federated States of Micronesia, Lao PDR = Lao People's Democratic Republic, PRC = People's Republic of China.
Source: Table 1.7.1, Key Indicators for Asia and the Pacific 2018.

SDG 8. Promote Sustained, Inclusive, and Sustainable Economic Growth; Full and Productive Employment; and Decent Work for All

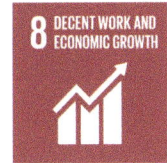

Economies aim for broad-based, inclusive, and sustainable economic growth to provide better prospects, welfare, and opportunities for their citizens. Providing access to better jobs is essential to ensure sustainable economic growth and development. It is the core objective of SDG 8. Sustaining high levels of economic growth, achieving full and productive employment, and ensuring decent work for all will be challenging if economies continue to deplete their natural resources and do not leverage technology.

In 2016, the annual growth rates of GDP per capita for economies in Asia and the Pacific ranged between -3.8% and 9.6%. Nauru (9.6%), the PRC (6.8%), Bhutan (6.6%), and Bangladesh (6.0%) registered the fastest growth rates in 2016, while Armenia (-0.1%), Fiji (-0.4%), Kazakhstan (-0.4%), the Federated States of Micronesia (-0.5%), Mongolia (-0.7%), Nepal (-0.7%), Azerbaijan (-3.6%), and Brunei Darussalam (-3.8%) experienced negative growth rates (Table 1.8.1). The economic performance of economies in Asia and the Pacific has been supported by robust domestic demand given slowdowns in external demand, and global trade.

Recent data on annual unemployment rates for 21 of 36 economies in Asia and the Pacific reported values below 5%, while unemployment was over 10% in 7 other economies. Unemployment rates for youth (15-24 years old) were higher than for adults 25 years or older (Figure 1.8.1). Further, gender disparities could be observed, especially within youth unemployment (Table 1.8.2). The sole use of the unemployment rate as a measure of success in providing decent work can be insufficient, especially in economies with large informal sectors, where women and the poor tend to occupy vulnerable employment. In these cases, examining underemployment, vulnerable employment, and the extent of unpaid family work is imperative. Due to their lower rates of labor force participation, higher levels of unemployment, and greater likelihood of being in vulnerable employment, women and the poor across Asia and the Pacific are less likely to have access to social protection coverage, unemployment benefits, pensions, and maternity leave (International Labour Organization 2018).

Figure 1.8.1: Unemployment Rate, by Age Group
(%)

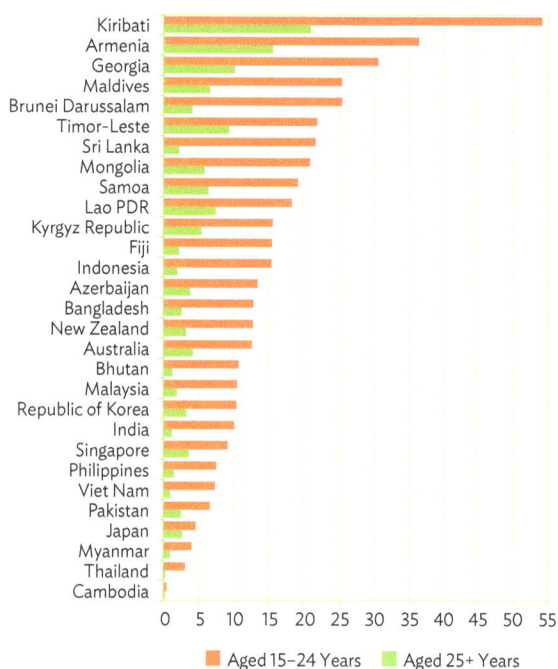

■ Aged 15–24 Years   ■ Aged 25+ Years

Lao PDR = Lao People's Democratic Republic.
Note: For Armenia, Fiji, Georgia, Indonesia, the Kyrgyz Republic, Mongolia, Singapore, and Sri Lanka, data refer to 2016; for Azerbaijan, Bhutan, Pakistan, and Thailand, data refer 2015; for Brunei Darussalam and Samoa, data refer to 2014; for Timor-Leste, data refer to 2013; for India, data refer to 2012; for Cambodia, Kiribati, and Maldives, data refer to 2010. For all other economies, data refer to 2017. Only economies with available data for both age groups 15–24 years and 25+ years are included.
Source: Table 1.8.2, Key Indicators for Asia and the Pacific 2018.

SDG 9. Build Resilient Infrastructure, Promote Inclusive and Sustainable Industrialization, and Foster Innovation

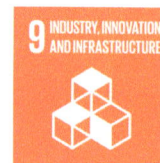

Amid the vastly changing landscape in manufacturing and trade brought about by technological innovations, SDG 9 seeks to strengthen supply chains and retrofit industries across economies. Investments in smart infrastructure and innovation are also needed to stimulate economic activity that ensures sustainable industrialization while achieving growth in wealth and productivity.

In developing Asia, among 16 of 43 economies the share of manufacturing value added as a proportion of GDP exceeded 15%, manufacturing value added per capita (at constant 2010 prices) was over $5,000 per person in Singapore ($8,780), and the Republic of Korea ($7,573) in 2017. Manufacturing value added per capita in 2017 was below $50 per person in Timor-Leste ($5.8), Tuvalu ($36.6), Nepal ($41.6), and the Marshall Islands ($48.8). From 2000 to 2017, negative growth in manufacturing value added per capita was reported in 10 developing economies. Since 2000, 14 of 43 reporting developing economies have doubled their manufacturing value added per capita, while increases of over $1,500 per person (at constant 2010 prices) were reported in the PRC, the Republic of Korea, Singapore, and Turkmenistan (Figure 1.9.1).

From 2000 to 2015, 23 of the 29 reporting economies in Asia and the Pacific lowered carbon dioxide (CO_2) emissions per unit of GDP (at 2010 PPP). In 2015, regional economies with the highest levels of CO_2 emissions per unit of GDP

Figure 1.9.1: Manufacturing Value Added per Capita (constant 2010 $)

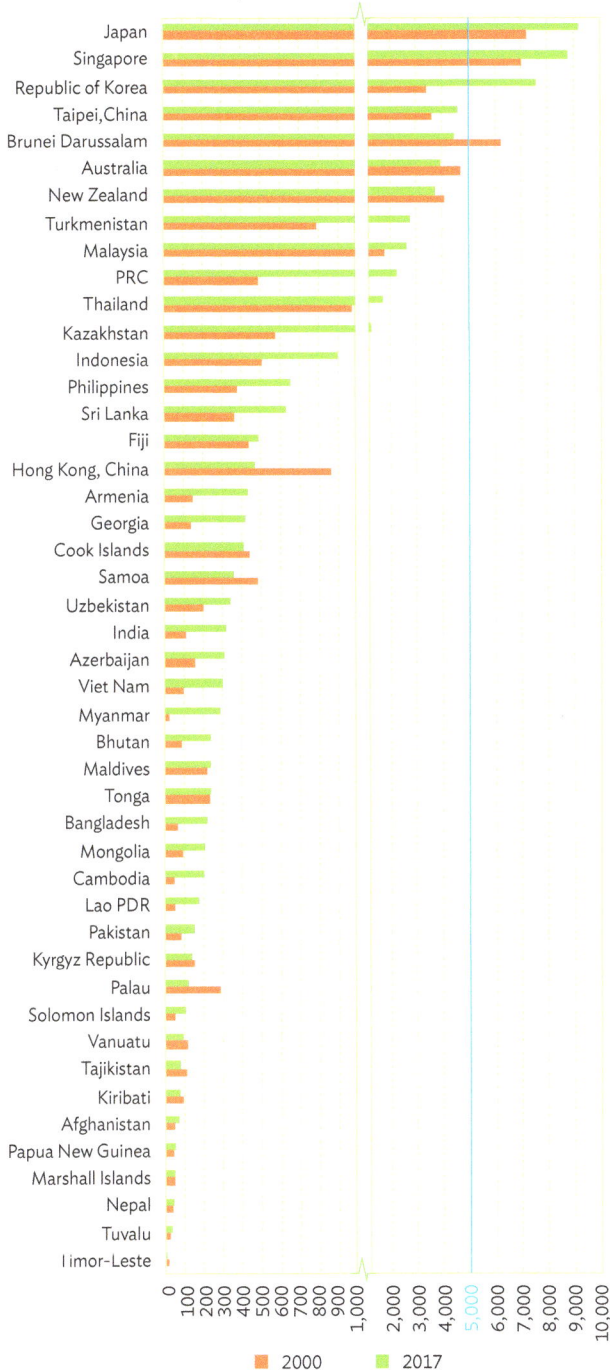

Japan
Singapore
Republic of Korea
Taipei,China
Brunei Darussalam
Australia
New Zealand
Turkmenistan
Malaysia
PRC
Thailand
Kazakhstan
Indonesia
Philippines
Sri Lanka
Fiji
Hong Kong, China
Armenia
Georgia
Cook Islands
Samoa
Uzbekistan
India
Azerbaijan
Viet Nam
Myanmar
Bhutan
Maldives
Tonga
Bangladesh
Mongolia
Cambodia
Lao PDR
Pakistan
Kyrgyz Republic
Palau
Solomon Islands
Vanuatu
Tajikistan
Kiribati
Afghanistan
Papua New Guinea
Marshall Islands
Nepal
Tuvalu
Timor-Leste

0 100 200 300 400 500 600 700 800 900 1,000 2,000 3,000 4,000 5,000 6,000 7,000 8,000 9,000 10,000

■ 2000   ■ 2017

$ = United States dollars, Lao PDR = Lao People's Democratic Republic, PRC = People's Republic of China.
Note: For Taipei,China, the latest available year is 2016. Only economies with data for both years 2000 and 2017 are included.
Source: Table 1.9.2, Key Indicators for Asia and the Pacific 2018.

(PPP) were the Central and West Asian economies of Turkmenistan, Uzbekistan, Kazakhstan, and the Kyrgyz Republic as well as the East Asian economies of Mongolia and the PRC. (Table 1.9.3). Data on CO_2 emissions per unit of GDP are compiled using emissions from fuel combustion compared to the value-added of associated economic activities.

SDG 10. Reduce Inequality Within and Among Countries

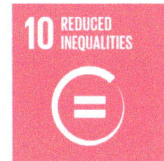

Across Asia and the Pacific, there remains unequal access to opportunities, public goods, and essential services among various groups. Inequality created by factors such as level of wealth, sex, residence, disability status, ethnicity, and migration status can create barriers to social mobility and economic growth. SDG 10 aims to provide more equitable access to opportunities, so that all people can be given a chance to participate in growth processes and fully realize their potential.

Based on the most recent data available, the growth rate of household expenditure or income per capita was faster among the bottom 40% of the population than it was for the overall population in 11 of 16 reporting economies. The PRC reported the largest increase (8.9%) in the income per capita of the bottom 40% of its population, while the Kyrgyz Republic reported the lowest increase at 0.6% (Figure 1.10.1). Conversely, Armenia, Bangladesh, the Lao PDR, Sri Lanka, and Tajikistan registered a lower growth rate of household expenditure or income per capita for the bottom 40% of the population than for the overall population.

Figure 1.10.1: Growth Rates of Household Expenditure or Income per Capita among the Bottom 40% and the Total Population, 2010–2015
(%)

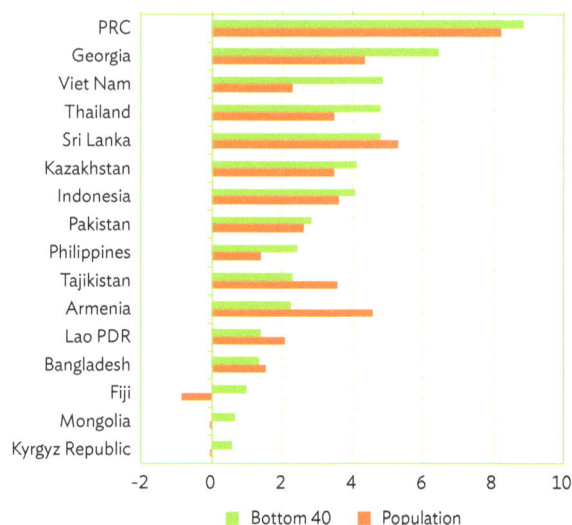

Lao PDR = Lao People's Democratic Republic, PRC = People's Republic of China.
Source: Table 1.10.1, Key Indicators for Asia and the Pacific 2018.

SDG 11. Make Cities and Human Settlements Inclusive, Safe, Resilient, and Sustainable

Nearly half the population of Asia and the Pacific resides in urban areas. As cities continue to be engines of economic growth and offer opportunities for improved welfare, urban populations in the region are expected to overtake those of rural areas by 2022 (United Nations Department of Economic and Social Affairs 2018). SDG 11, which aims to ensure access to safe housing and affordable transport and to build resilience in cities for all, will only be achieved if urban planning and management efforts are scaled up. These efforts must address the need to convert informal settlements into sustainable and resilient living communities and to bring air-pollution levels to internationally acceptable standards.

Notwithstanding growing urbanization, all economies of Asia and the Pacific with **available data have reduced the proportion of the urban population living in slums.** From 2000 to 2014, the Lao People's Democratic Republic (47.9 percentage points), Cambodia (23.8), Bangladesh (22.7), Mongolia (22.2) and Viet Nam (21.6) decreased the proportion of their urban populations that live in slum areas by at least 20 percentage points (Figure 1.11.1). However, the decline in the proportion of the urban population living in slums was fewer than 5 percentage points for Thailand (1.0), Pakistan (3.2), and Myanmar (4.6). Inadequate housing facilities persists in several developing economies of Asia and the Pacific, with the latest data suggesting that at least half of the urban population were living in slums, informal settlements, or inadequate housing in Afghanistan (62.7%), Cambodia (55.1%), Bangladesh (55.1%), and Nepal (54.3%) (Table 1.11.1).

Of 43 reporting economies, 19 were affected by pollution in cities, stemming from fine particulate matter above twice the suggested maximum level set by WHO. The concentration of people living in finite spaces, coupled with high and rising vehicle ownership in urban areas, can result in pollution of the surrounding environment. Air quality is generally monitored by the levels of fine particulate matter equal to 2.5 microns in diameter or less, or the levels of fine particulates together with coarse particles (between 2.5 microns and 10.0 microns). The maximum level set by the WHO for this indicator is 10 micrograms per cubic meter. According to the data for the year 2016, six economies—Nepal (99.5 micrograms per cubic meter), India (68.0), Afghanistan (59.9), Bangladesh (58.6), Pakistan (56.2), and the PRC (51.0)—had urban concentration levels of more than five times the WHO safety standards. The data also shows that four regional economies have managed to be within the WHO standards. These are the developing economies of Brunei Darussalam (5.8 micrograms per cubic meter) and Maldives (7.7), together with the two developed economies of New Zealand (5.8) and Australia (7.3).

Figure 1.11.1: Proportion of Urban Population Living in Slums, 2000 and 2014
(%)

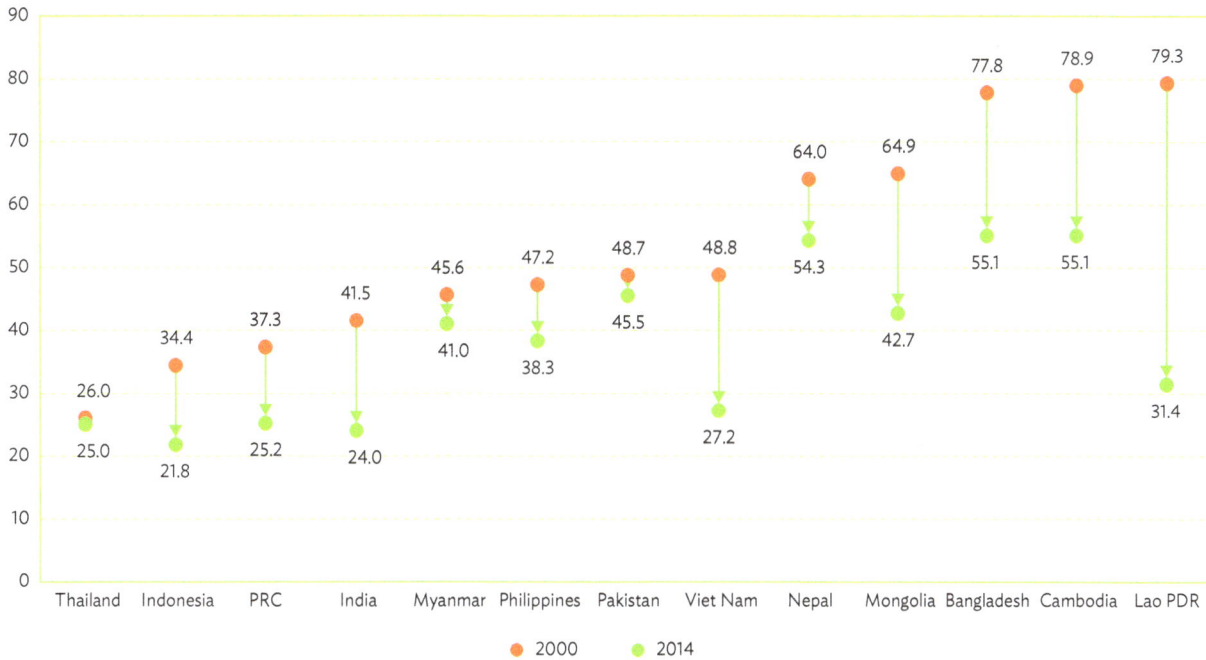

Lao PDR = Lao People's Democratic Republic, PRC = People's Republic of China.
Note: Only economies with available data for both 2000 and 2014 are included. For reference year 2000, data for Cambodia, the Lao People's Democratic
         Republic, Myanmar, and Thailand refer to 2005.
Source: Table 1.11.1, Key Indicators for Asia and the Pacific 2018.

SDG 12. Ensure Sustainable Consumption and Production Patterns

Across the world, increased demands for food, water, energy, and other vital necessities are driven by population growth and rising urbanization. Meeting these demands has affected past and present patterns of consumption and production. SDG 12 aims to reduce the world's ecological footprint by fostering sustainable ways to produce and consume goods, services, and resources. The efficient management of shared natural resources, and the reduction of toxic waste and pollutants throughout the entire production and consumption process, are critical to attaining sustainable development.

From 2000 to 2017, the material footprint of 36 economies in the Asia and Pacific region with available data increased by 127% from 20.7 billion metric tons in 2000 to 47.0 billion metric tons in 2017. As of 2017, seven regional economies had over a billion metric tons of material footprint: the PRC (27.7 billion metric tons), India (6.1), Japan (3.1), Indonesia (1.6), Republic of Korea (1.3), Australia (1.1), and Thailand (1.0). The PRC alone accounted for nearly three-fifths of the aggregate material footprint for Asia and the Pacific in 2017. In per capita terms, Singapore (70.4 metric tons), Australia (42.1), and New Zealand (24.4) had the highest material extraction per person in 2015. Three other economies also had material footprint per capita greater than 20 metric tons: Japan (23.8), Malaysia (22.3), and Turkmenistan (21.5). Among 35 economies with available data, only Japan decreased its total material footprint (by 401.1 million metric tons from 2000 to 2017) and its material footprint per capita (by 4.4 metric tons per person from 2000 to 2015) during the review periods for these indicators (Table 1.12.1).

Figure 1.12.1: Domestic Material Consumption per Capita
(t)

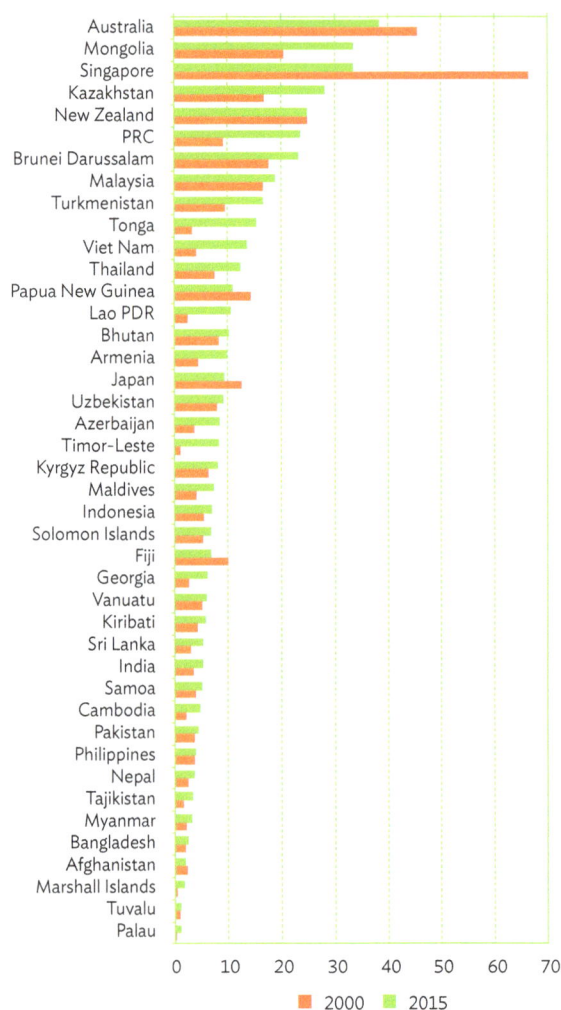

t = metric ton, Lao PDR = Lao People's Democratic Republic,
PRC = People's Republic of China.
Source: Table 1.12.1, Key Indicators for Asia and the Pacific 2018.

The total domestic material consumption of 43 economies in Asia and the Pacific increased by 134% from 22.9 billion metric tons in 2000 to 53.6 billion metric tons in 2017. In 2017, the PRC registered the highest total domestic material consumption at 35.2 billion metric tons. In per capita terms, Australia reported highest domestic material consumption at 38.4 metric tons per person in 2015, followed by Mongolia (33.5 metric tons per person), Singapore (33.4), Kazakhstan (28.2), New Zealand (24.9), PRC (23.6), and Brunei Darussalam (23.3) as shown in Figure 1.12.1. The Pacific economies of Palau (1.1 metric tons per person), Tuvalu (1.2), and the

Marshall Islands (1.8) had the lowest consumption of domestic materials per capita in 2015. From 2000 to 2015, 12 economies in Asia and the Pacific more than doubled their levels of consumption per capita. These included Armenia, Azerbaijan, Cambodia, Georgia, the Lao PDR, the Marshall Islands, Palau, the PRC, Tajikistan, Timor-Leste, Tonga, and Viet Nam. Conversely, consumption per capita was reduced over the same period in 6 of the 42 reporting economies, including the two developed economies—Australia and Japan.

SDG 13. Take Urgent Action to Combat Climate Change and its Impacts

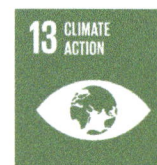

The increasing frequency and intensity of extreme weather events, rising sea levels, and other volatile climatic variables are of global concern. Among other issues, the impacts of climate change can affect livelihoods, food production, energy security, and social cohesion. Consequently, countries have committed to actions to combat climate change. SDG 13 focuses on development that is sensitive to climate change and its impacts, especially for the most vulnerable in society.

Across Asia and the Pacific, 28 of the region's 48 ADB member economies had, by at least in 2015, strategies and regulatory mechanisms for disaster risk reduction and management in line with the Sendai Framework (Table 1.13.1). The impact of disaster depends not only on the type of hazard, but also the extent of exposure to the hazard. The Sendai Framework for Disaster Risk Reduction 2015–2030, successor to the Hyogo Framework for Action 2005–2015, outlines seven targets and four priorities for action to build the resilience of nations and communities to disaster and climate risks. The Sendai Framework is a voluntary, nonbinding agreement among nations. It recognizes that the state has the primary role to reduce disaster risk, but that responsibility should be shared with other stakeholders, including local governments and the private sector. The monitoring and implementation of the Sendai Framework are targeted at devising initiatives for disaster risk reduction, especially for the many economies of Asia and the Pacific that are highly exposed to the harmful effects of climate-related disasters. For a discussion on the frequency of natural disasters, fatalities, and damage costs in Asia and the Pacific please refer to Box 1.13.1.

SDG 14. Conserve and Sustainably Use the Oceans, Seas, and Marine Resources for Sustainable Development

While seas and oceans cover nearly 70% of the planet's surface and play a critical role in the provision of vital ecosystems, their deterioration has been a result of overexploitation, pollution, and the impacts of climate change. SDG 14 emphasizes the use and conservation of the ocean and its resources, including coastal areas. This entails directing human behavior toward sustainable practices and actions to preserve the pristine nature of our oceans, seas, and marine environments.

In the Cook Islands and Palau, over 80% of marine areas were covered by some form of environmental protection. However, in 19 of 36 reporting economies, the corresponding coverage was below 1%. The remaining 15 economies had coverage rates of oceans reserved for long-term conservation ranging from 1% to around 41% (Figure 1.14.1). Globally, only about 7% of ocean areas are designated as marine protected areas (World Bank 2018). Protecting these marine areas is vital for curtailing declines in biodiversity, rebuilding depleted fish stocks, and ensuring long-term and sustainable use of marine natural resources.

Figure 1.14.1: Coverage of Protected Areas in Relation to Marine Areas, 2017
(%)

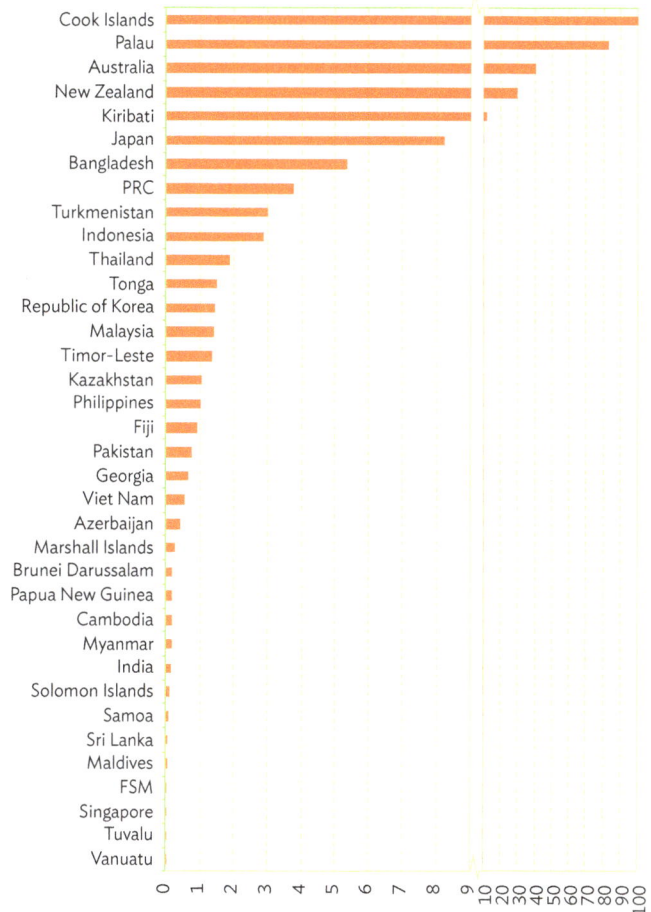

FSM = Federated States of Micronesia, PRC = People's Republic of China.
Source: Table 1.14.1, Key Indicators for Asia and the Pacific 2018.

SDG 15. Protect, Restore, and Promote Sustainable Use of Terrestrial Ecosystems; Sustainably Manage Forests; Combat Desertification; Halt and Reverse Land Degradation; and Halt Biodiversity Loss

Our lives, livelihoods, and continued sustenance hinge on the health of the earth's terrestrial

Box 1.13.1: Disaster Counts, Fatalities, and Damage Costs

While some economies have started compiling data on the number of disaster-related deaths, missing persons, and people affected by disasters, trends are difficult to establish, given the paucity of data and lack of disaggregation by type of disaster. Alternative disaster databases have been developed by other interested parties such as insurance companies and researchers. Of these databases, the most comprehensive, publicly available database on natural disasters is the Emergency Event (EM-DAT) database,[a] which suggests that over 4,800 natural disasters occurred in Asia and the Pacific from 1971 to 2015 (more information in the figure below). Of these, around half occurred from 2001 to 2015, of which 83% were climate-related disasters comprising meteorological (storms), hydrological (floods and wet mass movements), and climatological (drought and wildfire) disasters. It has been observed that over 9 out of 10 of climate-related disasters occurred in developing economies, while developed economies also have not been spared from these hazards (less than 10%).

From 2001 to 2015, Asia and the Pacific recorded an average of 127 reported fatalities per climate-related disaster. Fatality rates from disasters are sensitive to the chosen reference years, the severity of the hazard, and the coping capacity of an economy. A huge number of deaths were recorded as a result of Typhoon Nargis in Myanmar in 2008, which directly led to over 138,000 fatalities as well as 60,000 deaths in other countries from resulting tsunamis. Accounting for such outliers, fatalities from climate-related disasters do not appear to be increasing, unlike the incidence of climate-related disasters and their respective damages.

Damage costs[b] in absolute terms rose from 1971 to 2015 (more information in the figure below). Such a trend arises largely due to increasing populations and higher infrastructure costs (Economist Intelligence Unit 2012). In the same period, storms, floods, and other climate-related events accounted for 58% of the damages resulting from natural disasters and 42% of total damages due to geophysical disasters. Costs from both climate-related disasters and geophysical disasters have been rising in recent years compared to previous decades. From 2006 to 2015, climate-related damages were three times those of 2 decades earlier, while the damage costs for geophysical disasters in the corresponding period were 3.5 times the costs from 1986 to 1995. From 1971 to 2015, disaster costs in East Asia contributed over half of the total costs of climate-related disasters across Asia and the Pacific, and about a quarter of the costs across Asia and the Pacific from geophysical disasters. In the same period, economies of developed Asia carried a huge bulk (71%) of total disaster costs from geophysical hazards. The 2011 tsunami in Japan alone had a damage bill of $210 billion, or about 3.6% of the economy's gross domestic product.

More disaggregation of disaster data by location—as well as data on the sex or age of deaths, missing persons, and affected persons—would are needed to ensure better policies to reduce the exposure of vulnerable communities to climate disasters.

Frequency of Disasters in Asia and Pacific by Disaster Subgroup, 1971–2015

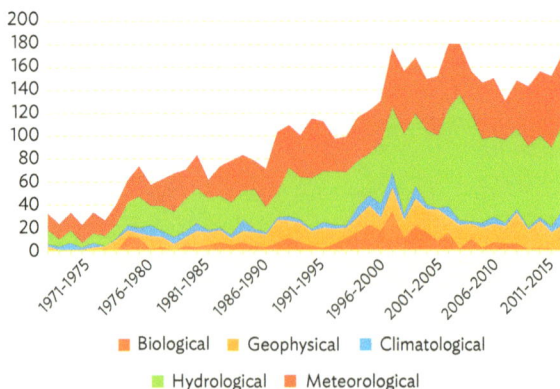

■ Biological   ■ Geophysical   ■ Climatological
■ Hydrological   ■ Meteorological

Source: Emergency Event Database (EM-DAT) http://www.emdat.be/.

Total Number of Deaths vs. Total Number of Damages: 1971–2015

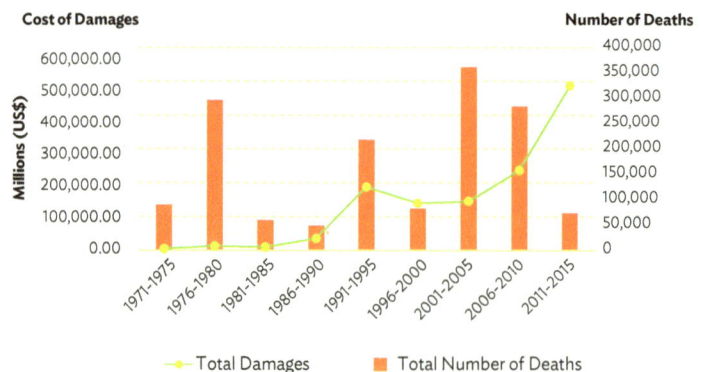

—— Total Damages   ■ Total Number of Deaths

Source: Emergency Event Database (EM-DAT) http://www.emdat.be/.

a   The Emergency Event Database (EM-DAT) http://www.emdat.be/ is maintained by the Centre for Research on the Epidemiology of Disasters (CRED).
b   EM-DAT's data on disaster damage costs (in nominal United States dollars) reflect both direct and indirect consequences of a disaster on the economy. These data are likely subject to issues of comparability across economies or even within an economy.

Sources: Economist Intelligence Unit. 2012. Counting the Cost of Calamities. *The Economist*. 14 Jan. http://www.economist.com/node/21542755 (accessed 15 July 2012). V. Thomas, J.R.G. Albert, and C. Hepburn. 2014. *Contributors to the Frequency of Intense Climate Disasters in Asia-Pacific Countries*. C. Climatic Change (2014) 126: 381. Springer-Verlag.

ecosystems. Human activity, however, can harm the planet's delicately poised habitats and ecosystems. Vigorous efforts are required for promoting the sustainable use of forests, wetlands, drylands, and mountains. Economies of the world must work to reduce the losses of natural habitats and biodiversity, halt and reverse land degradation, halt desertification and revitalize desert areas, and reduce the threat of extinction to many plant and animal species. SDG 15 emphasizes the need for urgent action to improve the management of natural resources to ensure that future generations will continue to benefit from terrestrial and related ecosystems.

In 2017, 25 of 47 reporting economies garnered a score of at least 0.8 on the Red List Index (RLI), a measure of change in aggregate extinction risk across groups of species. However, eight economies scored 0.7 or lower on the RLI. The RLI for each economy is a composite measure representing aggregate survival probability (the inverse of extinction risk) for all birds, mammals, amphibians, corals, and cycads occurring within the economy, weighted by the fraction of each species' distribution occurring within the economy. Values of the index range from 0.0 (indicating all species are categorized as "extinct") to 1.0 (indicating all species are categorized as "least concern"). The eight economies which had RLI scores of 0.7 or lower include Malaysia (0.69), the Federated States of Micronesia (0.69), India (0.68), Fiji (0.67), Vanuatu (0.67), the Philippines (0.65), New Zealand (0.63), and Sri Lanka (0.57) as shown in Figure 1.15.1. After Palau, which decreased its RLI score from 0.91 in 2000 to 0.75 in 2017, Malaysia and Sri Lanka registered the largest declines of 0.14 and 0.09 index points, respectively. The RLI scores of all member economies in Asia and the Pacific, except Nepal were lower in 2017 compared with 2000, although the increase in the index score for Nepal was negligible (Figure 1.15.1).

Figure 1.15.1: Red List Index

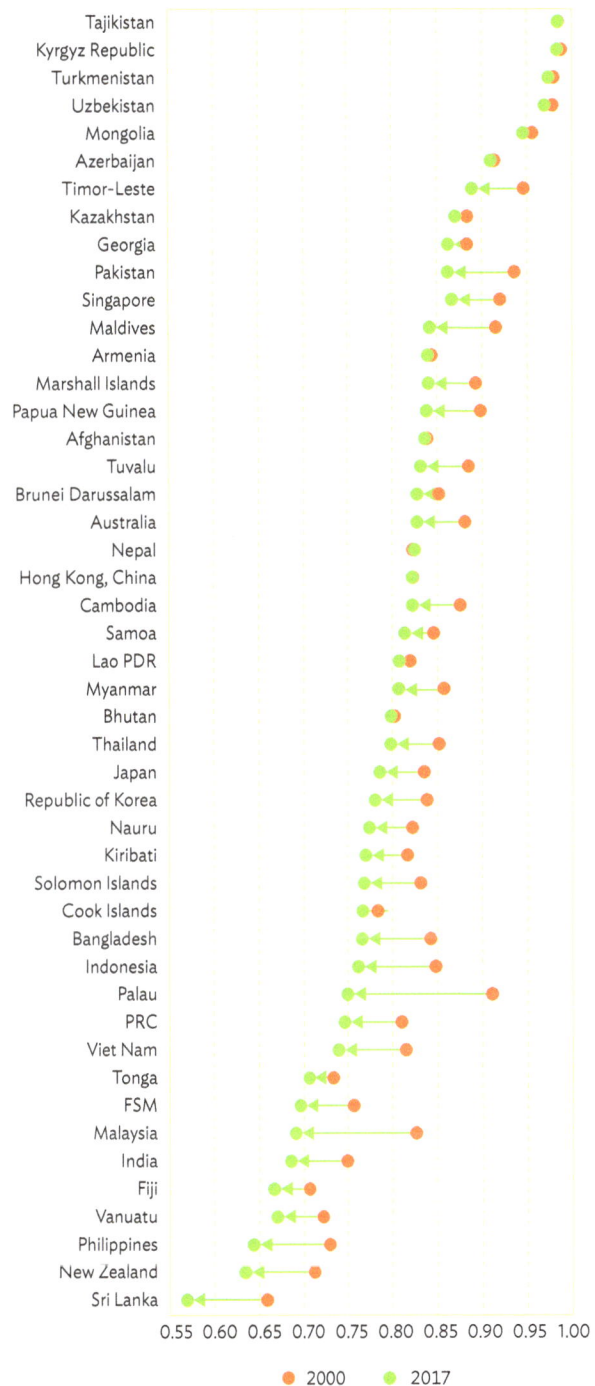

FSM = Federated States of Micronesia, Lao PDR = Lao People's Democratic Republic, PRC = People's Republic of China.
Source: Table 1.15.1, Key Indicators for Asia and the Pacific 2018.

SDG 16. Promote Peaceful and Inclusive Societies for Sustainable Development; Provide Access to Justice for All; and Build Effective, Accountable, and Inclusive Institutions at All Levels

SDG 16 aims to promote peaceful and inclusive societies by providing access to justice for all and building effective, transparent, and accountable institutions at all levels to uphold political stability, human rights, and the rule of law.

Intentional homicide rates ranged between 0 and 1 per 100,000 population in the three developed member economies of Australia, Japan, and New Zealand and in 11 economies in developing Asia to more than 10 per 100,000 population in two economies of Asia and the Pacific. Tuvalu (18.6 intentional homicides per 100,000 population) and the Philippines (11.0) recorded the highest rates among the 43 reporting economies in the most recent year (ranging from 2011 to 2016) (Figure 1.16.1 and Table 1.16.1). Across Asia and the Pacific, economies with intentional homicides between 0 and 1 for every 100,000 population include Georgia (1.0); New Zealand (1.0); Tonga (1.0); Australia (0.9); Maldives (0.8); Taipei,China (0.8); the Republic of Korea (0.7); the PRC (0.6); Brunei Darussalam (0.5); Indonesia (0.5); Hong Kong, China (0.4); Japan (0.3); Singapore (0.3); and Nauru (0.0). Although the rate of intentional homicides decreased in 29 economies since 2000, including in populous economies such as the PRC, India, Indonesia, and Pakistan, the rates increased in eight regional economies (Figure 1.16.1). Victims of intentional homicides across Asia and the Pacific are often men, with the share of male victims exceeding 85% for some economies (UNESCAP 2017). Empirical studies also suggest a correlation between crime rates, especially those of violent crime, and inequality (Rufrancos et al. 2013).

While the proportion of firms receiving at least one request for a bribe was not more than 5% in countries such as Bhutan and Georgia, the prevalence of bribery was as high as 25% or more in 15 of the 28 reporting economies. Bribery often enters the public consciousness through media reporting of scandals, investigations, or prosecutions. However, by its very nature, corruption can be challenging to measure. In its Enterprise Surveys, the World Bank asks firms if they are solicited for gifts or informal payments when meeting with public

Figure 1.16.1: Number of Victims of Intentional Homicide per 100,000 Population

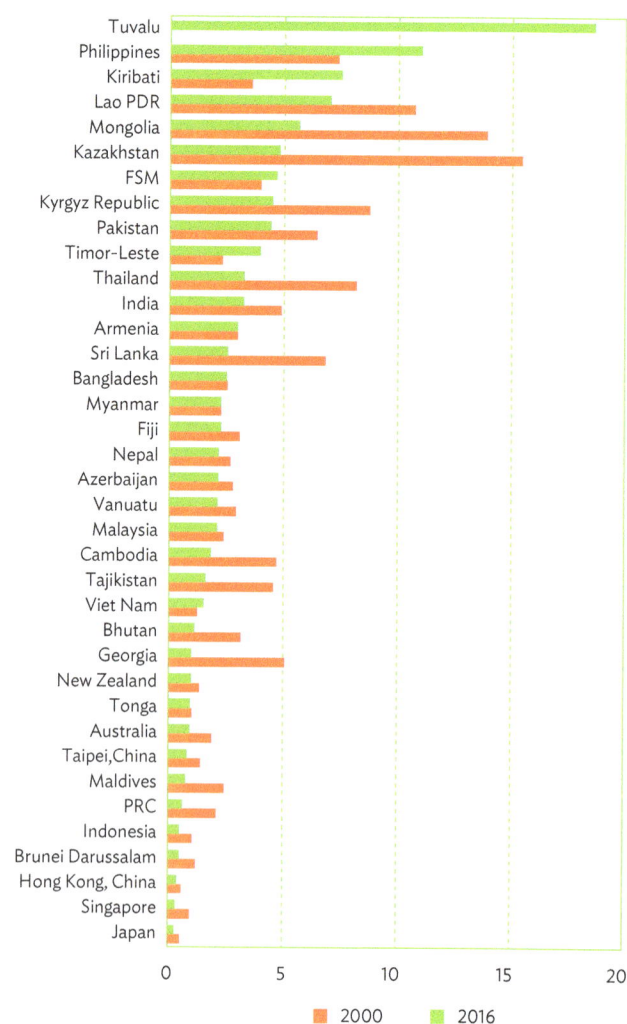

FSM = Federated States of Micronesia, Lao PDR = Lao People's Democratic Republic, PRC = People's Republic of China.
Note: This chart includes economies with available data for both 2000 and 2016. For 2000, data included are for 2000 to 2004. For 2016, data included are for 2011 to 2016.
Source: Table 1.16.1, Key Indicators for Asia and the Pacific 2018.

officials. The bribery prevalence rates resulting from these surveys give information on the experience of bribery occurring in the context of service delivery and/or transactions, but these do not cover other forms of corruption.

SDG 17. Strengthen the Means of Implementation and Revitalize the Global Partnership for Sustainable Development

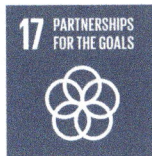

Ensuring that the targets and goals for sustainable development are achieved requires effective partnerships, since the SDGs are more ambitious and larger in scope than their predecessors, the Millennium Development Goals (MDGs). SDG 17 aims to ensure that no one is left behind as economies of the world grow and prosper. It is important that governments, development agencies, and other stakeholders work cohesively towards finding creative solutions to finance better quality statistical data, increase transparency in monitoring and accountability, and leverage partnerships to support the most vulnerable communities, including those in least developed economies, landlocked developing economies, and small-island developing states.

The dollar value of financial and technical assistance increased in 31 of 40 reporting economies when comparing averages over the periods 2000–2008 and 2009–2016. The dollar value of the average financial and technical assistance between the two periods of time grew by over 250% in Kazakhstan, Mongolia, Myanmar, and Uzbekistan (Figure 1.17.1). In absolute terms, Afghanistan ($897.3 million), Indonesia ($676.1 million), Pakistan ($480.2 million), and Viet Nam ($406.3 million) had the largest growth in average financial and technical assistance over the two periods of time. Meanwhile, four Pacific

Figure 1.17.1: Dollar Value of Financial and Technical Assistance Committed to Developing Countries
(constant 2016 $ million)

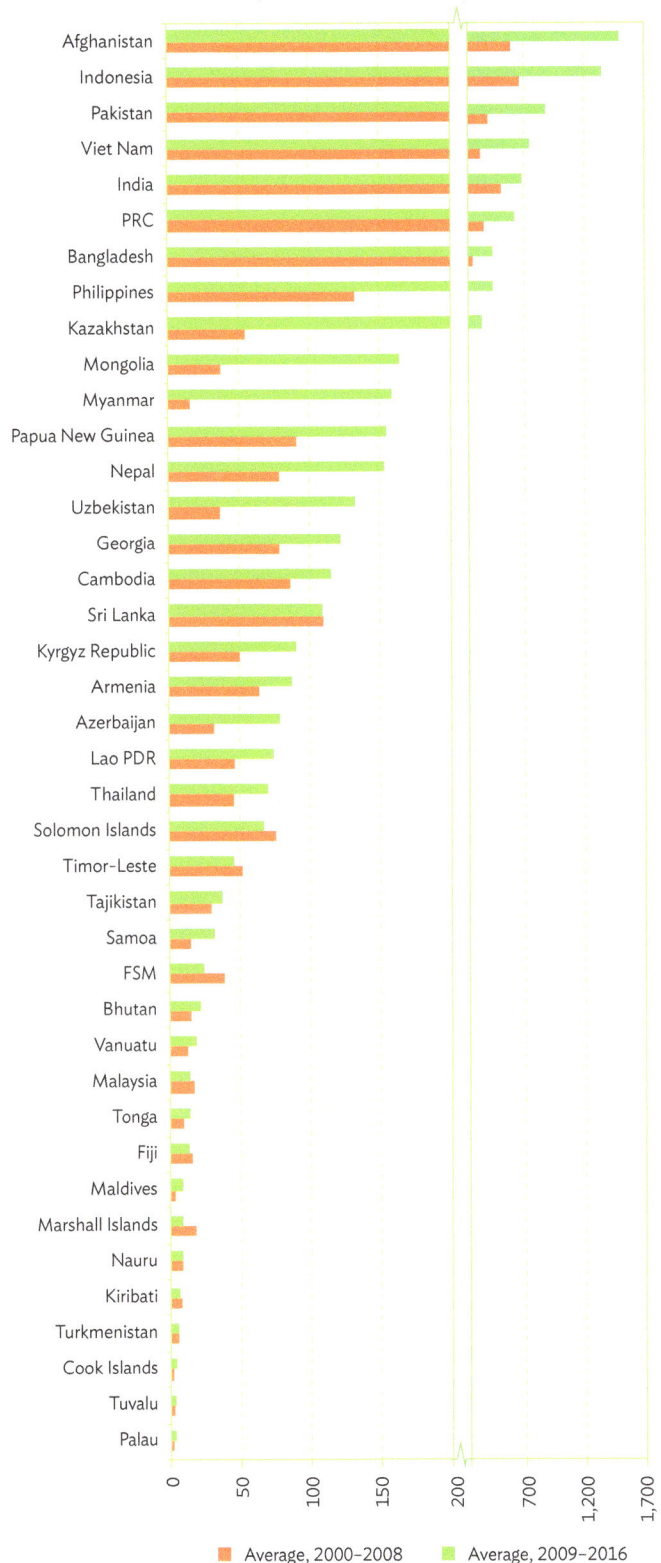

■ Average, 2000–2008   ■ Average, 2009–2016

$ = United States dollars, FSM = Federated States of Micronesia, Lao PDR = Lao People's Democratic Republic, PRC = People's Republic of China.
Source: Table 1.17.1, Key Indicators for Asia and the Pacific 2018.

economies—the Federated States of Micronesia, the Marshall Islands, Solomon Islands, and Timor-Leste—experienced reductions in average assistance of at least $5 million, comparing 2000–2008 with 2009–2016.

Resources made available to strengthen statistical capacity increased from $31.6 million in 2006 to $52.9 million in 2015. International resources to strengthen statistical capacity were increased in Central and West Asia, East Asia, South Asia, and Southeast Asia, with only the Pacific receiving fewer resources. In 2015, 20 of the 39 reporting economies had larger amounts of international resources relative to 2006, with increases of at least $1 million in nine economies: the Philippines ($5.8 million), the PRC ($4.7 million), Myanmar ($4.2 million), Azerbaijan ($3.6 million), Armenia ($3.3 million), the Kyrgyz Republic ($3.1 million), Georgia ($2.9 million), Bangladesh ($2.8 million), and Tajikistan ($1.7 million). The Philippines also reported the highest value for resources made available to statistical capacity development at $6.6 million in 2015, followed by the PRC ($6.3 million) and Myanmar ($5.4 million).

Data Gaps and Other Data-Related Issues

New and huge data demands. The approved framework for global monitoring of the SDGs consists of 232 indicators with greater disaggregation than the MDGs and across a wider spectrum of topics. This requires national statistical systems and the global statistical system to work closely with each other to identify strategies to produce more disaggregated and better-quality data. Currently, national statistical systems, with the assistance of their governments and the development community, are working towards addressing these data demands across all tiers of the SDG indicators.

Limited data availability for Sustainable Development Goal indicators. Since the launch of the SDGs in 2015, significant progress has been made towards closing the gap on data definitions and ensuring their timely availability. However, there is scope for further improvement. An assessment undertaken by ADB and UNESCAP on the extent of data availability for the SDG indicators across Asia and the Pacific revealed that only 52% of the SDG indicators had some data. Moreover, an assessment made by UNESCAP (2017) revealed that 11% of Tier I indicators, 34% of Tier II indicators, and 93% of Tier III indicators do not have any data available (Figure 1.18.1). Only 26% of all SDG indicators are amenable to trend analysis at the regional level, with two or more data points available for these indicators for 50% or more economies in Asia and the Pacific.

Figure 1.18.1: Distribution of Sustainable Development Goal Indicators, by Tier and by Data Availability
(number of indicators)

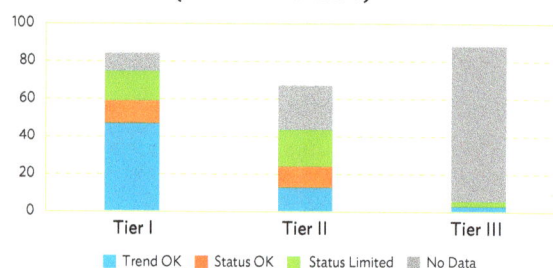

Notes:
1. Trend OK: if a particular indicator has two or more data points available for 50% (or more) of the economies in Asia and the Pacific or relevant economy grouping from 2000 to 2017.
2. Status OK: if a particular indicator has only one data point available for 50% (or more) of the economies in Asia and the Pacific or relevant economy grouping from 2000 to 2017.
3. Status Limited: if a particular indicator has at least one data point available but for less than 50% of the economies in Asia and the Pacific or relevant economy grouping from 2000 to 2017.
4. No Data: if no data points are available for any of the economies in Asia and the Pacific or relevant economy grouping from 2000 to 2017.

Source: United Nations Economic and Social Commission for Asia and the Pacific. 2017. *Statistical Yearbook for Asia and the Pacific 2017 Measuring SDG progress in Asia and the Pacific: Is There Enough Data?* Bangkok.

There may be disparities in data availability for SDG indicators across economic, social, and environmental dimensions as national statistics offices prioritize data production on economic indicators. Further, SDG indicators with a social dimension that overlap with indicators for the MDGs would be expected to have relatively good data availability. Most national statistics offices across Asia and the Pacific conduct population and housing censuses every decade, and such sources provide baseline data for socioeconomic information requirements, including SDG indicators with economic and social dimensions. Aside from censuses, data (and updates) on SDG indicators are sourced from household surveys—such as labor force surveys, household income, and expenditure surveys; demographic and health surveys, establishment surveys; agriculture surveys; etc.—as well as from administrative reporting systems, but the frequency of data on SDG indicators would depend on the regularity of these data collection activities.

Gaps in data granularity. Since the principle of the SDGs is to leave no one behind, many of the SDG indicators require disaggregation by location, sex, gender, age, income, ethnicity, migration status, disability status, and other relevant dimensions. Granular data can illustrate disparities within and across countries. However, the extent to which specific groups are disproportionately at risk, for example, to lack of housing and security of tenure in slums, is currently difficult to decipher given the lack of data disaggregation and interlinkages across indicators. Sex disaggregations, even for basic indicators such as extreme poverty rates based on the $1.90 a day (at 2011 purchasing power parity), are not currently available. Similarly, poverty numbers are currently unavailable for vulnerable groups, such as persons with disabilities or indigenous peoples, since the sample surveys that form the basis for poverty calculations are only designed to obtain an overall picture of welfare conditions. To obtain poverty data for groups that have a small share of the total population, investments in population registers and/ or special surveys need to be made.

With the growing use of information and communication technology, innovative data sources such as big data and crowdsourced data can potentially address gaps in data granularity in monitoring the SDGs. Unlike censuses, sample surveys, and administrative reporting systems (all

of which have well-defined target populations), some types of big data may not represent underlying populations of interest. Careful attention is needed when complementing surveys and other conventional data sources with big data to ensure that reliable statistical inferences can be made (Cox et al. 2018).

Lack of data comparability. SDG indicators, such as the proportion of the urban population living in slums or the proportion of the population with access to safely managed sanitation services, require data on housing conditions that may not be fully comparable across countries due to differences in definitions. Comparisons across economies are likewise difficult for urban–rural disaggregation of SDG indicators, due to variations in the definition of "urban" and "rural" across time and countries (Box 2.1.1).

Sparse data and irregular frequency. Indicators that provide a useful description of income inequality, such as the growth in household income of those in the bottom 40th percentile of income distribution in relation to national averages, are only currently available for a few economies. Indicators on material footprint and domestic material consumption, which are widely accepted as strategic sustainability indicators of production and consumption, are not produced annually. Data to monitor progress made towards addressing climate change are sparse.

Frequency is also of concern, and some indicators, such as the coverage of protected areas in relation to marine areas, are not regularly collected alongside other challenges such as difficulty in determining whether a site conforms to standards on the definition of a protected area. Further, some protected areas are not assigned management categories. While access to remote sensing data has improved in recent years, these data have their own limitations in assessing land use. For example, forest regrowth cannot easily be detected with remote-sensing techniques.

Data limitations. While the indicators included in the framework for monitoring the SDGs are carefully chosen, they may have some limitations. The labor share in GDP, for instance, does not include the income of the self-employed, and yet a sizeable proportion of the employed population in developing Asia is made up of people who are self-employed. Current measures of poverty used by economies are largely based on income or consumption data, while the SDG indicators include a multidimensional poverty measure, which has yet to be tested on a wider scale.

Cities face many challenges in relation to pollution, traffic, and inadequate housing for the poor, and these challenges are further fueled by migration and population growth, changes in family structures, inequalities of opportunity for excluded groups and rising insecurity. The interconnectedness of these issues is not easy to explore using currently available data.

As regards the Red List Index, since the composite index is aggregated across multiple taxonomic groups, it can be updated annually, but the index does not adequately capture the deteriorating status of common species that are abundant and widespread but are declining gradually. Other indicators for monitoring many targets under SDG 15 are also sparsely available. The absence of a framework of monitoring terrestrial ecosystems, low data availability, and the lack of good quality data has ecological implications and must be carefully addressed.

Measurement errors. The quality of data for all the SDG indicators needs to be considered when uncovering trends and patterns, as data are subject to measurement issues. Farmer self-reports of land area and production are known to have significant biases (Dillon and Rao 2018). Calculation of mortality rates in children under the age of 5 years requires complete counts of live births and child deaths by precise age, which are not always available due to lacking civil registration systems in some developing economies of Asia and the Pacific. Maternal deaths are likewise not always accounted for given incomplete or inaccurate records on causes of death. The measurement of quality education is a challenge given the lack of standard definitions for minimum competency. Anthropometric measures of malnutrition (including stunted heights) are subject to measurement errors and issues around reference standards, i.e., local versus international standards. Access to safely managed drinking water services, access to safely managed sanitation, and information on hygiene crucially depend on more and better data, particularly administrative data sources (WHO and UNICEF 2017).

As far as international support to statistics is concerned, full coverage of all statistical capacity development programs cannot be guaranteed in the data compiled by PARIS21 for measuring the dollar-value support for statistics development. Double counting of projects may happen. The data may also be inflated by working with project totals for multisector projects. Further, donor-side commitments do not necessarily translate to actual disbursements to the ODA-recipient economies.

Reliability of data on SDG indicators depends on the quality of the underlying data sources. Economies need to increase investment, look for innovative data sources, and form strategic partnerships with a range of stakeholders to ensure that data quality, comparability, measurement, and timeliness can be enhanced. The result will be good development data that can be used for evidence-based policymaking that eventually translates into better outcomes in sustainable development.

References

D.R. Cox, C. Kartsonaki, and R. H.Keogh. 2018. Big Data: Some Statistical Issues. *Statistics & Probability Letters* Volume 136, May 2018, pp. 111–115.

K.G. Dewey. 2016. Reducing Stunting by Improving Maternal, Infant and Young Child Nutrition in Regions such as South Asia: Evidence, Challenges and Opportunities. *Maternal & Child Nutrition*. John Wiley.

A. Dillon and L.N. Rao. 2018. Land Measurement Bias: Comparisons from Global Positioning System, Self-Reports, and Satellite Data. Asian Development Bank, Economics Working Paper Series. No. 540.

European Union and United Nations Human Settlements Programme (UN-Habitat). 2016. *The State of European Cities: Cities Leading the Way to a Better Future*. Brussels, Belgium: European Commission.

International Labour Organization (ILO). 2018. *World Employment and Social Outlook: Trends 2018*. Geneva, Switzerland: ILO.

N.M. Nour. 2009. Child Marriage: A Silent Health and Human Rights. Reviews in Obstetrics & Gynecology. Issue. Vol. 2 No. 1 pp. 51-56. Glastonbury, Connecticut, USA: MedReviews-CME.

https://www.ncbi.nlm.nih.gov/pmc/articles/PMC2672998/pdf/RIOG002001_0051.pdf (accessed 10 June 2018)

H.G. Rufrancos, M. Power, K.E. Pickett, and R. Wilkinson. 2013. Income Inequality and Crime: A Review and Explanation of the Time-Series Evidence. *Social Crimonol* 1: 103. doi: 10.4172/2375-4435.1000103.

Secretariat of the Partnership in Statistics for Development in the 21st Century (PARIS21).
2017. Partner Report on Support to Statistics PRESS 2017. Paris, France: PARIS21.

UN. 2015. Transforming Our World: the 2030 Agenda for Sustainable Development. A/RES/70/1. Resolution adopted by the General Assembly on 25 September 2015. New York, New York, USA: UN.

United Nations Department of Economic and Social Affairs (UNDESA). 2018. *World Urbanization Prospects 2018*. New York, New York, USA: UN.

UNDESA, Population Division. 2015. *World Urbanization Prospects: The 2014 Revision*. New York, New York, USA: UN.

United Nations Economic and Social Commission for Asia and the Pacific (UNESCAP). 2017. *Statistical Yearbook for Asia and the Pacific 2017*. Measuring SDG Progress in Asia and the Pacific: Is There Enough Data? Bangkok, Thailand: UNESCAP.

UNESCAP. 2017. *Economic and Social Survey of Asia and the Pacific 2017: Governance and Fiscal Management*. Bangkok, Thailand: UNESCAP.

UNESCAP. 2016. *Economic and Social Survey of Asia and the Pacific 2018: Nurturing Productivity for Inclusive Growth and Sustainable Development*. Bangkok, Thailand: UNESCAP.

WHO and UNICEF. 2017. *Progress on Drinking Water, Sanitation and Hygiene: 2017 Update and SDG Baselines*. (location and/or publisher).

World Bank. 2005. *Global Purchasing Power Parities and Real Expenditures 2005*. International Comparison Program. Washington, DC: World Bank.

World Bank. 2018. *Atlas of Sustainable Development Goals 2018: From World Development Indicators*. World Bank Atlas; Washington, DC: World Bank.

Table 1.1.1: Selected Indicators for Sustainable Development Goal 1—No Poverty

ADB Regional Member	Target 1.1: By 2030, eradicate extreme poverty for all people everywhere, measured as people living below the international poverty line of $1.90 a day (2011 PPP)							
	1.1.1a: Proportion of Population Living below the $1.90 a Day (2011 PPP) Poverty Line[a,b] (%)		1.1.1b: Proportion of Employed Population Living below the International Poverty Line, by Age Group and Sex[b,c] (%)					
			2017					
			Age Group					
				15+		15–24	25+
	2000	2016	Total	Female	Male		
Developing ADB Member Economies								
Central and West Asia								
Afghanistan	…	…	83.4	86.4	82.9	82.9	83.7
Armenia	19.3 (2001)	1.8	1.3	1.6	1.1	2.2	1.3
Azerbaijan[d]	2.7 (2001)	…	0.2	0.2	0.3	0.3	0.2
Georgia	21.0	4.2	5.5	4.0	6.8	6.6	5.4
Kazakhstan	10.5 (2001)	0.0 (2015)	…	…	…	…	…
Kyrgyz Republic	42.2	1.4	1.8	0.7	2.5	1.5	1.8
Pakistan	28.6 (2001)	6.1 (2013)	4.1	4.7	3.9	4.2	4.0
Tajikistan	30.8 (2003)	4.8 (2015)	4.0	3.9	4.0	4.1	3.9
Turkmenistan	…	…	0.8	0.2	1.2	0.7	0.8
Uzbekistan[d]	62.0	…	5.4	2.2	7.7	6.0	5.3
East Asia								
China, People's Republic of	31.9 (2002)	1.4 (2014)	3.0	3.2	2.9	4.0	2.9
Hong Kong, China[f]	…	…	…	…	…	…	…
Korea, Republic of[f]	0.3 (2006)	0.3 (2012)	…	…	…	…	…
Mongolia	10.6 (2002)	0.5	0.2	0.2	0.2	0.2	0.2
Taipei,China	…	…	…	…	…	…	…
South Asia								
Bangladesh	34.8	14.8	41.5	46.6	39.5	44.4	40.9
Bhutan	35.2 (2003)	2.2 (2012)	1.2	1.3	1.2	1.8	1.2
India	38.2 (2004)	21.2 (2011)	11.1	12.3	10.7	14.2	10.6
Maldives	10.0 (2002)	7.3 (2009)	1.6	2.0	1.5	2.0	1.5
Nepal	46.1 (2003)	15.0 (2010)	5.7	5.7	5.8	5.6	5.7
Sri Lanka	8.3 (2002)	0.7	1.1	1.0	1.1	1.3	1.1
Southeast Asia								
Brunei Darussalam	…	…	…	…	…	…	…
Cambodia	…	…	16.1	15.7	16.4	19.2	15.0
Indonesia	39.3	6.5	6.3	6.3	6.3	6.5	6.3
Lao People's Democratic Republic	33.8 (2002)	22.7 (2012)	47.7	47.4	48.0	52.2	46.3
Malaysia	0.4 (2004)	0.3 (2009)	0.1	0.1	0.1	0.1	0.1
Myanmar	…	6.4 (2015)	18.5	19.3	17.9	21.5	17.6
Philippines	14.5	8.3 (2015)	3.9	2.9	4.6	5.1	3.7
Singapore	…	…	…	…	…	…	…
Thailand	2.5	0.0 (2013)	…	…	…	…	…
Viet Nam	38.0 (2002)	2.6 (2014)	1.6	1.7	1.6	3.0	1.4
The Pacific								
Cook Islands	…	…	…	…	…	…	…
Fiji	4.9 (2002)	1.4 (2013)	1.2	1.3	1.2	1.5	1.1
Kiribati	12.9 (2006)	…	…	…	…	…	…
Marshall Islands	…	…	…	…	…	…	…
Micronesia, Federated States of	8.0 (2005)	16.0 (2013)	…	…	…	…	…
Nauru	…	…	…	…	…	…	…
Palau	…	…	…	…	…	…	…
Papua New Guinea	…	38.0 (2009)	19.4	18.3	20.5	23.5	18.2
Samoa	0.6 (2008)	…	…	…	…	…	…
Solomon Islands	45.6 (2005)	25.1 (2013)	17.8	17.8	17.8	21.8	16.4
Timor-Leste	42.5 (2001)	30.3 (2014)	2.7	2.5	2.7	3.6	2.5
Tonga	2.8 (2001)	1.1 (2009)	…	…	…	…	…
Tuvalu	…	3.3 (2010)	…	…	…	…	…
Vanuatu	…	13.2 (2010)	…	…	…	…	…
Developed ADB Member Economies								
Australia	…	…	…	…	…	…	…
Japan	…	…	…	…	…	…	…
New Zealand	…	…	…	…	…	…	…

continued on next page

Goal 1. End poverty in all its forms everywhere

Table 1.1.1: Selected Indicators for Sustainable Development Goal 1—No Poverty (continued)

ADB Regional Member	Target 1.2: By 2030, reduce at least by half the proportion of men, women, and children of all ages living in poverty in all its dimensions according to national definitions					
	1.2.1: Proportion of Population Living below the National Poverty Line, by Urban–Rural Location[a] (%)					
	2000			2016		
	Total	Urban	Rural	Total	Urban	Rural
Developing ADB Member Economies						
Central and West Asia						
Afghanistan	33.7 (2007)	...	...	54.5	41.6	58.5
Armenia	53.5 (2004)	...	...	29.4	28.8	30.4
Azerbaijan[d]	49.0 (2001)	...	...	5.9	...	...
Georgia	34.3 [e] (2004)	34.4 [e] (2004)	34.1 [e] (2004)	21.9 [e] (2017)	18.6 [e] (2017)	26.6 [e] (2017)
Kazakhstan	46.7 (2001)	36.0 (2001)	59.4 (2001)	2.6	...	...
Kyrgyz Republic	62.6	53.3	67.6	25.4	18.6	29.0
Pakistan	64.3 (2001)	50.0 (2001)	70.2 (2001)	29.5 (2013)	18.2 (2013)	35.6 (2013)
Tajikistan	72.4 (2003)	68.8 (2003)	73.8 (2003)	31.3 (2015)	23.2 (2015)	35.2 (2015)
Turkmenistan	...	...	...	...	...	...
Uzbekistan[d]	...	...	...	12.3	...	...
East Asia						
China, People's Republic of	...	...	49.8	...	...	4.5
Hong Kong, China[f]	...	...	...	14.7	...	...
Korea, Republic of[f]	...	...	...	17.9	...	...
Mongolia	36.1 (2003)	30.3 (2003)	43.4 (2003)	29.6	27.1	34.9
Taipei,China	0.7 [g]	...	...	1.4 [g]	...	...
South Asia						
Bangladesh	48.9	35.2	52.3	24.3	18.9	26.4
Bhutan	23.2 (2007)	1.7 (2007)	30.9 (2007)	8.2 (2017)	0.8 (2017)	11.9 (2017)
India	37.2 [h] (2004)	25.7 [h] (2004)	41.8 [h] (2004)	21.9 [h] (2011)	13.7 [h] (2011)	25.7 [h] (2011)
Maldives	21.0 [i] (2002)	...	...	15.0 [i] (2009)	...	...
Nepal	30.9 (2003)	9.6 (2003)	34.6 (2003)	25.2 (2010)	15.5 (2010)	27.4 (2010)
Sri Lanka	22.7 (2002)	7.9 (2002)	24.7 (2002)	4.1	1.9	4.3
Southeast Asia						
Brunei Darussalam	...	...	...	...	...	...
Cambodia	47.8 (2007)	...	53.2 (2007)	14.0 (2014)	...	...
Indonesia	19.1 [j]	14.6 [j]	22.4 [j]	10.6 [k] (2017)	7.7 [k] (2017)	13.9 [k] (2017)
Lao People's Democratic Republic	33.5 (2002)	19.7 (2002)	37.6 (2002)	23.2 (2012)	10.0 (2012)	28.6 (2012)
Malaysia	6.0 (2002)	2.3 (2002)	13.5 (2002)	0.4	0.2	1.0
Myanmar	48.2 (2004)	...	...	32.1 (2015)	14.5 (2015)	38.8 (2015)
Philippines	26.6 (2006)	...	...	21.6 (2015)	...	...
Singapore	...	...	...	...	...	...
Thailand	42.3	22.2	51.4	8.6	...	...
Viet Nam	28.9 (2002)	6.6 (2002)	35.6 (2002)	7.0 (2015)	2.5 (2015)	9.2 (2015)
The Pacific						
Cook Islands	28.4 [l] (2006)	...	...	...	...	...
Fiji	35.0 [l] (2002)	28.0 [l] (2002)	40.0 [l] (2002)	28.1 [l] (2013)	19.8 [l] (2013)	36.7 [l] (2013)
Kiribati	21.8 [l] (2006)	...	...	...	...	...
Marshall Islands	52.7 [l] (2002)	...	...	...	...	...
Micronesia, Federated States of	31.4 [l] (2005)	...	...	41.2 [l] (2013)	...	...
Nauru	25.1 [l] (2006)	...	...	24.0 (2013)	...	...
Palau	24.9 [l] (2006)	...	...	...	...	...
Papua New Guinea	...	...	...	39.9 [m] (2009)	29.3 [m] (2009)	41.6 [m] (2009)
Samoa	22.9 [l] (2002)	...	...	18.8 [l] (2013)	...	...
Solomon Islands	23.0 [m] (2005)	...	...	12.7 [m] (2012)	9.1 [m] (2012)	13.6 [m] (2012)
Timor-Leste	50.4 (2007)	38.3 (2007)	54.7 (2007)	41.8 (2014)	28.3 (2014)	47.1 (2014)
Tonga	16.2 [l] (2001)	...	...	22.1 [l] (2015)	...	...
Tuvalu	21.2 [l] (2004)	...	...	26.3 [l] (2010)	24.8 [l] (2010)	27.5 [l] (2010)
Vanuatu	13.0 [l] (2006)	...	11.5 [l] (2006)	12.7 [l] (2010)	...	10.0 [l] (2010)
Developed ADB Member Economies						
Australia	...	...	...	...	...	...
Japan	...	...	...	...	...	...
New Zealand	...	...	...	...	...	...

... = data not available, 0.0 = magnitude is less than half of unit employed or true zero, ADB = Asian Development Bank, PPP = purchasing power parity.

a For indicator 1.1.1a and indicator 1.2.1, the year indicated in the table refers to the year when the household survey data were collected. For economies where the household survey data collection period bridged two calendar years, the table reports the first year.

b For indicator 1.1.1a, data are consumption-based, except for Malaysia, where data are income-based. For indicator 1.1.1a and indicator 1.1.1b, the estimates are based on the international poverty line of $1.90 a day (2011 PPP).

c Data are taken from International Labour Organization modelled estimates and projections, which include both estimates and real values. All data reflected are modelled estimates.

d For Indicator 1.1.1a, the latest available estimate for Azerbaijan is for 2005: 0.0%. For Uzbekistan, the latest available estimate is for 2003: 62.1%

e Refers to absolute poverty or the share of the population under the absolute poverty line.

f For indicator 1.2.1, the earliest available estimate for Hong Kong, China is for 2009: 16.0%. For the Republic of Korea, the earliest available estimate is for 2012: 16.5%.

g Refers to the percentage of the low-income population to the total population.

h Based on Tendulkar methodology, using mixed reference period.

i Based on half the median of Atoll expenditure per person per day in 2009–2010 equivalent to 22 rufiyaa.

j Reference period is February 2000.

k Reference period is March 2017.

l Data refer to the percentage of the population living below the basic needs poverty line.

m Refers to poverty headcount ratio using the upper poverty line.

Sources: Economy sources; World Bank. PovcalNet Database. http://iresearch.worldbank.org/PovcalNet/povDuplicateWB.aspx (accessed 18 June 2018); United Nations. Sustainable Development Goals Indicators Database. http://unstats.un.org/sdgs/indicators/database/ (accessed 13 July 2018); World Bank. World Development Indicators. http://databank.worldbank.org/data/reports.aspx?source=world-development-indicators (accessed 15 July 2018); International Labour Organisation. ILOSTAT. http://www.ilo.org/ilostat (accessed 22 June 2018); and Pacific National Minimum Development Indicators. https://www.spc.int/nmdi/ (accessed 15 June 2018).

Table 1.2.1: Selected Indicators for Sustainable Development Goal 2—Zero Hunger

| ADB Regional Member | Target 2.1: By 2030, end hunger and ensure access by all people, in particular the poor and people in vulnerable situations, including infants, to safe, nutritious, and sufficient food all year round | | Target 2.2: By 2030, end all forms of malnutrition, including achieving, by 2025, the internationally agreed targets on stunting and wasting in children under 5 years of age, and address the nutritional needs of adolescent girls, pregnant and lactating women, and older persons | | | | | |
| | 2.1.1: Prevalence of Undernourishment (%) | | 2.2.1: Prevalence of Stunting among Children under 5 Years of Age[c] (%) | | 2.2.2a: Prevalence of Malnutrition (Wasting) among Children under 5 Years of Age[c] (%) | | 2.2.2b: Prevalence of Malnutrition (Overweight) among Children under 5 Years of Age[c] (%) | |
	2000[a]	2015[b]	2000	2016	2000	2016	2000	2016
Developing ADB Member Economies								
Central and West Asia								
Afghanistan	46.1	23.0	59.3 (2004)	40.9 (2013)	8.6 (2004)	9.5 (2013)	4.6 (2004)	5.4 (2013)
Armenia	23.8	4.4	17.7	9.4	2.5	4.2	16.0	13.6
Azerbaijan	23.2	<2.5	24.1	18.0 (2013)	9.0	3.1 (2013)	6.2	13.0 (2013)
Georgia	13.7	7.0	14.7 (2005)	11.3 (2009)	3.0 (2005)	1.6 (2009)	21.0 (2005)	19.9 (2009)
Kazakhstan	5.9	<2.5	17.5 (2006)	8.0 (2015)	4.9 (2006)	3.1 (2015)	16.9 (2006)	9.3 (2015)
Kyrgyz Republic	16.3	6.4	18.1 (2006)	12.9 (2014)	3.4 (2006)	2.8 (2014)	10.7 (2006)	7.0 (2014)
Pakistan	23.4	19.9	41.5 (2001)	45.0 (2012)	14.2 (2001)	10.5 (2012)	4.8 (2001)	4.8 (2012)
Tajikistan	42.4	30.1	42.1	26.8 (2012)	9.4	9.9 (2012)	6.7 (2005)	6.6 (2012)
Turkmenistan	8.2	5.5	28.1	11.5 (2015)	7.1	4.2 (2015)	4.5 (2006)	5.9 (2015)
Uzbekistan	16.4	6.3	25.3 (2002)	...	8.9 (2002)	...	11.1 (2002)	...
East Asia								
China, People's Republic of	16.1	9.7	17.8	8.1 (2013)	2.5	1.9 (2013)	3.4	6.6 (2010)
Hong Kong, China	2.4	<2.5	...	...	...	...	...	...
Korea, Republic of	<2.5	<2.5	2.5 (2003)	2.5 (2010)	0.9 (2003)	1.2 (2010)	6.2 (2003)	7.3 (2010)
Mongolia	35.1	19.6	29.8	10.8 (2013)	7.1	1.0 (2013)	12.7	10.5 (2013)
Taipei,China	4.0	5.2	...	...	...	...	...	...
South Asia								
Bangladesh	20.8	15.1	50.8	36.1 (2014)	12.5	14.3 (2014)	0.9	1.4 (2014)
Bhutan	...	...	34.9 (2008)	33.6 (2010)	4.7 (2008)	5.9 (2010)	4.4 (2008)	7.6 (2010)
India	17.2	14.5	47.9 (2006)	38.4 (2015)	20.0 (2006)	21.0 (2015)	1.9 (2006)	2.1 (2015)
Maldives	14.0	8.5	31.9 (2001)	20.3 (2009)	13.4 (2001)	10.2 (2009)	3.9 (2001)	6.5 (2009)
Nepal	22.0	8.1	57.1 (2001)	35.8	11.3 (2001)	9.7	0.7 (2001)	1.2
Sri Lanka	29.6	22.1	18.4	17.3	15.5	15.1	1.0	2.0
Southeast Asia								
Brunei Darussalam	3.1	<2.5	...	19.7 (2009)	...	2.9 (2009)	...	8.3 (2009)
Cambodia	29.2	15.3	49.2	32.4 (2014)	16.9	9.6 (2014)	4.0	2.0 (2014)
Indonesia	17.8	7.9	42.4	36.4 (2013)	5.5	13.5 (2013)	1.5	11.5 (2013)
Lao People's Democratic Republic	37.6	17.1	48.2	43.8 (2011)	17.5	6.4 (2011)	2.7	2.0 (2011)
Malaysia	2.8	<2.5	17.2 (2006)	20.7	...	11.5	...	6.0
Myanmar	48.4	16.9	40.8	29.2	10.7	7.0	2.4	1.3
Philippines	20.4	13.8	33.8 (2003)	33.4 (2015)	6.0 (2003)	7.1 (2015)	2.4 (2003)	3.9 (2015)
Singapore	...	...	4.4	...	3.6	...	2.6	...
Thailand	18.8	9.5	15.7 (2006)	10.5	4.7 (2006)	5.4	8.0 (2006)	8.2
Viet Nam	24.3	10.7	43.4	24.6 (2015)	6.1	6.4 (2015)	2.5	5.3 (2015)
The Pacific								
Cook Islands	...	...	...	...	...	...	...	...
Fiji	4.8	4.6	7.5 (2004)	...	6.3 (2004)	...	5.1 (2004)	...
Kiribati	4.4	3.3	...	...	...	...	...	...
Marshall Islands	...	...	...	...	...	...	...	...
Micronesia, Federated States of	...	...	...	...	...	...	...	...
Nauru	...	...	24.0 (2007)	...	1.0 (2007)	...	2.8 (2007)	...
Palau	...	...	...	...	...	...	...	...
Papua New Guinea	...	...	43.9 (2005)	49.5 (2010)	4.4 (2005)	14.3 (2010)	3.4 (2005)	13.8 (2010)
Samoa	5.3	3.2	...	4.7 (2014)	...	3.7 (2014)	...	5.4 (2014)
Solomon Islands	15.1	13.9	32.8 (2007)	31.6 (2015)	4.3 (2007)	7.9 (2015)	2.5 (2007)	3.9 (2015)
Timor-Leste	40.8	26.9	55.7 (2002)	50.2 (2013)	13.7 (2002)	11.0 (2013)	5.7 (2002)	1.5 (2013)
Tonga	...	...	...	8.1 (2012)	...	5.2 (2012)	...	17.3 (2012)
Tuvalu	...	...	10.0 (2007)	...	3.3 (2007)	...	6.3 (2007)	...
Vanuatu	8.2	6.9	25.9 (2007)	28.5 (2013)	5.9 (2007)	4.4 (2013)	4.7 (2007)	4.6 (2013)
Developed ADB Member Economies								
Australia	<2.5	<2.5	2.0 (2007)	...	...	...	7.7 (2007)	...
Japan	<2.5	<2.5	...	7.1 (2010)	...	2.3 (2010)	...	1.5 (2010)
New Zealand	<2.5	<2.5	...	...	...	...	...	...

... = data not available, < = less than, ADB = Asian Development Bank.

a Data refer to 3-year average for 1999–2001.

b Data refer to 3-year average for 2014–2016.

c According to the World Health Organization, for some economies the estimates were adjusted where necessary to be nationally representative and to cover the age range 0–5 years, which might result in slight differences in prevalence from the survey results reported. Estimates for some economies are also "pending reanalysis." Details can be found in the "Notes" column of the joint child malnutrition dataset.

Sources: For Indicator 2.1.1: Food and Agriculture Organization of the United Nations. http://www.fao.org/faostat/ (accessed 23 July 2018). For Indicator 2.2.1, Indicator 2.2.2.a, Indicator 2.2.2.b: United Nations Children's Fund, World Health Organization, World Bank: Joint Child Malnutrition Estimates. http://www.who.int/ (accessed 31 July 2018).

Goal 2. End hunger, achieve food security and improved nutrition, and promote sustainable agriculture

Table 1.2.2: Selected Indicators for Sustainable Development Goal 2—Improved Agricultural Investment

ADB Regional Member	Target 2.a: Increase investment, including through enhanced international cooperation, in rural infrastructure, agricultural research and extension services, technology development, and plant and livestock gene banks in order to enhance agricultural productive capacity in developing countries, in particular least developed countries					
	2.a.1: The Agriculture Orientation Index for Government Expenditures				2.a.2: Total Official Flows to the Agriculture Sector[a] (constant 2016 $ million)	
	2001		2016		2000	2016
Developing ADB Member Economies						
Central and West Asia						
Afghanistan	0.1	(2003)	0.2	(2013)	4.2	396.1
Armenia	...		0.2		15.0	81.6
Azerbaijan	0.4	(2008)	0.4	(2015)	73.4	26.1
Georgia	0.1	(2003)	0.3		36.0	47.4
Kazakhstan	0.6	(2005)	0.5	(2015)	3.5	4.0
Kyrgyz Republic	0.1		0.1	(2011)	79.9	20.6
Pakistan	0.0		0.0		58.1	235.8
Tajikistan	...		...		22.9	31.0
Turkmenistan	...		...		0.0	1.5
Uzbekistan	...		0.9	(2015)	0.2	143.5
East Asia						
China, People's Republic of	0.3	(2007)	0.3	(2015)	324.5	439.2
Hong Kong, China	...		...		...	...
Korea, Republic of	1.5		2.2		...	...
Mongolia	0.2		0.1	(2015)	4.3	19.6
Taipei,China	...		...		...	...
South Asia						
Bangladesh	0.2		0.5	(2015)	331.5	264.6
Bhutan	0.3		0.8		5.8	6.0
India	0.2		0.4	(2013)	219.2	909.5
Maldives	0.2		0.1		0.0	1.5
Nepal	0.2	(2002)	0.3		70.6	108.7
Sri Lanka	0.4		0.7		51.8	46.9
Southeast Asia						
Brunei Darussalam	...		...		...	...
Cambodia	...		...		155.2	84.0
Indonesia	0.2	(2004)	0.1	(2013)	195.7	287.6
Lao People's Democratic Republic	...		...		27.1	73.4
Malaysia	0.4		0.4		8.2	3.3
Myanmar	...		...		2.1	220.2
Philippines	0.3		0.4		354.2	94.0
Singapore	2.0		7.1	(2015)	...	...
Thailand	0.9		0.8	(2015)	27.0	7.8
Viet Nam	0.1	(2006)	0.2	(2014)	100.6	266.3
The Pacific						
Cook Islands	...		...		0.0	0.0
Fiji	0.3	(2005)	0.3	(2015)	1.0	8.7
Kiribati	...		...		7.8	1.5
Marshall Islands	0.1	(2008)	0.2		3.4	0.3
Micronesia, Federated States of	...		0.1	(2015)	10.0	0.7
Nauru	...		...		0.2 (2003)	0.3
Palau	0.1	(2008)	0.1	(2015)	0.2	0.8
Papua New Guinea	...		...		56.3	18.2
Samoa	...		0.3		2.5	5.0
Solomon Islands	...		0.1	(2015)	3.3	12.0
Timor-Leste	1.4	(2008)	0.4	(2015)	8.3	23.5
Tonga	...		...		0.2	1.8
Tuvalu	...		...		7.6 (2001)	2.1
Vanuatu	0.1	(2005)	0.2	(2012)	3.6	2.6
Developed ADB Member Economies						
Australia	0.2		0.2		...	...
Japan	...		...		...	...
New Zealand	0.3	(2004)	...		...	...

... = data not available, 0.0 = magnitude is less than half of unit employed, $ = United States dollars, ADB = Asian Development Bank.

a Total official flows refer to official development assistance plus other official flows. Data refer to gross disbursements.

Sources: United Nations. Sustainable Development Goals Indicators Database. http://unstats.un.org/sdgs/indicators/database/ (accessed 13 July 2018); and Food and Agriculture Organization of the United Nations. FAOSTAT. http://www.fao.org/faostat/en/#data/IG (accessed 23 July 2018).

Table 1.3.1: Selected Indicators for Sustainable Development Goal 3—Maternal and Child Health

ADB Regional Member	Target 3.1: By 2030, reduce the global maternal mortality ratio to less than 70 per 100,000 live births				Target 3.2: By 2030, end preventable deaths of newborns and children under 5 years of age, with all countries aiming to reduce neonatal mortality to at least as low as 12 per 1,000 live births and under-5 mortality to at least as low as 25 per 1,000 live births			
	3.1.1: Maternal Mortality Ratio (per 100,000 live births)[a]		3.1.2: Proportion of Births Attended by Skilled Health Personnel (%)[b]		3.2.1: Under-5 Mortality Rate (per 1,000 live births)[a]		3.2.2: Neonatal Mortality Rate (per 1,000 live births)[a]	
	2000	2015	2000	2016	2000	2016	2000	2016
Developing ADB Member Economies								
Central and West Asia	**366**	**174**			**104**	**66**	**53**	**38**
Afghanistan	1,100	396	15.0 [c] (2002)	50.5 [d] (2015)	130	70	61	40
Armenia	40	25	96.8 [c]	99.8 [d]	30	13	16	7
Azerbaijan	48	25	80.7 [c]	99.8 [e]	74	31	34	18
Georgia	37	36	95.5 [e]	99.9 [c] (2015)	36	11	22	7
Kazakhstan	65	12	98.3 [e]	99.4 [c] (2015)	43	11	20	6
Kyrgyz Republic	74	76	98.6 [e]	98.4 [c] (2014)	49	21	22	12
Pakistan	306	178	22.9 [c]	52.1 [d] (2013)	113	79	60	46
Tajikistan	68	32	70.7 [c]	90.3 [e] (2014)	93	43	30	20
Turkmenistan	59	42	97.2 [c]	100.0 [c]	83	51	31	22
Uzbekistan	34	36	94.9 [c]	100.0 [e] (2015)	63	24	29	14
East Asia	**57**	**27**			**36**	**10**	**20**	**5**
China, People's Republic of	58	27	96.6 [e]	99.9 [e] (2015)	37	10	21	5
Hong Kong, China	6	2 * (2017)	...	...	...	...	2 [f]	1 [f] (2013)
Korea, Republic of	16	11	99.9	100.0 (2015)	8	3	4	2
Mongolia	161	44	96.6 [d]	98.9 [c] (2013)	63	18	25	10
Taipei,China	8	12 (2016)	...	...	...	...	...	2
South Asia	**377**	**174**			**90**	**42**	**44**	**25**
Bangladesh	399	176	12.1 [d]	49.8 [d]	87	34	43	20
Bhutan	423	148	23.7 [e]	89.0 [e]	77	32	32	18
India	374	174	42.5 [e]	85.7 [d]	92	43	45	25
Maldives	163	68	84.0 [c] (2004)	95.6 [c] (2014)	44	9	25	5
Nepal	548	258	11.9 [e]	58.0 [d]	82	35	40	21
Sri Lanka	57	30	96.0 [d]	...	16	9	10	5
Southeast Asia	**200**	**110**			**49**	**27**	**21**	**13**
Brunei Darussalam	31	23	99.2 [e]	100.0 [e]	12	10	5	4
Cambodia	484	161	31.8 [c]	89.0 [d] (2014)	107	31	36	16
Indonesia	265	126	63.5 [d]	92.6 [c]	52	26	22	14
Lao People's Democratic Republic	546	197	16.7 [c]	40.1 [c] (2012)	117	64	43	29
Malaysia	58	40	96.6 [e]	99.4 [e] (2015)	10	8	5	4
Myanmar	308	178	57.0 [c] (2001)	60.2 [d]	90	51	38	25
Philippines	124	114	58.0 [c]	72.8 [c] (2013)	40	27	17	13
Singapore	18	10	99.7 [g]	99.6 [g]	4	3	2	1
Thailand	25	20	99.3 [e]	99.1 [d]	23	12	14	7
Viet Nam	81	54	58.8 [c]	93.8 [c] (2014)	30	22	15	12
The Pacific	**346**	**192**			**72**	**49**	**27**	**21**
Cook Islands	...	...	98.0 [d]	100.0 [e] (2009)	17	8	9	4
Fiji	42	30	96.9 [g]	99.9 [e] (2015)	22	22	11	9
Kiribati	166	90	85.0 [d]	98.3 [e] (2010)	71	54	29	23
Marshall Islands	...	...	86.2 [c] (2007)	90.1 [c] (2011)	41	35	18	16
Micronesia, Federated States of	153	100	82.8 [c]	100.0 [e] (2009)	53	33	24	17
Nauru	...	...	97.4 [d] (2007)	...	41	35	25	22
Palau	...	...	100.0 [e]	100.0 [c]	27	16	14	8
Papua New Guinea	342	215	41.0 [e]	40.0 [c]	77	54	30	24
Samoa	93	51	80.0 [d]	82.5 [d] (2014)	22	17	12	9
Solomon Islands	214	114	43.0 [d] (2003)	86.2 [d] (2015)	30	26	12	10
Timor-Leste	694	215	24.0 [d] (2002)	56.7 [d]	109	50	38	22
Tonga	97	124	95.0 [d]	95.5 [c] (2012)	17	16	8	7
Tuvalu	...	...	100.0 [d]	...	42	25	25	17
Vanuatu	144	78	88.0 [d]	89.4 [d] (2013)	29	28	12	12
Developed ADB Member Economies	**10**	**5**			**5**	**3**	**2**	**1**
Australia	9	6	99.3 [g]	99.7 [g] (2015)	6	4	4	2
Japan	10	5	99.8 [g]	99.9 [g] (2015)	5	3	2	1
New Zealand	12	11	97.3 [g]	96.3 [g] (2015)	7	5	4	3
DEVELOPING ADB MEMBER ECONOMIES	**269**	**126**			**71**	**34**	**35**	**19**
ALL ADB REGIONAL MEMBERS	**264**	**123**			**69**	**33**	**35**	**19**
WORLD	**341**	**216**			**76**	**43**	**31**	**19**

... = data not available, * = provisional, preliminary, ADB = Asian Development Bank.

a   Regional aggregates are weighted averages estimated using population of annual live births for the respective year headings. The data for maternal, under-5, and neonatal deaths are from UNICEF Global databases. Aggregates are derived for reporting economies only. For maternal mortality ratio, aggregates for East Asia exclude Hong Kong, China and Taipei,China.
b   Based on population-based national household survey data and routine health systems.
c   Estimates are aligned with the standard definition of doctor, nurse, and/or midwife.
d   Includes other health personnel not in alignment with the standard definition.
e   No clear definition of health personnel.
f   Calculated based on known births and deaths.
g   Institutional birth including all deliveries that occurred at a health facility.

Sources: For Indicator 3.1.1: World Health Organization. Trends in Maternal Mortality: 1990 to 2015 Estimates by WHO, UNICEF, UNFPA, World Bank Group and the United Nations Population Division. For Hong Kong, China: Government of Hong Kong, China, Centre for Health Protection. https://www.chp.gov.hk/en/statistics/data/10/27/110.html (accessed 3 July 2018); and Department of Health. Annual Report 2013/2014. Supplementary Tables. http://www.dh.gov.hk/english/pub_rec/pub_rec_ar/pdf/1314/supplementary_table2013.pdf. For Taipei,China: Government of Taipei,China, Directorate-General of Budget, Accounting and Statistics. https://eng.dgbas.gov.tw/public/data/dgbas03/bs2/yearbook_eng/Yearbook2016.pdf. For Indicator 3.1.2: United Nations. Sustainable Development Goals Indicators Database. http://unstats.un.org/sdgs/indicators/database/ (accessed 13 July 2018). For Indicator 3.2.1 and Indicator 3.2.2: United Nations Inter-agency Group for Child Mortality Estimation. http://childmortality.org/ (accessed 7 June 2018); and United Nations International Children's Emergency Fund. Global Databases. http://www.data.unicef.org (accessed 5 July 2018). For Hong Kong, China: Government of Hong Kong, China, Department of Health. Annual Report 2013/2014. Supplementary Tables. Official website: http://www.dh.gov.hk/english/pub_rec/pub_rec.html (accessed 5 July 2018). For Taipei,China: Government of Taipei,China, Ministry of Health and Welfare. 2017 Annual Report. Official website: https://www.mohw.gov.tw/lp-137-2.html (accessed 5 July 2018).

Goal 3. Ensure healthy lives and promote well-being for all at all ages

Table 1.3.2: Selected Indicators for Sustainable Development Goal 3—Incidence of Communicable Diseases

| ADB Regional Member | Target 3.3: By 2030, end the epidemics of AIDS, tuberculosis, malaria, and neglected tropical diseases; and combat hepatitis, water-borne diseases, and other communicable diseases | | | | | |
| | 3.3.1: Number of New HIV Infections (per 1,000 uninfected population) | | 3.3.2: Tuberculosis Incidence (per 100,000 population) | | 3.3.3: Malaria Incidence (per 1,000 population) | |
	2000	2016	2000	2016	2000	2016
Developing ADB Member Economies						
Central and West Asia						
Afghanistan	0.01	0.03	190.0	189.0	140.6	30.8
Armenia	0.18	0.09	54.0	44.0	...	...
Azerbaijan	0.05	0.10	80.0	66.0	19.2	–
Georgia	0.08	0.28	254.0	92.0	12.2	–
Kazakhstan	0.06	0.16	166.0	67.0	...	...
Kyrgyz Republic	0.06	0.13	244.0	145.0	7.2	–
Pakistan	<0.01	0.10	275.0	268.0	21.1	10.6
Tajikistan	0.09	0.15	219.0	85.0	40.0	–
Turkmenistan	...	...	112.0	60.0	...	...
Uzbekistan	...	...	99.0	76.0	6.0	–
East Asia						
China, People's Republic of	...	...	109.0	64.0	0.0	–
Hong Kong, China	...	...	104.0	69.0	...	...
Korea, Republic of	...	...	49.0	77.0	2.5	0.3
Mongolia	<0.01	0.01	162.0	183.0	...	...
Taipei,China	...	...	...	...	...	...
South Asia						
Bangladesh	<0.01	<0.01	221.0	221.0	11.0	0.6
Bhutan	...	...	249.0	178.0	23.8	0.0
India	0.25	0.06	289.0	211.0	42.1	18.8
Maldives	...	...	59.0	49.0	...	...
Nepal	0.23	0.03	163.0	154.0	14.3	0.9
Sri Lanka	<0.01	0.03	66.0	65.0	114.2	–
Southeast Asia						
Brunei Darussalam	...	...	106.0	66.0	...	...
Cambodia	0.72	0.04	575.0	345.0	152.7	8.9
Indonesia	0.11	0.19	449.0	391.0	14.6	9.2
Lao People's Democratic Republic	0.13	0.10	330.0	175.0	69.8	7.8
Malaysia	0.54	0.19	75.0	92.0	15.7	0.2
Myanmar	0.84	0.22	411.0	361.0	80.0	7.2
Philippines	<0.01	0.11	590.0	554.0	4.9	0.5
Singapore	...	...	51.0	51.0	...	...
Thailand	0.58	0.10	241.0	172.0	11.8	1.6
Viet Nam	0.32	0.12	197.0	133.0	7.3	0.1
The Pacific						
Cook Islands	...	...	6.3	13.0	...	...
Fiji	...	0.12	22.0	59.0	...	...
Kiribati	...	...	373.0	566.0	...	...
Marshall Islands	...	...	81.0	422.0	...	...
Micronesia, Federated States of	...	...	106.0	177.0	...	...
Nauru	...	...	46.0	112.0	...	...
Palau	...	...	65.0	123.0	...	...
Papua New Guinea	0.85	0.37	432.0	432.0	285.4	179.4
Samoa	...	...	28.0	7.7	...	...
Solomon Islands	...	...	91.0	84.0	655.4	144.8
Timor-Leste	...	...	498.0 (2002)	498.0	912.6	0.9
Tonga	...	...	28.0	8.6	...	...
Tuvalu	...	...	195.0	207.0	...	...
Vanuatu	...	...	110.0	56.0	144.9	14.7
Developed ADB Member Economies						
Australia	0.05	0.05	6.3	6.1	...	...
Japan	...	...	36.0	16.0	...	...
New Zealand	...	...	10.0	7.3	...	...

... = data not available, < = less than, – = magnitude equals zero, 0.0 = magnitude is less than half of unit employed, ADB = Asian Development Bank.

Sources: The Joint United Nations Programme on HIV/AIDS (UNAIDS) http://aidsinfo.unaids.org/ (accessed 7 June 2018); World Health Organization. http://www.who.int/tb/country/data/download/en/ (accessed 7 June 2018); and United Nations. Sustainable Development Goals Indicators Database. http://unstats.un.org/sdgs/indicators/database/ (accessed 13 July 2018).

Table 1.3.3: Selected Indicators for Sustainable Development Goal 3—Mortality Rates, Reproductive Health

| ADB Regional Member | Target 3.4: By 2030, reduce by one third premature mortality from noncommunicable diseases through prevention and treatment, and promote mental health and well-being | | | | | Target 3.6: By 2020, halve the number of global deaths and injuries from road traffic accidents | |
| | 3.4.1: Mortality Rate Attributed to Cardiovascular Disease, Cancer, Diabetes, or Chronic Respiratory Disease (%) | | 3.4.2 Suicide Mortality Rate[a] (per 100,000 population) | | | 3.6.1: Death Rate Due to Road Traffic Injuries (per 100,000 population) | |
	2000	2016	2016 Total	Female	Male	2000	2013
Developing ADB Member Economies							
Central and West Asia							
Afghanistan	34.4	29.8	4.7	1.5	7.6	15.7	15.5
Armenia	27.8	22.3	6.6	2.8	10.8	20.6	18.3
Azerbaijan	29.3	22.2	2.6	1.1	4.2	7.9	10.0
Georgia	24.7	24.9	8.2	2.7	14.2	10.5	11.8
Kazakhstan	39.1	26.8	22.5	7.6	38.3	14.1	24.2
Kyrgyz Republic	31.4	24.9	8.3	3.5	13.2	12.0	22.0
Pakistan	26.7	24.7	2.9	3.0	2.7	14.8	14.2
Tajikistan	27.3	25.3	2.5	1.3	3.7	19.7	18.8
Turkmenistan	34.0	29.5	6.7	3.5	10.1	18.0	17.4
Uzbekistan	29.3	24.5	7.4	4.8	9.9	9.7	11.2
East Asia							
China, People's Republic of	21.5	17.0	9.7	10.3	9.1	18.0	18.8
Hong Kong, China	...	...	...	...	...	...	...
Korea, Republic of	16.5	7.8	26.9	15.4	38.4	26.4	12.0
Mongolia	38.9	30.2	13.0	3.5	22.6	18.7	21.0
Taipei,China	...	...	...	...	...	...	...
South Asia							
Bangladesh	21.4	21.6	5.9	7.0	4.7	14.3	13.6
Bhutan	30.8	23.3	11.4	8.5	14.0	16.5	15.1
India	26.6	23.3	16.3	14.7	17.8	16.3	16.6
Maldives	26.8	13.4	2.3	1.3	3.0	2.9	3.5
Nepal	27.3	21.8	8.8	7.9	9.7	16.9	17.0
Sri Lanka	21.5	17.4	14.6	6.4	23.5	18.3	17.4
Southeast Asia							
Brunei Darussalam	20.5	16.6	4.6	2.7	6.4	16.3	8.1
Cambodia	25.5	21.1	5.3	2.9	7.8	17.8	17.4
Indonesia	26.3	26.4	3.4	2.0	4.8	15.2	15.3
Lao People's Democratic Republic	29.2	27.0	8.6	5.7	11.4	14.0	14.3
Malaysia	20.3	17.2	5.5	3.2	7.8	26.6	24.0
Myanmar	25.0	24.2	7.8	9.5	5.9	21.8	20.3
Philippines	26.8	26.8	3.2	2.0	4.3	9.9	10.5
Singapore	16.8	9.3	9.9	6.1	13.8	6.7	3.6
Thailand	19.2	14.5	14.4	5.9	23.4	37.7	36.2
Viet Nam	18.6	17.1	7.3	3.7	10.9	23.6	24.5
The Pacific							
Cook Islands	...	...	...	...	...	5.6	24.2
Fiji	36.4	30.6	5.0	2.4	7.5	9.6	5.8
Kiribati	29.5	28.4	14.4	5.0	24.1	8.5	2.9
Marshall Islands	...	...	...	...	...	17.3	5.7
Micronesia, Federated States of	27.4	26.1	11.1	6.3	15.8	16.8	1.9
Nauru	...	...	...	...	...	19.9	19.9
Palau	...	...	...	...	...	15.6	4.8
Papua New Guinea	31.2	30.0	6.0	3.3	8.6	17.3	16.8
Samoa	29.5	20.6	4.4	1.9	6.7	16.6	15.8
Solomon Islands	31.2	23.8	4.7	2.6	6.8	18.7	19.2
Timor-Leste	26.8	19.9	4.6	2.9	6.2	17.1	16.6
Tonga	26.1	23.3	3.5	2.7	4.3	15.3	7.6
Tuvalu	...	...	...	...	...	21.2	20.3
Vanuatu	27.9	23.3	4.5	2.2	6.6	15.7	16.6
Developed ADB Member Economies							
Australia	13.1	9.1	13.2	7.0	19.5	9.5	5.4
Japan	11.4	8.4	18.5	11.4	26.0	12.3	4.7
New Zealand	15.9	10.1	12.1	6.6	17.9	12.1	6.0

continued on next page

Goal 3. Ensure healthy lives and promote well-being for all at all ages

Table 1.3.3: Selected Indicators for Sustainable Development Goal 3—Mortality Rates, Reproductive Health
(*continued*)

ADB Regional Member	Target 3.7: By 2030, ensure universal access to sexual and reproductive health-care services, including for family planning, information, and education, and the integration of reproductive health into natural strategies and programs				Target 3.9: By 2030, substantially reduce the number of deaths and illnesses from hazardous chemicals and air, water, and soil pollution and contamination	
	3.7.1: Proportion of Women of Reproductive Age (Aged 15–49 Years) Who Have Their Need for Family Planning Satisfied with Modern Methods		3.7.2: Adolescent Birth Rate (Aged 15-19 Years) per 1,000 Women in That Age Group		3.9.1: Mortality Rate Attributed to Household and Ambient Air Pollution (per 100,000 population)	3.9.2: Mortality Rate Attributed to Unsafe Water, Unsafe Sanitation, and Lack of Hygiene (per 100,000 population)
	2000	2016	2000	2015	2016	2016
Developing ADB Member Economies						
Central and West Asia						
Afghanistan	...	42.1	193.8	87.0 (2013)	95.1	13.9
Armenia	28.4	40.2	31.6	24.1 (2016)	80.5	0.2
Azerbaijan	17.8 (2001)	...	29.0	52.8 (2016)	54.9	1.1
Georgia	30.8	52.8 (2010)	39.9	43.6 (2016)	184.0	0.2
Kazakhstan	...	79.6 (2011)	33.0	31.0	56.8	0.4
Kyrgyz Republic	...	62.1 (2012)	34.7	38.1 (2016)	74.0	0.8
Pakistan	33.3 (2001)	47.0 (2013)	60.0 (2002)	44.0 (2011)	113.0	19.6
Tajikistan	...	50.8 (2012)	37.3	54.0 (2011)	70.5	2.7
Turkmenistan	70.9	75.6	26.1	28.0 (2014)	51.4	4.0
Uzbekistan	...	...	21.1	29.5 (2010)	54.1	0.4
East Asia						
China, People's Republic of	96.6 (2001)	...	6.0	9.2	139.8	0.6
Hong Kong, China	...	...	5.0	2.9	...	...
Korea, Republic of	...	...	2.5	1.3 (2016)	35.0	1.8
Mongolia	79.3 (2003)	68.3 (2013)	27.3	26.7 (2014)	97.1	1.3
Taipei,China	...	...	...	...	...	...
South Asia						
Bangladesh	60.7	72.5 (2014)	134.0	78.0 (2016)	103.4	11.9
Bhutan	...	84.6 (2010)	61.7	28.4 (2012)	87.5	3.9
India	61.7 (2004)	72.0	79.1	28.1 (2013)	140.8	18.6
Maldives	...	42.7 (2009)	28.9	12.9 (2014)	14.2	0.3
Nepal	52.8 (2001)	56.1 (2017)	71.0	88.0	133.1	19.8
Sri Lanka	56.2	74.1	30.3	...	09.5	1.2
Southeast Asia						
Brunei Darussalam	...	...	31.2	11.4	8.5	0.1
Cambodia	33.1	56.4 (2014)	52.0 (2003)	57.0 (2013)	87.3	6.5
Indonesia	77.1 (2003)	77.9 (2017)	54.0	48.0 (2010)	80.8	7.1
Lao People's Democratic Republic	40.3	61.3 (2012)	96.0	75.6 (2014)	109.9	11.3
Malaysia	...	...	12.0	11.5	35.2	0.4
Myanmar	58.5 (2001)	75.0	22.7	36.0 (2014)	116.1	12.6
Philippines	46.6 (2003)	51.5 (2013)	55.0 (2001)	47.0 (2016)	116.7	4.2
Singapore	...	...	7.7	2.7	39.3	0.1
Thailand	94.8 (2006)	89.2	31.1	42.5 (2016)	84.6	3.5
Viet Nam	66.6 (2002)	69.7 (2014)	24.0	30.1 (2014)	65.1	1.6
The Pacific						
Cook Islands	...	...	47.0 (2001)	67.0	...	...
Fiji	...	...	34.8 (2002)	40.0 (2014)	76.2	2.9
Kiribati	...	35.8 (2009)	42.0	49.0 (2010)	88.1	16.7
Marshall Islands	80.5 (2007)	...	127.0 (2005)	84.5 (2011)	...	...
Micronesia, Federated States of	...	...	57.9	44.0 (2009)	92.7	3.6
Nauru	42.5 (2007)	...	71.0	94.0	...	...
Palau	...	...	23.0 (2001)	27.0	...	...
Papua New Guinea	40.6 (2007)	...	70.0	...	89.6	16.3
Samoa	...	39.4 (2014)	33.6 (2001)	39.2 (2011)	62.3	1.5
Solomon Islands	60.0 (2007)	38.0 (2015)	70.0 (2004)	78.0 (2013)	66.9	6.2
Timor-Leste	...	46.1	78.3 (2001)	50.0 (2010)	76.6	9.9
Tonga	...	47.9 (2012)	18.7	30.0 (2011)	56.6	1.4
Tuvalu	41.0 (2007)	...	42.0 (2007)	28.0 (2012)	...	...
Vanuatu	...	50.7 (2013)	...	78.0 (2011)	75.8	10.4
Developed ADB Member Economies						
Australia	...	...	17.8	11.9	16.8	0.1
Japan	...	...	5.4	4.1	42.9	0.2
New Zealand	...	...	28.2	16.0 (2016)	13.6	0.1

... = data not available, ADB = Asian Development Bank.

a   Data refers to crude suicide rates (per 100,000 population).

Sources: For Indicator 3.4.1: World Health Organization. http://apps.who.int/gho/data/view.main.2485 (accessed 8 June 2018). For Indicator 3.4.2: World Health Organization. http://apps.who.int/gho/data/view.main.MHSUICIDEv/ (accessed 8 June 2018). For Indicator 3.6.1, Indicator 3.7.1, and Indicator 3.7.2: United Nations. Sustainable Development Goals Indicators Database. http://unstats.un.org/sdgs/indicators/database/ (accessed 13 July 2018). For Indicator 3.9.1: World Health Organization. http://apps.who.int/gho/data/node.sdg.3-9-data?lang=en (accessed 8 June 2018). For Indicator 3.9.2: World Health Organization. http://apps.who.int/gho/data/node.main.INADEQUATEWSH?lang=en (accessed 8 June 2018).

Table 1.4.1: Selected Indicators for Sustainable Development Goal 4—Early Childhood Education

ADB Regional Member	Target 4.2: By 2030, ensure that all girls and boys have access to quality early childhood development, care, and pre-primary education, so that they are ready for primary education 4.2.2: Participation Rate in Organized Learning (1 Year before the Official Primary Entry Age)[a,b] (%)											
	2000						2016					
	Total		Female		Male		Total		Female		Male	
Developing ADB Member Economies												
Central and West Asia												
Afghanistan	...		...		...		...		...		...	
Armenia	...		...		...		...		...		...	
Azerbaijan	15.8		16.1		15.6		24.9		25.1		24.8	
Georgia	46.1	(2004)	49.1	(2004)	43.4	(2004)	...		...		...	
Kazakhstan	...		...		...		72.9	(2017)	74.6	(2017)	71.2	(2017)
Kyrgyz Republic	42.4		43.2		41.6		72.4		73.5		71.4	
Pakistan	...		...		...		...		...		...	
Tajikistan	...		...		...		12.5	(2017)	11.6	(2017)	13.4	(2017)
Turkmenistan	...		...		...		...		...		...	
Uzbekistan	...		...		...		36.9	(2017)	36.4	(2017)	37.4	(2017)
East Asia												
China, People's Republic of	...		...		...		...		...		...	
Hong Kong, China	...		...		...		99.9		99.8		100.0	
Korea, Republic of	49.6	(2005)	49.6	(2005)	49.6	(2005)	90.8	(2015)	90.6	(2015)	91.0	(2015)
Mongolia	96.5	(2007)	100.0	(2007)	93.1	(2007)	91.4		91.6		91.3	
Taipei,China	...		...		...		...		...		...	
South Asia												
Bangladesh	...		...		...		59.7	(2011)	59.3	(2011)	60.0	(2011)
Bhutan	...		...		...		...		...		...	
India	...		...		...		...		...		...	
Maldives	69.5		70.0		69.1		98.4		98.3		98.4	
Nepal	...		...		...		84.9	(2017)	82.1	(2017)	87.6	(2017)
Sri Lanka	...		...		...		...		...		...	
Southeast Asia												
Brunei Darussalam	97.5	(2006)	95.0	(2006)	100.0	(2006)	90.0		89.8		90.1	
Cambodia	26.6	(2006)	27.2	(2006)	26.0	(2006)	43.0	(2012)	43.6	(2012)	42.5	(2012)
Indonesia	...		...		...		96.4		100.0		92.9	
Lao People's Democratic Republic	...		...		...		61.1		61.7		60.6	
Malaysia	76.9	(2002)	79.3	(2002)	74.6	(2002)	86.2		87.8		84.8	
Myanmar	...		...		...		...		...		...	
Philippines	24.0	(2001)	23.8	(2001)	24.1	(2001)	84.6	(2015)	85.5	(2015)	83.7	(2015)
Singapore	...		...		...		...		...		...	
Thailand	98.9	(2006)	100.0	(2006)	97.9	(2006)	95.7	(2015)	91.0	(2015)	100.0	(2015)
Viet Nam	78.7	(2006)	...		...		89.6		87.9		91.1	
The Pacific												
Cook Islands	...		...		...		99.1		100.0		98.3	
Fiji	48.6	(2004)	50.2	(2004)	47.1	(2004)	...		...		...	
Kiribati	...		...		...		...		...		...	
Marshall Islands	...		...		...		65.6		64.8		66.4	
Micronesia, Federated States of	...		...		...		76.4	(2015)	72.8	(2015)	79.8	(2015)
Nauru	89.4	(2007)	78.5	(2007)	100.0	(2007)	74.8		84.3		67.3	
Palau	...		...		...		90.4	(2014)	80.4	(2014)	100.0	(2014)
Papua New Guinea	...		...		...		...		...		...	
Samoa	...		...		...		31.7		33.0		30.6	
Solomon Islands	...		...		...		65.4	(2015)	65.7	(2015)	65.1	(2015)
Timor-Leste	...		...		...		57.3		58.9		55.8	
Tonga	...		...		...		...		...		...	
Tuvalu	...		...		...		96.3	(2015)	100.0	(2015)	92.9	(2015)
Vanuatu	...		...		...		...		...		...	
Developed ADB Member Economies												
Australia	52.6	(2001)	53.3	(2001)	52.0	(2001)	90.6		90.0		91.3	
Japan	95.4		...		...		91.1	(2015)	...		...	
New Zealand	...		...		...		93.3	(2015)	94.0	(2015)	92.7	(2015)

... = data not available, ADB = Asian Development Bank.

a   Covers participation in early childhood education and pre-primary education.

b   The indicator measures the exposure of children to organized learning, but not to the intensity of the learning programs.

Source: United Nations Educational, Scientific and Cultural Organization Institute for Statistics. http://uis.unesco.org/ (accessed 19 June 2018).

Goal 4. Ensure inclusive and equitable quality education and promote lifelong learning opportunities for all

Table 1.4.2: Selected Indicators for Sustainable Development Goal 4—Teacher Training and Supply

ADB Regional Member	Target 4.c: By 2030, substantially increase the supply of qualified teachers, including through international cooperation for teacher training in developing countries, especially least developed countries and small island developing states							
	4.c.1a: Proportion of Teachers in Preprimary Education Who Have Received at least the Minimum Organized Teacher Training (% of total teachers)		4.c.1b: Proportion of Teachers in Primary Education Who Have Received at least the Minimum Organized Teacher Training (% of total teachers)		4.c.1c: Proportion of Teachers in Lower Secondary Education Who Have Received at least the Minimum Organized Teacher Training (% of total teachers)		4.c.1d: Proportion of Teachers in Upper Secondary Education Who Have Received at least the Minimum Organized Teacher Training (% of total teachers)	
	2000	2016	2000	2016	2000	2016	2000	2016
Developing ADB Member Economies								
Central and West Asia								
Afghanistan	97.1 (2002)	80.5	66.7 (2004)	...	...	...	...	...
Armenia	79.1	88.0	99.9	89.5	...	91.6	...	...
Azerbaijan	...	...	...	...	...	...	...	...
Georgia	99.1	...	94.7	94.6 (2009)	76.8	94.6 (2009)	93.0	94.8 (2009)
Kazakhstan	...	100.0 (2014)	...	100.0 (2017)	...	...	...	...
Kyrgyz Republic	32.1	46.2 (2011)	...	20.9	...	...	...	...
Pakistan	...	...	78.0 (2004)	75.4	...	57.9	...	...
Tajikistan	91.3 (2001)	100.0	81.6 (2001)	100.0 (2017)	94.0 (2003)	...	94.3 (2003)	...
Turkmenistan	...	...	...	...	...	...	...	...
Uzbekistan	100.0 (2006)	98.5 (2017)	100.0 (2006)	98.9 (2017)	...	99.0 (2017)	...	93.4 (2017)
East Asia								
China, People's Republic of	...	...	...	...	...	...	...	...
Hong Kong, China	...	...	87.5	96.6	...	...	...	...
Korea, Republic of	...	...	...	...	...	...	...	...
Mongolia	100.0	100.0	100.0	100.0	100.0	...	100.0	...
Taipei,China	...	...	...	...	...	...	...	...
South Asia								
Bangladesh	...	...	53.4 (2005)	50.4	36.8	67.2	22.4	58.5
Bhutan	93.8	100.0	94.8	100.0	93.5 (2005)	100.0	72.2 (2008)	100.0
India	...	...	...	69.5	...	77.0	...	...
Maldives	47.2	80.7 (2015)	66.5	82.8 (2015)	76.3	93.3 (2015)	54.3 (2002)	...
Nepal	72.6 (2008)	88.7 (2017)	15.4 (2001)	97.3 (2017)	32.6	89.5 (2017)	28.5 (2002)	88.0 (2017)
Sri Lanka	...	...	...	70.2	...	47.0	...	...
Southeast Asia								
Brunei Darussalam	64.4 (2005)	59.4	84.5 (2005)	84.9	...	92.6	...	90.6
Cambodia	98.1 (2001)	100.0	95.9 (2001)	100.0	99.7 (2001)	100.0	99.1 (2001)	...
Indonesia	...	...	...	...	...	...	...	...
Lao People's Democratic Republic	83.1	90.0	76.7	97.5	98.5	96.5	95.6	98.8
Malaysia	...	95.7	97.9	99.7	...	...	...	...
Myanmar	50.3 (2006)	48.4 (2014)	62.7	97.8 (2017)	62.1	89.1 (2017)	97.1	98.4 (2017)
Philippines	...	100.0 (2015)	...	100.0 (2015)	...	...	...	...
Singapore	...	...	...	...	...	...	...	...
Thailand	...	...	...	100.0 (2015)	...	100.0 (2015)	...	100.0 (2015)
Viet Nam	50.5	98.4	80.0	99.8	86.3	99.5	...	...
The Pacific								
Cook Islands	60.9 (2005)	78.1	79.2 (2007)	95.3	...	...	...	...
Fiji	...	...	97.8 (2008)	100.0 (2012)	...	100.0 (2012)	94.8 (2008)	100.0 (2012)
Kiribati	...	...	93.9 (2005)	72.7	83.6 (2005)	86.7 (2014)	43.1 (2005)	...
Marshall Islands	100.0 (2002)	...	...	...	...	...	...	...
Micronesia, Federated States of	...	...	...	...	...	...	...	...
Nauru	77.5 (2006)	100.0	74.2 (2007)	100.0	...	100.0	...	100.0
Palau	...	...	...	...	...	...	...	...
Papua New Guinea	...	...	...	100.0 (2012)	...	100.0 (2012)	...	100.0 (2012)
Samoa	...	100.0	...	...	...	...	...	79.5
Solomon Islands	...	59.5 (2014)	...	65.6	...	82.2	...	63.0 (2015)
Timor-Leste	...	...	...	...	...	...	...	...
Tonga	...	100.0 (2012)	...	97.1 (2014)	...	...	...	...
Tuvalu	...	74.6 (2014)	...	...	...	...	...	...
Vanuatu	100.0 (2007)	46.0 (2015)	100.0 (2007)	27.9 (2015)	...	21.5 (2015)	...	20.5 (2015)
Developed ADB Member Economies								
Australia	...	...	...	...	...	...	...	...
Japan	...	...	...	...	...	...	...	...
New Zealand	...	...	...	...	...	...	...	...

... = data not available, ADB = Asian Development Bank.

Source: United Nations Educational, Scientific and Cultural Organization. Institute for Statistics. http://data.uis.unesco.org/ (accessed 19 June 2018).

Table 1.5.1: Selected Indicators for Sustainable Development Goal 5—Early Marriage and Women in Leadership

ADB Regional Member	Target 5.3: Eliminate all harmful practices such as child, early, and forced marriage, and female genital mutilation				Target 5.5: Ensure women's full and effective participation in, and equal opportunities for leadership at, all levels of decision-making in political, economic, and public life		
	5.3.1: Proportion of Women Aged 20-24 Years Who Were Married or in a Union (%)				5.5.1.a: Proportion of Seats Held by Women in National Parliaments (%)		5.5.2: Proportion of Women in Managerial Positions (%)
	Before Age 15		Before Age 18				
	2000	2015	2000	2015	2000	2017	2016
Developing ADB Member Economies							
Central and West Asia							
Afghanistan	...	8.8	...	34.8	27.3 (2006)	27.7	...
Armenia	...	...	...	5.3 (2016)	3.1	18.1	29.1 (2015)
Azerbaijan	...	1.9 (2011)	...	11.0 (2011)	10.4	16.8	34.9
Georgia	...	1.1 (2010)	...	14.0 (2010)	7.2	16.0	...
Kazakhstan	...	0.2	...	7.0	10.4	27.1	37.1 (2015)
Kyrgyz Republic	...	0.9 (2014)	...	11.6 (2014)	2.3	19.2	34.9
Pakistan	...	2.8 (2013)	...	21.0 (2013)	21.6 (2003)	20.6	2.9
Tajikistan	...	0.1 (2012)	...	11.6 (2012)	15.0	19.0	14.8 (2009)
Turkmenistan	...	...	...	5.7 (2016)	26.0	25.8	...
Uzbekistan	0.3 (2006)	...	7.2 (2006)	...	7.2	16.0	...
East Asia							
China, People's Republic of	...	...	...	...	21.8	24.2	...
Hong Kong, China	...	...	...	...	...	...	...
Korea, Republic of	...	...	...	...	5.9	17.0	10.5 (2015)
Mongolia	...	0.1 (2013)	...	5.2 (2013)	10.5	17.1	40.8
Taipei,China	...	...	...	...	...	...	...
South Asia							
Bangladesh	...	22.4 (2014)	...	58.6 (2014)	9.1	20.3	11.5 (2017)
Bhutan	...	6.2 (2010)	...	25.8 (2010)	9.3	8.5	18.5 (2015)
India	...	6.6 (2016)	...	27.3 (2016)	9.0	11.8	12.9 (2012)
Maldives	...	0.3 (2009)	...	3.9 (2009)	6.0	5.9	18.5 (2014)
Nepal	...	7.0 (2016)	...	39.5 (2016)	5.9	29.6	...
Sri Lanka	1.7 (2007)	...	11.8 (2007)	...	4.9	5.8	24.8 (2014)
Southeast Asia							
Brunei Darussalam	...	...	...	...	...	9.1	33.6 (2014)
Cambodia	...	1.9 (2014)	...	18.5 (2014)	7.4	20.3	30.9 (2012)
Indonesia	...	1.1 (2013)	...	13.6 (2013)	8.0	19.8	22.4 (2015)
Lao People's Democratic Republic	...	8.9 (2012)	...	35.4 (2012)	25.2 (2007)	27.5	31.8 (2010)
Malaysia	...	...	...	...	10.4	10.4	20.4
Myanmar	...	1.9	...	16.0	...	10.2	28.4 (2015)
Philippines	...	2.0 (2013)	...	15.0 (2013)	11.3	29.5	49.0
Singapore	...	...	...	...	4.3	23.8	34.0 (2015)
Thailand	...	4.4	...	22.5	4.8	4.8	32.4
Viet Nam	...	0.9 (2014)	...	10.6 (2014)	26.0	26.7	26.1
The Pacific							
Cook Islands	...	...	...	...	...	...	...
Fiji	...	...	...	...	5.7 (2003)	16.0	38.9
Kiribati	...	2.8 (2009)	...	20.3 (2009)	4.9	6.5	36.5 (2010)
Marshall Islands	5.5 (2007)	...	26.3 (2007)	...	3.0	9.1	...
Micronesia, Federated States of	...	...	...	...	...	...	...
Nauru	1.9 (2007)	...	26.8 (2007)	...	...	10.5	...
Palau	...	...	...	...	...	12.5	...
Papua New Guinea	2.1 (2006)	...	21.3 (2006)	...	1.8	2.7	18.1 (2010)
Samoa	...	0.7 (2014)	...	10.8 (2014)	8.2	10.0	47.3 (2014)
Solomon Islands	...	5.6	...	21.3	2.0	2.0	...
Timor-Leste	...	3.0 (2010)	...	18.9 (2010)	29.2 (2007)	32.3	32.9 (2013)
Tonga	...	0.3 (2012)	...	5.6 (2012)	...	3.8	...
Tuvalu	...	...	9.9 (2007)	...	...	6.7	...
Vanuatu	...	2.5 (2013)	...	21.4 (2013)	...	...	28.5 (2009)
Developed ADB Member Economies							
Australia	...	...	...	...	23.0	28.7	36.6
Japan	...	...	...	...	7.3	10.1	13.0
New Zealand	...	...	...	...	30.8	38.3	...

... = data not available, ADB = Asian Development Bank.

Sources: United Nations. Sustainable Development Goals Indicators Database.https://unstats.un.org/sdgs/indicators/database (accessed 13 July 2018); and Women in National Parliaments. http://www.ipu.org/wmn-e/arc/classif011216.htm (accessed 9 July 2018). For the Cook Islands, the Federated States of Micronesia, the Marshall Islands, Nauru, Palau, Solomon Islands, Tonga, Tuvalu: National Minimum Development Indicators - Secretariat of the Pacific Community. http://www.spc.int/nmdi/mdg3 (accessed 17 June 2018).

Goal 6. Ensure availability and sustainable management of water and sanitation for all

Table 1.6.1: Selected Indicators for Sustainable Development Goal 6—Clean Water and Sanitation

| ADB Regional Member | Target 6.1: By 2030, achieve universal and equitable access to safe and affordable drinking water for all 6.1.1: Proportion of Population Using Safely Managed Drinking Water Services (%) | | | | | |
| | 2000 | | | 2015 | | |
	Total	Urban	Rural	Total	Urban	Rural
Developing ADB Member Economies						
Central and West Asia						
Afghanistan	...	...	...	...	...	...
Armenia	26.7	...	...	60.6	...	...
Azerbaijan	51.4	...	...	71.5	...	...
Georgia	73.9	...	...	73.0	...	...
Kazakhstan	...	...	...	...	...	...
Kyrgyz Republic	46.4	80.4	27.8	66.3	92.7	51.6
Pakistan	38.1	51.1	31.6	35.6	40.7	32.4
Tajikistan	37.2	...	...	47.4	...	...
Turkmenistan	67.3	87.3	50.2	86.1	85.5	86.8
Uzbekistan	51.4	83.5	32.3	51.2 (2012)	86.5 (2012)	31.1 (2012)
East Asia						
China, People's Republic of	...	93.9	...	...	91.3	...
Hong Kong, China	98.0	98.0	...	100.0	100.0	...
Korea, Republic of	96.8 (2002)	...	...	98.0	...	...
Mongolia	...	...	...	...	...	...
Taipei,China	...	...	...	...	...	...
South Asia						
Bangladesh	55.9	44.5	59.3	55.7	44.6	61.4
Bhutan	27.2	44.4	21.3	34.2	44.6	27.6
India	...	...	29.3	...	...	49.5
Maldives	...	...	...	...	...	...
Nepal	24.0	35.1	22.3	26.8	33.8	25.1
Sri Lanka	...	84.6	...	...	92.6	...
Southeast Asia						
Brunei Darussalam	...	...	...	...	...	...
Cambodia	16.9	43.3	10.8	24.1	55.3	15.9
Indonesia	...	...	...	...	...	...
Lao People's Democratic Republic	...	...	...	...	...	...
Malaysia	93.8	...	...	92.1	...	...
Myanmar	...	...	...	...	...	...
Philippines	...	...	...	...	...	...
Singapore	100.0	100.0	...	100.0	100.0	...
Thailand	...	...	...	...	...	...
Viet Nam	...	...	...	...	...	...
The Pacific						
Cook Islands	...	...	...	...	...	...
Fiji	...	...	...	...	...	...
Kiribati	...	...	...	...	...	...
Marshall Islands	...	...	...	...	...	...
Micronesia, Federated States of	...	...	...	...	...	...
Nauru	...	...	...	...	...	...
Palau	...	...	...	...	...	...
Papua New Guinea	...	...	...	...	...	...
Samoa	...	...	...	...	...	...
Solomon Islands	...	...	...	...	...	...
Timor-Leste	...	...	...	...	...	...
Tonga	...	...	...	...	...	...
Tuvalu	...	...	...	...	...	...
Vanuatu	...	...	...	...	...	...
Developed ADB Member Economies						
Australia	...	98.2	...	...	98.8	...
Japan	96.7	...	...	97.2	...	...
New Zealand	76.7	...	...	100.0	...	...

continued on next page

Goal 6. Ensure availability and sustainable management of water and sanitation for all

Table 1.6.1: Selected Indicators for Sustainable Development Goal 6—Clean Water and Sanitation (continued)

ADB Regional Member	Target 6.2: By 2030, achieve access to adequate and equitable sanitation and hygiene for all and end open defecation, paying special attention to the needs of women and girls and those in vulnerable situations					
	6.2.1a: Proportion of Population Using Safely Managed Sanitation Services (%)					
	2000			2015		
	Total	Urban	Rural	Total	Urban	Rural
Developing ADB Member Economies						
Central and West Asia						
Afghanistan	...	...	...	...	...	...
Armenia	...	...	...	...	...	...
Azerbaijan	...	71.2	...	...	73.4	...
Georgia	...	6.2	...	...	17.0	...
Kazakhstan	...	69.3	...	...	67.3	...
Kyrgyz Republic	...	...	...	...	...	...
Pakistan	...	...	...	...	...	...
Tajikistan	...	...	...	...	...	...
Turkmenistan	...	...	...	...	...	...
Uzbekistan	...	...	...	...	...	...
East Asia						
China, People's Republic of	29.1	26.1	30.5	59.7	73.4	42.0
Hong Kong, China	...	...	...	...	...	...
Korea, Republic of	85.6	...	...	98.5	...	...
Mongolia	...	...	...	...	...	...
Taipei,China	...	...	...	...	...	...
South Asia						
Bangladesh	...	...	15.2	...	...	32.1
Bhutan	...	...	...	...	...	...
India	...	...	9.5	...	...	30.5
Maldives	...	...	...	...	...	...
Nepal	...	...	...	...	...	...
Sri Lanka	...	...	...	...	...	...
Southeast Asia						
Brunei Darussalam	...	...	...	...	...	...
Cambodia	...	...	...	...	...	...
Indonesia	...	...	...	...	...	...
Lao People's Democratic Republic	...	...	...	...	...	...
Malaysia	78.1	...	...	81.9	...	...
Myanmar	...	...	...	...	...	...
Philippines	...	...	...	...	...	...
Singapore	100.0	100.0	...	100.0	100.0	...
Thailand	...	...	...	...	...	...
Viet Nam	...	...	...	...	...	...
The Pacific						
Cook Islands	...	...	...	...	...	...
Fiji	...	...	...	...	...	...
Kiribati	...	...	...	...	...	...
Marshall Islands	...	...	...	...	...	...
Micronesia, Federated States of	...	...	...	...	...	...
Nauru	...	...	...	...	...	...
Palau	16.8	12.1	...	19.6	16.0	...
Papua New Guinea	...	...	...	...	...	...
Samoa	...	...	...	...	...	...
Solomon Islands	...	...	...	...	...	...
Timor-Leste	...	...	...	...	...	...
Tonga	...	...	...	...	...	...
Tuvalu	7.6 (2001)	6.8 (2001)	8.3 (2001)	9.0	5.6	14.0
Vanuatu	...	...	...	...	...	...
Developed ADB Member Economies						
Australia	65.5	...	...	74.2	...	...
Japan	98.2	...	...	99.8	...	...
New Zealand	75.5	...	...	75.9	...	...

continued on next page

Goal 6. Ensure availability and sustainable management of water and sanitation for all

Table 1.6.1: Selected Indicators for Sustainable Development Goal 6—Clean Water and Sanitation (continued)

ADB Regional Member	Target 6.4: By 2030, substantially increase water-use efficiency across all sectors and ensure sustainable withdrawals and supply of freshwater to address water scarcity and substantially reduce the number of people suffering from water scarcity				Target 6.a: By 2030, expand international cooperation and capacity-building support to developing countries in water- and sanitation-related activities and programmes, including water harvesting, desalination, water efficiency, wastewater treatment, and recycling and reuse technologies			
	6.4.2: Level of Water Stress, Freshwater Withdrawal as a Proportion of Available Freshwater Resources (%)				6.a.1: Amount of Water- and Sanitation-Related Official Development Assistance Part of a Government-Coordinated Spending Plan ($ million)			
	2000		**2015**		**2000**		**2016**	
Developing ADB Member Economies								
Central and West Asia								
Afghanistan	43.7		...		4.3		152.6	
Armenia	35.0	(2002)	66.0		12.7		32.8	
Azerbaijan	44.7	(2002)	53.1	(2012)	48.4		88.5	
Georgia	4.5	(2005)	...		0.8		60.9	
Kazakhstan	26.3	(2002)	28.1	(2010)	7.0		0.2	
Kyrgyz Republic	57.5		...		13.8		39.0	
Pakistan	96.4		...		14.6		200.5	
Tajikistan	74.4		...		15.2		56.6	
Turkmenistan	145.5		...		0.0		0.2	(2011)
Uzbekistan	151.8	(2001)	...		2.2		108.3	
East Asia								
China, People's Republic of	27.2		29.4		996.2		86.8	
Hong Kong, China	...		...		...		...	
Korea, Republic of	57.8	(2002)	...		...		...	
Mongolia	2.4	(2006)	2.4	(2009)	0.3		6.5	
Taipei,China	...		...		...		...	
South Asia								
Bangladesh	3.8	(2008)	...		86.0		278.4	
Bhutan	0.6	(2008)	...		5.5		4.3	
India	42.0		44.5	(2010)	170.1		554.4	
Maldives	15.7	(2008)	...		0.6	(2001)	3.5	
Nepal	5.9		...		57.7		128.1	
Sri Lanka	34.2		...		31.7		121.8	
Southeast Asia								
Brunei Darussalam	...		1.9	(2014)	...		...	
Cambodia	0.6	(2006)	...		23.0		74.6	
Indonesia	9.2		...		82.6		138.8	
Lao People's Democratic Republic	1.4	(2005)	...		36.6		33.2	
Malaysia	2.8		...		543.4		22.0	
Myanmar	3.7		...		1.4		90.1	
Philippines	24.2	(2006)	25.1	(2009)	19.3		112.9	
Singapore	...		31.7	(2014)	...		...	
Thailand	17.5	(2007)	...		80.4		6.0	
Viet Nam	12.8	(2005)	...		216.0		610.6	
The Pacific								
Cook Islands	...		...		0.4		3.3	
Fiji	0.4		...		0.4		2.8	
Kiribati	...		...		0.1		3.5	
Marshall Islands	...		...		0.1		0.6	
Micronesia, Federated States of	...		...		0.0	(2003)	0.7	
Nauru	...		...		0.1		1.8	
Palau	...		...		0.0	(2003)	7.4	
Papua New Guinea	0.1		...		12.0		37.2	
Samoa	...		...		0.3		18.0	
Solomon Islands	...		...		2.1		5.3	
Timor-Leste	14.3	(2004)	...		3.7		15.3	
Tonga	...		...		10.6		1.4	
Tuvalu	...		...		0.1		1.3	
Vanuatu	...		...		0.1		2.5	
Developed ADB Member Economies								
Australia	5.9	(2001)	4.6		...		...	
Japan	29.6	(2002)	28.5	(2009)	...		...	
New Zealand	2.6	(2006)	2.7	(2010)	...		...	

... = data not available, 0.0 = magnitude is less than half of unit employed, $ = United States dollars, ADB = Asian Development Bank.

Sources: Food and Agriculture Organization of the United Nations. AQUASTAT. http://www.fao.org/nr/water/aquastat/data/query/results.html (accessed 2 August 2018); United Nations. Sustainable Development Goals Indicators Database. https://unstats.un.org/sdgs/indicators/database/ (accessed 13 July 2018); and World Health Organization and United Nations Children's Fund. Joint Monitoring Programme for Water Supply, Sanitation, and Hygiene. https://washdata.org/data/ (accessed 28 June 2018).

Goal 7. Ensure access to affordable, reliable, sustainable and modern energy for all

Table 1.7.1: Selected Indicators for Sustainable Development Goal 7—Affordable and Clean Energy

ADB Regional Member	Target 7.1: By 2030, ensure universal access to affordable, reliable, and modern energy services						7.1.2: Proportion of Population with Primary Reliance on Clean Fuels and Technology (%)		Target 7.2: By 2030, increase substantially the share of renewable energy in the global energy mix — 7.2.1: Renewable Energy Share in the Total Final Energy Consumption (%)		Target 7.3: By 2030, double the global rate of improvement in energy efficiency — 7.3.1: Energy Intensity Measured in Terms of Primary Energy and GDP (MJ/$ 2011 PPP GDP)	
	7.1.1: Proportion of Population with Access to Electricity (%)											
	Total		Urban		Rural							
	2000	2016	2000	2016	2000	2016	2000	2016	2000	2015	2000	2015
Developing ADB Member Economies												
Central and West Asia												
Afghanistan	23.0 [a]	84.1	74.0 [a]	98.0	13.0 [a]	79.0	8.8	32.4	54.2	18.4	1.7	2.5
Armenia	98.9	100.0	99.1	100.0	98.6	100.0	82.0	96.9	7.2	15.8	9.4	5.4
Azerbaijan	98.9	100.0	99.7	100.0	97.8	100.0	73.2	95.5	2.1	2.3	13.2	3.7
Georgia	98.8	100.0	99.0	100.0	98.5	100.0	41.2	77.8	47.3	28.7	8.3	5.8
Kazakhstan	99.0	100.0	99.7	100.0	98.2	100.0	82.9	95.3	2.5	1.6	10.1	7.9
Kyrgyz Republic	99.7	100.0	99.9	100.0	99.7	100.0	51.7	81.3	35.2	23.3	9.6	8.6
Pakistan	75.3	99.1	95.8	99.7	65.1	98.8	22.6	43.3	51.0	46.5	5.5	4.4
Tajikistan	98.5	100.0	99.7	100.0	98.0	100.0	38.7	80.4	62.4	44.7	12.3	5.0
Turkmenistan	99.6	100.0	99.7	100.0	99.6	100.0	96.3	99.3	0.1	0.0	25.9	13.9
Uzbekistan	99.6	100.0	99.9	100.0	99.5	100.0	79.6	92.1	1.2	3.0	34.5	10.0
East Asia												
China, People's Republic of	96.2	100.0	100.0	100.0	94.1	100.0	46.8	59.3	29.7	12.4	10.1	6.7
Hong Kong, China	100.0	100.0	100.0	100.0	100.0	100.0	...	...	0.6	0.9	2.5	1.5
Korea, Republic of	100.0	100.0	100.0	100.0	100.0	100.0	96.2	96.7	0.7	2.7	8.1	6.5
Mongolia	67.3	81.8	99.0	95.8	25.1	44.2	21.8	42.8	5.7	3.4	9.0	6.1
Taipei,China	...	...	...	...	...	...	...	...	1.3	2.1	...	...
South Asia												
Bangladesh	32.0	75.9	81.2	94.0	20.5	68.9	7.2	17.7	59.0	34.7	3.5	3.1
Bhutan	34.9	100.0	96.3	100.0	14.0	100.0	31.7	52.5	91.4	86.9	21.8	10.4
India	59.4	84.5	88.7	98.4	48.2	77.6	22.2	41.0	51.6	36.0	7.0	4.7
Maldives	83.8	100.0	98.3	100.0	78.2	100.0	32.2	93.8	2.1	1.0	3.6	3.8
Nepal	27.5	90.7	84.1	94.5	18.8	85.2	14.9	27.6	88.3	85.3	9.3	7.4
Sri Lanka	69.6	95.6	87.7	100.0	65.5	94.6	15.6	26.3	64.2	52.9	3.3	2.1
Southeast Asia												
Brunei Darussalam	100.0	100.0	100.0	100.0	100.0	100.0	100.0	100.0	–	0.0	3.7	3.7
Cambodia	16.6	49.8	60.6	100.0	9.0	36.5	4.7	17.7	81.1	64.9	8.5	5.8
Indonesia	86.3	97.6	95.4	100.0	79.7	94.8	5.4	58.4	45.6	36.9	5.3	3.5
Lao People's Democratic Republic	43.2	87.1	96.0	97.4	28.3	80.3	4.0	5.6	85.5	59.3	5.6	5.2
Malaysia	97.0	100.0	98.0	100.0	95.4	100.0	94.5	96.3	6.7	5.2	5.4	4.7
Myanmar	44.1	57.0	85.4	89.5	28.9	39.8	4.7	18.4	80.2	61.5	8.9	3.1
Philippines	73.5	91.0	89.7	96.9	58.5	86.3	36.3	43.2	34.8	27.5	5.1	3.1
Singapore	100.0	100.0	100.0	100.0	100.0	100.0	100.0	100.0	0.3	0.7	3.8	2.4
Thailand	82.1	100.0	99.9	99.9	87.0	100.0	68.0	74.4	22.0	22.9	5.2	5.4
Viet Nam	86.2	100.0	99.0	100.0	82.1	100.0	14.4	66.9	58.0	35.0	5.8	5.9
The Pacific												
Cook Islands	97.6	100.0	97.7	100.0	97.3	100.0	82.9	84.4	–	1.3	...	...
Fiji	75.4	98.6	91.4	99.2	60.7	98.0	31.1	39.6	52.9	31.3	4.0	4.9
Kiribati	52.3	84.9	93.3	88.4	21.5	82.2	2.3	5.5	4.8	4.3	2.8	4.1
Marshall Islands	68.3	93.1	89.2	94.6	23.2	89.1	13.2	65.4	19.6	11.2	10.6	11.3
Micronesia, Federated States of	46.0	75.4	70.0	91.9	10.0	70.7	10.9	12.0	1.2	1.2	5.5	6.6
Nauru	100.0	99.2	97.4	99.4	...	...	73.9	91.3	–	0.1	...	...
Palau	98.4	99.3	99.4	99.6	96.2	97.2	64.4	86.9	–	–	11.1	10.2
Papua New Guinea	12.2	22.9	63.3	72.7	4.4	15.5	6.8	13.4	66.4	52.5	9.9	9.3
Samoa	87.6	100.0	98.4	99.7	84.6	100.0	20.2	32.3	45.4	34.3	4.4	5.2
Solomon Islands	6.6	47.9	59.0	69.6	2.0	41.5	6.3	8.5	66.9	63.3	7.7	5.0
Timor-Leste	19.6	63.4	71.7	91.7	2.9	49.2	2.3	6.9	48.3 [b]	18.2	2.9	3.0
Tonga	85.4	97.0	96.9	98.6	82.0	96.6	48.0	59.2	2.5	1.9	3.2	3.0
Tuvalu	94.3	99.4	95.6	100.0	93.2	98.5	18.6	50.4	–	8.2	3.3	3.9
Vanuatu	22.3	57.8	78.3	91.4	6.8	46.4	11.8	12.6	48.7	36.1	4.0	3.9
Developed ADB Member Economies												
Australia	100.0	100.0	100.0	100.0	100.0	100.0	100.0	100.0	8.4	9.2	6.4	5.0
Japan	100.0	100.0	100.0	100.0	100.0	100.0	100.0	100.0	3.9	6.3	5.0	3.7
New Zealand	100.0	100.0	100.0	100.0	100.0	100.0	100.0	100.0	29.0	30.8	6.6	5.4

... = data not available, – = magnitude equals zero, 0.0 = magnitude is less than half of unit employed, $ = United States dollars, ADB = Asian Development Bank, GDP = gross domestic product, MJ = megajoule, PPP = purchasing power parity.

a   Data is for 2005.
b   Data is for 2002.

Sources: World Bank Group-administered Energy Sector Management Assistance Program. https://trackingsdg7.esmap.org/downloads (accessed 19 June 2018); World Bank. Sustainable Energy for All database. http://databank.worldbank.org/data/source/sustainable-energy-for-all# (accessed 19 June 2018); and United Nations. Sustainable Development Goals Indicators Database. http://unstats.un.org/sdgs/indicators/database/ (accessed 13 July 2018).

Goal 8. Promote sustained, inclusive, and sustainable economic growth; full and productive employment; and decent work for all

Table 1.8.1: Selected Indicators for Sustainable Development Goal 8—Decent Work and Economic Growth

| ADB Regional Member | Target 8.1: Sustain per capita economic growth in accordance with national circumstances and, in particular, at least 7% gross domestic product per annum in the least developed countries | | Target 8.2: Achieve higher levels of economic productivity through diversification, technological upgrading and innovation, including through a focus on high-value added and labor-intensive sectors | |
| | 8.1.1: Annual Growth Rate of Real GDP per Capita at Constant 2010 $ (%) | | 8.2.1: Annual Growth Rate of Real GDP per Employed Person at Constant 2010 $ (%) | |
	2000	2016	2000	2016
Developing ADB Member Economies				
Central and West Asia				
Afghanistan	-8.7	0.8	-8.2	-2.3
Armenia	6.6	-0.1	5.7	-0.4
Azerbaijan	10.2	-3.6	8.8	-4.9
Georgia	2.9	3.4	2.4	4.5
Kazakhstan	10.6	-0.4	9.4	0.4
Kyrgyz Republic	4.2	2.3	2.9	3.8
Pakistan	1.9	3.6	1.7	1.4
Tajikistan	6.5	4.6	5.0	4.6
Turkmenistan	4.3	4.4	2.8	4.8
Uzbekistan	2.5	4.4	1.0	5.3
East Asia				
China, People's Republic of	7.8	6.8	7.1	6.8
Hong Kong, China	6.3	1.2	4.4	1.7
Korea, Republic of	8.1	2.4	4.5	1.9
Mongolia	0.2	-0.7	-1.6	4.4
Taipei,China	…	…	…	…
South Asia				
Bangladesh	3.9	6.0	2.2	5.3
Bhutan	5.7	6.6	1.8	4.2
India	2.2	5.9	2.1	5.3
Maldives	1.7	3.8	1.3	3.2
Nepal	4.2	-0.7	4.2	-2.1
Sri Lanka	5.3	4.0	5.1	3.5
Southeast Asia				
Brunei Darussalam	0.7	-3.8	-0.8	-3.5
Cambodia	6.4	5.2	4.2	5.1
Indonesia	3.5	3.8	2.4	2.3
Lao People's Democratic Republic	4.1	5.5	3.5	4.9
Malaysia	6.4	2.7	5.3	2.6
Myanmar	12.4	4.7	12.2	5.4
Philippines	2.2	5.3	1.9	4.7
Singapore	6.2	0.4	4.6	0.6
Thailand	3.4	4.0	1.7	3.3
Viet Nam	5.6	5.1	4.3	5.4
The Pacific				
Cook Islands	13.9	4.1	…	…
Fiji	-2.3	-0.4	-1.6	1.4
Kiribati	10.1	2.4	…	…
Marshall Islands	5.8	2.8	…	…
Micronesia, Federated States of	5.0	-0.5	…	…
Nauru	-6.8	9.6	…	…
Palau	-2.7	0.9	…	…
Papua New Guinea	-4.9	0.4	-5.7	0.5
Samoa	6.6	5.1	8.1	6.1
Solomon Islands	-16.5	1.2	-18.2	0.4
Timor-Leste	12.6	2.7	24.2	2.3 (2015)
Tonga	2.6	2.6	3.5	2.2
Tuvalu	12.4	2.1	…	…
Vanuatu	3.1	1.8	3.8	1.2
Developed ADB Member Economies				
Australia	0.9	0.6	1.3	1.3
Japan	2.6	1.2	3.1	0.1
New Zealand	1.2	2.0	0.4	1.0

… = data not available, $ = United States dollars, ADB = Asian Development Bank, GDP = gross domestic product.

Source: United Nations. National Accounts Main Aggregates Database. https://unstats.un.org/unsd/snaama/dnlList.asp (accessed 13 July 2018).

Table 1.8.2: Selected Indicators for Sustainable Development Goal 8—Unemployment

ADB Regional Member	Target 8.5: By 2030, achieve full and productive employment and decent work for all women and men, including for young people and persons with disabilities, and equal pay for work of equal value					
	8.5.2a: Unemployment Rate for Age Group 15+, by Sex (%)					
	2000			2017		
	Total	Female	Male	Total	Female	Male
Developing ADB Member Economies						
Central and West Asia						
Afghanistan	8.5 (2005)	9.5 (2005)	7.6 (2005)	...	...	...
Armenia	28.3 (2007)	35.0 (2007)	21.9 (2007)	17.8	17.5	18.2
Azerbaijan	6.5 (2007)	5.3 (2007)	7.8 (2007)	5.0 (2016)	6.0 (2016)	4.2 (2016)
Georgia	10.8	10.5	11.1	11.8 (2016)	8.9 (2016)	14.2 (2016)
Kazakhstan	10.4 (2001)	12.1 (2001)	8.9 (2001)	4.9	...	...
Kyrgyz Republic	12.6 (2002)	14.3 (2002)	11.2 (2002)	7.2 (2016)	8.7 (2016)	6.2 (2016)
Pakistan	7.2	15.8	5.5	3.6 (2015)	6.1 (2015)	2.8 (2015)
Tajikistan	...	...	...	11.5 (2009)	10.5 (2009)	12.3 (2009)
Turkmenistan	...	...	...	4.0 (2010)	2.3 (2010)	5.3 (2010)
Uzbekistan	...	...	...	5.2 (2016)	...	...
East Asia						
China, People's Republic of	...	...	...	...	...	...
Hong Kong, China	...	...	...	...	...	...
Korea, Republic of	4.4	3.6	5.0	3.7	3.6	3.8
Mongolia	6.8 (2003)	6.4 (2003)	7.1 (2003)	7.2 (2016)	5.9 (2016)	8.4 (2016)
Taipei,China	...	...	...	...	...	...
South Asia						
Bangladesh	3.3	3.3	3.2	4.4	6.7	3.3
Bhutan	1.9 (2001)	3.2 (2001)	1.3 (2001)	2.5 (2015)	3.2 (2015)	1.8 (2015)
India	2.7	2.4	2.9	2.7 (2012)	3.7 (2012)	2.4 (2012)
Maldives	2.0	2.7	1.6	11.7 (2010)	13.8 (2010)	10.4 (2010)
Nepal	8.8 (2001)	10.7 (2001)	7.4 (2001)	3.0 (2014)	3.4 (2014)	2.6 (2014)
Sri Lanka	7.6	11.1	5.8	4.2	...	...
Southeast Asia						
Brunei Darussalam	...	...	...	7.0 (2014)	7.9 (2014)	6.3 (2014)
Cambodia	...	...	...	0.4 (2010)	0.3 (2010)	0.4 (2010)
Indonesia	10.3 (2006)	13.4 (2006)	8.5 (2006)	4.1 (2016)	3.7 (2016)	4.4 (2016)
Lao People's Democratic Republic	1.4 (2005)	1.4 (2005)	1.4 (2005)	9.4	7.8	10.8
Malaysia	3.0	3.1	3.0	3.4	3.9 (2016)	3.1 (2016)
Myanmar	...	...	...	1.6	2.0	1.2
Philippines	3.7 (2001)	4.0 (2001)	3.5 (2001)	2.6	2.7	2.5
Singapore	3.7	3.5	3.9	1.9	...	...
Thailand	3.7	3.9	3.5	0.7 (2016)	0.7 (2016)	0.7 (2016)
Viet Nam	2.3	2.1	2.4	1.9	1.7	2.1
The Pacific						
Cook Islands	...	...	...	...	...	...
Fiji	3.9 (2005)	5.2 (2005)	3.3 (2005)	4.3 (2016)	5.5 (2016)	3.7 (2016)
Kiribati	14.7 (2005)	18.2 (2005)	12.3 (2005)	30.6 (2010)	34.1 (2010)	27.6 (2010)
Marshall Islands	25.4 (2005)	...	...	...	...	...
Micronesia, Federated States of	...	...	...	...	...	...
Nauru	...	...	...	23.0 (2011)	25.5 (2011)	21.4 (2011)
Palau	3.3	3.5	3.1	...	...	...
Papua New Guinea	2.9	...	...	...	...	...
Samoa	...	...	...	8.7 (2014)	10.3 (2014)	7.8 (2014)
Solomon Islands	...	...	...	2.0 (2009)	1.8 (2009)	2.3 (2009)
Timor-Leste	...	...	...	11.0 (2013)	10.6 (2013)	11.2 (2013)
Tonga	5.2 (2003)	7.4 (2003)	3.8 (2003)	...	...	...
Tuvalu	6.5 (2002)	8.6 (2002)	5.0 (2002)	...	...	...
Vanuatu	...	...	...	...	...	...
Developed ADB Member Economies						
Australia	6.3	6.1	6.5	5.6	5.7	5.5
Japan	4.7	4.5	4.9	2.8	2.7	3.0
New Zealand	6.1	6.0	6.3	4.7	5.2	4.2

continued on next page

Goal 8. Promote sustained, inclusive, and sustainable economic growth; full and productive employment; and decent work for all

Table 1.8.2: Selected Indicators for Sustainable Development Goal 8—Unemployment (continued)

ADB Regional Member	Target 8.5: By 2030, achieve full and productive employment and decent work for all women and men, including for young people and persons with disabilities, and equal pay for work of equal value					
	8.5.2b: Unemployment Rate for Age Group 15-24, by Sex (%)					
	2000			**2017**		
	Total	**Female**	**Male**	**Total**	**Female**	**Male**
Developing ADB Member Economies						
Central and West Asia						
Afghanistan	...	...	...	...	...	...
Armenia	...	...	...	36.3 (2016)	45.7 (2016)	29.5 (2016)
Azerbaijan	14.0 (2007)	10.5 (2007)	18.2 (2007)	13.4 (2015)	15.8 (2015)	11.4 (2015)
Georgia	21.1	20.5	21.6	30.5 (2016)	28.9 (2016)	31.2 (2016)
Kazakhstan	17.3 (2002)	19.3 (2002)	15.7 (2002)	...	...	...
Kyrgyz Republic	20.1 (2002)	21.2 (2002)	19.3 (2002)	15.5 (2016)	20.6 (2016)	12.7 (2016)
Pakistan	13.3	29.2	11.1	6.6 (2015)	9.4 (2015)	5.7 (2015)
Tajikistan	...	...	...	...	...	...
Turkmenistan	...	...	...	...	...	...
Uzbekistan	...	...	...	...	...	...
East Asia						
China, People's Republic of	...	...	...	...	...	...
Hong Kong, China	...	...	...	...	...	...
Korea, Republic of	10.8	9.0	13.6	10.4	9.7	11.3
Mongolia	9.8 (2008)	8.8 (2008)	10.6 (2008)	20.8 (2016)	22.2 (2016)	20.0 (2016)
Taipei,China	...	...	...	...	...	...
South Asia						
Bangladesh	10.7	10.3	11.1	12.8	16.8	10.8
Bhutan	...	...	...	10.7 (2015)	12.7 (2015)	8.2 (2015)
India	8.1	7.0	8.4	10.1 (2012)	12.0 (2012)	9.5 (2012)
Maldives	4.4	5.1	4.0	25.4 (2010)	21.4 (2010)	29.1 (2010)
Nepal	...	...	...	...	...	...
Sri Lanka	26.4 (2005)	37.1 (2005)	20.4 (2005)	21.6 (2016)	29.2 (2016)	17.1 (2016)
Southeast Asia						
Brunei Darussalam	...	...	...	25.4 (2014)	28.1 (2014)	23.5 (2014)
Cambodia	...	...	...	0.5 (2010)	0.4 (2010)	0.7 (2010)
Indonesia	30.6 (2006)	34.7 (2006)	27.8 (2006)	15.4 (2016)	15.4 (2016)	15.3 (2016)
Lao People's Democratic Republic	...	...	...	18.2	15.5	20.8
Malaysia	10.9 (2007)	11.5 (2007)	10.5 (2007)	10.5 (2016)	11.4 (2016)	9.8 (2016)
Myanmar	...	...	...	4.0	4.8	3.3
Philippines	9.7 (2001)	12.8 (2001)	7.9 (2001)	7.5	8.9	6.6
Singapore	7.7 (2001)	10.7 (2001)	5.1 (2001)	9.1 (2016)	12.5 (2016)	6.2 (2016)
Thailand	6.6	6.0	7.0	3.1 (2015)	3.9 (2015)	2.6 (2015)
Viet Nam	4.6 (2004)	4.9 (2004)	4.4 (2004)	7.3	7.3	7.3
The Pacific						
Cook Islands	...	...	...	...	...	...
Fiji	9.8 (2005)	16.0 (2005)	7.1 (2005)	15.4 (2016)	22.4 (2016)	11.9 (2016)
Kiribati	39.3 (2005)	41.6 (2005)	37.2 (2005)	54.0 (2010)	61.8 (2010)	47.6 (2010)
Marshall Islands	...	...	...	...	...	...
Micronesia, Federated States of	...	...	...	...	...	...
Nauru	...	...	...	...	...	...
Palau	9.6	10.6	8.8	...	...	...
Papua New Guinea	5.3	...	...	...	...	...
Samoa	...	...	...	19.1 (2014)	25.3 (2014)	15.6 (2014)
Solomon Islands	...	...	...	...	...	...
Timor-Leste	...	...	...	21.8 (2013)	16.7 (2013)	25.1 (2013)
Tonga	...	...	...	...	...	...
Tuvalu	...	...	...	...	...	...
Vanuatu	...	...	...	...	...	...
Developed ADB Member Economies						
Australia	12.1	11.2	12.9	12.6	11.5	13.7
Japan	9.1	7.9	10.2	4.6	4.5	4.7
New Zealand	13.5	12.4	14.6	12.7	13.0	12.4

continued on next page

Goal 8. Promote sustained, inclusive, and sustainable economic growth; full and productive employment; and decent work for all

Table 1.8.2: Selected Indicators for Sustainable Development Goal 8—Unemployment (continued)

ADB Regional Member	Target 8.5: By 2030, achieve full and productive employment and decent work for all women and men, including for young people and persons with disabilities, and equal pay for work of equal value					
	8.5.2c: Unemployment Rate for Age Group 25+, by Sex (%)					
	2000			2017		
	Total	Female	Male	Total	Female	Male
Developing ADB Member Economies						
Central and West Asia						
Afghanistan	...	...	...	...	...	...
Armenia	...	...	...	15.5 (2016)	14.7 (2016)	16.3 (2016)
Azerbaijan	5.2 (2007)	4.3 (2007)	6.1 (2007)	3.8 (2015)	4.6 (2015)	3.0 (2015)
Georgia	9.7	9.5	9.8	10.1 (2016)	7.7 (2016)	12.3 (2016)
Kazakhstan	7.9 (2002)	9.9 (2002)	6.0 (2002)	...	...	...
Kyrgyz Republic	10.4 (2002)	12.4 (2002)	8.8 (2002)	5.4 (2016)	6.6 (2016)	4.6 (2016)
Pakistan	4.9	12.3	3.4	2.5 (2015)	4.8 (2015)	1.8 (2015)
Tajikistan	...	...	...	...	...	...
Turkmenistan	...	...	...	...	...	...
Uzbekistan	...	...	...	...	...	...
East Asia						
China, People's Republic of	...	...	...	...	...	...
Hong Kong, China	...	...	...	...	...	...
Korea, Republic of	3.7	2.7	4.3	3.3	3.0	3.5
Mongolia	4.7 (2008)	4.6 (2008)	4.9 (2008)	5.8 (2016)	4.5 (2016)	7.0 (2016)
Taipei,China	...	...	...	...	...	...
South Asia						
Bangladesh	0.9	0.7	1.0	2.6	4.4	1.8
Bhutan	...	...	...	1.3 (2015)	1.6 (2015)	1.1 (2015)
India	1.2	1.1	1.3	1.2 (2012)	2.1 (2012)	0.9 (2012)
Maldives	1.1	1.8	0.8	6.6 (2010)	9.9 (2010)	4.7 (2010)
Nepal	...	...	...	...	...	...
Sri Lanka	3.4 (2005)	5.6 (2005)	2.3 (2005)	2.2 (2016)	4.1 (2016)	1.1 (2016)
Southeast Asia						
Brunei Darussalam	...	...	...	4.1 (2014)	4.9 (2014)	3.5 (2014)
Cambodia	...	...	...	0.3 (2010)	0.2 (2010)	0.3 (2010)
Indonesia	4.9 (2006)	6.9 (2006)	3.8 (2006)	2.0 (2016)	1.4 (2016)	2.3 (2016)
Lao People's Democratic Republic	...	...	...	7.4	5.9	8.6
Malaysia	1.4 (2007)	1.3 (2007)	1.5 (2007)	1.9 (2016)	2.3 (2016)	1.7 (2016)
Myanmar	...	...	...	1.0	1.3	0.7
Philippines	2.0 (2001)	1.7 (2001)	2.2 (2001)	1.5	1.5	1.5
Singapore	3.3 (2001)	3.0 (2001)	3.5 (2001)	3.6 (2016)	3.7 (2016)	3.6 (2016)
Thailand	1.5	1.5	1.4	0.3 (2015)	0.3 (2015)	0.3 (2015)
Viet Nam	1.5 (2004)	1.8 (2004)	1.1 (2004)	1.0	0.9	1.2
The Pacific						
Cook Islands	...	...	...	...	...	...
Fiji	2.6 (2005)	2.7 (2005)	2.5 (2005)	2.2 (2016)	2.4 (2016)	2.2 (2016)
Kiribati	7.9 (2005)	10.1 (2005)	6.5 (2005)	20.9 (2010)	22.8 (2010)	19.2 (2010)
Marshall Islands	...	...	...	...	...	...
Micronesia, Federated States of	...	...	...	...	...	...
Nauru	...	...	...	...	...	...
Palau	2.6	2.8	2.5	...	...	...
Papua New Guinea	2.1	...	...	...	...	...
Samoa	...	...	...	6.4 (2014)	7.1 (2014)	6.0 (2014)
Solomon Islands	...	...	...	...	...	...
Timor-Leste	...	...	...	9.3 (2013)	9.5 (2013)	9.3 (2013)
Tonga	...	...	...	...	...	...
Tuvalu	...	...	...	...	...	...
Vanuatu	...	...	...	...	...	...
Developed ADB Member Economies						
Australia	4.9	4.7	5.1	4.2	4.5	4.0
Japan	4.2	3.9	4.3	2.7	2.5	2.8
New Zealand	4.6	4.6	4.6	3.2	3.8	2.7

... = data not available, ADB = Asian Development Bank.

Sources: United Nations. Sustainable Development Goals Indicators Database. https://unstats.un.org/sdgs/indicators/database/ (accessed 13 July 2018); and International Labour Organization. ILOSTAT. http://www.ilo.org/ilostat/ (accessed 28 June 2018).

Goal 8. Promote sustained, inclusive and sustainable economic growth, full and productive employment and decent work for all

Table 1.8.3: Selected Indicators for Sustainable Development Goal 8—Youth Participation in Education and Work, Child Labor

ADB Regional Member	Target 8.6: By 2020, substantially reduce the proportion of youth not in employment, education, or training 8.6.1: Proportion of Youth (Aged 15–24 Years) Not in Education, Employment, or Training (%)		Target 8.7: Take immediate and effective measures to eradicate forced labor, end modern slavery and human trafficking, and secure the prohibition and elimination of the worst forms of child labor, including recruitment and use of child soldiers; and, by 2025, end child labor in all its forms 8.7.1: Proportion of Children (Aged 5–17 Years) Engaged in Child Labor (%)	
	2000	**2016**	**2000**	**2015**
Developing ADB Member Economies				
Central and West Asia				
Afghanistan	...	...	...	16.6 (2013)
Armenia	...	36.6	...	3.9
Azerbaijan	...	...	6.1 (2005)	...
Georgia	...	...	...	1.5
Kazakhstan	18.6 (2001)	9.5	...	...
Kyrgyz Republic	...	20.4	36.3 (2007)	37.1 (2014)
Pakistan	36.2 (2006)	30.4 (2015)	...	...
Tajikistan	...	42.2 (2009)	...	...
Turkmenistan	...	...	...	0.3
Uzbekistan	...	...	...	...
East Asia				
China, People's Republic of	...	...	...	...
Hong Kong, China	...	...	...	...
Korea, Republic of	...	...	...	...
Mongolia	18.5 (2006)	20.5	6.2 (2002)	9.4 (2013)
Taipei,China	...	...	...	...
South Asia				
Bangladesh	31.0 (2005)	27.4 (2017)	15.1 (2003)	6.8 (2013)
Bhutan	...	...	...	...
India	32.2	27.5 (2012)	4.1 (2004)	2.1 (2012)
Maldives	...	23.5	...	...
Nepal	23.4 (2008)	...	27.6 (2008)	19.1 (2014)
Sri Lanka	...	27.7 (2014)	...	10.3 (2009)
Southeast Asia				
Brunei Darussalam	...	17.2 (2014)	...	...
Cambodia	...	12.7 (2012)	...	16.3 (2012)
Indonesia	29.4	21.5 (2017)	...	5.2 (2009)
Lao People's Democratic Republic	...	42.1 (2017)	...	11.9 (2010)
Malaysia	...	11.7	...	...
Myanmar	...	17.4 (2017)	...	...
Philippines	24.7 (2006)	21.7 (2017)	11.4 (2001)	4.3 (2011)
Singapore	...	4.0	...	...
Thailand	...	15.0	...	...
Viet Nam	10.6 (2007)	0.6	...	12.1 (2014)
The Pacific				
Cook Islands	...	...	...	...
Fiji	20.6 (2005)	20.1	...	...
Kiribati	...	...	...	...
Marshall Islands	...	...	...	...
Micronesia, Federated States of	...	...	...	...
Nauru	...	...	...	...
Palau	27.2	...	...	...
Papua New Guinea	...	27.7 (2010)	...	...
Samoa	...	38.9 (2012)	...	...
Solomon Islands	...	...	...	...
Timor-Leste	...	24.3 (2013)	...	...
Tonga	...	...	...	...
Tuvalu	...	...	...	...
Vanuatu	...	...	...	...
Developed ADB Member Economies				
Australia	...	8.7	...	...
Japan	...	3.5	...	...
New Zealand	10.8 (2004)	11.8 (2017)	...	...

... = data not available, ADB = Asian Development Bank.

Sources: United Nations. Sustainable Development Goals Indicators Database. https://unstats.un.org/sdgs/indicators/database/ (accessed 13 July 2018); and International Labour Organization. ILOSTAT. http://www.ilo.org/ilostat (accessed 29 June 2018).

Goal 8. Promote sustained, inclusive, and sustainable economic growth; full and productive employment; and decent work for all

Table 1.8.4: Selected Indicators for Sustainable Development Goal 8—Access to Banking, Insurance and Financial Services, and Trade

| ADB Regional Member | 8.10.1: Number of Commercial Bank Branches and ATMs per 100,000 Adults | | | | 8.10.2: Proportion of Adults (15 Years and Older) with an Account at a Bank or Other Financial Institution or with a Mobile-Money Service Provider (%) | |
| | Commercial Bank Branches | | ATMs | | | |
	2004	2016	2004	2016	2011	2017
Developing ADB Member Economies						
Central and West Asia						
Afghanistan	0.4	2.2	0.0	1.1	9.0	14.9
Armenia	10.8	23.1	3.0	61.1	17.5	47.8
Azerbaijan	6.5	10.7 (2015)	17.1 (2006)	32.7	14.9	28.6
Georgia	9.5	32.7	2.0	74.3	33.0	61.2
Kazakhstan	3.7	3.0	10.0	74.0	42.1	58.7
Kyrgyz Republic	5.1	8.4	0.6	31.2	3.8	39.9
Pakistan	7.7	10.4	0.8	9.8	10.3	21.3
Tajikistan	4.9	6.5 (2013)	0.6 (2005)	10.3 (2013)	2.5	47.0
Turkmenistan	...	...	...	...	0.4	40.6
Uzbekistan	39.1	36.1	0.9	21.6	22.5	37.1
East Asia						
China, People's Republic of	...	8.8	9.6 (2006)	81.5	63.8	80.2
Hong Kong, China	23.6	21.4	...	50.6	88.7	95.3
Korea, Republic of	16.8	16.3	208.2	276.3 (2015)	93.0	94.9
Mongolia	40.0	70.4	9.9 (2008)	88.6	77.7	93.0
Taipei,China	...	...	...	...	...	...
South Asia						
Bangladesh	6.9	8.4	0.1	7.8	31.7	50.0
Bhutan	14.4	15.3	0.5	32.3	...	33.7
India	9.0	14.1	2.3 (2005)	21.2	35.2	79.9
Maldives	10.1	14.1	7.2	30.0	...	...
Nepal	2.6	9.6	...	9.6	25.3	45.4
Sri Lanka	8.8	18.6 (2015)	9.4 (2007)	17.2 (2015)	68.5	73.6
Southeast Asia						
Brunei Darussalam	21.0	19.4	34.9	75.3	...	...
Cambodia	2.3 (2006)	6.1 (2015)	0.0 (2005)	13.3 (2015)	3.7	21.7
Indonesia	5.2	17.4	8.6	54.7	19.6	48.9
Lao People's Democratic Republic	...	3.0	2.6 (2008)	24.3	26.8	29.1
Malaysia	14.0	11.5	27.1	48.1	66.2	85.3
Myanmar	1.8	3.4	...	2.7	...	26.0
Philippines	8.2	8.9	10.3	27.1	26.6	34.5
Singapore	11.7	9.0	47.9	57.7	98.2	97.9
Thailand	7.8	12.4	19.9	113.1	72.7	81.6
Viet Nam	3.3 (2008)	3.9	1.4	24.5	21.4	30.8
The Pacific						
Cook Islands	...	...	...	...	...	...
Fiji	9.3	11.8	19.0	50.8	...	...
Kiribati	...	5.7 (2013)	...	14.3 (2013)	...	...
Marshall Islands	11.8	20.3	2.9 (2007)	5.8	...	...
Micronesia, Federated States of	12.3	14.3	3.1	14.3	...	...
Nauru	...	...	...	...	...	...
Palau	...	...	30.9 (2007)	46.3	...	...
Papua New Guinea	1.8	3.1	3.8	9.2	...	...
Samoa	17.6	22.7	12.1	47.1	...	...
Solomon Islands	7.5	4.1	1.5	11.5	...	...
Timor-Leste	1.2	5.0	2.1 (2008)	6.4	...	...
Tonga	24.2	29.7 (2015)	22.5	28.2 (2015)	...	...
Tuvalu	...	...	...	...	...	...
Vanuatu	19.6	20.8	4.9	40.5	...	...
Developed ADB Member Economies						
Australia	30.7	27.8	139.6	168.0	99.1	99.5
Japan	34.6	34.1	124.4	127.8	96.4	98.2
New Zealand	35.0	29.0 (2015)	59.0	69.3 (2015)	99.4	99.2

... = data not available, 0.0 = magnitude is less than half of unit employed, ADB = Asian Development Bank.

Sources: International Monetary Fund. Financial Access Survey database. http://data.imf.org/?sk=E5DCAB7E-A5CA-4892-A6EA-598B5463A34C (accessed 21 June 2018); United Nations. Sustainable Development Goals Indicators Database. http://unstats.un.org/sdgs/indicators/database/ (accessed 13 July 2018); and World Bank. Data Bank. Financial Inclusion. http://databank.worldbank.org/data/reports.aspx?source=1228# (accessed 26 June 2018).

Goal 9. Build resilient infrastructure, promote inclusive and sustainable industrialization, and foster innovation

Table 1.9.1: Selected Indicators for Sustainable Development Goal 9—Road and Air Transport, Passenger and Freight Volume

| ADB Regional Member | Target 9.1: Develop quality, reliable, sustainable and resilient infrastructure, including regional and transborder infrastructure, to support economic development and human well-being, with a focus on affordable and equitable access for all | | | |
	9.1.2: Passenger Volume, by Road Transport (passenger-km million) 2016	9.1.2: Freight Volume, by Road Transport (t-km million) 2016	9.1.2: Passenger Volume, by Air Transport (passenger-km million) 2016	9.1.2: Freight Volume, by Air Transport (t-km '000) 2016
Developing ADB Member Economies				
Central and West Asia				
Afghanistan	5,245.2	7,188.1	1,955.6	29,010.9
Armenia	3,175.3	565.6	...	...
Azerbaijan	47,259.2	16,486.0	3,511.8	732,789.8
Georgia	6,945.0	674.0	404.8	180.5
Kazakhstan	85,816.0	16,282.8	9,791.5	38,894.5
Kyrgyz Republic	1,609.9	1,370.0	1,024.1	88.3
Pakistan	64,018.8	177,297.6	23,358.7	175,474.4
Tajikistan	2,277.9	875.9	2,568.8	1,543.8
Turkmenistan	20,055.8	4,630.1	1,893.2	5,953.5
Uzbekistan	13,919.9	12,659.6	6,401.4	112,281.7
East Asia				
China, People's Republic of	4,864,144.7	6,903,998.0	836,515.6	21,304,585.1
Hong Kong, China	375,166.0	44,950.6	140,718.0	11,409,118.8
Korea, Republic of	394,760.5	108,428.3	131,890.0	11,484,878.5
Mongolia	5,294.9	12,462.1	1,073.6	8,070.2
Taipei,China	...	...	...	...
South Asia				
Bangladesh	58,354.7	18,113.9	7,773.2	53,979.2
Bhutan	1,999.3	1,027.0	466.9	659.1
India	16,950,000.0	2,210,850.0	163,966.8	1,893,881.5
Maldives	1,254.7	752.4	...	...
Nepal	6,663.0	16,444.5	779.0	4,895.1
Sri Lanka	43,843.8	12,443.8	14,546.4	403,075.6
Southeast Asia				
Brunei Darussalam	12,133.0	6,224.5	3,659.6	124,259.0
Cambodia	6,460.1	2,902.7	1,192.9	1,441.7
Indonesia	385,084.0	302,927.0	98,561.5	931,283.5
Lao People's Democratic Republic	3,757.8	583.4	875.9	1,496.0
Malaysia	368,275.9	28,607.8	96,740.9	1,149,877.0
Myanmar	17,683.2	4.2	1,206.9	5,065.3
Philippines	134,430.9	66,284.6	61,176.2	645,996.6
Singapore	237,188.8	...	126,618.0	6,423,166.2
Thailand	246,185.4	194,447.1	96,241.3	2,160,069.7
Viet Nam	62,611.9	40,916.0	47,565.4	458,977.2
The Pacific				
Cook Islands	...	...	30.8	153.2
Fiji	1,243.3	1,733.7	4,857.8	86,955.0
Kiribati	41.0	23.4	...	...
Marshall Islands	...	...	...	...
Micronesia, Federated States of	63.8	54.5	...	...
Nauru	...	...	185.0	9,718.5
Palau	299.4	79.0	...	...
Papua New Guinea	3,737.4	3,779.3	1,286.3	34,487.9
Samoa	161.7	138.8	25.1	17.6
Solomon Islands	266.0	182.0	320.5	3,595.6
Timor-Leste	219.4	...	...	...
Tonga	146.6	91.3	...	...
Tuvalu	6.2	3.1	...	...
Vanuatu	214.9	123.0	330.3	1,211.2
Developed ADB Member Economies				
Australia	302,436.8	216,425.3	149,409.9	1,902,075.5
Japan	1,046,661.9	259,116.1	179,932.0	9,360,892.0
New Zealand	46,995.8	23,313.0	33,276.9	1,232,650.7

... = data not available, ADB = Asian Development Bank, km = kilometer, t = metric ton.

Source: United Nations. Sustainable Development Goals Indicators Global Database. http://unstats.un.org/sdgs/indicators/database/ (accessed 13 July 2018).

Goal 9. Build resilient infrastructure, promote inclusive and sustainable industrialization, and foster innovation

Table 1.9.2: Selected Indicators for Sustainable Development Goal 9—Growth in Manufacturing

ADB Regional Member	Target 9.2: Promote inclusive and sustainable industrialization; and, by 2030, significantly raise industry's share of employment and GDP, in line with national circumstances, and double its share in least developed countries					
	9.2.1: Manufacturing Value Added[a]				9.2.2: Manufacturing Employment as a Proportion of Total Employment (%)	
	As a Proportion of GDP (%)		Per Capita (at constant 2010 $)			
	2000	2017	2000	2017	2000	2017
Developing ADB Member Economies						
Central and West Asia						
Afghanistan	17.2	11.6	46.3	70.3	4.6 (2008)	6.8 (2012)
Armenia	10.0	10.0	146.9	431.8	6.9 (2007)	8.3 (2016)
Azerbaijan	9.6	5.5	158.1	309.8	4.9 (2003)	5.1 (2016)
Georgia	10.2	10.0	137.5	419.7	5.9	...
Kazakhstan	13.0	10.1	575.1	1,079.0	7.7 (2001)	6.4 (2015)
Kyrgyz Republic	23.2	12.8	151.0	137.6	6.7 (2002)	7.6 (2016)
Pakistan	10.1	12.9	83.9	153.7	11.5	15.3 (2016)
Tajikistan	27.1	8.4	113.4	78.1	4.7 (2004)	5.5 (2009)
Turkmenistan	33.0	38.0	786.1	2,781.4	...	...
Uzbekistan	25.4	16.5	204.2	341.9	...	...
East Asia						
China, People's Republic of	28.2	31.6	489.3	2,265.6	...	...
Hong Kong, China	3.7	1.2	862.6	468.5	10.4	3.0 (2015)
Korea, Republic of	22.8	28.8	3,412.0	7,573.1	20.3	16.8
Mongolia	5.9	5.3	93.9	206.4	5.4 (2003)	7.5 (2016)
Taipei,China	24.6	22.5 (2016)	3,613.0	4,586.0 (2016)	...	...
South Asia						
Bangladesh	13.5	20.1	67.4	218.5	7.3	14.4
Bhutan	7.6	8.5	90.8	240.1	2.0 (2005)	6.5 (2015)
India	15.1	16.4	113.7	320.1	10.7	12.5 (2012)
Maldives	5.2	3.3	219.9	239.7	12.8	11.2 (2014)
Nepal	8.1	5.6	37.5	41.6	0.2 (2008)	...
Sri Lanka	20.1	15.8	366.2	630.1	16.5 (2002)	18.2 (2014)
Southeast Asia						
Brunei Darussalam	17.4	14.5	6,237.5	4,439.7	8.5 (2001)	3.8 (2014)
Cambodia	11.5	17.9	49.3	203.8	7.0	17.4 (2012)
Indonesia	23.7	21.7	508.3	896.6	13.0	14.1
Lao People's Democratic Republic	8.1	10.7	51.4	176.0	...	5.1 (2010)
Malaysia	25.8	22.9	1,807.8	2,629.2	22.8	16.9 (2016)
Myanmar	8.5	22.8	24.5	287.3	...	10.9 (2015)
Philippines	23.7	22.6	380.2	652.9	10.0	8.6
Singapore	20.4	16.7	7,010.3	8,779.8	20.7	11.1 (2015)
Thailand	28.5	28.3	985.2	1,722.4	14.7 (2002)	16.7 (2016)
Viet Nam	12.8	16.6	95.9	302.5	9.2	17.4
The Pacific						
Cook Islands	3.5	2.3	441.5	413.1	...	3.9 (2011)
Fiji	13.3	11.3	439.8	487.8	13.7 (2005)	5.6 (2016)
Kiribati	5.1	4.5	91.8	75.5	1.6	13.1 (2010)
Marshall Islands	1.8	1.4	47.6	48.8	...	0.7 (2010)
Micronesia, Federated States of	...	...	...	...	...	...
Nauru	...	...	...	...	...	...
Palau	2.8	1.2	290.4	122.7	0.7	...
Papua New Guinea	2.5	2.4	43.9	54.7	1.1	1.8 (2010)
Samoa	16.9	9.0	481.8	363.6	14.6 (2001)	6.8 (2014)
Solomon Islands	4.9	7.1	52.4	105.0	...	...
Timor-Leste	2.0	0.2	16.4	5.8	...	5.5 (2013)
Tonga	7.1	6.1	234.6	239.5	24.7 (2003)	...
Tuvalu	0.8	1.0	24.2	36.6	...	...
Vanuatu	4.3	3.3	117.2	95.6	...	1.9 (2009)
Developed ADB Member Economies						
Australia	9.4	6.2	4,677.3	3,929.4	12.1	7.2
Japan	17.1	19.1	7,188.8	9,197.2	20.5	16.1
New Zealand	14.1	9.8	4,081.7	3,736.9	15.8	9.8

... = data not available, $ = United States dollars, ADB = Asian Development Bank, GDP = gross domestic product.

a   United Nations Statistics Division data used for indicator 9.2.1 were calculated from GDP, manufacturing value added, and population data.

Sources: United Nations. Sustainable Development Goals Indicators Database. https://unstats.un.org/sdgs/indicators/database/ (accessed 13 July 2018); and United Nations Industrial Development Organization. Statistics Data Portal. https://stat.unido.org/SDG;jsessionid=A9681C75FAF7A7DC80C0DB7B2D5F1A31/ (accessed 21 June 2018).

Goal 9. Build resilient infrastructure, promote inclusive and sustainable industrialization, and foster innovation

Table 1.9.3: Selected Indicators for Sustainable Development Goal 9—Carbon Dioxide Emissions

ADB Regional Member	Target 9.4: By 2030, upgrade infrastructure and retrofit industries to make them sustainable, with increased resource-use efficiency and greater adoption of clean and environmentally sound technologies and industrial processes, with all countries taking action in accordance with their respective capabilities			
	9.4.1: Carbon Dioxide Emissions[a]			
	Per Unit of GDP (PPP) (kg of CO_2 equivalent per constant 2010 \$)		Per Unit of Manufacturing Value Added (kg of CO_2 equivalent per constant 2010 \$)	
	2000	2015	2000	2015
Developing ADB Member Economies				
Central and West Asia				
Afghanistan	...	...	...	...
Armenia	0.4	0.2	1.6	0.3
Azerbaijan	0.8	0.2	1.9	0.6
Georgia	0.3	0.3	0.9	0.9
Kazakhstan	0.7	0.5	2.1	2.2
Kyrgyz Republic	0.4	0.5	1.1	1.9
Pakistan	0.2	0.2	1.9	1.4
Tajikistan	0.3	0.2	–	–
Turkmenistan	1.6	0.8	0.2	0.2
Uzbekistan	1.9	0.6	3.0	1.2
East Asia				
China, People's Republic of	0.7	0.5	1.4	1.0
Hong Kong, China	0.2	0.1	0.7	1.8
Korea, Republic of	0.4	0.3	0.6	0.2
Mongolia	0.8	0.5	2.2	1.3
Taipei,China	...	...	0.5	0.4 (2014)
South Asia				
Bangladesh	0.1	0.1	0.5	0.6
Bhutan	...	...	...	...
India	0.3	0.3	1.5	1.4
Maldives	...	...	...	...
Nepal	0.1	0.1	1.2	1.9
Sri Lanka	0.1	0.1	0.1	0.2
Southeast Asia				
Brunei Darussalam	0.2	0.2	0.0	0.2
Cambodia	0.1	0.2	0.2	0.1
Indonesia	0.2	0.2	0.5	0.4
Lao People's Democratic Republic	...	...	...	...
Malaysia	0.3	0.3	0.6	0.4
Myanmar	0.1	0.1	2.1	0.3
Philippines	0.2	0.2	0.4	0.2
Singapore	0.2	0.1	0.1	0.2
Thailand	0.3	0.2	0.5	0.5
Viet Nam	0.2	0.3	1.9	2.1
The Pacific				
Cook Islands	...	...	...	...
Fiji	...	...	...	...
Kiribati	...	...	...	...
Marshall Islands	...	...	...	...
Micronesia, Federated States of	...	...	...	...
Nauru	...	...	...	...
Palau	...	...	...	...
Papua New Guinea	...	...	...	...
Samoa	...	...	...	...
Solomon Islands	...	...	...	...
Timor-Leste	...	...	...	...
Tonga	...	...	...	...
Tuvalu	...	...	...	...
Vanuatu	...	...	...	...
Developed ADB Member Economies				
Australia	0.5	0.4	0.5	0.3
Japan	0.3	0.3	0.2	0.2
New Zealand	0.3	0.2	0.4	0.3

... = data not available, – = magnitude equals zero, 0.0 = magnitude is less than half of unit employed, \$ = United States dollar, ADB = Asian Development Bank, CO_2 = carbon dioxide, GDP = gross domestic product, kg = kilogram, PPP = purchasing power parity.

a   Refers to carbon dioxide emissions from fuel combustion.

Sources: United Nations. Sustainable Development Goals Indicators Database. https://unstats.un.org/sdgs/indicators/database/ (accessed 13 July 2018); and United Nations Industrial Development Organization. Statistics Data Portal. https://stat.unido.org/SDG;jsessionid=A9681C75FAF7A7DC80C0DB7B2D5F1A31/ (accessed 21 June 2018).

Table 1.9.4: Selected Indicators for Sustainable Development Goal 9—Research and Development

ADB Regional Member	Target 9.5: Enhance scientific research, upgrade the technological capabilities of industrial sectors in all countries, in particular developing countries, including, by 2030, encouraging innovation and substantially increasing the number of research and development workers per 1 million people and public and private research and development spending							
	9.5.1: Research and Development Expenditure as a Proportion of GDP[a] (%)				9.5.2: Researchers (Full-Time Equivalent)[b] (per million inhabitants)			
	2000		2016		2000		2016	
Developing ADB Member Economies								
Central and West Asia								
Afghanistan	...		...		...		...	
Armenia	0.19		0.23		...		...	
Azerbaijan	0.34		0.21		...		...	
Georgia	0.22		0.30		...		1,718	
Kazakhstan	0.18		0.14		553	(2007)	926	
Kyrgyz Republic	0.16		0.12		...		...	
Pakistan	0.13		0.25	(2015)	345	(2005)	536	(2015)
Tajikistan	0.09	(2001)	0.11		...		...	
Turkmenistan	...		...		...		...	
Uzbekistan	0.36		0.22		1,030	(2002)	666	
East Asia								
China, People's Republic of	0.89		2.11		719		2,763	
Hong Kong, China	0.46		0.79		1,471		3,977	
Korea, Republic of	2.18		4.24		2,914		8,809	
Mongolia	0.19		0.18		...		...	
Taipei,China	...		...		...		...	
South Asia								
Bangladesh	...		...		...		...	
Bhutan	...		...		...		...	
India	0.77		0.62	(2015)	302		404	(2015)
Maldives	...		...		...		...	
Nepal	0.05	(2008)	0.30	(2010)	265	(2002)	...	
Sri Lanka	0.14		0.10	(2014)	283	(2004)	248	(2014)
Southeast Asia								
Brunei Darussalam	0.02	(2002)	...		404	(2002)	...	
Cambodia	0.05	(2002)	0.12	(2015)	39	(2002)	122	(2015)
Indonesia	0.06		0.08	(2013)	266		...	
Lao People's Democratic Republic	0.04	(2002)	...		49	(2002)	...	
Malaysia	0.47		1.30	(2015)	434		2,681	(2015)
Myanmar	0.11		...		94	(2001)	...	
Philippines	0.14	(2002)	0.14	(2013)	113	(2003)	270	(2013)
Singapore	1.82		2.18	(2014)	4,948		7,808	(2014)
Thailand	0.24		0.62	(2015)	504	(2001)	1,305	(2015)
Viet Nam	0.19	(2002)	0.44	(2015)	139	(2002)	868	(2015)
The Pacific								
Cook Islands	...		...		...		...	
Fiji	...		...		...		...	
Kiribati	...		...		...		...	
Marshall Islands	...		...		...		...	
Micronesia, Federated States of	...		...		...		...	
Nauru	...		...		...		...	
Palau	...		...		...		...	
Papua New Guinea	...		...		...		73	
Samoa	...		...		...		...	
Solomon Islands	...		...		...		...	
Timor-Leste	...		...		...		...	
Tonga	...		...		...		...	
Tuvalu	...		...		...		...	
Vanuatu	...		...		...		...	
Developed ADB Member Economies								
Australia	1.57		1.93	(2015)	5,015		...	
Japan	2.91		3.15		7,032		6,829	
New Zealand	1.10	(2001)	1.28	(2015)	3,829	(2001)	5,721	(2015)

... = data not available, ADB = Asian Development Bank, GDP = gross domestic product.

a   Research and development expenditure as a proportion of GDP is the amount of research and development expenditure divided by the total output of the economy.

b   The researchers (in full-time equivalent) per million inhabitants is a direct measure of the number of research and development workers per 1 million people.

Sources: United Nations Educational, Scientific and Cultural Organization Institute of Statistics, Organisation for Economic Co-operation and Development, Eurostat (Statistical Office of the European Union), and Network on Science and Technology Indicators – Ibero-American and Inter-American. African STI Indicators Initiative of AU/NEPAD. http://www.uis.unesco.org/ (accessed 27 July 2018).

Goal 9. Build resilient infrastructure, promote inclusive and sustainable industrialization, and foster innovation

Table 1.9.5: Selected Indicators for Sustainable Development Goal 9—Official International Support and Industry Value Added

ADB Regional Member	Target 9.a: Facilitate sustainable and resilient infrastructure development in developing countries through enhanced financial, technological, and technical support to African countries, least developed countries, landlocked developing countries, and small-island developing States		Target 9.b: Support domestic technology development, research and innovation in developing countries, including by ensuring a conducive policy environment for, inter alia, industrial diversification, and value addition to commodities	
	9.a.1: Total Official International Support to Infrastructure[a] (constant 2016 $ million)		9.b.1: Proportion of Medium and High-Tech Industry Value Added in Total Value Added (%)	
	2000	2016	2000	2015
Developing ADB Member Economies				
Central and West Asia				
Afghanistan	0.3	437.3	13.6	9.5
Armenia	132.0	287.0	9.5	3.7
Azerbaijan	23.7	713.2	16.5	13.7
Georgia	139.5	697.1	21.4	15.7
Kazakhstan	242.6	1,382.7	5.2	16.6
Kyrgyz Republic	90.8	100.0	5.9	4.1
Pakistan	471.0	1,229.0	25.2	24.6
Tajikistan	16.3	175.2	2.7	2.5
Turkmenistan	1.8	28.3	…	…
Uzbekistan	46.4	392.1	…	…
East Asia				
China, People's Republic of	2,145.9 (2002)	2,430.6	42.9	41.4
Hong Kong, China	…	…	39.5	36.1
Korea, Republic of	…	…	58.9	63.7
Mongolia	114.0	245.5	2.5	6.7
Taipei,China	…	…	56.2	70.8
South Asia				
Bangladesh	612.7	1,330.3	21.1	9.5
Bhutan	30.3	30.7	…	…
India	2,957.4	5,682.9	41.3	37.9
Maldives	11.3	10.3	2.6	2.6
Nepal	113.6	173.8	12.1	8.6
Sri Lanka	73.2	534.9	9.4	6.7
Southeast Asia				
Brunei Darussalam	…	…	3.3	3.3
Cambodia	44.6	226.4	0.3	0.3
Indonesia	105.6	1,463.1	35.7	35.1
Lao People's Democratic Republic	56.7 (2005)	96.2	…	…
Malaysia	587.2	4.9	51.2	42.6
Myanmar	0.0	259.2	12.4	6.6
Philippines	795.6	913.7	38.1	45.9
Singapore	…	…	78.5	80.4
Thailand	714.6	417.3	37.9	40.7
Viet Nam	1,125.1	2,567.4	23.5	40.4
The Pacific				
Cook Islands	0.9	0.5	…	…
Fiji	0.2	7.1	8.5	7.1
Kiribati	1.4	28.9	…	…
Marshall Islands	3.1	73.9	…	…
Micronesia, Federated States of	…	17.0	…	…
Nauru	0.0 (2002)	1.8	…	…
Palau	0.2	9.1	…	…
Papua New Guinea	206.7	221.1	12.6	12.6
Samoa	3.3	30.6	…	…
Solomon Islands	8.9	36.9	…	…
Timor-Leste	2.4	70.7	…	…
Tonga	4.7	30.9	1.6	1.6
Tuvalu	0.0 (2002)	8.0	…	…
Vanuatu	9.5	41.0	…	…
Developed ADB Member Economies				
Australia	…	…	27.2	28.2
Japan	…	…	52.0	55.3
New Zealand	…	…	12.5	17.2

… = data not available, 0.0 = magnitude is less than half of unit employed, $ = United States dollars, ADB = Asian Development Bank.

a   Gross disbursements of total official development assistance and other official flows from all donors in support of infrastructure.

Sources: United Nations. Sustainable Development Goals Indicators Database. http://unstats.un.org/sdgs/indicators/database/ (accessed 13 July 2018); The Organisation for Economic Co-operation and Development. https://stats.oecd.org/Index.aspx?DataSetCode=CRS1# (accessed 18 July 2018); and United Nations Industrial Development Organization. Statistics Data Portal. https://stat.unido.org/SDG;jsessionid=A9681C75FAF7A7DC80C0DB7B2D5F1A31 (accessed 2 July 2018).

Goal 9. Build resilient infrastructure, promote inclusive and sustainable industrialization, and foster innovation

Table 1.9.6: Selected Indicators for Sustainable Development Goal 9—Coverage by Mobile Networks

ADB Regional Member	Target 9.c: Significantly increase access to information and communications technology and strive to provide universal and affordable access to the Internet in least developed countries by 2020					
	9.c.1a: Proportion of Population Covered by 2G Mobile Networks[a] (%)		9.c.1b: Proportion of Population Covered by 3G Mobile Networks[b] (%)		9.c.1c: Proportion of Population Covered by LTE Mobile Networks[c] (%)	
	2000	2016	2008	2016	2012	2016
Developing ADB Member Economies						
Central and West Asia						
Afghanistan	72.0 (2007)	89.4	...	40.0	– (2014)	–
Armenia	38.0 (2001)	100.0	81.1 (2009)	100.0	17.5	52.5
Azerbaijan	93.5	100.0	32.2 (2009)	95.5	6.7	41.0
Georgia	79.0 (2001)	99.9	...	99.9	8.9 (2013)	92.0
Kazakhstan	94.0 (2001)	96.6	...	86.8	2.7	69.0
Kyrgyz Republic	5.2 (2004)	99.0	...	60.0	0.5 (2014)	40.0
Pakistan	27.1 (2001)	87.0	...	67.0	–	27.0
Tajikistan	– (2001)	...	...	90.0	8.4	73.6
Turkmenistan	12.4 (2001)	...	...	75.8	6.0 (2013)	46.1
Uzbekistan	75.0 (2002)	98.4	...	45.3	1.0 (2014)	16.9
East Asia						
China, People's Republic of	50.0 (2001)	99.5	...	98.0	10.0 (2013)	97.0
Hong Kong, China	100.0	100.0	99.0 (2009)	99.0	91.7	99.0
Korea, Republic of	99.0	99.9	99.0	99.0	99.0 (2014)	99.0
Mongolia	58.0	99.0	39.9	95.0	...	6.9
Taipei,China	...	...	...	...	...	...
South Asia						
Bangladesh	40.0 (2001)	99.5	...	91.4	59.0 (2014)	65.0
Bhutan	5.4 (2005)	98.0	15.0 (2010)	85.0	5.0 (2013)	53.0
India	21.1 (2001)	93.5 (2013)	–	79.7	2.0 (2014)	73.5
Maldives	40.0	100.0	41.8 (2009)	100.0	11.4 (2013)	80.0
Nepal	10.0 (2006)	82.0 (2015)	20.4 (2009)	90.0	– (2014)	20.7
Sri Lanka	57.9 (2001)	99.0	...	85.0	5.0	36.0
Southeast Asia						
Brunei Darussalam	...	98.7	...	92.5	5.0 (2013)	89.6
Cambodia	80.0	99.0	43.0 (2009)	80.0	9.0 (2014)	50.0
Indonesia	89.0	87.9	...	74.9	5.0 (2013)	22.6
Lao People's Democratic Republic	55.0 (2005)	98.0	–	69.0	2.0 (2014)	7.0
Malaysia	95.0 (2001)	96.0	74.0 (2009)	95.0	15.0 (2013)	88.0
Myanmar	10.0 (2006)	94.8	...	94.8	– (2014)	9.2
Philippines	70.0	99.0 (2014)	69.0 (2009)	93.0	6.0	80.0
Singapore	100.0	100.0	99.4	100.0	99.0 (2014)	100.0
Thailand	25.9 (2005)	98.0	...	98.0	– (2014)	98.0
Viet Nam	70.0 (2006)	94.0 (2015)	...	77.3	– (2014)	5.0
The Pacific						
Cook Islands	...	...	...	40.1	...	...
Fiji	40.0	88.0 (2015)	...	96.0	15.0 (2014)	90.0
Kiribati	...	70.0 (2015)	...	60.0	10.0 (2013)	40.0
Marshall Islands	...	...	...	...	40.0 (2014)	65.0 (2015)
Micronesia, Federated States of	–	80.0	...	15.0	...	–
Nauru	...	98.0 (2015)	98.0 (2010)	98.0	– (2014)	98.0
Palau	30.0 (2005)	98.0 (2015)	...	88.0	...	...
Papua New Guinea	...	89.0 (2015)	...	60.9	7.0 (2014)	35.0 (2015)
Samoa	...	96.8	...	84.5	...	37.0
Solomon Islands	35.0	93.0	...	72.0	...	13.3
Timor-Leste	38.0 (2003)	96.5	...	96.5	...	–
Tonga	70.0 (2001)	92.0 (2015)	...	95.0	– (2014)	41.1
Tuvalu	15.0 (2004)	...	...	...	...	...
Vanuatu	20.0 (2002)	95.0	...	80.0	...	25.0
Developed ADB Member Economies						
Australia	95.6	99.3	98.8	99.3	52.2	98.0
Japan	99.0	99.9	...	99.9	84.0	99.0
New Zealand	97.0	98.0	97.0	98.0	50.0 (2014)	90.0

... = data not available, – = magnitude equals zero, ADB = Asian Development Bank, LTE = Long-Term Evolution.

a The original indicator refers to "Percentage of the population covered by a 2G mobile-cellular network." This refers to the percentage of inhabitants within range of a mobile-cellular signal, irrespective of whether or not they are subscribers or users. This is calculated by dividing the number of inhabitants within range of a mobile-cellular signal by the total population and multiplying by 100.

b The original indicator refers to "Percentage of the population covered by at least a 3G mobile network." This refers to the percentage of inhabitants within range of at least a 3G mobile-cellular signal, irrespective of whether or not they are subscribers. This is calculated by dividing the number of inhabitants covered by at least a 3G mobile-cellular signal by the total population and multiplying by 100. It excludes people covered only by General Packet Radio Service, Enhanced Data for Global Evolution, or Code Division Multiple Access Single Carrier Radio Transmission Technology.

c The original indicator refers to "Percentage of the population covered by at least an LTE mobile network." This refers to the percentage of inhabitants within range of LTE/LTE-Advanced; mobile Worldwide Interoperability for Microwave Access (WiMAX)/WirelessMAN, or other more advanced mobile-cellular networks, irrespective of whether or not they are subscribers. This is calculated by dividing the number of inhabitants covered by the previously mentioned mobile-cellular technologies by the total population and multiplying by 100. It excludes people covered only by High Speed Packet Access, Universal Mobile Telecommunications Systems, Evolution-Data Optimized, and previous 3G technologies; and also excludes fixed WiMAX coverage.

Sources: International Telecommunication Union. Official communication, 18 June 2018; and United Nations. Sustainable Development Goals Indicators Global Database. http://unstats.un.org/sdgs/indicators/database/ (accessed 13 July 2018).

Goal 10. Reduce inequality within and among countries

Table 1.10.1: Selected Indicators for Sustainable Development Goal 10—Household Expenditure or Income Growth

| ADB Regional Member | Target 10.1: By 2030, progressively achieve and sustain income growth of the bottom 40% of the population at a rate higher than the national average | | | |
	10.1.1a: Growth Rates of Household Expenditure or Income per Capita among the Bottom 40% of the Population[a,b] (%)		10.1.1b: Growth Rates of Household Expenditure or Income per Capita[a,b] (%)	
Developing ADB Member Economies				
Central and West Asia				
Afghanistan	...		...	
Armenia	2.3	(2011–2016)	4.6	(2011–2016)
Azerbaijan	...		...	
Georgia	6.4	(2011–2016)	4.3	(2011–2016)
Kazakhstan	4.1	(2010–2015)	3.5	(2010–2015)
Kyrgyz Republic	0.6	(2011–2016)	-0.0	(2011–2016)
Pakistan	2.8	(2007–2013)	2.6	(2007–2013)
Tajikistan	2.3	(2009–2015)	3.6	(2009–2015)
Turkmenistan	...		...	
Uzbekistan	...		...	
East Asia				
China, People's Republic of	8.9	(2008–2012)	8.2	(2008–2012)
Hong Kong, China	...		...	
Korea, Republic of	...		...	
Mongolia	0.7	(2011–2016)	-0.0	(2011–2016)
Taipei,China	...		...	
South Asia				
Bangladesh	1.3	(2010–2016)	1.5	(2010–2016)
Bhutan	...		...	
India	...		...	
Maldives	...		...	
Nepal	...		...	
Sri Lanka	4.8	(2012–2016)	5.3	(2012–2016)
Southeast Asia				
Brunei Darussalam	...		...	
Cambodia	...		...	
Indonesia	4.1	(2011–2014)	3.6	(2011–2014)
Lao People's Democratic Republic	1.4	(2007–2012)	2.1	(2007–2012)
Malaysia	...		...	
Myanmar	...		...	
Philippines	2.4	(2009–2015)	1.4	(2009–2015)
Singapore	...		...	
Thailand	4.8	(2009–2013)	3.5	(2009–2013)
Viet Nam	4.8	(2010–2014)	2.3	(2010–2014)
The Pacific				
Cook Islands	...		...	
Fiji	1.0	(2008–2013)	-0.9	(2008–2013)
Kiribati	...		...	
Marshall Islands	...		...	
Micronesia, Federated States of	...		...	
Nauru	...		...	
Palau	...		...	
Papua New Guinea	...		...	
Samoa	...		...	
Solomon Islands	...		...	
Timor-Leste	...		...	
Tonga	...		...	
Tuvalu	...		...	
Vanuatu	...		...	
Developed ADB Member Economies				
Australia	...		...	
Japan	...		...	
New Zealand	...		...	

... = data not available, –0.0 = magnitude is less than half of unit employed, ADB=Asian Development Bank.

a Based on real mean per capita consumption or income measured at 2011 purchasing power parity using the World Bank's PovcalNet database (http://iresearch.worldbank.org/PovcalNet). Data reported are based on consumption, except for the Philippines, which collects income data.

b For the data collection periods, the initial year refers to the survey conducted between 3 and 7 years prior to the most recent survey, while the final year refers to the most recent survey available from 2012 to 2016.

Sources: World Bank. Global Database of Shared Prosperity. http://www.worldbank.org/en/topic/poverty/brief/global-database-of-shared-prosperity (accessed 8 June 2018); and World Bank. PovcalNet. http://iresearch.worldbank.org/PovcalNet/povOnDemand.aspx (accessed 31 July 2018).

Goal 11. Make cities and human settlements inclusive, safe, resilient, and sustainable

Table 1.11.1: Selected Indicators for Sustainable Development Goal 11—Sustainable Cities and Environment

ADB Regional Member	Target 11.1: By 2030, ensure access for all to adequate, safe, and affordable housing and basic services, and upgrade slums 11.1.1: Proportion of Urban Population Living in Slums, Informal Settlements, or Inadequate Housing (%)		Target 11.5: By 2030, significantly reduce the number of deaths and the number of people affected, and substantially decrease the direct economic losses relative to global gross domestic product caused by disasters, including water-related disasters, with a focus on protecting the poor and people in vulnerable situations 11.5.2: Direct Economic Loss Attributed to Disasters ($ million)		Target 11.6: By 2030, reduce the adverse per capita environmental impact of cities, including by paying special attention to air quality and municipal and other waste management 11.6.2: Annual Mean Levels (μg/m^3) of Fine Particulate Matter (e.g. PM$_{2.5}$ and PM$_{10}$) in Cities (Population Weighted)	
	2000	**2014**	**2017**		Total **2016**	Urban **2016**
Developing ADB Member Economies						
Central and West Asia						
Afghanistan	...	62.7	...		53.2	59.9
Armenia	...	14.4	13.3		30.5	32.9
Azerbaijan	...	...	...		18.2	18.5
Georgia	...	...	...		21.2	24.0
Kazakhstan	...	...	12.3		11.3	14.5
Kyrgyz Republic	...	...	0.1	(2016)	18.1	17.4
Pakistan	48.7	45.5	766.9	(2014)	55.2	56.2
Tajikistan	...	...	...		40.0	42.8
Turkmenistan	...	...	...		19.0	24.2
Uzbekistan	...	...	...		25.3	28.9
East Asia						
China, People's Republic of	37.3	25.2	...		49.2	51.0
Hong Kong, China	...	...	...		...	...
Korea, Republic of	...	...	17.2		24.6	24.7
Mongolia	64.9	42.7	...		40.4	49.5
Taipei,China	...	...	...		...	...
South Asia						
Bangladesh	77.8	55.1	...		58.3	58.6
Bhutan	...	...	8.0		35.3	35.4
India	41.5	24.0	...		65.2	68.0
Maldives	...	...	...		7.6	7.7
Nepal	64.0	54.3	139.3	(2013)	94.3	99.5
Sri Lanka	...	...	372.5		15.2	15.1
Southeast Asia						
Brunei Darussalam	...	...	...		5.8	5.8
Cambodia	78.9 (2005)	55.1	1,431.3		24.0	24.9
Indonesia	34.4	21.8	...		15.6	16.4
Lao People's Democratic Republic	79.3 (2005)	31.4	13.4	(2012)	24.5	25.5
Malaysia	...	...	408.1		16.0	17.3
Myanmar	45.6 (2005)	41.0	1,456.8		34.7	34.6
Philippines	47.2	38.3	...		18.4	18.7
Singapore	...	...	...		18.3	18.3
Thailand	26.0 (2005)	25.0	...		26.2	26.6
Viet Nam	48.8	27.2	945.0	(2010)	29.7	30.1
The Pacific						
Cook Islands	...	...	...		12.0	...
Fiji	...	...	...		10.2	10.5
Kiribati	...	...	0.3	(2014)	10.5	10.9
Marshall Islands	...	...	0.4	(2014)	9.4	...
Micronesia, Federated States of	...	...	...		10.2	10.5
Nauru	...	...	...		12.5	12.5
Palau	...	...	5.9	(2012)	12.2	12.4
Papua New Guinea	...	...	...		10.9	11.5
Samoa	...	...	...		10.6	10.9
Solomon Islands	...	...	...		10.7	11.5
Timor-Leste	...	...	0.7		17.9	18.2
Tonga	...	...	...		10.1	10.2
Tuvalu	...	...	...		11.4	...
Vanuatu	...	...	...		10.3	11.0
Developed ADB Member Economies						
Australia	...	...	...		7.2	7.3
Japan	...	...	...		11.4	11.8
New Zealand	...	...	12.5		5.7	5.8

... = data not available, $ = United States dollars, ADB = Asian Development Bank, m^3 = cubic meter, PM = particulate matter, μg = microgram.

Source: United Nations. Sustainable Development Goals Indicators Database. https://unstats.un.org/sdgs/indicators/database/ (accessed 13 July 2018).

Goal 12. Ensure sustainable consumption and production patterns

Table 1.12.1: Selected Indicators for Sustainable Development Goal 12—Responsible Consumption and Production

ADB Regional Member	Target 12.2: By 2030, achieve the sustainable management and efficient use of natural resources							
	12.2.1: Material Footprint				12.2.2: Domestic Material Consumption			
	All (t million)		Per Capita (t)		All (t million)		Per Capita (t)	
	2000	2017	2000	2015	2000	2017	2000	2015
Developing ADB Member Economies								
Central and West Asia								
Afghanistan	11.9	42.6	0.6	1.3	46.0	67.9	2.3	2.0
Armenia	7.2	24.0	2.3	7.4	13.8	32.5	4.5	10.0
Azerbaijan	20.4	61.8	2.5	5.9	30.2	90.1	3.7	8.4
Georgia	14.2	35.6	3.0	8.5	13.3	26.5	2.8	6.3
Kazakhstan	172.8	325.2	11.6	17.5	249.3	530.4	16.7	28.2
Kyrgyz Republic	29.2	48.1	5.9	7.9	32.0	50.7	6.5	8.2
Pakistan	354.7	627.0	2.6	3.2	514.4	875.8	3.7	4.4
Tajikistan	4.5	33.3	0.7	3.6	10.2	31.2	1.6	3.4
Turkmenistan	45.0	124.3	10.0	21.5	43.4	95.0	9.6	16.6
Uzbekistan	115.4	197.4	4.7	6.3	195.6	289.6	8.0	9.3
East Asia								
China, People's Republic of	8,864.7	27,670.5	7.0	18.8	11,805.8	35,194.1	9.3	23.6
Hong Kong, China	...	...	...	...	...	...	...	...
Korea, Republic of	1,056.5	1,346.1	...	...	...	...	...	...
Mongolia	9.1	42.6	3.8	13.3	49.0	106.2	20.4	33.5
Taipei,China	...	...	...	...	...	...	...	...
South Asia								
Bangladesh	228.2	387.7	1.7	2.3	255.8	438.3	1.9	2.6
Bhutan	2.6	8.4	4.5	10.3	4.7	8.4	8.4	10.2
India	2,941.9	6,135.9	2.8	4.4	3,868.5	7,417.2	3.7	5.3
Maldives	1.8	6.4	6.3	16.5	1.2	3.0	4.2	7.5
Nepal	30.3	79.2	1.3	2.6	61.7	114.4	2.6	3.8
Sri Lanka	37.0	79.7	2.0	3.7	58.0	116.8	3.1	5.4
Southeast Asia								
Brunei Darussalam	4.2	8.2	12.7	18.7	5.8	9.8	17.6	23.3
Cambodia	20.2	57.2	1.7	3.3	26.9	84.7	2.2	4.9
Indonesia	711.4	1,643.6	3.4	6.0	1,157.3	1,974.2	5.5	7.2
Lao People's Democratic Republic	6.7	50.6	1.3	6.5	13.7	82.2	2.6	10.6
Malaysia	445.0	714.9	19.0	22.3	388.5	609.4	16.6	18.9
Myanmar	24.5	79.9	0.5	1.4	106.9	187.6	2.2	3.3
Philippines	311.9	455.5	4.0	4.3	295.6	416.5	3.8	4.0
Singapore	200.2	417.0	51.1	70.4	260.0	186.3	66.4	33.4
Thailand	487.8	1,029.0	7.8	14.4	477.3	879.1	7.6	12.3
Viet Nam	274.9	956.6	3.4	9.3	332.8	1,400.7	4.1	13.6
The Pacific								
Cook Islands	...	...	...	...	...	...	...	...
Fiji	4.4	6.4	5.4	7.1	8.2	5.9	10.0	6.9
Kiribati	...	...	...	...	0.4	0.7	4.2	5.9
Marshall Islands	...	...	...	...	0.0	0.1	0.4	1.8
Micronesia, Federated States of	...	...	...	...	...	...	...	...
Nauru	...	...	...	...	...	...	...	...
Palau	...	...	...	...	0.0	0.0	0.2	1.1
Papua New Guinea	11.6	21.3	2.2	2.7	76.9	84.0	14.3	10.9
Samoa	0.7	1.7	4.1	8.1	0.7	1.0	4.0	5.1
Solomon Islands	...	...	...	...	2.2	4.3	5.4	6.9
Timor-Leste	...	...	...	...	0.9	10.0	1.1	8.3
Tonga	...	...	...	...	0.3	1.8	3.4	15.3
Tuvalu	...	...	...	...	0.0	0.0	0.9	1.2
Vanuatu	0.6	2.2	3.4	7.8	1.0	1.7	5.3	6.0
Developed ADB Member Economies								
Australia	643.6	1,050.7	33.7	42.1	868.4	927.4	45.5	38.4
Japan	3,539.6	3,138.5	28.2	23.8	1,575.4	1,141.6	12.5	9.4
New Zealand	82.0	114.5	21.2	24.4	95.8	113.7	24.8	24.9

... = data not available, 0.0 = magnitude is less than half of unit employed, ADB = Asian Development Bank, t = metric ton.

Source: United Nations Environment International Resource Panel Global Material Flows Database. http://www.resourcepanel.org/global-material-flows-database (accessed 7 August 2018).

Table 1.13.1: Selected Indicators for Sustainable Development Goal 13—Impact of Disasters and Risk Reduction Strategies

ADB Regional Member	Target 13.1: Strengthen resilience and adaptive capacity to climate-related hazards and natural disasters in all countries				13.1.2: Number of Countries that Adopt and Implement National Disaster Risk Reduction Strategies in Line with the Sendai Framework for Disaster Risk Reduction 2015–2030[a]
	13.1.1.a: Number of Persons Affected by Disaster		13.1.1.b: Number of Deaths Due to Disaster		
	2005	2017	2005	2017	
Developing ADB Member Economies					
Central and West Asia					
Afghanistan	...	...	...	...	2015
Armenia	...	6,067	...	302	2013
Azerbaijan	...	–	...	–	...
Georgia	...	...	...	...	2015
Kazakhstan	2,082	12,100	6	29	2013
Kyrgyz Republic	–	94 (2016)	–	2 (2016)	2015
Pakistan	1,546,357	58,321 (2014)	45,319	1,443 (2014)	2015
Tajikistan	...	...	...	...	...
Turkmenistan	...	...	...	...	...
Uzbekistan	...	–	...	–	...
East Asia					
China, People's Republic of	...	...	...	...	2013
Hong Kong, China	...	...	...	...	...
Korea, Republic of	...	1,975	...	55	2013
Mongolia	235 (2006)	5 (2016)	104 (2006)	2 (2016)	2015
Taipei,China	...	...	...	...	...
South Asia					
Bangladesh	...	...	...	...	2015
Bhutan	...	268	...	11	2015
India	...	...	...	...	2015
Maldives	2,278	–	1	–	...
Nepal	4,477	61,860 (2013)	333	626 (2013)	2015
Sri Lanka	93,228	375,572	123	356	2015
Southeast Asia					
Brunei Darussalam	...	...	...	...	...
Cambodia	9,939	73,590	29	98	...
Indonesia	...	...	...	...	2015
Lao People's Democratic Republic	6,306	1,400 (2012)	19	19 (2012)	...
Malaysia	...	399,859	...	31	2013
Myanmar	12,986	372,411	17	747	...
Philippines	...	...	...	...	2015
Singapore	...	...	...	...	...
Thailand	...	...	...	...	2015
Viet Nam	189,828	1,301,263 (2010)	675	60 (2010)	2015
The Pacific					
Cook Islands	2,241	3,523 (2010)	–	3 (2010)	...
Fiji	–	–	3	–	2015
Kiribati	–	352 (2014)	–	–	...
Marshall Islands	– (2006)	560 (2014)	– (2006)	–	...
Micronesia, Federated States of	– (2006)	– (2015)	– (2006)	10 (2015)	...
Nauru	...	...	...	...	2013
Palau	– (2006)	2,160 (2012)	– (2006)	–	...
Papua New Guinea	2	– (2015)	4	30 (2015)	2013
Samoa	–	– (2015)	18	– (2015)	2013
Solomon Islands	– (2006)	–	– (2006)	22 (2014)	...
Timor-Leste	6,416 (2006)	880	– (2006)	2	...
Tonga	–	–	–	1 (2014)	2013
Tuvalu	–	– (2015)	–	– (2015)	...
Vanuatu	–	– (2015)	–	11 (2015)	2013
Developed ADB Member Economies					
Australia	...	...	...	...	2015
Japan	...	...	...	...	2015
New Zealand	...	140	...	1	2015

... = data not available, – = magnitude equals zero, ADB = Asian Development Bank.

a Refers to the year in which countries made legislative and/or regulatory provisions to manage disaster risk.

Source: United Nations. Sustainable Development Goals Indicators Database. https://unstats.un.org/sdgs/indicators/database/ (accessed 13 July 2018).

Goal 14. Conserve and sustainably use the oceans, seas, and marine resources for sustainable development

Table 1.14.1: Selected Indicators for Sustainable Development Goal 14—Life Below Water

ADB Regional Member	Target 14.5: By 2020, conserve at least 10% of coastal and marine areas, consistent with national and international law and based on the best available scientific information		
	14.5.1a: Average Proportion of Marine Key Biodiversity Areas Covered by Protected Areas (%)	14.5.1b: Coverage of Protected Areas in Relation to Marine Areas (%)	14.5.1c: Protected Marine Areas (km²)
	2017	2017	2017
Developing ADB Member Economies			
Central and West Asia			
Afghanistan	...	...	...
Armenia	...	...	...
Azerbaijan	22.5	0.4	345.3
Georgia	–	0.7	153.0
Kazakhstan	43.4	1.0	1,249.5
Kyrgyz Republic	...	...	...
Pakistan	39.3	0.8	1,707.4
Tajikistan	...	...	...
Turkmenistan	25.8	3.0	2,331.8
Uzbekistan	...	...	...
East Asia			
China, People's Republic of	18.8	3.8	33,078.7
Hong Kong, China	49.9	...	77.6
Korea, Republic of	26.4	1.4	4,681.1
Mongolia	...	...	...
Taipei,China	...	...	...
South Asia			
Bangladesh	25.9	5.4	4,530.0
Bhutan	...	...	...
India	29.0	0.2	3,890.7
Maldives	–	0.1	474.9
Nepal	...	...	...
Sri Lanka	43.4	0.1	398.6
Southeast Asia			
Brunei Darussalam	60.9	0.2	51.7
Cambodia	21.7	0.2	89.1
Indonesia	27.7	2.9	171,449.6
Lao People's Democratic Republic	...	...	...
Malaysia	25.1	1.4	6,357.5
Myanmar	18.9	0.2	942.5
Philippines	44.9	1.0	18,998.8
Singapore	3.3	0.0	0.1
Thailand	64.1	1.9	5,773.8
Viet Nam	35.4	0.6	3,630.3
The Pacific			
Cook Islands	29.2	100.0	1,972,774.8
Fiji	12.9	0.9	11,953.0
Kiribati	40.2	11.8	408,796.5
Marshall Islands	12.3	0.3	5,388.4
Micronesia, Federated States of	1.8	0.0	475.1
Nauru	–	...	...
Palau	34.0	83.0	504,690.9
Papua New Guinea	2.4	0.2	4,585.5
Samoa	17.8	0.1	114.8
Solomon Islands	11.2	0.1	1,900.4
Timor-Leste	23.1	1.4	584.1
Tonga	5.9	1.5	10,055.2
Tuvalu	...	0.0	62.1
Vanuatu	4.7	0.0	47.5
Developed ADB Member Economies			
Australia	65.1	40.6	3,014,287.4
Japan	73.2	8.2	332,693.1
New Zealand	46.7	29.7	1,221,759.9

... = data not available, – = magnitude equals zero, 0.0 = magnitude is less than half of unit employed, ADB = Asian Development Bank, km² = square kilometer.

Source: United Nations. Sustainable Development Goals Indicators Database. http://unstats.un.org/sdgs/indicators/database/ (accessed 13 July 2018).

Goal 15. Protect, restore, and promote sustainable use of terrestrial ecosystems; sustainably manage forests; combat desertification and halt and reverse land degradation; and halt biodiversity loss

Table 1.15.1: Selected Indicators for Sustainable Development Goal 15—Protection of Ecosystems and Biodiversity

ADB Regional Member	Target 15.1: By 2020, ensure the conservation, restoration, and sustainable use of terrestrial and inland freshwater ecosystems and their services, in particular forests, wetlands, mountains, and drylands, in line with obligations under international agreements						Target 15.4: By 2030, ensure the conservation of mountain ecosystems, including their biodiversity, in order to enhance their capacity to provide benefits that are essential for sustainable development		Target 15.5: Take urgent and significant action to reduce the degradation of natural habitats, halt the loss of biodiversity and, by 2020, protect and prevent the extinction of threatened species	
	15.1.1: Forest Area as a Proportion of Total Land Area (%)		15.1.2: Proportion of Important Sites for Terrestrial and Freshwater Biodiversity that are Covered by Protected Areas				15.4.1: Coverage by Protected Areas of Important Sites for Mountain Biodiversity (%)		15.5.1: Red List Index[a]	
			Terrestrial (%)		Freshwater (%)					
	2000	2015	2000	2017	2000	2017	2000	2017	2000	2017
Developing ADB Member Economies										
Central and West Asia										
Afghanistan	2.1	2.1	0.0	6.1	0.1	0.1	0.1	12.3	0.84	0.84
Armenia	11.7	11.7	22.1	30.5	25.1	26.9	17.5	28.0	0.85	0.84
Azerbaijan	10.6	13.8	20.4	39.4	6.1	24.5	30.5	58.8	0.91	0.91
Georgia	39.7	40.6	15.4	28.4	1.8	27.3	15.6	30.1	0.88	0.86
Kazakhstan	1.3	1.2	9.6	16.3	8.4	17.4	28.0	30.2	0.88	0.87
Kyrgyz Republic	4.5	3.3	21.7	22.6	29.8	31.1	28.5	30.2	0.99	0.98
Pakistan	2.7	1.9	35.0	36.6	36.3	37.0	36.0	36.0	0.93	0.86
Tajikistan	3.0	3.0	17.6	21.0	27.2	34.6	15.9	19.5	0.99	0.98
Turkmenistan	8.8	8.8	14.4	14.6	12.7	13.1	21.3	21.3	0.98	0.97
Uzbekistan	7.6	7.6	11.1	15.9	1.8	10.4	37.5	37.5	0.98	0.97
East Asia										
China, People's Republic of	18.8	22.1	44.2	47.6	31.1	36.1	62.2	65.0	0.81	0.75
Hong Kong, China	...	...	56.7	56.7	...	...	83.6	83.6	0.82	0.82
Korea, Republic of	64.5	63.4	25.3	36.6	29.7	36.8	...	...	0.84	0.78
Mongolia	7.5	8.1	33.1	43.7	30.7	42.1	42.5	47.0	0.96	0.95
Taipei,China	58.1 (2001)	60.7 (2016)	...	...	...	...	...	...	...	...
South Asia										
Bangladesh	11.3	11.0	37.8	48.0	20.8	20.8	...	...	0.83	0.77
Bhutan	68.4	72.3	38.6	42.9	23.1	34.3	38.6	42.9	0.80	0.80
India	22.0	23.8	21.7	26.1	13.2	15.2	28.0	35.4	0.75	0.68
Maldives	3.3	3.3	...	...	...	...	...	...	0.91	0.85
Nepal	27.2	25.4	42.2	54.6	21.9	36.5	57.1	67.1	0.82	0.82
Sri Lanka	35.0	33.0	41.6	49.8	72.6	79.9	25.9	40.2	0.66	0.57
Southeast Asia										
Brunei Darussalam	75.3	72.1	62.9	62.9	50.0	50.0	...	...	0.85	0.83
Cambodia	65.4	53.6	35.8	39.5	28.0	33.0	92.3	92.3	0.88	0.82
Indonesia	54.9	50.2	19.2	23.5	33.0	39.3	19.8	23.4	0.84	0.76
Lao People's Democratic Republic	71.6	81.3	44.0	45.5	19.9	19.9	56.7	56.7	0.82	0.81
Malaysia	65.7	67.6	38.9	39.5	76.6	76.6	37.3	37.6	0.83	0.69
Myanmar	53.4	44.5	15.6	22.9	14.8	18.5	23.3	42.2	0.86	0.81
Philippines	23.6	27.0	29.9	41.7	48.1	48.1	28.3	43.9	0.73	0.65
Singapore	23.1	23.1	19.0	21.1	...	...	...	...	0.91	0.86
Thailand	33.3	32.1	67.2	71.7	43.4	43.6	85.6	91.9	0.85	0.80
Viet Nam	37.8	47.6	12.0	40.9	11.6	33.2	13.3	48.1	0.82	0.74
The Pacific										
Cook Islands	62.9	62.9	7.6	22.4	...	...	...	...	0.80	0.77
Fiji	53.7	55.7	2.9	4.9	0.1 (2004)	0.1	5.7	11.4	0.70	0.67
Kiribati	15.0	15.0	12.5	52.5	...	...	...	...	0.82	0.77
Marshall Islands	70.2	70.2	10.6	25.4	...	...	...	...	0.89	0.84
Micronesia, Federated States of	91.2	91.8	1.3	1.3	...	...	...	...	0.76	0.69
Nauru	...	...	...	...	...	...	...	...	0.82	0.77
Palau	86.1	87.6	17.9	36.6	...	...	...	...	0.91	0.75
Papua New Guinea	74.2	74.1	6.9	7.3	...	...	6.3	6.8	0.90	0.84
Samoa	60.4	60.4	16.3	36.5	...	...	19.0	51.3	0.84	0.82
Solomon Islands	81.0	78.1	3.9	9.5	...	...	0.3	0.3	0.83	0.77
Timor-Leste	57.4	46.1	14.9	38.7	...	...	13.5	42.0	0.95	0.89
Tonga	12.5	12.5	0.7	9.3	...	...	...	...	0.73	0.71
Tuvalu	33.3	33.3	...	...	...	...	...	...	0.89	0.83
Vanuatu	36.1	36.1	6.2	6.4	...	...	9.2	9.3	0.72	0.67
Developed ADB Member Economies										
Australia	16.8	16.2	34.9	54.3	24.1	35.1	59.6	82.5	0.88	0.83
Japan	68.2	68.5	59.9	68.5	60.8	67.0	71.4	74.3	0.84	0.79
New Zealand	38.5	38.6	40.2	44.3	20.0	26.7	20.9	29.0	0.71	0.63

... = data not available, 0.0 = magnitude is less than half of unit employed, ADB = Asian Development Bank.

a   The Red List Index midpoint value ranges from 1, which means all species are categorized as 'Least Concern' hence that none are expected to go extinct in the near future, to 0 meaning all species are categorized as 'Extinct'. The index therefore indicates how far the set of species has moved overall towards extinction.

Sources: United Nations. Sustainable Development Goals Indicators Database. https://unstats.un.org/sdgs/indicators/database/ (accessed 13 July 2018). For Taipei,China: Government of Taipei,China, Directorate-General of Budget, Accounting and Statistics. https://eng.stat.gov.tw/ (accessed 20 August 2018).

Sustainable Development Goals

Goal 16. Promote peaceful and inclusive societies for sustainable development; provide access to justice for all; and build effective, accountable, and inclusive institutions at all levels

Table 1.16.1: Selected Indicators for Sustainable Development Goal 16—Peace, Justice, and Strong Institutions

ADB Regional Member	Target 16.1: Significantly reduce all forms of violence and related death rates everywhere — 16.1.1: Number of Victims of Intentional Homicide (per 100,000 population)		Target 16.3: Promote the rule of law at the national and international levels and ensure equal access to justice for all — 16.3.2: Unsentenced Detainees as a Proportion of Overall Prison Population (%)		Target 16.5: Substantially reduce corruption and bribery in all their forms — 16.5.2: Proportion of Firms Experiencing at least One Bribe Payment Request (%)	Target 16.9: By 2030, provide legal identity for all, including birth registration — 16.9.1: Proportion of Children Under 5 Years of Age Whose Births have been Registered with a Civil Authority[a] (%)
	2000	2016	2005	2016	2013	2016
Developing ADB Member Economies						
Central and West Asia						
Afghanistan	...	6.3 (2012)	55.3 (2006)	31.3 (2014)	46.8 (2014)	42.3 (2015)
Armenia	3.0	3.0	29.6 (2003)	31.3	7.1	99.3
Azerbaijan	2.8	2.1	11.6 (2004)	19.4	15.9	...
Georgia	5.1	1.0	45.7 (2003)	11.8	2.2	99.6 (2015)
Kazakhstan	15.4 [b]	4.8 [b] (2015)	15.6	13.8 (2015)	26.7	99.7 (2015)
Kyrgyz Republic	8.7	4.5	16.1 (2003)	18.9	59.8	97.7 (2014)
Pakistan	6.4	4.4	58.0 (2004)	69.1 (2015)	30.8	33.6 (2013)
Tajikistan	4.6	1.6 (2011)	18.6 (2006)	...	36.3	88.4 (2012)
Turkmenistan	5.9	...	5.9 (2003)	...	...	99.6
Uzbekistan	4.3	...	12.2 (2003)	...	7.0	...
East Asia						
China, People's Republic of	2.1	0.6	...	...	...	...
Hong Kong, China	0.6	0.4	11.2 (2003)	18.8	...	...
Korea, Republic of	...	0.7	36.6 (2003)	36.8	...	...
Mongolia	13.9 (2003)	5.7	22.6 (2004)	19.8	33.4	99.3 (2013)
Taipei,China	1.4 (2001)	0.8 (2015)	10.6	5.2 (2014)	...	...
South Asia						
Bangladesh	2.5	2.5 (2015)	66.2	75.8 (2015)	47.7	20.2 (2014)
Bhutan	3.1	1.1	...	...	0.9 (2015)	99.9 (2010)
India	4.9	3.2	65.5 (2004)	67.2 (2015)	22.7 (2014)	71.9 (2014)
Maldives	2.4 (2001)	0.8 (2013)	...	...	...	92.5 (2009)
Nepal	2.7	2.2	...	...	14.4	56.2
Sri Lanka	6.8 [b] (2003)	2.5 [b]	50.7	52.8 (2015)	10.0 (2011)	...
Southeast Asia						
Brunei Darussalam	1.2	0.5 (2013)	5.3 (2003)	7.1 (2015)	...	...
Cambodia	4.7	1.8 (2011)	29.8	58.2 (2014)	64.7 (2016)	73.3 (2014)
Indonesia	1.0	0.5	42.9	35.2	30.6 (2015)	72.5
Lao People's Democratic Republic	10.7	7.0 (2015)	...	...	...	...
Malaysia	2.4	2.1 (2013)	37.5	22.7 (2013)	28.2 (2015)	...
Myanmar	2.3	2.3	11.4 (2007)	10.8 (2009)	29.3 (2016)	81.3
Philippines	7.4 [b]	11.0 [b]	63.5 (2004)	68.3 (2015)	17.2 (2015)	90.2 (2010)
Singapore	0.9	0.3	4.8 (2003)	10.0	...	...
Thailand	8.2	3.2	25.0	18.6 (2015)	9.9 (2016)	99.5
Viet Nam	1.2 (2001)	1.5 (2011)	...	17.6 (2015)	...	96.1 (2014)
The Pacific						
Cook Islands	...	3.5 (2012)	3.7	21.6 (2015)	...	...
Fiji	3.1 (2003)	2.3 (2014)	8.5	23.2 (2014)	10.5 (2009)	...
Kiribati	3.6	7.5 (2012)	2.7	5.4	...	93.5 (2009)
Marshall Islands	...	...	...	11.4 (2014)	...	...
Micronesia, Federated States of	4.0	4.7 (2015)	...	18.7 (2013)	...	...
Nauru	...	–	...	...	...	...
Palau	...	3.1 (2012)	4.1	...	...	...
Papua New Guinea	8.3	...	31.3	37.8 (2015)	26.4 (2015)	...
Samoa	...	3.1 (2013)	...	...	30.5 (2009)	58.6 (2014)
Solomon Islands	4.4 (2004)	...	34.2	61.3 (2015)	43.8 (2015)	88.0 (2015)
Timor-Leste	2.3 (2004)	3.9 (2015)	64.7 (2003)	78.3 (2015)	44.2 (2015)	55.2 (2010)
Tonga	1.0	1.0 (2012)	2.5	7.4 (2014)	24.9 (2009)	93.4 (2012)
Tuvalu	– (2002)	18.6 (2012)	...	0.0 (2014)	...	...
Vanuatu	2.9	2.1 (2015)	18.8	12.4 (2012)	11.9 (2009)	43.4 (2013)
Developed ADB Member Economies						
Australia	1.9	0.9	20.5 (2003)	31.2	...	100.0
Japan	0.5	0.3	16.5 (2003)	11.2	...	100.0
New Zealand	1.3 [b]	1.0 [b] (2014)	17.3	18.4	...	100.0

... = data not available, – = magnitude equals zero, ADB = Asian Development Bank.

a Changes in the definition of birth registration were made from the second and third rounds of Multiple Indicator Cluster Surveys (MICS2 and MICS3) to the fourth round (MICS4). In order to allow for comparability with the latter round, data from MICS2 and MICS3 on birth registration were recalculated according to the MICS4 indicator definition. Therefore, the recalculated data presented here may differ from estimates included in MICS2 and MICS3 national reports.

b For Kazakhstan, the Philippines, and Sri Lanka: changes in definitions and/or counting rules are reported by the Member State to indicate a break in the time series. For New Zealand: data for 2000–2006 refer to offences, data for 2007 onwards refer to victims of intentional homicide.

Sources: For Indicator 16.1.1 and Indicator 16.3.2: United Nations Office on Drugs and Crime. UNODC Statistics Online https://dataunodc.un.org/ (accessed 22 June 2018).
For Indicator 16.5.2: World Bank World Development Indicator. https://data.worldbank.org/indicator/ (accessed 22 June 2018). For Indicator 16.9.1: United Nations. Sustainable Development Goals Indicators Database. https://unstats.un.org/sdgs/indicators/database/ (accessed 13 July 2018).

Table 1.17.1: Selected Indicators for Sustainable Development Goal 17—Financial Sustainability of Developing Countries

ADB Regional Member	Target 17.4: Assist developing countries in attaining long-term debt sustainability through coordinated policies aimed at fostering debt financing, debt relief, and debt restructuring, as appropriate, and address the external debt of highly indebted poor countries to reduce debt distress			Target 17.9: Enhance international support for implementing effective and targeted capacity-building in developing countries to support national plans to implement all the Sustainable Development Goals, including through North-South, South-South, and triangular cooperation	
	17.4.1: Debt Service as a Proportion of Exports of Goods and Services (%)			17.9.1: Dollar Value of Financial and Technical Assistance Committed to Developing Countries[a] (constant 2016 $ million)	
	2000		2016	Average, 2000–2008	Average, 2009–2016
Developing ADB Member Economies					
Central and West Asia					
Afghanistan	0.3	(2008)	3.4	551.9	1,449.2
Armenia	8.7		5.4	63.8	87.1
Azerbaijan	5.5		4.4	31.6	78.4
Georgia	12.2		6.9	79.0	121.9
Kazakhstan	8.8		2.7	54.8	312.4
Kyrgyz Republic	9.8		6.5	50.2	90.5
Pakistan	21.1		13.3	360.1	840.4
Tajikistan	9.2	(2002)	7.5	29.4	37.7
Turkmenistan	...		...	6.0	6.0
Uzbekistan	...		...	36.7	132.6
East Asia					
China, People's Republic of	7.1		0.7	329.8	579.8
Hong Kong, China	...		...	...	...
Korea, Republic of	...		...	...	...
Mongolia	6.5		4.0	37.7	164.0
Taipei,China	...		...	...	...
South Asia					
Bangladesh	10.3		3.1	233.0	402.0
Bhutan	2.5	(2006)	11.4	14.9	22.4
India	15.4		5.1	472.4	645.3
Maldives	4.0		2.5	3.6	9.2
Nepal	7.4		8.6	78.8	153.2
Sri Lanka	10.9		16.5	109.7	108.8
Southeast Asia					
Brunei Darussalam	...		...	...	...
Cambodia	0.7		1.4	86.1	114.8
Indonesia	11.2		9.4	630.1	1,306.2
Lao People's Democratic Republic	7.9		8.6	46.6	74.5
Malaysia	2.8		1.7	17.8	14.3
Myanmar	0.4		0.6	15.7	158.6
Philippines	14.6		7.7	132.6	397.3
Singapore	...		...	...	...
Thailand	5.8		0.3	45.7	70.5
Viet Nam	7.2		1.8	301.5	707.7
The Pacific					
Cook Islands	...		...	2.2	4.3
Fiji	2.5		5.6	16.1	13.8
Kiribati	...		...	8.1	7.0
Marshall Islands	...		...	18.1	9.0
Micronesia, Federated States of	...		...	38.5	24.3
Nauru	...		...	8.7	8.8
Palau	...		...	1.7	3.3
Papua New Guinea	8.0		7.7	90.8	154.3
Samoa	5.5	(2004)	8.7	15.0	31.7
Solomon Islands	2.8		1.9	75.3	67.6
Timor-Leste	...		...	52.3	46.0
Tonga	8.9	(2001)	16.2	10.1	14.3
Tuvalu	...		...	3.1	3.8
Vanuatu	1.4		1.6	12.7	19.2
Developed ADB Member Economies					
Australia	...		...	...	...
Japan	...		...	...	...
New Zealand	...		...	...	...

... = data not available, $ = United States dollars, ADB = Asian Development Bank.

a Technical assistance includes assistance through North-South, South-South, and triangular cooperation. United Nations Statistics Division dataset and metadata refer to this indicator as total official development assistance (gross disbursements) for technical cooperation.

Sources: For Indicator 17.4.1: World Bank. World Development Indicators. https://data.worldbank.org (accessed 22 June 2018). For Indicator 17.9.1: United Nations. Sustainable Development Goals Indicators Database. http://unstats.un.org/sdgs/indicators/database/ (accessed 13 July 2018).

Sustainable Development Goals

Goal 17. Strengthen the means of implementation and revitalize the Global Partnership for Sustainable Development

Table 1.17.2: Selected Indicators for Sustainable Development Goal 17—Statistical Capacity Building

ADB Regional Member	17.18.3: Availability of National Statistical Plan[a] 2017	17.19.1: Value of All Resources Made Available to Strengthen Statistical Capacity in Developing Countries (current $) 2006		2015		17.19.2: Countries that Have Conducted at Least One Population and Housing Census in the Last 10 Years[b] 2017
Developing ADB Member Economies						
Central and West Asia						
Afghanistan	...	2,069,400.0		55,747.8		...
Armenia	A, B, C, D	56,731.7		3,384,659.9		2011
Azerbaijan	...	140,534.9		3,769,583.2		2009
Georgia	A, B, C	342,978.7		3,233,049.7		2014
Kazakhstan	...	372,625.0		1,750.0		2009
Kyrgyz Republic	B	260,060.6		3,315,161.0		2009
Pakistan	A, B, C	4,933,085.6		3,250,979.0		2017
Tajikistan	C, D, E	2,411,705.8		4,158,210.0		2010
Turkmenistan	...	279,722.6		18,738.0	(2014)	2012
Uzbekistan	A, B, C, D, E	272,261.8		3,000.0		...
East Asia						
China, People's Republic of	A, B, C	1,568,187.0		6,267,282.8		2010
Hong Kong, China	A, B, C	...		...		2016
Korea, Republic of	A, B, C	...		...		2015
Mongolia	A, B, C, D	2,994,147.0		529,933.5		2010
Taipei,China	...	...		...		2010
South Asia						
Bangladesh	A, B, C, D	1,245,957.7		4,020,075.5		2011
Bhutan	B	598,515.6		16,199.8		2016
India	...	1,171,518.6		1,284,777.8		2011
Maldives	B, C, D	136,444.6		615,424.0	(2013)	2014
Nepal	B, C, D	568,917.5		631,806.1		2011
Sri Lanka	...	361,402.2		686,644.6		2012
Southeast Asia						
Brunei Darussalam	A, B	...		...		2011
Cambodia	C, D	5,058,884.8		2,118,802.9		2008
Indonesia	...	795,895.3		71,663.0	(2013)	2010
Lao People's Democratic Republic	B	468,513.1		689,052.1		2015
Malaysia	...	274,242.8		92,130.2	(2012)	2010
Myanmar	...	1,187,054.1		5,379,831.8		2014
Philippines	B	773,000.7		6,576,861.0		2015
Singapore	A, B, C	...		...		2010
Thailand	B	510,883.2		105,030.1		2010
Viet Nam	B	...		...		2009
The Pacific						
Cook Islands	B	43,363.3		212,521.3	(2014)	2016
Fiji	...	151,154.8		306,012.2	(2014)	2017
Kiribati	...	50,302.5	(2007)	59,903.9	(2013)	2015
Marshall Islands	...	53,283.3		4,029.0		2011
Micronesia, Federated States of	...	210,191.8		20,551.9	(2013)	2010
Nauru	...	34,046.5	(2007)	5,089.9	(2013)	2011
Palau	...	120,972.2		34,808.8		2015
Papua New Guinea	...	1,018,702.0		386,062.3	(2014)	2011
Samoa	B	174,911.1		616,894.3	(2014)	2016
Solomon Islands	...	66,377.7		14,937.1		2009
Timor-Leste	B, C, D	172,795.8		819,371.6		2015
Tonga	...	123,480.6		13,906.9		2016
Tuvalu	...	7,618.0	(2007)	89,478.9	(2013)	2012
Vanuatu	B, C	489,116.6		32,838.9	(2013)	2016
Developed ADB Member Economies						
Australia	A, B, C	...		...		2016
Japan	A, B, C	...		...		2015
New Zealand	A, B, C, E	...		...		2013

... = data not available, $ = United States dollars, ADB = Asian Development Bank.

a A represents a national statistical plan fully funded, B represents a national statistical plan under implementation, C represents a national statistical plan with funding from government, D represents a national statistical plan with funding from donors, E represents a national statistical plan with funding from others.

b Refers to the most recent year that population and housing census was conducted.

Sources: United Nations. Sustainable Development Goals Indicators Global Database. http://unstats.un.org/sdgs/indicators/database/ (accessed 13 July 2018). For Taipei,China: Government of Taipei,China. Directorate-General of Budget, Accounting and Statistics. https://eng.stat.gov.tw/ (accessed 7 August 2018).

PART II
Regional Trends and Tables

Introduction

The *Key Indicators for Asia and the Pacific 2018* contains 101 regional tables depicting trends in social, economic, and environmental developments across Asia and the Pacific. The statistical tables in Part II are grouped into eight themes, each with a short commentary highlighting important recent developments in selected indicators. Each theme concludes with a section on data issues and comparability, wherein issues surrounding the collection and presentation of indicators are detailed.

Data patterns for key indicators are summarized and/or visualized through charts and figures. These charts and figures compare indicators across Asian Development Bank (ADB) member economies for the latest year available, which is generally 2017. In some cases, indicators for the latest year available are compared with either the previous year (e.g., 2016) or an earlier year (e.g., 2000 or 2005). Such comparisons help the reader identify regional, subregional, and economy-level trends.

The eight themes are People; Economy and Output; Money, Finance, and Prices; Globalization; Transport and Communications; Energy and Electricity; Environment; and Government and Governance.

People brings together standard demographic indicators such as population size and age structure, as well as primary educational attainment levels. The regional tables in this section present data on birth, death, and fertility rates; age dependency ratios; urbanization and employment; poverty and inequality; health and education resources; international migration; and the Human Development Index.

Economy and Output presents figures comparing the relative size of economies, both within the region and across the world, using data on gross domestic product (GDP) expressed at purchasing power parity (PPP) and current United States (US) dollars. Regional members' economic growth rates and gross fixed capital formation levels and growth are also discussed. Statistical tables generated from the national accounts, include gross domestic product, value added, consumption expenditure, capital formation, exports and imports, and gross domestic saving. Other tables present production indicators and trends in external trade and domestic consumption.

Money, Finance, and Prices summarizes the latest statistics on consumer price inflation (food and nonfood), the money supply, and nonperforming loans. Other monetary and financial statistics include producer price inflation, interest rates, bank lending, official exchange rates, and stock market capitalization and growth rates.

Globalization focuses on trends in remittances, foreign direct investment, and merchandise exports. The statistical tables cover external trade, balance of payments, international reserves, capital flows, external indebtedness, and tourism. This theme also includes a box discussion on the monitoring of public and private flows to developing Asia, which comprise net private capital flows (including migrant workers remittances), net official loans and grants, and other official flows.

Transport and Communications features a discussion on air carrier departures and passenger traffic, as well as the global surge in mobile telephone subscriptions, particularly in Asia and the Pacific. Other data topics include container port traffic; road and rail networks; motor vehicle ownership, injuries, and fatalities; fixed telephone subscriptions; and broadband internet penetration rates.

Energy and Electricity comprises statistics on energy demand, supplies and uses of primary energy, and electricity consumption and generation. The discussion focuses on trends across the region in energy productivity, total production and sources, and energy imports.

Environment includes a discussion on deforestation and greenhouse gas emissions. Indicators related to land use, forest resources, air and water pollution, and per capita freshwater resources are presented in the tables.

Government and Governance presents statistics on the tax revenues and expenditures of governments; fiscal balances; and expenditures on health and education services, and on social security and welfare. It also includes statistics on the time and cost required to register a new business in each economy, as well as the latest global rankings for Transparency International's Corruption Perceptions Index. The discussion focuses on regional trends in fiscal performance, total government expenditure, and the number of days required to start a business.

I.   People

Snapshot

- The combined population of Asia and the Pacific reached 4,141 million in 2017, or 54.8% of the world's total population, down from 56.0% in 2000. In 2017, 5 of the 10 most populous economies in the world were located in Asia and the Pacific, including the two most populous, the People's Republic of China (PRC), with 1,390 million people, and India, with 1,316 million people.

- The region's population is gradually aging amid increasing life expectancy and decreasing fertility rates. In 2050, the number of people in Asia and the Pacific over the age of 65 is expected to exceed the number under the age of 15.

- Within Asia and the Pacific, there has been a shift in employment away from agriculture and toward sectors with higher productivity and pay, such as industry and services.

- Asia and the Pacific has made great strides in education, particularly in improving access to primary education.

Key Trends

The combined population in Asia and the Pacific reached 4,141 million in 2017, or 54.8% of the world's total population, down from 56.0% in 2000. Figure 2.1.1 shows percentage distribution of population by global regions and economies in Asia and the Pacific.

As of 2017, the two most populous economies in the world—the People's Republic of China (PRC) (1,390 million people) and India (1,316 million) of Asia and the Pacific—accounted for 35.8% of global population. Indonesia (262 million), Pakistan (208 million), and Bangladesh (163 million) were also among the world's 10 most populous economies in 2017. The economies with the smallest populations

Figure 2.1.1: Percentage Distribution of Population by Global Region, and by Economy in Asia and the Pacific, 2017

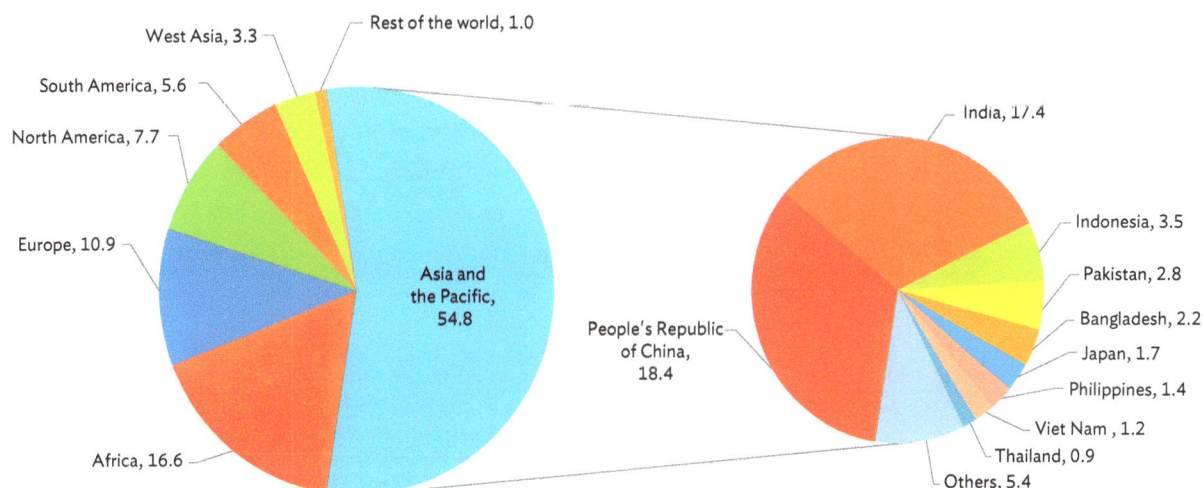

Note: The aggregate for the West Asia region was adjusted to exclude Armenia, Azerbaijan, and Georgia, which are included in the total for Asia and the Pacific.
Source: Table 2.1.1, Key Indicators for Asia and the Pacific 2018.

in the region were all located in the Pacific: Tuvalu (11,400), Nauru (13,300), Palau (17,900), and the Cook Islands (18,200).

South Asia was the most populous region within Asia and the Pacific, comprising 36.9% of the regional total in 2017 (Table 2.1.1). This was followed by East Asia (35.6%), Southeast Asia (15.5%), Central and West Asia (7.9%), and the Pacific (0.3%). Developed member economies accounted for 3.8% of the regional total in 2017.

The United Nations (UN) projects that, by around 2024, the population of India will surpass that of the PRC. The UN also projects that half of the world's population growth from 2017 to 2050 will be concentrated in just nine countries, three of which are in Asia—India, Pakistan, and Indonesia (ordered by their projected contribution to total growth). The world's population in 2050 is projected to reach 9.77 billion, with Asia and the Pacific comprising 53.8% of the total (UN 2017).

The region's population is gradually aging amid increasing life expectancy and decreasing fertility rates. In 2050, the number of people in Asia and the Pacific over the age of 65 is expected to exceed the number under the age of 15. The decline in fertility rates and increase in life expectancy are combining to alter the region's population structure so that, by 2050, the number of people over the age of 65 is expected to exceed the number under the age of 15 (Smith and Majmunder 2012). In 2000, the most populous 5-year age cohort among the region's male and female populations was 10–14 years old. By 2016, this had shifted to 25–29 years old. By 2050, the UN projects the most populous 5-year age cohort will be 35–39 years old for men and 60–64 years old for women (Smith and Majmunder 2012). Population aging will continue to place fiscal and political pressures on the governments of Asia and the Pacific, as they address the increasing costs of health care, old-age pensions, and social protection systems (ADB 2017a).

Within Asia and the Pacific, there has been a shift in employment away from agriculture toward industry and services. New technologies are raising productivity and shifting employment patterns. As some sectors see net job losses, others are experiencing gains, often in the form of better-paid jobs that can drive economic growth (ADB 2018a). From 2000 to 2017, industry's share of total employment increased in 24 of 36 economies and services' share increased in 28 of 36 economies, mostly at the expense of agriculture's share of total employment, which declined in 34 of 36 economies (Table 2.1.6).

Asia and the Pacific has made great strides in education, particularly in improving access to primary education. In the 1970s, Asia and the Pacific was home to two-thirds of the world's out-of-school children. In 2017, 9 out of 10 children in the region were enrolled in primary school.[1] Increased educational attainment reduces an individual's risk of remaining in, or falling into, poverty and improves employment opportunities and the likelihood for participation in civic and political affairs (McMahon 1998).

Figure 2.1.2 shows the gross intake levels for the last grade of primary education for both males and females.[2] The most recent available data ranging from 2012 to 2017 show that only 19 of 42 economies had a gross intake level for the last year of primary education that met or exceeded 100% for all students. A total of 20 economies met this threshold for female students only, while 20 met it for male students only. The gross intake level for the last year of primary education met or exceeded 100% in 4 of 8 economics

---

[1] This information was sourced from https://www.adb.org/sectors/education/issues.

[2] These calculations include all new entrants regardless of age. Therefore, the ratio can exceed 100% due to inclusion in the numerator, but not in the denominator, of overaged and underaged children who enter school late or early, and/or repeat grades. United Nations Educational, Scientific and Cultural Organization (UNESCO) Institute for Statistics. Glossary. http://uis.unesco.org/en/glossary-term/gross-intake-ratio-last-grade-primary-education (accessed 25 July 2018).

Regional Trends and Tables

Figure 2.1.2: Primary Education Completion Rate, by Sex: Latest Year

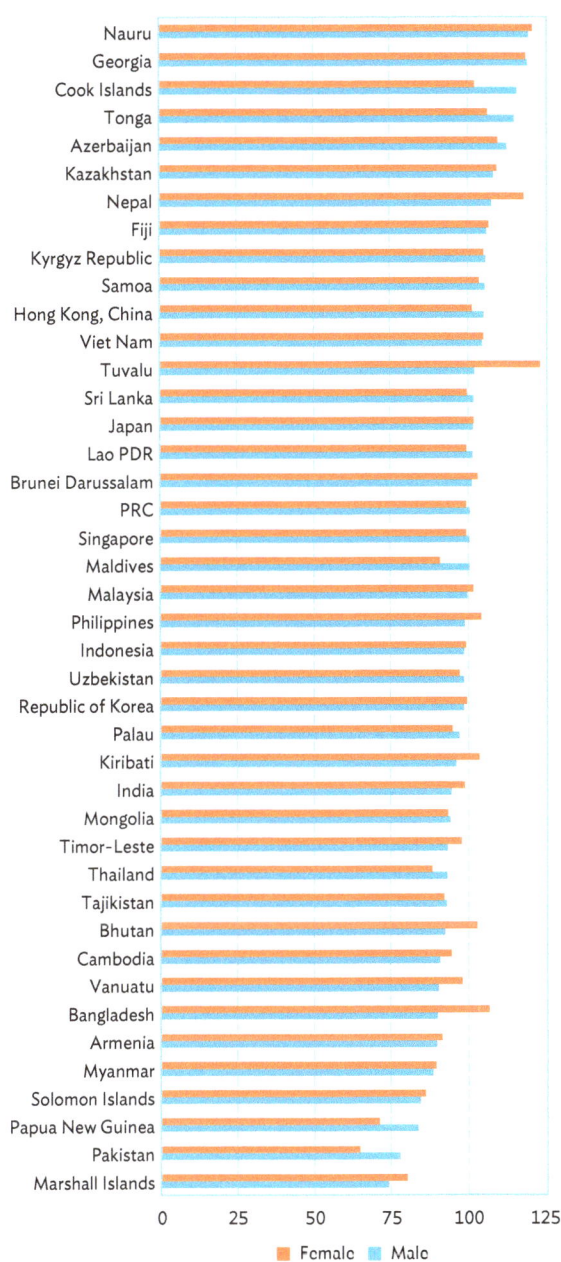

Lao PDR = Lao People's Democratic Republic, PRC = People's Republic of China.
Note: This chart includes economies with available data between 2012 and 2017.
Source: Table 2.1.11, Key Indicators for Asia and the Pacific 2018.

in Central and West Asia, 1 of 4 in East Asia, 2 of 6 in South Asia, 5 of 10 in Southeast Asia, and 6 of 13 in the Pacific (Table 2.1.11).

The lowest average (male and female) levels of primary educational attainment in the latest year for which data is available were observed in Pakistan (71.3%), the Marshall Islands (76.9%), and Papua New Guinea (77.4%).

Data Issues and Comparability

Demographic data are based on vital registration records, censuses, and surveys. Since vital registration records in many of ADB's developing member economies are incomplete, they cannot be used for statistical purposes. In most economies, population censuses, which are used to provide more accurate estimates of population sizes, are conducted every 10 years. Population numbers in between census years are products of imputation methods that use various population distributional assumptions.

The UN Department of Economics and Social Affairs' Population Division uses future trends on fertility, mortality, and international migration to project population numbers through to 2100. The medium-fertility variant included in *World Population Prospects 2017 Revision* assumes a decline in global fertility from over 2.5 births per woman in 2010–2015 to about 2.4 in 2025–2030 and 2.0 in 2095–2100.

Urban population statistics are compiled according to each economy's national definition, as there is no agreed international standard for defining an urban area, which poses constraints in comparability of urban and city indicators across countries (Box 2.1.1). Data from *World Urbanization Prospects* are used when national estimates are not available.

Household surveys, which are the best source of labor force data, are not carried out in all economies on a regular basis. Some economies rely on census data supplemented by enterprise surveys and unemployment registration records, which are often incomplete and may refer only to formal employment. Furthermore, a breakdown by economic activities also may not be available. An initiative is underway to adopt new standards for work and employment statistics, following the recommendations of the 19th International Conference of Labour Statisticians in 2013, which included the need for more in-depth statistics on forced labor, cooperatives, and labor migration as well as guidelines on a statistical definition of employment in the environment sector. The conceptual definitions used here are, however, based on the old framework.

Box 2.1.1: Disaggregation of Urban and Rural Indicators

Overview

As outlined by the United Nations (UN), the number of people in the world living in urban areas surpassed those living in rural areas in 2009 (UN 2009). It is, however, hard to provide conclusive statements about precisely where the majority of the global population lives, since each economy has its own definition of an urban area. The world's estimated total urban population, whether in 2008 or today, is really the aggregate of the individual urban population estimates of 232 different economies. These estimates, however, are based on varying definitions that include factors such as population size, population density, type of economic activity, physical characteristics, and level of infrastructure, or a combination of these and other criteria (World Bank 2015). The national definitions of rural-urban are developed to suit national context, but the differences in definitions pose problems when comparing issues related to, say, urbanization across countries.

There have been attempts to standardize the definition of an urban area. For example, the Organisation for Economic Co-operation and Development (OECD) employs a three-step methodology: (i) identifying contiguous or highly interconnected densely inhabited urban cores, (ii) grouping these into functional areas, and (iii) defining the hinterland of the functional urban area (OECD 2012). The World Bank is using map layers to build on this core-and-hinterland approach to develop standard, comparable definitions of urban areas (World Bank 2015).

From a development standpoint, the definition of urban areas, based on a common set of standards, can help facilitate the collection and effective utilization of the socioeconomic data that are needed to manage the urbanization process (Population Reference Bureau 2015). At the same time, the data collection process in rural areas presents unique challenges that impact research outcomes and subsequent policy recommendations (International Labour Organization 2018). For example, rural areas are more likely to not provide administrative data in digital format, making analysis difficult (German Development Institute 2018).

Data Disaggregation and the Sustainable Development Goals

As country-level data can mask disparities between rural and urban areas, the comprehensive collection of disaggregated data can help to inform and promote evidence-based policymaking (World Bank 2013). Insufficiently disaggregated data might miss trends in development at the intracountry level or among different sections of the population. A failure to account for geographic differences can impede the implementation of the Sustainable Development Goals (SDGs) and violate their principle of "leave no one behind" (German Development Institute 2018).

Working on behalf of the United Nations secretary-general, the Independent Expert Advisory Group on the Data Revolution for Sustainable Development (IEAG) has established three working groups—on statistical data and metadata exchange, geospatial information, and interlinkages—and one workstream on data disaggregation (UN 2017a). The IEAG has called for data collection that provides for granularity and disaggregation of the SDG indicators based on geography, where appropriate, to better understand urban–rural disparities (UN 2017b).

Under SDG Target 17.18, the IEAG is seeking, by 2020, enhanced capacity-building support to developing countries to increase the availability of high-quality, timely, and reliable data disaggregated by geographic location, among other characteristics relevant in national contexts (IEAG 2014). To realize this objective, new sources and methods will be needed to complement existing data collection and disaggregation strategies.

continued on next page

Box 2.1.1 continued

The Application of Satellite Imagery in Defining Rural-Urban

To address the varying definitions of urban and rural areas across economies, the European Union—together with the Food and Agricultural Organization, the Organisation for Economic Co-operation and Development, and the World Bank—is developing a global people-based definition of cities and settlements, based on a 1 square kilometer population grid. Satellite imagery of areas covered by buildings is aggregated into 1 square kilometer grids that are layered with population census data. Based on the conditions detailed in the table below, the following classifications are applied: urban centers (cities) and urban clusters (towns and suburbs), which are collectively known as urban areas; and rural grid cells (rural areas) (European Commission 2017).

Three Types of Grid Cells

Urban centers	Contiguous cells with at least 1,500 inhabitants per km^2 and at least 50,000 inhabitants in the center
Urban clusters	Contiguous cells with at least 300 inhabitants per km^2 and at least 5,000 inhabitants in the cluster
Rural grid cells	All cells outside urban clusters

km^2 = square kilometer.
Source: European Commission. 2017. *Developing a Global, People-Based Definition of Cities and Settlements.* 2030 Agenda for Sustainable Development Forum. 10–12 May. Kunming.

A potential flaw in this approach may arise if populations are not reported accurately or if building detection methods overestimate or underestimate the presence of buildings. To address these concerns, pilot initiatives are underway in partnership with national statistical offices using economy-level data.

Sources:

European Commission. 2017. *Developing a Global, People-Based Definition of Cities and Settlements.* 2030 Agenda for Sustainable Development Forum. 10–12 May. Kunming.

German Development Institute. 2018. *Data for Development: An Agenda for German Development Cooperation.* https://www.die-gdi.de/uploads/media/BP_12.2018.pdf.

IEAG. 2014. A *World That Counts: Mobilising the Data Revolution for Sustainable Development.* https://www.undatarevolution.org/wp-content/uploads/2014/12/A-World-That-Counts2.pdf.

International Labour Organization. 2018. *Rural Labour Statistics.* http://www.ilo.org/global/statistics-and-databases/statistics-overview-and-topics/rural-labour/lang--en/index.htm (accessed 18 July 2018).

OECD. 2012. iLibrary. Redefining Urban. https://www.oecd-ilibrary.org/urban-rural-and-regional-development/redefining-urban_9789264174108-en.

Population Reference Bureau. 2015. *The Urban–Rural Divide in Health and Development.* https://www.prb.org/wp-content/uploads/2015/05/urban-rural-datasheet-1.pdf.

UN. 2009. Department of Economic and Social Affairs, Population Division. *Urban and Rural Areas.* http://www.un.org/en/development/desa/population/publications/pdf/urbanization/urbanization-wallchart2009.pdf.

UN. 2017a. Economic and Social Council. *Report of the Inter-Agency and Expert Group on Sustainable Development Goal Indicators.* New York. 8–11 March 2017.

UN. 2017b. Department of Economic and Social Affairs, Statistics Division. *Data Disaggregation and the SDGs: An Overview.* https://psa.gov.ph/system/files/Plenary%20Session%204_Min.pdf.

World Bank. 2013. *Global Monitoring Report: Rural–Urban Disparities and Dynamics.* Washington, DC.

World Bank. 2015. Sustainable Cities. What Does Urban Mean? http://blogs.worldbank.org/sustainablecities/what-does-urban-mean.

Population

Table 2.1.1:   Midyear Population

ADB Regional Member	Population (million)				Population Growth Rates[a] (%)			
	2000	2005	2010	2017	2000	2005	2010	2017
Developing ADB Member Economies								
Central and West Asia	**231.5**	**253.2**	**278.3**	**325.2**	**1.8**	**1.8**	**2.0**	**4.5**
Afghanistan[b]	21.0	23.6	26.0	29.7	1.4	1.7	2.0	1.7
Armenia	3.2	3.1	3.0	3.0	-0.3	-0.6	-0.7	-0.4
Azerbaijan	8.1	8.5	9.1	9.9	1.1	1.2	1.2	1.0
Georgia[b]	4.1	3.9	3.8	3.7	-1.9	-0.6	-0.7	0.0
Kazakhstan	14.9	15.1	16.3	18.0	-0.3	0.9	1.4	1.3
Kyrgyz Republic[b]	4.9	5.1	5.4	6.1	1.4	1.2	1.3	2.0
Pakistan	140.0	156.0	173.5	207.8	2.4	2.2	2.1	2.4
Tajikistan	6.2	6.8	7.5	8.8	2.3	1.2	2.5	2.2
Turkmenistan	4.5	4.8	5.1	5.8	1.1	1.1	1.6	1.7
Uzbekistan	24.7	26.2	28.6	32.4	1.4	1.2	2.9	1.7
East Asia	**1,345.7**	**1,387.8**	**1,423.4**	**1,475.6**	**0.8**	**0.6**	**0.5**	**0.5**
China, People's Republic of[b]	1,267.4	1,307.6	1,340.9	1,390.1	0.8	0.6	0.5	0.5
Hong Kong, China	6.7	6.8	7.0	7.4	0.9	0.4	0.7	0.8
Korea, Republic of	47.0	48.2	49.6	51.4	0.8	0.2	0.5	0.4
Mongolia	2.4	2.5	2.7	3.1	1.3	1.1	1.8	1.9
Taipei,China	22.2	22.7	23.1	23.6	0.8	0.4	0.3	0.2
South Asia	**1,189.6**	**1,290.5**	**1,382.6**	**1,530.1**	**1.6**	**1.5**	**1.4**	**1.3**
Bangladesh	129.3	138.6	148.6	162.7	1.4	1.4	1.3	1.2
Bhutan	0.6	0.6	0.7	0.7	1.3	1.3	1.8	1.3
India[b]	1,019.0	1,106.0	1,186.0	1,316.0	1.8	1.5	1.4	1.3
Maldives	0.3	0.3	0.4	0.5	1.5	3.3	2.3	4.3
Nepal	21.0	25.3	26.3	28.7	3.0	2.3	1.4	1.4
Sri Lanka	19.4	19.6	20.7	21.4	1.3	0.9	1.0	1.1
Southeast Asia	**513.9**	**548.6**	**588.9**	**641.7**	**1.5**	**1.3**	**2.0**	**1.1**
Brunei Darussalam	0.3	0.4	0.4	0.4	2.5	1.8	1.8	1.0
Cambodia	12.5	13.3	14.1	15.4	1.3	1.3	1.3	1.3
Indonesia	206.3	219.9	238.5	261.9	1.2	1.3	2.7	1.2
Lao People's Democratic Republic	5.1	5.6	6.0	6.7	2.0	2.0	1.5	1.4
Malaysia	23.5	26.0	28.6	32.0	2.5	2.1	1.8	1.3
Myanmar[b]	46.1	48.5	50.2	53.4	1.2	0.9	0.7	0.9
Philippines	76.8	84.7	93.1	104.9	2.3	1.9	2.3	1.6
Singapore	4.0	4.3	5.1	5.6	1.7	2.4	1.8	0.1
Thailand	62.2	64.1	65.9	67.7	1.1	0.6	0.6	0.4
Viet Nam	77.1	81.9	86.9	93.7	1.4	1.2	1.1	1.1
The Pacific[c]	**8.0**	**9.2**	**10.4**	**12.5**	**4.5**	**2.7**	**2.6**	**2.7**
Cook Islands	18.0	21.5	23.7	18.2	9.1	5.9	4.9	-6.6
Fiji	802.0	827.0	850.7	884.9	0.6	0.7	0.6	1.3
Kiribati[b]	84.5	92.5	103.1	113.1	1.7	1.8	2.2	1.3
Marshall Islands	51.2	51.2	52.9	54.4	0.8	1.4	1.2	0.4
Micronesia, Federated States of[b]	107.0	105.6	102.8	102.5	0.2	-0.3	-0.5	0.1
Nauru	10.1	9.5	9.7	13.3	1.0	-2.2	1.9	2.3
Palau	18.9	19.8	18.3	17.9	0.3	0.8	-1.9	0.2
Papua New Guinea	5,190.8	6,051.7	7,055.4	8,746.3	3.3	3.1	3.1	3.1
Samoa	175.1	179.9	186.4	197.5	1.0	0.6	0.6	0.9
Solomon Islands	418.6	470.1	528.0	620.8	2.3	2.3	2.3	2.3
Timor-Leste	871.6	1,026.5	1,109.6	1,296.3	1.0	3.0	1.6	2.2
Tonga	99.1	101.2	102.8	100.1	0.4	0.4	0.2	-0.5
Tuvalu	9.5	10.3	11.1	11.4	1.3	3.1	0.5	1.2
Vanuatu	190.9	214.0	239.7	278.4	2.3	2.3	2.4	2.2
Developed ADB Member Economies	**149.7**	**152.1**	**154.5**	**156.2**	**0.2**	**0.2**	**0.3**	**0.2**
Australia	19.0	20.2	22.0	24.6	1.2	1.2	1.6	1.6
Japan	126.8	127.8	128.1	126.8	0.2	0.0	0.0	-0.2
New Zealand	3.9	4.1	4.4	4.8	0.6	1.1	1.1	2.1
DEVELOPING ADB MEMBER ECONOMIES[d]	**3,288.6**	**3,489.3**	**3,683.5**	**3,985.0**	**1.3**	**1.1**	**1.2**	**1.2**
ALL ADB REGIONAL MEMBERS[d]	**3,438.3**	**3,641.4**	**3,838.0**	**4,141.2**	**1.2**	**1.1**	**1.1**	**1.2**
WORLD	**6,145.0**	**6,542.2**	**6,958.2**	**7,550.3**	**1.3**	**1.3**	**1.2**	**1.1**

0.0 = magnitude is less than half of unit employed, ADB = Asian Development Bank.

a   The annual population growth rate is calculated as the percentage change of the population between the reference year and the year prior to the reference year. For example, the population growth rates under the column heading "2017" refer to population growth between 2016 and 2017.

b   Estimates of population size are as of 1 January for Georgia and the Kyrgyz Republic; 1 May for Afghanistan; 1 April for 2000, 4 April for 2010, and 30 September for 2005 and 2017 for the Federated States of Micronesia; 1 October for India and Myanmar; 7 November for Kiribati; and 31 December for the People's Republic of China.

c   Estimates of population size for ADB developing member economies in the Pacific are in thousands while the total population for the Pacific region is expressed in millions.

d   For reporting economies only.

Sources: Economy sources; and United Nations Population Division, Department of Economic and Social Affairs. World Population Prospects, The 2017 Revision. https://esa.un.org/unpd/wpp/ (accessed 14 June 2018).

Table 2.1.2: Migration and Urbanization

ADB Regional Member	Net International Migration Rate[a] (per 1,000 population)				Urban Population (% of total population)			
	2000–2005	2005–2010	2010–2015	2015–2020[b]	2000	2005	2010	2017
Developing ADB Member Economies								
Central and West Asia								
Afghanistan	8.2	-5.8	2.9	-1.7	20.0	20.3	21.9	24.0
Armenia	-10.6	-12.5	-2.1	-1.7	64.8	64.0	63.5	63.7
Azerbaijan	0.9	1.2	0.0	0.0	51.1	52.5	53.0	53.0
Georgia	-12.1	-13.7	-14.9	-2.5	55.4	56.7	56.7	58.0
Kazakhstan	0.6	-0.4	1.9	0.0	56.5	57.1	54.5	57.3
Kyrgyz Republic	-6.9	-2.9	-4.9	-3.3	34.7	34.8	34.1	32.6 (2016)
Pakistan	-0.9	-1.7	-1.3	-1.1	33.0	34.6	36.3	36.4
Tajikistan	-2.5	-2.0	-2.5	-2.2	26.6	26.4	26.4	27.0
Turkmenistan	-5.4	-2.5	-1.9	-0.9	45.9	47.1	48.5	51.2
Uzbekistan	-1.9	-1.0	-0.4	-0.3	37.2	36.1	51.3	50.7
East Asia								
China, People's Republic of	-0.3	-0.4	-0.2	-0.2	36.2	43.0	50.0	58.5
Hong Kong, China	1.9	2.6	2.1	4.0	100.0	100.0	100.0	100.0
Korea, Republic of	0.3	-0.6	0.7	0.8	79.6	81.3	81.9	82.7
Mongolia	-1.2	-1.1	-1.1	-1.0	56.6	61.9	69.2	67.6
Taipei,China[c]	1.8	2.2	1.5	1.3	55.8	57.7	59.3	61.1
South Asia								
Bangladesh	-2.2	-4.8	-3.2	-2.8	23.1	24.2	25.9	35.9
Bhutan	9.4	4.9	2.6	0.0	21.0	30.9	34.8	37.8
India	-0.4	-0.5	-0.4	-0.4	27.7	28.8	29.9	33.6
Maldives	9.2	10.5	11.2	4.4	27.7	33.8	36.4	39.4
Nepal	-6.5	-7.8	-2.7	-2.4	14.1	14.6	16.6	20.1
Sri Lanka	-4.7	-5.2	-4.7	-4.3	14.6 (2001)	15.1	18.2 (2012)	19.4
Southeast Asia								
Brunei Darussalam	1.9	-1.1	1.0	0.8	71.2	73.2	75.0	77.3
Cambodia	-0.6	-4.3	-2.0	-1.9	18.6	19.2	20.3	23.0
Indonesia	-0.8	-0.6	-0.7	-0.6	42.0	45.9	49.9	54.7
Lao People's Democratic Republic	-5.3	-3.7	-5.5	-2.1	22.0	27.2	30.1	34.4
Malaysia	5.3	5.3	5.3	1.6	62.0	66.5	71.0	75.5
Myanmar	-5.3	-5.9	-1.9	-0.4	27.0	27.9	28.9	29.5
Philippines	-2.7	-3.3	-1.3	-1.2	46.1	45.7	45.3	46.7
Singapore	20.7	18.8	12.7	10.4	100.0	100.0	100.0	100.0
Thailand	1.2	0.2	0.5	0.3	31.1	32.5	42.0	49.2
Viet Nam	-1.6	-2.0	-0.4	-0.4	24.2	27.1	30.5	35.0
The Pacific								
Cook Islands	...	...	...	...	65.2	71.0	73.3	74.8
Fiji	-15.1	-6.8	-6.6	-4.4	47.9	49.9	51.8	55.9
Kiribati	-4.6	-1.2	-4.0	-3.6	43.0	43.6	43.8	44.4 (2016)
Marshall Islands	...	...	...	...	68.4	69.9	71.3	72.9 (2016)
Micronesia, Federated States of	-24.1	-23.1	-15.8	-11.3	22.3	22.3	22.3	22.6
Nauru	...	...	...	...	100.0	100.0	100.0	100.0
Palau	...	...	...	...	69.5	77.4	77.0	78.7 (2015)
Papua New Guinea	-0.0	-0.0	-0.0	-0.0	13.2	13.1	13.0	13.1
Samoa	-17.7	-16.8	-13.4	-12.7	22.0	21.2	20.1	18.5
Solomon Islands	-2.2	-4.8	-4.3	-3.9	15.8	17.8	20.0	23.3
Timor-Leste	0.8	-17.6	-8.5	-7.6	24.3	26.0	27.7	30.2
Tonga	-16.3	-16.0	-15.4	-8.9	23.0	23.2	23.4	23.2
Tuvalu	...	...	...	...	46.0	49.7	54.8	61.5
Vanuatu	-0.5	1.0	0.5	0.4	21.8	23.2	24.4	24.9
Developed ADB Member Economies								
Australia	5.9	10.6	8.0	6.9	84.1 (2001)	84.6	85.7	86.7
Japan	0.3	0.4	0.6	0.4	78.6	86.0	90.8	91.5
New Zealand	6.7	2.9	4.0	3.2	85.7	86.1	86.2	86.5

... = data not available, -0.0 or 0.0 = magnitude is less than half of unit employed, ADB = Asian Development Bank.

a Refers to annual average.
b For 2015–2020, the United Nations Population Division projected the country's population based on the medium-fertility variant where fertility is above 2.5 children per woman in 2010 to 2015 censuses.
c For urban population, refers to localities of 100,000 or more inhabitants.

Sources: Economy sources; United Nations Population Division, Department of Economic and Social Affairs. World Urbanization Prospects, the 2018 Revision – Data Query. https://esa.un.org/unpd/wup/DataQuery/ (accessed 14 June 2018); and World Population Prospects. The 2017 Revision https://esa.un.org/unpd/wpp/Download/Standard/Migration/ (accessed 14 June 2018).

Population

Table 2.1.3:   Population Aged 0–14 Years and Aged 15–64 Years
(% of total population)

ADB Regional Member	Population Aged 0–14 Years				Population Aged 15–64 Years			
	2000	2005	2010	2017[a]	2000	2005	2010	2017[a]
Developing ADB Member Economies								
Central and West Asia	**39.3**	**36.5**	**34.8**	**33.9**	**56.2**	**58.8**	**60.6**	**61.5**
Afghanistan	48.6	47.6	47.8	43.2	49.2	50.2	49.9	54.2
Armenia	25.8	21.5	19.5	20.0	64.2	66.6	69.5	68.8
Azerbaijan	31.1	26.2	22.8	23.3	63.0	67.2	71.3	70.7
Georgia	22.6	19.5	18.0	19.2	65.0	66.2	67.7	66.0
Kazakhstan	27.6	24.5	24.0	27.9	65.6	67.8	69.1	65.1
Kyrgyz Republic	34.9	31.0	29.9	31.8	59.6	63.4	65.6	63.7
Pakistan	41.1	38.2	36.2	34.8	54.8	57.6	59.4	60.7
Tajikistan	42.5	38.1	35.7	35.3	53.9	58.0	60.8	61.3
Turkmenistan	36.3	32.6	29.5	30.9	59.5	62.8	66.3	64.8
Uzbekistan	37.3	32.6	29.1	28.0	58.1	62.6	66.4	67.5
East Asia	**24.4**	**19.8**	**17.7**	**17.5**	**68.6**	**72.4**	**73.7**	**71.7**
China, People's Republic of	24.6	19.9	17.8	17.7	68.5	72.4	73.8	71.7
Hong Kong, China	16.9	14.4	11.9	11.5	72.1	73.4	75.1	72.2
Korea, Republic of	20.6	18.8	16.1	13.5	72.2	72.3	73.2	72.6
Mongolia	34.8	28.9	27.0	29.7	61.5	67.3	69.2	66.3
Taipei,China	21.4	19.2	16.1	13.3	70.1	71.2	73.2	73.2
South Asia	**35.0**	**33.0**	**31.1**	**27.9**	**60.7**	**62.3**	**63.8**	**66.2**
Bangladesh	37.1	34.4	32.1	28.4	59.1	61.3	63.2	66.5
Bhutan	41.4	34.9	30.6	26.5	55.1	61.3	65.3	68.6
India	34.7	32.8	30.9	27.8	60.9	62.4	64.0	66.2
Maldives	40.7	31.6	25.5	23.4	55.6	64.2	70.1	72.5
Nepal	41.0	39.7	37.0	30.9	55.2	56.0	58.1	63.3
Sri Lanka	26.8	25.6	25.4	24.0	67.0	67.6	67.3	65.9
Southeast Asia	**31.8**	**29.9**	**28.0**	**26.2**	**63.3**	**64.9**	**66.6**	**67.5**
Brunei Darussalam	30.6	27.8	26.0	23.0	67.0	69.2	70.6	72.4
Cambodia	41.6	37.1	33.3	31.3	55.3	59.5	62.9	64.3
Indonesia	30.7	30.0	29.0	27.4	64.6	65.2	66.2	67.3
Lao People's Democratic Republic	43.4	40.3	36.3	32.9	53.1	56.1	60.0	63.1
Malaysia	33.4	30.5	27.9	24.3	62.7	65.1	67.1	69.4
Myanmar	32.1	30.9	30.0	26.8	63.0	64.3	65.1	67.4
Philippines	38.5	37.1	33.9	31.7	58.3	59.4	62.0	63.5
Singapore	21.5	19.1	17.3	15.0	71.2	72.6	73.6	72.1
Thailand	24.0	21.3	19.2	17.3	69.5	70.9	71.9	71.3
Viet Nam	31.7	27.2	23.7	23.1	61.9	66.3	69.8	69.8
The Pacific	**40.5**	**39.5**	**38.3**	**36.3**	**56.3**	**57.1**	**58.1**	**59.7**
Cook Islands	34.7	31.4	28.0	27.1	59.1	61.3	64.0	62.9
Fiji	35.0	30.5	29.0	28.5	61.5	65.4	66.2	65.3
Kiribati	40.0	36.9	36.1	35.0	56.7	59.5	60.4	61.1
Marshall Islands	42.3	41.3	41.8	39.2	55.5	56.5	55.9	57.6
Micronesia, Federated States of	40.3	38.8	36.9	33.1	56.0	57.2	59.3	62.1
Nauru	40.1	37.1	35.6	39.7	58.6	61.2	63.1	58.2
Palau	23.9	24.1	20.5	19.5	70.7	70.2	73.7	71.5
Papua New Guinea	39.7	39.1	38.3	35.9	57.1	57.6	58.3	60.3
Samoa	40.7	39.6	38.3	36.6	54.8	55.6	56.7	57.8
Solomon Islands	41.9	41.3	40.8	38.8	55.2	55.7	55.9	57.7
Timor-Leste	50.4	49.2	45.6	43.6	47.4	48.3	51.3	52.8
Tonga	38.4	38.2	37.4	35.8	55.8	55.8	56.8	58.3
Tuvalu	37.1	34.3	32.0	32.7	57.0	60.1	62.7	61.5
Vanuatu	41.5	39.7	38.2	35.9	55.2	57.0	57.9	59.7
Developed ADB Member Economies	**15.8**	**14.8**	**14.4**	**14.0**	**68.0**	**66.6**	**64.7**	**61.1**
Australia	20.9	19.8	19.0	19.0	66.8	67.3	67.5	65.5
Japan	14.8	13.8	13.4	12.9	68.2	66.5	64.1	60.1
New Zealand	22.7	21.5	20.5	19.8	65.5	66.4	66.4	64.9
DEVELOPING ADB MEMBER ECONOMIES	**30.5**	**27.6**	**25.8**	**24.2**	**64.0**	**66.4**	**67.8**	**68.1**
ALL ADB REGIONAL MEMBERS	**29.9**	**27.1**	**25.3**	**23.9**	**64.2**	**66.4**	**67.7**	**67.8**
WORLD	**30.2**	**28.0**	**26.7**	**25.9**	**63.0**	**64.7**	**65.7**	**65.4**

ADB = Asian Development Bank.

a   Data for 2017 are based on projections from the United Nations Population Division. These projections follow the medium-fertility variant wherein fertility is estimated to be above 2.5 children per woman in 2010 to 2015 censuses.

Sources: United Nations, Department of Economic and Social Affairs, Population Division. World Population Prospects, The 2017 Revision. https://esa.un.org/unpd/wpp/ (accessed 13 June 2018). For the Cook Islands, the Marshall Islands, Nauru, Palau, and Tuvalu: Statistics for Development Division. http://sdd.spc. int/en/ (accessed 13 June 2018).

Table 2.1.4: Population Aged 65 Years and Over and Age Dependency Ratio

ADB Regional Member	Population Aged 65 Years and Over (% of total population)				Age Dependency Ratio			
	2000	2005	2010	2017[a]	2000	2005	2010	2017[a]
Developing ADB Member Economies								
Central and West Asia	**4.5**	**4.7**	**4.6**	**4.6**	**78.0**	**70.0**	**65.0**	**62.6**
Afghanistan	2.2	2.2	2.3	2.6	103.3	99.0	100.4	84.6
Armenia	10.0	11.9	11.0	11.2	55.8	50.1	43.8	45.4
Azerbaijan	5.8	6.6	5.9	6.0	58.7	48.8	40.3	41.4
Georgia	12.4	14.3	14.3	14.9	53.9	51.1	47.8	51.6
Kazakhstan	6.8	7.7	6.8	7.0	52.4	47.4	44.6	53.7
Kyrgyz Republic	5.5	5.6	4.5	4.5	67.9	57.7	52.5	57.1
Pakistan	4.1	4.3	4.4	4.5	82.4	73.6	68.4	64.7
Tajikistan	3.6	3.9	3.4	3.5	85.6	72.3	64.4	63.2
Turkmenistan	4.3	4.6	4.1	4.3	68.2	59.2	50.7	54.3
Uzbekistan	4.6	4.8	4.5	4.5	72.1	59.8	50.7	48.0
East Asia	**7.0**	**7.8**	**8.5**	**10.8**	**45.7**	**38.1**	**35.6**	**39.4**
China, People's Republic of	6.9	7.7	8.4	10.6	46.1	38.1	35.6	39.5
Hong Kong, China	11.0	12.3	13.0	16.3	38.6	36.2	33.2	38.5
Korea, Republic of	7.2	8.9	10.7	13.9	38.5	38.3	36.6	37.7
Mongolia	3.7	3.7	3.8	4.0	62.5	48.5	44.4	50.8
Taipei,China	8.5	9.6	10.7	13.4	42.7	40.4	36.5	36.5
South Asia	**4.4**	**4.7**	**5.1**	**5.9**	**64.9**	**60.6**	**56.6**	**51.0**
Bangladesh	3.8	4.3	4.7	5.1	69.2	63.1	58.2	50.3
Bhutan	3.5	3.8	4.2	4.9	81.4	63.2	53.2	45.8
India	4.4	4.8	5.1	6.0	64.3	60.1	56.3	51.0
Maldives	3.7	4.3	4.5	4.1	79.9	55.9	42.7	38.0
Nepal	3.8	4.3	4.9	5.8	81.0	78.4	72.2	58.0
Sri Lanka	6.2	6.8	7.3	10.1	49.2	48.0	48.7	51.7
Southeast Asia	**4.9**	**5.2**	**5.5**	**6.3**	**57.9**	**54.1**	**50.2**	**48.1**
Brunei Darussalam	2.4	3.0	3.4	4.6	49.4	44.5	41.6	38.2
Cambodia	3.1	3.4	3.7	4.4	80.7	67.9	58.9	55.5
Indonesia	4.7	4.8	4.8	5.3	54.8	53.5	51.1	48.5
Lao People's Democratic Republic	3.6	3.7	3.7	4.0	88.5	78.4	66.6	58.5
Malaysia	3.9	4.4	4.9	6.3	59.4	53.5	49.0	44.1
Myanmar	4.8	4.8	4.9	5.7	58.6	55.6	53.6	48.3
Philippines	3.3	3.5	4.1	4.8	71.6	68.2	61.4	57.5
Singapore	7.3	8.2	9.0	12.9	40.5	37.7	35.8	38.7
Thailand	6.5	7.8	8.9	11.4	43.9	41.0	39.1	40.2
Viet Nam	6.4	6.6	6.6	7.1	61.5	50.9	43.3	43.3
The Pacific	**3.1**	**3.3**	**3.6**	**4.0**	**77.5**	**75.0**	**72.1**	**67.6**
Cook Islands	6.2	7.3	8.0	9.9	69.3	63.1	56.2	58.9
Fiji	3.4	4.1	4.8	6.2	62.5	53.0	51.1	53.1
Kiribati	3.3	3.6	3.5	3.9	76.3	68.0	65.6	63.6
Marshall Islands	2.1	2.2	2.3	3.1	80.0	76.9	78.8	73.5
Micronesia, Federated States of	3.7	4.0	3.8	4.8	78.7	74.8	68.8	61.1
Nauru	1.3	1.7	1.3	2.0	70.7	63.4	58.5	71.8
Palau	5.4	5.7	5.8	9.0	41.4	42.5	35.7	39.8
Papua New Guinea	3.2	3.3	3.4	3.8	75.1	73.7	71.5	66.0
Samoa	4.5	4.8	5.1	5.6	82.5	79.9	76.5	73.0
Solomon Islands	2.8	3.0	3.3	3.5	81.0	79.6	78.8	73.5
Timor-Leste	2.2	2.6	3.1	3.6	111.1	107.1	94.9	89.3
Tonga	5.7	6.0	5.9	5.8	79.1	79.2	76.1	71.4
Tuvalu	5.9	5.6	5.3	5.9	75.4	66.5	59.5	62.7
Vanuatu	3.3	3.3	3.9	4.4	81.2	75.4	72.9	67.5
Developed ADB Member Economies	**16.3**	**18.6**	**20.9**	**24.9**	**47.1**	**50.1**	**54.6**	**63.8**
Australia	12.3	12.9	13.4	15.5	49.7	48.6	48.1	52.7
Japan	17.0	19.7	22.5	27.0	46.6	50.3	55.9	66.5
New Zealand	11.8	12.1	13.1	15.3	52.7	50.6	50.5	54.1
DEVELOPING ADB MEMBER ECONOMIES	**5.5**	**6.0**	**6.4**	**7.7**	**56.3**	**50.6**	**47.5**	**46.9**
ALL ADB REGIONAL MEMBERS	**6.0**	**6.5**	**7.0**	**8.3**	**55.8**	**50.6**	**47.7**	**47.5**
WORLD	**6.8**	**7.3**	**7.6**	**8.7**	**58.7**	**54.6**	**52.3**	**52.9**

ADB = Asian Development Bank.

a Data for 2017 are based on projections from the United Nations Population Division. These projections follow the medium-fertility variant wherein fertility is estimated to be above 2.5 children per woman in 2010 to 2015 censuses.

Sources: United Nations, Department of Economic and Social Affairs, Population Division. World Population Prospects, The 2017 Revision. https://esa.un.org/unpd/wpp/ (accessed 13 June 2018). For the Cook Islands, the Marshall Islands, Nauru, Palau, and Tuvalu: Statistics for Development Division. http://sdd.spc. int/en/ (accessed 13 June 2018).

Labor Force and Employment

Table 2.1.5:   Labor Force Participation Rates[a]
(%)

ADB Regional Member	2000	2005	2010	2012	2013	2014	2015	2016	2017
Developing ADB Member Economies									
Central and West Asia									
Afghanistan	...	...	...	...	55.4	...	...	53.9	...
Armenia	61.4	57.7	61.2	62.7	63.4	63.1	62.5	61.0	60.9*
Azerbaijan	77.6	68.4	64.8	64.5	64.7	65.1	65.4	66.0	66.2
Georgia	65.2	62.7	63.3	65.6	65.2	65.5	66.8	66.3	65.8
Kazakhstan	66.0	69.4	71.2	71.7	71.7	70.7	69.7	70.0	69.7
Kyrgyz Republic	76.4 (2002)	75.8	73.4	73.2	71.3	71.2	71.5	70.7	...
Pakistan	42.8	43.7	45.9	45.7	45.7	45.5	45.2	...	...
Tajikistan	56.3	55.0	50.3	48.9	48.6	47.8	47.7	46.7	...
Turkmenistan	63.4	63.5	64.2	64.7	65.0	65.3	65.4	65.5	65.5
Uzbekistan	62.9	63.2	64.1	64.6	64.9	65.2	65.4	65.5	65.7
East Asia									
China, People's Republic of	77.2	73.4	71.0	70.5	70.3	70.0	69.7	69.4	68.9
Hong Kong, China	61.4	60.9	59.6	60.5	61.2	61.1	61.1	61.1	61.1
Korea, Republic of	61.2	62.2	61.1	61.6	61.7	62.7	62.8	62.9	63.2
Mongolia	62.9	63.5	61.6	63.5	61.9	62.1	61.5	60.5	61.1
Taipei,China	57.7	57.8	58.1	58.4	58.4	58.5	58.7	58.8	58.8
South Asia									
Bangladesh	54.9	58.5 (2006)	59.3	...	57.1	...	...	58.5	58.2
Bhutan	56.5 (2001)	60.4	68.6	64.4	65.3	62.6	63.1	62.2	63.3
India	37.6	39.2	37.4 (2009)	...	...	...	...	...	...
Maldives[b]	47.7	57.7 (2006)	52.1	...	...	63.8	...	...	...
Nepal	...	77.2 (2004)	83.4 (2008)	74.3	77.2	72.2	...	...	...
Sri Lanka	50.3	49.3	48.6	52.5	53.7	53.2	53.8	53.8	54.1
Southeast Asia									
Brunei Darussalam	67.9 (2001)	...	...	...	...	65.6	...	...	...
Cambodia	65.2	74.6 (2004)	87.0	84.2	83.0	82.6	...	...	...
Indonesia	67.8	66.8	67.7	67.8	66.8	66.6	65.8	66.3	66.7
Lao People's Democratic Republic	79.9 (2001)	66.6	79.2	...	...	...	...	...	...
Malaysia	65.4	63.3	63.7	65.6	67.3	67.6	67.9	67.7	68.0
Myanmar	...	...	...	...	...	67.0	64.7	...	61.5
Philippines	64.9	65.1	64.1	64.2	63.9	64.6	63.7	63.5	61.2
Singapore[c]	63.2	63.0	66.2	66.6	66.7	67.0	68.3	68.0	67.7
Thailand[d]	71.5	72.5	72.3	71.8	71.1	70.3	69.8	68.8	68.1
Viet Nam[e]	49.6	52.5 |	69.5	70.0	70.3	70.3	71.1	70.6	68.5*
The Pacific									
Cook Islands	69.0 (2001)	70.2 (2006)	...	...	...	...	...	...	...
Fiji	...	...	...	...	...	55.2	...	58.3	57.1
Kiribati	80.9	63.6	59.3	...	...	...	66.0	...	...
Marshall Islands	51.1	51.1	...	...	...	...	...	...	...
Micronesia, Federated States of	58.6	...	57.3	...	...	...	...	...	...
Nauru	...	75.8 (2006)	...	...	65.6	...	...	...	...
Palau	67.5	69.1	...	68.1	...	...	77.4	...	...
Papua New Guinea	72.0	72.4	71.6	70.8	70.6	70.3	70.0	70.0	69.9
Samoa	50.6 (2001)	49.8 (2006)	...	...	...	...	...	...	...
Solomon Islands	...	...	62.9 (2009)	...	...	...	...	...	...
Timor-Leste	56.0 (2001)	60.2 (2004)	41.7	...	30.6	...	...	...	...
Tonga	...	94.8 (2003)	...	...	...	...	...	63.7	...
Tuvalu	58.2 (2002)	...	...	59.4	...	...	...	52.3	...
Vanuatu	69.6	70.4	70.4	70.4	70.4	70.4	70.6	70.5	70.5
Developed ADB Member Economies									
Australia	63.1	64.4	65.4	65.2	64.9	64.7	65.0	64.9	65.2
Japan	62.4	60.4	59.6	59.1	59.3	59.4	59.6	60.0	60.5
New Zealand	65.2	67.7	68.0	68.0	67.8	68.7	68.7	69.8	70.7

... = data not available, * = preliminary, | = marks break in series, ADB = Asian Development Bank.

a Based on labor force concepts and definitions of each economy and these may vary. For International Labour Organization modelled estimates, based on the International Labour Organization's Labour Force Estimates and Projections model.
b Includes local population only.
c Refers to Singapore residents only.
d Includes seasonally inactive labor force.
e For 2005 onwards, data refer to urban areas only.

Sources: Economy sources. For Papua New Guinea, the People's Republic of China, Turkmenistan, Uzbekistan, and Vanuatu: International Labour Organization. ILOSTAT. http://www.ilo.org/ilostat/ (accessed 23 July 2018). For the Lao People's Democratic Republic for 2001: International Labour Organization. ILOSTAT. http://www.ilo.org/ilostat/ (accessed July 2016). For Nauru and Tuvalu: Secretariat of the Pacific Community. National Minimum Development Indicator Database. http://www.spc.int/nmdi/ (accessed 23 July 2018). For Timor-Leste for 2001: United Nations Development Programme. 2002. East Timor Human Development Report 2002. http://www.tl.undp.org/content/timor_leste/en/home/library/poverty/human-development-report-2002-timor-leste.html (accessed 23 July 2018).

Table 2.1.6:   Employment in Agriculture, Industry, and Services[a]
(% of total employment)

ADB Regional Member	Agriculture			
	2000	2005	2010	2017
Developing ADB Member Economies				
Central and West Asia				
Afghanistan	69.6 (2001)	69.6 (2004)	...	39.5 (2016)
Armenia	44.4	46.2	38.6	31.3*
Azerbaijan	39.1	38.7	38.2	36.4
Georgia[b]	52.8 (2001)	50.0	48.0	43.1
Kazakhstan	31.4	31.9	28.3	15.4
Kyrgyz Republic	53.1	38.5	31.2	26.8 (2016)
Pakistan[c]	48.4	43.0	45.0	42.3 (2015)
Tajikistan	65.0	67.5	65.9	64.5 (2016)
Turkmenistan	47.6	...	...	...
Uzbekistan	34.4	29.1	26.8	27.3
East Asia				
China, People's Republic of[d]	50.0	44.8	36.7	27.7 (2016)
Hong Kong, China[e]	0.3	0.3	0.0	0.0
Korea, Republic of[f]	10.7	8.0	6.6	4.8
Mongolia	48.6	39.9	33.5	28.8
Taipei,China	7.8	5.9	5.2	4.9
South Asia				
Bangladesh	50.8	48.1 (2006)	47.5	40.6
Bhutan[g]	46.5 (2001)	43.6	59.4	43.9
India	59.9	56.1	53.2 (2009)	...
Maldives[h]	13.7	15.9 (2007)	4.3	10.4
Nepal	...	...	64.0 (2011)	...
Sri Lanka[i]	36.0	32.8	32.5	26.1
Southeast Asia				
Brunei Darussalam	...	...	...	...
Cambodia	73.7	60.3	72.3	...
Indonesia	45.3	44.0	38.3	29.7
Lao People's Democratic Republic	...	76.3	72.2	...
Malaysia[j]	16.7	14.6	13.6	11.3
Myanmar	...	...	...	48.9
Philippines	37.1	35.7	33.2	25.4
Singapore[k]	0.1	0.1	0.2	0.1
Thailand	44.2	38.6	38.2	31.5
Viet Nam[l]	65.1	55.1	49.5	40.2*
The Pacific				
Cook Islands[m]	7.2 (2001)	4.9 (2006)	4.3 (2011)	...
Fiji[n]	1.5	1.1	1.7	19.2 (2016)
Kiribati[o]	...	2.7	22.1	24.3 (2015)
Marshall Islands[p]	20.5	...	11.0	...
Micronesia, Federated States of	52.2	...	...	...
Nauru	...	...	...	...
Palau[q]	7.1	7.8	...	6.4 (2015)
Papua New Guinea	...	...	...	...
Samoa	39.9 (2001)	35.4 (2006)	37.0 (2011)	...
Solomon Islands[r]	...	...	41.5 (2009)	...
Timor-Leste	...	...	51.0	40.5 (2013)
Tonga	...	27.9 (2006)	...	24.1 (2016)
Tuvalu	...	...	...	...
Vanuatu	...	...	...	...
Developed ADB Member Economies				
Australia	4.8	3.6	3.2	2.6
Japan	5.1	4.4	4.0	3.4
New Zealand	8.8	6.9	6.7	6.2

continued on next page

Table 2.1.6:   Employment in Agriculture, Industry, and Services[a] *(continued)*
(% of total employment)

ADB Regional Member	Industry			
	2000	**2005**	**2010**	**2017**
Developing ADB Member Economies				
Central and West Asia				
Afghanistan	6.2 (2001)	6.2 (2004)	...	14.8 (2016)
Armenia	20.6	15.9	17.4	16.8*
Azerbaijan	12.1	12.4	13.7	14.4
Georgia[b]	5.8 (2001)	7.5	7.2	13.2
Kazakhstan	18.2	17.9	18.7	19.9
Kyrgyz Republic	10.5	17.6	21.1	22.1 (2016)
Pakistan[c]	11.5	20.3	20.9	23.6 (2015)
Tajikistan	9.1	8.7	7.9	6.5 (2016)
Turkmenistan	13.0	...	...	...
Uzbekistan	12.7	13.2	22.7	23.0
East Asia				
China, People's Republic of[d]	22.5	23.8	28.7	28.8 (2016)
Hong Kong, China[e]	19.6	14.4	11.2	11.8
Korea, Republic of[f]	20.4	26.7	25.0	25.3
Mongolia	14.1	16.8	16.2	19.2
Taipei,China	28.1	36.4	35.9	35.8
South Asia				
Bangladesh	13.1	14.6 (2006)	17.6	20.4
Bhutan[g]	5.6 (2001)	17.2	6.6	19.9
India	16.3	18.8	21.5 (2009)	...
Maldives[h]	19.0	27.9 (2007)	9.4	18.8
Nepal	...	...	9.5 (2011)	...
Sri Lanka[i]	23.6	25.4	24.6	28.4
Southeast Asia				
Brunei Darussalam	...	...	...	...
Cambodia	7.0	9.7	9.2	...
Indonesia	17.4	18.8	19.3	22.3
Lao People's Democratic Republic	...	...	8.1	...
Malaysia[j]	32.5	29.7	27.8	27.7
Myanmar	...	...	...	18.1
Philippines	16.2	15.4	15.0	18.3
Singapore[k]	25.7	21.7	21.8	15.8
Thailand	20.2	22.4	20.8	22.8
Viet Nam[l]	13.1	17.6	21.0	25.8*
The Pacific				
Cook Islands[m]	6.0 (2001)	14.2 (2006)	11.7 (2011)	...
Fiji[n]	30.8	30.8	23.9	14.4 (2016)
Kiribati[o]	...	3.2	16.1	18.2 (2015)
Marshall Islands[p]	7.8	...	0.7	...
Micronesia, Federated States of	...	...	...	...
Nauru	...	...	...	...
Palau[q]	0.7	2.6	...	11.7 (2015)
Papua New Guinea	...	...	...	...
Samoa	19.7 (2001)	21.8 (2006)	12.2 (2011)	...
Solomon Islands[r]	...	...	13.0 (2009)	...
Timor-Leste	...	...	8.8	12.7 (2013)
Tonga	...	27.8 (2006)	...	25.6 (2016)
Tuvalu	...	...	...	...
Vanuatu	...	...	...	...
Developed ADB Member Economies				
Australia	21.5	21.1	21.0	19.5
Japan	31.2	27.5	25.4	24.2
New Zealand	12.6	22.4	20.6	20.4

continued on next page

Table 2.1.6: **Employment in Agriculture, Industry, and Services**[a] (*continued*)
(% of total employment)

ADB Regional Member	Services			
	2000	2005	2010	2017
Developing ADB Member Economies				
Central and West Asia				
Afghanistan	24.2 (2001)	24.2 (2004)	...	45.7 (2016)
Armenia	35.0	37.8	44.0	51.8*
Azerbaijan	48.7	48.8	48.1	49.3
Georgia[b]	41.4 (2001)	42.5	44.8	43.7
Kazakhstan	50.5	50.2	53.0	64.8
Kyrgyz Republic	36.5	43.9	47.7	51.1 (2016)
Pakistan[c]	40.0	36.7	34.2	34.2 (2015)
Tajikistan	26.0	23.9	26.3	28.9 (2016)
Turkmenistan	39.4	...	...	...
Uzbekistan	52.8	57.7	50.5	49.7
East Asia				
China, People's Republic of[d]	27.5	31.4	34.6	43.5 (2016)
Hong Kong, China[e]	79.8	85.1	88.9	88.1
Korea, Republic of[f]	68.9	65.4	68.4	69.9
Mongolia	37.2	43.3	50.2	52.0
Taipei,China	64.1	57.7	58.8	59.3
South Asia				
Bangladesh	36.2	37.6 (2006)	35.3	38.9
Bhutan[g]	47.9 (2001)	39.2	33.7	36.2
India	23.7	25.1	25.3 (2009)	...
Maldives[h]	67.3	56.2 (2007)	...	70.8
Nepal	...	...	25.7 (2011)	...
Sri Lanka[i]	40.3	41.8	42.9	45.5
Southeast Asia				
Brunei Darussalam	...	...	...	...
Cambodia	19.3	30.0	18.6	...
Indonesia	37.3	37.3	42.3	48.1
Lao People's Democratic Republic	...	...	19.7	...
Malaysia[j]	50.8	55.6	58.7	61.0
Myanmar	...	...	...	27.2
Philippines	46.7	48.1	51.8	56.3
Singapore[k]	74.2	78.2	77.9	84.1
Thailand	35.6	39.0	41.0	45.7
Viet Nam[l]	21.8	27.3	29.5	34.1*
The Pacific				
Cook Islands[m]	86.7 (2001)	80.9 (2006)	84.0 (2011)	...
Fiji[n]	67.7	68.1	74.4	66.4 (2016)
Kiribati[o]	...	30.7	61.8	57.5 (2015)
Marshall Islands[p]	72.3	...	88.2	...
Micronesia, Federated States of	...	...	...	...
Nauru	...	...	...	...
Palau[q]	92.2	89.6	...	82.0 (2015)
Papua New Guinea	...	...	...	...
Samoa	40.4 (2001)	42.8 (2006)	50.9 (2011)	...
Solomon Islands[r]	...	...	44.8 (2009)	...
Timor-Leste	...	...	39.8	46.7 (2013)
Tonga	...	44.3 (2006)	...	50.3 (2016)
Tuvalu	...	...	...	...
Vanuatu	...	...	...	...
Developed ADB Member Economies				
Australia	73.7	75.3	75.9	77.9
Japan	63.7	68.1	70.5	72.4
New Zealand	...	70.7	72.6	73.3

... = data not available, * = preliminary, ADB = Asian Development Bank.

a Data are based on labor force concepts and definitions adopted by economies. Some values may not add up to 100 due to limitations on data availability.
b For years prior to 2017, services includes employment in the construction industry.
c For 2000, services includes employment in the electricity, gas, and water industries.
d Refers to persons engaged in social labor and receiving remuneration or earning business income.
e Industry includes employment in public administration and social and personal services.
f For 2000, services includes employment in the electricity, gas, water, and construction industries.
g For 2005 and 2017, data are from the census of population. For other years, data are from labor force surveys. Data prior to, and after, the census years may not be directly comparable to 2005 and 2017 figures.
h Figures include local population only.
i Some data may not add up because (i) for 2005 and 2011–2013, data cover all islands; (ii) for 2003, data exclude northern provinces; (iii) for 2004, data exclude Mullaitivu and Kilinochchi districts; and (iv) for 2006–2010 and years prior to 2003, data exclude northern and eastern provinces.
j For 2005 and 2010, services includes employment in water supply; sewerage, waste management, and remediation activities.
k Refers to Singapore residents only.
l Refers to total number of persons engaged in any activity, regardless of age.
m Covers all wage and salary earners from all islands. For 2001, services includes employment in the electricity, gas, water, and construction industries.
n Refers to paid employment as of end of June, except for 2000 and 2005, which refer to end of December.
o Refers to cash work and unpaid village work. For 2005, employment figures by industry include only paid (cash work) workers. For 2010, agriculture includes employment in mining and quarrying.
p Services includes employment in the electricity, gas, water, and construction industries.
q For 2000 and 2005, services includes employment in the electricity, gas, water, and construction industries.
r For 2009, the figure refers to paid employment.

Source: Economy sources.

Table 2.1.7:   Poverty and Inequality[a]

ADB Regional Member	Proportion of Population Living on Less Than $1.90 a Day (2011 PPP) (%)		Proportion of Population Living on Less Than $3.20 a Day (2011 PPP) (%)		Income Ratio of Highest 20% to Lowest 20%[b]		Gini Coefficient	
	2000	2016	2000	2016	2000	2016	2000	2016
Developing ADB Member Economies								
Central and West Asia								
Afghanistan	...	...	...	...	...	...	...	...
Armenia	19.3 (2001)	1.8	55.6 (2001)	14.1	5.7 (2001)	5.1	0.354 (2001)	0.325
Azerbaijan[c]	2.7 (2001)	...	17.7 (2001)	...	6.0 (2001)	...	0.365 (2001)	...
Georgia	21.0	4.2	46.7	17.1	8.6	6.5	0.405	0.365
Kazakhstan	10.5 (2001)	0.0 (2015)	32.5 (2001)	0.3 (2015)	6.4 (2001)	3.7 (2015)	0.360 (2001)	0.269 (2015)
Kyrgyz Republic	42.2	1.4	77.6	19.1	4.7	3.7	0.310	0.268
Pakistan	28.6 (2001)	6.1 (2013)	72.4 (2001)	39.7 (2013)	4.3 (2001)	4.4 (2013)	0.304 (2001)	0.307 (2013)
Tajikistan	30.8 (2003)	4.8 (2015)	66.8 (2003)	20.3 (2015)	5.2 (2003)	5.6 (2015)	0.327 (2003)	0.340 (2015)
Turkmenistan	...	...	...	...	...	...	...	...
Uzbekistan[d]	62.0	...	86.7	...	6.2	...	0.361	...
East Asia								
China, People's Republic of	31.9 (2002)	1.4 (2014)	57.9 (2002)	9.5 (2014)	9.5 (2008)	9.2 (2012)	0.428 (2008)	0.422 (2012)
Hong Kong, China	...	...	...	...	...	...	...	...
Korea, Republic of	0.3 (2006)	0.3 (2012)	0.7 (2006)	0.7 (2012)	5.4 (2006)	5.3 (2012)	0.317 (2006)	0.316 (2012)
Mongolia	10.6 (2002)	0.5	35.5 (2002)	6.5	5.4 (2002)	5.1	0.329 (2002)	0.323
Taipei,China[e]	...	...	...	...	4.2	3.9	0.294	0.278
South Asia								
Bangladesh	34.8	14.8	72.7	52.9	5.0	4.8	0.334	0.324
Bhutan	35.2 (2003)	2.2 (2012)	62.3 (2003)	14.5 (2012)	9.8 (2003)	6.9 (2012)	0.468 (2003)	0.388 (2012)
India	38.2 (2004)	21.2 (2011)	75.2 (2004)	60.4 (2011)	...	5.3 (2011)	...	0.351 (2011)
Maldives	10.0 (2002)	7.3 (2009)	39.2 (2002)	24.4 (2009)	7.2 (2002)	7.0 (2009)	0.413 (2002)	0.384 (2009)
Nepal	46.1 (2003)	15.0 (2010)	75.5 (2003)	50.8 (2010)	7.9 (2003)	5.0 (2010)	0.438 (2003)	0.328 (2010)
Sri Lanka	8.3 (2002)	0.7	36.0 (2002)	9.5	7.1 (2002)	6.8	0.410 (2002)	0.398
Southeast Asia								
Brunei Darussalam	...	...	...	...	...	...	...	...
Cambodia	...	...	...	...	...	...	...	...
Indonesia	39.3	6.5	79.9	30.9	...	6.6 (2013)	...	0.395 (2013)
Lao People's Democratic Republic	33.8 (2002)	22.7 (2012)	72.1 (2002)	58.7 (2012)	4.8 (2002)	5.9 (2012)	0.326 (2002)	0.364 (2012)
Malaysia	0.4 (2004)	0.3 (2009)	2.6 (2004)	3.1 (2009)	10.9 (2004)	11.2 (2009)	0.461 (2004)	0.463 (2009)
Myanmar	...	6.4 (2015)	...	29.8 (2015)	...	6.3 (2015)	...	0.381 (2015)
Philippines	14.5	8.3 (2015)	43.1	33.7 (2015)	8.0	7.2 (2015)	0.428	0.401 (2015)
Singapore	...	...	...	...	...	...	...	...
Thailand	2.5	0.0 (2013)	18.6	1.1 (2013)	8.0	6.5 (2013)	0.428	0.378 (2013)
Viet Nam	38.0 (2002)	2.6 (2014)	70.8 (2002)	11.2 (2014)	6.1 (2002)	5.9 (2014)	0.370 (2002)	0.348 (2014)
The Pacific								
Cook Islands	...	...	...	...	...	...	...	...
Fiji	4.9 (2002)	1.4 (2013)	21.8 (2002)	14.3 (2013)	6.8 (2002)	5.8 (2013)	0.381 (2002)	0.364 (2013)
Kiribati	12.9 (2006)	...	34.6 (2006)	...	6.7 (2006)	...	0.370 (2006)	...
Marshall Islands	...	...	...	...	...	...	...	...
Micronesia, Federated States of	8.0 (2005)	16.0 (2013)	24.3 (2005)	39.5 (2013)	8.7 (2005)	8.4 (2013)	0.424 (2005)	0.401 (2013)
Nauru	...	...	...	...	...	...	...	...
Palau	...	...	...	...	...	...	...	...
Papua New Guinea	...	38.0 (2009)	...	65.6 (2009)	...	9.3 (2009)	...	0.419 (2009)
Samoa	0.6 (2008)	...	9.7 (2008)	...	7.7 (2008)	...	0.420 (2008)	...
Solomon Islands	45.6 (2005)	25.1 (2013)	70.6 (2005)	58.8 (2013)	10.4 (2005)	6.4 (2013)	0.461 (2005)	0.371 (2013)
Timor-Leste	42.5 (2001)	30.3 (2014)	73.5 (2001)	73.2 (2014)	6.0 (2001)	4.1 (2014)	0.359 (2001)	0.287 (2014)
Tonga	2.8 (2001)	1.1 (2009)	8.4 (2001)	8.9 (2009)	7.1 (2001)	6.7 (2009)	0.377 (2001)	0.375 (2009)
Tuvalu	...	3.3 (2010)	...	17.6 (2010)	...	7.0 (2010)	...	0.391 (2010)
Vanuatu	...	13.2 (2010)	...	39.5 (2010)	...	6.7 (2010)	...	0.376 (2010)
Developed ADB Member Economies								
Australia	...	...	...	...	5.5 (2001)	5.8 (2010)	0.335 (2001)	0.347 (2010)
Japan	...	...	...	...	5.4 (2008)	...	0.321 (2008)	...
New Zealand[f]	...	...	...	...	...	...	...	0.349 (2014)

... = Data not available, 0.0 = magnitude is less than half the unit employed or true zero, ADB = Asian Development Bank, PPP = purchasing power parity.

a Poverty and inequality estimates are consumption-based, except for Malaysia; New Zealand; and Taipei,China, which are income-based. For the Gini coefficient, the data for New Zealand are based on disposable income post taxes and transfers. The estimates for the Gini coefficient for Taipei,China are based on per capita disposable income. The year indicated in the table refers to the year when the household survey data were collected. For economies where the household survey data collection period bridged 2 calendar years, the table reports the first year.

b Derived from income or expenditure share of the highest 20% and lowest 20% groups.

c The latest available data for Azerbaijan are for 2005: 0.0% for proportion of population living on less than $1.90 a day (2011 PPP); 0.0% for proportion of population living on less than $3.20 a day (2011 PPP); 2.3 for income ratio of highest 20% to lowest 20%; and 0.166 for Gini coefficient.

d The latest available data for Uzbekistan are for 2003: 62.1% for proportion of population living on less than $1.90 a day (2011 PPP); 86.4% for proportion of population living on less than $3.20 a day (2011 PPP); 5.9 for income ratio of highest 20% to lowest 20%; and 0.353 for Gini coefficient.

e The Gini coefficient for Taipei,China reflected in the table refers to Gini coefficient using per capita disposable income. The estimates using disposable income of households are 0.326 for 2000 and 0.336 for 2016.

f The earliest available estimate for the Gini coefficient using the new income definition for New Zealand is 0.323 for 2011.

Sources: World Bank. World Development Indicators. http://data.worldbank.org/data-catalog/world-development-indicators (accessed 16 June 2018) and Organisation for Economic Co-operation and Development. Income Distribution and Poverty. https://stats.oecd.org/index.aspx?queryid=66670 (accessed 16 June 2018). For Taipei,China: Government of Taipei,China, Directorate-General of Budget, Accounting and Statistics. http://eng.dgbas.gov.tw/mp.asp?mp=2 (accessed 16 June 2018).

Table 2.1.8:   Human Development Index[a]

ADB Regional Member	2000	2005	2010	2011	2012	2013	2014	2015	Rank in 2015[b]
Developing ADB Member Economies									
Central and West Asia	**0.573**	**0.618**	**0.653**	**0.659**	**0.665**	**0.671**	**0.676**	**0.678**	
Afghanistan	0.340	0.405	0.454	0.463	0.470	0.476	0.479	0.479	169
Armenia	0.644	0.692	0.729	0.732	0.736	0.739	0.741	0.743	84
Azerbaijan	0.642	0.682	0.741	0.742	0.745	0.752	0.758	0.759	78
Georgia	0.673	0.714	0.742	0.749	0.755	0.759	0.768	0.769	70
Kazakhstan	0.685	0.747	0.766	0.774	0.782	0.789	0.793	0.794	56
Kyrgyz Republic	0.593	0.613	0.632	0.638	0.647	0.656	0.662	0.664	120
Pakistan	0.450	0.501	0.525	0.529	0.538	0.542	0.548	0.550	147
Tajikistan	0.535	0.579	0.608	0.613	0.617	0.622	0.625	0.627	129
Turkmenistan	...	...	0.665	0.672	0.678	0.683	0.688	0.692	111
Uzbekistan	0.594	0.626	0.664	0.673	0.681	0.690	0.697	0.701	105
East Asia	**0.706**	**0.774**	**0.811**	**0.817**	**0.822**	**0.829**	**0.833**	**0.835**	
China, People's Republic of	0.592	0.646	0.700	0.703	0.713	0.723	0.734	0.738	90
Hong Kong, China	0.825	0.870	0.898	0.905	0.907	0.913	0.916	0.917	12
Korea, Republic of	0.820	0.860	0.884	0.889	0.891	0.896	0.899	0.901	18
Mongolia	0.588	0.649	0.701	0.712	0.720	0.729	0.733	0.735	92
Taipei,China	...	0.846	0.873	0.874	0.879	0.882	0.882	0.885	...
South Asia	**0.536**	**0.572**	**0.606**	**0.616**	**0.623**	**0.630**	**0.636**	**0.639**	
Bangladesh	0.468	0.506	0.545	0.557	0.565	0.570	0.575	0.579	139
Bhutan	...	...	0.572	0.581	0.589	0.596	0.604	0.607	132
India	0.494	0.536	0.580	0.590	0.599	0.607	0.615	0.624	131
Maldives	0.587	0.622	0.663	0.675	0.683	0.693	0.701	0.701	105
Nepal	0.446	0.476	0.529	0.538	0.545	0.551	0.555	0.558	144
Sri Lanka	0.686	0.718	0.746	0.752	0.757	0.760	0.764	0.766	73
Southeast Asia	**0.612**	**0.645**	**0.684**	**0.690**	**0.696**	**0.701**	**0.705**	**0.708**	
Brunei Darussalam	0.819	0.837	0.846	0.852	0.860	0.863	0.864	0.865	30
Cambodia	0.412	0.483	0.533	0.540	0.546	0.553	0.558	0.563	143
Indonesia	0.604	0.632	0.662	0.669	0.677	0.682	0.686	0.689	113
Lao People's Democratic Republic	0.463	0.503	0.542	0.554	0.563	0.573	0.582	0.586	138
Malaysia	0.725	0.732	0.774	0.776	0.779	0.783	0.787	0.789	59
Myanmar	0.427	0.474	0.526	0.533	0.540	0.547	0.552	0.556	145
Philippines	0.622	0.646	0.669	0.666	0.671	0.676	0.679	0.682	116
Singapore	0.820	0.839	0.911	0.917	0.920	0.922	0.924	0.925	5
Thailand	0.649	0.686	0.720	0.729	0.733	0.737	0.738	0.740	87
Viet Nam	0.576	0.618	0.655	0.662	0.668	0.675	0.678	0.683	115
The Pacific	**0.585**	**0.603**	**0.630**	**0.634**	**0.637**	**0.639**	**0.639**	**0.641**	
Cook Islands	...	...	...	...	...	...	...	...	...
Fiji	0.683	0.695	0.709	0.714	0.719	0.727	0.734	0.736	91
Kiribati	...	0.576	0.585	0.581	0.589	0.597	0.586	0.588	137
Marshall Islands	...	...	...	...	...	...	...	...	...
Micronesia, Federated States of	0.604	0.622	0.638	0.640	0.641	0.639	0.637	0.638	127
Nauru	...	...	...	...	...	...	...	...	...
Palau	0.741	0.758	0.770	0.775	0.779	0.782	0.783	0.788	60
Papua New Guinea	0.422	0.454	0.494	0.501	0.506	0.511	0.515	0.516	154
Samoa	0.645	0.677	0.693	0.698	0.700	0.701	0.702	0.704	104
Solomon Islands	0.442	0.470	0.497	0.505	0.509	0.512	0.514	0.515	156
Timor-Leste	0.470	0.511	0.607	0.618	0.620	0.612	0.603	0.606	133
Tonga	0.674	0.695	0.712	0.717	0.718	0.716	0.718	0.721	101
Tuvalu	...	...	...	...	...	...	...	...	...
Vanuatu	...	0.572	0.591	0.592	0.591	0.596	0.598	0.597	134
Developed ADB Member Economies	**0.874**	**0.892**	**0.904**	**0.908**	**0.912**	**0.915**	**0.917**	**0.919**	
Australia	0.899	0.915	0.927	0.930	0.933	0.936	0.937	0.939	2
Japan	0.856	0.873	0.884	0.889	0.894	0.899	0.902	0.903	17
New Zealand	0.868	0.888	0.901	0.904	0.908	0.910	0.913	0.915	13

... = data not available, ADB = Asian Development Bank.

a   The regional indexes are calculated as simple averages of the indexes for their member economies.
b   Rank among the 188 countries presented in Human Development Report 2016 of the United Nations Development Programme.

Sources: United Nations Development Programme. Human Development Data (1990–2015). http://hdr.undp.org/en/data# (accessed 21 June 2018). For Taipei,China: Government of Taipei,China, Directorate-General of Budget, Accounting and Statistics. http://eng.stat.gov.tw/ct.asp?xItem=25280&ctNode=6032&mp=5 (accessed 21 June 2018). For the ranking: United Nations Development Programme. 2016. Human Development Report 2016. New York.

Table 2.1.9:   **Life Expectancy at Birth**
(years)

ADB Regional Member	Both Sexes		Female		Male	
	2000	2016	2000	2016	2000	2016
Developing ADB Member Economies						
Central and West Asia						
Afghanistan	55.5	63.7	56.7	65.0	54.4	62.4
Armenia	71.4	74.6	74.5	77.6	68.1	71.3
Azerbaijan	66.8	72.0	69.9	75.0	63.6	69.0
Georgia	71.9	73.3	75.4	77.5	68.1	69.0
Kazakhstan	65.5	72.3	71.1	76.6	60.2	68.1
Kyrgyz Republic	68.6	71.0	72.4	75.1	64.9	67.0
Pakistan	62.7	66.5	63.6	67.5	62.0	65.5
Tajikistan	65.5	71.1	68.8	74.2	62.5	68.3
Turkmenistan	63.6	67.8	67.7	71.3	59.6	64.4
Uzbekistan	67.2	71.3	70.4	74.1	64.0	68.6
East Asia						
China, People's Republic of	72.0	76.3	73.7	77.8	70.4	74.8
Hong Kong, China	80.9	84.2*	83.9	87.3*	78.0	81.3 *
Korea, Republic of	75.9	82.0	79.7	85.2	72.3	79.0
Mongolia	62.9	69.3	65.9	73.5	60.1	65.3
Taipei,China	76.5	80.0	79.6	83.4	73.8	76.8
South Asia						
Bangladesh	65.3	72.5	65.7	74.3	65.0	70.9
Bhutan	60.8	70.2	60.9	70.5	60.6	69.9
India	62.6	68.6	63.4	70.2	61.8	67.1
Maldives	69.9	77.3	71.1	78.5	69.2	76.4
Nepal	62.4	70.3	63.4	71.9	61.3	68.7
Sri Lanka	71.0	75.3	74.9	78.6	67.5	71.9
Southeast Asia						
Brunei Darussalam	75.2	77.2	76.9	78.9	73.7	75.6
Cambodia	58.4	69.0	60.6	70.9	56.2	66.8
Indonesia	66.3	69.2	68.0	71.4	64.6	67.2
Lao People's Democratic Republic	58.9	66.7	60.3	68.2	57.5	65.1
Malaysia	72.8	75.3	75.0	77.7	70.8	73.2
Myanmar	62.1	66.6	64.2	68.9	60.1	64.2
Philippines	67.2	69.1	70.3	72.7	64.2	65.8
Singapore	78.0	82.8	80.0	85.1	76.0	80.6
Thailand	70.6	75.3	74.5	79.1	66.9	71.6
Viet Nam	73.3	76.3	78.1	80.9	68.4	71.5
The Pacific						
Cook Islands	71.9	76.0 (2017)	74.7	79.0 (2017)	69.2	73.2 (2017)
Fiji	67.6	70.3	70.2	73.5	65.2	67.4
Kiribati	64.0	66.3	67.0	69.6	61.1	63.0
Marshall Islands	68.4	73.4 (2017)	70.4	75.7 (2017)	66.6	71.2 (2017)
Micronesia, Federated States of	67.3	69.2	67.9	70.4	66.7	68.0
Nauru	60.9	67.4 (2017)	64.5	70.9 (2017)	57.4	63.3 (2017)
Palau	68.5	73.4 (2017)	71.7	76.8 (2017)	65.4	70.2 (2017)
Papua New Guinea	61.8	65.5	64.4	68.1	59.5	63.1
Samoa	69.3	75.0	72.8	78.3	66.3	72.0
Solomon Islands	63.1	70.7	64.0	72.3	62.3	69.3
Timor-Leste	59.4	68.9	60.6	70.8	58.1	67.1
Tonga	70.8	73.0	72.8	76.1	68.8	70.0
Tuvalu	61.6	66.9 (2017)	63.6	69.2 (2017)	59.7	64.7 (2017)
Vanuatu	67.4	72.1	69.3	74.4	65.9	70.0
Developed ADB Member Economies						
Australia	79.2	82.5	82.0	84.6	76.6	80.5
Japan	81.1	84.0	84.6	87.1	77.7	81.0
New Zealand	78.6	81.6	81.3	83.4	76.1	79.9
WORLD	**67.7**	**72.0**	**69.9**	**74.3**	**65.6**	**70.0**

* = preliminary, ADB = Asian Development Bank.

Sources: World Bank. World Development Indicators. http://databank.worldbank.org/data/source/world-development-indicators/preview/on# (accessed 8 June 2018). For the Cook Islands, the Marshall Islands, Nauru, Palau, and Tuvalu: United States Census Bureau Online. https://www.census.gov/data-tools/demo/idb/informationGateway.php (accessed 8 June 2018). For Taipei,China: Government of Taipei,China, Directorate-General of Budget, Accounting and Statistics. http://eng.dgbas.gov.tw/mp.asp?mp=2 (accessed 8 June 2018).

Table 2.1.10: Births, Deaths, and Fertility Rates

ADB Regional Member	Crude Birth Rate (per 1,000 people)		Crude Death Rate (per 1,000 people)		Total Fertility Rate (births per woman)	
	2000	2016	2000	2016	2000	2016
Developing ADB Member Economies						
Central and West Asia						
Afghanistan	48.4	33.2	12.0	6.7	7.5	4.6
Armenia	12.9	13.5	8.6	9.7	1.6	1.6
Azerbaijan	14.5	16.3	5.8	5.8	2.0	1.9
Georgia	12.0	13.5	9.9	13.2	1.6	2.0
Kazakhstan	14.9	22.5	10.1	7.4	1.8	2.7
Kyrgyz Republic	19.8	26.0	7.0	5.5	2.4	3.1
Pakistan	32.0	28.2	8.7	7.3	4.6	3.5
Tajikistan	30.2	28.8	7.0	5.2	3.9	3.4
Turkmenistan	23.6	25.4	7.8	7.1	2.8	2.9
Uzbekistan	21.4	22.8	5.5	4.9	2.6	2.5
East Asia						
China, People's Republic of	14.0	12.0	6.5	7.3	1.5	1.6
Hong Kong, China	8.1	8.3	5.1	6.4	1.0	1.2
Korea, Republic of	13.3	7.9	5.2	5.5	1.5	1.2
Mongolia	19.3	24.0	7.7	6.3	2.1	2.8
Taipei,China	13.8	8.2 (2017)	5.7	7.3 (2017)	1.7	1.1 (2017)
South Asia						
Bangladesh	27.6	19.0	6.9	5.3	3.2	2.1
Bhutan	28.0	18.2	8.5	6.0	3.6	2.1
India	26.5	19.0	8.7	7.3	3.3	2.3
Maldives	22.6	18.3	4.7	3.3	2.9	2.1
Nepal	32.1	19.7	8.5	6.3	4.0	2.1
Sri Lanka	18.5	15.3	7.0	6.9	2.2	2.0
Southeast Asia						
Brunei Darussalam	21.4	15.9	2.9	3.6	2.2	1.9
Cambodia	28.1	23.3	9.4	6.1	3.8	2.6
Indonesia	21.8	19.0	7.3	7.1	2.5	2.4
Lao People's Democratic Republic	31.8	23.9	9.8	6.7	4.3	2.7
Malaysia	22.0	17.1	4.5	4.9	2.8	2.0
Myanmar	24.5	17.8	9.1	8.1	2.9	2.2
Philippines	29.6	23.2	6.0	6.5	3.8	2.9
Singapore	13.7	9.4	4.5	4.8	1.6	1.2
Thailand	14.5	10.3	6.9	7.9	1.7	1.5
Viet Nam	17.5	16.7	5.5	5.8	2.0	2.0
The Pacific						
Cook Islands	23.1	14.0 (2017)	6.3	8.4 (2017)	3.2	2.2 (2017)
Fiji	24.7	19.4	6.1	7.1	3.1	2.5
Kiribati	30.6	28.2	7.6	7.0	4.1	3.7
Marshall Islands	35.0	24.4 (2017)	5.3	4.2 (2017)	4.4	3.0 (2017)
Micronesia, Federated States of	29.9	23.7	6.3	6.2	4.3	3.1
Nauru	27.9	24.0 (2017)	7.2	5.9 (2017)	3.5	2.8 (2017)
Palau	14.5	12.0	6.5	10.0	1.8	2.2 (2015)
Papua New Guinea	34.0	27.6	8.3	7.1	4.5	3.7
Samoa	30.6	24.7	6.1	5.0	4.5	4.0
Solomon Islands	35.6	28.7	7.5	4.8	4.7	3.9
Timor-Leste	43.5	35.0	9.4	5.5	7.1	5.5
Tonga	28.2	24.0	6.2	6.0	4.3	3.6
Tuvalu	24.6	23.7 (2017)	10.8	8.5 (2017)	3.6	3.0 (2017)
Vanuatu	32.4	25.9	6.2	4.8	4.4	3.3
Developed ADB Member Economies						
Australia	13.0	12.5	6.7	6.5	1.8	1.8
Japan	9.4	7.8	7.7	10.5	1.4	1.4
New Zealand	14.7	12.7	6.9	6.6	2.0	1.9
WORLD	**21.6**	**18.9**	**8.5**	**7.6**	**2.7**	**2.4**

ADB = Asian Development Bank.

Sources: World Bank. World Development Indicators. http://databank.worldbank.org/data/source/world-development-indicators/preview/on (accessed 7 June 2018). For the Cook Islands, the Marshall Islands, Nauru, and Tuvalu: United States Census Bureau Online. http://www.census.gov/ (accessed 6 June 2018). For Taipei,China: Government of Taipei,China, Directorate-General of Budget, Accounting and Statistics. http://eng.dgbas.gov.tw/mp.asp?mp=2 (accessed 6 June 2018).

Table 2.1.11:   Primary Education Completion Rate[a]
(%)

ADB Regional Member	Both Sexes		Female		Male	
	2000	2016	2000	2016	2000	2016
Developing ADB Member Economies						
Central and West Asia						
Afghanistan	...	...	...	...	...	...
Armenia	93.7 (2002)	90.4	94.1 (2002)	91.3	93.3 (2002)	89.6
Azerbaijan	89.5	111.3	85.5	109.7	93.8	112.7
Georgia	96.2	119.1	96.4	118.8	96.0	119.4
Kazakhstan	92.1	108.8 (2017)	92.0	109.4 (2017)	92.2	108.3 (2017)
Kyrgyz Republic	93.7	105.5	93.2	105.1	94.1	105.8
Pakistan	64.3 (2005)	71.3	53.5 (2005)	64.6	74.5 (2005)	77.6
Tajikistan	92.7	92.4 (2017)	...	92.0 (2017)	...	92.7 (2017)
Turkmenistan	...	...	...	...	...	...
Uzbekistan	100.4 (2001)	97.7 (2017)	100.3 (2001)	97.0 (2017)	100.5 (2001)	98.4 (2017)
East Asia						
China, People's Republic of	89.1 (2006)	99.9 (2013)	89.0 (2006)	99.2 (2013)	89.2 (2006)	100.5 (2013)
Hong Kong, China	...	103.2	...	101.2	...	105.1
Korea, Republic of	103.2	98.9 (2015)	105.0	99.4 (2015)	101.6	98.4 (2015)
Mongolia	87.0	93.6	89.3	93.2	84.6	94.0
Taipei,China	...	...	...	...	...	...
South Asia						
Bangladesh	64.3 (2005)	98.1 (2015)	66.8 (2005)	106.6 (2015)	61.9 (2005)	89.9 (2015)
Bhutan	49.5	97.4	46.1	102.7	52.9	92.3
India	71.8	96.3	63.5	98.6	79.4	94.3
Maldives	177.8 (2001)	95.6 (2015)	183.9 (2001)	90.8 (2015)	172.0 (2001)	100.3 (2015)
Nepal	67.3	112.8 (2017)	57.2	118.1 (2017)	77.0	107.6 (2017)
Sri Lanka	107.3 (2001)	100.6	106.6 (2001)	99.5	108.0 (2001)	101.7
Southeast Asia						
Brunei Darussalam	114.8	102.1 (2015)	109.9	103.0 (2015)	119.5	101.2 (2015)
Cambodia	51.3 (2001)	92.4	46.1 (2001)	94.3	56.3 (2001)	90.6
Indonesia	93.8 (2001)	98.8	94.2 (2001)	99.1	93.4 (2001)	98.6
Lao People's Democratic Republic	67.3	100.4	61.4	99.4	73.0	101.3
Malaysia	100.6	100.6	100.7	101.5	100.5	99.6
Myanmar	78.2	88.9 (2017)	75.9	89.3 (2017)	80.6	88.4 (2017)
Philippines	100.3 (2001)	101.3 (2015)	105.4 (2001)	104.1 (2015)	95.5 (2001)	98.8 (2015)
Singapore	...	99.8	...	99.2	...	100.4
Thailand	84.9	90.6 (2015)	84.3	88.2 (2015)	85.4	92.9 (2015)
Viet Nam	99.0	104.8	96.6	105.0	101.3	104.5
The Pacific						
Cook Islands	112.0 (2007)	108.9	...	102.1	...	115.9
Fiji	95.0	106.4 (2015)	93.9	106.7 (2015)	96.0	106.1 (2015)
Kiribati	99.0	99.5	95.1	103.5	102.7	95.8
Marshall Islands	114.3 (2002)	76.9	118.1 (2002)	80.0	110.8 (2002)	74.0
Micronesia, Federated States of	...	...	...	...	...	...
Nauru	87.0 (2001)	120.4	90.1 (2001)	121.0	84.3 (2001)	119.8
Palau	104.5 (2004)	95.9 (2014)	...	94.7 (2014)	...	96.9 (2014)
Papua New Guinea	52.5	77.4 (2012)	48.1	71.0 (2012)	56.7	83.5 (2012)
Samoa	94.0	104.6	95.5	103.5	92.7	105.5
Solomon Islands	...	85.1 (2012)	...	86.0 (2012)	...	84.3 (2012)
Timor-Leste	76.6 (2008)	95.3	76.1 (2008)	97.6	77.2 (2008)	93.1
Tonga	105.5 (2001)	111.0 (2013)	104.0 (2001)	106.5 (2013)	107.0 (2001)	115.1 (2013)
Tuvalu	101.7 (2001)	112.2 (2015)	108.3 (2001)	123.4 (2015)	96.1 (2001)	101.9 (2015)
Vanuatu	92.1	93.8 (2013)	94.4	97.8 (2013)	89.9	90.2 (2013)
Developed ADB Member Economies						
Australia	...	...	...	...	...	...
Japan	98.5	101.7 (2012)	98.6	101.8 (2012)	98.4	101.5 (2012)
New Zealand	...	...	...	...	...	...

... = data not available, ADB = Asian Development Bank.

a   The total number of new entrants in the last grade of primary education, regardless of age, expressed as a percentage of the population at the theoretical age to enter the last grade of primary education.

Source: United Nations Educational, Scientific and Cultural Organization, Institute for Statistics Database. UIS.Stat. http://data.uis.unesco.org/ (accessed 6 June 2018).

Table 2.1.12:   Adult (15 Years and Older) Literacy Rate
(%)

ADB Regional Member	Both Sexes		Female		Male	
	2000	2011	2000	2011	2000	2011
Developing ADB Member Economies						
Central and West Asia						
Afghanistan	...	31.7	...	17.6	...	45.4
Armenia	99.4 (2001)	99.7	99.2 (2001)	99.7	99.7 (2001)	99.8
Azerbaijan	99.6 (2007)	99.8 (2016)	99.4 (2007)	99.7 (2016)	99.8 (2007)	99.9 (2016)
Georgia	99.7 (2002)	99.6 (2014)	99.6 (2002)	99.5 (2014)	99.8 (2002)	99.7 (2014)
Kazakhstan	...	99.8 (2010)	...	99.7 (2010)	...	99.8 (2010)
Kyrgyz Republic	...	99.2 (2009)	...	99.0 (2009)	...	99.5 (2009)
Pakistan	49.9 (2005)	57.0 (2014)	35.4 (2005)	44.3 (2014)	64.1 (2005)	69.1 (2014)
Tajikistan	99.5	...	99.2	...	99.7	...
Turkmenistan	...	...	...	...	...	...
Uzbekistan	98.6	100.0 (2015)	98.1	100.0 (2015)	99.2	100.0 (2015)
East Asia						
China, People's Republic of	90.9	95.1 (2010)	86.5	92.7 (2010)	95.1	97.5 (2010)
Hong Kong, China	...	...	...	...	...	...
Korea, Republic of	...	...	...	...	...	...
Mongolia	97.8	98.3 (2010)	97.5	98.3 (2010)	98.0	98.2 (2010)
Taipei,China	...	...	...	...	...	...
South Asia						
Bangladesh	47.5 (2001)	72.8 (2016)	40.8 (2001)	69.9 (2016)	53.9 (2001)	75.6 (2016)
Bhutan	52.8 (2005)	57.0 (2012)	38.7 (2005)	48.0 (2012)	65.0 (2005)	66.0 (2012)
India	61.0 (2001)	69.3	47.8 (2001)	59.3	73.4 (2001)	78.9
Maldives	98.4 (2006)	98.6 (2014)	98.4 (2006)	98.7 (2014)	98.4 (2006)	98.5 (2014)
Nepal	48.6 (2001)	59.6	34.9 (2001)	48.8	62.7 (2001)	71.7
Sri Lanka	90.7 (2001)	91.2 (2010)	89.1 (2001)	90.0 (2010)	92.3 (2001)	92.6 (2010)
Southeast Asia						
Brunei Darussalam	92.7 (2001)	96.1	90.2 (2001)	94.7	95.2 (2001)	97.4
Cambodia	73.6 (2004)	73.9 (2009)	64.1 (2004)	65.9 (2009)	84.7 (2004)	82.8 (2009)
Indonesia	90.4 (2004)	95.4 (2016)	86.8 (2004)	93.6 (2016)	94.0 (2004)	97.2 (2016)
Lao People's Democratic Republic	69.6	58.3	58.5	49.7	81.4	67.4
Malaysia	88.7	93.1 (2010)	85.4	90.7 (2010)	92.0	95.4 (2010)
Myanmar	89.9	75.6 (2016)	86.4	71.8 (2016)	93.9	80.0 (2016)
Philippines	92.6	96.4 (2013)	92.7	96.8 (2013)	92.5	96.0 (2013)
Singapore	92.5	97.0 (2016)	88.6	95.4 (2016)	96.6	98.7 (2016)
Thailand	92.6	92.9 (2015)	90.5	91.2 (2015)	94.9	94.7 (2015)
Viet Nam	90.2	93.5 (2009)	86.6	91.4 (2009)	93.9	95.8 (2009)
The Pacific						
Cook Islands	...	...	...	...	...	...
Fiji	...	...	...	...	...	...
Kiribati	...	...	...	...	...	...
Marshall Islands	...	98.3	...	98.2	...	98.3
Micronesia, Federated States of	...	...	...	...	...	...
Nauru	...	...	...	...	...	...
Palau	...	96.6 (2015)	...	96.3 (2015)	...	96.8 (2015)
Papua New Guinea	57.3	...	50.9	...	63.4	...
Samoa	...	99.0	...	99.1	...	98.9
Solomon Islands	...	...	...	...	...	...
Timor–Leste	37.6 (2001)	58.3 (2010)	30.0 (2001)	53.0 (2010)	45.3 (2001)	63.6 (2010)
Tonga	99.0 (2006)	99.4	99.1 (2006)	99.4	99.0 (2006)	99.3
Tuvalu	...	...	...	...	...	...
Vanuatu	...	...	...	...	...	...
Developed ADB Member Economies						
Australia	...	...	...	...	...	...
Japan	...	...	...	...	...	...
New Zealand	...	...	...	...	...	...
WORLD	81.5	86.2 (2016)	76.4	82.7 (2016)	86.6	89.8 (2016)

... = data not available, ADB = Asian Development Bank.

Source: United Nations Educational, Scientific and Cultural Organization, Institute for Statistics Database. UIS.Stat. http://data.uis.unesco.org/ (accessed 11 July 2018).

Table 2.1.13:   Education Resources

ADB Regional Member	Primary Pupil–Teacher Ratio		Secondary Pupil–Teacher Ratio	
	2000	2016	2000	2016
Developing ADB Member Economies				
Central and West Asia				
Afghanistan	42.3 (2006)	44.3 (2017)	31.6 (2007)	38.9 (2017)
Armenia[a]	20.3 (2001)	...	...	...
Azerbaijan	18.7	15.5	...	...
Georgia	16.8	8.8	7.5	7.4
Kazakhstan[b]	18.7 (2001)	20.8 (2017)	...	6.6 (2017)
Kyrgyz Republic	24.1	25.0	13.3	11.0
Pakistan	33.0	47.6	24.2 (2003)	21.4
Tajikistan	21.8	22.3 (2017)	16.4	15.4 (2011)
Turkmenistan	...	...	...	...
Uzbekistan	21.4	21.2 (2017)	11.5	10.3 (2017)
East Asia				
China, People's Republic of	22.2 (2001)	16.5	17.1	13.5
Hong Kong, China	21.5	13.7	18.8 (2001)	12.4
Korea, Republic of	32.1	16.6 (2015)	21.0	14.4 (2015)
Mongolia	32.6	29.7	19.9	14.1
Taipei,China[c]	19.0	12.2 (2017)	17.6	13.3 (2017)
South Asia				
Bangladesh	47.0 (2005)	33.9	38.4	36.2
Bhutan	41.1	38.0	28.1 (2005)	11.4
India	40.0	35.2	33.6	28.5
Maldives[d]	22.7	10.3	15.3	...
Nepal	38.0	20.9 (2017)	30.2	28.8 (2017)
Sri Lanka[e]	26.3 (2001)	23.2	...	17.4
Southeast Asia				
Brunei Darussalam	13.7	10.2	10.9	8.6
Cambodia[f]	50.1	42.5	18.5	...
Indonesia	22.1	14.0	14.6	14.1
Lao People's Democratic Republic	30.1	23.0	21.3	18.3
Malaysia	19.6	11.6	...	13.2
Myanmar	32.8	22.0 (2017)	31.9	24.0 (2017)
Philippines	35.3	30.3 (2015)	36.4 (2001)	26.2 (2015)
Singapore	20.4 (2007)	17.4 (2009)	17.0 (2007)	14.9 (2009)
Thailand	20.8	16.9 (2015)	24.0 (2001)	28.2 (2015)
Viet Nam	29.5	19.6	...	...
The Pacific				
Cook Islands	17.8	17.4	13.9	15.7
Fiji	28.1	28.0 (2012)	20.2	19.3 (2012)
Kiribati[g]	31.7	25.7	21.0 (2001)	...
Marshall Islands[h]	16.9 (2002)	...	16.7 (2002)	...
Micronesia, Federated States of	...	19.7 (2015)	...	...
Nauru	21.5	40.2	17.4	24.8
Palau	15.7	...	15.1	...
Papua New Guinea	35.4	45.2 (2012)	...	27.4 (2012)
Samoa	24.0	30.2 (2010)	21.2	27.7
Solomon Islands[i]	...	25.2	10.1	25.9 (2012)
Timor-Leste	61.9 (2001)	31.4 (2011)	28.0 (2001)	24.3 (2011)
Tonga	22.1	21.9 (2014)	14.6	13.4 (2014)
Tuvalu	19.7	12.7 (2015)	...	6.2 (2015)
Vanuatu	22.5	26.6 (2015)	24.7	20.6 (2015)
Developed ADB Member Economies				
Australia	...	...	...	...
Japan	20.7	16.2 (2015)	14.0	11.4 (2015)
New Zealand	18.4	14.5 (2015)	15.5	13.8 (2015)

... = data not available, ADB = Asian Development Bank.

a   The latest available data for Armenia is for 2007: 19.3 for primary pupil-teacher ratio.
b   The earliest available data for Kazakhstan is for 2015: 7.5 for secondary pupil-teacher ratio.
c   For 2017, data for secondary pupil–teacher ratio include those for vocational secondary schools.
d   The latest available data for Maldives is for 2003: 13.7 for secondary pupil-teacher ratio.
e   The earliest available data for Sri Lanka is for 2011: 17.3 for secondary pupil-teacher ratio.
f   The latest available data for Cambodia is for 2007: 28.9 for secondary pupil-teacher ratio.
g   The latest available data for Kiribati is for 2008: 17.4 for secondary pupil-teacher ratio.
h   The latest available data for the Marshall Islands is for 2003: 14.9 for secondary pupil-teacher ratio.
i   The earliest available data for Solomon Islands is for 2010: 19.9 for primary pupil-teacher ratio.

Sources: United Nations Educational, Scientific and Cultural Organization, Institute for Statistics Database. UIS.Stat. http://data.uis.unesco.org/ (accessed 5 June 2018). For Taipei,China: Government of Taipei,China, Directorate-General of Budget, Accounting and Statistics. Social Indicators. http://eng.dgbas.gov.tw/mp.asp?mp=2 (accessed 4 June 2018).

Table 2.1.14: Health Care Resources
(per 1,000 population)

ADB Regional Member	Physicians		Hospital Beds	
	2000	2015	2000	2015
Developing ADB Member Economies				
Central and West Asia				
Afghanistan	0.20 (2001)	0.30 (2016)	0.3	0.5
Armenia	2.99	2.80 (2014)	6.4	4.2
Azerbaijan	3.61	3.40 (2014)	8.7	4.7 (2013)
Georgia	4.73	4.78 (2014)	4.8	2.6 (2013)
Kazakhstan	3.29	3.27 (2014)	7.2	6.7 (2013)
Kyrgyz Republic	2.82	1.85 (2014)	7.0	4.5 (2013)
Pakistan	0.66	0.98	0.7	0.6 (2014)
Tajikistan	2.18	1.71 (2014)	6.5	4.8 (2013)
Turkmenistan	4.36 (2002)	2.29 (2014)	9.1	7.4 (2013)
Uzbekistan	2.95	2.45 (2014)	5.3	4.0 (2013)
East Asia				
China, People's Republic of	1.26	3.63	2.5	4.2 (2012)
Hong Kong, China	...	...	...	...
Korea, Republic of	1.30	2.33 (2016)	12.3 (2008)	11.5
Mongolia	2.76 (2002)	3.26	7.5 (2002)	7.0 (2012)
Taipei,China	1.54 (2001)	2.18 (2016)	5.7 (2001)	6.9 (2016)
South Asia				
Bangladesh	0.24 (2001)	0.47	0.3 (2005)	0.8
Bhutan	0.19 (2004)	0.38 (2016)	1.7 (2006)	1.7 (2012)
India	0.53	0.76 (2016)	0.9 (2005)	0.7 (2011)
Maldives	0.78	3.61	2.6 (2005)	4.3 (2009)
Nepal	0.05 (2001)	0.60 (2014)	5.0 (2006)	0.3 (2012)
Sri Lanka	0.42	0.88	3.1 (2004)	3.5 (2010)
Southeast Asia				
Brunei Darussalam	1.02	1.75	2.7 (2008)	2.7
Cambodia	0.17	0.14 (2014)	0.6 (2001)	0.8
Indonesia	0.16	0.20 (2012)	0.6 (2002)	1.2
Lao People's Democratic Republic	0.28	0.49 (2014)	1.2 (2005)	1.5 (2012)
Malaysia	0.69	1.53	1.8 (2001)	1.9
Myanmar	0.30	0.57 (2012)	0.6 (2006)	0.9 (2012)
Philippines	0.57	...	0.5 (2006)	0.5 (2010)
Singapore	1.43 (2001)	2.28 (2016)	3.1 (2008)	2.4
Thailand	0.37	0.47	2.2 (2002)	2.1 (2010)
Viet Nam	0.52 (2001)	0.82 (2016)	2.9 (2008)	2.6 (2014)
The Pacific				
Cook Islands	0.78 (2001)	1.19 (2009)	6.3 (2005)	...
Fiji	0.47 (2003)	0.84	2.1 (2008)	2.3 (2011)
Kiribati	0.25 (2008)	0.20 (2013)	1.5 (2004)	1.9
Marshall Islands	0.47	0.46 (2012)	...	2.7 (2010)
Micronesia, Federated States of	0.60	0.18 (2010)	2.8	3.2 (2009)
Nauru	0.99 (2004)	1.39 (2011)	3.5 (2007)	5.0 (2010)
Palau	1.58	1.19 (2014)	5.9 (2006)	4.8 (2010)
Papua New Guinea	0.05	0.06 (2010)	...	...
Samoa	0.28 (2003)	0.34 (2010)	1.0 (2005)	...
Solomon Islands	0.13 (2003)	0.19 (2013)	2.2 (2003)	1.4 (2012)
Timor-Leste	0.00 (2001)	0.08 (2011)	...	5.9 (2010)
Tonga	0.50	0.56 (2010)	2.4 (2008)	2.6 (2010)
Tuvalu	0.63 (2002)	1.09 (2010)	5.6 (2001)	...
Vanuatu	0.15 (2004)	0.19 (2012)	1.7 (2008)	...
Developed ADB Member Economies				
Australia	2.50	3.50	7.8	3.8 (2014)
Japan	2.04	2.37 (2014)	13.8 (2008)	13.4 (2012)
New Zealand	2.31 (2001)	3.06	6.2 (2002)	2.8 (2013)

... = data not available, 0.00 = magnitude is less than half of unit employed, ADB = Asian Development Bank.

Sources: For number of physicians per 1,000 population: World Bank. World Development Indicators. http://databank.worldbank.org (accessed 5 June 2018); for the Cook Islands: World Health Organization. Global Health Observatory. http://apps.who.int/gho/data/view.main.HS07v (accessed 5 June 2018). For number of hospital beds per 1,000 population: World Health Organization. Global Health Observatory. http://apps.who.int/gho/data/view.main.HS07v (accessed 5 June 2018); and for initial year data of Australia, Cambodia, the Federated States of Micronesia, Kiribati, Malaysia, Mongolia, Palau, the People's Republic of China, and Solomon Islands: World Bank. World Development Indicators. http://databank.worldbank.org (accessed 5 June 2018). For Taipei,China: Government of Taipei,China, Directorate-General of Budget, Accounting and Statistics. Statistical Yearbook of the Republic of China 2016. https://eng.dgbas.gov.tw/lp.asp?ctNode=2351&CtUnit=1072&BaseDSD=36&MP=2 (accessed 4 June 2018).

Table 2.1.15:   Estimated Number of Adults Aged 15 Years and Over Living with HIV[a]

('000)

ADB Regional Member	Adults		Women	
	2000	2016	2000	2016
Developing ADB Member Economies				
Central and West Asia				
Afghanistan	1.8	7.2	0.5	2.1
Armenia	1.4	3.3	0.4	1.0
Azerbaijan	1.5	9.1	0.5	2.8
Georgia	2.2	11.4	0.6	3.5
Kazakhstan	4.0	25.1	0.5	7.5
Kyrgyz Republic	1.3	8.3	0.4	2.7
Pakistan	0.4	130.3	0.1	39.7
Tajikistan	1.3	13.7	0.3	3.5
Turkmenistan	...	...	...	...
Uzbekistan	...	...	...	...
East Asia				
China, People's Republic of	...	...	...	...
Hong Kong, China	...	...	...	...
Korea, Republic of	...	...	...	...
Mongolia	0.0	0.5	0.0	0.1
Taipei,China	...	...	...	...
South Asia				
Bangladesh	1.4	11.4	0.3	3.9
Bhutan	...	...	...	...
India	1,949.2	1,977.1	674.8	799.1
Maldives	...	...	...	...
Nepal	26.3	31.2	7.8	11.8
Sri Lanka	0.5	4.0	0.1	0.8
Southeast Asia				
Brunei Darussalam	...	...	...	...
Cambodia	107.1	66.8	42.2	35.4
Indonesia	79.6	606.3	14.6	215.0
Lao People's Democratic Republic	1.7	10.7	0.6	4.9
Malaysia	101.1	96.4	3.6	12.7
Myanmar	190.9	221.4	45.4	80.5
Philippines	1.1	55.8	0.4	5.5
Singapore	...	...	...	...
Thailand	665.0	444.8	222.0	197.7
Viet Nam	111.8	243.2	19.3	78.0
The Pacific				
Cook Islands	...	...	...	...
Fiji	0.1	0.7	0.0	0.2
Kiribati	...	...	...	...
Marshall Islands	...	...	...	...
Micronesia, Federated States of	...	...	...	...
Nauru	...	...	...	...
Palau	...	...	...	...
Papua New Guinea	21.9	42.4	12.0	24.5
Samoa	...	...	...	...
Solomon Islands	...	...	...	...
Timor-Leste	...	...	...	...
Tonga	...	...	...	...
Tuvalu	...	...	...	...
Vanuatu	...	...	...	...
Developed ADB Member Economies				
Australia	14.8	24.8	1.2	2.6
Japan	...	...	...	...
New Zealand	...	...	...	...

... = data not available, 0.0 = magnitude is less than half of unit employed, ADB = Asian Development Bank.

a   The modeled HIV estimates are calculated by the Joint United Nations Programme on HIV/AIDS (UNAIDS) using the software Spectrum developed by Avenir Health (www.avenirhealth.org), and the Estimates and Projections Package developed by the East–West Center (www.eastwestcenter.org). The UNAIDS Reference Group on Estimates, Modelling and Projections (www.epidem.org) provides technical guidance on the development of the HIV component of the software.

Source: Joint United Nations Programme on HIV/AIDS (UNAIDS). AIDSinfo Epidemiological estimates database. http://www.aidsinfoonline.org/epi/libraries/aspx/Home.aspx (accessed 4 June 2018).

II.   Economy and Output

Snapshot

- The Asia and Pacific region, which accounts for a growing share of global GDP at purchasing power parity (PPP), saw its share of this measure rise from 30.1% in 2000 to 42.6% in 2017. The region's three largest economies—the People's Republic of China (PRC), India, and Japan—accounted for more than 70% of the region's GDP at PPP in 2017, up from about 63% in 2000.

- From 2000 to 2017, gross capital formation as a share of GDP increased in 25 of 37 regional economies.

- In 2017, 36 of 38 economies in Asia and the Pacific experienced real GDP growth, compared to 2016. The most rapid average annual growth rates were in Armenia and Nepal (7.5% each).

Key Trends

The Asia and Pacific region now accounts for more than two-fifths of the share of global GDP in purchasing power parity (PPP) terms. Figure 2.2.1 presents global GDP shares by region at PPP in 2000 and 2017. Asia and the Pacific's growing share of global output, which increased from 30.1% to 42.6% during the review period, came at the expense of the global shares of North America, Europe, South America, and the rest of the world, which declined by

6.8, 4.7, 1.3, and 0.3 percentage points, respectively. Meanwhile, Africa's share of global GDP rose from 4.4% to 5.0% during the review period.

The three largest economies in Asia and the Pacific—the PRC, India, and Japan—accounted for more than 70% of the region's GDP at PPP in 2017, up from about 63% in 2000. The PRC accounted for 42.7% of the region's total output at PPP in 2017, compared with 25.1% in 2000. The next largest regional share of GDP at PPP in 2017 was

Figure 2.2.1: Distribution of Gross Domestic Product at Purchasing Power Parity, Asia and Pacific Region in the World Economy (%)

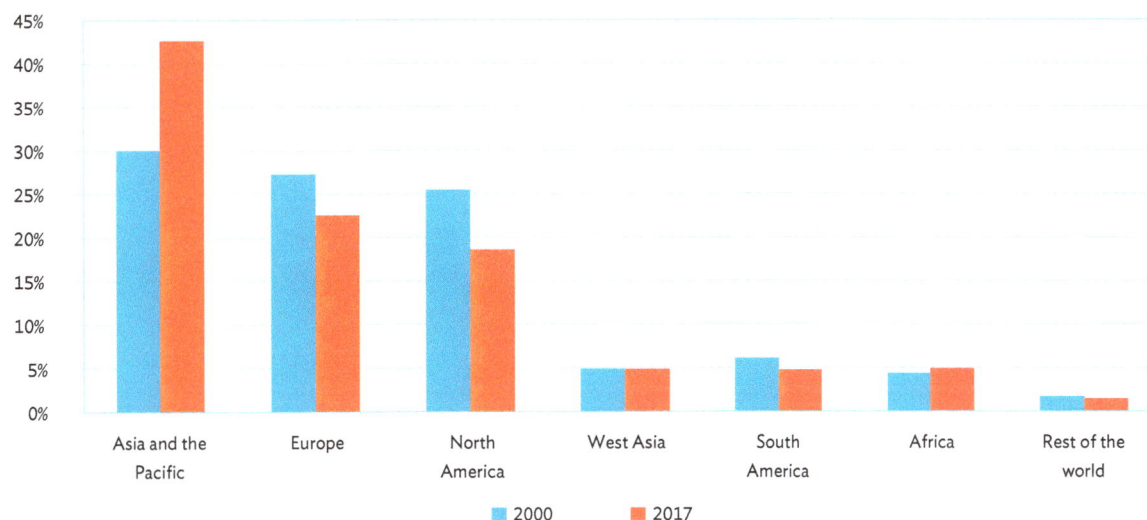

Sources: Table 2.2.1, Key Indicators for Asia and the Pacific 2018; and World Bank. World Development Indicators. http//data.worldbank.org/ (accessed 3 August 2018).

**Figure 2.2.2: Share of Gross Capital Formation
to Gross Domestic Product**
(%)

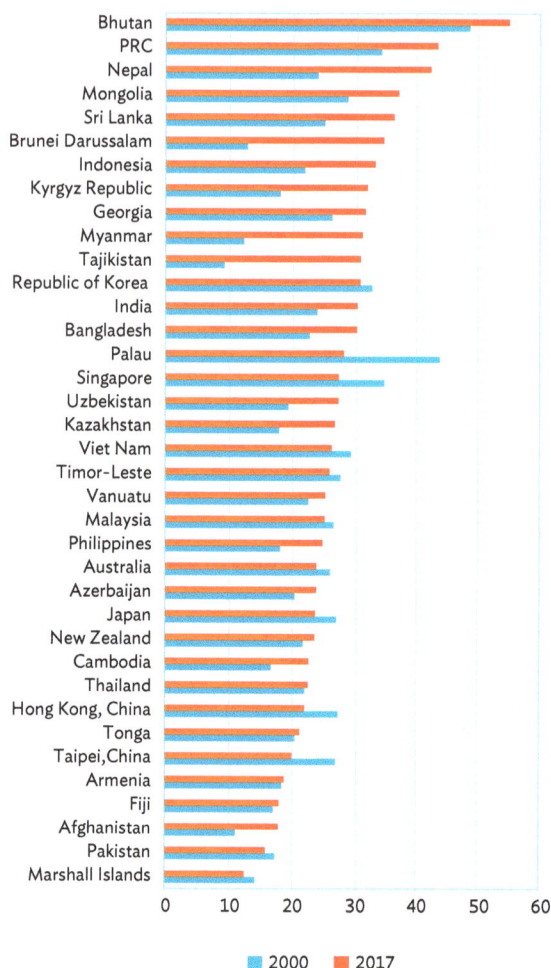

PRC = People's Republic of China.

Note: This chart includes economies with available data between 2000 and
          2017. For 2000, data included are for 2000 to 2005. For 2017, data
          included are for 2015 to 2017.

Source: Table 2.2.8, Key Indicators for Asia and the Pacific 2018.

the economy for accelerated growth (ADB 2018a). Gross capital formation as a share of GDP was also relatively high in the PRC (43.6%), Nepal (42.5%), and Mongolia (37.3%). While most economies with high shares are building modern infrastructure, many of those with lower shares include more mature economies with much of infrastructure already in place.

Capital formation comprises fixed investment in the form of buildings, civil engineering, machinery, and equipment. Many developing economies seek to increase their stock of capital assets and incorporate more modern technology to spur growth (ADB 2017b).

Figure 2.2.2 shows gross capital formation as a percentage of each member economy's GDP in 2000 and 2017.

In 2017, 36 of 38 economies in Asia and the Pacific experienced real annual GDP growth. The most rapid annual growth rates were in Armenia and Nepal (7.5% each). In 2017, every economy in Asia and the Pacific recorded real GDP growth, except for Palau (–3.7%) and Samoa (–0.4%), as shown in Figure 2.2.3. In Palau, an ongoing slump in tourism contributed to the contraction in real GDP, while in Samoa declines in construction, communications, and fishing offset expansion elsewhere (ADB 2018a).

The region's most rapidly growing economies in 2017 were Armenia and Nepal, both of which recorded annual GDP growth of 7.5%. Expansion in industry and services buttressed economic growth in Armenia in 2017, following GDP growth of only 0.2% in 2016. In Nepal, the economy continued to recover from the devastating 2015 earthquake, with the normalization of disrupted trade, better management of the electricity supply, and improved harvests all contributing to growth in 2017 (ADB 2018a). The two most populous economies of Asia— the PRC and India—witnessed 6.9% and 6.7% GDP growth in 2017.

that of India at 17.3%, up from 14.6% in 2000. Japan was third, with a 10.2% share in 2017, down from 23.1% in 2000.

From 2000 to 2017, gross capital formation as a share of GDP increased in 25 of 37 regional economies. Across the region in 2017 (or the most recent year for which data were available), gross capital formation as a percentage of GDP ranged from a low of 12.7% in the Marshall Islands to a high of 55.0% in Bhutan, where increased fixed capital investment in the hydropower sector has positioned

Figure 2.2.3: Growth Rates of Real Gross Domestic Product, 2017
(%)

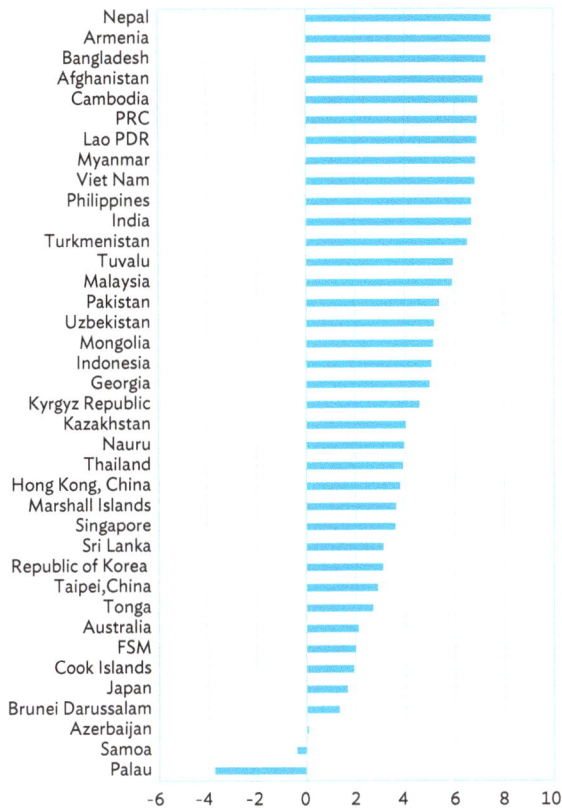

FSM = Federated States of Micronesia, Lao PDR = Lao People's Democratic Republic,
PRC = People's Republic of China.
Source: Table 2.2.11, Key Indicators for Asia and the Pacific 2018.

Data Issues and Comparability

Indicators in this theme are derived from national accounts statistics compiled in accordance with the UN System of National Accounts. As national statistical offices gradually adopt the latest 2008 System of National Accounts framework with regard to data compilation frameworks and methodologies, these indicators will become more consistent across economies. Currently, economies in the region have varying reference periods (e.g., calendar year versus fiscal year) and price valuation methods. Due to a lack of reliable data and limited technical and financial resources dedicated for national accounts compilation, some economies with small statistical offices are not able to provide timely estimates, while some are dependent upon the estimates of external institutions.

Table 2.2.1:   Gross Domestic Product at Purchasing Power Parity
(current international dollars, million)

ADB Regional Member	2000	2005	2010	2012	2013	2014	2015	2016	2017
Developing ADB Member Economies									
Central and West Asia									
Afghanistan	21,014 (2002)	26,690	46,614	58,848	63,424	65,489	66,685	70,015	72,445
Armenia	7,116	14,219	18,896	20,672	23,141	24,404	25,458	25,834	28,271
Azerbaijan	28,446	60,164	141,499	150,415	161,702	167,897	171,584	168,386	171,589
Georgia	11,430	18,288	25,902	30,701	32,254	34,351	35,723	37,210	39,768
Kazakhstan	117,400	215,982	321,378	375,997	404,994	429,577	439,446	449,948	476,366
Kyrgyz Republic	8,054	10,895	14,893	16,388	18,471	19,559	20,537	21,701	23,104
Pakistan	425,583	603,006	715,834	791,333	839,466	894,478	946,956	1,012,041	1,088,982
Tajikistan	5,813	10,417	15,770	18,926	20,654	22,434	24,041	26,028	28,373
Turkmenistan	18,749	27,498	49,556	65,641	73,505	82,458	88,985	95,561	92,769
Uzbekistan	48,918	71,507	118,646	144,515	158,597	174,024	189,984	208,585	226,717
East Asia									
China, People's Republic of	3,703,735	6,639,265	12,484,971	15,331,833	16,788,019	18,336,442	19,814,240	21,411,515	23,300,778
Hong Kong, China	179,705	248,256	331,083	366,845	384,331	402,036	416,100	430,511	454,887
Korea, Republic of	850,052	1,165,894	1,505,299	1,611,273	1,644,777	1,704,458	1,795,917	1,877,123	1,969,106
Mongolia	8,846	13,603	20,488	28,055	31,829	34,956	36,176	37,103	38,753
Taipei,China	481,040	658,502	894,069	984,588	1,022,483	1,082,688	1,103,238	1,133,100	1,186,865
South Asia									
Bangladesh	151,207	213,938	364,141	429,253	462,416	499,245	537,727	583,327	637,078
Bhutan	1,608	2,644	4,577	5,393	5,597	6,025	6,492	7,101	7,721
India	2,147,733	3,339,659	5,478,661	6,209,846	6,713,105	7,339,970	8,024,587	8,705,012	9,460,762
Maldives	2,171	2,633	4,288	4,960	5,407	5,908	6,106	6,568	7,277
Nepal	28,974	38,453	52,582	59,229	62,670	67,616	70,620	71,817	78,591
Sri Lanka	84,448	112,586	168,798	207,597	218,113	233,041	247,365	261,716	274,718
Southeast Asia									
Brunei Darussalam	21,672	26,976	30,674	33,380	33,198	33,000	33,169	32,764	33,797
Cambodia	13,260	23,268	35,370	42,195	46,205	50,569	54,470	58,903	63,943
Indonesia	973,477	1,377,638	2,003,952	2,344,875	2,515,160	2,688,485	2,851,492	3,031,818	3,242,769
Lao People's Democratic Republic	9,942	15,850	24,427	31,322	34,382	37,663	40,839	44,265	48,167
Malaysia	299,741	424,428	581,369	671,120	713,970	770,439	817,953	863,345	930,746
Myanmar	47,733	98,203	182,865	215,424	237,348	260,914	282,187	302,576	319,894
Philippines	261,128	367,111	513,961	590,801	642,751	694,494	744,615	805,965	875,311
Singapore	165,079	235,389	358,705	412,729	440,828	466,169	481,785	499,625	527,022
Thailand	458,555	671,403	888,080	998,288	1,041,670	1,070,804	1,115,105	1,166,404	1,233,958
Viet Nam	163,044	255,657	382,113	444,114	475,754	513,271	553,492	595,368	647,125
The Pacific									
Cook Islands	...	...	...	...	...	...	...	...	...
Fiji	4,276	5,387	6,195	6,706	7,137	7,673	8,054	8,187	8,651
Kiribati	135	162	177	193	203	211	235	241	253
Marshall Islands	121	153	182	196	205	208	209	215	248
Micronesia, Federated States of	266	308	335	352	344	343	364	368	384
Nauru	...	...	79	96	113	157	163	182	193
Palau	188	252	238	273	273	286	318	322	316
Papua New Guinea	12,124	15,157	22,228	24,446	25,792	30,230	35,887	35,923	36,139
Samoa	532	797	1,020	1,082	1,096	1,149	1,167	1,277	1,317
Solomon Islands	390	728	989	1,028	1,119	1,158	1,196	1,249	1,313
Timor-Leste	2,285	5,752	9,633	11,754	10,630	8,002	9,777	9,984	9,350
Tonga	358	449	508	547	538	560	588	615	643
Tuvalu	23	25	30	33	35	36	40	45	49
Vanuatu	416	486	683	731	757	789	814	850	905
Developed ADB Member Economies									
Australia	504,049	663,626	865,291	971,872	1,059,955	1,098,649	1,102,388	1,117,187	1,157,294
Japan	3,404,323	4,045,734	4,482,491	4,746,699	4,967,052	4,986,566	5,176,842	5,370,229	5,560,098
New Zealand	82,978	106,148	136,027	145,406	160,892	168,135	174,015	184,306	195,186
DEVELOPING ADB MEMBER ECONOMIES[a]	10,766,791	17,019,679	27,821,756	32,743,995	35,364,466	38,263,664	41,101,887	44,100,695	47,647,416
ALL ADB REGIONAL MEMBERS[a]	14,758,140	21,835,187	33,305,566	38,607,973	41,552,364	44,517,014	47,555,133	50,772,417	54,559,994

... = data not available, ADB = Asian Development Bank.

a   For reporting economies only.

Source: Asian Development Bank estimates.

Table 2.2.2:   Gross Domestic Product[a]
(current $ million)

ADB Regional Member	2000	2005	2010	2012	2013	2014	2015	2016	2017
Developing ADB Member Economies									
Central and West Asia									
Afghanistan	4,285 (2002)	6,622	16,078	21,331	21,610	21,331	20,607	20,234	21,517
Armenia	1,912	4,900	9,260	9,958	11,121	11,610	10,553	10,546	11,537
Azerbaijan	5,273	13,245	52,906	69,680	74,161	75,239	53,076	37,867	40,749
Georgia	3,058	6,411	11,638	15,847	16,141	16,510	13,993	14,378	15,159
Kazakhstan	18,292	57,124	148,047	207,999	236,635	221,416	184,388	137,278	159,407
Kyrgyz Republic	1,370	2,460	4,794	6,605	7,335	7,468	6,678	6,813	7,565
Pakistan	79,097	119,739	174,508	214,642	220,269	248,949	267,035	277,521	303,092
Tajikistan	861	2,312	5,642	7,633	8,506	9,237	7,855	6,953	7,146
Turkmenistan	4,932	17,175	22,583	35,164	39,198	43,486	35,855	36,180	37,926
Uzbekistan	13,759	14,396	39,526	51,608	57,691	63,111	66,904	67,446	49,677
East Asia									
China, People's Republic of	1,211,332	2,285,960	6,100,647	8,560,506	9,607,286	10,482,320	11,064,684	11,191,026	12,237,773
Hong Kong, China	171,669	181,569	228,639	262,629	275,697	291,460	309,386	320,874	341,447
Korea, Republic of	561,634	898,137	1,094,499	1,222,807	1,305,605	1,411,334	1,382,764	1,414,804	1,530,751
Mongolia	1,137	2,523	7,189	12,293	12,582	12,227	11,750	11,187	11,135
Taipei,China	331,503	375,920	446,217	495,946	511,614	530,554	525,759	530,729	572,659
South Asia									
Bangladesh	45,468	57,627	114,508	128,899	153,505	173,062	194,466	220,316	245,633
Bhutan	439	819	1,585	1,824	1,798	1,959	2,059	2,213	...
India	484,498	837,499	1,702,346	1,860,877	1,917,054	2,042,939	2,145,537	2,270,056	2,575,667
Maldives	624	1,163	2,588	2,886	3,295	3,697	4,007	4,224	...
Nepal	5,338	8,259	16,281	17,927	18,227	20,138	20,801	20,929	24,870
Sri Lanka	16,717	24,406	56,726	68,434	74,318	79,356	80,604	81,787	87,175
Southeast Asia									
Brunei Darussalam	6,001	9,531	13,707	19,048	18,094	17,098	12,930	11,400	12,128
Cambodia	3,668	6,293	11,242	14,038	15,268	16,805	18,080	20,017	22,121
Indonesia	165,021	285,869	755,094	917,870	912,524	890,815	861,256	932,259	1,015,539
Lao People's Democratic Republic	1,638	2,717	6,744	10,191	11,942	13,268	14,390	15,806	16,853
Malaysia	93,790	143,534	255,017	314,443	323,276	338,066	296,434	296,536	314,497
Myanmar	...	...	...	...	62,140	66,300	62,543	64,560	67,102
Philippines	81,026	103,072	199,591	250,092	271,836	284,585	292,774	304,889	313,595
Singapore	95,836	127,418	236,420	290,678	304,454	311,552	304,091	309,753	323,900
Thailand	126,392	189,318	341,105	397,558	420,334	407,339	401,399	411,755	455,303
Viet Nam	31,173	57,633	115,932	155,820	171,222	186,205	193,241	205,276	223,780
The Pacific									
Cook Islands	92	183	255	302	302	316	286	288	309
Fiji	1,678	2,981	3,140	3,972	4,190	4,484	4,362	4,671	...
Kiribati	68	112	156	190	185	179	169	182	...
Marshall Islands	112	140	168	187	192	185	181	196	222
Micronesia, Federated States of	233	250	297	326	316	318	315	330	338
Nauru	...	26	63	121	102	115	90	104	116
Palau	145	185	183	215	225	246	293	303	292
Papua New Guinea	3,499	4,866	14,251	21,295	21,261	23,004	22,962	21,480	22,006
Samoa	231	434	680	800	805	824	774	822	856
Solomon Islands	286	428	696	918	1,015	1,047	1,027	1,093	...
Timor-Leste	440	1,814	3,999	6,671	5,650	4,045	3,104	2,521	...
Tonga	189	264	374	465	439	435	402	401	427
Tuvalu	14	22	31	37	37	37	35	40	44
Vanuatu	273	395	701	782	802	815	760	804	...
Developed ADB Member Economies									
Australia	383,144	703,607	1,191,641	1,549,803	1,480,810	1,438,465	1,218,102	1,233,714	1,344,863
Japan	4,887,520	4,755,410	5,700,098	6,203,213	5,155,717	4,850,414	4,394,978	4,949,965	4,869,751
New Zealand	54,444	114,723	146,584	176,193	190,786	200,955	177,620	188,354	...
DEVELOPING ADB MEMBER ECONOMIES[b]	3,575,003	5,855,754	12,216,056	15,681,516	17,120,258	18,335,484	18,900,662	19,288,847	21,070,312
ALL ADB REGIONAL MEMBERS[b]	8,900,110	11,429,493	19,254,378	23,610,726	23,947,571	24,825,317	24,691,361	25,660,879	27,284,927

... = data not available, $ = United States dollars, ADB = Asian Development Bank.

a Gross domestic product at local currency units are obtained from economy sources and are converted to United States dollars using the official exchange rates from the International Monetary Fund. The exchange rates used are expressed as the average rate for a period of time (average of period), calculated as annual averages based on the monthly averages (local currency units relative to the United States dollar).

b For reporting economies only.

Source: Asian Development Bank estimates.

Table 2.2.3:   Gross Domestic Product per Capita at Purchasing Power Parity
(current international dollars)

ADB Regional Member	2000	2005	2010	2012	2013	2014	2015	2016	2017
Developing ADB Member Economies									
Central and West Asia									
Afghanistan	964 (2002)	1,131	1,793	2,180	2,306	2,331	2,332	2,398	2,439
Armenia	2,209	4,519	6,206	6,836	7,657	8,097	8,473	8,634	9,489
Azerbaijan	3,523	7,078	15,628	16,191	17,166	17,612	17,781	17,257	17,420
Georgia	2,804	4,686	6,840	8,233	8,676	9,236	9,589	9,983	10,667
Kazakhstan	7,888	14,259	19,690	22,392	23,774	24,847	25,054	25,278	26,465
Kyrgyz Republic	1,652	2,121	2,749	2,952	3,262	3,386	3,484	3,605	3,763
Pakistan	3,041	3,864	4,126	4,379	4,554	4,757	4,940	5,180	5,241
Tajikistan	938	1,536	2,097	2,396	2,558	2,717	2,845	3,010	3,211
Turkmenistan	4,152	5,783	9,741	12,461	13,698	15,085	15,989	16,876	16,111
Uzbekistan	1,984	2,733	4,154	4,854	5,244	5,658	6,070	6,550	6,997
East Asia									
China, People's Republic of	2,922	5,078	9,311	11,323	12,338	13,406	14,414	15,485	16,762
Hong Kong, China	26,963	36,437	47,135	51,306	53,536	55,610	57,068	58,680	61,540
Korea, Republic of	18,083	24,196	30,377	32,097	32,616	33,588	35,204	36,630	38,275
Mongolia	3,704	5,363	7,481	9,880	10,979	11,797	11,952	12,012	12,307
Taipei,China	21,684	28,971	38,636	42,311	43,799	46,262	47,021	48,184	50,386
South Asia									
Bangladesh	1,169	1,544	2,450	2,811	2,989	3,184	3,384	3,628	3,916
Bhutan	2,702	4,164	6,577	7,483	7,636	8,086	8,576	9,239	10,619
India	2,108	3,020	4,619	5,028	5,366	5,793	6,255	6,701	7,189
Maldives	6,331	7,776	10,894	11,887	12,614	13,503	13,437	13,936	14,802
Nepal	1,377	1,520	2,003	2,206	2,303	2,451	2,526	2,535	2,737
Sri Lanka	4,362	5,731	8,173	10,164	10,599	11,220	11,798	12,343	12,811
Southeast Asia									
Brunei Darussalam	66,725	75,246	79,302	83,658	82,316	80,962	80,430	78,533	80,220
Cambodia	1,064	1,746	2,504	2,912	3,148	3,402	3,618	3,863	4,140
Indonesia	4,720	6,266	8,402	9,554	10,108	10,662	11,162	11,719	12,382
Lao People's Democratic Republic	1,954	2,819	4,043	5,037	5,450	5,885	6,290	6,721	7,209
Malaysia	12,760	16,295	20,336	22,742	23,641	25,096	26,216	27,321	29,086
Myanmar	1,036	2,026	3,646	4,225	4,613	5,019	5,380	5,718	5,992
Philippines	3,401	4,335	5,518	6,122	6,546	6,953	7,332	7,806	8,344
Singapore	40,984	55,181	70,657	77,692	81,647	85,227	87,043	89,103	93,905
Thailand	7,368	10,482	13,472	15,014	15,604	15,981	16,585	17,292	18,227
Viet Nam	2,114	3,121	4,396	5,003	5,300	5,657	6,035	6,423	6,909
The Pacific									
Cook Islands	...	...	...	...	...	...	...	...	...
Fiji	5,332	6,514	7,282	7,816	8,279	8,863	9,263	9,376	9,777
Kiribati	1,595	1,756	1,721	1,828	1,897	1,943	2,138	2,161	2,238
Marshall Islands	2,367	2,980	3,445	3,673	3,826	3,863	3,869	3,978	4,569
Micronesia, Federated States of	2,482	2,916	3,255	3,448	3,373	3,359	3,556	3,594	3,749
Nauru	...	...	8,178	9,361	10,451	13,185	13,061	14,019	14,529
Palau	9,948	12,686	12,992	15,504	15,702	16,467	18,007	18,040	17,646
Papua New Guinea	2,336	2,505	3,150	3,259	3,334	3,790	4,363	4,235	4,132
Samoa	3,038	4,431	5,474	5,712	5,736	5,967	6,006	6,516	6,668
Solomon Islands	932	1,548	1,873	1,858	1,977	1,999	2,017	2,058	2,114
Timor-Leste	2,622	5,604	8,682	10,161	8,975	6,598	7,879	7,872	7,213
Tonga	3,616	4,436	4,944	5,327	5,265	5,509	5,810	6,115	6,421
Tuvalu	2,398	2,479	2,727	3,033	3,191	3,243	3,538	3,999	4,273
Vanuatu	2,179	2,274	2,847	2,913	2,950	3,004	3,031	3,121	3,249
Developed ADB Member Economies									
Australia	26,489	32,891	39,275	42,734	45,795	46,743	46,220	46,144	47,047
Japan	26,839	31,663	35,000	37,191	38,974	39,179	40,717	42,287	43,854
New Zealand	21,509	25,677	31,266	32,986	36,220	37,283	37,865	39,271	40,715
DEVELOPING ADB MEMBER ECONOMIES[a]	**3,274**	**4,878**	**7,553**	**8,668**	**9,266**	**9,922**	**10,550**	**11,204**	**11,957**
ALL ADB REGIONAL MEMBERS[a]	**4,292**	**5,996**	**8,678**	**9,818**	**10,462**	**11,096**	**11,738**	**12,408**	**13,175**

... = data not available, ADB = Asian Development Bank.

a For reporting economies only.

Source: Asian Development Bank estimates.

Table 2.2.4: **Gross National Income per Capita, Atlas Method**[a]
(current $)

ADB Regional Member	2000	2005	2010	2012	2013	2014	2015	2016	2017
Developing ADB Member Economies									
Central and West Asia									
Afghanistan	...	250	500	670	680	650	600	580	570
Armenia	660	1,540	3,470	3,880	4,120	4,150	4,030	3,770	4,000
Azerbaijan	610	1,270	5,410	6,480	7,450	7,700	6,550	4,760	4,080
Georgia	750	1,410	3,000	3,870	4,240	4,490	4,120	3,830	3,790
Kazakhstan	1,260	2,950	7,440	9,940	11,840	12,090	11,420	8,800	7,890
Kyrgyz Republic	280	450	850	1,040	1,190	1,250	1,180	1,110	1,130
Pakistan	490	730	1,080	1,260	1,360	1,390	1,430	1,500	1,580
Tajikistan	170	320	910	1,140	1,320	1,340	1,240	1,110	990
Turkmenistan	600	1,590	4,070	5,560	6,510	7,200	7,030	6,820	6,650
Uzbekistan	630	530	1,340	1,740	1,970	2,110	2,170	2,220	1,980
East Asia									
China, People's Republic of	940	1,760	4,340	5,940	6,800	7,520	7,950	8,250	8,690
Hong Kong, China	26,930	28,890	33,620	36,340	38,570	40,240	41,180	42,970	46,310
Korea, Republic of	10,740	17,790	21,260	24,550	25,760	26,800	27,250	27,690	28,380
Mongolia	470	900	2,000	3,660	4,350	4,240	3,850	3,590	3,290
Taipei,China	13,921	17,644	20,034	21,901	22,620	23,369	23,075	23,013	23,836
South Asia									
Bangladesh	420	530	780	940	1,010	1,070	1,190	1,330	1,470
Bhutan	770	1,210	1,970	2,290	2,300	2,330	2,340	2,510	2,720
India	440	700	1,220	1,480	1,520	1,560	1,600	1,680	1,820
Maldives	2,070	3,470	5,980	6,820	7,110	7,800	8,190	8,740	9,570
Nepal	230	310	540	690	720	730	740	730	790
Sri Lanka	880	1,210	2,420	3,360	3,490	3,640	3,760	3,790	3,840
Southeast Asia									
Brunei Darussalam	14,680	23,080	33,300	42,290	45,180	42,930	38,590	32,890	29,600
Cambodia	300	460	750	880	970	1,020	1,060	1,140	1,230
Indonesia	580	1,220	2,520	3,570	3,730	3,620	3,430	3,410	3,540
Lao People's Democratic Republic	280	460	1,000	1,380	1,620	1,840	2,000	2,150	2,270
Malaysia	3,460	5,280	8,290	10,150	10,760	11,010	10,450	9,860	9,650
Myanmar	170 (2002)	270	860	1,140	1,230	1,230	1,190	1,190	1,190
Philippines	1,220	1,430	2,470	2,980	3,300	3,470	3,520	3,580	3,660
Singapore	23,670	28,370	44,790	51,110	54,730	56,370	54,020	52,350	54,530
Thailand	1,980	2,790	4,580	5,520	5,720	5,760	5,710	5,700	5,960
Viet Nam	410	630	1,250	1,530	1,710	1,860	1,950	2,060	2,170
The Pacific									
Cook Islands	6,129	8,475	9,790	15,060	16,207	17,110	16,575	15,623	16,397*
Fiji	2,230	3,590	3,650	4,100	4,640	4,750	4,810	4,800	4,970
Kiribati	1,330	1,730	1,990	2,450	2,840	3,230	3,460	2,800	2,780
Marshall Islands	2,850	3,580	3,790	3,980	4,300	4,500	4,720	4,630	4,800
Micronesia, Federated States of	2,210	2,550	2,880	3,180	3,230	3,240	3,640	3,550	3,590
Nauru	...	...	5,800	9,190	13,330	14,730	11,850	10,750	10,220
Palau	7,370 (2002)	9,270	8,970	9,880	9,780	10,670	11,790	12,550	12,530
Papua New Guinea	600	670	1,780	2,310	2,630	3,010	2,780	2,530	2,410
Samoa	1,600	2,370	3,200	3,780	3,920	4,040	4,070	4,120	4,100
Solomon Islands	1,010	890	900	1,510	1,790	1,880	1,920	1,880	1,920
Timor-Leste	790	710	2,810	3,230	3,540	2,870	2,980	2,290	1,790
Tonga	2,050	2,450	3,560	4,220	4,330	4,360	4,280	4,060	4,010
Tuvalu	2,700 (2001)	3,620	4,400	4,440	5,580	4,700	5,490	5,130	4,970
Vanuatu	1,430	1,780	2,690	2,950	3,200	3,170	2,860	2,870	2,920
Developed ADB Member Economies									
Australia	21,110	30,270	46,550	60,060	65,870	64,980	60,360	54,130	51,360
Japan	36,230	40,560	43,440	49,480	48,280	43,950	38,880	38,000	38,550
New Zealand	14,020	25,380	29,770	36,840	39,730	41,490	40,270	38,560	38,970

... = data not available, * = provisional, preliminary, estimate, $ = United States dollars, ADB = Asian Development Bank.

a   Refers to a conversion factor that averages the exchange rate for a given year and the 2 preceding years, adjusted for differences in rates of inflation between the member economy and the G5 economies.

Sources: World Bank. World Development Indicators Online. http://data.worldbank.org (accessed 9 July 2018). For the Cook Islands and Taipei,China: Asian Development Bank estimates using the Atlas method based on economy sources.

Table 2.2.5:   Gross Domestic Product per Capita
(current $)

ADB Regional Member	2000	2005	2010	2012	2013	2014	2015	2016	2017
Developing ADB Member Economies									
Central and West Asia									
Afghanistan	197 (2002)	281	618	790	786	759	721	693	724
Armenia	593	1,557	3,041	3,293	3,680	3,852	3,512	3,524	3,872
Azerbaijan	653	1,558	5,843	7,500	7,873	7,892	5,500	3,881	4,137
Georgia	750	1,643	3,073	4,250	4,342	4,439	3,756	3,857	4,066
Kazakhstan	1,229	3,771	9,071	12,387	13,891	12,807	10,512	7,712	8,856
Kyrgyz Republic	281	479	885	1,190	1,295	1,293	1,133	1,132	1,232
Pakistan	565	767	1,006	1,188	1,195	1,324	1,393	1,420	1,459
Tajikistan	139	341	750	967	1,053	1,119	929	804	809
Turkmenistan	1,092	3,612	4,439	6,675	7,304	7,955	6,443	6,389	6,587
Uzbekistan	558	550	1,384	1,733	1,908	2,052	2,138	2,118	1,533
East Asia									
China, People's Republic of	956	1,748	4,550	6,322	7,060	7,664	8,049	8,094	8,804
Hong Kong, China	25,757	26,650	32,550	36,731	38,404	40,315	42,432	43,736	46,193
Korea, Republic of	11,948	18,640	22,087	24,359	25,890	27,811	27,105	27,608	29,754
Mongolia	476	995	2,625	4,329	4,340	4,126	3,882	3,622	3,536
Taipei,China	14,943	16,539	19,283	21,312	21,916	22,670	22,408	22,569	24,311
South Asia									
Bangladesh	352	416	771	844	992	1,104	1,224	1,370	1,510
Bhutan	738	1,290	2,279	2,531	2,453	2,629	2,720	2,879	...
India	475	757	1,435	1,507	1,532	1,612	1,672	1,748	1,957
Maldives	2,311	3,436	6,576	6,916	7,687	8,450	8,817	8,963	...
Nepal	254	326	620	668	670	730	744	739	866
Sri Lanka	863	1,242	2,747	3,351	3,611	3,821	3,845	3,857	4,065
Southeast Asia									
Brunei Darussalam	18,477	26,587	35,437	47,740	44,865	41,947	31,354	27,326	28,788
Cambodia	294	472	796	969	1,040	1,131	1,201	1,313	1,432
Indonesia	800	1,300	3,166	3,740	3,667	3,533	3,371	3,604	3,878
Lao People's Democratic Republic	322	483	1,116	1,639	1,893	2,073	2,216	2,400	2,522
Malaysia	3,993	5,511	8,920	10,655	10,705	11,012	9,501	9,384	9,828
Myanmar	...	...	...	...	1,208	1,275	1,192	1,220	1,257
Philippines	1,055	1,217	2,143	2,591	2,768	2,849	2,883	2,953	2,989
Singapore	23,793	29,870	46,570	54,717	56,389	56,960	54,940	55,241	57,713
Thailand	2,031	2,956	5,174	5,979	6,297	6,079	5,970	6,104	6,725
Viet Nam	404	704	1,334	1,755	1,908	2,052	2,107	2,215	2,389
The Pacific									
Cook Islands	5,091	8,491	10,766	15,491	16,213	16,987	15,268	14,769	16,996
Fiji	2,093	3,604	3,692	4,629	4,861	5,179	5,017	5,349	...
Kiribati	799	1,212	1,515	1,796	1,726	1,646	1,536	1,627	...
Marshall Islands	2,195	2,741	3,180	3,497	3,591	3,445	3,361	3,624	4,090
Micronesia, Federated States of	2,179	2,370	2,883	3,190	3,095	3,114	3,081	3,220	3,299
Nauru	...	2,780	6,476	11,794	9,466	9,658	7,233	8,017	8,702
Palau	7,647	9,314	9,998	12,185	12,945	14,156	16,595	16,945	16,288
Papua New Guinea	674	804	2,020	2,839	2,748	2,884	2,791	2,532	2,516
Samoa	1,319	2,414	3,649	4,224	4,212	4,278	3,985	4,196	4,331
Solomon Islands	682	911	1,318	1,661	1,793	1,807	1,732	1,801	...
Timor-Leste	504	1,767	3,604	5,767	4,770	3,336	2,502	1,988	...
Tonga	1,907	2,607	3,636	4,525	4,298	4,280	3,972	3,989	4,261
Tuvalu	1,450	2,108	2,816	3,450	3,401	3,331	3,135	3,497	3,837
Vanuatu	1,432	1,846	2,923	3,116	3,124	3,104	2,828	2,952	...
Developed ADB Member Economies									
Australia	20,135	34,872	54,087	68,146	63,977	61,201	51,072	50,957	54,672
Japan	38,532	37,218	44,508	48,603	40,454	38,109	34,568	38,978	38,409
New Zealand	14,113	27,752	33,692	39,970	42,949	44,561	38,649	40,133	...
DEVELOPING ADB MEMBER ECONOMIES[a]	**1,103**	**1,702**	**3,362**	**4,208**	**4,485**	**4,754**	**4,852**	**4,900**	**5,287**
ADB REGIONAL MEMBERS[a]	**2,624**	**3,181**	**5,083**	**6,083**	**6,029**	**6,188**	**6,095**	**6,271**	**6,589**

...= data not available, $ = United States dollars, ADB = Asian Development Bank.

a   For reporting economies only.

Source: Asian Development Bank estimates using economy sources and official exchange rates from the International Monetary Fund.

Table 2.2.6: Agriculture, Industry, and Services Value Added
(% of GDP)[a]

ADB Regional Member	Agriculture				Industry				Services			
	2000	2005	2010	2017	2000	2005	2010	2017	2000	2005	2010	2017
Developing ADB Member Economies												
Central and West Asia												
Afghanistan	43.7 (2002)	35.2	28.8	24.8	21.7 (2002)	26.0	21.3	22.0	34.6 (2002)	38.8	49.8	53.2
Armenia	25.1	20.6	18.8	16.3	38.3	44.7	36.3	27.6	36.5	34.6	45.0	56.1
Azerbaijan	17.1	9.8	5.9	6.1	45.3	63.3	64.3	53.5	37.5	26.9	29.8	40.4
Georgia	21.9	16.7	8.4	8.2	22.4	26.8	22.2	25.8	55.7	56.5	69.4	66.0
Kazakhstan	8.6	6.6	4.7	4.7	40.1	39.2	41.9	34.3	51.3	54.2	53.4	61.0
Kyrgyz Republic	36.6	31.3	18.7	13.8	31.3	22.0	28.2	29.7	32.1	46.7	53.1	56.5
Pakistan	27.4	24.4	24.3	24.4	18.8	21.1	20.6	19.1	53.8	54.5	55.1	56.5
Tajikistan	27.3	23.8	21.8	23.6	38.4	30.7	27.9	29.6	34.3	45.6	50.3	46.8
Turkmenistan	22.9	18.8	14.5	9.3 (2015)	41.8	37.6	48.4	56.9 (2015)	35.2	43.6	37.0	33.8 (2015)
Uzbekistan	34.4	29.5	19.8	19.7	23.1	29.1	33.3	34.2	42.5	41.4	46.9	46.2
East Asia												
China, People's Republic of	14.9	12.0	9.8	8.2	45.7	47.2	46.6	40.6	39.4	40.9	43.6	51.2
Hong Kong, China	0.1	0.1	0.1	0.1 (2016)	12.6	8.7	7.0	7.7 (2016)	87.3	91.3	93.0	92.2 (2016)
Korea, Republic of	4.4	3.1	2.5	2.2	38.1	37.5	38.3	39.6	57.5	59.4	59.3	58.3
Mongolia	30.9	22.1	13.1	10.6	25.0	36.2	37.0	39.4	44.1	41.7	50.0	50.0
Taipei,China	2.0	1.6	1.6	1.7	31.3	32.3	33.8	35.4	66.7	66.1	64.6	62.9
South Asia												
Bangladesh	25.5	20.1	17.8	14.2	25.3	27.2	26.1	29.3	49.2	52.6	56.0	56.5
Bhutan	27.4	23.2	17.5	17.3 (2016)	36.0	37.3	44.6	43.5 (2016)	36.6	39.5	37.9	39.2 (2016)
India	23.0	18.8	18.2	17.1	26.0	28.1	27.2	29.1	51.0	53.1	54.6	53.9
Maldives	6.9 (2001)	8.7	6.1	6.8 (2016)	13.2 (2001)	13.2	10.2	11.2 (2016)	79.9 (2001)	78.1	83.8	82.0 (2016)
Nepal	39.6	35.2	35.4	29.4	21.5	17.1	15.1	14.6	38.9	47.7	49.5	56.0
Sri Lanka	17.6	11.8	9.5	8.5	29.9	30.2	29.7	30.0	52.5	58.0	60.9	61.5
Southeast Asia												
Brunei Darussalam	1.0	0.9	0.7	1.1	63.7	71.6	67.4	58.7	35.3	27.5	31.9	40.2
Cambodia	37.9	32.4	36.1	25.0	23.0	26.4	23.2	32.7	39.1	41.2	40.8	42.3
Indonesia	15.6	13.1	14.3	13.7	45.9	46.5	43.9	41.0	38.5	40.3	41.8	45.4
Lao People's Democratic Republic	48.5	36.7	30.6	18.3	19.1	23.5	29.8	34.9	32.4	39.8	39.6	46.8
Malaysia	8.3	8.4	10.2	8.9	46.8	46.9	40.9	39.4	44.9	44.7	48.9	51.7
Myanmar	57.2	46.7	36.8	23.7	9.7	17.5	26.5	36.2	33.1	35.8	36.7	40.1
Philippines	14.0	12.7	12.3	9.7	34.5	33.8	32.6	30.5	51.5	53.5	55.1	59.9
Singapore	0.1	0.1	0.0	0.0	34.8	32.4	27.6	24.8	65.1	67.6	72.3	75.2
Thailand	8.5	9.2	10.5	8.7	36.7	38.5	39.9	35.1	54.8	52.3	49.6	56.3
Viet Nam	24.5	19.3	21.0	17.0	36.7	38.1	36.7	37.1	38.7	42.6	42.2	45.8
The Pacific												
Cook Islands	10.3	6.9	4.9	6.1	8.3	9.6	8.5	8.6	81.4	83.5	86.6	85.3
Fiji	16.5	14.1	11.0	13.6 (2016)	21.6	19.2	20.9	17.5 (2016)	61.9	66.8	68.1	68.9 (2016)
Kiribati	20.0	21.8	24.2	25.4 (2016)	12.2	9.3	11.9	15.8 (2016)	67.8	68.9	63.9	58.9 (2016)
Marshall Islands	10.3	9.0	15.4	19.8	12.0	10.0	12.4	13.0	77.7	80.9	72.2	67.2
Micronesia, Federated States of	25.3	24.2	26.7	28.8 (2016)	8.7	5.7	7.8	6.5 (2016)	66.0	70.1	65.5	64.8 (2016)
Nauru	...	7.8	4.3	...	...	-6.5	47.8	...	...	98.7	47.9	...
Palau	4.3	4.2	4.2	3.5	16.1	15.2	11.0	10.3	79.6	80.6	84.8	86.2
Papua New Guinea	35.2	34.0	20.2	...	40.7	44.3	34.2	...	24.1	21.7	45.5	...
Samoa	16.7	12.3	9.1	10.6	26.8	30.6	25.9	21.6	56.6	57.2	65.0	67.8
Solomon Islands	...	32.4	30.3	27.3 (2016)	...	9.5	13.3	14.7 (2016)	...	58.0	56.4	58.0 (2016)
Timor-Leste[b]	24.2	7.4	5.7	11.4 (2016)	31.7	76.1	79.1	45.1 (2016)	44.1	16.4	15.2	43.4 (2016)
Tonga	22.2	20.0	18.2	19.3 (2016)	20.7	19.0	20.0	19.4 (2016)	57.1	61.0	61.8	61.3 (2016)
Tuvalu	20.4	22.2	27.3	20.0	7.4	8.3	5.7	17.8	72.2	69.4	67.0	62.2
Vanuatu	25.4	24.1	21.9	22.2 (2016)	12.2	8.5	13.0	11.1 (2016)	62.3	67.4	65.0	66.6 (2016)
Developed ADB Member Economies												
Australia	3.1	2.9	2.2	2.8	24.6	24.6	25.1	23.0	72.2	72.5	72.7	73.8
Japan	1.5	1.1	1.1	1.1	32.7	30.1	28.5	29.1	65.8	68.8	70.4	69.7
New Zealand	8.3	4.9	7.1	5.0 (2015)	25.3	25.8	23.0	23.4 (2015)	66.4	69.3	69.9	71.7 (2015)

... = data not available, 0.0 = magnitude is less than half of the unit employed, ADB = Asian Development Bank, GDP = gross domestic product.

a   Calculated as a share of GDP at current prices.
b   GDP estimates released by the Government of Timor-Leste's General Directorate of Statistics include the value added by the oil sector.

Source: Economy sources.

National Accounts

Table 2.2.7:   Household and Government Consumption Expenditure
(% of GDP)[a]

ADB Regional Member	Household Final Consumption				Government Final Consumption			
	2000	2005	2010	2017	2000	2005	2010	2017
Developing ADB Member Economies								
Central and West Asia								
Afghanistan	111.2 (2002)	115.7	97.4	76.0	7.7 (2002)	10.0	14.0	11.9
Armenia[b]	97.1	75.5	82.0	77.3	11.8	10.6	13.1	14.2
Azerbaijan	63.0	41.6	38.9	57.2	15.2	10.4	10.9	11.5
Georgia	80.5	64.6	72.3	60.9	8.5	17.3	21.1	17.1
Kazakhstan[b]	61.9	49.9	45.4	52.8	12.1	11.2	10.8	11.1
Kyrgyz Republic[b]	65.7	84.5	84.6	82.8 (2016)	20.0	17.5	18.1	17.4 (2016)
Pakistan[b]	75.5	78.4	79.7	82.0	8.1	7.5	10.3	11.3
Tajikistan[b]	87.7	81.1	84.7	78.8 (2016)	11.6	14.6	11.3	14.1 (2016)
Turkmenistan[b]	37.1	46.6	5.0	...	14.5	13.2	9.3	...
Uzbekistan[b]	61.9	46.7	47.9	52.3	18.7	17.6	15.8	16.7
East Asia								
China, People's Republic of	46.9	40.2	35.4	38.4	16.6	14.0	12.8	14.3
Hong Kong, China[b]	58.6	57.5	61.4	67.0	9.4	9.2	8.9	9.9
Korea, Republic of	52.5	50.7	48.6	45.8	11.3	13.3	14.5	15.3
Mongolia	75.1	55.2	55.2	50.7	15.3	12.1	12.7	12.7
Taipei,China[b]	55.1	56.1	53.1	53.0	15.7	15.3	14.9	14.1
South Asia								
Bangladesh	77.5	74.4	74.1	68.7	4.6	5.5	5.1	6.0
Bhutan[b]	47.7	40.4	46.6	50.9 (2016)	21.9	21.9	20.0	16.9 (2016)
India[b]	64.6	58.3	56.0	59.1	12.6	10.9	11.4	11.4
Maldives	...	...	...	...	22.9	...	...	...
Nepal[b]	75.9	79.5	78.6	78.0	8.9	8.9	10.0	11.7
Sri Lanka	70.9	69.0	68.5	62.2	13.7	13.1	8.5	8.5
Southeast Asia								
Brunei Darussalam[b]	24.8	22.5	14.7	20.5	25.8	18.4	22.2	26.5
Cambodia[b]	86.7	84.3	81.3	73.6	5.2	5.8	6.3	5.1
Indonesia[c]	61.7	64.4	55.2	56.1	6.5	8.1	9.0	9.1
Lao People's Democratic Republic	...	...	...	...	...	...	...	...
Malaysia[c]	43.8	44.2	48.1	55.4	10.2	11.5	12.6	12.2
Myanmar[d]	87.7	86.9	67.3	71.6	...	...	...	...
Philippines[b]	72.2	75.0	71.6	73.5	11.4	9.0	9.7	11.3
Singapore	41.5	39.1	35.5	35.6	10.7	10.2	10.2	10.9
Thailand[b]	53.1	54.9	51.2	47.8	13.6	13.7	15.8	16.4
Viet Nam	66.5	65.5	66.6	68.0	6.4	5.5	6.0	6.5
The Pacific								
Cook Islands	...	...	...	...	...	...	...	...
Fiji[e]	57.2	73.3	70.3	63.3 (2016)	17.3	15.9	15.0	19.8 (2016)
Kiribati	...	...	...	...	...	...	...	...
Marshall Islands	...	68.1	69.4	65.3 (2016)	...	58.1	54.9	57.0 (2016)
Micronesia, Federated States of	...	...	...	...	...	...	...	...
Nauru	...	...	...	...	...	...	...	...
Palau	...	66.4	68.3	67.2	...	31.3	37.6	29.2
Papua New Guinea[b]	44.6	48.0	...	...	16.6	16.1	...	...
Samoa	...	...	...	...	...	...	...	...
Solomon Islands	...	62.6	60.2	58.5 (2016)	...	45.3	40.7	29.7 (2016)
Timor-Leste[f]	70.7	22.6	15.1	37.5 (2016)	111.3	13.4	22.8	36.3 (2016)
Tonga	87.3	93.0	91.3	96.6 (2015)	18.2	15.5	18.1	19.9 (2015)
Tuvalu	...	...	...	...	...	...	...	...
Vanuatu	62.4	65.8	60.6	63.6 (2016)	16.4	13.2	17.5	14.5 (2016)
Developed ADB Member Economies								
Australia	58.1	57.7	56.3	57.1	17.7	17.5	18.0	18.5
Japan[b]	54.4	55.6	57.8	55.5	16.9	18.1	19.5	19.6
New Zealand[b]	58.0	58.2	58.1	57.5 (2016)	17.0	17.9	19.5	18.1 (2016)

... = data not available, ADB = Asian Development Bank, GDP = gross domestic product.

a   Calculated as a share of GDP at current prices.
b   Data for household consumption include nonprofit institution serving households.
c   Prior to 2010, data for household consumption include nonprofit institution serving households.
d   Data for household consumption include government consumption.
e   For 2000–2004, data for household consumption include nonprofit institution serving households.
f   GDP estimates released by the Government of Timor-Leste's General Directorate of Statistics include the value added by the oil sector.

Source: Economy sources.

Table 2.2.8:   Gross Capital Formation and Changes in Inventories
(% of GDP)[a]

ADB Regional Member	Gross Capital Formation				Changes in Inventories			
	2000	2005	2010	2017	2000	2005	2010	2017
Developing ADB Member Economies								
Central and West Asia								
Afghanistan	11.3 (2002)	21.8	17.5	18.2	...	...	5.3	34.9
Armenia	18.6	30.5	32.9	19.0	0.2	0.7	-0.6	1.7
Azerbaijan	20.7	41.5	18.1	24.1	-2.5	0.2	-0.1	0.5
Georgia	26.6	33.5	21.6	31.9	1.1	5.4	2.3	2.4
Kazakhstan	18.1	31.0	25.4	27.1	0.8	3.0	1.0	4.8
Kyrgyz Republic	18.3	16.2	28.1	32.2 (2016)	1.7	0.2	-0.7	1.7 (2016)
Pakistan	17.6	17.7	15.8	16.1	1.6	1.6	1.6	1.6
Tajikistan	9.4	11.6	23.8	31.1 (2016)	2.0	0.5	-0.6	0.4 (2016)
Turkmenistan	35.4	22.9	51.9	...	...	...	...	...
Uzbekistan	19.6	26.5	26.6	27.6	-4.4	4.5	-0.8	1.5
East Asia								
China, People's Republic of	34.4	41.4	47.6	43.6	1.0	0.9	2.6	1.7
Hong Kong, China	27.6	21.1	23.9	22.3	1.1	-0.3	2.1	0.4
Korea, Republic of	32.9	32.2	32.0	31.1	1.3	1.3	1.5	-0.0
Mongolia	29.0	37.5	42.1	37.3	3.8	9.6	7.6	12.8
Taipei,China	27.2	24.5	25.0	20.3	0.9	0.3	1.3	-0.2
South Asia								
Bangladesh	23.0	24.5	26.2	30.5	...	...	...	...
Bhutan	48.7	52.0	61.7	55.0 (2016)	-1.8	-0.0	0.5	0.6 (2016)
India	24.3	34.7	36.5	30.6	0.7	2.8	3.5	0.6
Maldives	...	...	...	...	...	...	...	...
Nepal	24.3	26.5	38.3	42.5	5.0	6.5	16.1	8.7
Sri Lanka	25.4	26.1	30.4	36.5	0.6	2.8	5.9	9.2
Southeast Asia								
Brunei Darussalam	13.1	11.4	23.7	34.8	0.1	0.0	0.2	0.2
Cambodia	16.9	18.5	17.4	22.9	-1.4	-0.4	1.2	1.0
Indonesia	22.2	25.1	32.9	33.4	2.4	1.4	1.9	1.3
Lao People's Democratic Republic	...	...	...	...	...	...	...	...
Malaysia	26.9	22.4	23.4	25.5	1.6	0.1	1.0	0.2
Myanmar	12.4	13.2	23.2	31.4	0.7	0.5	0.3	0.7
Philippines	18.4	21.6	20.5	25.1	-3.7	1.6	0.0	0.1
Singapore	34.9	21.4	28.2	27.6	2.9	-1.7	2.1	2.8
Thailand	22.3	30.4	25.4	22.8	0.7	2.7	1.4	-0.3
Viet Nam	29.6	33.8	35.7	26.6	2.0	2.5	3.0	2.8
The Pacific								
Cook Islands	...	...	...	...	...	...	...	...
Fiji	17.3	21.0	18.7	18.3 (2016)	1.9	1.4	2.9	0.0 (2016)
Kiribati	...	...	...	...	...	...	...	...
Marshall Islands	...	14.4	37.3	12.7 (2016)	...	0.2	0.1	0.2 (2016)
Micronesia, Federated States of	...	...	...	...	...	...	...	...
Nauru	...	...	...	...	...	...	...	...
Palau	...	44.0	26.8	28.4	...	0.4	0.7	–
Papua New Guinea	21.9	17.5	...	...	1.5	1.0	...	...
Samoa	...	...	...	...	...	...	...	...
Solomon Islands	...	...	...	...	...	...	...	...
Timor-Leste[b]	28.0	4.0	12.0	26.2 (2016)	-3.7	0.0	0.0	1.1 (2016)
Tonga	20.7	22.3	30.1	21.5 (2015)	0.5	0.3	0.5	0.4 (2015)
Tuvalu	...	...	...	...	...	...	...	...
Vanuatu	22.9	24.1	34.7	25.6 (2016)	0.5	0.7	0.8	0.9 (2016)
Developed ADB Member Economies								
Australia	26.3	27.5	26.8	24.2	0.3	0.5	-0.2	0.2
Japan	27.3	24.7	21.3	24.0	-0.1	0.1	-0.0	-0.0
New Zealand	22.0	25.4	20.1	23.9 (2016)	1.2	0.7	0.4	0.3 (2016)

... = data not available, -0.0 or 0.0 = magnitude is less than half of unit employed, - = magnitude equals zero, ADB = Asian Development Bank, GDP = gross domestic product.

a   Calculated as a share of GDP at current prices.
b   GDP estimates released by the Government of Timor-Leste's General Directorate of Statistics include the value added by the oil sector.

Source: Economy sources.

Table 2.2.9: Exports and Imports of Goods and Services
(% of GDP)[a]

ADB Regional Member	Exports of Goods and Services				Imports of Goods and Services			
	2000	2005	2010	2017	2000	2005	2010	2017
Developing ADB Member Economies								
Central and West Asia								
Afghanistan	29.7 (2002)	26.0	9.8	8.1	59.8 (2002)	73.6	43.9	49.0
Armenia	23.4	28.8	20.8	38.1	50.5	43.2	45.3	50.4
Azerbaijan	40.2	62.9	54.3	48.7	38.4	52.9	20.7	42.0
Georgia	23.0	33.7	35.0	50.4	39.7	51.6	52.8	62.2
Kazakhstan	56.6	53.2	44.2	35.1	49.1	44.6	29.9	26.8
Kyrgyz Republic	41.8	38.3	51.6	35.8 (2016)	47.6	56.8	81.7	70.0 (2016)
Pakistan	12.1	14.3	13.5	8.2	13.2	17.8	19.4	17.6
Tajikistan	92.4	54.3	26.8	13.3 (2016)	100.2	72.8	59.0	42.8 (2016)
Turkmenistan	97.2	65.0	76.3	...	82.4	47.8	44.5	...
Uzbekistan	26.5	37.9	33.1	28.9	26.7	28.7	24.5	26.4
East Asia								
China, People's Republic of	20.9	33.8	26.3	19.7	18.5	28.4	22.6	17.8
Hong Kong, China	126.0	177.5	205.3	188.0	121.6	165.2	199.4	187.1
Korea, Republic of	35.0	36.8	49.4	43.1	32.9	34.4	46.2	37.7
Mongolia	54.0	58.8	46.7	61.4	67.9	63.6	56.7	58.9
Taipei,China	51.9	60.6	70.9	65.2	49.9	56.4	63.9	52.6
South Asia								
Bangladesh	14.0	16.6	16.0	15.0	19.2	23.0	21.8	20.3
Bhutan	29.4	38.2	42.5	29.7 (2016)	48.3	64.4	70.7	53.1 (2016)
India	12.8	19.3	22.0	19.0	13.7	22.0	26.3	22.0
Maldives	89.5	...	...	...	71.6	...	...	...
Nepal	23.3	14.6	9.6	9.8	32.4	29.5	36.4	42.0
Sri Lanka	38.2	32.3	19.6	21.9	48.4	41.3	26.8	29.1
Southeast Asia								
Brunei Darussalam	67.4	70.2	67.4	49.6	35.8	27.3	28.0	35.6
Cambodia	49.9	64.1	54.1	60.8	61.7	72.7	59.5	64.3
Indonesia	41.0	34.1	24.3	20.4	30.5	29.9	22.4	19.2
Lao People's Democratic Republic	...	...	...	...	...	...	...	...
Malaysia	119.8	112.9	86.9	71.5	100.6	91.0	71.0	64.4
Myanmar	0.5	0.2	19.6	19.4	0.6	0.1	15.1	23.7
Philippines	51.4	46.1	34.8	31.0	53.4	51.7	36.6	40.9
Singapore	189.2	226.2	199.7	173.3	176.9	196.4	173.7	149.1
Thailand	64.8	68.4	66.5	68.2	56.5	69.5	60.8	54.6
Viet Nam	55.0	63.7	72.0	101.6	57.5	67.0	80.2	98.8
The Pacific								
Cook Islands	...	...	...	...	...	...	...	...
Fiji	65.4	54.1	57.4	47.1 (2016)	70.5	63.7	63.8	53.4 (2016)
Kiribati	...	...	...	...	...	...	...	...
Marshall Islands	...	36.3	43.8	41.3 (2016)	...	93.9	92.5	76.8 (2016)
Micronesia, Federated States of	...	...	...	...	...	...	...	...
Nauru	...	...	...	...	...	...	...	...
Palau	...	43.0	49.7	50.2	...	77.6	76.9	76.4
Papua New Guinea	66.2	74.5	...	...	49.2	56.1	...	...
Samoa	...	...	...	...	...	...	...	...
Solomon Islands	...	33.0	47.4	50.1 (2016)	...	45.2	78.7	57.3 (2016)
Timor-Leste[b]	27.2	82.8	100.2	57.8 (2016)	139.5	23.7	50.7	60.2 (2016)
Tonga	15.4	17.7	13.2	17.0 (2015)	46.8	57.8	57.9	63.4 (2015)
Tuvalu	...	...	...	...	...	...	...	...
Vanuatu	34.7	45.4	46.6	47.4 (2016)	43.7	54.8	52.7	58.9 (2016)
Developed ADB Member Economies								
Australia	19.4	18.3	19.8	21.2	21.6	21.0	20.9	20.6
Japan	10.6	14.0	15.0	17.7	9.2	12.5	13.6	16.8
New Zealand	35.7	28.3	30.3	26.1 (2016)	32.8	29.7	28.0	25.7 (2016)

... = data not available, ADB = Asian Development Bank, GDP = gross domestic product.

a Computed as a share of GDP at current prices.
b GDP estimates released by the Government of Timor-Leste's General Directorate of Statistics include the value added by the oil sector.

Source: Economy sources.

Table 2.2.10: Gross Domestic Saving
(% of GDP)[a]

ADB Regional Member	2000	2005	2010	2012	2013	2014	2015	2016	2017
Developing ADB Member Countries									
Central and West Asia									
Afghanistan	-18.8 (2002)	-25.8	-11.4	3.8	7.8	8.0	5.0	8.2	12.1
Armenia	-8.9	14.0	4.9	-1.2	0.9	2.4	8.8	9.2	8.5
Azerbaijan	20.4	47.5	49.8	50.0	47.8	43.7	30.9	28.5	30.9
Georgia	9.9	15.7	3.8	9.3	11.8	12.3	14.0	17.0	20.1
Kazakhstan	26.0	38.9	43.8	43.5	39.9	40.8	34.6	33.9	...
Kyrgyz Republic	14.3	-2.1	-2.7	-15.9	-15.6	-13.5	-8.3	-0.2	...
Pakistan	16.5	14.2	10.0	7.1	8.2	8.2	9.3	8.7	6.8
Tajikistan	0.6	4.3	4.0	-13.5	-13.6	-12.7	2.5	5.9	...
Turkmenistan	48.4	40.2	85.6	76.1	81.6	...	...	...	...
Uzbekistan	19.4	35.7	35.2	32.6	31.0	29.5	27.1	25.3	30.1
East Asia									
China, People's Republic of	36.8	46.8	51.3	49.9	49.8	49.5	48.9	46.6	45.5
Hong Kong, China	32.0	33.3	29.8	26.4	24.6	24.0	23.9	23.8	23.2
Korea, Republic of	34.9	34.5	35.2	33.8	34.1	34.5	35.7	36.2	36.6
Mongolia	9.6	32.7	32.1	33.5	30.7	30.4	27.4	34.2	39.7
Taipei,China	29.4	29.1	31.7	28.8	30.7	32.2	33.5	32.9	32.9
South Asia									
Bangladesh	17.9	20.0	20.8	21.2	22.0	22.1	22.2	25.0	25.3
Bhutan	29.7	25.9	33.4	43.6	24.1	30.7	25.4	31.7	...
India	...	...	...	...	...	...	...	...	...
Maldives	...	...	...	...	...	...	...	...	...
Nepal	15.2	11.6	11.5	11.0	10.6	11.9	9.2	3.8	10.3
Sri Lanka	15.4	17.9	23.1	27.2	24.6	24.2	23.6	27.6	29.3
Southeast Asia									
Brunei Darussalam	49.4	59.1	39.4	34.9	25.0	35.7	19.9	...	...
Cambodia	8.1	9.9	12.4	16.0	17.9	19.4	19.8	20.4	23.0
Indonesia	31.8	27.5	34.8	34.4	33.7	33.4	32.9	32.7	33.6
Lao People's Democratic Republic	...	...	...	...	...	...	...	...	...
Malaysia	46.1	44.3	39.3	36.5	34.5	34.3	32.8	32.6	32.5
Myanmar	12.3	13.1	32.7	36.6	33.8	32.6	31.8	26.7	...
Philippines	16.4	15.9	18.7	14.9	15.8	17.0	15.2	15.1	15.2
Singapore	47.2	51.2	54.3	53.3	53.1	53.4	52.9	53.2	51.9
Thailand	31.7	30.3	32.0	30.0	31.3	31.8	34.9	36.9	37.4
Viet Nam	27.1	29.0	27.4	29.6	28.4	27.9	25.7	24.9	25.2
The Pacific									
Cook Islands	...	...	...	...	...	...	...	...	...
Fiji	25.6	7.1	12.7	14.2	15.0	15.4	17.1	13.9	...
Kiribati	...	...	...	...	...	...	...	...	...
Marshall Islands	...	-27.5	-25.4	-22.4	-19.1	-21.4	-26.3	-24.0	...
Micronesia, Federated States of	...	...	...	...	...	...	...	...	...
Nauru	...	...	...	...	...	...	...	...	...
Palau	...	0.4	-8.2	-5.0	-4.3	-1.9	9.5	6.5	1.1
Papua New Guinea	38.8	35.9	...	...	...	...	...	...	...
Samoa	...	...	...	...	...	...	...	...	...
Solomon Islands	...	...	...	...	...	...	...	...	...
Timor-Leste[b]	-84.4	63.1	61.8	74.0	68.8	53.3	39.1	24.7	...
Tonga	-10.0	-16.3	-16.1	-12.8	-19.8	-21.3	...	...	...
Tuvalu	...	...	...	...	...	...	...	...	...
Vanuatu	21.2	13.9	27.0	20.9	23.3	24.0	...	...	...
Developed ADB Member Economies									
Australia	24.2	24.8	25.7	27.4	26.5	26.2	24.6	23.0	24.4
Japan	29.0	26.8	22.9	21.1	20.9	21.4	23.3	24.0	...
New Zealand	19.7	17.6	27.2	17.3	19.5	19.4	20.5	21.8	...

... = data not available, ADB = Asian Development Bank, GDP = gross domestic product.

a   Calculated as a share of GDP at current prices.
b   GDP estimates released by the Government of Timor-Leste's General Directorate of Statistics include the value added by the oil sector.

Source: Economy sources.

National Accounts

Table 2.2.11:   Growth Rates of Real Gross Domestic Product
(%)

ADB Regional Member	2000	2005	2010	2012	2013	2014	2015	2016	2017
Developing ADB Member Economies									
Central and West Asia									
Afghanistan	...	9.9	3.2	10.9	6.5	3.1	-1.8	3.6	7.2
Armenia	5.9	13.9	2.2	7.2	3.3	3.6	3.2	0.2	7.5
Azerbaijan	11.1	26.4	5.0	2.2	5.8	2.8	1.1	-3.1	0.1
Georgia	1.8	9.6	6.2	6.4	3.4	4.6	2.9	2.8	5.0
Kazakhstan	9.8	9.7	7.3	4.8	6.0	4.2	1.2	1.1	4.0
Kyrgyz Republic	5.4	-0.2	-0.5	-0.1	10.9	4.0	3.9	4.3	4.6
Pakistan	3.6 (2001)	6.5	1.6	3.5	4.4	4.7	4.7	4.6	5.4
Tajikistan	8.3	6.7	6.5	7.5	7.4	6.7	6.0	6.9	...
Turkmenistan	5.5	13.0	9.2	11.1	10.2	10.3	6.5	6.2	6.5
Uzbekistan	4.0	7.0	8.5	8.2	8.0	8.0	7.9	6.2	5.2
East Asia									
China, People's Republic of	8.5	11.4	10.6	7.9	7.8	7.3	6.9	6.7	6.9
Hong Kong, China	7.7	7.4	6.8	1.7	3.1	2.8	2.4	2.2	3.8
Korea, Republic of	8.9	3.9	6.5	2.3	2.9	3.3	2.8	2.9	3.1
Mongolia	1.1	7.3	17.3 (2011)	12.3	11.6	7.9	2.4	1.2	5.1
Taipei,China	6.4	5.4	10.6	2.1	2.2	4.0	0.8	1.4	2.9
South Asia									
Bangladesh	6.0	6.0	5.6	6.5	6.0	6.1	6.6	7.1	7.3
Bhutan	6.9	7.1	11.7	5.1	2.1	5.7	6.6	8.0	...
India	3.8	9.3	10.3	5.5	6.4	7.4	8.2	7.1	6.7
Maldives	3.8	-13.1	7.3	2.5	7.3	7.3	2.2	6.2	...
Nepal	6.0	3.5	4.8	4.8	4.1	6.0	3.3	0.4	7.5
Sri Lanka	6.0	6.2	8.0	9.1	3.4	5.0	5.0	4.5	3.1
Southeast Asia									
Brunei Darussalam	2.8	0.4	3.7 (2011)	0.9	-2.1	-2.5	-0.4	-2.5	1.3
Cambodia	8.4	13.3	6.0	7.3	7.6	7.1	6.9	7.0	6.9
Indonesia	4.9	5.7	6.2	6.0	5.6	5.0	4.9	5.0	5.1
Lao People's Democratic Republic	6.3	6.8	8.1	8.0 (2011)	8.0	7.6	7.3	7.0	6.9
Malaysia	8.9	5.3	7.4	5.5	4.7	6.0	5.0	4.2	5.9
Myanmar	13.7	13.6	9.6	7.3	8.4	8.0	7.0	5.9	6.8
Philippines	4.4	4.8	7.6	6.7	7.1	6.1	6.1	6.9	6.7
Singapore	8.9	7.5	15.2	4.1	5.1	3.9	2.2	2.4	3.6
Thailand	4.5	4.2	7.5	7.2	2.7	1.0	3.0	3.3	3.9
Viet Nam	6.8	7.5	6.4	5.2	5.4	6.0	6.7	6.2	6.8
The Pacific									
Cook Islands	13.9	-1.1	-3.0	4.7	-1.4	6.2	4.0	5.7	1.9
Fiji	-1.7	-1.3	3.0	1.4	4.7	5.6	3.8	0.4	...
Kiribati	5.3	-0.0 (2006)	-0.9	4.6	4.3	-0.6	10.3	1.1	...
Marshall Islands	6.0	3.6	7.1	3.0	2.8	-0.5	-0.6	2.0	3.6
Micronesia, Federated States of	4.9	2.1	2.0	-2.0	-3.9	-2.2	4.9	-0.1	2.0
Nauru	...	-9.8	20.1	20.2	34.2	36.5	2.8	10.4	4.0
Palau	5.6 (2001)	6.1	-0.9	4.0	-1.5	2.7	10.1	0.1	-3.7
Papua New Guinea	-2.5	3.9	10.1	4.7	3.8	12.5	...	...	...
Samoa	8.6	4.7	4.4	-2.3	0.5	1.9	2.9	6.5	-0.4
Solomon Islands	-14.2	7.4	9.7	2.4	2.8	1.8	2.6	3.4	...
Timor-Leste[a]	9.2 (2001)	35.9	-1.2	5.0	-11.0	-26.0	20.9	0.8	...
Tonga	-0.8	1.6	3.3	0.8	-3.1	2.0	2.5	4.7	2.7
Tuvalu	1.5 (2001)	-4.1	-3.3	-3.9	4.9	1.2	9.2	5.9	5.9
Vanuatu	5.9	5.3	1.6	1.8	2.0	2.3	0.2	3.5	...
Developed ADB Member Economies									
Australia	3.9	3.2	2.1	3.9	2.6	2.6	2.4	2.8	2.1
Japan	2.8	1.7	4.2	1.5	2.0	0.4	1.4	1.0	1.7
New Zealand	2.9	3.3	1.6	2.3	2.6	3.7	3.6	3.7	...

... = data not available, -0.0 or 0.0 = magnitude is less than half of unit employed, ADB = Asian Development Bank.

a   Gross domestic product estimates released by the Government of Timor-Leste's General Directorate of Statistics include the value added by the oil sector.

Source: Economy sources.

Table 2.2.12: Growth Rates of Real Gross Domestic Product per Capita
(%)

ADB Regional Member	2000	2005	2010	2012	2013	2014	2015	2016	2017
Developing ADB Member Economies									
Central and West Asia									
Afghanistan	...	8.0	1.3	8.9	4.5	0.9	-3.5	1.4	5.4
Armenia	6.2	14.5	2.9	7.3	3.3	3.9	3.6	0.6	8.0
Azerbaijan	9.8	24.9	3.8	0.9	4.5	1.5	-0.1	-4.2	-0.9
Georgia	3.8	10.3	7.0	7.1	3.7	4.6	2.7	2.8	5.0
Kazakhstan	10.2	8.7	5.7	3.3	4.4	2.7	-0.3	-0.4	2.7
Kyrgyz Republic	4.0	-1.4	-1.8	-1.4	8.7	2.0	1.8	2.2	2.5
Pakistan	1.5 (2001)	4.2	-0.5	1.4	2.3	2.6	2.7	2.6	2.9
Tajikistan	5.8	5.5	3.9	5.1	5.1	4.3	3.5	4.5	...
Turkmenistan	4.3	11.8	7.5	9.1	8.2	8.3	4.6	4.4	4.7
Uzbekistan	2.6	5.7	5.5	6.6	6.4	6.2	6.0	4.4	3.4
East Asia									
China, People's Republic of	7.7	10.7	10.1	7.4	7.3	6.7	6.4	6.1	6.3
Hong Kong, China	6.8	6.9	6.0	0.6	2.7	2.1	1.5	1.6	3.0
Korea, Republic of	8.0	3.7	6.0	1.8	2.4	2.7	2.3	2.4	2.7
Mongolia	-0.2	6.1	15.3 (2011)	10.2	9.4	5.6	0.2	-0.8	3.1
Taipei,China	5.6	5.0	10.3	1.7	2.0	3.8	0.6	1.2	2.7
South Asia									
Bangladesh	4.5	4.5	4.2	5.1	4.6	4.6	5.1	5.8	6.0
Bhutan	5.6	5.7	9.7	3.3	0.4	4.0	4.9	6.4	...
India	2.0	7.7	8.8	4.1	5.1	6.1	6.9	5.8	5.3
Maldives	2.3	-15.9	4.9	-0.2	4.4	5.2	-1.6	2.4	...
Nepal	2.9	1.2	3.4	3.4	2.7	4.5	1.9	-0.9	6.1
Sri Lanka	4.6	5.3	7.0	11.5	2.6	4.0	4.0	3.3	2.0
Southeast Asia									
Brunei Darussalam	0.3	-1.3	2.0 (2011)	-0.5	-3.2	-3.5	-1.6	-3.6	0.3
Cambodia	7.0	11.7	4.6	6.0	6.2	5.7	5.5	5.6	5.6
Indonesia	3.7	4.3	3.4	4.5	4.1	3.6	3.5	3.7	3.8
Lao People's Democratic Republic	4.2	4.7	6.6	6.5 (2011)	6.5	6.1	5.7	5.5	5.4
Malaysia	6.2	3.2	5.5	3.9	2.3	4.2	3.4	2.9	4.5
Myanmar	12.4	12.6	8.9	6.4	7.4	7.1	6.1	5.0	5.9
Philippines	2.0	2.8	5.2	4.8	5.3	4.4	4.3	5.1	5.0
Singapore	7.1	5.0	13.2	1.6	3.4	2.6	1.0	1.1	3.5
Thailand	3.3	3.6	6.9	6.8	2.3	0.6	2.7	2.9	3.5
Viet Nam	5.3	6.3	5.3	4.1	4.3	4.9	5.5	5.1	5.7
The Pacific									
Cook Islands	4.4	-6.7	-7.5	3.6	3.4	6.2	3.5	1.3	9.1
Fiji	-2.3	-2.0	2.3	1.0	4.2	5.2	3.4	-0.1	...
Kiribati	3.5	-2.2 (2006)	-3.0	3.3	2.9	-1.9	8.8	-0.2	...
Marshall Islands	5.2	2.1	5.8	2.6	2.5	-0.9	-1.0	1.7	3.2
Micronesia, Federated States of	4.6	2.3	2.6	-1.7	-3.7	-2.2	4.8	-0.2	1.9
Nauru	...	-7.8	17.9	17.7	28.0	23.9	-1.9	5.9	1.6
Palau	4.1 (2001)	5.3	1.0	5.9	-0.3	3.0	8.2	-1.1	-3.9
Papua New Guinea	-5.5	0.8	6.8	1.5	0.7	9.1	...	...	...
Samoa	7.5	4.1	3.8	-3.1	-0.3	1.0	2.1	5.6	-1.2
Solomon Islands	-16.2	4.9	7.2	0.0	0.5	-0.5	0.2	1.1	...
Timor-Leste[a]	6.6 (2001)	31.9	-2.7	2.7	-13.1	-27.8	18.1	-1.3	...
Tonga	-1.2	1.1	3.1	1.4	-2.6	2.5	3.0	5.2	3.2
Tuvalu	1.1 (2001)	-7.0	-3.8	-5.7	3.7	-0.0	7.9	4.6	4.7
Vanuatu	3.5	2.9	-0.8	-0.5	-0.3	0.0	-2.1	2.0	...
Developed ADB Member Economies									
Australia	2.8	1.9	0.5	2.1	0.9	1.0	0.9	1.3	0.5
Japan	2.6	1.7	4.2	1.7	2.1	0.5	1.5	1.1	1.8
New Zealand	2.3	2.2	0.4	1.7	1.8	2.1	1.7	1.6	...

...= data not available, -0.0 or 0.0 = magnitude is less than half of unit employed, ADB = Asian Development Bank.

a   Gross domestic product estimates released by the Government of Timor-Leste's General Directorate of Statistics include the value added by the oil sector.

Source: Asian Development Bank estimates using economy sources.

National Accounts

Table 2.2.13: **Growth Rates of Agriculture Real Value Added**
(%)

ADB Regional Member	2000	2005	2010	2012	2013	2014	2015	2016	2017
Developing ADB Member Economies									
Central and West Asia									
Afghanistan	...	12.2	-18.0	3.2	8.3	3.7	-16.9	12.4	21.4
Armenia	-1.0	11.2	-16.0	9.5	7.6	6.1	13.2	-5.0	-5.3
Azerbaijan	12.1	6.7	-4.7	6.6	4.9	-2.6	6.6	2.6	4.2
Georgia	-12.0	11.7	-4.2	-3.8	11.3	1.6	1.5	0.3	-2.7
Kazakhstan	-3.2	7.1	-12.9	-17.4	11.2	1.3	3.5	5.4	2.8
Kyrgyz Republic	2.6	-4.2	-2.6	1.2	2.7	-0.5	6.2	2.9	2.2
Pakistan	-0.7 (2001)	7.0	0.2	3.6	2.7	2.5	2.1	0.2	2.1
Tajikistan	8.0 (2001)	2.8	6.8	9.5	7.7	9.2	3.4	5.2	...
Turkmenistan	-2.6	14.1	27.3	8.1	9.9	1.7	...	...	...
Uzbekistan	3.2	5.9	6.4	7.2	6.8	6.9	6.8	6.8	2.0
East Asia									
China, People's Republic of	2.3	5.1	4.3	4.5	3.8	4.1	3.9	3.3	3.9
Hong Kong, China	0.3 (2001)	-0.2	3.9	-3.2	4.9	-6.0	-6.8	-2.0	-0.5
Korea, Republic of	1.1	1.4	-4.3	-0.9	3.1	3.6	-0.4	-2.8	0.3
Mongolia	-16.3	11.3	-0.3 (2011)	21.1	19.2	13.7	10.7	6.2	2.3
Taipei,China	1.8	-3.9	2.3	-3.2	1.4	1.6	-8.4	-10.1	7.3
South Asia									
Bangladesh	7.4	2.2	6.2	3.0	2.5	4.4	3.3	2.8	3.0
Bhutan	5.4	1.1	0.9	2.3	2.4	2.4	5.1	3.6	...
India	-0.0	5.1	8.6	1.5	5.6	-0.2	0.6	6.3	3.4
Maldives	-0.8	11.4	-3.5	-0.2	6.9	-0.3	-0.5	1.4	...
Nepal	4.9	3.5	2.0	4.6	1.1	4.5	1.1	0.0	5.3
Sri Lanka	2.3	1.8	7.0	3.9	3.2	4.6	4.7	-3.8	-0.8
Southeast Asia									
Brunei Darussalam	6.6	1.3	-2.6 (2011)	8.1	-1.2	4.7	6.4	-3.6	-1.6
Cambodia	-1.2	15.7	4.0	4.3	1.6	0.3	0.2	1.4	1.9
Indonesia	1.9	2.7	3.0	4.6	4.2	4.2	3.8	3.4	3.8
Lao People's Democratic Republic	4.2	0.7	3.2	2.7 (2011)	2.8	4.1	3.6	2.8	2.9
Malaysia	6.1	2.6	2.4	1.0	2.0	2.0	1.3	-5.1	7.2
Myanmar	11.0	12.1	4.7	1.7	3.6	2.8	3.4	-0.4	2.0
Philippines	3.4	2.2	-0.2	2.8	1.2	1.7	0.1	-1.2	4.0
Singapore[a]	-4.8	7.1	2.4	3.6	4.5	7.3	-7.0	-1.5	-8.4
Thailand	6.8	-0.1	-0.5	2.7	0.7	-0.3	-6.3	-2.5	6.3
Viet Nam	4.6	4.2	0.5	2.9	2.6	3.4	2.4	1.4	2.9
The Pacific									
Cook Islands	0.1	-3.5	1.9	14.9	3.9	8.5	-1.5	3.5	-13.9
Fiji	-1.2	0.9	-2.6	-1.9	6.7	1.9	6.3	-7.5	...
Kiribati	-7.2	10.4 (2006)	-3.9	2.1	-0.7	5.9	2.7	11.4	...
Marshall Islands	22.6	-9.2	28.4	9.7	3.4	-1.5	0.2	-2.3	5.1
Micronesia, Federated States of	7.1	4.4	-3.9	-1.7	-6.4	6.0	10.7	-7.3	...
Nauru	...	-0.6	3.0	2.1	28.8	22.0	-38.8	94.3	1.6
Palau	-0.6 (2001)	7.0	-5.3	-4.1	3.4	-8.0	-5.2	7.8	11.0
Papua New Guinea	2.1	5.6	2.8	6.0	4.7	3.3	...	...	...
Samoa	8.1	2.4	-6.1	-12.6	8.9	1.1	5.6	6.4	-4.9
Solomon Islands	-17.1	-1.5	14.8	0.4	-1.3	5.8	2.5	5.8	...
Timor-Leste[b]	-1.0 (2001)	2.3	4.3	18.4	-5.2	-3.1	-4.3	3.0	...
Tonga	-2.5	-2.1	0.5	0.5	3.7	3.1	-2.7	2.1	...
Tuvalu	-2.2 (2001)	-1.1	12.8	-3.6	-2.7	-0.5	-1.8	2.9	0.8
Vanuatu	4.3	2.3	4.8	2.2	4.8	4.2	-15.8	5.1	...
Developed ADB Member Economies									
Australia	6.7	4.3	-0.7	1.0	-0.7	1.1	1.3	-6.4	17.4
Japan	7.3	-0.0	-5.8	0.6	0.3	-3.1	-4.8	-13.1	...
New Zealand	3.6	5.2	-7.9	5.0	-2.6	5.5	4.6	-0.8	...

... = data not available, -0.0 or 0.0 = magnitude is less than half of unit employed, ADB = Asian Development Bank.

a Refers to other goods industries comprising agriculture, forestry, and fishing; and mining and quarrying.
b Gross domestic product estimates released by the Government of Timor-Leste's General Directorate of Statistics include the value added by the oil sector.

Source: Economy sources.

Table 2.2.14: Growth Rates of Industry Real Value Added
(%)

ADB Regional Member	2000	2005	2010	2012	2013	2014	2015	2016	2017
Developing ADB Member Economies									
Central and West Asia									
Afghanistan	...	13.0	6.3	7.8	4.5	2.4	4.5	-1.8	0.9
Armenia	12.8	14.8	5.7	5.7	0.5	-2.3	2.8	-0.3	5.4
Azerbaijan	5.7	43.6	3.7	-1.0	4.3	0.4	-3.4	-5.7	-3.6
Georgia	4.9	9.6	8.2	9.6	2.4	4.6	4.1	6.2	5.7
Kazakhstan	15.3	10.7	9.5	1.8	3.1	1.5	-0.4	1.1	6.3
Kyrgyz Republic	8.8	-9.8	2.5	-11.4	30.2	5.7	2.9	7.1	9.3
Pakistan	5.8 (2001)	6.5	3.4	2.5	0.8	4.5	5.2	5.7	5.4
Tajikistan	15.6 (2001)	7.7	5.6	-2.6	4.0	14.9	16.3	22.2	...
Turkmenistan	1.0	10.6	-2.9	10.7	8.0	11.6	...	...	...
Uzbekistan	1.8	5.3	6.5	7.1	9.2	8.0	8.2	5.6	4.8
East Asia									
China, People's Republic of	9.5	12.1	12.7	8.4	8.0	7.4	6.2	6.3	6.1
Hong Kong, China	-3.8 (2001)	-1.4	7.7	4.4	1.5	7.4	2.4	3.0	1.7
Korea, Republic of[a]	...	...	...	...	...	...	...	...	...
Mongolia	1.5	4.2	8.8 (2011)	14.8	14.6	12.7	9.9	-0.4	-1.3
Taipei,China	7.1	7.6	20.8	3.3	1.7	7.2	-0.5	2.8	3.8
South Asia									
Bangladesh	6.2	8.3	7.0	9.4	9.6	8.2	9.7	11.1	10.2
Bhutan	7.3	3.8	12.5	6.8	3.9	3.7	8.2	6.8	...
India	6.0	9.7	7.6	3.3	3.8	7.0	9.8	6.8	5.5
Maldives	-3.8	14.3	7.3	4.1	-6.0	16.2	16.5	15.1	...
Nepal	8.6	3.0	4.0	3.0	2.7	7.1	1.4	-6.3	10.9
Sri Lanka	9.0	8.0	8.4	9.0	4.1	4.7	2.2	5.8	3.9
Southeast Asia									
Brunei Darussalam	3.0	-1.8	3.2 (2011)	-1.4	-5.6	-4.4	-0.0	-2.9	1.5
Cambodia	31.2	12.7	13.0	10.4	11.5	9.8	11.7	10.5	10.1
Indonesia	5.9	4.7	4.9	5.3	4.3	4.2	3.0	3.8	4.1
Lao People's Democratic Republic	9.3	10.6	17.5	14.6 (2011)	7.7	7.3	7.0	12.0	11.6
Malaysia	13.6	3.6	8.4	4.9	3.6	5.9	5.3	4.3	4.7
Myanmar	21.3	19.9	18.6	8.0	11.4	12.1	8.3	8.9	9.0
Philippines	6.5	4.2	11.6	7.3	9.2	7.8	6.4	8.0	7.2
Singapore[b]	11.6	8.2	25.3	2.2	2.0	3.6	-2.7	3.2	5.7
Thailand[a]	2.6	5.3	10.5	7.3	1.6	-0.1	3.0	2.8	1.8
Viet Nam	10.1	8.4	-9.9	7.4	5.1	6.4	9.6	7.6	8.0
The Pacific									
Cook Islands	18.2	-6.3	-8.4	11.0	-6.3	-13.5	-10.2	8.1	24.2
Fiji	-5.5	-6.7	6.5	-2.2	4.4	1.2	3.5	0.9	...
Kiribati	-6.4	15.0 (2006)	9.5	20.9	16.6	-1.9	21.3	11.6	...
Marshall Islands	-14.6	10.1	0.1	-4.1	5.8	-12.9	-4.0	16.7	4.2
Micronesia, Federated States of	6.6	-3.0	17.9	-1.2	-19.6	-28.3	-6.0	5.8	...
Nauru	...	-13.3	56.5	43.1	-3.7	-19.2	-67.5	95.7	3.1
Palau	29.3 (2001)	6.2	4.2	-5.3	-13.2	4.9	28.4	13.2	-8.3
Papua New Guinea	-0.8	4.1	12.0	-2.2	2.0	36.7	...	...	...
Samoa	14.4	4.7	10.1	-1.1	0.1	-1.9	1.5	2.8	-4.9
Solomon Islands	-29.7	-3.1	15.4	-1.4	-2.0	-13.0	-5.0	0.9	...
Timor-Leste[c]	-14.3 (2001)	73.9	-6.4	2.9	-14.8	-44.5	41.7	-1.1	...
Tonga	-0.4	-2.8	11.6	1.2	-14.3	1.3	11.2	7.8	...
Tuvalu	5.0 (2001)	-18.2	-41.6	-25.8	40.5	-5.8	36.7	20.2	21.1
Vanuatu	46.4	5.3	12.6	-22.2	9.8	3.2	35.4	4.2	...
Developed ADB Member Economies									
Australia[a]	...	...	...	...	...	...	...	...	...
Japan[a]	...	...	...	...	...	...	...	...	...
New Zealand[a]	...	...	...	...	...	...	...	...	...

.... = data not available, -0.0 or 0.0 = magnitude is less than half of unit employed, ADB = Asian Development Bank.

a National accounts are compiled using chain volume measures.
b Refers to manufacturing, construction, and utilities.
c Gross domestic product estimates released by the Government of Timor-Leste's General Directorate of Statistics include the value added by the oil sector.

Source: Economy sources.

National Accounts

Table 2.2.15:   Growth Rates of Services Real Value Added
(%)

ADB Regional Member	2000	2005	2010	2012	2013	2014	2015	2016	2017
Developing ADB Member Economies									
Central and West Asia									
Afghanistan	...	5.4	18.1	16.0	6.4	4.0	1.4	2.3	3.3
Armenia	3.1	14.7	4.7	6.9	2.8	6.7	1.0	3.4	12.1
Azerbaijan	9.6	9.6	8.8	7.6	8.6	7.6	6.8	-0.8	3.5
Georgia	5.5	6.5	8.2	5.9	3.6	4.5	3.0	2.1	5.4
Kazakhstan	8.4	10.4	6.0	10.4	6.9	5.7	3.1	0.9	2.7
Kyrgyz Republic	5.8	8.4	-1.3	6.3	4.8	4.6	3.5	3.0	2.6
Pakistan	5.1 (2001)	8.1	3.2	4.4	5.1	4.5	4.4	5.7	6.5
Tajikistan	3.9 (2001)	7.7	7.1	11.9	9.4	1.7	1.9	-1.5	...
Turkmenistan	18.0	27.1	16.1	-10.9	-9.2	-13.2	...	...	...
Uzbekistan	5.4	7.6	10.4	9.3	7.8	8.5	8.4	6.6	6.4
East Asia									
China, People's Republic of	9.8	12.4	9.7	8.0	8.3	7.8	8.2	7.7	8.0
Hong Kong, China	1.8 (2001)	7.8	6.9	1.8	2.7	2.5	1.7	2.3	3.5
Korea, Republic of	7.3	3.9	4.4	2.8	2.9	3.3	2.8	2.5	2.1
Mongolia	10.5	9.7	17.8 (2011)	10.3	7.8	7.8	0.6	1.1	8.6
Taipei,China	6.5	4.1	6.3	1.3	2.3	3.3	1.2	1.3	2.3
South Asia									
Bangladesh	5.5	6.4	5.5	6.6	5.5	5.6	5.8	6.3	6.7
Bhutan	8.7	14.8	12.1	0.7	1.6	8.2	8.3	10.0	...
India	5.1	10.9	9.7	8.3	7.7	9.8	9.6	7.5	7.9
Maldives	5.1	-17.7	7.3	2.6	8.8	7.0	1.4	5.2	...
Nepal	5.9	3.3	5.8	5.0	5.7	6.2	4.6	2.1	6.9
Sri Lanka	6.1	6.4	8.0	11.2	3.8	4.8	6.0	4.7	3.2
Southeast Asia									
Brunei Darussalam	2.5	4.1	4.9 (2011)	5.5	4.7	0.6	-1.2	-1.6	1.1
Cambodia	8.9	13.1	3.3	7.4	8.7	8.7	7.1	6.8	6.6
Indonesia	5.2	7.9	8.4	6.8	6.4	6.0	5.5	5.7	5.7
Lao People's Democratic Republic	6.9	10.8	7.6	8.4 (2011)	9.7	8.1	8.0	4.7	4.5
Malaysia	6.0	7.3	7.4	6.6	6.0	6.8	5.2	5.6	6.4
Myanmar	13.4	13.1	9.5	12.0	10.3	9.1	8.7	8.0	8.4
Philippines	3.3	5.8	7.2	7.1	7.0	6.0	6.9	7.5	6.8
Singapore[a]	7.5	7.4	11.3	4.9	7.1	4.3	3.6	1.6	2.9
Thailand[b]	4.8	12.1	7.0	8.2	4.0	2.0	4.8	4.5	4.9
Viet Nam	5.3	8.6	-7.7	6.7	6.7	6.2	6.3	7.0	7.4
The Pacific									
Cook Islands	15.4	-0.3	-2.6	2.3	-0.6	7.6	5.4	6.6	0.6
Fiji	0.8	-17.0	2.9	3.0	4.5	7.4	3.6	1.4	...
Kiribati	1.7	0.9 (2006)	-0.1	2.3	2.6	-0.3	8.0	4.9	...
Marshall Islands	6.6	3.3	3.6	1.9	1.7	2.6	1.7	1.2	3.2
Micronesia, Federated States of	3.3	0.8	2.3	-1.7	-0.7	-1.3	3.0	2.4	...
Nauru	...	-10.0	3.1	1.7	63.5	64.5	32.4	1.1	3.8
Palau	2.6 (2001)	5.1	-2.0	2.9	-1.0	5.4	9.0	-1.3	-3.4
Papua New Guinea	-12.7	3.6	12.4	6.0	4.3	0.2	...	...	...
Samoa	6.2	5.2	4.0	-0.9	-0.2	3.3	3.1	8.0	1.8
Solomon Islands	-5.7	19.4	6.4	4.8	7.6	3.9	5.0	3.3	...
Timor-Leste[c]	42.2 (2001)	4.3	13.7	7.0	1.4	7.5	4.9	5.9	...
Tonga	0.0	3.6	1.0	0.5	-0.5	1.6	2.7	3.7	...
Tuvalu	-0.5 (2001)	-4.9	2.3	0.2	0.0	2.4	7.1	2.0	3.2
Vanuatu	2.2	6.6	3.0	4.4	0.1	2.4	2.0	2.9	...
Developed ADB Member Economies									
Australia[b]	...	...	...	...	...	...	...	...	...
Japan[b]	...	...	...	...	...	...	...	...	...
New Zealand[b]	...	...	...	...	...	...	...	...	...

.... = data not available, 0.0 = magnitude is less than half of unit employed, ADB = Asian Development Bank.

a Refers to services-producing industries, including ownership of dwellings.
b National accounts are compiled using chain volume measures.
c Gross domestic product estimates released by the Government of Timor-Leste's General Directorate of Statistics include the value added by the oil sector.

Source: Economy sources.

Table 2.2.16:   Growth Rates of Real Household Final Consumption
(%)

ADB Regional Member	2000	2005	2010	2012	2013	2014	2015	2016	2017
Developing ADB Member Economies									
Central and West Asia									
Afghanistan	...	...	...	...	...	...	...	...	...
Armenia[a]	8.3	8.8	3.9	9.1	0.9	1.0	-7.7	-1.0	8.9
Azerbaijan[a]	10.0	13.2	10.8	8.4	8.6	8.1	8.5	1.7	0.9
Georgia[a]	...	...	6.7 (2011)	4.5	-0.1	3.2	0.1	-0.6	...
Kazakhstan[a]	1.2	10.7	11.5	10.1	18.7	1.1	1.8	1.2	1.6
Kyrgyz Republic[a]	-5.0	8.3	2.7	11.2	8.0	3.0	-0.9	-0.6	...
Pakistan[a]	3.5 (2001)	10.8	2.2	5.0	2.1	5.6	2.9	7.6	8.7
Tajikistan[a]	8.6 (2001)	20.6	10.5	15.0	9.3	1.8	-15.0	6.4	...
Turkmenistan[a]	-48.3	-15.2	-61.3	...	...	...	...	...	...
Uzbekistan	...	...	...	...	...	...	...	...	...
East Asia									
China, People's Republic of	...	...	...	...	...	...	...	...	...
Hong Kong, China[a]	4.5	3.5	6.1	4.1	4.6	3.3	4.8	2.0	5.5
Korea, Republic of	9.1	4.4	4.4	1.2	1.4	1.7	2.2	2.4	2.7
Mongolia	...	12.4 (2006)	15.8 (2011)	13.0	15.4	6.3	8.1	-9.5	5.0
Taipei,China	5.1	3.3	3.8	1.8	2.4	3.2	2.9	2.4	...
South Asia									
Bangladesh	4.1	3.9	4.6	4.1	5.1	4.0	5.8	3.0	7.4
Bhutan[a]	0.4	1.3	5.5	-2.4	58.0	-6.4	9.9	-2.6	...
India[a]	3.4	8.6	8.7	5.5	7.3	6.4	7.4	7.3	6.6
Maldives	...	...	...	...	...	...	...	...	...
Nepal[a]	3.5 (2002)	4.7	6.2	15.9	2.7	4.2	2.9	-0.9	2.4
Sri Lanka	4.0	1.7	9.9 (2011)	2.3	7.8	3.7	7.5	-3.9	1.3
Southeast Asia									
Brunei Darussalam[a]	-7.0	-0.6	5.4 (2011)	8.7	6.0	-3.7	5.2	-1.3	4.1
Cambodia[a]	4.9	12.3	9.7	6.4	4.0	4.5	2.6	6.8	7.9
Indonesia[b]	1.6	4.0	4.7	5.5	5.4	5.1	5.0	5.0	4.9
Lao People's Democratic Republic	...	...	...	...	...	...	...	...	...
Malaysia	13.0	9.1	6.9	8.4	7.3	7.0	6.0	6.0	7.0
Myanmar[c]	4.3	14.6	2.6	8.1	13.7	11.1	4.7	2.2	6.2
Philippines[a]	5.2	4.4	3.4	6.6	5.6	5.6	6.3	7.1	5.9
Singapore	14.7	3.4	5.9	3.9	3.6	3.4	4.9	1.7	3.1
Thailand[a]	7.0	4.2	5.5	6.7	0.9	0.8	2.3	3.0	3.2
Viet Nam	3.1	5.8	8.2	4.9	5.2	6.1	9.3	7.3	7.3
The Pacific									
Cook Islands	...	...	...	...	...	...	...	...	...
Fiji	...	...	...	...	...	...	...	...	...
Kiribati	...	...	...	...	...	...	...	...	...
Marshall Islands	...	-0.4	1.9	-2.0	-2.9	-1.2	1.3	5.0	...
Micronesia, Federated States of	...	...	...	...	...	...	...	...	...
Nauru	...	...	...	...	...	...	...	...	...
Palau	...	1.1 (2006)	-1.3	4.0	0.0	3.0	4.0	6.4	0.7
Papua New Guinea[a]	-28.5	9.8	...	...	...	...	...	...	...
Samoa	...	...	...	...	...	...	...	...	...
Solomon Islands	...	9.3	8.7	3.1	4.8	4.8	4.4	2.2	...
Timor-Leste[d]	12.9 (2001)	-1.2	5.2	7.1	3.0	6.0	2.9	6.0	...
Tonga	3.5	2.2	-1.3	1.6	...	...	...	...	...
Tuvalu	...	...	...	...	...	...	...	...	...
Vanuatu	...	2.4	2.6	3.0	3.5	3.9	1.3	8.9	...
Developed ADB Member Economies									
Australia	4.3	4.5	3.3	3.0	1.8	2.4	2.4	2.8	2.6
Japan[a]	1.6	1.2	2.4	2.0	2.4	-0.9	-0.0	-2.6	...
New Zealand[a]	1.4	4.6	2.3	2.3	3.8	3.2	3.9	5.4	...

... = data not available, -0.0 or 0.0 = magnitude is less than half of unit employed, ADB = Asian Development Bank.

a   Includes expenditure of nonprofit institutions serving households.
b   Prior to 2010, includes expenditure of nonprofit institutions serving households.
c   Includes government final consumption expenditure.
d   Gross domestic product estimates released by the Government of Timor-Leste's General Directorate of Statistics include the value added by the oil sector.

Source: Economy sources.

Table 2.2.17:   Growth Rates of Real Government Consumption Expenditure
(%)

ADB Regional Member	2000	2005	2010	2012	2013	2014	2015	2016	2017
Developing ADB Member Economies									
Central and West Asia									
Afghanistan	...	...	...	...	...	...	...	...	...
Armenia	2.8	19.0	3.9	-1.4	7.6	-1.2	4.7	-2.4	13.1
Azerbaijan	2.3	3.4	3.4	3.1	3.6	3.7	1.3	6.8	1.1
Georgia	...	...	1.0 (2011)	7.3	4.3	11.2	22.1	6.5	...
Kazakhstan	15.0	10.8	2.7	13.5	1.7	9.8	2.4	2.3	2.1
Kyrgyz Republic	5.9	-2.7	-1.1	2.1	-0.4	-0.5	0.9	1.5	...
Pakistan	-6.7 (2001)	3.4	-0.6	7.3	10.1	1.5	8.1	8.2	5.3
Tajikistan	10.8 (2001)	0.4	0.9	2.1	2.3	4.1	3.3	3.9	...
Turkmenistan	28.0	17.9	3.8	...	...	...	...	...	...
Uzbekistan	...	...	...	...	...	...	...	...	...
East Asia									
China, People's Republic of	...	...	...	...	...	...	...	...	...
Hong Kong, China	2.4	-2.6	3.4	3.6	2.7	3.1	3.4	3.3	3.4
Korea, Republic of	0.9	4.5	3.8	3.4	3.3	3.0	3.0	4.5	3.4
Mongolia	...	5.5 (2006)	15.3 (2011)	19.9	15.8	12.2	-4.7	8.9	-1.3
Taipei,China	0.6	0.4	1.1	2.2	-0.8	3.7	-0.1	3.7	-1.2
South Asia									
Bangladesh	0.9	7.7	6.8	3.1	5.8	7.9	8.8	8.4	7.8
Bhutan	–	2.8	7.5	-0.8	-10.1	2.4	10.8	4.2	...
India	1.4	8.9	5.8	0.6	0.6	7.6	6.8	12.2	10.9
Maldives	...	...	...	...	...	...	...	...	...
Nepal	7.8 (2002)	1.2	1.3	15.9	-6.7	10.0	7.4	-0.4	12.2
Sri Lanka	5.3	12.0	-2.1 (2011)	6.0	0.1	6.0	10.2	2.3	-5.2
Southeast Asia									
Brunei Darussalam	7.7	-1.0	5.3 (2011)	0.4	3.6	1.9	-3.6	-6.5	7.4
Cambodia	12.4	3.9	-6.2	4.7	6.3	2.4	4.4	5.7	6.5
Indonesia	-0.9	6.6	0.3	4.5	6.7	1.2	5.3	-0.1	2.1
Lao People's Democratic Republic	...	...	...	...	...	...	...	...	...
Malaysia	1.6	6.5	3.4	5.4	5.8	4.4	4.4	0.9	5.4
Myanmar	...	...	...	...	...	...	...	...	...
Philippines	-1.0	2.1	4.0	15.5	5.0	3.3	7.6	9.0	7.0
Singapore	20.9	5.0	10.7	-1.5	11.4	0.2	7.8	3.5	4.1
Thailand	2.8	8.0	8.9	7.2	1.5	2.8	2.5	2.2	0.5
Viet Nam	5.0	8.2	12.3	7.2	7.3	7.0	7.0	7.5	7.4
The Pacific									
Cook Islands	...	...	...	...	...	...	...	...	...
Fiji	...	...	...	...	...	...	...	...	...
Kiribati	...	...	...	...	...	...	...	...	...
Marshall Islands	...	2.5	-0.0	4.7	0.3	-1.7	7.0	7.9	...
Micronesia, Federated States of	...	...	...	...	...	...	...	...	...
Nauru	...	...	...	...	...	...	...	...	...
Palau	...	6.0 (2006)	-1.5	-2.2	0.6	1.9	1.3	3.7	-2.0
Papua New Guinea	3.7	1.1	...	...	...	...	...	...	...
Samoa	...	...	...	...	...	...	...	...	...
Solomon Islands	...	80.6	10.0	-9.0	14.7	8.2	-1.4	2.0	...
Timor-Leste[a]	33.8 (2001)	-28.1	2.1	-2.5	-16.5	12.0	3.2	-0.2	...
Tonga	-2.8	-1.5	-8.6	10.7	...	...	...	...	...
Tuvalu	...	...	...	...	...	...	...	...	...
Vanuatu	...	-0.1	4.3	-1.3	2.2	-3.7	16.9	-1.4	...
Developed ADB Member Economies									
Australia	3.1	3.2	1.7	3.6	0.3	1.5	2.4	4.2	3.9
Japan	3.9	0.8	1.9	1.7	1.5	0.5	1.5	1.3	0.2
New Zealand	1.3	7.2	1.9	-0.2	2.0	3.2	2.5	2.0	...

... = data not available, -0.0 or 0.0 = magnitude is less than half of unit employed, – = magnitude equals zero, ADB = Asian Development Bank.

a   Gross domestic product estimates released by the Government of Timor-Leste's General Directorate of Statistics include the value added by the oil sector.

Source: Economy sources.

Table 2.2.18:   Growth Rates of Real Gross Capital Formation
(%)

ADB Regional Member	2000	2005	2010	2012	2013	2014	2015	2016	2017
Developing ADB Member Economies									
Central and West Asia									
Afghanistan	...	...	...	...	...	...	...	-8.7	...
Armenia	5.2	26.9	0.5	0.5	-9.1	-3.0	-1.2	-8.7	13.9
Azerbaijan	2.6	5.8	2.0	4.0	4.5	-1.7	-11.1	-19.0	-1.0
Georgia	...	...	...	19.1	-11.7	26.9	9.3	8.1	...
Kazakhstan	10.7	35.0	2.0	12.7	6.7	8.6	5.5	2.5	2.4
Kyrgyz Republic	22.1	13.7	-5.2	42.4	5.1	15.7	-2.3	8.1	...
Pakistan	2.5 (2001)	13.2	-6.5	2.5	2.8	2.8	14.6	7.3	9.5
Tajikistan	39.2 (2001)	2.6	7.5	-21.9	15.1	17.6	25.3	19.1	...
Turkmenistan	-6.0	12.4	21.6	...	...	...	...	...	...
Uzbekistan	...	...	...	...	...	...	...	...	...
East Asia									
China, People's Republic of	...	...	...	...	...	...	...	...	...
Hong Kong, China	16.1	–	11.3	3.5	3.1	1.6	-8.1	4.0	5.7
Korea, Republic of	14.5	2.4	17.8	-2.3	-0.1	5.3	7.3	5.6	10.1
Mongolia	...	15.0 (2006)	62.8 (2011)	17.4	1.4	-30.1	-26.5	13.2	39.3
Taipei,China	9.0	1.3	35.8	-2.6	5.3	2.1	1.5	1.0	-1.2
South Asia									
Bangladesh	7.3	10.7	8.6	10.6	5.4	9.9	7.1	8.9	10.1
Bhutan	26.5	-12.2	46.1	3.5	-35.7	24.4	16.5	12.0	...
India	-5.5	16.2	14.1	6.9	-5.2	8.5	7.5	...	...
Maldives	...	...	...	...	...	...	...	...	...
Nepal	-14.0 (2002)	9.5	34.4	-21.6	23.5	22.8	9.4	10.4	29.1
Sri Lanka	8.7	9.4	20.2 (2011)	21.7	-8.8	11.5	3.8	27.1	17.2
Southeast Asia									
Brunei Darussalam	6.7 (2001)	0.5	37.0 (2011)	28.8	11.9	-31.2	6.6	-11.1	8.0
Cambodia	8.6	29.9	-18.6	6.2	25.0	8.8	9.9	10.0	6.0
Indonesia	12.9	12.4	8.8	11.0	2.8	5.7	3.0	5.0	5.3
Lao People's Democratic Republic	...	...	...	...	...	...	...	...	...
Malaysia	29.2	-2.5	25.3	18.3	4.9	2.5	6.6	3.3	6.2
Myanmar	11.3	29.8	34.6	13.6	12.3	7.5	16.1	4.3	-0.2
Philippines	1.1	3.0	31.6	-4.3	27.9	4.2	18.4	24.5	9.4
Singapore	26.3	-0.4	24.2	14.1	5.3	1.8	-7.0	4.8	8.7
Thailand	8.0	21.7	32.0	11.1	3.2	-12.3	1.8	-4.0	...
Viet Nam	10.1	11.2	10.4	2.4	5.5	8.9	9.0	9.7	9.8
The Pacific									
Cook Islands	...	...	...	...	...	...	...	...	...
Fiji	...	...	...	...	...	...	...	...	...
Kiribati	...	...	...	...	...	...	...	...	...
Marshall Islands	...	2.5	18.8	-34.1	92.9	-18.4	1.1	-20.4	...
Micronesia, Federated States of	...	...	...	...	...	...	...	...	...
Nauru	...	...	...	...	...	...	...	...	...
Palau	...	-10.9 (2006)	9.0	2.1	-11.2	37.9	-1.7	14.6	-3.6
Papua New Guinea	36.8	-9.8	...	...	...	...	...	...	...
Samoa	...	...	...	...	...	...	...	...	...
Solomon Islands	...	71.1	88.7	3.6	1.9	3.3	10.2	-5.0	...
Timor-Leste[a]	10.7 (2001)	-7.8	-4.5	-12.5	-20.3	3.3	-10.3	16.2	...
Tonga	1.3	4.7	11.7	-3.7	...	...	...	...	...
Tuvalu	...	...	...	...	...	...	...	...	...
Vanuatu	...	7.7	-5.2	-16.6	17.0	9.0	33.2	-21.5	...
Developed ADB Member Economies									
Australia	...	...	...	...	...	...	...	...	...
Japan	2.9	2.3	2.9	3.7	3.2	3.4	2.9	...	...
New Zealand	-3.9	4.0	7.4	3.3	8.1	8.7	3.1	5.3	...

... = data not available, – = magnitude equals zero, ADB = Asian Development Bank.

a   Gross domestic product estimates released by the Government of Timor-Leste's General Directorate of Statistics include the value added by the oil sector.

Source: Economy sources.

Table 2.2.19:　Growth Rates of Real Exports of Goods and Services
(%)

ADB Regional Member	2000	2005	2010	2012	2013	2014	2015	2016	2017
Developing ADB Member Economies									
Central and West Asia									
Afghanistan	...	...	...	...	...	...	...	...	...
Armenia	19.0	15.9	26.5	8.4	8.6	6.4	4.9	19.1	19.7
Azerbaijan	15.4	52.8	9.1	-4.9	2.1	-1.9	-0.1	11.4	-2.2
Georgia	...	...	15.5 (2011)	14.4	20.3	0.4	6.0	7.7	...
Kazakhstan	27.9	0.4	3.1	4.8	2.7	-2.5	-4.1	-4.5	2.2
Kyrgyz Republic	10.5	-11.0	-11.7	-19.2	12.3	-6.2	-5.6	-3.8	...
Pakistan	12.2 (2001)	11.7	15.7	-15.0	13.6	-1.5	-6.3	-1.6	-0.8
Tajikistan	-20.8 (2001)	2.9	23.0	1.0	-10.0	–	–	–	...
Turkmenistan	82.7	19.2	11.7	...	...	...	...	...	...
Uzbekistan	...	...	...	...	...	...	...	...	...
East Asia									
China, People's Republic of	...	...	...	...	...	...	...	...	...
Hong Kong, China	16.9	12.2	17.6	3.2	7.8	1.0	-1.4	0.7	5.5
Korea, Republic of	17.2	7.8	12.7	5.1	4.3	2.0	-0.1	2.6	1.9
Mongolia	...	6.1 (2006)	18.2 (2011)	8.3	12.8	53.2	0.1	15.9	11.3
Taipei,China	18.0	7.6	25.7	0.4	3.5	5.9	-0.4	1.9	7.5
South Asia									
Bangladesh	14.4	15.6	0.9	12.5	2.5	3.2	-2.8	2.2	-2.3
Bhutan	3.3	34.3	7.5	-2.4	3.9	-5.8	-3.5	-1.8	...
India	18.2	26.1	19.6	6.8	7.8	1.8	-5.6	5.0	5.6
Maldives	...	...	...	...	...	...	...	...	...
Nepal	-23.2 (2002)	-3.0	-10.4	1.9	10.3	18.8	6.8	-13.7	16.9
Sri Lanka	17.1	6.6	10.2 (2011)	-0.2	6.6	4.3	4.7	-0.7	7.5
Southeast Asia									
Brunei Darussalam	11.9	-1.3	-3.0 (2011)	1.2	-5.7	0.9	-10.8	-9.2	5.1
Cambodia	39.4	16.4	16.0	7.9	20.9	11.3	7.2	8.6	5.3
Indonesia	26.5	16.6	15.3	1.6	4.2	1.1	-2.1	-1.6	9.1
Lao People's Democratic Republic	...	...	...	...	...	...	...	...	...
Malaysia	16.1	8.3	11.1	-1.7	0.3	5.0	0.3	1.1	9.6
Myanmar	79.3	3.6	10.9	6.5	12.9	18.7	15.1	0.7	17.2
Philippines	13.7	5.0	21.0	8.6	-1.0	12.6	8.5	11.6	19.5
Singapore	14.6	12.5	17.4	1.7	5.9	3.4	4.7	1.1	4.1
Thailand	15.8	7.8	14.2	4.9	2.7	0.3	1.6	2.8	5.5
Viet Nam	11.0 (2002)	7.8	14.6	15.7	17.4	11.6	12.6	13.9	16.7
The Pacific									
Cook Islands	...	...	...	...	...	...	...	...	...
Fiji	...	...	...	...	...	...	...	...	...
Kiribati	...	...	...	...	...	...	...	...	...
Marshall Islands	...	14.5	22.4	2.1	8.5	1.1	8.4	-8.6	...
Micronesia, Federated States of	...	...	...	...	...	...	...	...	...
Nauru	...	...	...	...	...	...	...	...	...
Palau	...	-1.6 (2006)	6.9	9.4	-2.9	13.1	10.6	-2.2	-11.5
Papua New Guinea	7.1	6.8	...	...	...	...	...	...	...
Samoa	...	...	...	...	...	...	...	...	...
Solomon Islands	...	10.5	34.8	11.6	-4.8	-8.9	1.8	3.6	...
Timor-Leste	-19.2 (2001)	74.0	-6.7	10.9	-13.2	-26.4	12.7	-9.2	...
Tonga	-14.7	-2.8	-8.8	-0.8	...	...	...	...	...
Tuvalu	...	...	...	...	...	...	...	...	...
Vanuatu	...	7.1	0.4	-1.2	4.2	-0.7	4.9	19.5	...
Developed ADB Member Economies									
Australia	9.9	3.5	4.7	4.6	5.3	6.0	6.8	6.9	5.5
Japan	12.7	7.2	24.9	-0.1	0.8	9.3	2.9	1.7	6.7
New Zealand	6.1	-0.4	2.8	3.0	0.0	4.3	5.6	0.7	...

... = data not available, – = magnitude equals zero, 0.0 = magnitude is less than half of unit employed, ADB = Asian Development Bank.

Source:　Economy sources.

Table 2.2.20: Growth Rates of Real Imports of Goods and Services
(%)

ADB Regional Member	2000	2005	2010	2012	2013	2014	2015	2016	2017
Developing ADB Member Economies									
Central and West Asia									
Afghanistan	...	...	...	...	...	...	...	7.6	...
Armenia	7.2	14.3	12.8	-2.8	-2.1	-1.0	-15.1	7.6	26.8
Azerbaijan	17.3	19.8	12.4	-3.1	1.1	-2.1	-0.5	11.3	-1.6
Georgia	...	...	17.9 (2011)	15.6	2.9	11.1	10.4	6.3	...
Kazakhstan	28.0	12.1	2.9	24.8	7.8	-4.0	-0.1	-2.0	-4.5
Kyrgyz Republic	0.4	6.5	-6.9	12.4	4.1	1.6	-13.2	-1.1	...
Pakistan	2.2 (2001)	39.5	4.3	-3.1	1.8	0.3	-1.6	16.0	21.0
Tajikistan	-14.5 (2001)	16.5	8.0	1.2	1.1	1.0	–	–	...
Turkmenistan	4.1	-9.3	7.4	...	...	...	...	...	...
Uzbekistan	...	...	...	...	...	...	...	...	...
East Asia									
China, People's Republic of	...	...	...	...	...	...	...	...	...
Hong Kong, China	17.1	9.3	18.2	4.2	8.3	1.0	-1.8	0.9	6.3
Korea, Republic of	21.8	7.8	17.3	2.4	1.7	1.5	2.1	4.7	7.0
Mongolia	...	6.7 (2006)	49.5 (2011)	15.4	7.6	6.8	-11.4	13.3	24.1
Taipei,China	14.9	2.9	28.0	-1.8	3.4	5.7	1.1	3.5	5.2
South Asia									
Bangladesh	10.2	19.1	0.7	10.5	1.2	1.2	3.2	-7.1	2.9
Bhutan	4.2	13.0	28.7	-7.1	-1.8	-3.2	13.4	-5.5	...
India	4.6	32.6	15.6	6.0	-8.1	0.9	-5.9	4.0	12.4
Maldives	...	...	...	...	...	...	...	...	...
Nepal	-15.1 (2002)	6.9	28.3	3.4	14.1	21.0	9.6	2.8	22.0
Sri Lanka	14.8	2.7	23.6 (2011)	0.5	-1.5	9.6	10.6	7.9	19.3
Southeast Asia									
Brunei Darussalam	-6.2	10.2	33.7 (2011)	20.6	14.5	-30.9	-11.7	1.8	2.2
Cambodia	30.6	17.3	10.3	8.1	24.5	10.1	6.5	8.6	4.1
Indonesia	25.9	17.8	17.3	8.0	1.9	2.1	-6.2	-2.4	8.1
Lao People's Democratic Republic	...	...	...	...	...	...	...	...	...
Malaysia	24.4	8.9	15.6	2.9	1.7	4.0	0.8	1.1	11.0
Myanmar	-8.0	2.2	51.9	3.7	54.4	22.3	21.6	-11.3	2.2
Philippines	11.8	3.3	22.5	5.6	4.4	9.9	14.6	20.2	18.1
Singapore	20.5	11.5	16.3	2.7	6.0	2.9	4.1	0.1	5.2
Thailand	26.0	16.2	23.0	5.6	1.7	-5.3	0.0	-1.0	6.8
Viet Nam	15.8 (2002)	5.9	13.7	9.1	17.3	12.8	18.1	15.3	17.5
The Pacific									
Cook Islands	...	...	...	...	...	...	...	...	...
Fiji	...	...	...	...	...	...	...	...	...
Kiribati	...	...	...	...	...	...	...	...	...
Marshall Islands	...	7.3	-6.2	-0.9	16.5	-8.5	11.6	1.9	...
Micronesia, Federated States of	...	...	...	...	...	...	...	...	...
Nauru	...	...	...	...	...	...	...	...	...
Palau	...	1.3 (2006)	3.9	8.4	1.3	16.6	0.7	10.3	-1.7
Papua New Guinea	-4.7	4.7	...	...	...	...	...	...	...
Samoa	...	...	...	...	...	...	...	...	...
Solomon Islands	...	14.0	51.7	2.0	6.6	-5.9	3.9	1.2	...
Timor-Leste	26.7 (2001)	-19.1	-6.6	1.3	-13.8	19.6	-15.6	-5.3	...
Tonga	-0.6	1.8	-4.5	2.6	...	...	...	...	...
Tuvalu	...	...	...	...	...	...	...	...	...
Vanuatu	...	2.9	-2.2	0.8	6.5	0.2	26.2	2.3	...
Developed ADB Member Economies									
Australia	12.0	12.5	7.1	11.4	0.3	-2.3	0.9	-0.1	4.9
Japan	9.3	6.1	11.2	5.4	3.3	8.3	0.8	-1.6	3.4
New Zealand	-1.1	4.9	11.5	1.3	8.1	7.4	2.1	5.1	...

... = data not available, – = magnitude equals zero, 0.0 = magnitude is less than half of unit employed, ADB = Asian Development Bank.

Source: Economy sources.

Table 2.2.21:   Growth Rates of Agriculture Production Index
(%)

ADB Regional Member	2000	2005	2010	2011	2012	2013	2014	2015	2016
Developing ADB Member Economies									
Central and West Asia									
Afghanistan	-15.9	10.7	-0.8	-4.4	10.1	-2.2	3.6	-3.7	5.3
Armenia	4.7	36.9	-18.3	16.1	13.3	4.3	0.3	6.1	-10.0
Azerbaijan	10.1	15.8	-0.7	6.3	4.5	1.9	-3.4	6.4	1.9
Georgia	-13.7	17.1	-6.2	9.1	-6.2	19.2	-15.7	2.1	-5.2
Kazakhstan	-8.5	8.0	-13.7	31.8	-22.6	13.8	1.2	4.9	7.6
Kyrgyz Republic	4.8	-3.1	0.5	2.2	-2.2	1.2	0.0	6.8	2.9
Pakistan	1.3	3.1	-2.1	7.2	-0.4	5.4	1.7	1.3	-0.5
Tajikistan	12.6	-6.8	1.1	3.4	11.2	10.4	-1.8	6.0	-2.7
Turkmenistan	7.4	3.4	2.8	0.4	5.1	6.2	-4.0	-5.2	3.2
Uzbekistan	3.1	5.0	4.5	5.7	3.5	5.9	-2.1	6.8	-1.4
East Asia									
China, People's Republic of	5.1	3.8	2.4	3.1	3.6	1.5	1.4	2.9	2.2
Hong Kong, China	2.4	13.5	–	6.7	6.3	–	-5.9	–	6.3 (2017)
Korea, Republic of	0.8	0.6	-5.9	-3.2	1.3	4.3	2.5	-1.7	-1.4
Mongolia	-1.8	-7.1	-20.2	7.5	5.4	9.4	8.6	-1.9	5.6
Taipei,China	2.2	-5.7	2.1	3.7	-1.7	-1.2	1.1	-3.4	5.4 (2017)
South Asia									
Bangladesh	6.1	13.0	5.9	3.4	0.6	1.7	4.3	0.7	2.3
Bhutan	-10.2	23.5	4.5	12.3	-5.3	-4.2	2.1	0.1	3.4
India	-1.1	5.7	8.6	6.4	2.0	3.8	2.7	-1.2	2.3
Maldives	5.9	-20.0	-3.9	-8.1	-6.5	-3.2	3.9	2.4	0.2
Nepal	5.1	2.0	1.0	7.2	15.2	-6.6	4.3	-0.2	1.4
Sri Lanka	2.3	8.7	10.5	-3.7	3.8	9.5	-9.5	4.5	0.6
Southeast Asia									
Brunei Darussalam	13.0	-26.6	4.9	7.3	3.0	8.4	-0.2	2.1	-0.3
Cambodia	1.8	26.7	8.7	13.9	2.7	1.5	0.3	1.4	5.0
Indonesia	3.3	2.7	2.6	2.5	7.3	0.9	2.0	2.2	0.5
Lao People's Democratic Republic	14.3	4.0	6.9	9.4	10.6	4.4	17.1	11.0	4.0
Malaysia	3.5	4.6	0.5	8.2	-0.1	1.9	-0.8	0.9	0.6
Myanmar	10.3	7.2	2.1	-3.5	0.2	2.0	1.3	2.3	0.1 (2017)
Philippines	2.7	2.2	-0.8	4.5	3.2	0.9	-3.3	-1.3	-2.2
Singapore	-59.2	-22.8	0.5	9.6	3.8	6.7	-0.3	-2.0	4.9
Thailand	8.8	-1.9	-0.2	7.8	9.0	-0.7	-1.4	-5.4	-2.9
Viet Nam	3.2	3.7	2.7	4.3	6.5	1.5	2.2	2.4	-1.5
The Pacific									
Cook Islands	-3.3	3.3	-2.5	-2.2	-1.5	3.4	-0.5	-0.2	-1.8
Fiji	-0.1	1.6	-6.9	14.8	-17.7	12.1	2.2	-3.3	-2.1
Kiribati	-5.5	1.1	-48.4	0.8	–	-0.9	0.7	0.1	-0.2
Marshall Islands	-74.9	15.2	-5.0	-13.2	11.9	6.1	–	-4.3	-5.6
Micronesia, Federated States of	-0.0	-3.5	-0.4	-0.4	-1.4	6.1	12.2	13.1	-20.8
Nauru	0.8	1.2	1.0	-3.4	5.6	2.1	0.9	1.0	0.7
Palau	...	...	...	...	...	...	...	...	...
Papua New Guinea	3.2	1.8	-1.4	4.2	-0.6	2.3	1.2	0.8	1.1
Samoa	3.1	2.1	0.0	2.4	2.2	1.5	1.1	4.1	-1.1
Solomon Islands	2.9	12.2	2.9	1.2	0.1	2.6	1.7	-0.8	-3.1
Timor-Leste	6.0	6.0	-0.7	-12.6	9.2	-3.4	-0.4	0.2	-1.3
Tonga	-3.3	-0.2	-1.4	1.4	-1.3	-1.0	0.8	3.6	-1.5
Tuvalu	6.1	1.4	-1.3	0.8	1.5	2.3	-0.4	0.9	1.0
Vanuatu	-4.6	1.9	24.0	-2.7	1.4	6.0	-8.8	0.2	1.0
Developed ADB Member Economies									
Australia	-1.4	-0.4	-2.0	9.8	7.1	-1.0	-0.3	0.5	-3.5
Japan	-0.5	1.0	-2.4	-1.7	1.7	-0.4	-0.2	-1.1	-3.8
New Zealand	6.9	-2.1	1.2	0.6	4.6	0.5	5.8	1.9	-0.8

... = data not available, – = magnitude equals zero, -0.0 or 0.0 = magnitude is less than half of unit employed, ADB = Asian Development Bank.

Sources: Food and Agricultural Organization of the United Nations. FAOSTAT. http://www.fao.org/faostat/en/#home (accessed 1 June 2018). For Hong Kong, China;
            Myanmar (2010–2017); and Taipei,China: Economy sources.

Table 2.2.22: Growth Rates of Manufacturing Production Index
(%)

ADB Regional Member	2000	2005	2010	2012	2013	2014	2015	2016	2017
Developing ADB Member Economies									
Central and West Asia									
Afghanistan	...	...	...	...	...	...	...	...	...
Armenia	...	...	...	...	...	...	...	...	...
Azerbaijan	...	...	...	...	...	...	...	...	...
Georgia	...	...	...	...	...	...	...	...	...
Kazakhstan	17.3	15.9	15.1	1.2	1.9	1.1	0.2	0.6	5.1
Kyrgyz Republic[a]	3.4	-15.6	10.1	-25.8	45.8	-3.0	-7.8	5.4	...
Pakistan	1.0 (2001)	18.2	0.5	1.2	4.4	5.4	3.4	3.2	6.5
Tajikistan	12.0	10.5	-6.2 (2009)	...	...	...	...	...	...
Turkmenistan	13.4	...	...	...	...	...	...	...	...
Uzbekistan	7.1	10.2 (2004)	...	...	...	...	...	...	...
East Asia									
China, People's Republic of	...	18.2 (2006)	16.6	10.5	10.5	9.4	7.0	6.8	7.2
Hong Kong, China	-0.5	3.0	3.6	-0.8	0.1	-0.4	-1.5	-0.5	0.4
Korea, Republic of	10.4	3.3	7.9	2.1	1.7	1.6	0.9	2.4	1.6
Mongolia	...	...	...	...	...	...	...	...	...
Taipei,China	7.8	3.2	29.7	0.6	3.4	6.8	-1.2	1.9	5.3
South Asia									
Bangladesh	4.9	8.5	6.3	10.8	11.6	9.2	10.7	13.5	11.2
Bhutan	...	...	...	...	...	...	...	...	...
India	5.3	10.3	9.0	4.8	3.6	3.8	3.0	4.1	4.5
Maldives	...	...	...	...	...	...	...	...	...
Nepal	6.5	2.6	2.6	3.8	4.0	7.0	0.3	-13.3	26.2
Sri Lanka	...	...	...	...	...	...	...	...	...
Southeast Asia									
Brunei Darussalam	...	...	...	...	...	...	...	...	...
Cambodia	48.8	...	...	...	...	...	...	...	...
Indonesia	3.6	1.3	4.8	4.1	6.0	4.8	4.8	4.0	4.7
Lao People's Democratic Republic	...	...	...	...	...	...	...	...	...
Malaysia	24.9	5.1	11.0	5.3	4.2	6.0	4.8	4.3	6.1
Myanmar	...	...	10.1 (2011)	6.8	8.8	9.4	10.2	9.1	9.8
Philippines	16.0	1.1	23.3	7.7	15.2	6.2	2.4	14.5	-2.9
Singapore	15.3	9.5	29.8	0.4	1.7	2.7	-5.1	3.7	10.5
Thailand	6.9	5.0	14.2	10.6	2.4	-5.1	0.3	2.7	1.2
Viet Nam	...	...	...	...	2.0	1.0	1.8	0.5	...
The Pacific									
Cook Islands	...	...	...	...	...	...	...	...	...
Fiji	-5.6	2.3 (2006)	7.6	-25.7	5.2	2.9	4.0	-1.0	0.1
Kiribati	...	...	...	...	...	...	...	...	...
Marshall Islands	...	...	...	...	...	...	...	...	...
Micronesia, Federated States of	...	...	...	...	...	...	...	...	...
Nauru	...	...	...	...	...	...	...	...	...
Palau	...	...	...	...	...	...	...	...	...
Papua New Guinea	...	...	...	...	...	...	...	...	...
Samoa[a]	2.8	–	15.2	7.7	3.2	...	...	...	...
Solomon Islands	...	...	...	...	...	...	...	...	...
Timor-Leste	...	...	...	...	...	...	...	...	...
Tonga	...	...	...	...	...	...	...	...	...
Tuvalu	...	...	...	...	...	...	...	...	...
Vanuatu	...	...	...	...	...	...	...	...	...
Developed ADB Member Economies									
Australia	1.3	-1.0	0.4	0.9	-3.2	-1.0	-1.4	-2.3	-1.7
Japan	5.7	1.3	15.6	0.6	-0.8	2.1	-1.2	-0.1	4.5
New Zealand	4.3	0.6	4.3	1.3	0.9	1.3	2.0	2.7	2.2

... = data not available, – = magnitude equals zero, ADB = Asian Development Bank.

a   Refers to volume indices of industrial production.

Source: Economy sources.

III.   Money, Finance, and Prices

Snapshot

- Inflation, as measured by the consumer price index (CPI), exceeded 5.0% in 13 of 47 regional economies in 2017.

- In 2017, the money supply expanded on an annual basis in 38 of 41 economies in Asia and the Pacific.

- The ratio of nonperforming loans (NPLs) to total gross loans decreased in 16 of 29 regional economies from 2016 to 2017.

Key Trends

Inflation, as measured by the CPI, exceeded 5.0% in 13 of 47 regional economies in 2017. Consumer price inflation in 2017 increased most rapidly in three economies of Central and West Asia: Azerbaijan (12.9%), Uzbekistan (9.5%), and Turkmenistan (8.0%) as shown in Figure 2.3.1. In Azerbaijan, inflation accelerated as a result of the lagged effect of currency devaluation and increased fuel and electricity tariffs. In Turkmenistan, the government cut subsidies for utilities and raised prices for public transportation, and the manat depreciated steeply against the US dollar on the parallel market, driving inflation higher (ADB 2018a). In Uzbekistan, inflation was driven higher by the impact on import prices and production costs of the devaluation of the national currency by nearly 50% in September. In addition, an expanded list of goods and services used to monitor prices impacted the calculation of the CPI (ADB 2018b).

Deflation was recorded in the Cook Islands (–0.1%) and Brunei Darussalam (–0.2%). In both cases, nonfood inflation of –0.3% drove the CPI into negative territory.

The rise in the food CPI in 2017 outpaced growth in the total CPI in 26 of 45 regional economies in 2017, while growth in the nonfood CPI exceeded the growth in the total CPI in 15 of the region's 40 economies (Tables 2.3.1, 2.3.2, and 2.3.3).

Figure 2.3.1: Inflation Rate
(% annual change)

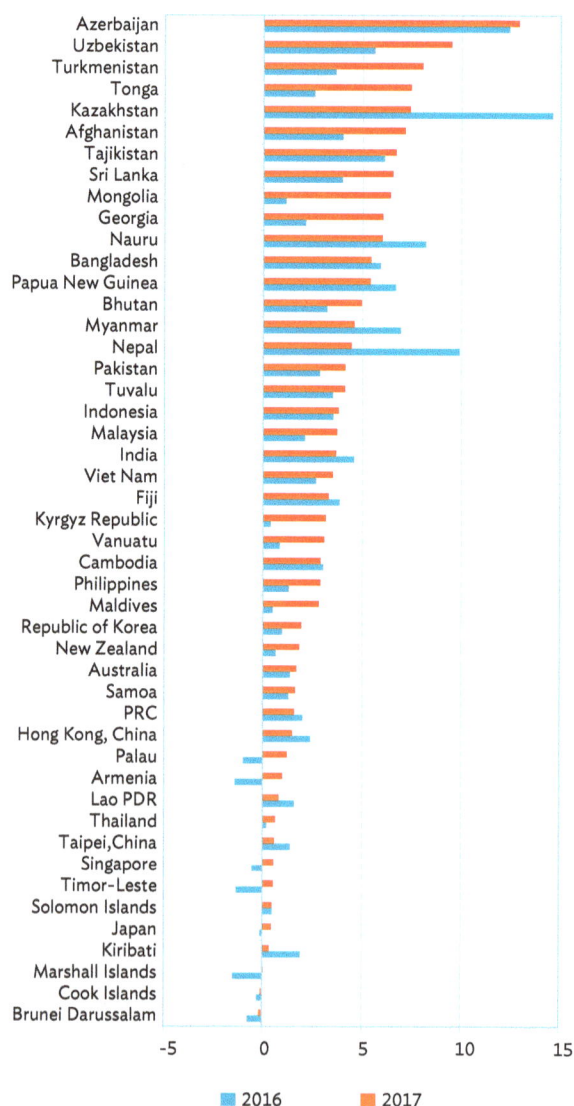

Lao PDR = Lao People's Democratic Republic, PRC = People's Republic of China.
Note: This chart includes economies with available data for both 2016 and 2017.
Source: Table 2.3.1, Key Indicators for Asia and the Pacific 2018.

In 2017, the money supply expanded on an annual basis in 38 of 41 economies in Asia and the Pacific. The money supply comprises the total currency in circulation and the value of deposits held in banks, including transferable funds, current accounts, and term deposits. Most governments seek to keep the growth of the money supply in line with that of nominal GDP. Financial authorities have traditionally influenced the money supply through government borrowing and setting interest rates, and more recently through quantitative easing (International Monetary Fund 2016).

Figure 2.3.2 presents the expansion (or contraction) in the money supply from 2016 to 2017 for the 41 regional economies for which data were available. The (arithmetic) average rate of expansion was 13.4%. The largest increase in 2017 was recorded in Uzbekistan (40.2%), where the expansion of broad money was driven by foreign currency deposits (ADB 2018a). Other sizeable annual increases in the money supply were observed in Tajikistan (36.6%) and Mongolia (30.5%).

In 2017, the following economies experienced a contraction in the money supply: Kazakhstan (–1.7%), Papua New Guinea (–0.7%), and Brunei Darussalam (–0.4%).

The ratio of NPLs to total gross loans decreased in 16 of 29 regional economies from 2016 to 2017. The largest percentage-point decline in the ratio of NPLs to total gross loans among reporting regional economies occurred in Pakistan (from 10.1% to 8.4%) as shown in Figure 2.3.3. Armenia (from 6.7% to 5.4%) and Brunei Darussalam (from 4.7% to 3.5%) had the next largest declines during the review period.

Significant increases in the ratio of NPLs to total gross loans were observed in Kazakhstan (from 6.7% to 12.7%) and Vanuatu (from 10.8% to 14.0%).

Figure 2.3.2: Growth in Money Supply, 2016–2017 (%)

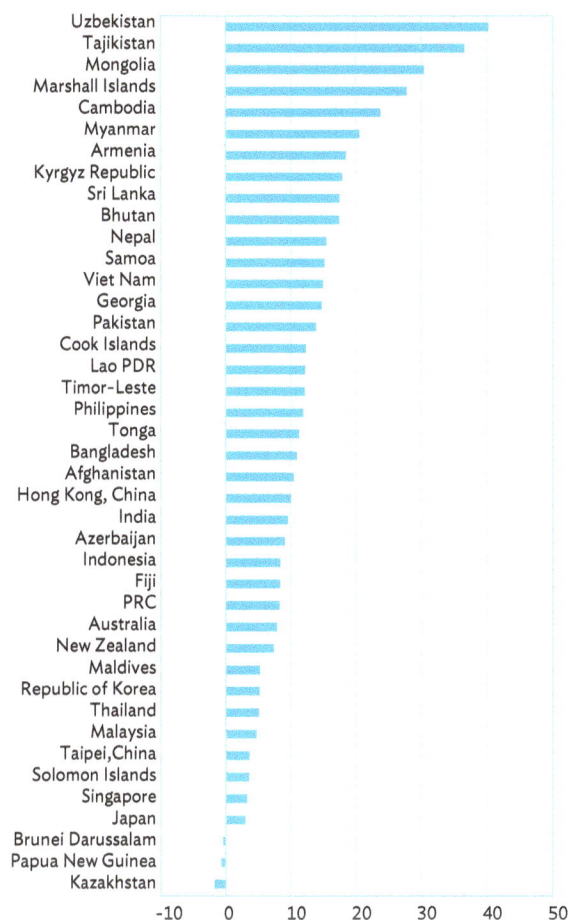

Lao PDR = Lao People's Democratic Republic, PRC = People's Republic of China.
Note: Australia, Azerbaijan, Fiji, Georgia, India, Japan, Kazakhstan, Malaysia, Papua New Guinea, Philippines, Solomon, and Turkmenistan use M3 while the rest use M2.
Source: Table 2.3.6, Key Indicators for Asia and the Pacific 2018.

Data Issues and Comparability

Not all reporting economies meet the standards and classifications of the International Monetary Fund (IMF) on the compilation of monetary and financial statistics available on the fund's Dissemination Standards Bulletin Board.[3]

___
3   The IMF's Dissemination Standards Bulletin Board can be found at http://dsbb.imf.org/Pages/SDDS/StatMethod.aspx.

CPI coverage differs across economies. Most economies try to follow the Classification of Individual Consumption by Purpose guidelines, but the implementation varies across economies. In some instances, the basket of goods and services in the index is outdated or represents only urban areas (or the capital city). Other price measurements, such as the wholesale price index and the producer price index, are not available in Pacific economies.

Broad money supply in most economies relates to M2, which includes cash, checking deposits, savings deposits, money market securities, mutual funds, and other time deposits. However, 12 of the 43 economies for which data were available reported M3, thereby posing limits to comparability as M3 also includes less liquid financial assets. Not all countries publish the same types of aggregates, and even when aggregates have the same name (i.e. M1, M2, M3, etc.) their asset composition often differs significantly. For example, the definition of M2 in one country may include time deposits with maturities of 1 year or less, whereas another country's M2 definition may include time deposits with maturities of 2 years or less.

Finally, some economies use the central bank policy rate, while others use commercial bank rates in measuring banks' average deposit and lending rates.

Figure 2.3.3: Nonperforming Bank Loans
(% of total gross loans)

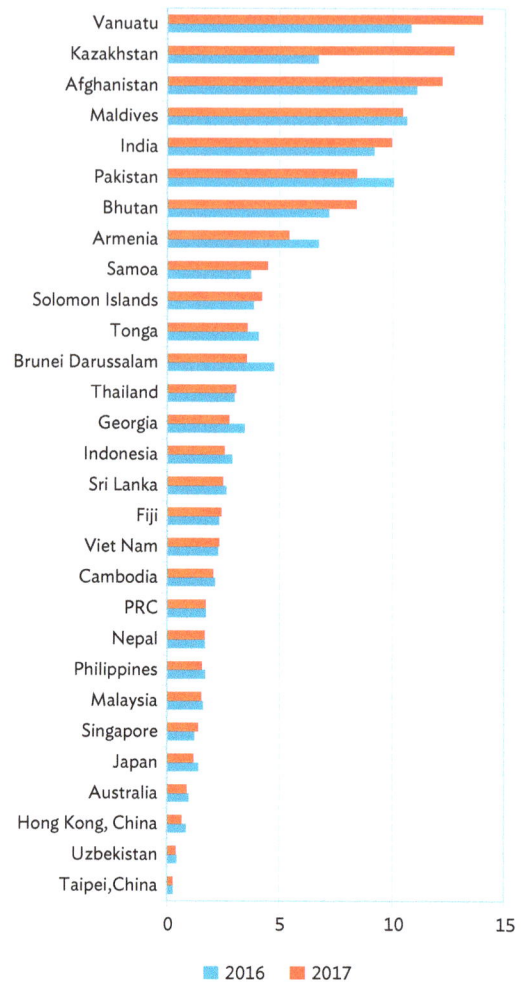

PRC = People's Republic of China.
Source: World Bank. World Development Indicators Online. http://data.worldbank.org/ (accessed 6 July 2018). For Taipei,China: Central bank of Taipei,China. http://www.cbc.gov.tw (accessed 8 August 2018).

Table 2.3.1: Growth Rates of Consumer Price Index[a]
(%)

ADB Regional Member	2000	2005	2010	2012	2013	2014	2015	2016	2017
Developing ADB Member Economies									
Central and West Asia									
Afghanistan	...	11.9	-4.5	8.4	6.4	5.6	-0.6	4.0	7.2
Armenia	-0.8	0.6	8.2	2.6	5.8	3.0	3.7	-1.4	1.0
Azerbaijan	1.8	9.6	5.7	1.1	2.4	1.4	4.0	12.4	12.9
Georgia	4.6	8.2	7.1	-0.9	-0.5	3.1	4.0	2.1	6.0
Kazakhstan	13.2	7.6	7.1	5.1	5.8	6.7	6.6	14.6	7.4
Kyrgyz Republic	18.7	4.3	8.0	2.8	6.6	7.5	6.5	0.4	3.2
Pakistan	3.6	9.3	10.1	11.0	7.4	8.6	4.5	2.9	4.2
Tajikistan	60.6	7.1	9.8	6.4	3.7	7.4	5.1	6.1	6.7
Turkmenistan	8.0	10.7	4.4	5.3	6.8	6.0	7.4	3.6	8.0
Uzbekistan	24.9	6.4	7.6	7.2	7.0	6.4	5.5	5.6	9.5
East Asia									
China, People's Republic of	0.4	1.8	3.3	2.6	2.6	2.0	1.4	2.0	1.6
Hong Kong, China	-3.7	0.8	2.3	4.1	4.3	4.4	3.0	2.4	1.5
Korea, Republic of[b]	2.3	2.8	2.9	2.2	1.3	1.3	0.7	1.0	1.9
Mongolia	8.0 (2001)	9.5	13.0	14.0	12.5	10.5	1.9	1.1	6.4
Taipei,China	1.3	2.3	1.0	1.9	0.8	1.2	-0.3	1.4	0.6
South Asia									
Bangladesh	2.8	6.5	6.8	8.7	6.8	7.3	6.4	5.9	5.4
Bhutan	4.0	5.3	7.0	10.9	8.8	8.3	4.5	3.2	5.0
India	3.7	4.2	10.4	9.9	12.2	5.8	4.9	4.6	3.7
Maldives	-1.2	1.3	6.1	10.9	3.8	2.1	1.0	0.5	2.8
Nepal	3.4	4.6	9.5	8.3	9.9	9.1	7.2	9.9	4.5
Sri Lanka[c]	6.2	11.0	6.2	7.5	6.9	5.1	2.2	4.0	6.5
Southeast Asia									
Brunei Darussalam	1.2	1.1	0.4	0.1	0.4	-0.2	-0.4	-0.7	-0.2
Cambodia[c]	-0.8	5.8	4.0	2.9	2.9	3.9	1.2	3.0	2.9
Indonesia[d]	3.8	10.5	5.1	4.3	7.0	6.4	6.4	3.5	3.8
Lao People's Democratic Republic	23.2	7.2	6.0	4.3	6.4	4.1	1.3	1.6	0.8
Malaysia	1.5	2.9	1.7	1.6	2.1	3.2	2.1	2.1	3.7
Myanmar	-0.2	9.4	7.7	1.5	8.9	5.0	9.5	6.9	4.6
Philippines	6.7	6.5	3.8	3.2	2.6	3.6	0.7	1.3	2.9
Singapore	1.3	0.5	2.8	4.6	2.4	1.0	-0.5	-0.5	0.6
Thailand	1.6	4.4	3.3	3.0	2.2	1.9	-0.9	0.2	0.7
Viet Nam	-0.3 (2001)	8.3	9.2	9.2	6.6	4.1	0.6	2.7	3.5
The Pacific									
Cook Islands	3.2	2.5	-0.3	3.0	1.9	2.1	1.9	-0.3	-0.1
Fiji	1.1	2.5 (2006)	3.7	3.4	2.9	0.6	1.4	3.9	3.3
Kiribati[c]	0.4	-0.3	-3.0	-3.0	-1.5	2.1	0.6	1.9	0.4
Marshall Islands[c]	0.9	3.5	1.8	4.3	1.9	1.1	-2.2	-1.5	0.0[d]
Micronesia, Federated States of	1.8	4.1	3.6	6.3	2.1	0.7	0.0	-1.0	...
Nauru	2.3	9.8	-4.6	-0.8	-1.1	0.3	9.8	8.2	6.0
Palau	-1.8 (2001)	3.9	1.4	3.6	3.4	4.2	0.9	-1.0	1.2
Papua New Guinea	15.6	1.8	6.0	4.6	5.0	5.2	6.0	6.7	5.4
Samoa	0.9	1.9	0.8	2.1	0.6	-0.4	0.7	1.3	1.6
Solomon Islands[c]	7.1	7.2	0.9	5.9	5.4	5.2	-0.6	0.5	0.5
Timor-Leste	...	1.6	5.2	10.9	9.5	0.7	0.6	-1.3	0.6
Tonga	6.3	8.7	3.5	1.1	0.8	2.5	-1.1	2.6	7.4
Tuvalu	3.9	3.2	-1.9	1.4	2.0	1.1	3.1	3.5	4.1
Vanuatu	2.5	0.8	2.8	1.4	1.5	0.8	2.5	0.8	3.1
Developed ADB Member Economies									
Australia	2.4	2.4	2.3	2.3	2.3	2.7	1.7	1.4	1.7
Japan	-0.7	-0.3	-0.7	-0.1	0.3	2.8	0.8	-0.1	0.5
New Zealand	2.6	3.0	2.3	1.1	1.1	1.2	0.3	0.6	1.9

... = data not available, 0.0 = magnitude is less than half of unit employed, * = preliminary, ADB = Asian Development Bank.

a Data refer to the whole economy, unless otherwise indicated.
b Data refer to all cities.
c Data refer to capital city.
d Consumer price index data for Indonesia for 2000–2002 refer to the consumer price indexes for 43 cities; for 2003–2007, 45 cities; for 2008–2013, 66 cities; and for 2014–2017, 82 cities.

Source: Economy sources.

Table 2.3.2:   Growth Rates of Food Consumer Price Index[a]
(%)

ADB Regional Member	2000	2005	2010	2012	2013	2014	2015	2016	2017
Developing ADB Member Economies									
Central and West Asia									
Afghanistan	...	9.1	-9.1	7.0	5.2	10.0	-0.6	4.9	10.0
Armenia	-2.2	0.7	8.6	2.3	5.8	2.2	3.0	-3.0	4.0
Azerbaijan	2.3	10.9	7.2	0.8	2.2	1.0	6.1	14.7	16.4
Georgia	7.5	8.3	22.2	-2.8	6.0	2.6	4.8	3.5	9.1
Kazakhstan	16.0	8.1	6.2	4.5	4.3	6.6	6.4	12.7	8.6
Kyrgyz Republic	18.5	7.0	6.5	-4.1	5.3	8.2	3.7	-6.5	2.5
Pakistan	2.2	12.5	12.9	11.0	7.1	9.0	3.5	2.1	3.8
Tajikistan	66.3	8.3	13.4	5.6	3.2	9.7	4.3	6.8	7.5
Turkmenistan	...	...	...	...	...	...	...	...	...
Uzbekistan	18.9	4.2	4.8	5.1	4.9	3.9	2.8	-0.4	7.8
East Asia									
China, People's Republic of	-2.6	2.9	7.2	4.8	4.7	3.1	2.3	3.8	-0.4
Hong Kong, China	-2.2	1.7	3.4	6.2	4.3	3.7	3.2	3.5	1.1
Korea, Republic of[b]	1.1	3.1	5.9	3.8	0.9	0.3	5.5	2.1	3.2
Mongolia	...	26.3 (2007)	17.0	20.9	13.3	7.0	-5.1	1.4	6.8
Taipei,China	0.4	8.4	1.7	5.0	1.2	3.8	3.6	7.3	-1.1
South Asia									
Bangladesh	2.6	7.9	6.3	7.7	5.2	8.6	6.7	4.9	6.0
Bhutan	1.0	5.7	8.8	13.9	8.7	10.4	3.2	3.9	7.1
India	1.6	4.2	10.0	11.2	15.8	6.2	4.6	4.4	1.9
Maldives	-4.8	7.8	7.5	17.6	7.2	0.7	0.5	0.6	5.6
Nepal	0.6	3.8	15.3	7.7	9.6	11.6	9.6	10.9	1.9
Sri Lanka[c]	4.5	11.4	6.9	4.7	7.9	4.3	5.5	6.1	9.2
Southeast Asia									
Brunei Darussalam	–	0.5	1.0	-0.0	0.1	-0.2	0.8	-0.9	0.3
Cambodia[c]	-3.4	8.4	4.4	3.3	3.9	4.9	4.1	5.7	3.4
Indonesia[d]	-4.8	10.0	9.4	5.9	12.0	...	7.2	7.2	2.1
Lao People's Democratic Republic	18.0	7.7	7.7	5.9	12.1	6.9	4.4	3.9	0.1
Malaysia	2.1	3.7	2.5	2.7	3.6	3.4	3.6	3.9	4.5
Myanmar	-2.6	9.3	7.2	-1.5	5.4	6.9	13.1	9.2	4.4
Philippines	3.0	6.4	4.0	2.4	2.5	5.9	1.8	1.6	3.0
Singapore	0.5	1.3	1.4	2.3	2.1	2.9	1.9	2.1	1.4
Thailand	-1.1	4.8	5.4	4.8	3.4	3.9	1.1	1.6	–
Viet Nam	...	8.7 (2006)	10.7	8.1	2.7	4.0	1.5	2.5	-1.5
The Pacific									
Cook Islands	3.4	1.1	2.9	3.1	2.6	3.3	-0.1	1.3	0.3
Fiji	-3.2	1.8 (2006)	4.1	4.3	3.5	1.9	4.7	6.0	-2.1
Kiribati[c]	0.7	-4.8	-11.1	-2.4	-0.6	0.0	-0.5	1.2	-0.2
Marshall Islands[c]	-0.8	1.1	-1.4	4.7	2.5	1.9	2.2	-1.3	-0.5*
Micronesia, Federated States of	1.1	3.4	2.2	4.5	2.6	0.8	0.8	-1.3	...
Nauru	...	...	-0.4	-0.0	0.8	...	...	...	...
Palau	-4.6 (2001)	0.8	0.8	4.0	2.9	5.1	6.7	-2.0	1.1
Papua New Guinea	13.6	3.5	5.4	-1.4	-0.9	4.8	4.9	5.1	2.8
Samoa	-0.1	0.3	-6.6	1.9	0.7	-3.4	3.3	5.9	1.1
Solomon Islands[c]	6.6	5.6	-1.4	4.4	3.6	5.3	-2.3	2.0	0.7
Timor-Leste	...	0.4	6.0	12.4	12.0	0.8	0.6	-1.8	0.8
Tonga	0.4	6.0	3.0	1.5	1.8	3.7	1.9	1.3	8.6
Tuvalu	1.1	5.5	-5.9	0.2	0.1	0.6	4.0	3.4	4.5
Vanuatu	2.0	0.5	4.5	2.1	1.5	1.7	3.6	2.3	6.8
Developed ADB Member Economies									
Australia	2.1	1.6	1.6	0.7	0.5	1.3	2.1	0.1	1.8
Japan	-2.0	-0.9	-0.2	0.1	-0.2	3.9	3.1	1.7	0.7
New Zealand	3.3	2.0	2.4	1.1	1.6	1.1	1.5	0.6	2.9

... = data not available, – = magnitude equals zero, -0.0 or 0.0 = magnitude is less than half of unit employed, * = preliminary, ADB = Asian Development Bank.

a Coverage of food varies by economy. Data refer to the whole economy, unless otherwise indicated.
b Refers to all cities.
c Refers to capital city.
d Consumer price index data for Indonesia for 2000–2002 refer to the consumer price indexes for 43 cities; for 2003–2007, 45 cities; for 2008–2013, 66 cities; and for 2014–2017, 82 cities.

Source: Economy sources.

Table 2.3.3:   Growth Rates of Nonfood Consumer Price Index[a]
(%)

ADB Regional Member	2000	2005	2010	2012	2013	2014	2015	2016	2017
Developing ADB Member Economies									
Central and West Asia									
Afghanistan	...	16.3	3.9	10.4	7.7	1.1	-0.5	3.2	4.5
Armenia	3.0	0.5	9.6	4.6	4.6	1.7	5.6	-2.5	-1.8
Azerbaijan	1.9	5.4	2.3	1.0	0.8	3.2	3.8	16.7	11.6
Georgia	0.4	3.7	2.9	-0.6	0.3	1.6	4.9	0.8	5.4
Kazakhstan	11.5	6.3	6.4	4.3	3.1	6.9	8.1	22.4	8.4
Kyrgyz Republic	18.1	3.7	11.4	10.1	7.4	6.9	10.1	5.9	1.8
Pakistan	4.3	7.1	8.3	11.0	7.5	8.3	5.3	3.4	4.4
Tajikistan	44.2	2.7	5.5	6.7	6.1	2.9	7.8	5.7	4.4
Turkmenistan	...	...	...	...	...	...	...	...	...
Uzbekistan	36.6	4.9	5.3	4.9	5.5	7.6	6.3	10.2	11.7
East Asia									
China, People's Republic of	...	...	...	...	...	...	...	1.3	2.4
Hong Kong, China	-4.1	0.5	2.1	3.7	4.4	4.5	3.0	2.4	1.5
Korea, Republic of[b]	2.4	2.7	2.4	1.9	1.4	1.5	-0.1	0.8	1.7
Mongolia	...	10.3 (2007)	8.4	10.8	12.1	12.2	5.4	1.0	6.2
Taipei,China	1.6	0.7	0.8	1.1	0.7	0.7	-1.1	0.1	1.0
South Asia									
Bangladesh	3.0	4.3	7.7	10.2	9.2	5.5	6.0	7.4	4.6
Bhutan	9.2	5.1	6.1	9.3	8.7	6.9	5.4	2.8	3.6
India	...	...	...	...	...	...	...	...	...
Maldives	...	...	...	...	1.4	2.7	1.1	0.5	1.7
Nepal	7.1	5.0	4.8	9.0	10.0	6.8	5.2	9.2	6.5
Sri Lanka[c]	10.1	10.7	5.4	13.2	6.1	5.4	1.0	3.1	5.5
Southeast Asia									
Brunei Darussalam	...	...	...	0.3	0.4	-0.2	-0.7	-0.7	-0.3
Cambodia[c]	1.2	3.9	3.8	2.7	2.0	2.7	-2.7	-3.0	4.1
Indonesia	...	...	...	...	...	...	...	...	...
Lao People's Democratic Republic	30.4	6.7	4.2	3.1	2.0	1.8	-1.4	-0.7	1.6
Malaysia	1.3	2.7	1.4	1.3	1.6	3.0	1.2	1.4	3.7
Myanmar	...	9.4	8.8	7.4	12.9	2.1	3.8	3.1	4.9
Philippines	9.3	6.8	3.8	3.7	2.0	2.2	-0.3	1.0	2.6
Singapore	1.7	0.2	3.2	5.2	2.4	0.5	-1.2	-1.3	0.3
Thailand	3.2	4.3	2.1	1.8	1.5	0.8	-2.0	-0.6	1.2
Viet Nam	...	6.4 (2006)	9.1	8.4	4.6	2.9	-2.2	-1.3	3.5
The Pacific									
Cook Islands	3.1	3.0	-1.6	2.9	1.5	1.6	2.8	-0.9	-0.3
Fiji	3.7	3.4 (2006)	3.5	3.0	2.7	-0.3	0.3	3.4	6.4
Kiribati[c]	-7.7	-1.9	4.5	-3.6	-2.2	3.7	1.4	2.4	0.8
Marshall Islands[c]	3.1	5.0	3.8	4.1	1.5	0.6	-5.0	-1.6	0.4*
Micronesia, Federated States of	2.5	4.7	4.6	7.5	1.8	0.7	-0.5	-0.8	...
Nauru	...	...	-9.5	-0.4	1.0	...	...	...	...
Palau	0.3 (2001)	6.3	1.8	3.2	3.8	3.4	-4.0	-0.1	1.3
Papua New Guinea	17.0	0.6	6.5	8.0	8.0	5.4	6.5	7.4	...
Samoa	1.6	3.3	3.4	2.1	0.6	2.9	-2.8	-3.2	2.1
Solomon Islands[c]	8.1	8.4	3.4	7.4	7.1	5.1	1.0	-0.8	0.5
Timor-Leste	...	2.5	2.7	7.1	2.8	1.0	1.1	-0.5	-0.3
Tonga	11.5	10.9	4.0	0.9	-0.1	1.6	-3.7	3.7	6.4
Tuvalu	5.4	2.1	1.8	2.3	3.4	1.4	2.5	3.6	3.9
Vanuatu	...	...	...	...	...	...	...	...	...
Developed ADB Member Economies									
Australia	2.5	2.6	2.5	2.6	2.6	3.0	1.6	1.6	1.7
Japan	...	...	...	...	...	...	...	...	...
New Zealand	2.3	3.4	2.3	1.1	0.9	1.3	-0.1	0.7	1.6

... = data not available, * = preliminary, ADB = Asian Development Bank.

a   Coverage of nonfood varies by economy. Data refer to the whole economy, unless otherwise indicated.
b   Refers to all cities.
c   Refers to capital city.

Sources: Economy sources; and Asian Development Bank estimates based on consumer price index weights from economy sources.

Table 2.3.4:   Growth Rates of Wholesale and/or Producer Price Indexes
(%)

ADB Regional Member	2000	2005	2010	2012	2013	2014	2015	2016	2017
Developing ADB Member Economies									
Central and West Asia									
Afghanistan	...	...	...	...	...	...	...	...	...
Armenia	0.8	7.7	22.6	7.0	4.7	8.5	-0.8	1.5	3.9
Azerbaijan	3.3 (2001)	17.3	30.5	4.5	-3.9	-5.1	-30.6	27.5	36.8
Georgia	5.8	7.5	11.3	1.6	-2.0	2.9	7.5	-0.1	11.0
Kazakhstan	38.0	23.7	25.2	3.5	-0.3	9.5	-20.5	16.8	15.3
Kyrgyz Republic	29.6	2.8	22.8	5.3	-2.1	1.5	8.8	6.4	1.7
Pakistan	1.8	6.8	13.8	10.4	7.4	8.2	-0.3	-1.0	4.0
Tajikistan	39.2	10.4	27.2	6.1	2.1	4.7	3.0	14.7	...
Turkmenistan	...	...	...	...	...	...	...	...	...
Uzbekistan	60.9	25.6	15.6	14.5	11.7	13.6	13.5	14.8	17.5
East Asia									
China, People's Republic of	2.8	4.9	5.5	-1.7	-1.9	-1.9	-5.2	-2.0	...
Hong Kong, China	0.2	0.8	6.0	0.1	-3.1	-1.7	-2.7	1.3	3.8
Korea, Republic of	2.1	2.1	3.8	0.7	-1.6	-0.5	-4.0	-1.8	3.5
Mongolia	...	...	...	...	...	...	...	...	...
Taipei,China	1.8	0.6	5.5	-1.2	-2.4	-0.6	-8.9	-3.0	0.9
South Asia									
Bangladesh[a]	-0.4	3.4	...	...	...	...	...	...	...
Bhutan	...	...	...	...	...	...	...	...	...
India	7.2	4.5	9.6	6.9	5.2	1.3	-3.7	1.7	...
Maldives	-2.4 (2002)	4.6	3.9	...	0.3	2.1	-2.4	...	...
Nepal	1.4 (2001)	7.3	12.6	6.4	9.0	8.3	6.1	6.3	2.7
Sri Lanka	1.7	11.5	2.6	3.5	9.2	3.2	1.0	4.2	...
Southeast Asia									
Brunei Darussalam	...	...	...	...	...	...	...	...	...
Cambodia	...	...	...	...	...	...	...	...	...
Indonesia[b]	12.5	15.3	4.9	5.1	-1.6	5.4	4.4	7.9	4.6
Lao People's Democratic Republic	...	...	...	...	...	...	...	...	...
Malaysia	-1.8 (2001)	3.8 (2006)	12.3 (2011)	-0.4	-2.7	1.5	-7.4	-1.1	6.7
Myanmar	...	...	...	...	...	...	...	...	...
Philippines	5.8	11.4	5.9	1.1	1.6	2.7	-3.9	1.2	4.4
Singapore	10.0	9.6	4.7	0.5	-2.7	-3.3	-15.3	-6.9	7.0
Thailand	3.9	9.1	9.4	1.0	0.3	0.1	-4.1	-1.2	0.7
Viet Nam	-0.2	4.4	12.6	3.4	5.3	3.3	-0.6	-0.6	2.8
The Pacific									
Cook Islands	...	...	...	...	...	...	...	...	...
Fiji	...	...	...	...	...	...	...	...	...
Kiribati	...	...	...	...	...	...	...	...	...
Marshall Islands	...	...	...	...	...	...	...	...	...
Micronesia, Federated States of	...	...	...	...	...	...	...	...	...
Nauru	...	...	...	...	...	...	...	...	...
Palau	...	...	...	...	...	...	...	...	...
Papua New Guinea	...	...	...	...	...	...	...	...	...
Samoa	...	...	...	...	...	...	...	...	...
Solomon Islands	...	...	...	...	...	...	...	...	...
Timor-Leste	...	...	...	...	...	...	...	...	...
Tonga	...	...	...	...	...	...	...	...	...
Tuvalu	...	...	...	...	...	...	...	...	...
Vanuatu	...	...	...	...	...	...	...	...	...
Developed ADB Member Economies									
Australia	2.6	3.6	-0.1	2.0	1.2	2.1	1.0	1.5	1.0
Japan	0.0	1.6	-0.1	-0.9	1.3	1.1	-3.0	-3.5	2.3
New Zealand	5.2	3.4	2.3	0.2	2.2	1.1	-1.3	0.8	4.8

... = data not available, 0.0 = magnitude is less than half of unit employed, ADB = Asian Development Bank.

a   For agricultural and industrial products only.
b   Change of the wholesale price index for 2013 was estimated by rebasing January–October 2013 and 2012 data to 2005.

Source: Economy sources.

Table 2.3.5: Growth Rates of Gross Domestic Product Deflator
(%)

ADB Regional Member	2000	2005	2010	2012	2013	2014	2015	2016	2017
Developing ADB Member Economies									
Central and West Asia									
Afghanistan	...	11.6	14.3	9.3	3.5	-1.0	5.1	5.2	-0.5
Armenia	-1.4	3.2	7.8	-1.2	3.4	2.3	1.2	0.3	2.2
Azerbaijan	12.5	16.1	13.6	2.9	0.4	-1.3	-8.9	14.7	16.0
Georgia	4.7	7.9	8.5	1.1	-0.8	3.8	5.9	4.2	6.5
Kazakhstan	17.4	17.9	19.6	4.8	9.5	5.8	1.9	13.6	5.6
Kyrgyz Republic	27.2	7.1	10.0	8.7	3.2	8.4	3.4	6.1	4.6*
Pakistan	5.3 (2001)	7.8	10.9	6.0	7.0	7.4	4.1	0.4	4.0
Tajikistan	22.7	9.5	12.4	11.8	4.3	5.5	0.2	5.2	...
Turkmenistan	21.3	7.0	2.3	8.3	1.2	0.6	-4.9	-5.0	-1.6
Uzbekistan	47.1	21.4	16.5	14.9	14.2	11.7	9.2	9.6	20.8
East Asia									
China, People's Republic of	2.0	3.8	6.7	2.4	2.2	0.8	0.1	...	...
Hong Kong, China	-3.4	-0.2	0.3	3.5	1.8	2.9	3.6	1.7	2.9
Korea, Republic of	1.1	1.0	3.2	1.0	0.9	0.6	2.4	2.0	2.3
Mongolia	12.0	20.1	...	12.8	2.9	7.4	1.7	2.2	8.0
Taipei,China	7.6	-1.5	-1.5	0.5	1.5	1.7	3.3	0.9	-1.2
South Asia									
Bangladesh	1.9	5.1	7.1	8.2	7.2	5.7	5.9	6.7	6.3
Bhutan	3.7	5.9	6.0	9.2	5.9	7.6	3.4	7.9	...
India	3.6	4.2	9.0	7.9	6.2	3.3	2.1	3.5	3.1
Maldives	...	9.2	2.9	6.8	6.4	4.6	5.9	-0.7	...
Nepal	4.6	5.8	14.4	6.6	6.1	9.0	5.1	5.0	8.0
Sri Lanka	6.7	10.4	7.3	10.8	6.2	2.9	0.6	4.1	8.3
Southeast Asia									
Brunei Darussalam	29.0	18.8	5.3	1.2	-2.8	-1.8	-17.6	-9.2	5.0
Cambodia	-3.1	6.1	3.1	1.3	1.0	3.1	1.2	3.5	3.1
Indonesia	9.6	14.3	8.2	3.8	5.0	5.4	4.0	2.4	4.2
Lao People's Democratic Republic	21.8	7.8	3.1	...	6.5	5.7	2.3	3.0	1.5
Malaysia	-1.6 (2001)	4.0 (2006)	5.4 (2011)	1.0	0.2	2.5	-0.4	2.0	3.8
Myanmar	2.5	19.2	7.0	3.1	4.4	4.2	4.1	3.6	7.2
Philippines	5.7	5.8	4.2	2.0	2.0	3.2	-0.6	1.7	2.3
Singapore	3.7	2.2	0.0	0.6	-0.2	-0.3	3.6	0.0	0.9
Thailand	1.3	5.1	4.1	1.9	1.8	1.4	0.9	2.4	2.3
Viet Nam	3.4	9.0	12.1	10.9	4.8	3.7	-0.2	1.1	4.1
The Pacific									
Cook Islands	2.2	-2.6	6.2	-1.7	0.0	-2.4	3.3	-4.4	3.2
Fiji	-2.4	3.1 (2006)	2.5	3.3	2.3	4.1	3.7	4.9	...
Kiribati	3.2	-0.3 (2006)	1.2	-0.4	0.1	4.1	2.9	7.3	...
Marshall Islands	-3.0	2.0	1.5	3.2	0.2	-3.2	-1.5	6.1	9.3*
Micronesia, Federated States of	1.1	2.1	3.8	7.2	0.8	2.8	-5.5	4.7	0.5*
Nauru	...	1.6	-18.4	16.4	-32.8	-11.8	-8.4	5.7	3.6
Palau	1.7 (2001)	6.0	1.0	6.8	6.6	6.1	8.4	3.2	0.0
Papua New Guinea	13.1	7.9	9.9	-0.6	3.6	5.8	5.0	6.6	5.8*
Samoa	1.1	5.1	2.0	2.9	0.8	1.5	0.2	-0.1	3.0
Solomon Islands	6.9	8.8	1.8	4.2	6.8	1.9	4.0	2.9	...
Timor-Leste	7.9 (2001)	23.8	26.5	11.9	-4.8	-3.2	-36.5	-19.5	...
Tonga	7.4	6.7	3.7	2.3	0.6	1.1	2.7	0.4	3.0
Tuvalu	6.1 (2001)	0.7	2.5	0.8	2.0	4.9	4.6	7.7	1.7
Vanuatu	2.4	0.4	2.6	0.4	2.7	2.0	4.5	1.8	...
Developed ADB Member Economies									
Australia	2.6	3.7	1.2	1.8	-0.1	1.4	-0.7	-0.5	3.8
Japan	-1.4	-1.0	-1.9	-0.8	-0.3	1.7	2.1	0.3	-0.2
New Zealand	2.3	2.5	2.9	-0.3	3.3	2.3	0.2	1.8	3.4

... = data not available, 0.0 = magnitude is less than half of unit employed, * = preliminary, ADB = Asian Development Bank.

Source: Economy sources.

Money and Finance

Table 2.3.6:   Growth Rates of Money Supply[a]
(%)

ADB Regional Member	2000	2005	2010	2012	2013	2014	2015	2016	2017
Developing ADB Member Economies									
Central and West Asia									
Afghanistan	...	38.3 (2006)	39.3	14.3	7.1	6.0	3.7	5.5	10.4
Armenia	38.6	27.8	11.8	19.5	14.8	8.3	10.8	17.5	18.5
Azerbaijan[b]	21.8	22.3	24.3	20.7	15.0	11.8	-1.3	-1.9	9.0
Georgia[b]	39.2	27.9	30.1	11.4	24.5	13.8	19.3	20.2	14.8
Kazakhstan[b]	45.0	25.2	13.3	7.9	10.2	10.4	33.8	15.6	-1.7
Kyrgyz Republic	12.1	9.9	21.1	23.8	22.8	3.0	14.9	14.6	17.9
Pakistan	9.4	19.8	13.0	13.4	16.9	12.6	12.8	14.5	13.9
Tajikistan	43.3	62.9	17.6	22.8	18.6	3.5	12.2	56.7	36.6
Turkmenistan[b]	94.6	5.6	74.2	37.4	26.0	10.0	18.0	...	...
Uzbekistan	37.1	54.4	52.4	29.2	23.0	14.9	25.2	23.5	40.2
East Asia									
China, People's Republic of	12.3	16.5	19.7	14.4	13.6	11.0	13.3	11.3	8.2
Hong Kong, China	7.8	5.1	8.1	11.1	12.4	9.5	5.5	7.7	10.0
Korea, Republic of	5.2	7.0	6.0	4.8	4.6	8.1	8.2	7.1	5.1
Mongolia	17.6	34.6	62.5	18.7	24.2	12.5	-5.5	21.0	30.5
Taipei,China	6.5	6.6	5.5	3.5	5.8	6.1	5.8	3.6	3.6
South Asia									
Bangladesh	18.6	16.7	22.4	17.4	16.7	16.1	12.4	16.3	10.9
Bhutan	16.1	13.2	16.5	5.9	3.3	26.0	3.8	23.0	17.4
India[b]	16.8	21.1	16.1	13.6	13.4	10.9	13.4	6.9	9.5
Maldives	4.2	10.6	14.6	4.9	18.4	14.9	12.1	-0.2	5.2
Nepal	21.8	8.3	14.1	22.7	16.4	19.1	19.9	19.5	15.5
Sri Lanka	12.9	19.1	18.0	18.3	18.0	13.1	17.2	18.9	17.5
Southeast Asia									
Brunei Darussalam	1.9 (2002)	-4.5	4.8	0.9	1.5	3.2	-1.8	1.5	-0.4
Cambodia	26.9	16.1	20.0	20.9	14.6	29.9	14.7	17.9	23.8
Indonesia	15.6	16.3	15.4	15.0	12.8	11.9	9.0	10.0	8.3
Lao People's Democratic Republic	45.9	8.2	39.5	31.0	17.0	25.2	14.7	10.9	12.2
Malaysia[b]	5.1	8.3	6.8	9.0	7.3	7.0	2.7	3.1	4.7
Myanmar	42.2	27.3	42.5	32.6	31.4	21.0	30.7	17.4	20.5
Philippines[b]	4.6	16.8	10.0	9.4	31.8	11.2	9.4	12.8	11.9
Singapore	-2.0	6.2	8.6	7.2	4.3	3.3	1.5	8.0	3.2
Thailand	4.0	6.1	10.9	10.4	7.3	4.7	4.4	4.2	5.0
Viet Nam	56.2	29.7	33.3	18.5	18.8	17.7	16.2	18.4	15.0
The Pacific									
Cook Islands	4.8	-5.2	-2.8	19.2	-25.6	3.0	9.6	-2.7	12.3
Fiji[b]	-2.1	15.2	3.5	6.3	19.0	10.1	14.3	4.8	8.2
Kiribati	...	...	...	...	...	...	...	...	...
Marshall Islands	16.6	-0.8	9.4	-13.4	6.8	31.0	28.6	19.9	27.8
Micronesia, Federated States of	...	...	...	...	...	...	...	...	...
Nauru	...	...	...	...	...	...	...	...	...
Palau	...	...	...	...	...	...	...	...	...
Papua New Guinea[b]	5.4	29.5	11.4	11.0	6.7	3.4	8.0	10.9	-0.7
Samoa	16.4	15.6	6.4	-1.6	6.4	9.6	6.0	9.2	15.2
Solomon Islands[b]	0.4	46.1	13.3	17.4	12.4	5.1	15.5	13.4	3.5
Timor-Leste	155.5 (2001)	17.6	18.2	26.2	22.9	19.9	7.1	14.2	12.1
Tonga	8.3	12.1	5.1	-1.6	7.0	8.0	2.4	12.6	11.3
Tuvalu	...	...	...	...	...	...	...	...	...
Vanuatu	5.5	11.6	-6.0	-0.6	-5.6	8.6	11.4	10.6	...
Developed ADB Member Economies									
Australia[b]	7.3	8.9	4.5	9.1	6.5	7.0	6.7	5.8	7.8
Japan[c]	1.9	0.4	1.9	2.2	3.4	2.8	2.5	3.2	2.9
New Zealand[d]	6.6	7.8	3.2	6.0	5.0	6.3	8.1	6.4	7.3

... = data not available, ADB = Asian Development Bank.

a   Data are based on M2 unless otherwise stated.
b   Refers to M3.
c   Refers to M3, except for 2000 (M2).
d   Refers to M3, except for 2017 (M2).

Source: Economy sources.

Table 2.3.7:   Money Supply[a]
(% of GDP)

ADB Regional Member	2000	2005	2010	2012	2013	2014	2015	2016	2017
Developing ADB Member Economies									
Central and West Asia									
Afghanistan	11.0 (2002)	17.9	30.3	29.3	28.5	29.6	29.7	28.8	29.8
Armenia	14.7	16.3	26.3	33.7	33.9	34.7	36.8	43.0	46.4
Azerbaijan[b]	10.8	14.7	24.8	30.6	33.2	36.5	39.1	34.6	32.5
Georgia[b]	10.1	16.9	29.9	30.2	36.6	38.4	42.0	47.2	48.4
Kazakhstan[b]	15.3	27.2	38.9	33.9	32.2	32.3	41.9	42.2	37.7
Kyrgyz Republic	11.3	21.1	31.4	31.7	34.0	31.1	33.3	34.4	37.1
Pakistan	33.0	41.6	37.7	37.0	38.8	38.9	40.2	43.5	45.0
Tajikistan	5.8	11.2	12.0	13.1	13.9	12.8	13.5	18.8	22.9
Turkmenistan[b]	19.4	10.5	17.3	36.9	41.7	41.4	48.2	...	...
Uzbekistan	12.2	14.4	22.4	24.4	24.3	23.2	24.6	26.1	28.8
East Asia									
China, People's Republic of	134.2	158.0	175.7	180.3	185.9	190.7	202.1	208.5	202.7
Hong Kong, China	272.9	310.1	401.7	439.4	470.3	487.2	484.4	502.2	516.9
Korea, Republic of	111.4	111.1	131.2	133.3	134.4	139.8	143.7	146.6	146.2
Mongolia	21.1	37.5	48.0	45.6	49.3	47.8	43.4	50.8	58.4
Taipei,China	182.6	201.9	219.2	228.6	233.2	234.0	237.8	240.8	245.4
South Asia									
Bangladesh	31.5	40.9	45.5	49.0	50.3	52.1	52.0	52.9	51.4
Bhutan	50.8	57.8	70.5	57.8	55.2	61.4	57.7	63.0	65.6
India[b]	60.3	73.6	83.6	84.3	84.7	84.6	86.9	83.9	83.6
Maldives	41.1	45.2	47.9	45.1	46.8	47.8	49.5	46.9	44.7
Nepal	49.0	51.0	60.3	74.0	77.6	79.7	88.2	99.9	99.7
Sri Lanka	37.6	41.7	28.3	29.7	31.9	33.4	37.1	40.5	42.6
Southeast Asia									
Brunei Darussalam	77.8 (2001)	57.8	67.3	58.7	62.6	67.5	80.8	92.6	86.7
Cambodia	13.0	19.5	41.4	50.5	53.3	62.7	66.5	70.9	79.5
Indonesia	53.8	43.4	36.0	38.4	39.1	39.5	39.4	40.3	39.9
Lao People's Democratic Republic	17.4	18.7	38.0	43.8	44.5	49.0	51.2	51.5	53.1
Malaysia[b]	128.6	123.8	132.2	139.3	142.6	140.4	137.7	133.6	127.2
Myanmar	32.7	21.6	23.6	31.7	36.8	39.5	46.4	49.7	52.3
Philippines[b]	39.9	41.8	49.8	49.7	60.0	61.0	63.3	65.6	67.3
Singapore	103.4	103.6	125.0	130.9	130.2	129.8	124.4	131.3	129.7
Thailand	122.4	104.1	109.0	121.1	124.4	127.0	127.7	125.9	124.3
Viet Nam	50.5	75.6	129.3	114.1	122.8	131.5	143.6	158.3	163.7
The Pacific									
Cook Islands	42.0	44.0	62.6	61.4	46.3	46.1	47.0	45.3	48.3
Fiji[b]	42.4	58.9	67.6	67.7	74.2	74.7	78.7	77.1	76.7
Kiribati	...	...	...	...	...	...	...	...	...
Marshall Islands	54.6	52.9	60.7	45.6	47.2	64.2	84.3	93.4	105.4
Micronesia, Federated States of	...	...	...	...	...	...	...	...	...
Nauru	...	...	...	...	...	...	...	...	...
Palau	...	...	...	...	...	...	...	...	...
Papua New Guinea[b]	31.2	33.6	34.0	38.2	37.9	33.1	32.5	33.1	30.1
Samoa	38.2	41.1	45.0	38.3	40.2	42.6	43.8	45.0	50.5
Solomon Islands[b]	31.7	40.5	44.0	50.1	46.5	46.9	51.4	54.6	52.3
Timor-Leste	4.6	4.2	7.4	6.1	8.9	14.8	20.7	29.1	...
Tonga	29.2	39.0	40.9	36.8	40.4	42.3	41.1	44.0	46.3
Tuvalu	...	...	...	...	...	...	...	...	...
Vanuatu	89.7	98.6	83.3	78.6	70.9	73.7	78.5	82.5	...
Developed ADB Member Economies									
Australia[b]	65.4	73.6	94.7	97.8	101.7	104.5	109.8	113.5	115.5
Japan[c]	123.4	198.7	218.8	232.1	236.0	237.4	235.2	239.7	243.2
New Zealand[d]	86.3	98.7	110.5	116.6	114.5	116.9	120.1	100.8	...

... = data not available, ADB = Asian Development Bank, GDP = gross domestic product.

a   Refers to M2, unless otherwise stated.
b   Refers to M3.
c   Refers to M3, except for 2000 (M2).
d   Refers to M3 until 2015.

Source: Economy sources.

Money and Finance

Table 2.3.8:   Interest Rates on Savings and Time Deposits
(% per annum, period averages)

ADB Regional Member	Savings Deposits				Time Deposits[a]			
	2000	2005	2010	2017	2000	2005	2010	2017
Developing ADB Member Economies								
Central and West Asia								
Afghanistan	...	4.26 (2006)	5.10	1.56	...	4.72 (2006)	8.94	2.11
Armenia	...	...	...	...	20.72	6.66	10.70	9.64
Azerbaijan	...	...	...	...	10.40	9.38	10.96	12.13
Georgia[b]	10.98	6.79	8.71	4.02	9.85	10.23	11.60	6.06
Kazakhstan[b]	...	...	...	...	7.53	10.29	9.84	11.21
Kyrgyz Republic[c]	...	...	...	...	28.07	9.78	11.47	10.84
Pakistan[b]	5.75	1.24	5.02	3.50	7.37	4.21	7.21	4.30
Tajikistan[d]	5.28 (2002)	3.63	3.83	1.40	14.84 (2002)	20.16	17.78	14.60
Turkmenistan	...	...	...	...	...	...	...	...
Uzbekistan	...	...	...	...	...	...	...	17.95
East Asia								
China, People's Republic of	0.99	0.72	0.36	0.35	2.25	2.25	2.33	1.50
Hong Kong, China	4.50	0.97	0.01	0.01	5.40	1.73	0.16	0.15
Korea, Republic of	7.08	3.57	3.18	1.52	7.94	3.72	3.86	1.67
Mongolia	13.80	12.60	10.70	13.00	...	...	...	...
Taipei,China	3.50	0.55	0.24	0.23	4.98	1.77	1.03	0.77
South Asia								
Bangladesh	5.81	4.19	4.88	3.16	8.97	8.31	9.00	6.43
Bhutan[e]	6.00	4.50	4.75	5.50	9.50	6.50	6.75	7.00
India	4.00	3.50	3.50	4.00 (2016)	7.10	5.32	7.50	5.49 (2016)
Maldives[f]	5.50	2.25	2.25	1.48	6.50	4.50	3.75	2.66
Nepal	5.25	3.38	7.00	4.01	6.88	3.63	8.13	10.39
Sri Lanka	8.40	5.00	5.00	4.00	15.00	9.00	8.50	11.00
Southeast Asia								
Brunei Darussalam	...	1.01	0.47	0.29	...	1.61	0.75	0.70
Cambodia	6.13	2.08	1.18	1.39	7.20	6.83	6.58	5.90
Indonesia	8.86	4.32	3.92	1.47	12.17	10.95	7.88	6.79
Lao People's Democratic Republic	...	...	...	...	...	...	...	...
Malaysia	2.72	1.41	0.94	0.96	4.24	3.70	2.81	3.09
Myanmar	...	...	...	...	...	...	...	...
Philippines[g]	7.40	3.80	1.60	0.69	10.50	6.00	2.07	2.82
Singapore	1.30	0.24	0.14	0.16	2.45	0.76	0.48	0.33
Thailand	2.50	1.88	0.50	0.47	3.50	3.00	1.55	1.40
Viet Nam	0.20	3.00	3.00	0.67 (2015)	6.24	8.40	11.50	6.32 (2015)
The Pacific								
Cook Islands	...	...	...	...	...	...	...	...
Fiji	...	...	...	...	...	...	...	...
Kiribati	...	...	...	...	...	...	...	...
Marshall Islands	...	...	...	...	...	...	...	...
Micronesia, Federated States of	...	...	...	...	...	...	...	...
Nauru	...	...	...	...	...	...	...	...
Palau	...	...	...	...	...	...	...	...
Papua New Guinea	3.88	1.80	1.00	...	9.38	1.30	4.80	...
Samoa	3.00	2.75	0.88	1.00	7.35	6.38	2.25	2.90
Solomon Islands	...	...	...	...	...	...	...	...
Timor-Leste	0.20 (2002)	0.75	0.75	0.27	–	1.28	1.33	0.71
Tonga	3.15	3.36	1.51	2.35	5.13	5.93	3.45	5.36
Tuvalu	...	...	...	...	...	...	...	...
Vanuatu	...	...	...	...	...	...	...	...
Developed ADB Member Economies								
Australia	...	5.40	4.50	1.65	5.90	4.55	6.00	2.25
Japan[h]	0.09	0.01	0.04	0.00	0.24	0.03	0.10	0.03
New Zealand[i]	...	...	...	...	6.49	6.90	4.72	3.30

... = data not available, – = magnitude equals zero, 0.00 = magnitude is less than half of unit employed, ADB = Asian Development Bank.

a   Refers to interest rate on time deposits of 12 months, unless otherwise indicated.
b   Refers to interest rate on time deposits of over 12 months.
c   Rates for time deposits refer to interest rates of commercial banks in national currency for 6–12 months.
d   Refers to savings and time deposits as of end of period.
e   Rates for time deposits refer to rates for fixed deposits of 1 year to less than 3 years.
f   Refers to interest rate on time deposits of 2–3 years.
g   Rates for time deposits refer to rates charged on interest-bearing deposits with maturities of over 1 year.
h   Refers to time deposits from 12 months to less than 2 years, calculated as the arithmetic average of the monthly figures.
i   Refers to interest rate on time deposits of 6 months.

Sources: Economy sources. For the People's Republic of China: CEIC database (accessed 30 July 2018).

Table 2.3.9: Yields on Short-Term Treasury Bills and Lending Interest Rates
(% per annum, period averages)

ADB Regional Member	Yields on Short-Term Treasury Bills[a]				Lending Interest Rates			
	2000	2005	2010	2017	2000	2005	2010	2017
Developing ADB Member Economies								
Central and West Asia								
Afghanistan	...	...	...	...	...	18.0 (2006)	15.6	14.8
Armenia[b]	20.6 (2001)	4.1	10.6	6.7	31.6	18.0	19.2	14.4
Azerbaijan	16.7	7.5	1.8	14.3	19.7	17.0	20.7	16.5
Georgia	29.9 (2001)	12.6	9.6	7.3	...	17.6	15.8	11.5
Kazakhstan	11.6	3.3	...	...	...	...	...	...
Kyrgyz Republic	32.3	4.4	10.4	5.0	57.0	21.7	23.7	19.8
Pakistan[c]	8.4	7.2	12.5	6.0	...	9.1	14.0	8.2
Tajikistan[d]	...	...	6.7	1.0	1.6	23.3	23.4	29.6
Turkmenistan	...	...	...	...	...	...	...	...
Uzbekistan	...	...	...	...	...	...	...	...
East Asia								
China, People's Republic of[e]	2.6	1.9	2.6	...	5.9	5.6	5.8	4.4
Hong Kong, China	5.7	3.7	0.3	0.7	9.5	7.8	5.0	5.0
Korea, Republic of[f]	7.1	3.6	2.7	1.4	8.5	5.6	5.5	3.5
Mongolia[g]	...	13.7	12.9 (2012)	15.0	37.0	30.6	20.1	20.0
Taipei,China[h]	...	1.3	0.3	0.3	7.7	3.8	2.7	2.6
South Asia								
Bangladesh[d]	6.3	6.7	2.2	3.8	12.8	10.6	12.2	9.5
Bhutan[d]	7.3	3.5	2.0	0.7	16.0	14.5	13.9	14.3
India[d,i]	9.0	5.7	6.2	6.2	12.3	10.8	8.3	9.5
Maldives[j]	...	5.0 (2006)	4.9	3.5	13.0	13.0	10.4	10.2
Nepal[d]	5.3	3.0	6.9	1.6	9.5	8.1	8.0	...
Sri Lanka[k]	13.7 (2001)	9.0	8.6	10.1	14.3 (2001)	10.8	10.2	11.6
Southeast Asia								
Brunei Darussalam	...	...	...	...	5.5	5.5	5.5	5.5
Cambodia	...	...	...	...	...	...	...	...
Indonesia	...	...	...	...	18.5	14.1	13.3	11.1
Lao People's Democratic Republic[l]	29.9	18.6	8.0	...	32.0	26.8	22.6	...
Malaysia	2.9	2.5	2.6	2.8 (2016)	7.7	6.0	5.0	4.6
Myanmar	...	...	...	...	15.3	15.0	17.0	13.0
Philippines[d]	9.9	6.1	3.5	2.1	10.9	10.2	7.7	5.6
Singapore	2.2	2.1	0.3	...	5.8	5.3	5.4	5.3
Thailand[d]	2.3 (2001)	2.7	1.4	1.3	7.8	4.7	4.3	4.4
Viet Nam[m]	5.4	6.1	11.1	...	10.6	11.0	13.1	7.4
The Pacific								
Cook Islands	...	...	...	...	...	...	...	...
Fiji	3.5	1.9	3.4	1.4	8.4	6.8	7.5	5.7
Kiribati	...	...	...	...	...	...	...	...
Marshall Islands	...	...	...	...	...	...	...	...
Micronesia, Federated States of	...	...	...	...	15.3	16.4	15.1	16.1
Nauru	...	...	...	...	...	...	...	...
Palau	...	...	...	...	...	...	...	...
Papua New Guinea[n]	17.0	3.8	4.6	4.7	17.5	11.5	10.4	8.4
Samoa	...	...	...	...	11.6 (2001)	11.4	10.7	8.8
Solomon Islands	7.0	4.5	3.7	0.5	10.3	9.3	14.4	10.7
Timor-Leste	...	...	...	...	17.4 (2002)	16.7	11.0	13.3
Tonga	...	...	...	...	11.3	11.4	11.5	7.9
Tuvalu	...	...	...	...	...	...	...	...
Vanuatu	...	...	...	...	9.9	7.5	5.5	3.2
Developed ADB Member Economies								
Australia[o]	6.0	...	4.4	...	7.7	7.3	7.3	5.2
Japan	0.2	0.0	0.1	-0.2	2.1	1.7	1.6	1.0
New Zealand	6.4	6.5	2.8	1.8	7.8	7.8	6.3	5.0 (2016)

... = data not available, 0.0 = magnitude is less than half of unit employed, ADB = Asian Development Bank.

a Refers to 3-month Treasury bills, unless otherwise indicated.
b Refers to average yield on 9-month to 12-month Treasury bills since March 2001.
c Refers to weighted average yield on 6-month Treasury securities.
d Refers to 91-day Treasury bills.
e Refers to 3-month Treasury bonds trading rate.
f Refers to 91-day certificates of deposit.
g Refers to weighted average rate on Treasury bills of all maturities. From December 2012 onward, refers to yield on 12-week Treasury bills.
h Refers to prime lending rates.
i Figures are for fiscal year ending March.
j Refers to rate on 28-day Treasury bills.
k Refers to weighted average rate on the last monthly issuance of 364-day Treasury bills since December 2001.
l Refers to weighted average auction rate for 12-month Treasury bills.
m Refers to average monthly yield on 360-day Treasury bills sold at auction.
n Refers to rate on 182-day Treasury bills.
o Refers to estimated closing yield in the secondary market on 13-week Treasury notes.

Sources: International Monetary Fund. International Financial Statistics. http://data.imf.org/ (accessed 27 July 2018); and Organisation for Economic Co-operation and Development. Main Economic Indicators. http://dx.doi.org/10.1787/data-00043-en (accessed 31 July 2018). For Taipei,China; Bangladesh; Bhutan; and India: Economy sources.

Table 2.3.10:   Domestic Credit Provided by the Banking Sector and Bank Nonperforming Loans

ADB Regional Member	Domestic Credit Provided by the Banking Sector[a] (% of GDP)				Bank Nonperforming Loans[b] (% of total gross loans)	
	2000	2005	2010	2017	2010	2017
Developing ADB Member Economies						
Central and West Asia						
Afghanistan	...	-4.8 (2006)	4.8	-2.4	49.9	12.2
Armenia	11.5	8.8	27.8	58.2	3.0	5.4
Azerbaijan	9.6	11.2	23.0	29.5	...	...
Georgia	21.5	21.6	35.5	61.6	5.9	2.8
Kazakhstan	12.3	39.0	45.4	41.9	20.9	12.7
Kyrgyz Republic	12.2	13.8	12.5	20.5	14.8	...
Pakistan	41.6	46.5	46.2	53.9	14.7	8.4
Tajikistan	17.9	13.0	7.6	15.8	7.4	19.1 (2015)
Turkmenistan	...	...	...	...	...	...
Uzbekistan	...	...	...	...	1.0	0.4
East Asia						
China, People's Republic of	118.4	132.6	142.2	215.2	1.1	1.7 (2015)
Hong Kong, China	134.0	139.8	195.4	210.6 (2016)	0.8	0.7
Korea, Republic of	70.9	125.5	151.0	170.1	0.6	0.5 (2014)
Mongolia	9.0	26.6	25.7	65.3	...	...
Taipei,China	1.8	1.9	0.9	...	0.6	0.3
South Asia						
Bangladesh	30.2	47.7	57.4	63.7	5.8 (2011)	8.4 (2015)
Bhutan	2.9	21.8	45.6	53.5 (2016)	5.2	8.4
India	52.8	60.2	74.3	75.0 (2016)	2.4	10.0
Maldives	34.8	47.0	76.9	68.5	20.9 (2012)	10.5
Nepal	40.8	42.2	67.4	87.1	...	1.7
Sri Lanka	43.7	43.5	35.5	71.9 (2016)	3.8 (2011)	2.5
Southeast Asia						
Brunei Darussalam	38.6	10.4	22.7	28.6	6.9	3.5
Cambodia	6.4	7.2	22.7	74.4	3.1	2.1
Indonesia	60.7	46.2	34.2	47.0	2.5	2.6
Lao People's Democratic Republic	9.0	8.1	26.7	...	...	...
Malaysia	138.4	117.7	123.3	145.3 (2016)	3.4	1.5
Myanmar	31.2	23.1	25.2	41.1	...	...
Philippines	58.3	47.2	49.2	66.3	3.4	1.6
Singapore	76.7	61.2	80.8	140.8	1.4	1.4
Thailand	134.3	111.0	133.4	164.7	3.9	3.1
Viet Nam	35.1	65.4	124.7	141.8	2.1	2.3
The Pacific						
Cook Islands	...	...	...	...	...	...
Fiji	37.9	111.6	132.3	120.9	4.4	2.4
Kiribati	...	...	...	...	...	...
Marshall Islands	...	...	...	...	...	...
Micronesia, Federated States of	-42.3	-24.5	-14.7	...	...	...
Nauru	...	...	...	...	...	...
Palau	...	...	...	...	...	...
Papua New Guinea	28.2	22.2	23.7	44.3	1.9	3.1 (2015)
Samoa	18.3	31.8	63.4	78.7	...	4.5
Solomon Islands	26.5	29.4	26.8	28.5	9.3	4.2
Timor-Leste	-7.6 (2002)	-2.5	-5.5	-7.2	...	...
Tonga	38.8	48.3	39.9	32.6	14.4 (2012)	3.6
Tuvalu	...	...	...	...	...	...
Vanuatu	35.6	44.5	63.7	58.0	4.8	14.0
Developed ADB Member Economies						
Australia	93.4	113.4	154.0	177.1	2.1	0.9
Japan	295.0	296.8	313.8	345.1 (2016)	2.5	1.2
New Zealand	108.0	126.4	150.7	...	...	...

... = data not available, ADB = Asian Development Bank, GDP = gross domestic product.

a Domestic credit provided by the financial sector includes all credit to various sectors on a gross basis, with the exception of credit to the central government, which is net. The financial sector includes monetary authorities and deposit money banks, as well as other financial corporations where data are available (including corporations that do not accept transferable deposits, but do incur such liabilities as time and savings deposits). Examples of other financial corporations are finance and leasing companies, money lenders, insurance corporations, pension funds, and foreign exchange companies.
b Bank nonperforming loans to total gross loans are the value of nonperforming loans divided by the total value of the loan portfolio (including nonperforming loans before the deduction of specific loan-loss provisions). The loan amount recorded as nonperforming should be the gross value of the loan as recorded on the balance sheet, not just the amount that is overdue.

Sources: World Bank. World Development Indicators Online. http://data.worldbank.org/ (accessed 6 July 2018). For Taipei,China: Central bank of Taipei,China. http://www.cbc.gov.tw (accessed 8 August 2018).

Table 2.3.11: Growth Rates of Stock Market Price Index[a]
(%)

ADB Regional Member	2000	2005	2010	2012	2013	2014	2015	2016	2017
Developing ADB Member Economies									
Central and West Asia									
Afghanistan	...	...	...	...	...	...	...	...	...
Armenia	...	...	...	...	...	...	...	...	...
Azerbaijan	...	...	...	...	...	...	...	...	...
Georgia	...	...	...	...	...	...	...	...	...
Kazakhstan	...	...	...	...	...	...	...	...	...
Kyrgyz Republic	...	...	...	...	...	...	...	...	...
Pakistan[b]	7.0	53.7	28.2	49.0	49.4	27.2	2.1	45.7	...
Tajikistan	...	...	...	...	...	...	...	...	...
Turkmenistan	...	...	...	...	...	...	...	...	...
Uzbekistan	...	...	...	...	...	...	...	...	...
East Asia									
China, People's Republic of	37.3	-22.1	3.4	-16.8	-1.1	1.5	66.0	-19.0	6.7
Hong Kong, China	26.5	11.1	19.3	-4.4	10.4	2.7	4.8	-12.0	22.3
Korea, Republic of	-8.7	28.5	23.6	-2.6	1.5	1.1	1.4	-1.2	16.5
Mongolia	...	18.7	88.7	-11.0	-21.0	4.2	-14.6	-14.0	33.5
Taipei,China	5.7	1.0	23.1	-8.3	8.2	11.1	-0.4	-2.2	16.5
South Asia									
Bangladesh[b]	31.8	-14.9	82.8	-19.7	1.1	14.0	-4.8	8.8	24.0
Bhutan	...	...	...	...	...	...	...	...	...
India	11.2	32.6	29.8	-2.5	11.4	25.2	10.9	-3.6	8.6
Maldives	...	51.8	-20.4	-6.9	-5.3	-4.8	8.9	4.8	7.4
Nepal	...	...	...	...	...	...	...	...	...
Sri Lanka[b]	...	27.6	96.0	-7.1	4.8	23.4	-5.5	-9.7	...
Southeast Asia									
Brunei Darussalam	...	...	...	...	...	...	...	...	...
Cambodia	...	...	...	...	...	...	...	...	...
Indonesia[b]	-38.5	16.2	46.1	12.9	-1.0	22.3	-12.1	15.3	20.0
Lao People's Democratic Republic	...	...	...	...	...	...	...	...	...
Malaysia	21.4	6.4	27.1	6.5	8.7	5.5	-6.1	-3.8	...
Myanmar	...	...	...	...	...	...	...	...	...
Philippines	-6.3	17.5	43.1	14.7	16.0	1.8	5.5	0.9	8.0
Singapore	8.6	16.7	30.3	0.7	7.6	1.2	-2.5	-11.6	10.3
Thailand	-18.7	4.2	45.6	17.3	21.3	-0.2	0.2	-2.1	12.7
Viet Nam[b]	...	8.3	12.2	-4.2	22.1	8.1	6.1	14.8	...
The Pacific									
Cook Islands	...	...	...	...	...	...	...	...	...
Fiji	...	13.5	-11.1	-0.0	2.6	0.5	20.8	27.6	22.4
Kiribati	...	...	...	...	...	...	...	...	...
Marshall Islands	...	...	...	...	...	...	...	...	...
Micronesia, Federated States of	...	...	...	...	...	...	...	...	...
Nauru	...	...	...	...	...	...	...	...	...
Palau	...	...	...	...	...	...	...	...	...
Papua New Guinea	...	52.5	26.2	-28.0	-15.3	-12.3	-6.3	...	...
Samoa	...	...	...	...	...	...	...	...	...
Solomon Islands	...	...	...	...	...	...	...	...	...
Timor-Leste	...	...	...	...	...	...	...	...	...
Tonga	...	...	...	...	...	...	...	...	...
Tuvalu	...	...	...	...	...	...	...	...	...
Vanuatu	...	...	...	...	...	...	...	...	...
Developed ADB Member Economies									
Australia[b]	1.7	17.6	-2.6	14.6	15.1	1.1	-2.1	7.0	7.0
Japan	11.6	13.5	2.0	-6.5	46.0	12.6	22.7	-12.6	...
New Zealand	2.3	19.4	9.7	6.9	25.5	14.1	12.7	17.4	11.1

... = data not available, -0.0 = magnitude is less than half of unit employed, ADB = Asian Development Bank.

a Refers to growth rates of stock market prices (period average), unless otherwise indicated.
b Refers to growth rates of end-of-period stock market prices.

Sources: International Monetary Fund. 2018. International Financial Statistics. http://data.imf.org/IFS (accessed 8 August 2018). For Taipei,China: Annual statistics from the stock exchange corporation in Taipei,China. http://www.twse.com.tw/en/statistics/statisticsList?type=07&subType=240 (accessed 9 July 2018).

Table 2.3.12:   Stock Market Capitalization

ADB Regional Member	Stock Market Capitalization ($ million)				Stock Market Capitalization (% of GDP)			
	2000	2005	2010	2017	2000	2005	2010	2017
Developing ADB Member Economies								
Central and West Asia								
Afghanistan	...	...	...	...	...	...	...	...
Armenia	...	...	...	...	...	...	...	...
Azerbaijan	...	...	...	...	...	...	...	...
Georgia	...	...	...	...	...	...	...	...
Kazakhstan	802	10,529	26,673	45,558	4.4	18.4	18.0	28.6
Kyrgyz Republic	...	...	...	...	...	...	...	...
Pakistan	6,625	45,317	38,007	91,864 (2016)	9.0	41.4	21.4	33.0 (2016)
Tajikistan	...	...	...	...	...	...	...	...
Turkmenistan	...	...	...	...	...	...	...	...
Uzbekistan	...	...	...	...	...	...	...	...
East Asia								
China, People's Republic of	...	401,852	4,027,840	8,711,267	...	17.6	66.0	71.2
Hong Kong, China	623,398	1,054,999	2,711,316	4,350,515	363.1	581.0	1,185.9	1,274.1
Korea, Republic of	171,262	718,011	1,091,911	1,771,768	30.5	79.9	99.8	115.7
Mongolia	...	...	...	...	...	...	...	...
Taipei,China	262,295	485,825	752,335	1,045,727	79.1	129.3	168.6	182.6
South Asia								
Bangladesh	2,192	3,300	41,617	86,179	4.1	4.8	36.1	34.5
Bhutan	53	101	219	338 (2016)	12.0	12.4	13.8	15.3 (2016)
India	...	553,074	1,631,830	2,331,567	...	68.4	98.5	89.8
Maldives	...	...	...	...	...	...	...	...
Nepal	...	...	...	...	...	...	...	...
Sri Lanka	1,074	5,720	19,924	18,960	6.5	23.4	35.1	21.7
Southeast Asia								
Brunei Darussalam	...	...	...	...	...	...	...	...
Cambodia	...	...	...	...	...	...	...	...
Indonesia	26,813	81,428	360,388	520,687	16.2	28.5	47.7	51.3
Lao People's Democratic Republic	...	...	...	...	...	...	...	...
Malaysia	113,156	180,518	408,689	455,772	120.6	125.8	160.3	144.9
Myanmar	...	...	...	...	...	...	...	...
Philippines	25,981	39,799	157,321	290,401	32.1	38.6	78.8	92.6
Singapore	152,826	257,340	647,226	787,255	159.5	202.0	273.8	243.0
Thailand	29,217	123,885	277,732	548,795	23.1	65.4	81.4	120.6
Viet Nam	...	...	30,115	116,657	...	...	26.0	52.1
The Pacific								
Cook Islands	...	...	...	...	...	...	...	...
Fiji	...	...	...	...	...	...	...	...
Kiribati	...	...	...	...	...	...	...	...
Marshall Islands	...	...	...	...	...	...	...	...
Micronesia, Federated States of	...	...	...	...	...	...	...	...
Nauru	...	...	...	...	...	...	...	...
Palau	...	...	...	...	...	...	...	...
Papua New Guinea	...	6,138	11,027	...	...	126.2	77.4	...
Samoa	...	...	...	...	...	...	...	...
Solomon Islands	...	...	...	...	...	...	...	...
Timor-Leste	...	...	...	...	...	...	...	...
Tonga	...	...	...	...	...	...	...	...
Tuvalu	...	...	...	...	...	...	...	...
Vanuatu	...	...	...	...	...	...	...	...
Developed ADB Member Economies								
Australia	372,794	804,015	1,454,491	1,508,463	89.8	116.1	127.1	114.0
Japan	3,157,222	4,572,901	3,827,774	6,222,825	64.6	96.2	67.2	127.7
New Zealand	18,613	40,592	43,516	94,691	35.4	35.4	29.7	46.0

... = data not available, $ = United States dollars, ADB = Asian Development Bank, GDP = gross domestic product.

Sources: World Bank. World Development Indicators Online. http://databank.worldbank.org/data (accessed 1 July 2018). For Bhutan and Taipei,China: Asian Development Bank estimates using data from economy sources.

Table 2.3.13:   Official Exchange Rates
(local currency units per $, period averages)

ADB Regional Member	2000	2005	2010	2012	2013	2014	2015	2016	2017
Developing ADB Member Economies									
Central and West Asia									
Afghanistan	47.36	49.49	46.45	50.92	55.38	57.25	61.14	67.87	68.03
Armenia	539.53	457.69	373.66	401.76	409.63	415.92	477.92	480.49	482.72
Azerbaijan	0.89	0.95	0.80	0.79	0.78	0.78	1.02	1.60	1.72
Georgia	1.98	1.81	1.78	1.65	1.66	1.77	2.27	2.37	2.51
Kazakhstan	142.13	132.88	147.36	149.11	152.13	179.19	221.73	342.16	326.00
Kyrgyz Republic	47.70	41.01	45.96	47.00	48.44	53.65	64.46	69.91	68.87
Pakistan	53.65	59.51	85.19	93.40	101.63	101.10	102.77	104.77	105.46
Tajikistan	2.08	3.12	4.38	4.74	4.76	4.94	6.16	7.84	8.55
Turkmenistan	1.04	1.04	2.85	2.85	2.85	2.85	3.50	3.50	3.50
Uzbekistan[a]	236.61	1,106.10	1,578.42	1,897.56	2,094.99	2,310.95	2,567.99	2,965.25	5,113.88
East Asia									
China, People's Republic of	8.28	8.19	6.77	6.31	6.20	6.14	6.23	6.64	6.76
Hong Kong, China	7.79	7.78	7.77	7.76	7.76	7.75	7.75	7.76	7.79
Korea, Republic of	1,130.96	1,024.12	1,156.06	1,126.47	1,094.85	1,052.96	1,131.16	1,160.43	1,130.42
Mongolia	1,076.67	1,205.25	1,357.06	1,357.58	1,523.93	1,817.94	1,970.31	2,140.29	2,439.78
Taipei,China	31.23	32.17	31.64	29.61	29.77	30.37	31.90	32.32	30.44
South Asia									
Bangladesh	52.14	64.33	69.65	81.86	78.10	77.64	77.95	78.65	80.44
Bhutan	44.94	44.10	45.73	53.44	58.60	61.03	64.15	67.20	65.12
India	44.94	44.10	45.73	53.44	58.60	61.03	64.15	67.20	65.12
Maldives	11.77	12.80	12.80	15.36	15.37	15.38	15.37	15.37	15.39
Nepal	71.09	71.37	73.26	85.20	92.99	97.55	102.41	107.38	104.51
Sri Lanka	77.01	100.50	113.06	127.60	129.07	130.56	135.86	145.58	152.45
Southeast Asia									
Brunei Darussalam	1.72	1.66	1.36	1.25	1.25	1.27	1.37	1.38	1.38
Cambodia	3,840.75	4,092.50	4,184.92	4,033.00	4,027.25	4,037.50	4,067.75	4,058.69	4,050.58
Indonesia	8,421.78	9,704.74	9,090.43	9,386.63	10,461.24	11,865.21	13,389.41	13,308.33	13,380.87
Lao People's Democratic Republic	7,887.64	10,655.17	8,258.77	8,007.76	7,860.14	8,048.96	8,147.91	8,179.27	8,351.53
Malaysia	3.80	3.79	3.22	3.09	3.15	3.27	3.91	4.15	4.30
Myanmar[b]	6.52	5.82	5.63	640.65	933.57	984.35	1,162.62	1,234.87	1,360.36
Philippines	44.19	55.09	45.11	42.23	42.45	44.40	45.50	47.49	50.40
Singapore	1.72	1.66	1.36	1.25	1.25	1.27	1.37	1.38	1.38
Thailand	40.11	40.22	31.69	31.08	30.73	32.48	34.25	35.30	33.94
Viet Nam	14,167.75	15,858.92	18,612.92	20,828.00	20,933.42	21,148.00	21,697.57	21,935.00	22,370.09
The Pacific									
Cook Islands	2.20	1.42	1.39	1.23	1.22	1.21	1.43	1.44	1.41
Fiji	2.13	1.69	1.92	1.79	1.84	1.89	2.10	2.09	2.07
Kiribati	1.72	1.31	1.09	0.97	1.04	1.11	1.33	1.35	1.30
Marshall Islands[c]	1.00	1.00	1.00	1.00	1.00	1.00	1.00	1.00	1.00
Micronesia, Federated States of[c]	1.00	1.00	1.00	1.00	1.00	1.00	1.00	1.00	1.00
Nauru	1.72	1.31	1.09	0.97	1.04	1.11	1.33	1.35	1.30
Palau[c]	1.00	1.00	1.00	1.00	1.00	1.00	1.00	1.00	1.00
Papua New Guinea	2.78	3.10	2.72	2.08	2.24	2.46	2.77	3.13	3.19
Samoa	3.29	2.71	2.48	2.29	2.31	2.33	2.56	2.56	2.53
Solomon Islands	5.09	7.53	8.06	7.36	7.30	7.38	7.91	7.95	7.89
Timor-Leste[c]	1.00	1.00	1.00	1.00	1.00	1.00	1.00	1.00	1.00
Tonga	1.76	1.94	1.91	1.72	1.77	1.85	2.11	2.22	2.21
Tuvalu	1.72	1.31	1.09	0.97	1.04	1.11	1.33	1.35	1.30
Vanuatu	137.64	109.25	96.91	92.64	94.54	97.07	108.99	108.48	106.18
Developed ADB Member Economies									
Australia	1.72	1.31	1.09	0.97	1.04	1.11	1.33	1.35	1.30
Japan	107.77	110.22	87.78	79.79	97.60	105.94	121.04	108.79	112.17
New Zealand	2.20	1.42	1.39	1.23	1.22	1.21	1.43	1.44	1.41

$ = United States (US) dollars, ADB = Asian Development Bank.

a Data show weighted averages of the official, bank, and parallel market rates.
b Beginning 1 April 2012, the Central Bank of Myanmar adopted the managed float exchange rate regime for kyat vis-à-vis the US dollar.
c Unit of currency is the US dollar.

Sources: International Monetary Fund. International Financial Statistics. http://data.imf.org/ (accessed 18 May 2018). For Turkmenistan: United Nations National
Accounts Main Aggregates Database and Interstate Statistical Committee of the Commonwealth of Independent States. For Uzbekistan: Economy source; United
Nations National Accounts Main Aggregates Database, and Interstate Statistical Committee of the Commonwealth of Independent States. For Taipei,China:
Central bank of Taipei,China. http://www.cbc.gov.tw (accessed 2 July 2018).

Table 2.3.14:   Purchasing Power Parity Conversion Factor[a]
(local currency units per $, period averages)

ADB Regional Member	2000	2005	2010	2012	2013	2014	2015	2016	2017
Developing ADB Member Economies									
Central and West Asia									
Afghanistan	9.64 (2002)	12.28	16.02	18.46	18.87	18.65	18.89	19.61	20.21
Armenia	144.93	157.74	183.12	193.53	196.87	197.86	198.12	196.15	196.98
Azerbaijan	0.17	0.21	0.30	0.36	0.36	0.35	0.32	0.36	0.41
Georgia	0.53	0.64	0.80	0.85	0.83	0.85	0.89	0.91	0.96
Kazakhstan	22.15	35.14	67.88	82.49	88.89	92.36	93.04	104.39	109.09
Kyrgyz Republic	8.11	9.26	14.80	18.94	19.24	20.49	20.96	21.95	22.55
Pakistan	9.97	11.82	20.77	25.33	26.67	28.14	28.98	28.73	29.35
Tajikistan	0.31	0.69	1.57	1.91	1.96	2.03	2.01	2.09	2.15
Turkmenistan	0.27	0.65	1.30	1.53	1.52	1.50	1.41	1.33	1.43
Uzbekistan	66.55	222.68	525.83	677.64	762.07	838.08	904.33	958.81	1,120.53
East Asia									
China, People's Republic of	2.71	2.82	3.31	3.52	3.55	3.51	3.48	3.47	3.55
Hong Kong, China	7.44	5.69	5.37	5.55	5.56	5.62	5.76	5.79	5.85
Korea, Republic of	747.23	788.92	840.57	854.89	869.08	871.88	870.93	874.63	878.77
Mongolia	138.38	223.58	476.22	594.84	602.41	635.87	639.95	645.30	701.02
Taipei,China	21.52	18.36	15.79	14.92	14.90	14.88	15.20	15.14	14.69
South Asia									
Bangladesh	15.68	17.33	21.90	24.58	25.93	26.91	28.19	29.71	31.01
Bhutan	12.27	13.66	15.84	18.07	18.83	19.84	20.34	20.94	22.12
India	10.14	11.06	14.21	16.01	16.73	16.99	17.15	17.52	17.73
Maldives	3.38	5.66	7.73	8.94	9.36	9.63	10.08	9.88	9.71
Nepal	13.10	15.33	22.68	25.79	27.05	29.05	30.16	31.29	33.07
Sri Lanka	15.24	21.79	38.00	42.06	43.98	44.46	44.27	45.49	48.37
Southeast Asia									
Brunei Darussalam	0.48	0.59	0.61	0.71	0.68	0.66	0.54	0.48	0.50
Cambodia	1,062.54	1,106.83	1,330.18	1,341.80	1,330.80	1,341.74	1,350.17	1,379.24	1,401.31
Indonesia	1,427.63	2,013.80	3,425.30	3,674.27	3,795.44	3,931.47	4,044.10	4,092.20	4,190.49
Lao People's Democratic Republic	1,299.25	1,826.40	2,280.01	2,605.55	2,730.14	2,835.59	2,871.06	2,920.57	2,922.08
Malaysia	1.19	1.28	1.41	1.43	1.45	1.44	1.42	1.42	1.45
Myanmar	53.48	125.12	217.52	237.95	244.42	250.13	257.68	263.48	285.35
Philippines	13.71	15.47	17.52	17.88	17.95	18.19	17.89	17.97	18.06
Singapore	1.00	0.90	0.90	0.88	0.86	0.85	0.87	0.86	0.85
Thailand	11.06	11.34	12.17	12.38	12.40	12.36	12.33	12.46	12.52
Viet Nam	2,708.76	3,575.10	5,647.10	7,307.63	7,533.85	7,672.08	7,575.29	7,562.94	7,735.71
The Pacific									
Cook Islands	...	...	...	...	...	...	...	...	...
Fiji	0.84	0.94	0.97	1.06	1.08	1.10	1.14	1.20	1.21
Kiribati	0.86	0.90	0.96	0.95	0.94	0.94	0.96	1.01	1.01
Marshall Islands	0.93	0.92	0.92	0.95	0.94	0.89	0.87	0.91	0.90
Micronesia, Federated States of	0.88	0.81	0.89	0.93	0.92	0.93	0.87	0.90	0.88
Nauru	...	...	0.86	1.22	0.94	0.81	0.74	0.77	0.78
Palau	0.77	0.73	0.77	0.79	0.82	0.86	0.92	0.94	0.92
Papua New Guinea	0.80	1.00	1.74	1.82	1.85	1.87	1.77	1.87	1.94
Samoa	1.43	1.48	1.66	1.70	1.70	1.67	1.70	1.65	1.64
Solomon Islands	3.73	4.43	5.68	6.57	6.62	6.67	6.80	6.95	6.94
Timor-Leste	0.19	0.32	0.42	0.57	0.53	0.51	0.32	0.25	0.32
Tonga	0.93	1.14	1.40	1.46	1.45	1.43	1.44	1.45	1.46
Tuvalu	1.04	1.11	1.13	1.10	1.10	1.14	1.18	1.18	1.17
Vanuatu	90.42	88.70	99.50	99.10	100.12	100.30	101.69	102.61	103.39
Developed ADB Member Economies									
Australia	1.31	1.39	1.50	1.54	1.45	1.45	1.47	1.49	1.52
Japan	154.72	129.55	111.62	104.27	101.30	103.05	102.76	100.28	98.24
New Zealand	1.44	1.54	1.50	1.50	1.45	1.44	1.46	1.47	1.48

... = data not available, $ = United States dollars, ADB = Asian Development Bank.

a Purchasing power parity figures are extrapolated from the 2011 International Comparison Program (ICP) benchmark estimates or imputed using a statistical model based on the 2011 ICP.

Sources: World Bank. World Development Indicators. http://databank.worldbank.org/data/home.aspx (accessed 2 July 2018). For Taipei,China: Asian Development Bank estimates using data from economy sources and World Bank data.

Table 2.3.15: Price Level Indexes
(PPPs to official exchange rates, period averages, United States = 100)

ADB Regional Member	2000	2005	2010	2012	2013	2014	2015	2016	2017
Developing ADB Member Economies									
Central and West Asia									
Afghanistan	20.39 (2002)	24.81	34.49	36.25	34.07	32.57	30.90	28.90	29.70
Armenia	26.86	34.46	49.01	48.17	48.06	47.57	41.45	40.82	40.81
Azerbaijan	18.54	22.02	37.39	46.32	45.86	44.81	30.93	22.49	23.75
Georgia	26.75	35.05	44.93	51.62	50.04	48.06	39.17	38.64	38.12
Kazakhstan	15.58	26.45	46.07	55.32	58.43	51.54	41.96	30.51	33.46
Kyrgyz Republic	17.01	22.58	32.19	40.30	39.71	38.18	32.52	31.40	32.74
Pakistan	18.59	19.86	24.38	27.12	26.24	27.83	28.20	27.42	27.83
Tajikistan	14.80	22.20	35.78	40.33	41.19	41.17	32.67	26.71	25.18
Turkmenistan	26.31	62.46	45.57	53.57	53.33	52.74	40.29	37.86	40.88
Uzbekistan	28.13	20.13	33.31	35.71	36.38	36.27	35.22	32.33	21.91
East Asia									
China, People's Republic of	32.71	34.43	48.86	55.83	57.23	57.17	55.84	52.27	52.52
Hong Kong, China	95.53	73.14	69.06	71.59	71.73	72.50	74.35	74.53	75.06
Korea, Republic of	66.07	77.03	72.71	75.89	79.38	82.80	76.99	75.37	77.74
Mongolia	12.85	18.55	35.09	43.82	39.53	34.98	32.48	30.15	28.73
Taipei,China	68.91	57.09	49.91	50.37	50.04	49.00	47.66	46.84	48.25
South Asia									
Bangladesh	30.07	26.94	31.45	30.03	33.20	34.66	36.16	37.77	38.56
Bhutan	27.30	30.97	34.64	33.82	32.13	32.51	31.71	31.16	33.97
India	22.56	25.08	31.07	29.97	28.56	27.83	26.74	26.08	27.22
Maldives	28.76	44.19	60.36	58.18	60.93	62.58	65.61	64.31	63.12
Nepal	18.42	21.48	30.96	30.27	29.08	29.78	29.46	29.14	31.64
Sri Lanka	19.80	21.68	33.61	32.97	34.07	34.05	32.59	31.25	31.73
Southeast Asia									
Brunei Darussalam	27.69	35.33	44.69	57.07	54.50	51.81	38.98	34.79	35.89
Cambodia	27.66	27.05	31.79	33.27	33.04	33.23	33.19	33.98	34.60
Indonesia	16.95	20.75	37.68	39.14	36.28	33.13	30.20	30.75	31.32
Lao People's Democratic Republic	16.47	17.14	27.61	32.54	34.73	35.23	35.24	35.71	34.99
Malaysia	31.29	33.82	43.86	46.85	45.28	43.88	36.24	34.35	33.79
Myanmar[a]	7.70	20.17	36.20	37.14	26.18	25.41	22.16	21.34	20.98
Philippines	31.03	28.08	38.83	42.33	42.29	40.98	39.32	37.83	35.83
Singapore	58.05	54.13	65.91	70.43	69.06	66.83	63.12	62.00	61.46
Thailand	27.56	28.20	38.41	39.82	40.35	38.04	36.00	35.30	36.90
Viet Nam	19.12	22.54	30.34	35.09	35.99	36.28	34.91	34.48	34.58
The Pacific									
Cook Islands	...	...	...	...	...	...	...	...	...
Fiji	39.24	55.33	50.70	59.23	58.71	58.44	54.16	57.05	58.50
Kiribati	50.08	69.03	88.02	98.29	91.00	84.69	71.83	75.27	77.48
Marshall Islands	92.73	91.97	92.31	95.23	93.86	89.17	86.88	91.11	89.51
Micronesia, Federated States of	87.81	81.27	88.57	92.53	91.78	92.72	86.64	89.60	88.00
Nauru	...	...	79.19	125.99	90.57	73.25	55.38	57.19	59.89
Palau	76.87	73.42	76.96	78.60	82.44	85.97	92.16	93.93	92.30
Papua New Guinea	28.86	32.11	64.11	87.11	82.43	76.10	63.98	59.79	60.89
Samoa	43.43	54.47	66.67	73.95	73.43	71.70	66.36	64.38	64.96
Solomon Islands	73.23	58.87	70.39	89.37	90.66	90.37	85.88	87.50	88.04
Timor-Leste	19.23	31.53	41.51	56.76	53.15	50.56	31.75	25.25	31.60
Tonga	52.72	58.77	73.53	84.94	81.64	77.69	68.35	65.23	66.35
Tuvalu	60.47	85.04	103.28	113.76	106.58	102.72	88.61	87.44	89.80
Vanuatu	65.69	81.19	102.68	106.98	105.90	103.33	93.31	94.59	97.37
Developed ADB Member Economies									
Australia	76.01	106.02	137.72	159.47	139.70	130.93	110.50	110.43	116.21
Japan	143.57	117.54	127.16	130.68	103.80	97.27	84.90	92.17	87.58
New Zealand	65.61	108.08	107.76	121.17	118.58	119.52	102.07	102.20	104.95

... = data not available, PPP = purchasing power parity, ADB = Asian Development Bank.

a   The Central Bank of Myanmar devalued the local currency effective 1 April 2012. To achieve a consistent price series, the exchange rate used for estimating the price level index in prior years was extrapolated using the pre-devaluation exchange rate series.

Source: Asian Development Bank estimates using economy sources and World Bank data.

IV.   Globalization

Snapshot

- The aggregate level of remittances to developing ADB member economies increased from $35.3 billion in 2000 to $266.8 billion in 2017. On a global basis, remittance flows to low- and middle-income economies increased 8.5% in 2017, following 2 consecutive years of decline.

- Foreign direct investment (FDI) flows to developing Asia were mostly stable in 2017, following a 17% decline in the previous year. The People's Republic of China (PRC) ($168.2 billion); Hong Kong, China ($122.4 billion); and Singapore ($63.6 billion) were among the world's top 10 recipients of FDI.

- As global trade expanded in 2017 at its most rapid rate in 6 years, Asia and the Pacific accounted for more than a third of global exports.

The aggregate level of remittances to developing ADB member economies increased from $35.3 billion in 2000 to $266.8 billion in 2017. On a global basis, remittance flows to low- and middle-income countries increased 8.5% in 2017, following 2 consecutive years of decline. In 2017, the aggregate level of remittances to all developing member economies of the Asia and Pacific region topped $266 billion (Table 2.4.4). The top three recipient economies—in US dollar terms—in the region were India ($69.0 billion), the PRC ($63.9 billion), and the Philippines ($32.8 billion) as illustrated by Figure 2.4.1. These three economies are also globally the top three recipient of remittances (World Bank 2018).

South Asia received the largest share of developing Asia's total remittances at 36.2%, followed by East Asia (27.0%), Southeast Asia (24.4%), Central and West Asia (12.1%), and the Pacific (0.2%).

The 8.5% increase in remittances to the world's low- and middle-income countries in 2017, following 2 years of decline, was driven by economic growth in the European Union, the Russian Federation, and the US, as well as rising oil prices and the relative weakening of the US dollar against the euro and the ruble. Excluding the PRC, remittance flows to low- and middle-income countries are significantly larger

Figure 2.4.1: Worker's Remittances and Compensation of Employees, Receipts
($ million)

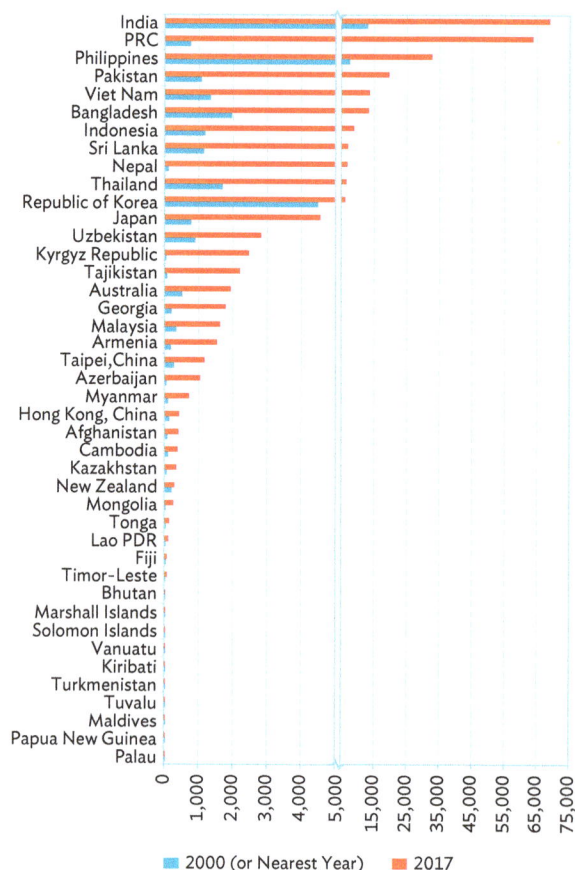

■ 2000 (or Nearest Year)   ■ 2017

$= United States dollars, Lao PDR = Lao People's Democratic Republic, PRC = People's Republic of China.

Note: Only economies with both two data points, 2000 and 2017, are presented in this chart. For 2000, includes data from 2000 to 2008.

Source: Table 2.4.4, Key Indicators for Asia and the Pacific 2018.

than FDI. Such flows are also more stable than cyclical private debt and equity flows. However, this stability is at risk as anti-immigration sentiments are rising and immigration policies are becoming stricter in some economies that are the largest sources of remittances.[4]

As a share of GDP, the top recipients of remittances in Asia and the Pacific in 2017 were smaller economies, including Tonga (34.2%), the Kyrgyz Republic (32.9%), and Tajikistan (31.1%) as shown in Table 2.4.5.

In addition to FDI and remittances, aggregate net resource flows to developing ADB member economies include official development assistance and other official flows, among others. For a discussion on the monitoring of public and private flows to developing Asia, please refer to Box 2.4.1.

Box 2.4.1: Public and Private Flows to Developing ADB Member Economies: Tracking Trends

Overview

The 2030 Agenda for Sustainable Development calls for the eradication of all forms of poverty, including extreme poverty. The relevant indicator for Sustainable Development Goal (SDG) Target 17.9 is the "dollar value of financial and technical assistance (including through North–South, South–South, and triangular cooperation) committed to developing countries."[a] Therefore, tracking the dollar value of such assistance to developing economies is necessary to assess progress toward the achievement of SDG Target 17.9. Private flows to developing economies can also promote productive employment, economic growth, social inclusion, and environmental sustainability in developing Asian Development Bank (ADB) member economies (United Nations 2017a). Hence, monitoring private flows over time helps inform decision-making and steer efforts toward attracting additional flows with the greatest potential for positive impacts on other SDG targets.

There is some reason for caution concerning a possible slowdown in public and/or private flows to developing economies. Over the past 2 decades, Asia and the Pacific has seen private flows plummet (at least temporarily) as a result of financial crises. Ongoing cuts to aid budgets in some developed economies pose a risk to those developing economies that are most dependent on foreign assistance. At the same time, rising anti-migrant sentiments in places that serve as a valuable source of remittances can threaten the financial lifeline of many poor communities in developing economies. While the governments of these economies may have little influence over such global trends, monitoring public and private flows to developing economies and identifying key trends remain important aspects of the development process.

Definitions and Distinctions

Aggregate net resource flows from all sources to developing economies can be split into official development assistance (ODA), other official flows (OOFs), and private direct investment and other private capital (private). ODA refers to government aid (bilateral or multilateral) to promote the economic development and welfare of developing countries. Such aid includes grants, soft loans (grant element of at least 25%), and technical assistance. Loans and credits for military purposes are excluded from ODA, as defined by the Organisation for Economic Co-operation and Development (OECD).[b] ODA eligibility is determined every 3 years by the OECD's Development Assistance Committee based on gross national income per capita.[c] Countries that have exceeded the World Bank's high-income threshold for 3 consecutive years are no longer eligible.

OOFs are official sector transactions that do not meet ODA criteria, including grants to developing countries for commercial purposes, official bilateral transactions to promote development (grant element of less than 25%), and official bilateral transactions to facilitate exports. OOFs also include the purchase by governments and central monetary institutions of securities issued by multilateral development banks at market terms.[d]

Net private financial flows are private financial flows at market terms that result in changes in the holdings of private, long-term assets held by residents of the reporting country, and private grants. Examples include foreign direct investment (FDI), portfolio equity (buying and selling of stocks and shares), migrant remittances, and private sector borrowing.[e]

continued on next page

[4] SDG Target 17.9 is "the enhancement of international support for implementing effective and targeted capacity building in developing countries to support national plans to implement all SDGs United Nations." Sustainable Development Knowledge Platform. SDGS. https://sustainabledevelopment.un.org/sdg17.

Box 2.4.1 continued

Crises and Recovery

The total receipts of developing ADB member economies increased steadily for nearly a decade following the 1997–1998 Asian financial crisis, with the exception of dips of about 4.3% in 2002 and 5.0% in 2006, which were driven by a decline in combined ODA and OOFs (Tables 2.4.16, 2.4.17, 2.4.19). Total receipts recovered in 2007, led by soaring private flows, before the global financial crisis resulted in a collapse in such flows in 2008. The recovery in total receipts of developing ADB member economies in the aftermath of the global financial crisis was generally robust, notwithstanding declines in 2012 (–22.6%) and 2015 (–38.8%). In each case, the decline was driven by falling private flows, which recovered the following year.

Short-term portfolio investments comprise the majority of private cross-border flows, both globally and in Asia and the Pacific (United Nations 2017b). Within Asia and the Pacific, the main recipients of longer-term, and therefore more stable, investments such as FDI, include the two most populous economies, India and the PRC, and economies in Southeast Asia (Table 2.4.18). Led by these economies, the region's global share of inward FDI has risen from less than 20% in 2000–2005 to almost 30% in 2016 (Asia Regional Integration Center 2017).

On an aggregate level, the region's overall level of ODA and OOFs in 2016 were roughly on par with their respective levels prior to the onset of the global financial crisis (2000–2005). By individual economy, India was the largest recipient in 2016 with combined ODA and OOFs of $4,614 million (12.8% of the total for developing ADB member economies). Afghanistan was the second largest recipient in 2016 with $4,165 million in ODA and OOFs, or 11.6% of the total amount received by all developing member economies. Afghanistan has consistently been one of the recipients of large amount of ODA since 2002. The third largest recipient in 2016 was Pakistan, with combined ODA and OOFs of $4,042 million (11.2% of the total for developing ADB member economies).

On the other hand, the People's Republic of China and Indonesia had the largest declines in their ODA since 2000, when they were the recipients of $1,749 million and $1,663 million, respectively. In 2011, the People's Republic of China became a net donor of ODA and, in 2014, Indonesia achieved this same distinction.

Conclusion

Total receipts of developing ADB member economies recovered rapidly after the 1997–1998 Asian financial crisis and have been either mostly stable (ODA, OOFs) or increasing (private flows) since the 2008 global financial crisis. However, these trends are not irreversible. Stagnant, or in some cases, declining, aid budgets in the United States and parts of Europe could lead to a decrease in vital ODA and OOFs for Asia and the Pacific's least developed and/or smallest economies. There is also the slim possibility of global capital flight from developing ADB member economies triggered by an emerging market crisis elsewhere e.g., in Argentina (ADB 2018). Finally, interrupted remittance flows are a potential outcome of rising anti-migrant sentiments in some developed economies. This could jeopardize the much-needed economic contributions of migrant workers in a number of developing economies.

While these global trends may be beyond the control of individual developing member governments, monitoring aid to developing ADB member economies over time remains important for tracking progress toward the achievement of SDG Target 17.9 and in assessing the characteristics and impacts of private flows. Informed policymakers are better prepared to make crucial decisions related to poverty eradication, inclusive growth, and social and environmental development.

---

[a] SDG Target 17.9 is "the enhancement of international support for implementing effective and targeted capacity building in developing countries to support national plans to implement all SDGs, United Nations." Sustainable Development Knowledge Platform. SDGS. https://sustainabledevelopment.un.org/sdg17.
[b] The full definition can be found at https://data.oecd.org/oda/net-oda.htm.
[c] The full definition can be found at http://www.oecd.org/dac/stats/What-is-ODA.pdf.
[d] The full definition can be found at https://data.oecd.org/drf/other-official-flows-oof.htm.
[e] The full definition can be found at https://data.oecd.org/drf/private-flows.htm#indicator-chart.

Sources:
ADB. 2018. *Asia Bond Monitor June 2018*. Manila.

Asia Regional Integration Center. 2017. *Cross-Border Investment*. https://aric.adb.org/pdf/aeir/AEIR2017_3_cross-border-investment.pdf.

United Nations. 2017a. *Development Issues No. 10 on International Financial Flows and External Debt*. 24 March.

United Nations. 2017b. Sustainable Development Knowledge Platform. SDGS. https://sustainabledevelopment.un.org/sdg17.

At $503 billion, FDI flows to developing Asia were mostly stable in 2017, following a 17% decline in the previous year, making once again developing Asia the largest recipient in the world. The PRC ($168.2 billion); Hong Kong, China ($122.4 billion); and Singapore ($63.6 billion) ranked among the world's top 10 recipients of FDI in 2017 as shown in Figure 2.4.2. The next largest FDI recipients in Asia and the Pacific in 2017 included Australia ($48.8 billion), India ($40.0 billion), and Indonesia ($22.1 billion) as illustrated by Figure 2.4.3. East Asia was the destination for the majority of FDI in developing member economies, with a regional share of 62.1%, followed by Southeast Asia (26.5%), South Asia (8.8%), Central and West Asia (2.5%), and the Pacific (0.1%).

Figure 2.4.2: Top 10 Global Economies in Terms of Net Inflows of Foreign Direct Investments, 2017
($ million)

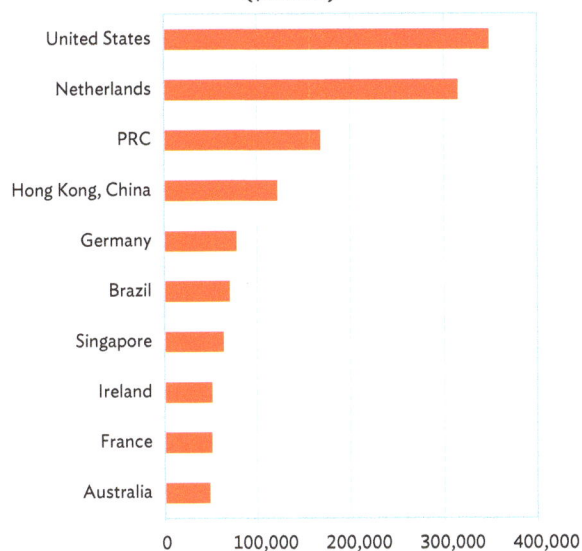

$ = United States dollars, PRC = People's Republic of China.
Source: World Bank. World Development Indicators. http://data.worldbank.org/indicator/BX.KLT.DINV.CD.WD?locations=MH (accessed 6 July 2018).

Figure 2.4.3: Top 10 Economies in Asia and the Pacific in Terms of Net Inflows of Foreign Direct Investment, 2017
($ million)

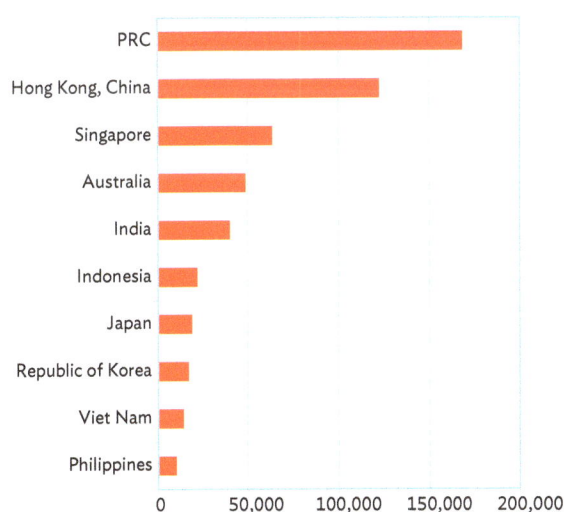

$ = United States dollars, PRC = People's Republic of China.
Source: World Bank. World Development Indicators. http://data.worldbank.org/indicator/BX.KLT.DINV.CD.WD?locations=MH (accessed 6 July 2018).

Global FDI flows fell by 23.9% to $1.86 trillion in 2017, with growth in cross-border investment near zero in developing economies, despite accelerated growth in global GDP and trade. A major contributing factor to declining FDI has been falling rates of return in recent years, including in developing Asia, where the average rate of return on inward FDI fell from 10.5% in 2012 to 9.1% in 2017. In the near term, global FDI flows are expected to remain well below their 2007 peak. Policymakers in developing economies will have to contend with the impacts of escalating trade tensions on investments in global value chains as well as the implementation of tax reforms in the US, which could affect global investment patterns (UN 2018).

As global trade expanded in 2017 at its most rapid rate in 6 years, Asia and the Pacific accounted for more than a third of global exports. As global merchandise exports grew 10.7% in 2017, its most rapid expansion in 6 years, based on accelerated growth in global GDP and investment, Asia and the Pacific accounted for 36.5% of the global exports, up from 28.7% in 2000. The PRC is by far the region's largest exporter, accounting for 35.4% of total exports from Asia and the Pacific in 2017. The next largest exporters in 2017 were Japan (10.9%) and the Republic of Korea (9.0%) (Table 2.4.8). On the other hand, the Asia and Pacific region was the recipient of 33.2% of the world's exports in 2017, up from 32.2% in the previous year and 25.4% in 2000. As an export destination, Asia and the Pacific is second only to Europe, which accounted for 36.9% of global exports in 2017 (Figure 2.4.4 and Table 2.4.13).

Figure 2.4.4: Destination of Merchandise Exports by Global Region and Major Merchandise Export Destinations in Asia and the Pacific, 2017
(%)

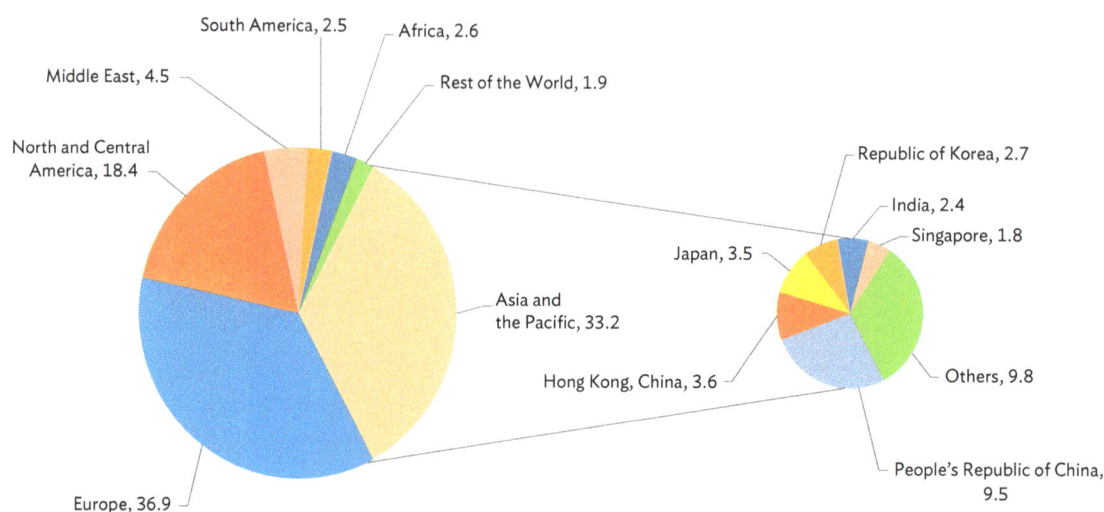

Sources: Table 2.4.13, Key Indicators for Asia and the Pacific 2018; International Monetary Fund. May 2018. *Direction of Trade Statistics* (CD-ROM). Washington DC.

Data Issues and Comparability

Most of the data on international transactions presented in this section are taken from balance-of-payments statistics as reported by individual economies. IMF guidelines are followed by most governments in compiling these statistics. However, authorities have difficulty accurately recording nonofficial transactions such as migrant workers' remittances and private capital flows, which is one of the reasons that the IMF's Balance of Payments Manual (BPM) was updated to the sixth edition (BPM6) in 2009. A majority of economies use BPM5, some have shifted to BPM6, and a few continue to use BPM4. This affects the comparability of data across economies.

The World Trade Organization and other international agencies closely monitor international trade statistics. Common definitions are used by all economies, with the larger economies across Asia and the Pacific using standard forms and procedures for data processing.

Data on official development assistance, other official flows, and private direct investment and other private capital are compiled by the Organisation for Co-operation and Economic Development's Development Assistance Committee. These data are standardized on a calendar-year basis for all donors, but may have discrepancies for some economies owing to the fiscal-year data available in budget documents. Donor-side commitments do not necessarily translate to actual disbursements to recipient economies of official development assistance.

Table 2.4.1:   Trade in Goods Balance
(% of GDP)

ADB Regional Member	2000	2005	2010	2012	2013	2014	2015	2016	2017
Developing ADB Member Economies									
Central and West Asia									
Afghanistan[a]	-28.4	-65.5	-28.1	-28.1	-37.9	-30.0	-34.1	-29.5	-29.3
Armenia	-24.4	-13.0	-22.3	-21.2	-19.7	-17.7	-11.2	-9.0	-12.8
Azerbaijan	6.1	24.9	37.3	31.8	28.8	25.2	11.0	11.1	15.0
Georgia	-17.5	-19.0	-22.6	-26.7	-21.7	-26.0	-28.3	-27.0	-25.4
Kazakhstan	12.2	18.1	19.3	18.3	14.7	16.4	6.9	6.7	11.0
Kyrgyz Republic	0.3	-17.0	-25.1	-39.0	-37.9	-37.6	-33.6	-31.4	-31.0
Pakistan	-1.8	-3.7	-6.6	-7.3	-7.0	-6.7	-6.5	-6.9	-8.8
Tajikistan	-9.5	-14.0	-36.0	-45.3	-45.9	-32.5	-29.1	-27.1	-21.2
Turkmenistan	...	11.6	9.9	18.6	10.3	9.5	-5.3	-15.6	...
Uzbekistan	3.6	10.1	7.6	1.5	0.7	-0.7	0.1	-0.1	1.8
East Asia									
China, People's Republic of	2.5	5.4	3.9	3.6	3.7	4.2	5.2	4.4	3.9
Hong Kong, China	11.9	17.1	1.4	-7.2	-10.1	-11.1	-7.4	-5.2	-7.0
Korea, Republic of	2.8	3.6	4.4	4.0	6.3	6.3	8.8	8.4	7.8
Mongolia	-6.4	-3.9	-2.4	-24.6	-20.7	1.5	4.8	12.0	13.4
Taipei,China	5.8	6.5	8.3	10.0	10.7	11.3	13.9	13.3	14.1
South Asia									
Bangladesh	-4.0	-5.5	-4.5	-7.0	-4.7	-3.9	-3.6	-2.8	-3.8
Bhutan	-15.6	-30.7	-17.3	-20.4	-19.7	-20.2	-20.2	-23.9	-18.6
India	-2.7	-6.2	-7.4	-10.7	-7.9	-7.1	-6.2	-4.9	-6.1
Maldives	-37.4	-42.4	-40.9	-43.7	-41.6	-44.9	-41.3	-43.5	...
Nepal	-14.4	-14.6	-25.5	-24.4	-27.2	-30.4	-31.3	-30.2	-35.3
Sri Lanka	...	-10.3	-8.5	-13.8	-10.2	-10.4	-10.4	-10.9	-11.0
Southeast Asia									
Brunei Darussalam[b]	45.4	43.5	45.3	46.0	38.2	43.5	22.3	21.6	...
Cambodia	-14.7	-16.1	-23.9	-25.1	-23.8	-22.9	-21.8	-19.2	-19.3
Indonesia	15.2	6.0	4.1	0.9	0.6	0.8	1.6	1.6	1.9
Lao People's Democratic Republic	-12.5	-12.1	-4.7	-8.4	-6.6	-12.8	-14.1	-7.1	-6.4
Malaysia	...	23.9	15.1	11.6	9.5	10.2	9.4	8.2	8.7
Myanmar	-0.1	0.1	0.1	1.0	0.2	-2.8	-6.1	-5.5	-8.9
Philippines	-7.4	-11.8	-8.4	-7.6	-6.5	-6.1	-8.0	-11.7	-13.1
Singapore	16.9	37.4	26.2	25.0	25.0	27.3	29.5	27.6	26.2
Thailand	4.3	1.8	7.8	0.0	0.0	4.2	6.7	8.9	7.0
Viet Nam	1.2	-4.2	-4.4	5.6	5.1	6.5	3.8	5.4	4.8
The Pacific									
Cook Islands	...	...	-23.8	-27.5	-23.8	-22.0	-25.0	-26.5	...
Fiji	-14.0	-23.0	-23.5	-19.4	-27.7	-22.9	-20.8	-21.4	...
Kiribati	-52.2	-62.8	-40.9	-49.4	-48.8	-50.3	-53.8	-53.1	...
Marshall Islands	-54.7	-40.4	-55.5	-26.9	-36.2	-37.5	-34.4	...	...
Micronesia, Federated States of	-38.2	-42.8	-43.3	-38.5	-40.7	-36.9	-40.6	-33.4	...
Nauru	...	...	...	...	...	...	...	...	...
Palau	-80.0	-52.0	-49.9	-57.5	-58.4	-64.6	-48.3	-46.3	-49.1
Papua New Guinea	31.4	36.8	15.6	7.4	1.1	8.4	10.2	9.0	9.9
Samoa	-120.7	-31.5	-31.2	-34.6	-37.5	-38.1	-34.1	-33.6	-33.5
Solomon Islands	-8.1	-5.6	-19.7	7.2	-1.7	-0.5	-1.7	1.3	0.5
Timor-Leste[c]	...	-3.9	-7.0	-9.6	-11.0	-14.9	-20.5	-21.4	...
Tonga	-25.5	-33.8	-27.6	-29.9	-31.9	-30.6	-34.0	-34.0	-36.5
Tuvalu[c]	-64.9	-40.5	-54.3	-4.2	-35.1	-24.5	-29.6	...	...
Vanuatu	-18.2	-23.3	-27.1	-25.4	-27.9	-22.9	-31.5	-32.4	...
Developed ADB Member Economies									
Australia	-1.9	-2.6	-0.7	0.6	-0.2	0.6	-0.8	-1.6	0.8
Japan	2.4	2.2	1.9	-0.9	-1.7	-2.0	-0.2	1.0	0.9
New Zealand	1.6	-3.0	1.4	0.2	1.2	-0.2	-1.0	-1.1	...

... = data not available, 0.0 = magnitude is less than half of unit employed, ADB = Asian Development Bank, GDP = gross domestic product.

a   For 2000, data refer to 2002.
b   For 2000, data refer to 2001.
c   For 2005, data refer to 2006.

Source: Economy sources.

Table 2.4.2:   Trade in Services Balance
(% of GDP)

ADB Regional Member	2000	2005	2010	2012	2013	2014	2015	2016	2017
Developing ADB Member Economies									
Central and West Asia									
Afghanistan[a]	...	-8.2	6.4	-0.3	-3.0	-0.1	-0.8	-1.8	-3.1
Armenia	-3.4	-3.0	-2.8	-1.0	-1.1	-1.0	-0.9	-0.7	-0.5
Azerbaijan	-4.3	-14.9	-3.3	-4.2	-5.6	-8.1	-8.0	-8.3	-8.3
Georgia	2.4	1.6	4.7	7.0	8.8	7.9	10.5	11.4	13.7
Kazakhstan	-5.3	-9.5	-4.9	-3.8	-3.0	-2.8	-2.8	-3.5	-2.8
Kyrgyz Republic[a]	-12.2	-4.9	-4.2	-5.1	-0.7	-4.4	-2.8	-3.0	-0.4
Pakistan[a]	-3.5	-2.8	-1.0	-1.5	-0.7	-1.1	-1.1	-1.2	-1.4
Tajikistan	-1.7	-4.5	-2.0	-2.9	-3.3	-3.3	-3.1	-2.0	-4.0
Turkmenistan	...	...	...	...	...	...	...	...	...
Uzbekistan[b,c]	...	-1.1	-1.4	-0.1	-0.4	-0.1	1.5	1.7	3.6
East Asia									
China, People's Republic of	-0.1	0.0	-0.2	-0.9	-1.3	-2.0	-2.0	-2.1	-2.2
Hong Kong, China	-7.5	-4.9	4.4	8.3	10.7	11.3	9.8	7.5	7.8
Korea, Republic of	-0.2	-1.0	-1.3	-0.4	-0.5	-0.3	-1.1	-1.3	-2.3
Mongolia[a]	-8.5	0.7	-6.2	-14.7	-12.0	-12.2	-6.3	-12.4	-12.4
Taipei,China	-3.8	-3.8	-2.5	-3.7	-3.0	-2.2	-2.0	-1.9	-1.5
South Asia									
Bangladesh	-1.4	-1.5	-1.1	-2.3	-2.1	-2.4	-1.6	-1.2	-1.3
Bhutan[a]	-1.8	-4.8	-4.5	-4.7	-3.0	-3.3	-3.3	-2.8	...
India[a]	0.3	2.8	2.6	3.5	3.8	3.7	3.2	3.0	3.0
Maldives[a]	33.4	6.8	34.8	55.5	57.1	59.6	50.7	42.3	...
Nepal[d]	7.2	-0.4	-1.3	1.0	0.5	1.1	1.3	0.4	0.1
Sri Lanka[a]	0.2	1.4	1.2	1.8	1.6	2.4	2.9	3.5	3.8
Southeast Asia									
Brunei Darussalam[a,e]	11.0	0.6	-5.9	-11.3	-13.1	-9.5	-7.8	-9.8	...
Cambodia[a]	-0.6	2.9	9.0	11.4	11.2	10.3	9.5	8.0	8.5
Indonesia[a]	-11.1	-3.1	-1.3	-1.2	-1.3	-1.1	-1.0	-0.8	-0.8
Lao People's Democratic Republic[a]	5.1	2.5	2.4	-0.9	-2.3	-2.9	-1.6	-1.2	-1.6
Malaysia[a]	-11.1	-2.0	0.8	-0.9	-0.9	-1.0	-1.8	-1.6	-1.7
Myanmar[a,f]	-0.0	-0.1	-0.0	-0.4	0.4	1.4	2.2	2.0	1.7
Philippines[a]	-2.3	2.1	2.9	2.5	2.6	1.6	1.9	2.3	3.0
Singapore	-4.6	-7.6	-0.2	-1.5	-2.5	-4.0	-3.8	-1.5	-1.9
Thailand	3.7	-3.6	-2.1	1.0	2.7	2.5	4.8	5.9	6.5
Viet Nam[a]	-1.8	-0.5	-2.1	-0.9	-1.8	-2.1	-2.5	-2.1	-1.8
The Pacific									
Cook Islands	...	...	39.1	52.4	49.9	48.8	49.7	56.4	...
Fiji[a]	7.1	13.4	17.1	16.3	15.0	15.0	15.8	15.1	...
Kiribati[a]	-27.4	-30.3	-25.4	-27.5	-27.2	-41.3	-39.8	-31.4	...
Marshall Islands[d]	-20.1	-21.8	-19.5	-20.5	-21.4	-19.0	-19.3	-19.2	-21.3
Micronesia, Federated States of	-15.4	-15.5	-14.2	-13.3	-12.1	-10.4	-10.6	-12.4	...
Nauru	...	...	...	-11.6	-7.4	-23.5	-13.4	-15.1	-15.2
Palau	14.9	17.9	22.6	31.5	33.2	36.1	34.6	28.1	22.9
Papua New Guinea[d]	-21.2	-17.8	-17.2	-15.3	-16.4	-9.0	-5.1	-4.4	-4.9
Samoa[a]	44.1	10.9	9.4	13.8	14.5	15.0	16.1	15.1	17.0
Solomon Islands[a]	-8.2	1.5	-13.8	-9.2	-12.0	-10.6	-7.4	-8.4	...
Timor-Leste	...	...	-24.0	-13.8	-7.6	-14.7	-18.7	-20.9	...
Tonga[g]	1.0	-3.8	-1.1	-0.5	0.8	-0.4	0.6	2.0	2.9
Tuvalu[a,h]	-51.2	5.6	-3.8	-62.3	-63.7	-52.2	-60.9	...	...
Vanuatu[a]	17.1	14.9	17.6	19.9	24.8	19.3	12.9	21.9	...
Developed ADB Member Economies									
Australia	-0.2	-0.2	-0.3	-0.9	-1.1	-1.1	-0.7	-0.6	-0.2
Japan	-1.0	-0.8	-0.5	-0.8	-0.7	-0.6	-0.4	-0.2	-0.1
New Zealand	1.4	1.5	0.9	0.5	0.4	0.9	1.7	1.5	...

... = data not available, | = marks break in series due to change in compilation methodology, -0.0 or 0.0 = magnitude is less than half of the unit employed, ADB = Asian Development Bank, GDP = gross domestic product.

a Change in methodology from the International Monetary Fund's Balance of Payments Manual (fifth edition) [BPM5] to the International Monetary Fund's Balance of Payment Manual (sixth edition) [BPM6].
b Refers to the methodology of the International Monetary Fund's Balance of Payments Manual (fourth edition) [BPM4].
c For 2005 onwards, includes other goods and income.
d Refers to the methodology in BPM5.
e For 2000, data refer to 2001.
f Change in methodology from BPM4 to BPM5.
g Change in methodology from BPM4 to BPM6.
h For 2005, data refer to 2006.

Source: Economy sources.

Table 2.4.3:   Current Account Balance
(% of GDP)

ADB Regional Members	2000	2005	2010	2012	2013	2014	2015	2016	2017
Developing ADB Member Economies									
Central and West Asia									
Afghanistan[a]	-3.5	-2.7	-10.1	-20.3	-26.1	-18.5	-22.8	-18.0	-21.8
Armenia	-15.8	-2.5	-13.6	-10.6	-7.3	-7.6	-2.6	-2.3	-3.5
Azerbaijan	-3.2	1.3	28.4	21.4	17.6	13.9	-0.4	-3.6	4.1
Georgia	-5.8	-10.9	-10.3	-11.9	-5.9	-10.8	-12.1	-12.9	-8.6
Kazakhstan	2.0	-1.8	0.9	0.5	0.5	2.8	-2.8	-6.5	-3.4
Kyrgyz Republic	-5.5	-1.4	-6.6	-15.4	-13.9	-17.0	-15.9	-11.6	-3.1*
Pakistan	-0.3	-1.3	-2.3	-2.2	-1.1	-1.3	-1.0	-1.8	-4.2
Tajikistan	-7.2	-0.8	-3.9	-9.0	-7.8	-2.8	-6.4	-5.2	-0.5
Turkmenistan	8.4	5.1	-12.9	-0.9	-7.3	-6.1	-15.6	-19.9	...
Uzbekistan	1.6	13.5	6.1	2.7	3.4	4.1	2.0	2.2	6.2
East Asia									
China, People's Republic of	1.7	5.8	3.9	2.5	1.5	2.3	2.7	1.8	1.3
Hong Kong, China	4.4	11.9	7.0	1.6	1.5	1.4	3.3	4.0	4.2
Korea, Republic of	1.9	1.4	2.6	4.2	6.2	6.0	7.7	7.0	5.1
Mongolia	-6.1	3.5	-12.3	-43.8	-37.6	-15.8	-8.1	-6.3	-10.4
Taipei,China	2.5	4.0	8.3	8.7	9.7	11.4	14.2	13.7	14.5
South Asia									
Bangladesh	-0.9	-1.0	3.7	-0.3	1.6	0.8	1.8	2.0	-0.6
Bhutan	-9.4	-29.0	-20.5	-20.0	-24.4	-24.8	-27.0	-27.7	-21.7
India	-0.6	-1.2	-2.8	-4.8	-1.7	-1.3	-1.1	-0.6	-1.9
Maldives	-8.2	-23.5	-13.8	-6.4	-3.9	-3.2	-7.5	-24.4	...
Nepal	-2.2	2.0	-2.3	4.8	3.4	4.6	5.1	6.2	-0.4
Sri Lanka	-6.4	-2.7	-1.9	-5.8	-3.4	-2.5	-2.3	-2.1	-2.6
Southeast Asia									
Brunei Darussalam[b]	51.5	47.3	36.5	29.8	20.9	30.7	16.5	15.5	...
Cambodia	-2.7	-3.6	-8.7	-8.7	-8.4	-8.4	-8.7	-8.5	-8.1
Indonesia	4.8	0.1	0.7	-2.7	-3.2	-3.1	-2.0	-1.8	-1.7
Lao People's Democratic Republic	-0.3	-7.1	0.4	-7.3	-7.9	-14.5	-15.8	-8.8	-8.6
Malaysia	9.0	14.4	10.1	5.2	3.5	4.4	3.0	2.4	3.0
Myanmar	-0.1	0.0	0.0	-1.5	-0.8	-2.9	-4.3	-2.2	-8.6
Philippines	-2.7	1.9	3.6	2.8	4.2	3.8	2.5	-0.4	-0.8
Singapore	10.8	22.1	23.4	17.0	16.5	18.7	18.6	19.0	18.8
Thailand	7.4	-4.0	3.4	-0.4	-1.2	3.7	8.0	11.7	10.6
Viet Nam	4.2	-1.0	-3.7	5.9	4.5	4.6	0.1	3.0	2.1
The Pacific									
Cook Islands	...	...	14.6	27.3	29.9	30.9	30.5	37.3	...
Fiji	-1.6	-7.0	-4.7	-1.4	-9.7	-7.6	-3.6	-5.0	...
Kiribati	-3.2	-32.4	0.1	1.9	20.0	53.7	46.7	19.4	...
Marshall Islands	-10.9	7.7	-17.8	-6.2	-9.2	-1.2	15.0	7.6	-0.3
Micronesia, Federated States of	-13.5	-9.1	-15.7	-13.6	-10.4	1.3	3.0	3.9	2.8
Nauru	...	...	...	38.1	18.8	-13.5	-9.5	1.7	0.5
Palau	-50.2	-23.7	-10.9	-13.6	-14.6	-17.8	-10.6	-14.3	-20.3
Papua New Guinea	10.1	13.3	-4.4	-10.8	-1.5	-0.6	-0.5	0.0	0.1
Samoa	-3.3	-8.5	-5.4	0.1	-5.6	-0.1	-0.0	-0.0	-0.0
Solomon Islands	-12.9	-1.9	-20.8	2.9	-3.8	-4.7	-3.4	-5.0	-3.9
Timor-Leste[c]	...	20.5	42.0	41.0	43.5	27.0	6.4	-20.7	...
Tonga	-4.8	-2.2	-7.4	-6.9	-8.5	-5.0	-3.7	2.4	3.4
Tuvalu[c]	54.5	-1.6	-3.8	18.4	1.3	19.6	7.1	...	...
Vanuatu	-5.0	-3.5	-5.8	-8.8	-0.5	-0.2	-8.3	-3.6	...
Developed ADB Member Economies									
Australia	-5.1	-6.6	-5.0	-3.4	-3.9	-3.2	-3.7	-4.5	-2.1
Japan	2.7	3.6	3.9	1.0	0.9	0.8	3.1	3.9	4.0
New Zealand	-2.3	-7.8	-2.8	-3.7	-2.6	-3.5	-2.8	-2.9	...

... = data not available, * = provisional, preliminary, estimate, -0.0 or 0.0 = magnitude is less than half of the unit employed, ADB = Asian Development Bank, GDP = gross
domestic product.

a   For 2000, data refers to 2002.
b   For 2000, data refers to 2001.
c   For 2005, data refers to 2006.

Source: Economy sources.

Balance of Payments

Table 2.4.4:   Workers' Remittances and Compensation of Employees, Receipts[a]
($ million)

ADB Regional Member	2000	2005	2010	2012	2013	2014	2015	2016	2017
Developing ADB Member Economies									
Central and West Asia	**1,669**	**8,108**	**20,701**	**31,096**	**33,725**	**35,137**	**31,046**	**30,320**	**32,367**
Afghanistan	...	90 (2008)	342	252	314	268	301	387	410
Armenia	182	915	1,669	1,915	2,192	2,079	1,491	1,382	1,539
Azerbaijan	57	623	1,410	1,990	1,733	1,846	1,270	643	1,050
Georgia	206	446	1,184	1,770	1,945	1,986	1,459	1,521	1,794
Kazakhstan	67	62	226	178	207	229	194	275	355
Kyrgyz Republic	2	313	1,266	2,031	2,278	2,243	1,688	1,995	2,486
Pakistan	1,075	4,280	9,690	14,007	14,629	17,244	19,306	19,761	19,665
Tajikistan	79 (2002)	467	2,021	3,222	3,698	3,384	2,259	1,867	2,220
Turkmenistan	...	14 (2006)	35	37	40	30	16	9	10
Uzbekistan	...	898 (2006)	2,858	5,693	6,689	5,828	3,062	2,479	2,839
East Asia	**5,675**	**29,601**	**59,401**	**65,936**	**67,356**	**70,370**	**71,944**	**69,160**	**72,074**
China, People's Republic of	758	23,626	52,460	57,987	59,491	62,332	63,938	61,000	63,860
Hong Kong, China	136	297	340	367	360	372	387	399	430
Korea, Republic of	4,507	5,178	5,836	6,571	6,455	6,551	6,444	6,504	6,332
Mongolia	1	177	266	324	257	255	261	260	269
Taipei,China	274	323	500	688	792	860	915	997	1,183
South Asia	**16,119**	**29,959**	**71,929**	**93,754**	**95,864**	**98,319**	**97,958**	**90,196**	**96,618**
Bangladesh	1,968	4,642	10,850	14,120	13,867	14,988	15,296	13,544	13,469
Bhutan	...	2 (2006)	8	18	12	14	20	34	40
India	12,883	22,125	53,480	68,821	69,970	70,389	68,910	62,744	68,968
Maldives	2	2	3	3	3	3	4	4	4
Nepal	111	1,212	3,464	4,793	5,589	5,889	6,730	6,612	6,947
Sri Lanka	1,154	1,976	4,123	6,000	6,422	7,036	7,000	7,257	7,190
Southeast Asia	**11,699**	**24,900**	**42,578**	**49,278**	**55,219**	**58,041**	**61,077**	**60,940**	**65,183**
Brunei Darussalam	...	...	...	...	...	...	...	...	...
Cambodia	103	164	153	172	176	377	400	371	386
Indonesia	1,190	5,420	6,916	7,212	7,614	8,551	9,659	8,891	8,997
Lao People's Democratic Republic	1	1	42	59	60	40	93	116	124
Malaysia	342	1,117	1,103	1,294	1,423	1,580	1,644	1,585	1,634
Myanmar	102	129	115	275	1,644	279	387	682	723
Philippines	6,924	13,733	21,557	24,610	26,717	28,691	29,799	31,145	32,808
Singapore	...	...	...	...	...	...	...	...	...
Thailand	1,697	1,187	4,433	5,657	6,585	6,524	5,895	6,270	6,729
Viet Nam	1,340	3,150	8,260	10,000	11,000	12,000	13,200	11,880	13,781
The Pacific	**...**	**419**	**620**	**731**	**651**	**678**	**721**	**552**	**580**
Cook Islands	...	...	...	...	...	...	...	...	...
Fiji	43	203	176	191	204	221	251	80	86
Kiribati	...	13 (2006)	16	18	17	17	16	17	18
Marshall Islands	...	24	22	23	25	26	27	28	29
Micronesia, Federated States of	...	...	18	21	22	23	23	23	24
Nauru	...	...	...	...	...	...	...	...	...
Palau	...	1	2	2	2	2	2	2	2
Papua New Guinea	7	7	3	14	14	10	10	3	3
Samoa	...	82	139	178	165	158	144	136	143
Solomon Islands	4	7	14	21	21	16	19	20	20
Timor-Leste	...	4 (2006)	137	120	34	44	62	80	85
Tonga	53 (2001)	69	77	118	121	129	138	138	146
Tuvalu	...	5	4	4	4	4	4	4	4
Vanuatu	14	5	12	22	24	28	24	19	19
Developed ADB Member Economies	**1,507**	**2,197**	**3,919**	**5,407**	**5,212**	**6,297**	**5,751**	**6,144**	**6,816**
Australia	518	940	1,864	2,405	2,389	2,258	2,141	2,051	1,941
Japan	773	905	1,684	2,540	2,364	3,734	3,325	3,819	4,578
New Zealand	215	352	371	462	459	305	285	274	297
DEVELOPING ADB MEMBER ECONOMIES[b]	**35,327**	**92,988**	**195,229**	**240,795**	**252,815**	**262,546**	**262,747**	**251,168**	**266,822**
ALL ADB REGIONAL MEMBERS[b]	**36,834**	**95,185**	**199,148**	**246,202**	**258,027**	**268,843**	**268,498**	**257,312**	**273,639**
WORLD[b]	**116,306**	**274,675**	**467,503**	**545,604**	**576,407**	**597,859**	**582,053**	**573,131**	**613,466**

... = data not available, $ = United States dollars, ADB = Asian Development Bank.

a For 2005 onward, figures are based on the IMF's Balance of Payments and International Investment Position Manual (sixth edition). Prior to 2005, figures are based on the IMF's Balance of Payments Manual (fifth edition).
b For reporting economies only.

Sources: World Bank. http://www.worldbank.org/en/topic/migrationremittancesdiasporaissues/brief/migration-remittances-data (accessed 7 June 2018). For Taipei,China: Central bank of Taipei,China. https://www.cbc.gov.tw/ct.asp?xItem=1061&ctNode=535&mp=2 (accessed 7 June 2018).

Table 2.4.5: Workers' Remittances and Compensation of Employees, Receipts
(% of GDP)

ADB Regional Member	2000	2005	2010	2012	2013	2014	2015	2016	2017
Developing ADB Member Economies									
Central and West Asia									
Afghanistan	...	0.8 (2008)	2.1	1.2	1.5	1.3	1.5	1.9	1.9
Armenia	9.5	18.7	18.0	19.2	19.7	17.9	14.1	13.1	13.3
Azerbaijan	1.1	4.7	2.7	2.9	2.3	2.5	2.4	1.7	2.6
Georgia	6.7	7.0	10.2	11.2	12.1	12.0	10.4	10.6	11.8
Kazakhstan	0.4	0.1	0.2	0.1	0.1	0.1	0.1	0.2	0.2
Kyrgyz Republic	0.2	12.7	26.4	30.8	31.1	30.0	25.3	29.3	32.9
Pakistan	1.4	3.6	5.6	6.5	6.6	6.9	7.2	7.1	6.5
Tajikistan	6.4 (2002)	20.2	35.8	42.2	43.5	36.6	28.8	26.9	31.1
Turkmenistan	...	0.1 (2006)	0.2	0.1	0.1	0.1	0.0	0.0	0.0
Uzbekistan	...	5.2 (2006)	7.2	11.0	11.6	9.2	4.6	3.7	5.7
East Asia									
China, People's Republic of	0.1	1.0	0.9	0.7	0.6	0.6	0.6	0.5	0.5
Hong Kong, China	0.1	0.2	0.1	0.1	0.1	0.1	0.1	0.1	0.1
Korea, Republic of	0.8	0.6	0.5	0.5	0.5	0.5	0.5	0.5	0.4
Mongolia	0.1	7.0	3.7	2.6	2.0	2.1	2.2	2.3	2.4
Taipei,China	0.1	0.1	0.1	0.1	0.2	0.2	0.2	0.2	0.2
South Asia									
Bangladesh	4.3	8.1	9.5	11.0	9.0	8.7	7.9	6.1	5.5
Bhutan	...	0.2 (2006)	0.5	1.0	0.7	0.7	1.0	1.6	...
India	2.7	2.6	3.1	3.7	3.6	3.4	3.2	2.8	2.7
Maldives	0.4	0.2	0.1	0.1	0.1	0.1	0.1	0.1	...
Nepal	2.1	14.7	21.3	26.7	30.7	29.2	32.4	31.6	27.9
Sri Lanka	6.9	8.1	7.3	8.8	8.6	8.9	8.7	8.9	8.2
Southeast Asia									
Brunei Darussalam	...	...	...	...	...	...	...	...	...
Cambodia	2.8	2.6	1.4	1.2	1.2	2.2	2.2	1.9	1.7
Indonesia	0.7	1.9	0.9	0.8	0.8	1.0	1.1	1.0	0.9
Lao People's Democratic Republic	0.0	0.0	0.6	0.6	0.5	0.3	0.6	0.7	0.7
Malaysia	0.4	0.8	0.4	0.4	0.4	0.5	0.6	0.5	0.5
Myanmar	0.0	0.0	0.0	0.3	2.6	0.4	0.6	1.1	1.1
Philippines	8.5	13.3	10.8	9.8	9.8	10.1	10.2	10.2	10.5
Singapore	...	...	...	...	...	...	...	...	...
Thailand	1.3	0.6	1.3	1.4	1.6	1.6	1.5	1.5	1.5
Viet Nam	4.3	5.5	7.1	6.4	6.4	6.4	6.8	5.8	6.2
The Pacific									
Cook Islands	...	...	...	...	...	...	...	...	...
Fiji	2.6	6.8	5.6	4.8	4.9	4.9	5.8	1.7	...
Kiribati	...	11.8 (2006)	10.0	9.3	9.3	9.4	9.5	9.6	...
Marshall Islands	...	16.9	13.2	12.5	12.8	14.1	15.1	14.4	13.2
Micronesia, Federated States of	...	...	6.1	6.4	7.0	7.3	7.4	7.1	7.1
Nauru	...	...	...	...	...	...	...	...	...
Palau	...	0.8	0.9	1.1	1.0	0.9	0.8	0.8	0.8
Papua New Guinea	0.2	0.1	0.0	0.1	0.1	0.0	0.0	0.0	0.0
Samoa	...	18.8	20.4	22.2	20.5	19.1	18.6	16.5	16.7
Solomon Islands	1.5	1.7	2.1	2.3	2.0	1.6	1.8	1.9	...
Timor-Leste	...	0.1 (2006)	3.4	1.8	0.6	1.1	2.0	3.2	...
Tonga	31.5 (2001)	26.0	20.7	25.3	27.5	29.6	34.4	34.4	34.2
Tuvalu	...	22.7	12.5	10.3	10.9	11.0	11.6	10.3	9.8
Vanuatu	4.9	1.3	1.7	2.8	3.0	3.5	3.2	2.3	...
Developed ADB Member Economies									
Australia	0.1	0.1	0.2	0.2	0.2	0.2	0.2	0.2	0.1
Japan	0.0	0.0	0.0	0.0	0.0	0.1	0.1	0.1	0.1
New Zealand	0.4	0.3	0.3	0.3	0.2	0.2	0.2	0.1	...
DEVELOPING ADB MEMBER ECONOMIES[a]	0.9	1.2	1.0	1.5	1.5	1.4	1.4	1.3	1.3
ALL ADB REGIONAL MEMBERS[a]	0.4	0.7	0.8	1.0	1.1	1.1	1.1	1.0	1.0

... = data not available, 0.0 = magnitude is less than half of unit employed, ADB = Asian Development Bank, GDP = gross domestic product.

a For reporting economies only.

Sources: Economy sources; International Monetary Fund. International Financial Statistics. http://data.imf.org/ (accessed 18 May 2018); and World Bank. http://www.worldbank.org/en/topic/migrationremittancesdiasporaissues/brief/migration-remittances-data (accessed 7 June 2018).

Balance of Payments

Table 2.4.6:   Foreign Direct Investment, Net Inflows
($ million)

ADB Regional Member	2000	2005	2010	2012	2013	2014	2015	2016	2017
Developing ADB Member Economies									
Central and West Asia	**2,271**	**10,946**	**20,273**	**25,490**	**20,485**	**21,242**	**19,949**	**31,255**	**12,620**
Afghanistan	0	271	191	57	48	43	169	94	53
Armenia	104	292	529	497	346	404	178	338	246
Azerbaijan	130	4,476	3,353	5,293	2,619	4,430	4,048	4,500	2,867
Georgia	131	453	900	943	1,028	1,818	1,659	1,608	1,802
Kazakhstan	1,371	2,546	7,456	13,648	10,011	7,225	6,379	16,780	4,542
Kyrgyz Republic	-2	43	473	261	612	343	1,144	619	94
Pakistan	308	2,201	2,022	859	1,333	1,868	1,621	2,488	2,815
Tajikistan	24	54	79	239	125	309	426	241	200
Turkmenistan	131	418	3,632	3,130	3,732	4,170	4,259	4,522	...
Uzbekistan	75	192	1,636	563	629	632	65	67	...
East Asia	**129,082**	**160,528**	**340,093**	**333,076**	**386,210**	**410,384**	**430,126**	**325,218**	**312,459**
China, People's Republic of	42,095	104,109	243,703	241,214	290,928	268,097	242,489	174,750	168,224
Hong Kong, China	70,496	40,963	82,709	74,887	76,857	129,847	181,047	133,259	122,401
Korea, Republic of	11,509	13,643	9,497	9,496	12,767	9,274	4,104	12,104	17,053
Mongolia	54	188	1,691	4,272	2,060	338	94	-4,156	1,494
Taipei,China	4,928	1,625	2,492	3,207	3,598	2,828	2,391	9,261	3,287
South Asia	**4,062**	**8,364**	**29,486**	**26,866**	**32,144**	**38,402**	**47,881**	**48,253**	**44,207**
Bangladesh	280	761	1,232	1,584	2,603	2,539	2,831	2,327	2,151
Bhutan	2 (2002)	6	75	24	20	29	11	8	-11
India	3,584	7,269	27,397	23,996	28,153	34,577	44,009	44,459	39,978
Maldives	22	53	216	228	361	333	298	457	517
Nepal	-0	2	88	92	74	30	52	106	196
Sri Lanka	173	272	478	941	933	894	680	897	1,375
Southeast Asia	**21,371**	**43,000**	**108,073**	**115,097**	**132,962**	**130,574**	**133,976**	**122,620**	**133,159**
Brunei Darussalam	61 (2001)	175	481	865	776	568	171	-151	...
Cambodia	118	377	1,342	1,835	1,872	1,720	1,701	2,287	...
Indonesia	-4,550	8,336	15,292	21,201	23,282	25,121	19,779	4,542	22,078
Lao People's Democratic Republic	34	28	279	294	427	913	1,421	997	...
Malaysia	3,788	3,925	10,886	8,896	11,296	10,619	9,857	13,470	9,512
Myanmar	255	235	901	1,334	2,255	2,175	4,084	3,278	4,685
Philippines	1,487	1,664	1,070	3,215	3,737	5,740	5,639	8,280	10,049
Singapore	15,515	18,090	55,076	56,189	64,482	69,543	70,595	74,253	63,633
Thailand	3,366	8,216	14,747	12,899	15,936	4,975	8,928	3,063	9,101
Viet Nam	1,298	1,954	8,000	8,368	8,900	9,200	11,800	12,600	14,100
The Pacific	**259**	**253**	**641**	**495**	**524**	**490**	**687**	**331**	**...**
Cook Islands	...	...	...	...	...	...	...	...	...
Fiji	1	185	356	376	265	348	308	282	300
Kiribati	1	3	-7	-2	-0	1	1	2	...
Marshall Islands	126	3	-9	21	33	9	-5	-3	...
Micronesia, Federated States of	-0 (2001)	0	1	1	1	20	1	...	...
Nauru	1	1	1 (2009)	...	...	...	...	...	...
Palau	3	4	3	22	18	40	35	35	...
Papua New Guinea	96	32	29	-64	18	-30	203	-40	...
Samoa	-1	4	-1	14	14	23	27	3	...
Solomon Islands	2	1	166	24	53	21	32	37	37
Timor-Leste	1 (2002)	1	30	40	56	34	43	5	7
Tonga	9	7	9	2	7	10	12	9	...
Tuvalu	-0 (2001)	-0	0	1	0	0	0	0	...
Vanuatu	20	13	63	60	59	13	31	...	...
Developed ADB Member Economies	**24,073**	**-17,727**	**42,938**	**61,944**	**64,576**	**68,980**	**42,662**	**83,838**	**70,937**
Australia	14,893	-25,093	35,211	57,550	53,997	45,979	37,419	42,580	48,752
Japan	10,688	5,460	7,441	547	10,648	19,752	5,252	39,323	18,838
New Zealand	-1,508	1,907	286	3,847	-70	3,249	-10	1,935	3,347
DEVELOPING ADB MEMBER ECONOMIES[a]	**157,045**	**223,091**	**498,567**	**501,024**	**572,324**	**601,092**	**632,619**	**527,677**	**502,788**
ALL ADB REGIONAL MEMBERS[a]	**181,118**	**205,364**	**541,505**	**562,968**	**636,901**	**670,072**	**675,281**	**611,515**	**573,725**
WORLD[a]	**1,460,994**	**1,543,154**	**1,860,424**	**2,115,523**	**2,130,718**	**1,791,461**	**2,408,672**	**2,448,814**	**1,862,732**

... = data not available, -0 or 0 = magnitude is less than half of unit employed, $ = United States dollars, ADB = Asian Development Bank.

a   For reporting economies only.

Sources: World Bank. World Development Indicators. http://data.worldbank.org/indicator/BX.KLT.DINV.CD.WD?locations=MH (accessed 6 July 2018). For Taipei,China: Central bank of Taipei,China. https://www.cbc.gov.tw/ct.asp?xItem=1061&ctNode=535&mp=2 (accessed 19 June 2018).

Table 2.4.7: Foreign Direct Investment, Net Inflows
(% of GDP)

ADB Regional Member	2000	2005	2010	2012	2013	2014	2015	2016	2017
Developing ADB Member Economies									
Central and West Asia									
Afghanistan	0.0 (2002)	4.1	1.2	0.3	0.2	0.2	0.8	0.5	0.2
Armenia	5.5	6.0	5.7	5.0	3.1	3.5	1.7	3.2	2.1
Azerbaijan	2.5	33.8	6.3	7.6	3.5	5.9	7.6	11.9	7.0
Georgia	4.3	7.1	7.7	6.0	6.4	11.0	11.9	11.2	11.9
Kazakhstan	7.5	4.5	5.0	6.6	4.2	3.3	3.5	12.2	2.8
Kyrgyz Republic	-0.2	1.7	9.9	4.0	8.3	4.6	17.1	9.1	1.2
Pakistan	0.4	1.8	1.2	0.4	0.6	0.8	0.6	0.9	0.9
Tajikistan	2.7	2.4	1.4	3.1	1.5	3.3	5.4	3.5	2.8
Turkmenistan	2.7	2.4	16.1	8.9	9.5	9.6	11.9	12.5	...
Uzbekistan	0.5	1.3	4.1	1.1	1.1	1.0	0.1	0.1	...
East Asia									
China, People's Republic of	3.5	4.6	4.0	2.8	3.0	2.6	2.2	1.6	1.4
Hong Kong, China	41.1	22.6	36.2	28.5	27.9	44.6	58.5	41.5	35.8
Korea, Republic of	2.0	1.5	0.9	0.8	1.0	0.7	0.3	0.9	1.1
Mongolia	4.7	7.4	23.5	34.8	16.4	2.8	0.8	-37.2	13.4
Taipei,China	1.5	0.4	0.6	0.6	0.7	0.5	0.5	1.7	0.6
South Asia									
Bangladesh	0.6	1.3	1.1	1.2	1.7	1.5	1.5	1.1	0.9
Bhutan	0.5 (2002)	0.8	4.7	1.3	1.1	1.5	0.5	0.4	...
India	0.7	0.9	1.6	1.3	1.5	1.7	2.1	2.0	1.6
Maldives	3.6	4.6	8.4	7.9	11.0	9.0	7.4	10.8	...
Nepal	-0.0	0.0	0.5	0.5	0.4	0.2	0.2	0.5	0.8
Sri Lanka	1.0	1.1	0.8	1.4	1.3	1.1	0.8	1.1	1.6
Southeast Asia									
Brunei Darussalam	1.0	1.8	3.5	4.5	4.3	3.3	1.3	-1.3	...
Cambodia	3.2	6.0	11.9	13.1	12.3	10.2	9.4	11.4	...
Indonesia	-2.8	2.9	2.0	2.3	2.6	2.8	2.3	0.5	2.2
Lao People's Democratic Republic	2.1	1.0	4.1	2.9	3.6	6.9	9.9	6.3	...
Malaysia	4.0	2.7	4.3	2.8	3.5	3.1	3.3	4.5	3.0
Myanmar	0.1	0.0	0.0	1.7	3.6	3.3	6.5	5.1	7.0
Philippines	1.8	1.6	0.5	1.3	1.4	2.0	1.9	2.7	3.2
Singapore	16.2	14.2	23.3	19.3	21.2	22.3	23.2	24.0	19.6
Thailand	2.7	4.3	4.3	3.2	3.8	1.2	2.2	0.7	2.0
Viet Nam	4.2	3.4	6.9	5.4	5.2	4.9	6.1	6.1	6.3
The Pacific									
Cook Islands	...	...	...	...	...	...	...	...	...
Fiji	0.0	6.2	11.3	9.5	6.3	7.8	7.1	6.0	...
Kiribati	1.1	2.3	-4.2	-1.3	-0.1	0.7	0.5	1.1	...
Marshall Islands	111.8	2.3	-5.6	11.5	16.9	4.9	-3.0	-1.6	...
Micronesia, Federated States of	-0.1 (2001)	0.0	0.3	0.3	0.3	6.4	0.3	...	...
Nauru	...	3.8	2.5 (2009)	...	...	...	...	...	...
Palau	2.2	2.2	1.5	10.1	8.0	16.2	11.8	11.6	...
Papua New Guinea	2.8	0.7	0.2	-0.3	0.1	-0.1	0.9	-0.2	...
Samoa	-0.5	0.9	-0.2	1.7	1.7	2.8	3.5	0.3	...
Solomon Islands	0.7	0.1	23.8	2.6	5.3	2.0	3.1	3.4	...
Timor-Leste	0.2 (2002)	0.1	0.8	0.6	1.0	0.8	1.4	0.2	...
Tonga	4.9	2.7	2.4	0.4	1.5	2.4	2.9	2.2	...
Tuvalu	-0.1 (2001)	-0.1	1.4	3.6	0.9	0.7	0.6	0.6	...
Vanuatu	7.4	3.4	9.0	7.7	7.4	1.6	4.1	...	...
Developed ADB Member Economies									
Australia	3.9	-3.6	3.0	3.7	3.6	3.2	3.1	3.5	3.6
Japan	0.2	0.1	0.1	0.0	0.2	0.4	0.1	0.8	0.4
New Zealand	-2.8	1.7	0.2	2.2	-0.0	1.6	-0.0	1.0	...
DEVELOPING ADB MEMBER ECONOMIES[a]	**4.0**	**2.8**	**2.6**	**3.2**	**3.3**	**3.3**	**3.3**	**2.7**	**2.4**
ALL ADB REGIONAL MEMBERS[a]	**2.0**	**1.5**	**2.1**	**2.4**	**2.7**	**2.7**	**2.7**	**2.4**	**2.1**

... = data not available, -0.0 or 0.0 = magnitude is less than half of the unit employed, ADB = Asian Development Bank, GDP = gross domestic product.

a   For reporting economies with data available for both foreign direct investment and GDP.

Sources: Economy sources; International Monetary Fund. International Financial Statistics. http://data.imf.org/ (accessed 18 May 2018); and World Bank. World Development Indicators. http://data.worldbank.org/indicator/BX.KLT.DINV.CD.WD?locations=MH (accessed 6 July 2018).

External Trade

Table 2.4.8: Merchandise Exports
($ million)

ADB Regional Member	2000	2005	2010	2012	2013	2014	2015	2016	2017
Developing ADB Member Economies									
Central and West Asia	**26,716**	**64,110**	**134,665**	**182,663**	**181,036**	**174,603**	**116,374**	**97,479**	**111,469**
Afghanistan	137	384	388	414	515	571	571	596	723
Armenia	300	974	1,041	1,380	1,479	1,547	1,485	1,792	2,243
Azerbaijan	1,745	7,649	26,374	32,374	31,703	28,260	15,586	13,211	15,152
Georgia	324	865	1,677	2,377	2,910	2,861	2,205	2,113	2,728
Kazakhstan	8,812	27,849	60,271	86,449	84,700	79,460	45,956	36,737	48,342
Kyrgyz Republic	505	674	1,756	1,928	2,007	1,884	1,483	1,573	...
Pakistan	8,335	14,453	19,261	22,797	23,383	25,715	23,526	20,859	20,566
Tajikistan	784	909	1,195	1,358	1,162	977	891	899	...
Turkmenistan	2,508	4,944	9,679	19,987	18,854	19,782	12,164	7,520	7,788
Uzbekistan	3,265	5,409	13,023	13,600	14,323	13,546	12,508	12,179	13,928
East Asia	**775,319**	**1,536,567**	**2,714,594**	**3,350,013**	**3,542,100**	**3,713,254**	**3,553,456**	**3,339,763**	**3,658,070**
China, People's Republic of	249,203	761,953	1,577,754	2,048,714	2,209,004	2,342,293	2,273,468	2,097,631	2,263,522
Hong Kong, China	201,855	289,325	390,134	442,775	458,959	473,654	465,092	462,269	497,340
Korea, Republic of	172,268	284,419	466,384	547,870	559,632	572,665	526,757	495,426	573,694
Mongolia	536	1,064	2,909	4,385	4,269	5,774	4,669	4,916	6,201
Taipei,China	151,458	199,807	277,413	306,269	310,236	318,869	283,470	279,521	317,313
South Asia	**56,445**	**119,305**	**276,096**	**340,721**	**364,635**	**353,716**	**310,213**	**320,096**	**345,864**
Bangladesh	4,780	8,259	16,099	23,508	27,619	30,217	30,590	33,275	33,461
Bhutan	103	214	535	580	511	539	561	488	566
India	45,297	103,496	249,951	305,839	325,099	310,742	267,549	275,232	299,773
Maldives	109	162	62	162	166	144	144	139	...
Nepal	701	823	830	872	827	943	833	653	699
Sri Lanka	5,456	6,351	8,618	9,761	10,413	11,130	10,536	10,309	11,364
Southeast Asia	**427,614**	**655,107**	**1,048,726**	**1,257,284**	**1,279,221**	**1,298,529**	**1,172,522**	**1,152,424**	**1,305,504**
Brunei Darussalam	3,906	6,247	8,887	12,980	11,436	10,601	6,338	4,917	5,585
Cambodia	1,397	2,908	3,903	5,684	7,044	8,170	9,336	10,273	11,224
Indonesia	62,124	85,660	157,779	190,032	182,552	175,981	150,366	145,186	168,811
Lao People's Democratic Republic	330	553	1,746	2,191	2,264	3,276	3,653	4,245	4,275
Malaysia	98,229	141,595	198,325	227,480	228,503	233,868	199,041	189,708	217,511
Myanmar	1,961	3,558	8,861	8,977	11,204	12,524	11,137	11,952	13,480
Philippines	38,078	41,255	51,498	52,100	56,698	62,102	58,827	57,406	62,875
Singapore	137,954	230,523	352,553	415,590	419,969	415,191	357,729	337,962	372,938
Thailand	69,152	110,360	192,937	227,721	227,518	226,601	214,077	214,195	234,787
Viet Nam	14,483	32,447	72,237	114,529	132,033	150,217	162,017	176,581	214,019
The Pacific	**2,880**	**4,348**	**7,167**	**8,294**	**7,809**	**10,742**	**10,056**	**9,909**	**11,443**
Cook Islands	9	5	5	5	11	18	14	14	21
Fiji	543	705	837	1,219	1,151	1,220	982	925	994
Kiribati	4	4	4	7	7	10	9	..	..
Marshall Islands	25	34	..	..	..	..	..	..	..
Micronesia, Federated States of	17	13	30	52	35	32	40	63	..
Nauru[a]	68	44	189	..	56	46	19	26	25
Palau	12	14	16	21	21	19	18	...	..
Papua New Guinea	2,089	3,311	5,737	6,323	5,951	8,794	8,425	8,202	9,872
Samoa	14	12	23	31	24	27	34	36	38
Solomon Islands	65	105	227	488	448	455	421	432	469
Timor-Leste	...	43	42	77	53	39	38	162	24
Tonga	9	10	8	16	14	19	18	..	..
Tuvalu	0	0	0	0	0	0	0	..	..
Vanuatu	26	46	48	55	39	63	39	50	..
Developed ADB Member Economies	**556,592**	**723,605**	**1,011,217**	**1,092,780**	**1,007,225**	**971,166**	**846,359**	**869,646**	**966,980**
Australia	63,980	106,211	212,027	256,522	252,894	239,708	187,525	192,140	230,928
Japan	479,320	595,696	767,825	798,937	714,931	689,916	624,681	643,753	697,951
New Zealand	13,292	21,698	31,365	37,321	39,399	41,541	34,152	33,753	38,102
DEVELOPING ADB MEMBER ECONOMIES[b]	**1,288,974**	**2,379,437**	**4,181,247**	**5,138,974**	**5,374,802**	**5,550,845**	**5,162,621**	**4,919,671**	**5,432,350**
ALL ADB REGIONAL MEMBERS[b]	**1,845,566**	**3,103,042**	**5,192,464**	**6,231,754**	**6,382,026**	**6,522,010**	**6,008,980**	**5,789,317**	**6,399,330**
WORLD	**6,431,713**	**10,438,127**	**15,148,157**	**18,310,958**	**18,700,945**	**18,798,310**	**16,384,868**	**15,829,792**	**17,519,034**

... = data not available, 0 = magnitude is less than half of unit employed, $ = United States dollars, ADB = Asian Development Bank.

a Prior to 2012, ADB estimates were derived from the International Monetary Fund's Direction of Trade Statistics. For 2012 onward, estimates are based on International Monetary Fund Staff Country Reports.
b For reporting economies only.

Sources: Economy sources; and International Monetary Fund. International Financial Statistics. http://data.imf.org/ (accessed 18 May 2018). For world merchandise exports: International Monetary Fund. May 2018. *International Financial Statistics* (CD-ROM). Washington, DC.

Table 2.4.9: Growth Rates of Merchandise Exports[a]
(%)

ADB Regional Member	2000	2005	2010	2012	2013	2014	2015	2016	2017
Developing ADB Member Economies									
Central and West Asia									
Afghanistan	-17.4	25.9	-3.7	10.1	24.4	10.9	–	4.5	21.2
Armenia	29.7	34.7	46.6	3.4	7.1	4.6	-4.0	20.6	25.2
Azerbaijan	87.7	111.6	25.3	-5.9	-2.1	-10.9	-44.8	-15.2	14.7
Georgia	36.1	33.8	48.0	8.7	22.5	-1.7	-22.9	-4.2	29.1
Kazakhstan	50.1	38.6	39.5	2.5	-2.0	-6.2	-42.2	-20.1	31.6
Kyrgyz Republic	11.2	-6.5	5.0	-14.0	4.1	-6.1	-21.3	6.1	…
Pakistan	4.8	14.9	12.0	-8.5	2.6	10.0	-8.5	-11.3	-1.4
Tajikistan	13.9	-0.7	18.3	8.0	-14.4	-15.9	-8.9	0.9	…
Turkmenistan	115.5	28.3	3.8	19.3	-5.7	4.9	-38.5	-38.2	3.6
Uzbekistan	0.9	11.5	10.6	-9.5	5.3	-5.4	-7.7	-2.6	14.4
East Asia									
China, People's Republic of	27.8	28.4	31.3	7.9	7.8	6.0	-2.9	-7.7	7.9
Hong Kong, China	16.1	11.6	22.5	3.3	3.7	3.2	-1.8	-0.6	7.6
Korea, Republic of	19.9	12.0	28.3	-1.3	2.1	2.3	-8.0	-5.9	15.8
Mongolia	18.0	22.4	54.3	-9.0	-2.6	35.3	-19.1	5.3	26.1
Taipei,China	22.6	8.6	35.1	-1.9	1.3	2.8	-11.1	-1.4	13.5
South Asia									
Bangladesh	12.5	11.3	3.7	6.6	17.5	9.4	1.2	8.8	0.6
Bhutan	-11.3	35.8	6.5	-10.2	-11.9	5.5	4.1	-13.0	16.0
India	22.2	25.0	43.1	-2.6	6.3	-4.4	-13.9	2.9	8.9
Maldives	18.8	-10.5	-63.6	40.6	2.8	-13.0	-0.6	-3.2	…
Nepal	34.0	12.4	-4.9	0.3	-5.1	14.0	-11.6	-21.6	7.0
Sri Lanka	18.5	10.1	21.7	-7.6	6.7	6.9	-5.3	-2.2	10.2
Southeast Asia									
Brunei Darussalam	53.1	23.3	23.9	4.1	-11.9	-7.3	-40.2	-22.4	13.6
Cambodia	23.6	12.3	24.4	12.8	23.9	16.0	14.3	10.0	9.3
Indonesia	27.7	19.7	35.4	-6.6	-3.9	-3.6	-14.6	-3.4	16.3
Lao People's Democratic Republic	9.6	52.2	65.9	0.1	3.3	44.7	11.5	16.2	0.7
Malaysia	16.1	11.8	26.5	-0.3	0.4	2.3	-14.9	-4.7	14.7
Myanmar	72.3	21.5	16.8	-1.7	24.8	11.8	-11.1	7.3	12.8
Philippines	8.7	4.0	34.0	7.9	8.8	9.5	-5.3	-2.4	9.5
Singapore	20.3	15.7	30.5	-0.1	1.1	-1.1	-13.8	-5.5	10.3
Thailand	18.0	14.6	27.3	3.5	-0.1	-0.4	-5.5	0.1	9.6
Viet Nam	25.5	22.5	26.5	18.2	15.3	13.8	7.9	9.0	21.2
The Pacific									
Cook Islands	154.4	-26.9	88.0	69.9	100.6	65.8	-20.3	-2.9	52.8
Fiji	-12.1	1.4	24.9	13.6	-5.6	6.0	-19.5	-5.8	7.5
Kiribati	-59.1	58.2	-38.0	-18.3	-4.9	51.9	-11.0	…	…
Marshall Islands	48.7	14.0	5.6 (2009)	…	…	…	…	…	…
Micronesia, Federated States of	688.9	-7.3	63.5	20.2	-33.3	-7.8	23.0	59.9	…
Nauru[a]	-7.9	-15.3	58.0	-71.2	-19.5	-18.7	-58.9	36.2	-4.1
Palau	65.9	116.9	15.9	12.2	-0.5	-8.7	-5.3	…	…
Papua New Guinea	7.3	26.8	30.9	-8.5	-5.9	47.8	-4.2	-2.6	20.4
Samoa	-24.9	0.6	114.4	26.8	-23.2	14.7	23.8	6.3	4.2
Solomon Islands	-48.1	22.3	37.4	19.7	-8.3	1.7	-7.6	2.7	8.6
Timor-Leste	…	-58.9	20.7	44.4	-30.7	-26.7	-1.7	321.2	-85.1
Tonga	-27.1	-35.2	7.1	-1.2	-9.2	34.2	-6.5	…	…
Tuvalu	-91.5	-54.0	55.5	-83.7	4.4	464.8	-12.0	…	…
Vanuatu	2.8	-6.5	-14.8	-18.5	-29.4	62.6	-38.0	28.8	…
Developed ADB Member Economies									
Australia	14.1	22.6	38.3	-5.0	-1.4	-5.2	-21.8	2.5	20.2
Japan	14.8	5.4	32.6	-2.7	-10.5	-3.5	-9.5	3.1	8.4
New Zealand	6.5	6.6	26.6	-1.0	5.6	5.4	-17.8	-1.2	12.9
DEVELOPING ADB MEMBER ECONOMIES[b]	**21.0**	**18.3**	**30.2**	**3.2**	**4.6**	**3.3**	**-7.0**	**-4.7**	**10.4**
ALL ADB REGIONAL MEMBERS[b]	**19.0**	**15.6**	**30.8**	**2.0**	**2.4**	**2.2**	**-7.9**	**-3.7**	**10.5**
WORLD	**13.6**	**13.8**	**22.3**	**0.8**	**2.1**	**0.5**	**-12.8**	**-3.4**	**10.7**

… = data not available, – = magnitude equals zero, ADB = Asian Development Bank.

a   Growth rates are based on the value of exports in United States dollars.

b   For reporting economies only.

Sources: Economy sources; and International Monetary Fund. International Financial Statistics. http://data.imf.org/ (accessed 18 May 2018). For world merchandise exports: International Monetary Fund. May 2018. *International Financial Statistics* (CD-ROM). Washington, DC.

Table 2.4.10: Merchandise Imports
($ million)

ADB Regional Member	2000	2005	2010	2012	2013	2014	2015	2016	2017
Developing ADB Member Economies									
Central and West Asia	24,868	58,649	109,356	155,070	163,205	157,857	138,055	128,494	133,558
Afghanistan	1,176	2,470	5,154	8,932	8,724	7,729	7,723	6,534	7,065
Armenia	885	1,802	3,749	4,261	4,386	4,424	3,239	3,273	4,183
Azerbaijan	1,172	4,350	6,662	10,192	10,321	9,332	9,774	9,004	9,037
Georgia	710	2,488	5,236	8,056	8,023	8,602	7,300	7,295	7,983
Kazakhstan	5,040	17,353	31,127	46,358	48,806	41,296	30,568	25,377	29,305
Kyrgyz Republic	554	1,189	3,223	5,576	5,987	5,735	4,154	4,000	...
Pakistan	9,967	20,630	34,169	42,960	42,802	45,820	45,394	44,665	52,742
Tajikistan	675	1,330	2,657	1,779	4,121	4,297	3,436	3,031	...
Turkmenistan	1,742	2,947	8,204	14,138	16,090	16,638	14,051	13,177	10,189
Uzbekistan	2,947	4,091	9,176	12,817	13,947	13,984	12,417	12,138	13,055
East Asia	739,620	1,407,134	2,513,437	3,126,375	3,272,375	3,314,814	2,877,443	2,743,744	3,142,290
China, People's Republic of	225,094	659,953	1,396,244	1,818,405	1,949,989	1,959,235	1,679,565	1,587,926	1,840,982
Hong Kong, China	212,800	299,520	433,102	504,377	523,558	544,107	522,001	516,395	559,074
Korea, Republic of	160,481	261,238	425,212	519,584	515,586	525,515	436,499	406,193	478,478
Mongolia	615	1,177	3,200	6,738	6,358	5,237	3,798	3,358	4,337
Taipei,China	140,630	185,245	255,679	277,269	276,884	280,722	235,581	229,872	259,419
South Asia	68,758	174,440	412,017	561,767	528,719	519,180	455,085	452,877	529,257
Bangladesh	8,080	12,575	23,581	35,219	38,738	41,031	37,530	39,703	42,778
Bhutan[a]	193	466	810	952	864	936	977	1,046	1,044
India	51,372	149,753	368,166	499,495	463,402	448,486	388,187	383,608	454,979
Maldives	389	683	909	1,554	1,728	1,988	1,890	2,121	...
Nepal	1,526	2,094	5,110	5,419	5,987	7,323	7,565	7,204	9,474
Sri Lanka	7,198	8,869	13,441	19,129	17,999	19,417	18,935	19,195	20,982
Southeast Asia	368,357	583,476	954,710	1,202,318	1,233,183	1,224,425	1,088,950	1,072,156	1,226,882
Brunei Darussalam	1,107	1,448	2,535	3,565	3,613	3,596	3,235	2,671	3,083
Cambodia[a]	1,936	3,918	6,588	9,212	10,680	12,022	13,285	14,119	15,502
Indonesia	33,515	57,701	135,663	191,691	186,629	178,179	142,695	135,653	156,925
Lao People's Democratic Republic	535	882	2,060	3,046	3,051	4,976	5,675	5,372	5,350
Malaysia	81,963	114,302	164,177	196,412	205,875	208,667	175,593	168,459	194,897
Myanmar	2,319	1,984	6,413	9,069	13,760	16,633	16,578	17,211	17,010
Philippines	34,491	47,418	54,933	62,129	62,411	65,398	71,067	84,108	92,660
Singapore	134,675	200,861	312,668	385,851	388,053	377,714	307,967	291,922	327,389
Thailand	62,180	118,200	184,834	227,564	227,079	209,392	187,079	177,662	202,962
Viet Nam	15,637	36,761	84,839	113,780	132,033	147,849	165,776	174,978	211,104
The Pacific	2,715	4,486	7,251	9,585	11,524	9,773	7,746	6,754	6,822
Cook Islands	51	81	91	112	116	121	110	106	130
Fiji	856	1,610	1,806	2,252	2,823	2,656	2,268	2,310	2,408
Kiribati	39	76	73	109	107	107	103	...	...
Marshall Islands	116	132	...	...	...	...	...	...	...
Micronesia, Federated States of	107	128	168	194	188	161	160	186	...
Nauru[b]	78	51	42	35	52	77	57	65	72
Palau	127	108	103	136	145	149	156	...	...
Papua New Guinea	999	1,519	3,522	4,757	6,196	4,548	3,005	2,381	2,826
Samoa	91	187	280	308	326	341	298	312	324
Solomon Islands	92	185	405	497	510	505	485	465	508
Timor-Leste	...	109	298	670	529	554	491	512	554
Tonga	70	121	158	199	198	219	209	...	...
Tuvalu	5	13	22	21	21	22	37	...	...
Vanuatu	84	165	284	296	314	314	367	416	...
Developed ADB Member Economies	461,654	661,780	915,836	1,174,604	1,104,784	1,081,268	885,005	832,052	933,140
Australia	67,806	118,836	193,071	250,419	232,685	227,859	200,643	189,075	220,981
Japan	379,884	516,697	692,242	885,928	832,440	810,886	647,744	607,043	672,032
New Zealand	13,963	26,248	30,523	38,256	39,659	42,523	36,618	35,935	40,127
DEVELOPING ADB MEMBER ECONOMIES[c]	1,204,318	2,228,185	3,996,771	5,055,116	5,209,006	5,226,049	4,567,280	4,404,024	5,038,810
ALL ADB REGIONAL MEMBERS[c]	1,665,972	2,889,966	4,912,607	6,229,720	6,313,790	6,307,317	5,452,285	5,236,076	5,971,950
WORLD	6,603,642	10,680,260	15,398,312	18,535,058	18,809,348	18,919,308	16,579,814	16,178,586	17,807,501

... = data not available, $ = United States dollars, ADB = Asian Development Bank.

a Compilation methodology shifted from cost, insurance, and freight to free on board for Bhutan from 2004 onward and for Cambodia from 2005 onward.
b Prior to 2012, ADB estimates were derived from the International Monetary Fund's Direction of Trade Statistics. For 2012 onward, estimates are based on International Monetary Fund Staff Country Reports.
c For reporting economies only.

Sources: Economy sources; and International Monetary Fund. International Financial Statistics. http://data.imf.org/ (accessed 18 May 2018). For world merchandise imports: International Monetary Fund. May 2018. International Financial Statistics (CD-ROM). Washington, DC.

Table 2.4.11: Growth Rates of Merchandise Imports[a]
(%)

ADB Regional Member	2000	2005	2010	2012	2013	2014	2015	2016	2017
Developing ADB Member Economies									
Central and West Asia									
Afghanistan	16.2	13.5	54.5	39.8	-2.3	-11.4	-0.1	-15.4	8.1
Armenia	9.1	33.4	12.9	2.8	2.9	0.9	-26.8	1.1	27.8
Azerbaijan	13.1	23.7	6.9	1.4	1.3	-9.6	4.7	-7.9	0.4
Georgia	2.9	34.9	17.0	13.9	-0.4	7.2	-15.1	-0.1	9.4
Kazakhstan	37.9	35.8	9.6	25.6	5.3	-15.4	-26.0	-17.0	15.5
Kyrgyz Republic	-7.6	25.5	6.0	30.9	7.4	-4.2	-27.6	-3.7	...
Pakistan	5.7	33.7	2.5	7.3	-0.4	7.1	-0.9	-1.6	18.1
Tajikistan	1.8	11.7	3.4	-44.5	131.6	4.3	-20.1	-11.8	...
Turkmenistan	26.8	-6.4	-8.8	24.4	13.8	3.4	-15.5	-6.2	-22.7
Uzbekistan	-5.2	7.2	-2.8	13.0	8.8	0.3	-11.2	-2.2	7.6
East Asia									
China, People's Republic of	35.8	17.6	38.8	4.3	7.2	0.5	-14.3	-5.5	15.9
Hong Kong, China	18.5	10.5	24.7	4.3	3.8	3.9	-4.1	-1.1	8.3
Korea, Republic of	34.0	16.4	31.6	-0.9	-0.8	1.9	-16.9	-6.9	17.8
Mongolia	19.8	15.5	49.7	2.1	-5.6	-17.6	-27.5	-11.6	29.2
Taipei,China	26.3	7.8	44.3	-3.4	-0.1	1.4	-16.1	-2.4	12.9
South Asia									
Bangladesh	3.1	16.5	4.4	1.5	10.0	5.9	-8.5	5.8	7.7
Bhutan[b]	2.9	77.2	40.7	-12.9	-9.2	8.3	4.4	7.0	-0.1
India	2.8	35.4	30.7	-0.6	-7.2	-3.2	-13.4	-1.2	18.6
Maldives	-3.4	21.3	-5.6	16.9	11.2	15.0	-4.9	12.2	...
Nepal	19.0	13.2	39.3	1.2	10.5	22.3	3.3	-4.8	31.5
Sri Lanka	20.5	10.7	31.8	-5.6	-5.9	7.9	-2.5	1.4	9.3
Southeast Asia									
Brunei Darussalam	-16.7	1.5	5.6	-1.0	1.4	-0.5	-10.0	-17.4	15.4
Cambodia[b]	21.6	...	35.0	13.1	15.9	12.6	10.5	6.3	9.8
Indonesia	39.6	24.0	40.1	8.0	-2.6	-4.5	-19.9	-4.9	15.7
Lao People's Democratic Republic	-3.4	23.8	41.0	26.7	0.1	63.1	14.1	-5.3	-0.4
Malaysia	25.3	8.7	33.1	4.8	4.8	1.4	-15.9	-4.1	15.7
Myanmar	-11.0	0.6	53.4	0.4	51.7	20.9	-0.3	3.8	-1.2
Philippines	5.9	7.7	27.5	2.7	0.5	4.8	8.7	18.4	10.2
Singapore	21.3	15.4	26.9	3.6	0.6	-2.7	-18.5	-5.2	12.1
Thailand	23.3	25.1	37.7	-0.6	-0.2	-7.8	-10.7	-5.0	14.2
Viet Nam	33.2	15.0	21.3	6.6	16.0	12.0	12.1	5.6	20.6
The Pacific									
Cook Islands	21.9	7.0	11.2	1.9	3.9	4.1	-9.3	-3.0	21.8
Fiji	-8.3	11.5	16.9	3.2	25.4	-5.9	-14.6	1.9	4.2
Kiribati	-4.2	28.7	5.4	18.4	-1.2	0.0	-3.7	...	...
Marshall Islands	16.7	15.3	...	...	...	...	...	...	...
Micronesia, Federated States of	...	-3.2	-1.8	3.0	-3.1	-14.3	-0.3	16.0	...
Nauru[c]	104.9	52.3	-79.4	-43.7	48.7	48.6	-25.3	12.9	10.4
Palau	-5.7	0.7	9.3	8.4	6.7	3.1	4.4	...	...
Papua New Guinea	-7.0	4.5	23.0	12.4	30.3	-26.6	-33.9	-20.8	18.7
Samoa	-21.7	20.7	36.6	-3.3	5.6	4.8	-12.7	4.8	3.7
Solomon Islands	-16.1	52.4	51.2	5.1	2.7	-1.0	-4.1	-4.1	9.4
Timor-Leste	...	-25.3	1.0	97.3	-21.1	4.7	-11.3	4.2	8.2
Tonga	-3.8	15.3	10.3	3.7	-0.5	10.4	-4.4	...	...
Tuvalu	-36.0	13.3	59.2	-22.9	-1.2	7.1	66.3	...	...
Vanuatu	-12.6	22.4	-2.5	-2.7	5.8	-0.0	17.0	13.5	...
Developed ADB Member Economies									
Australia	3.5	14.4	23.4	7.0	-7.1	-2.1	-11.9	-5.8	16.9
Japan	22.7	13.6	25.8	3.8	-6.0	-2.6	-20.1	-6.3	10.7
New Zealand	-2.7	13.4	21.5	3.3	3.7	7.2	-13.9	-1.9	11.7
DEVELOPING ADB MEMBER ECONOMIES[d]	**24.3**	**16.3**	**32.7**	**2.9**	**3.0**	**0.3**	**-12.6**	**-3.6**	**14.4**
ALL ADB REGIONAL MEMBERS[d]	**22.6**	**15.7**	**31.2**	**3.2**	**1.3**	**-0.1**	**-13.6**	**-4.0**	**14.1**
WORLD	**13.5**	**13.2**	**21.5**	**1.2**	**1.5**	**0.6**	**-12.4**	**-2.4**	**10.1**

... = data not available, -0.0 or 0.0 = magnitude is less than half of unit employed, ADB = Asian Development Bank.

a   Growth rates are based on the value of imports in United States dollars.
b   Compilation methodology shifted from cost, insurance, and freight to free on board for Bhutan in 2004 and Cambodia in 2005.
c   Prior to 2012, ADB estimates were derived from the International Monetary Fund's Direction of Trade Statistics. For 2012 onward, estimates are based on International Monetary Fund Staff Country Reports.
d   For reporting economies only.

Sources: Economy sources; and International Monetary Fund. International Financial Statistics. http://data.imf.org/ (accessed 18 May 2018). For world merchandise imports: International Monetary Fund. May 2018. *International Financial Statistics* (CD-ROM). Washington, DC.

Table 2.4.12:   **Trade in Goods**[a]
(% of GDP)

ADB Regional Member	2000	2005	2010	2012	2013	2014	2015	2016	2017
Developing ADB Member Economies									
Central and West Asia									
Afghanistan	...	43.1	34.5	43.8	42.8	38.9	40.2	35.2	36.2
Armenia	62.0	56.6	51.7	56.7	52.7	51.4	44.8	48.0	55.7
Azerbaijan	55.3	90.6	62.4	61.1	56.7	50.0	47.8	58.7	59.4
Georgia	33.8	52.3	59.4	65.8	67.7	69.4	67.9	65.4	70.7
Kazakhstan	75.7	79.1	61.7	63.9	56.4	54.5	41.5	45.2	48.7
Kyrgyz Republic	77.3	75.7	103.8	113.6	109.0	102.0	84.4	81.8	...
Pakistan	23.1	29.3	30.6	30.6	30.0	28.7	25.8	23.6	24.2
Tajikistan	169.6	96.8	68.3	41.1	62.1	57.1	55.1	56.5	...
Turkmenistan	86.2	45.9	79.2	97.0	89.1	83.8	73.1	57.2	47.4
Uzbekistan	45.1	66.0	56.2	51.2	49.0	43.6	37.3	36.1	54.3
East Asia									
China, People's Republic of	39.2	62.2	48.7	45.2	43.3	41.0	35.7	32.9	33.5
Hong Kong, China	241.5	324.3	360.1	360.6	356.4	349.2	319.0	305.0	309.4
Korea, Republic of	59.2	60.8	81.5	87.3	82.4	77.8	69.7	63.7	68.7
Mongolia	101.2	88.8	85.0	90.5	84.5	90.1	72.1	74.0	94.6
Taipei,China	88.1	102.4	119.5	117.7	114.8	113.0	98.7	96.0	100.7
South Asia									
Bangladesh	28.3	36.2	34.7	45.6	43.2	41.2	35.0	33.1	31.0
Bhutan	67.3	83.1	84.9	84.0	76.5	75.3	74.7	69.3	...
India	20.0	30.2	36.3	43.3	41.1	37.2	30.6	29.0	29.3
Maldives	79.7	72.6	37.5	59.4	57.5	57.7	50.8	53.5	...
Nepal	41.7	35.3	36.5	35.1	37.4	41.0	40.4	37.5	40.9
Sri Lanka	75.7	62.4	38.9	42.2	38.2	38.5	36.6	36.1	37.1
Southeast Asia									
Brunei Darussalam	83.5	80.7	83.3	86.9	83.2	83.0	74.0	66.6	71.5
Cambodia[b]	90.9	108.5	93.3	106.1	116.1	120.2	125.1	121.9	120.8
Indonesia	58.0	50.1	38.9	41.6	40.5	39.8	34.0	30.1	32.1
Lao People's Democratic Republic	52.9	52.8	56.5	51.4	44.5	62.2	64.8	60.8	57.1
Malaysia	192.1	178.3	142.1	134.8	134.4	130.9	126.4	120.8	131.1
Myanmar	1.1	0.3	0.22	22.55	40.2	44.0	44.3	45.2	45.4
Philippines	89.6	86.0	53.3	45.7	43.8	44.8	44.4	46.4	49.6
Singapore[c]	284.5	338.6	281.4	275.7	265.4	254.5	218.9	203.4	216.2
Thailand	103.9	120.7	110.7	114.5	108.2	107.0	99.9	95.2	96.1
Viet Nam	96.6	120.1	135.5	146.5	154.2	160.1	169.6	171.3	190.0
The Pacific									
Cook Islands	65.3	47.3	37.5	38.7	42.0	43.8	43.3	41.7	48.6
Fiji	83.3	77.7	84.2	87.4	94.9	86.4	74.5	69.3	...
Kiribati	63.6	72.0	49.3	60.8	61.5	65.6	66.4	...	...
Marshall Islands	125.4	118.1	...	...	...	...	...	...	...
Micronesia, Federated States of	53.0	56.5	66.7	75.4	70.4	60.7	63.4	75.5	...
Nauru	...	360.0	366.6	...	105.6	106.7	84.5	86.8	83.1
Palau	96.1	66.1	64.9	72.9	73.5	68.5	59.3	...	...
Papua New Guinea	88.3	99.3	65.0	52.0	57.1	58.0	49.8	49.3	57.7
Samoa	45.1	45.9	44.5	42.4	43.5	44.7	42.9	42.4	42.3
Solomon Islands	55.1	67.7	90.8	107.3	94.4	91.8	88.1	82.1	...
Timor-Leste	...	8.4	8.5	11.2	10.3	14.7	17.1	26.7	...
Tonga	41.9	49.6	44.6	46.2	48.3	54.6	56.5	...	...
Tuvalu	37.3	59.8	72.5	56.4	55.9	60.9	105.7	...	...
Vanuatu	40.5	53.5	47.4	44.9	43.9	46.2	53.4	58.0	...
Developed ADB Member Economies									
Australia	34.4	32.0	34.0	32.7	32.8	32.5	31.9	30.9	33.6
Japan	17.6	23.4	25.6	27.2	30.0	30.9	29.0	25.3	28.1
New Zealand	50.1	41.8	42.2	42.9	41.4	41.8	39.8	37.0	...
DEVELOPING ADB MEMBER ECONOMIES[d]	**62.9**	**57.8**	**42.4**	**64.7**	**61.8**	**58.8**	**51.5**	**48.3**	**49.7**
ALL ADB REGIONAL MEMBERS[d]	**37.8**	**44.3**	**38.4**	**52.6**	**53.0**	**51.7**	**46.4**	**43.0**	**45.3**

... = data not available, ADB = Asian Development Bank, GDP = Gross Domestic Product.

a   The sum of merchandise exports and imports in US dollar values.
b   For 2005 onward, the compilation methodology for imports shifted from cost, insurance, and freight to free on board.
c   Prior to 2003, data excluded Indonesia.
d   For reporting economies only.

Sources: Economy sources; and International Monetary Fund. International Financial Statistics. http://data.imf.org/ (accessed 18 May 2018).

Table 2.4.13: **Direction of Trade: Merchandise Exports**
(% of total merchandise exports)

To From ADB Regional Member	Asia and the Pacific		Europe		North and Central America		Middle East		South America		Africa		Rest of the World	
	2000	2017	2000	2017	2000	2017	2000	2017	2000	2017	2000	2017	2000	2017
Developing ADB Member Economies														
Central and West Asia														
Afghanistan	39.2	87.8	49.0	2.4	2.9	0.3	0.5	6.3	2.4	0.3	0.3	0.7	5.7	2.2
Armenia	8.2	13.9	56.0	65.2	12.9	3.7	12.5	16.3	0.0	0.0	0.0	0.0	10.3	0.9
Azerbaijan	7.4	18.6	76.4	55.2	0.5	3.8	8.6	7.2	0.4	0.0	0.6	1.8	6.1	13.6
Georgia	16.1	33.0	52.7	46.7	2.7	5.1	4.0	6.2	0.1	0.2	1.4	0.9	23.1	7.9
Kazakhstan	12.4	24.8	48.3	68.5	14.8	1.4	2.5	2.6	0.1	0.1	0.1	0.3	21.8	2.4
Kyrgyz Republic	38.2	32.5	58.1	57.2	0.6	0.2	1.7	2.7	0.0	0.0	0.1	0.1	1.5	7.4
Pakistan	24.8	26.1	28.6	36.3	28.1	19.6	12.4	8.9	1.2	1.2	3.6	6.3	1.2	1.5
Tajikistan	16.6	26.4	72.6	32.1	0.1	0.0	1.7	10.4	0.7	0.0	0.8	7.2	7.5	23.9
Turkmenistan	6.0	88.9	74.8	5.7	1.1	0.2	10.2	0.0	0.0	0.1	0.2	0.0	7.7	5.1
Uzbekistan	28.1	36.1	62.6	53.2	2.1	0.2	2.2	1.8	1.1	0.1	0.1	0.1	3.6	8.6
East Asia														
China, People's Republic of	52.0	45.6	18.0	18.9	23.6	22.8	2.9	4.8	1.4	3.4	1.7	3.7	0.4	0.8
Hong Kong, China	53.9	75.7	16.5	11.3	26.1	9.0	1.4	2.3	1.1	0.7	0.7	0.8	0.2	0.2
Korea, Republic of	49.1	63.8	15.5	11.3	26.4	15.9	4.3	4.2	2.2	1.9	1.5	1.7	1.0	1.3
Mongolia	57.7	86.7	17.5	12.8	24.6	0.2	0.1	0.2	0.0	0.0	0.0	0.0	0.1	0.0
Taipei,China	53.6	73.5	15.7	9.2	26.1	13.3	1.7	2.0	1.2	0.8	0.9	0.6	0.8	0.5
South Asia														
Bangladesh	7.0	11.3	41.0	50.4	33.8	15.1	2.4	2.0	0.2	0.7	0.6	0.6	14.9	19.8
Bhutan	93.0	97.1	2.0	2.8	1.4	0.1	0.0	0.0	0.3	0.0	3.2	0.0	0.0	0.0
India	26.5	33.4	27.8	18.6	23.8	18.1	12.2	17.8	1.3	2.3	4.3	7.5	4.0	2.3
Maldives	36.7	64.9	18.6	28.0	44.2	6.0	0.0	0.2	0.0	0.0	0.5	0.9	0.0	0.0
Nepal	46.1	61.8	24.0	14.0	28.0	12.9	0.1	0.6	0.0	0.2	0.0	0.1	1.7	10.4
Sri Lanka	14.8	25.0	29.6	32.1	43.5	28.5	7.7	9.1	0.6	1.5	0.7	1.7	3.1	2.0
Southeast Asia														
Brunei Darussalam	87.1	94.0	0.5	5.3	12.3	0.6	0.1	0.1	0.0	0.0	0.0	0.0	0.0	0.0
Cambodia	28.3	27.6	17.2	41.1	54.4	28.8	0.0	0.8	0.0	0.9	0.0	0.2	0.0	0.6
Indonesia	64.1	69.2	14.8	11.4	15.1	11.9	3.4	3.4	0.9	1.2	1.4	2.1	0.4	0.7
Lao People's Democratic Republic	58.3	91.1	38.0	6.2	3.2	2.3	0.1	0.1	0.0	0.0	0.2	0.1	0.2	0.1
Malaysia	60.0	70.4	14.3	11.2	22.3	11.0	2.0	2.9	0.6	0.7	0.6	2.4	0.2	1.3
Myanmar	66.7	87.8	8.9	9.6	23.8	0.6	0.1	1.2	0.3	0.5	0.3	0.3	0.0	0.1
Philippines	48.8	65.8	18.6	15.3	31.7	16.4	0.5	1.5	0.2	0.6	0.1	0.3	0.1	0.1
Singapore	62.6	77.6	14.5	9.6	19.2	8.9	1.7	2.0	0.4	0.5	1.1	1.1	0.5	0.3
Thailand	53.2	65.6	17.3	12.4	23.3	13.4	3.1	3.5	0.6	1.7	1.7	2.5	0.8	0.8
Viet Nam	65.9	48.5	22.9	20.1	6.3	22.8	3.0	4.1	0.3	2.1	0.8	1.2	0.7	1.1
The Pacific														
Cook Islands	87.1	82.4	0.0	0.0	7.8	0.1	0.0	0.0	0.0	0.0	0.0	0.0	5.1	17.6
Fiji	52.7	61.6	20.2	13.1	23.7	22.1	0.0	0.2	0.1	0.0	0.0	0.1	3.3	2.9
Kiribati	85.3	87.5	2.8	0.4	0.1	11.8	0.0	0.0	11.8	0.0	0.0	0.1	0.0	0.2
Marshall Islands[a]	0.1	28.0	99.9	42.5	0.0	6.7	0.0	13.1	0.0	0.3	0.0	3.8	0.0	5.6
Micronesia, Federated States of	41.9	77.5	0.4	0.1	57.7	1.6	0.0	0.0	0.0	3.1	0.0	0.0	0.0	17.6
Nauru	84.1	54.9	1.3	0.3	7.5	3.8	0.0	0.2	0.1	0.1	7.0	40.6	0.0	0.1
Palau	64.7	70.2	7.0	2.0	12.2	15.9	0.0	0.0	1.4	1.9	14.7	1.9	0.0	8.0
Papua New Guinea	71.9	84.3	19.9	11.2	6.9	2.4	0.2	0.1	0.0	1.9	1.1	0.1	0.1	0.0
Samoa	72.1	66.3	1.6	1.3	26.0	6.4	0.2	0.6	0.0	0.2	0.1	0.2	0.0	25.0
Solomon Islands	97.9	85.6	0.7	13.5	0.0	0.5	0.0	0.1	0.0	0.0	1.0	0.3	0.3	0.0
Timor-Leste[a]	75.5	25.7	17.1	24.6	6.7	16.5	0.0	13.6	0.0	0.0	0.6	19.6	0.0	0.0
Tonga	57.0	82.6	1.2	1.5	21.5	14.5	0.1	0.0	0.0	0.0	15.6	0.2	4.7	1.2
Tuvalu	6.0	17.5	77.4	35.8	0.6	19.4	0.0	0.3	8.5	5.8	7.5	21.2	0.0	0.0
Vanuatu	28.6	51.1	66.9	4.6	3.0	36.1	0.0	0.1	0.1	6.2	0.0	0.5	1.3	1.3
Developed ADB Member Economies														
Australia	66.0	81.5	12.2	6.2	11.6	4.6	5.1	2.8	0.8	0.7	1.9	1.0	2.4	3.2
Japan	43.4	57.8	17.7	12.9	34.3	23.5	2.3	3.1	1.2	1.2	0.9	0.9	0.3	0.5
New Zealand	58.1	67.8	16.5	9.8	18.0	12.4	2.8	4.4	1.5	0.9	0.9	2.7	2.1	2.0
DEVELOPING ADB MEMBER ECONOMIES	**52.7**	**56.3**	**17.5**	**16.2**	**23.6**	**17.2**	**2.9**	**4.6**	**1.1**	**2.1**	**1.3**	**2.7**	**0.9**	**1.0**
ALL ADB REGIONAL MEMBERS	**50.8**	**57.4**	**17.4**	**15.4**	**26.0**	**17.4**	**2.8**	**4.3**	**1.1**	**2.0**	**1.2**	**2.4**	**0.8**	**1.1**
WORLD	**24.5**	**33.2**	**41.6**	**36.9**	**25.3**	**18.4**	**3.0**	**4.5**	**2.2**	**2.5**	**1.7**	**2.6**	**1.7**	**1.9**

0.0 = magnitude is less than half of unit employed, ADB = Asian Development Bank.

a   For 2000, data refer to 2004.

Sources: International Monetary Fund. May 2018. *International Financial Statistics* (CD-ROM). Washington, DC. For the Cook Islands and Taipei,China: Economy sources.

External Trade

Table 2.4.14:   Direction of Trade: Merchandise Imports
(% of total merchandise imports)

From / To / ADB Regional Member	Asia and the Pacific		Europe		North and Central America		Middle East		South America		Africa		Rest of the World	
	2000	2017	2000	2017	2000	2017	2000	2017	2000	2017	2000	2017	2000	2017
Developing ADB Member Economies														
Central and West Asia														
Afghanistan	91.9	67.8	3.4	4.6	0.1	1.3	3.7	24.1	0.0	0.2	0.3	0.6	0.6	1.4
Armenia	4.3	21.7	55.8	56.5	14.6	5.4	15.4	7.1	0.0	2.2	0.0	0.9	9.9	6.1
Azerbaijan	14.5	20.9	54.1	48.7	10.5	8.9	7.3	3.9	0.5	2.6	2.1	0.2	11.1	14.8
Georgia	17.9	28.0	51.2	44.7	10.2	3.8	4.2	3.7	0.9	2.2	0.1	0.3	15.5	17.2
Kazakhstan	11.7	27.6	75.7	62.7	7.0	5.2	1.1	0.9	1.0	0.6	0.5	0.5	3.0	2.5
Kyrgyz Republic	39.3	52.4	40.6	35.7	11.7	3.6	2.9	0.6	0.1	0.1	0.0	0.1	5.5	7.6
Pakistan	31.2	49.5	19.0	12.5	7.0	6.2	38.3	25.7	1.0	2.1	2.7	3.4	0.8	0.5
Tajikistan	56.5	36.7	40.0	51.3	0.1	1.6	1.6	5.3	0.0	1.6	1.1	0.0	0.6	3.5
Turkmenistan	17.7	19.7	44.8	34.5	3.5	7.1	13.5	0.1	0.1	0.1	0.0	14.4	20.4	24.2
Uzbekistan	34.0	50.2	49.6	42.4	10.9	1.2	1.1	0.2	0.1	0.1	0.0	0.0	4.3	5.9
East Asia														
China, People's Republic of	58.2	48.5	17.6	17.5	11.9	10.3	4.5	6.1	2.1	6.1	2.4	3.9	3.2	7.5
Hong Kong, China	80.5	82.2	10.2	9.3	7.6	5.7	0.8	1.3	0.5	0.7	0.3	0.7	0.1	0.1
Korea, Republic of	48.1	53.0	12.5	15.7	20.0	12.7	15.9	14.4	1.6	2.5	1.8	1.3	0.1	0.4
Mongolia	47.1	52.2	47.7	40.6	4.8	5.9	0.2	0.1	0.0	0.3	0.0	0.1	0.2	0.7
Taipei,China	58.9	62.7	13.6	12.1	19.4	12.9	4.8	8.6	1.0	1.8	2.3	1.4	0.0	0.4
South Asia														
Bangladesh	60.8	65.8	12.1	9.6	3.7	4.4	5.2	5.3	1.4	4.7	0.9	2.4	16.0	7.8
Bhutan	91.3	97.2	8.1	2.2	0.4	0.2	0.0	0.2	0.2	0.0	0.0	0.1	0.0	0.2
India	23.6	40.5	28.8	17.3	7.2	7.7	9.4	20.6	1.4	4.2	6.1	7.7	23.5	2.0
Maldives	76.0	64.7	10.5	9.5	3.7	3.5	8.9	18.6	0.1	0.8	0.4	0.7	0.5	2.1
Nepal	71.6	84.6	12.6	5.6	2.0	2.5	5.7	4.3	0.8	1.8	0.1	0.8	7.2	0.4
Sri Lanka	70.4	72.5	14.1	10.8	4.6	5.0	9.4	9.1	0.5	0.7	0.5	1.5	0.4	0.4
Southeast Asia														
Brunei Darussalam	74.7	75.7	13.7	13.8	10.7	9.4	0.3	0.3	0.1	0.5	0.0	0.1	0.4	0.1
Cambodia	88.8	92.6	8.2	5.3	2.8	1.6	0.1	0.2	0.1	0.1	0.0	0.1	0.1	0.1
Indonesia	60.5	72.7	13.9	9.8	12.3	6.5	8.4	5.5	1.5	2.4	2.3	2.8	1.0	0.4
Lao People's Democratic Republic	92.2	95.6	7.0	3.9	0.7	0.5	0.0	0.0	0.0	0.1	0.0	0.0	0.0	0.0
Malaysia	65.2	73.5	12.5	11.0	17.3	8.3	2.0	3.7	0.6	2.0	0.4	1.2	1.9	0.3
Myanmar	89.3	86.7	8.4	2.9	2.3	0.9	0.0	8.7	0.0	0.6	0.0	0.2	0.0	0.2
Philippines	58.4	78.6	10.7	7.7	19.4	8.5	10.5	3.8	0.7	1.2	0.2	0.1	0.0	0.1
Singapore	60.7	59.8	14.1	16.9	15.8	12.0	8.2	9.3	0.3	1.1	0.4	0.7	0.6	0.2
Thailand	60.2	65.8	12.6	14.1	12.6	7.4	10.2	8.3	1.1	1.5	1.3	1.2	2.0	1.6
Viet Nam	82.9	83.5	11.8	6.7	2.6	3.9	1.3	1.2	0.4	2.4	0.3	1.3	0.7	0.9
The Pacific														
Cook Islands	87.0	72.4	0.2	0.1	8.6	6.4	0.0	0.0	0.0	0.0	0.0	0.0	4.3	21.0
Fiji	84.6	90.6	3.8	4.3	5.5	3.7	0.1	0.3	0.3	0.1	0.2	0.4	5.5	0.7
Kiribati	85.2	90.8	2.5	1.8	12.3	6.9	0.0	0.0	0.0	0.1	0.0	0.4	0.0	0.0
Marshall Islands[a]	0.2	86.5	99.8	8.7	0.0	2.2	0.0	1.1	0.0	0.0	0.0	0.3	0.0	1.1
Micronesia, Federated States of	98.0	58.2	2.0	0.2	0.0	11.3	0.0	0.0	0.0	0.1	0.0	0.5	0.0	29.7
Nauru	32.3	98.5	7.9	0.3	10.6	1.2	0.0	0.0	0.0	0.0	49.2	0.0	0.0	0.0
Palau	40.1	48.0	0.7	2.3	59.3	33.5	0.0	0.0	0.0	0.3	0.0	0.1	0.0	15.8
Papua New Guinea	94.1	91.3	3.2	4.2	2.3	2.6	0.0	1.2	0.2	0.3	0.1	0.4	0.0	0.1
Samoa	80.3	85.6	0.7	2.7	18.5	10.7	0.0	0.0	0.2	0.3	0.0	0.0	0.2	0.6
Solomon Islands	90.6	96.2	3.0	1.5	6.1	2.1	0.0	0.0	0.1	0.1	0.2	0.1	0.0	0.0
Timor-Leste[a]	94.0	89.4	5.3	6.8	0.6	0.0	0.0	0.2	0.1	2.9	0.1	0.4	0.0	0.3
Tonga	88.7	86.0	0.5	1.5	10.3	11.0	0.0	0.2	0.2	0.9	0.1	0.1	0.2	0.2
Tuvalu	66.1	82.8	32.5	1.6	0.2	3.9	0.0	0.3	1.0	6.5	0.0	4.9	0.2	0.0
Vanuatu	87.4	57.0	7.4	38.6	0.7	2.5	0.0	0.1	0.2	0.1	0.6	0.3	3.7	1.4
Developed ADB Member Economies														
Australia	49.4	58.8	23.3	19.1	22.1	12.7	2.8	1.5	0.8	0.9	0.9	1.2	0.6	5.9
Japan	46.3	55.9	15.0	15.3	22.2	13.8	13.0	11.0	2.0	2.8	1.3	1.2	0.1	0.1
New Zealand	53.1	60.7	18.6	19.9	19.6	12.8	5.6	4.5	1.1	1.2	1.2	0.5	0.7	0.4
DEVELOPING ADB MEMBER ECONOMIES	**60.4**	**58.9**	**14.6**	**14.9**	**13.6**	**9.0**	**6.7**	**7.7**	**1.1**	**3.5**	**1.5**	**2.7**	**2.2**	**3.3**
ALL ADB REGIONAL MEMBERS	**56.7**	**58.6**	**15.1**	**15.1**	**15.9**	**9.7**	**7.9**	**7.8**	**1.3**	**3.3**	**1.4**	**2.5**	**1.6**	**3.0**
WORLD	**29.2**	**36.0**	**40.2**	**37.4**	**20.0**	**13.7**	**4.2**	**4.7**	**2.6**	**3.0**	**2.2**	**2.4**	**1.7**	**2.8**

0.0 = magnitude is less than half of unit employed, ADB = Asian Development Bank.

a   For 2000, data refer to 2004.

Sources: International Monetary Fund. May 2018. International Financial Statistics (CD-ROM). Washington, DC. For the Cook Islands and Taipei,China: Economy sources.

Table 2.4.15:   International Reserves and Ratio of International Reserves to Imports

ADB Regional Member	International Reserves, End of Year[a] ($ million)				Ratio of International Reserves to Imports[b] (months)			
	2000	2005	2010	2017	2000	2005	2010	2017
Developing ADB Member Economies								
Central and West Asia								
Afghanistan	7 (2002)	0	5,147	8,075	0.0 (2002)	0.0	12.4	13.6
Armenia	314	669	1,866	2,314	4.8	4.8	6.9	7.2
Azerbaijan	680	1,178	6,409	6,681	5.3	3.2	11.5	8.9
Georgia	116	479	2,264	3,039	1.4	2.2	5.4	4.9
Kazakhstan	2,096	7,070	28,275	30,747	3.6	4.7	10.3	11.6
Kyrgyz Republic	262	612	1,720	2,177	6.2	6.6	6.9	6.2
Pakistan	2,056	10,948	17,210	18,455	2.6	6.9	6.6	4.5
Tajikistan	94	189	403	1,292	1.2	1.6	1.9	6.5
Turkmenistan	1,808	4,457	...	...	12.5	18.1	...	...
Uzbekistan	1,273	2,900	14,600	28,077	30.9	24.0	58.3	386.2
East Asia								
China, People's Republic of	168,855	825,588	2,872,090	3,235,350	10.8	17.5	27.8	22.3
Hong Kong, China	107,560	124,278	268,743	431,383	7.9	6.1	8.4	9.2
Korea, Republic of	96,198	210,391	291,571	389,248	7.5	10.0	8.4	10.2
Mongolia	202	333	2,288	3,016	4.0	3.4	8.9	8.3
Taipei,China	111,370	257,952	387,207	438,984 (2016)	9.7	17.0	18.4	22.0 (2016)
South Asia								
Bangladesh	1,516	2,825	11,178	33,424	2.4	2.9	6.3	9.2
Bhutan	318	467	1,002	1,127 (2016)	20.6	12.2	15.1	12.8 (2016)
India	40,155	136,026	296,730	409,772	8.3	10.4	9.3	10.5
Maldives	123	189	364	597	4.3	3.5	3.5	3.2
Nepal	952	1,504	2,939	29	7.3	8.9	7.2	0.0
Sri Lanka	1,147	2,735	7,196	7,959	1.9	3.7	6.4	4.6
Southeast Asia								
Brunei Darussalam	382 (2001)	492	1,563	3,489 (2016)	4.2 (2001)	4.2	7.3	15.7 (2016)
Cambodia	611	1,159	3,802	12,200	3.8	3.5	6.9	9.4
Indonesia	29,268	34,731	96,211	130,203	8.7	6.5	9.7	10.4
Lao People's Democratic Republic	140	239	713	1,270	3.1	3.3	4.2	2.8
Malaysia	28,624	70,152	106,525	102,446	4.4	7.8	8.6	7.7
Myanmar	234	782	5,729	5,214	1.3	5.3	16.0	4.0
Philippines	15,063	18,494	62,373	81,565	4.2	5.9	14.0	10.9
Singapore	80,170	116,172	225,715	279,902	6.9	7.2	8.8	10.8
Thailand	32,661	52,065	172,129	202,562	6.3	5.9	12.4	12.0
Viet Nam	3,510	9,216	12,926	49,497	3.0	3.2	2.0	2.9
The Pacific								
Cook Islands	...	...	...	...	...	...	...	...
Fiji	412	321	721	1,116	6.4	2.8	5.6	6.4
Kiribati	0	0	8	7 (2016)	0.0	0.0	1.3	0.8 (2016)
Marshall Islands	0	0	5	5	0.0	0.0	0.5	0.5
Micronesia, Federated States of	113	50	56	157 (2016)	12.4	4.8	4.2	11.8 (2016)
Nauru	...	...	...	1	...	...	...	0.2
Palau	0	0	5	4	0.0	0.0	0.5	0.3
Papua New Guinea	296	749	3,092	13	3.5	5.9	10.5	0.1
Samoa	64	77	189	133	2.4	6.3	11.3	4.9
Solomon Islands	32	95	266	574	4.2	9.4	8.9	14.9
Timor-Leste	...	...	...	281 (2016)	...	...	...	6.0 (2016)
Tonga	25	47	105	199	4.7	5.0	11.5	14.3
Tuvalu	0	0 (2006)	3	2	0.0	0.0 (2006)	1.8	...
Vanuatu	39	67	161	267 (2016)	6.1	6.2	8.1	10.4 (2016)
Developed ADB Member Economies								
Australia	18,817	43,257	42,268	66,584	3.5	4.5	2.6	3.8
Japan	361,639	846,896	1,096,185	1,264,141	12.9	21.9	21.0	23.5
New Zealand	3,952	8,893	16,723	17,808 (2016)	3.7	4.2	6.5	5.8 (2016)
DEVELOPING ADB MEMBER ECONOMIES[c]	**728,742**	**1,895,701**	**4,911,499**	**5,922,853**	**7.7**	**11.1**	**15.8**	**14.7**
ALL ADB REGIONAL MEMBERS[c]	**1,113,150**	**2,794,746**	**6,066,674**	**7,271,387**	**8.6**	**12.7**	**15.9**	**15.2**

... = data not available, 0 or 0.0 = magnitude is less than half of the unit employed, $ = United States dollars, ADB = Asian Development Bank.

a Data refer to international reserves with gold at national valuation, unless otherwise specified. For Afghanistan (up to 2007), Kiribati, Palau, Samoa, Solomon Islands, Tonga, Turkmenistan, and Vanuatu, data refer to international reserves without gold.

b Merchandise imports from the balance of payments were used in the calculation.

c For reporting economies only.

Sources: International Monetary Fund. International Financial Statistics. http://data.imf.org/ (accessed 16 May 2018); and economy sources.

Table 2.4.16:   Net Official Development Assistance from All Sources to Developing Member Economies[a]
($ million)

ADB Regional Member	2000	2005	2010	2011	2012	2013	2014	2015	2016
Developing ADB Member Economies									
Central and West Asia									
Afghanistan	136	2,838	6,470	6,866	6,667	5,153	4,943	4,237	4,068
Armenia	216	173	343	396	271	280	267	347	326
Azerbaijan	141	211	162	287	287	-71	217	70	78
Georgia	172	293	627	587	659	646	564	449	463
Kazakhstan	189	225	212	201	132	91	93	83	60
Kyrgyz Republic	215	267	384	523	470	539	627	770	515
Pakistan	707	1,617	3,021	3,498	2,017	2,194	3,616	3,748	2,949
Tajikistan	124	252	433	349	394	391	356	426	334
Turkmenistan	36	29	44	41	38	36	34	24	33
Uzbekistan	186	169	234	204	256	295	325	448	457
East Asia									
China, People's Republic of	1,749	1,799	672	-603	-181	-657	-947	-332	-792
Hong Kong, China	...	...	...	...	...	...	...	...	...
Korea, Republic of	...	...	...	...	...	...	...	...	...
Mongolia	218	221	303	351	447	431	317	236	326
Taipei,China	...	...	...	...	...	...	...	...	...
South Asia									
Bangladesh	1,174	1,320	1,405	1,495	2,154	2,634	2,423	2,570	2,503
Bhutan	53	90	131	141	162	137	131	97	52
India	1,383	1,876	2,831	3,270	1,682	2,456	2,992	3,174	2,679
Maldives	19	77	112	54	57	22	23	27	27
Nepal	386	423	814	887	770	873	884	1,225	1,063
Sri Lanka	278	1,165	580	613	491	403	492	427	366
Southeast Asia									
Brunei Darussalam	...	...	...	...	...	...	...	...	...
Cambodia	396	539	734	792	808	808	803	679	728
Indonesia	1,663	2,537	1,390	402	69	69	-382	-33	-111
Lao People's Democratic Republic	281	297	413	400	411	423	474	471	399
Malaysia	49	29	-6	41	18	-113	20	-1	-52
Myanmar	106	145	355	380	505	3,936	1,384	1,169	1,535
Philippines	575	568	541	-184	-3	192	677	515	283
Singapore	...	...	...	...	...	...	...	...	...
Thailand	699	-167	-20	-134	-131	29	355	59	228
Viet Nam	1,683	1,911	2,948	3,619	4,113	4,086	4,216	3,157	2,895
The Pacific									
Cook Islands	4	8	14	27	21	16	28	26	17
Fiji	29	66	76	75	105	91	94	102	117
Kiribati	18	28	23	65	66	65	81	65	61
Marshall Islands	57	57	33	82	84	94	56	57	13
Micronesia, Federated States of	102	106	63	133	143	143	117	81	51
Nauru	4	9	28	38	36	29	23	31	23
Palau	39	24	29	28	15	35	23	14	18
Papua New Guinea	275	267	512	613	670	657	582	591	532
Samoa	28	44	148	98	117	113	94	94	89
Solomon Islands	68	198	340	339	305	290	201	190	176
Timor-Leste	231	185	291	279	284	259	250	212	224
Tonga	19	32	70	93	78	81	80	68	83
Tuvalu	4	9	14	39	25	28	34	50	24
Vanuatu	46	40	108	91	102	91	100	187	129
DEVELOPING ADB MEMBER ECONOMIES[b]	13,760	19,977	26,883	26,479	24,613	27,276	26,664	25,811	22,969
DEVELOPING ECONOMIES[c]	50,072	108,542	131,574	141,810	133,752	151,138	161,730	152,740	157,668

... = data not available, $ = United States dollars, ADB = Asian Development Bank.

a Net official development assistance refers to concessional flows to developing economies and multilateral institutions provided by official agencies, including state and local governments, or by their executing agencies, administered with the objective of promoting the economic development and welfare of developing economies, and containing a grant element of at least 25%. Net flow takes into account principal repayments for loans, offsetting entries for forgiven debt, and recoveries made on grants.
b For reporting economies only.
c Includes data for all developing economies as reported in the Organisation for Economic Co-operation and Development's OECD.Stat database.

Source: Organisation for Economic Co-operation and Development. OECD.Stat. http://stats.oecd.org (accessed 6 July 2018).

Table 2.4.17: Net Other Official Flows from All Sources to Developing Member Economies[a]
($ million)

ADB Regional Member	2000	2005	2010	2011	2012	2013	2014	2015	2016
Developing ADB Member Economies									
Central and West Asia									
Afghanistan	...	56.9	71.2	70.6	29.1	60.5	-24.2	127.4	97.2
Armenia	16.9	7.8	288.3	156.0	133.4	112.1	103.6	111.1	197.2
Azerbaijan	314.3	226.5	179.9	637.1	411.8	391.0	630.1	801.8	1,114.7
Georgia	62.7	86.3	250.2	325.1	146.6	-0.7	2.9	342.4	486.6
Kazakhstan	-41.7	-502.3	2,247.2	1,191.7	606.9	1,548.0	549.5	1,256.7	441.4
Kyrgyz Republic	-4.0	56.3	18.3	50.5	73.7	69.7	16.5	0.4	-43.2
Pakistan	-592.9	127.4	345.3	593.9	414.3	-236.7	-97.1	-343.9	1,092.7
Tajikistan	0.7	22.8	6.4	8.6	9.2	6.6	-5.5	68.1	13.6
Turkmenistan	130.3	-74.1	647.4	235.2	-333.2	135.4	1,143.9	2,356.6	926.1
Uzbekistan	272.1	-48.7	16.0	-277.8	122.9	754.6	743.9	530.5	1,204.2
East Asia									
China, People's Republic of	-1,782.4	423.1	3,196.3	2,043.4	1,474.0	742.1	343.0	1,215.8	139.9
Hong Kong, China	...	...	...	...	...	...	...	...	...
Korea, Republic of	...	...	...	...	...	...	...	...	...
Mongolia	-8.5	-14.6	159.3	92.8	283.9	255.0	509.8	213.3	756.4
Taipei,China	...	...	...	...	...	...	...	...	...
South Asia									
Bangladesh	-30.5	186.8	35.1	430.4	129.3	187.7	247.0	417.9	1,421.5
Bhutan	-1.1	4.8	24.0	8.6	3.7	-5.0	-6.0	-2.8	8.0
India	-196.4	2,322.3	5,967.5	5,292.9	4,011.4	3,010.8	4,029.7	1,811.5	1,935.6
Maldives	-4.8	44.0	-33.9	-25.7	-105.3	13.3	-3.7	-8.1	-24.7
Nepal	23.7	-8.3	-6.9	-8.2	3.9	16.2	-2.4	-7.4	0.7
Sri Lanka	-22.7	39.8	189.3	127.6	491.3	436.0	350.5	320.8	312.6
Southeast Asia									
Brunei Darussalam	...	...	...	...	...	...	...	...	...
Cambodia	-0.4	7.6	-5.0	14.8	33.4	89.3	96.3	84.6	-12.3
Indonesia	100.1	1,443.8	1,783.7	2,313.4	-2,036.8	120.8	-1,715.7	3,775.4	3,708.7
Lao People's Democratic Republic	-8.8	59.4	-120.5	-39.1	29.7	4.6	194.8	73.1	38.6
Malaysia	519.9	-1,369.3	159.2	1,349.7	552.9	-126.4	1,339.4	-231.8	-1,494.5
Myanmar	20.1	-31.5	30.9	8.7	-32.7	227.2	107.6	427.5	100.6
Philippines	499.6	-945.9	-680.3	1,157.8	603.5	-1,245.5	1,029.6	1,148.5	203.1
Singapore	...	...	...	...	...	...	...	...	...
Thailand	-2,112.2	1,629.6	-71.5	287.2	1,474.9	2,454.4	-349.0	138.7	-39.3
Viet Nam	-546.4	248.4	2,815.4	1,625.2	2,005.8	4,828.3	2,133.3	2,782.1	580.6
The Pacific									
Cook Islands	-0.2	-0.3	9.7	5.2	7.1	4.9	-1.3	-0.6	-1.2
Fiji	-11.8	1.2	14.2	21.6	20.3	73.6	66.1	-11.4	40.6
Kiribati	0.1 (2002)	0.2	0.5	0.9	0.8	0.6	0.2	0.2	0.3
Marshall Islands	-0.2	-0.1	-0.6	131.3	-57.2	-21.1	146.2	7.6	36.7
Micronesia, Federated States of	-0.1	0.3	0.8	2.6	3.5	-1.0	1.1	0.2	2.3
Nauru	-5.6	0.2	0.3	0.1	0.3	-0.1	...	...	62.5
Palau	-1.5	-2.1	0.1 (2008)	6.4	14.7	6.4	-11.1	0.3	6.6
Papua New Guinea	85.4	-9.1	4,892.3	1,600.2	843.2	1,025.2	-2,991.6	19.4	-320.7
Samoa	0.4	-0.1	4.1	3.5	-5.7	4.2	-0.9	-1.3	5.6
Solomon Islands	1.2	-11.7	59.2	7.9	0.6	37.4	25.0	0.7	19.1
Timor-Leste	417.8	1.1	4.6	-11.8	2.0	5.7	9.9	7.8	24.8
Tonga	0.0	0.4	0.3	0.8	1.0	0.3	0.0	2.1	2.5
Tuvalu	...	0.5 (2006)	-0.1	...	0.2	0.2	0.2	0.2	0.2
Vanuatu	-16.2	0.8	1.3	1.3	2.6	1.7	0.8	0.7	0.9
DEVELOPING ADB MEMBER ECONOMIES[b]	-2,922.9	3,980.2	22,499.3	19,440.1	11,370.6	14,987.2	8,612.3	17,436.0	13,046.0
DEVELOPING ECONOMIES[c]	9,856.9	9,605.9	70,855.8	33,003.2	38,758.7	38,737.1	22,530.7	50,967.9	29,513.4

... = data not available, 0.0 = magnitude is less than half of unit employed, $ = United States dollars, ADB = Asian Development Bank.

a Net other official flows refer to official sector transactions with economies on the Development Assistance Committee List of Official Development Assistance Recipients, which do not meet the conditions for eligibility as official development assistance, either because they are not primarily aimed at development or because they have a grant element of less than 25%. The Development Assistance Committee List of Official Development Assistance Recipients is available at http://www.oecd.org/dac/financing-sustainable-development/development-finance-standards/daclist.htm. Also includes net export credits. Net flow takes into account principal repayments for loans, offsetting entries for forgiven debt, and recoveries made on grants.

b For reporting economies only.

c Includes data for all developing economies as reported in the Organisation for Economic Co-operation and Development's OECD.Stat.

Source: Organisation for Economic Co-operation and Development. OECD.Stat. http://stats.oecd.org (accessed 6 July 2018).

Capital Flows

Table 2.4.18:   Net Private Flows from All Sources to Developing Member Economies[a]
($ million)

ADB Regional Member	2000	2005	2010	2011	2012	2013	2014	2015	2016
Developing ADB Member Economies									
Central and West Asia									
Afghanistan	21	-14	-21	7	-12	26	32	-6	-5
Armenia	-21	35	-69	-23	-91	208	-0	57	190
Azerbaijan	219	1,082	798	714	326	869	-129	436	449
Georgia	23	-32	22	152	182	52	-59	1,249	190
Kazakhstan	603	2,252	-1,511	1,774	194	2,947	1,251	3,090	-12
Kyrgyz Republic	12	7	23	15	15	18	10	6	-23
Pakistan	60	833	-75	73	298	-172	155	131	135
Tajikistan	-8	-1	18	5	15	47	4	-8	-2
Turkmenistan	124	1	-46	32	43	103	42	-11	285
Uzbekistan	-10	-84	39	112	153	-117	-478	110	112
East Asia									
China, People's Republic of	923	21,125	46,301	48,549	17,987	53,925	61,702	17,154	44,354
Hong Kong, China	...	...	...	...	...	...	...	...	...
Korea, Republic of	...	...	...	...	...	...	...	...	...
Mongolia	3	-2	22	15	417	511	42	216	587
Taipei,China	...	...	...	...	...	...	...	...	...
South Asia									
Bangladesh	93	186	-3	90	858	-105	249	100	-383
Bhutan	-8	1	18	-1	107	-163	9	16	-5
India	1,099	4,548	19,976	11,501	14,426	6,292	10,655	7,288	14,591
Maldives	-4	8	38	-68	38	-16	100	112	18
Nepal	-4	-2	-11	-7	78	115	7	-3	6
Sri Lanka	98	35	218	243	199	447	427	387	492
Southeast Asia									
Brunei Darussalam	...	...	...	...	...	...	...	...	...
Cambodia	9	9	256	127	276	310	399	380	404
Indonesia	606	4,012	3,348	8,222	10,084	7,291	13,343	9,678	8,215
Lao People's Democratic Republic	14	0	172	62	363	59	50	-19	44
Malaysia	-872	2,064	6,573	6,068	9,684	9,719	6,165	3,689	2,062
Myanmar	-70	17	260	489	357	534	566	865	356
Philippines	330	3,496	2,424	2,037	4,785	2,510	4,839	1,908	2,750
Singapore	...	...	...	...	...	...	...	...	...
Thailand	32	10,944	6,394	10,241	5,356	6,096	10,076	-2,337	2,815
Viet Nam	237	224	2,038	3,134	3,412	5,002	3,467	2,790	4,657
The Pacific									
Cook Islands	-31	-29	-0	8	-1	3	-2	-2	-1
Fiji	6	51	-3	51	163	2	49	53	-15
Kiribati	0	1	-0	3	0	0	3	3	-9
Marshall Islands	108	2,737	974	2,836	2,179	-1,048	-365	2,245	10
Micronesia, Federated States of	-0 (2001)	0	3	599	4	93	320	798	714
Nauru	4	2	2 (2009)	-0	...	...	...	...	-0
Palau	18	1	3	6	7	2	6	7	9
Papua New Guinea	-27	238	-40	-173	3,063	879	65	-2,931	211
Samoa	1	30	17	5	14	-36	37	3	9
Solomon Islands	-15	-17	3	8	-463	4	23	11	-1
Timor-Leste	54 (2001)	0	-3	-1	3	25	2	17	-34
Tonga	-7	2	-10	-3	0	1	1	-1	-0
Tuvalu	-4	-1	0 (2007)	1	-0	-2	-1	0	0
Vanuatu	41	11	31	-23	86	43	15	-5	1
DEVELOPING ADB MEMBER ECONOMIES[b]	3,656	53,772	88,180	96,879	74,604	96,475	113,076	47,476	83,176
DEVELOPING ECONOMIES[c]	75,170	173,009	324,145	327,099	300,041	251,983	414,725	119,676	127,974

... = data not available, –0 or 0 = magnitude is less than half of unit employed, $ = United States dollars, ADB = Asian Development Bank.

a   Net private flows refer to the sum of direct investments and portfolio investments.
b   For reporting economies only.
c   Includes data for all developing economies as reported in the Organisation for Economic Co-operation and Development's OECD.Stat.

Source: Organisation for Economic Co-operation and Development. OECD.Stat. http://stats.oecd.org (accessed 6 July 2018).

Table 2.4.19: Aggregate Net Resource Flows from All Sources to Developing Member Economies[a]
($ million)

ADB Regional Member	2000	2005	2010	2011	2012	2013	2014	2015	2016
Developing ADB Member Economies									
Central and West Asia									
Afghanistan	157	2,881	6,520	6,943	6,684	5,239	4,951	4,359	4,160
Armenia	211	216	561	528	313	600	371	515	713
Azerbaijan	673	1,519	1,140	1,639	1,024	1,189	718	1,308	1,641
Georgia	258	347	899	1,064	987	698	508	2,040	1,140
Kazakhstan	751	1,975	948	3,167	933	4,586	1,893	4,430	490
Kyrgyz Republic	223	331	425	588	559	627	653	776	449
Pakistan	174	2,577	3,291	4,165	2,730	1,786	3,673	3,534	4,177
Tajikistan	117	274	458	363	418	444	355	486	345
Turkmenistan	290	-44	645	308	-253	274	1,220	2,370	1,244
Uzbekistan	448	37	290	38	532	933	590	1,089	1,774
East Asia									
China, People's Republic of	889	23,347	50,169	49,989	19,280	54,011	61,098	18,037	43,702
Hong Kong, China	...	...	...	...	...	...	...	...	...
Korea, Republic of	...	...	...	...	...	...	...	...	...
Mongolia	213	204	484	459	1,147	1,196	869	665	1,669
Taipei,China	...	...	...	...	...	...	...	...	...
South Asia									
Bangladesh	1,237	1,694	1,437	2,015	3,141	2,717	2,918	3,088	3,542
Bhutan	44	96	174	149	273	-32	133	110	55
India	2,286	8,746	28,774	20,064	20,120	11,760	17,676	12,274	19,206
Maldives	11	128	116	-40	-10	19	119	131	20
Nepal	406	413	797	871	851	1,005	888	1,215	1,070
Sri Lanka	354	1,240	987	984	1,181	1,286	1,269	1,135	1,171
Southeast Asia									
Brunei Darussalam	...	...	...	...	...	...	...	...	...
Cambodia	405	556	985	934	1,117	1,207	1,298	1,144	1,120
Indonesia	2,370	7,992	6,522	10,937	8,116	7,481	11,245	13,420	11,813
Lao People's Democratic Republic	286	357	465	422	803	487	719	526	482
Malaysia	-304	724	6,726	7,459	10,255	9,480	7,524	3,457	516
Myanmar	56	131	646	878	829	4,697	2,058	2,460	1,992
Philippines	1,405	3,118	2,285	3,011	5,385	1,457	6,546	3,571	3,236
Singapore	...	...	...	...	...	...	...	...	...
Thailand	-1,382	12,406	6,302	10,394	6,700	8,579	10,081	-2,139	3,004
Viet Nam	1,374	2,383	7,801	8,378	9,531	13,916	9,816	8,729	8,133
The Pacific									
Cook Islands	-27	-22	23	41	28	23	25	23	15
Fiji	24	118	87	148	289	166	210	144	143
Kiribati	18	29	24	69	67	66	84	68	52
Marshall Islands	165	2,794	1,006	3,050	2,205	-975	-163	2,309	59
Micronesia, Federated States of	102	107	68	735	150	236	438	879	767
Nauru	2	12	28	37	36	29	23	31	85
Palau	55	22	32	40	37	44	18	21	33
Papua New Guinea	333	496	5,364	2,040	4,576	2,562	-2,344	-2,320	422
Samoa	29	73	169	106	126	81	130	95	103
Solomon Islands	55	170	403	356	-158	331	249	202	194
Timor-Leste	649	186	293	266	288	290	262	238	214
Tonga	12	34	61	92	79	83	82	70	85
Tuvalu	-0	8	14	40	26	26	34	50	25
Vanuatu	71	52	140	69	191	136	117	182	131
DEVELOPING ADB MEMBER ECONOMIES[b]	14,440	77,729	137,559	142,798	110,587	138,738	148,353	90,722	119,191
DEVELOPING ECONOMIES[c]	135,099	291,157	526,575	501,912	472,551	441,858	598,986	323,384	315,156

... = data not available, -0 or 0 = magnitude is less than half of unit employed, $ = United States dollars, ADB = Asian Development Bank.

a Aggregate net resource flows refer to the sum of net official development assistance, net other official flows, and net private flows.
b For reporting economies only.
c Includes data for all developing economies as reported in the Organisation for Economic Co-operation and Development's OECD.Stat.

Source: Organisation for Economic Co-operation and Development. OECD.Stat. http://stats.oecd.org (accessed 6 July 2018).

External Indebtness

Table 2.4.20:   Total External Debt of Developing ADB Member Economies[a]
($ million)

ADB Regional Member	Total External Debt				External Debt, Public and Publicly Guaranteed			
	2000	2005	2010	2016	2000	2005	2010	2016
Developing ADB Member Economies								
Central and West Asia								
Afghanistan	...	969 (2006)	2,425	2,404	...	911 (2006)	1,966	1,921
Armenia	1,010	1,968	6,305	9,953	675	923	2,557	4,469
Azerbaijan	1,585	2,247	7,159	14,085	794	1,491	3,720	10,518
Georgia	1,826	2,151	9,656	15,987	1,274	1,531	4,141	5,907
Kazakhstan	12,890	43,857	119,145	163,758	3,623	2,177	3,845	21,426
Kyrgyz Republic	1,938	2,257	4,114	7,876	1,220	1,665	2,442	3,564
Pakistan	33,022	34,018	62,801	72,697	27,192	30,089	43,403	51,600
Tajikistan	1,141	1,121	3,562	4,877	755	826	1,806	1,862
Turkmenistan	2,627	1,153	529	509	2,271	878	359	236
Uzbekistan	4,948	4,632	7,802	16,283	3,766	3,626	3,423	7,434
East Asia								
China, People's Republic of	145,666	283,310	734,465	1,429,468	94,489	84,212	94,003	158,675
Hong Kong, China[b]	208,260	470,288	879,034	1,563,924 (2017)	...	...	...	...
Korea, Republic of	135,208	161,956	355,911	418,824 (2017)	52,128	39,665	120,636	169,751 (2014)
Mongolia	960	1,396	5,928	23,912	833	1,267	1,782	4,506
Taipei,China	34,757	86,732	101,581	181,938 (2017)	23	222	8,035	317 (2017)
South Asia								
Bangladesh	15,603	18,506	26,881	41,126	14,992	17,441	21,453	28,650
Bhutan	212	657	935	2,348	202	636	919	2,221
India	101,131	121,195	290,428	456,140	81,196	54,726	100,563	166,883
Maldives	203	362	917	1,155	185	300	628	898
Nepal	2,878	3,191	3,789	4,251	2,826	3,112	3,509	3,623
Sri Lanka	9,250	11,300	21,684	46,608	7,945	9,658	16,430	29,725
Southeast Asia								
Brunei Darussalam	...	...	...	...	...	...	...	...
Cambodia	1,946	2,769	3,685	10,230	1,853	2,666	2,874	5,646
Indonesia	144,032	142,120	198,269	316,431	70,025	77,705	103,388	177,067
Lao People's Democratic Republic	2,531	3,279	6,505	14,160	2,474	2,354	3,751	7,301
Malaysia	41,946	64,911	133,800	200,364	19,125	34,387	61,858	65,721
Myanmar	5,875	6,674	8,217	6,453	5,328	5,815	6,646	5,314
Philippines	58,456	58,693	65,358	77,319	33,744	35,364	45,094	33,395
Singapore	...	...	...	...	...	...	...	...
Thailand	79,830	58,467	106,358	121,497	29,462	12,602	15,929	23,192
Viet Nam	12,785	18,530	44,902	86,952	11,584	16,219	32,764	48,038
The Pacific								
Cook Islands	59	68	99	72 (2017)	...	...	...	...
Fiji	195	303	570	868	174	185	388	679
Kiribati	8	11	14	36 (2015)	...	...	...	...
Marshall Islands	105	92	105	83 (2017)	...	...	...	...
Micronesia, Federated States of	63	62	86	81 (2015)	...	...	...	...
Nauru	...	...	...	...	...	...	...	...
Palau	58	60	66	86 (2017)	...	...	...	...
Papua New Guinea	2,325	1,871	5,987	19,688	1,454	1,264	1,042	1,919
Samoa	139	169	325	417	138	167	299	390
Solomon Islands	156	167	231	240	121	144	125	87
Timor-Leste	...	...	...	...	...	...	...	...
Tonga	74	89	154	160	65	80	144	151
Tuvalu	4	10 (2006)	16	14 (2013)	...	...	...	...
Vanuatu	112	100	178	213	73	72	103	137
DEVELOPING ADB MEMBER ECONOMIES[c]	1,065,815	1,611,713	3,219,973	5,333,489	472,010	444,378	710,025	1,043,223
DEVELOPING ECONOMIES WORLDWIDE[d]	2,467,352	3,243,852	5,870,450	9,042,006	1,320,923	1,323,339	1,796,096	2,696,785

... = Data not available, $ = United States dollars, ADB = Asian Development Bank.

a   Refers to the sum of public and publicly guaranteed long-term debt, private nonguaranteed long-term debt, use of International Monetary Fund credit, and estimated short-term debt.
b   Data prior to 2005 are not comparable with the rest of the series due to a change in coverage or compilation methodology.
c   For reporting economies only.
d   Refers to all low- and middle-income countries as classified by the World Bank. For developing member economies not covered by the World Bank, data are from economy sources.

Sources: World Bank. International Debt Statistics Online. http://data.worldbank.org/data-catalog/international-debt-statistics (accessed 10 July 2018); and Asian Development Bank estimates using economy sources.

Table 2.4.21: Total External Debt of Developing ADB Member Economies

(% of GNI)

ADB Regional Member	Total External Debt				External Debt, Public and Publicly Guaranteed			
	2000	2005	2010	2016	2000	2005	2010	2016
Developing ADB Member Economies								
Central and West Asia								
Afghanistan	...	13.6 (2006)	15.2	12.2	...	12.8 (2006)	12.3	9.8
Armenia	51.4	38.5	64.9	92.4	34.4	18.1	26.3	41.5
Azerbaijan	31.8	19.4	14.4	39.8	15.9	12.9	7.5	29.7
Georgia	57.5	33.2	85.6	118.0	40.1	23.7	36.7	43.2
Kazakhstan	75.7	84.7	92.6	135.1	21.3	4.2	3.0	17.2
Kyrgyz Republic	150.5	95.1	91.7	125.3	94.8	70.2	54.4	55.2
Pakistan	45.2	30.4	34.1	24.1	37.2	26.9	23.6	17.4
Tajikistan	138.4	50.2	51.1	59.7	91.6	37.0	25.9	22.8
Turkmenistan	96.3	15.3	2.6	1.5	83.3	11.6	1.7	0.7
Uzbekistan	36.5	32.4	19.3	23.8	27.8	25.4	8.4	10.9
East Asia								
China, People's Republic of	12.2	12.5	12.1	12.8	7.9	3.7	1.5	1.4
Hong Kong, China[a]	120.3	257.7	376.5	439.5 (2017)	...	...	...	...
Korea, Republic of	24.2	18.2	32.5	27.4 (2017)	9.3	4.5	11.0	12.0 (2014)
Mongolia	84.8	56.5	89.9	232.0	73.6	51.2	27.0	43.2
Taipei,China	10.3	22.5	22.1	30.9 (2017)	0.0	0.1	1.7	0.1 (2017)
South Asia								
Bangladesh	28.3	25.5	21.6	17.6	27.2	24.1	17.2	12.2
Bhutan	48.2	81.3	62.4	113.8	46.1	78.7	61.4	109.5
India	22.1	15.1	17.7	20.4	17.8	6.8	6.1	7.4
Maldives	34.2	33.3	45.6	35.5	31.1	26.5	27.6	23.2
Nepal	52.2	39.1	23.5	19.7	51.2	38.2	21.8	16.9
Sri Lanka	57.8	46.9	38.6	59.0	48.8	40.1	29.3	37.4
Southeast Asia								
Brunei Darussalam	...	...	...	...	...	...	...	...
Cambodia	55.1	46.1	34.3	54.4	52.4	44.4	26.8	30.1
Indonesia	93.5	52.3	27.0	35.1	45.4	28.6	14.1	19.6
Lao People's Democratic Republic	152.4	122.8	97.4	93.1	149.0	88.2	56.2	48.3
Malaysia	48.7	47.3	54.2	69.6	22.2	25.1	25.1	22.8
Myanmar	66.0	55.7	16.6	...	59.9	48.5	13.4	8.7
Philippines	61.6	45.2	24.6	21.1	35.5	28.9	18.7	9.1
Singapore	...	...	...	...	...	...	...	...
Thailand	64.4	32.3	32.5	31.4	23.8	7.0	4.9	5.9
Viet Nam	38.5	32.8	40.3	45.6	34.9	28.7	29.4	24.4
The Pacific								
Cook Islands[b]	64.3	37.4	38.7	23.4 (2017)	...	...	...	...
Fiji	11.3	9.9	18.7	19.6	10.1	6.1	12.8	15.1
Kiribati	...	7.1	6.3	10.7 (2015)	...	...	...	...
Marshall Islands	70.5	50.9	52.0	29.0 (2017)	...	...	...	...
Micronesia, Federated States of	26.4	23.9	27.8	21.9 (2015)	...	...	...	...
Nauru	...	...	...	...	...	...	...	...
Palau[b]	40.4	32.3	36.4	29.5 (2017)	...	...	...	...
Papua New Guinea	70.4	41.3	65.6	123.6 (2014)	44.0	27.9	8.0	10.0
Samoa	51.7	38.6	52.0	54.4	51.2	38.2	47.9	50.8
Solomon Islands	35.9	40.3	46.5	20.8	27.7	34.7	25.2	7.5
Timor-Leste	...	...	...	...	...	...	...	...
Tonga	36.7	33.8	40.3	40.4	32.2	30.3	37.6	37.3
Tuvalu[b]	28.9	45.7 (2006)	49.8	...	...	...	...	...
Vanuatu	43.3	27.2	26.3	26.8 (2014)	28.2	19.5	15.2	17.6

... = data not available, 0.0 = magnitude is less than half of unit employed, ADB = Asian Development Bank, GNI = gross national income.

a Data prior to 2005 are not comparable with the rest of the series due to a change in coverage or compilation methodology.
b For total external debt as a percentage of GNI, gross domestic product is used in lieu of GNI.

Sources: World Bank. World Development Indicators and International Debt Statistics. http://data.worldbank.org/data-catalog/world-development-indicators (accessed 10 July 2018); and Asian Development Bank estimates using economy sources.

Table 2.4.22:   Total External Debt of Developing ADB Member Economies
(% of exports of goods, services, and primary income)

ADB Regional Member	2000	2005	2010	2011	2012	2013	2014	2015	2016
Developing ADB Member Economies									
Central and West Asia									
Afghanistan	...	...	91.6	78.3	126.7	147.1	86.1	164.7	190.4
Armenia	181.0	101.3	193.4	194.6	189.4	196.6	188.8	222.0	228.7
Azerbaijan	72.9	26.9	24.8	19.2	27.3	27.2	34.4	62.1	76.1
Georgia	183.7	89.1	210.3	189.3	174.7	166.3	174.0	211.1	223.3
Kazakhstan	123.0	139.8	174.7	135.5	144.4	160.6	176.9	277.6	357.2
Kyrgyz Republic	328.5	234.4	181.0	169.6	170.6	176.5	219.2	306.0	327.5
Pakistan	326.5	172.1	218.5	199.7	194.2	189.5	196.6	224.7	264.5
Tajikistan	...	88.7	158.3	132.8	130.9	130.4	162.5	195.1	214.5
Turkmenistan	...	...	...	...	...	...	...	...	...
Uzbekistan	...	...	...	...	...	...	...	...	...
East Asia									
China, People's Republic of	71.9	34.9	42.1	48.5	48.6	57.9	65.5	51.3	59.0
Hong Kong, China[a, b]	76.8	121.2	149.2	148.1	145.6	152.0	166.2	168.8	190.4 (2017)
Korea, Republic of[a]	64.6	46.5	62.5	56.7	55.5	56.3	56.4	59.6	60.8 (2017)
Mongolia	153.3	93.6	173.3	208.3	340.8	416.9	339.4	414.6	421.5
Taipei,China[a]	19.3	35.9	29.9	32.1	29.2	38.4	39.6	39.1	42.4 (2017)
South Asia									
Bangladesh	214.0	163.4	123.5	100.5	102.8	107.0	107.6	110.2	108.9
Bhutan	...	...	154.0	140.6	194.2	233.9	270.6	274.5	353.9
India	161.9	75.6	81.1	73.2	86.5	89.1	91.8	108.1	102.3
Maldives	43.4	73.1	45.6	36.0	35.7	30.9	32.1	30.6	34.2
Nepal	212.5	224.2	212.7	178.0	193.9	159.5	148.6	154.4	165.3
Sri Lanka	141.7	141.9	189.8	182.8	260.5	258.5	250.2	257.3	265.3
Southeast Asia									
Brunei Darussalam	...	...	...	...	...	...	...	...	...
Cambodia	102.8	67.6	61.5	54.0	70.7	70.6	69.9	74.4	76.4
Indonesia	197.1	146.5	117.6	101.9	118.2	127.8	145.8	177.0	184.2
Lao People's Democratic Republic	493.1	430.1	281.9	306.8	279.7	314.3	328.2	350.2	327.9
Malaysia	36.7	38.9	57.2	53.4	73.7	72.8	74.0	86.0	94.5
Myanmar	273.9	173.9	104.7	94.6	80.5	58.5	46.6	47.0	48.6
Philippines	189.8	152.4	106.7	102.0	92.4	86.9	93.4	98.6	92.5
Singapore	...	...	...	...	...	...	...	...	...
Thailand	92.8	44.4	45.7	40.8	47.0	46.9	46.7	46.2	42.3
Viet Nam	73.1	50.1	56.0	50.7	49.4	45.8	44.8	44.8	45.9
The Pacific									
Cook Islands	...	...	...	...	...	...	...	...	...
Fiji	19.0	17.9	30.2	36.2	29.7	32.2	34.0	39.5	38.1
Kiribati[a]	16.3	17.6	...	...	11.1	9.6	7.5	17.8	
Marshall Islands[a]	141.1	98.0	98.9	76.9	70.5	65.8	68.5	61.7	52.1 (2017)
Micronesia, Federated States of[a]	100.3	98.2	91.9	88.9	69.3	65.7	66.0	52.0	50.3
Nauru	...	...	...	...	...	...	...	...	...
Palau[a]	86.5	70.1	67.7	53.6	50.3	45.9	43.0	35.5	52.9 (2017)
Papua New Guinea	98.2	51.3	98.2	170.5	217.7	337.3	227.4	210.4	253.5
Samoa	...	114.8	161.1	173.9	177.7	179.4	185.3	195.5	158.7
Solomon Islands	121.3	108.1	68.9	45.5	35.0	33.7	30.5	35.9	40.3
Timor-Leste	...	...	...	...	...	...	...	...	...
Tonga	...	151.0	224.7	191.6	174.9	177.4	266.6	228.3	175.0
Tuvalu[a]	85.9	54.9	65.0	67.6	48.1	47.3	...	...	...
Vanuatu	63.9	49.0	49.0	45.4	91.8	52.2	50.4	60.6	50.8

... = data not available, ADB = Asian Development Bank.

a External debt as a percentage of exports of goods, services, and primary income was derived using balance-of-payments data. For Tuvalu, data for 2005 refer to 2006.
b Data prior to 2005 are not comparable with the rest of the series due to a change in coverage or compilation methodology.

Sources: World Bank. World Development Indicators and International Debt Statistics. http://data.worldbank.org/data-catalog/world-development-indicators (accessed 11 July 2018); Asian Development Bank estimates using economy sources.

Table 2.4.23: Total Debt Service Paid

ADB Regional Member	Debt Service Payment ($ million)				Debt Service Payment (% of exports of goods, services, and primary income)			
	2000	2005	2010	2016	2000	2005	2010	2016
Developing ADB Member Economies								
Central and West Asia								
Afghanistan	...	11 (2006)	10	44	...	...	0.4	3.5
Armenia	51	142	969	1,483	9.1	7.3	29.7	34.1
Azerbaijan	138	242	432	1,499	6.4	2.9	1.5	8.1
Georgia	126	195	803	2,694	12.7	8.1	17.5	37.6
Kazakhstan	3,392	13,158	39,474	20,310	32.4	41.9	57.9	44.3
Kyrgyz Republic	178	143	557	446	30.2	14.8	24.5	18.6
Pakistan	2,871	2,466	4,310	4,220	28.4	12.5	15.0	15.4
Tajikistan	68	73	695	639	...	5.8	30.9	28.1
Turkmenistan	472	310	155	40	...	...	...	...
Uzbekistan	908	795	618	1,363	...	...	...	...
East Asia								
China, People's Republic of	26,610	27,469	51,992	127,363	13.1	3.4	3.0	5.3
Hong Kong, China	...	...	...	...	...	...	...	...
Korea, Republic of[a, b]	22,905	7,224	2,843	...	10.9	2.1	0.5	...
Mongolia	41	45	239	1,614	6.6	3.0	7.0	28.5
Taipei,China[a, b]	45	11,006	3,630	7,613 (2017)	0.0	4.6	1.1	1.8 (2017)
South Asia								
Bangladesh	773	812	1,129	1,776	10.6	7.2	5.2	4.7
Bhutan	7	7	87	77	...	...	14.4	11.6
India	10,668	23,922	24,413	77,145	17.1	14.9	6.8	17.3
Maldives	20	31	81	124	4.2	6.3	4.0	3.7
Nepal	103	120	188	230	7.6	8.5	10.6	8.9
Sri Lanka	791	441	1,408	3,151	12.1	5.5	12.3	17.9
Southeast Asia								
Brunei Darussalam	...	...	...	...	...	...	...	...
Cambodia	13	30	65	797	0.7	0.7	1.1	6.0
Indonesia	16,696	20,281	31,569	67,973	22.8	20.9	18.7	39.6
Lao People's Democratic Republic	41	136	302	556	8.0	17.8	13.1	12.9
Malaysia	6,441	9,381	5,575	10,385	5.6	5.6	2.4	4.9
Myanmar	9	5	4	100	0.4	0.1	0.0	0.8
Philippines	7,066	9,528	11,461	10,532	22.9	24.7	18.7	12.6
Singapore	...	...	...	...	...	...	...	...
Thailand	14,013	18,044	10,965	14,310	16.3	13.7	4.7	5.0
Viet Nam	1,306	946	1,873	7,342	7.5	2.6	2.3	3.9
The Pacific								
Cook Islands[a]	1	3	2	...	...	...	...	...
Fiji	26	15	24	131	2.6	0.9	1.2	5.7
Kiribati[b]	1	1	1	...	1.7	1.9	0.9	0.2 (2015)
Marshall Islands[b]	22	4	9	7 (2017)	29.8	4.8	8.1	4.4 (2017)
Micronesia, Federated States of[b]	23	2	5	6	36.1	3.9	5.3	4.0
Nauru	...	...	...	...	...	...	...	...
Palau[a]	...	...	...	...	...	...	...	...
Papua New Guinea	305	308	812	3,815	12.9	8.4	13.3	49.1
Samoa	6	6	11	23	...	3.9	5.3	8.7
Solomon Islands	9	14	21	23	7.1	9.1	6.2	3.9
Timor-Leste	...	...	...	...	...	...	...	...
Tonga	5	5	5	15	...	8.8	7.4	16.2
Tuvalu	...	...	...	...	...	...	...	...
Vanuatu	3	3	6	7	1.6	1.6	1.6	1.8

... = data not available, 0.0 = magnitude is less than half of unit employed, $ = United States dollars, ADB = Asian Development Bank.

a   Refers to principal repayments on long-term debts plus interests on short-term and long-term debts.
b   Debt service payment as a percentage of exports of goods, services, and primary income was derived from balance-of-payments data.

Sources: World Bank. World Development Indicators and International Debt Statistics. http://data.worldbank.org/data-catalog/world-development-indicators (accessed 11 July 2018); Asian Development Bank estimates using economy sources.

Table 2.4.24:   International Tourist Arrivals[a]
('000)

ADB Regional Member	2000	2005	2010	2015	2016	2017
Developing ADB Member Economies						
Central and West Asia[b]	**3,404**	**5,514**	**8,922**	**14,386**	...	...
Afghanistan	...	...	...	...	...	...
Armenia	45	319	687	1,192	1,260	1,495
Azerbaijan	576 (2002)	693	1,280	1,922	2,045	2,454
Georgia	387	...	1,067	2,282	2,721	3,479
Kazakhstan	1,471	3,143	2,991	4,560 (2014)	...	...
Kyrgyz Republic	59	319	855	3,051	2,930	...
Pakistan	557	798	907	965 (2014)	...	...
Tajikistan	4	...	160	414	...	...
Turkmenistan	3	...	...	...	...	...
Uzbekistan	302	242	975	...	...	...
East Asia	**48,126**	**71,322**	**90,571**	**107,630**	**114,159**	**113,170**
China, People's Republic of	31,229	46,809	55,665	56,886	59,270	60,740
Hong Kong, China	8,814	14,773	20,085	26,686	26,553	27,885
Korea, Republic of	5,322	6,023	8,798	13,232	17,242	13,336
Mongolia	137	339	456	386	404	469
Taipei,China	2,624	3,378	5,567	10,440	10,690	10,740
South Asia[b]	**4,187**	**5,460**	**8,169**	**17,135**	**18,870**	**20,244**
Bangladesh	199	208	303	125 (2014)	...	...
Bhutan	8	14	41	155	210	255
India	2,649	3,919	5,776	13,284	14,570	15,543
Maldives	467	395	792	1,234	1,286	1,390
Nepal	464	375	603	539	753	940
Sri Lanka	400	549	654	1,798	2,051	2,116
Southeast Asia[b]	**35,458**	**48,971**	**70,431**	**104,181**	**110,764**	**100,639**
Brunei Darussalam	...	126	214	218	219	259
Cambodia	...	1,333	2,508	4,775	5,012	5,602
Indonesia	5,064	5,002	7,003	9,963	11,072	...
Lao People's Democratic Republic	191	672	1,670	3,543	3,315	...
Malaysia	10,222	16,431	24,577	25,721	26,757	25,948
Myanmar	208	660	792	4,681	2,907	...
Philippines	1,992	2,623	3,520	5,361	5,967	6,621
Singapore	6,062	7,079	9,161	12,052	12,914	13,906
Thailand	9,579	11,567	15,936	29,923	32,588	35,381
Viet Nam	2,140	3,478	5,050	7,944	10,013	12,922
The Pacific[b]	**701**	**1,031**	**1,345**	**1,628**	**1,681**	**1,553**
Cook Islands	73	88	104	125	146	161
Fiji	294	545	632	755	792	843
Kiribati	5	4	5	4	6	...
Marshall Islands	5	9	5	6	10	6
Micronesia, Federated States of	21	19	45	31	30	...
Nauru	...	...	...	...	...	...
Palau	58	81	85	164	138	123
Papua New Guinea	58	69	140	185	179	...
Samoa	88	102	122	128	134	146
Solomon Islands	5	9	21	22	22	26
Timor-Leste	...	...	40	62	66	74
Tonga	35	42	47	54	61	62
Tuvalu	1	1	2	2	2	3
Vanuatu	58	62	97	90	95	109
Developed ADB Member Economies	**11,475**	**14,544**	**16,918**	**30,226**	**35,678**	**41,061**
Australia	4,931	5,463	5,872	7,450	8,269	8,815
Japan	4,757	6,728	8,611	19,737	24,039	28,691
New Zealand	1,787	2,353	2,435	3,039	3,370	3,555
DEVELOPING ADB MEMBER ECONOMIES[b]	**91,876**	**132,298**	**179,438**	**244,960**	**254,430**	**243,034**
ALL ADB REGIONAL MEMBERS[b]	**103,351**	**146,842**	**196,356**	**275,186**	**290,108**	**284,095**
WORLD	**676,655**	**808,570**	**952,156**	**1,194,581**	**1,239,036**	**1,322,702**

... = data not available, | = marks break in the series, ADB = Asian Development Bank.

a   For Australia; Japan; the Republic of Korea; the Kyrgyz Republic; Taipei,China; Tajikistan; and Viet Nam, data refer to international visitor arrivals at frontiers (including tourists and same-day visitors). For the rest of the economies, data refer to international tourist arrivals at frontiers (overnight visitors, i.e., excluding same-day visitors).
b   For reporting economies only. Regional aggregates include data for nearest years as reported in the table.

Source: World Tourism Organization. June 2018. UNWTO *World Tourism Barometer and Statistical Annex*. Volume 16.

Table 2.4.25: International Tourism Receipts
($ million)

ADB Regional Member	2000	2005	2010	2015	2016	2017*
Developing ADB Member Economies						
Central and West Asia[a]	**679**	**1,528**	**3,642**	**7,541**	**8,204**	**9,024**
Afghanistan	...	...	86	82	49	...
Armenia	38	223	646	936	968	1,120
Azerbaijan	63	78	657	2,309	2,714	3,012
Georgia	97	241	659	1,936	2,166	2,751
Kazakhstan	356	701	1,005	1,534	1,549	1,781
Kyrgyz Republic	15	73	160	426	432	...
Pakistan	81	182	306	317	322	352
Tajikistan	2 (2002)	2	2	1	4	8
Turkmenistan	...	...	...	...	...	...
Uzbekistan	27	28	121	...	...	...
East Asia	**32,707**	**50,550**	**87,307**	**110,966**	**108,301**	**92,016**
China, People's Republic of	16,231	29,296	45,814	44,969	44,432	32,617
Hong Kong, China	5,868	10,294	22,200	36,150	32,846	33,243
Korea, Republic of	6,834	5,806	10,328	15,214	17,332	13,427
Mongolia	36	177	244	246	316	396
Taipei,China	3,738	4,977	8,721	14,387	13,375	12,333
South Asia	**4,247**	**8,974**	**17,243**	**27,288**	**29,201**	**35,102**
Bangladesh	50	75	81	150	213	337
Bhutan	10	19	40	94	91	103
India	3,460	7,493	14,490	21,013	22,427	27,365
Maldives	321	826	1,713	2,569	2,506	2,742
Nepal	158	132	343	481	446	630
Sri Lanka	248	429	576	2,981	3,518	3,925
Southeast Asia[a]	**25,502**	**34,986**	**68,423**	**108,608**	**116,651**	**123,874**
Brunei Darussalam	155 (2001)	191	...	147	144	...
Cambodia	304	840	1,519	3,130	3,207	...
Indonesia	4,975	4,522	6,958	10,761	11,206	12,520
Lao People's Democratic Republic	114	147	382	724	712	...
Malaysia	5,011	8,847	18,115	17,584	18,075	18,323
Myanmar	162	67	72	2,101	2,177	...
Philippines	2,156	2,287	2,645	5,272	5,143	6,986
Singapore	5,142	6,209	14,178	16,617	18,945	19,707
Thailand	7,483	9,576	20,104	44,922	48,792	57,477
Viet Nam	...	2,300	4,450	7,350	8,250	8,861
The Pacific[a]	**416**	**839**	**1,296**	**1,607**	**1,373**	...
Cook Islands	36	91	111	154	179	...
Fiji	189	485	634	763	777	885
Kiribati	3	4	4	2	3	...
Marshall Islands	3	3	4	1	5	...
Micronesia, Federated States of	17	16	24	25	...	...
Nauru	...	...	...	...	...	...
Palau	53	60	73	149	141	...
Papua New Guinea	7	4	2	2	1	1
Samoa	41	73	123	141	153	165
Solomon Islands	4	2	44	51	56	67
Timor-Leste	...	...	31	51	58	73
Tonga	7	15	27	40	...	...
Tuvalu[b]	...	1	2	...	...	...
Vanuatu	56	85	217	228	...	...
Developed ADB Member Economies	**14,934**	**31,526**	**52,305**	**68,278**	**77,194**	**86,077**
Australia	9,289	18,423	32,584	34,246	37,040	41,738
Japan	3,373	6,630	13,199	24,982	30,679	34,054
New Zealand	2,272	6,473	6,522	9,050	9,475	10,285
DEVELOPING ADB MEMBER ECONOMIES[a]	63,550	96,877	177,911	256,010	263,730	261,207
ALL ADB REGIONAL MEMBERS[a]	78,484	128,403	230,216	324,288	340,924	347,284
WORLD	475,510	703,779	976,638	1,216,794	1,238,602	1,332,391

... = data not available, * = provisional or preliminary, $ = United States dollars, ADB = Asian Development Bank.

a For reporting economies only. Regional aggregates include data for nearest years as reported in the table.
b Data is sourced from World Tourism Organization's *UNWTO World Tourism Barometer and Statistical Annex*, Volume 15 (June 2017).

Source: World Tourism Organization. June 2018. UNWTO *World Tourism Barometer and Statistical Annex*. Volume 16.

V.   Transport and Communications

Snapshot

- From 2000 to 2017, air carrier departures and the total number of passengers carried across Asia and the Pacific grew faster than the global averages for these two measures.

- In 2016, three of the world's top five developing economies in terms of mobile phone subscriptions were located in Asia and the Pacific—the People's Republic of China (PRC), India, and Indonesia, together accounting for 38% of total global subscriptions.

Key Trends

From 2000 to 2017, air carrier departures and the total number of passengers carried across Asia and the Pacific grew faster than the global averages for these two measures. On average, air carrier departures in the region increased by 7.6% annually, while the total number of passengers carried increased by 8.4% annually, for economies with data available for both 2000 and 2017 (Figure 2.5.1). The growth of air travel in the region grew faster than the global average over this period. Based on the World Bank's World Development Indicators database, global air carrier departures and the total number of passengers carried increased by annual averages of 2.9% and 5.2%, respectively. Afghanistan, Bhutan, India, Indonesia, Kazakhstan, Myanmar, Philippines, the PRC, and Viet Nam were among the economies in which air carrier departures and the total number of passengers carried both grew by an average of more than 10% per year.

In 2016, three of the world's top five developing economies in terms of mobile phone subscriptions were located in Asia and the Pacific—the PRC, India, and Indonesia. The PRC (1,365 million subscriptions) and India (1,128 million) led the world in terms of mobile phone subscriptions in 2016 (Figure 2.5.2). Together with Indonesia (385.6 million), these economies accounted for 38.3% of the global total for subscriptions (Table 2.5.8). Other

Figure 2.5.1: Annual Change in Air Carrier Departures and Number of Passengers Carried, 2000–2017
(%)

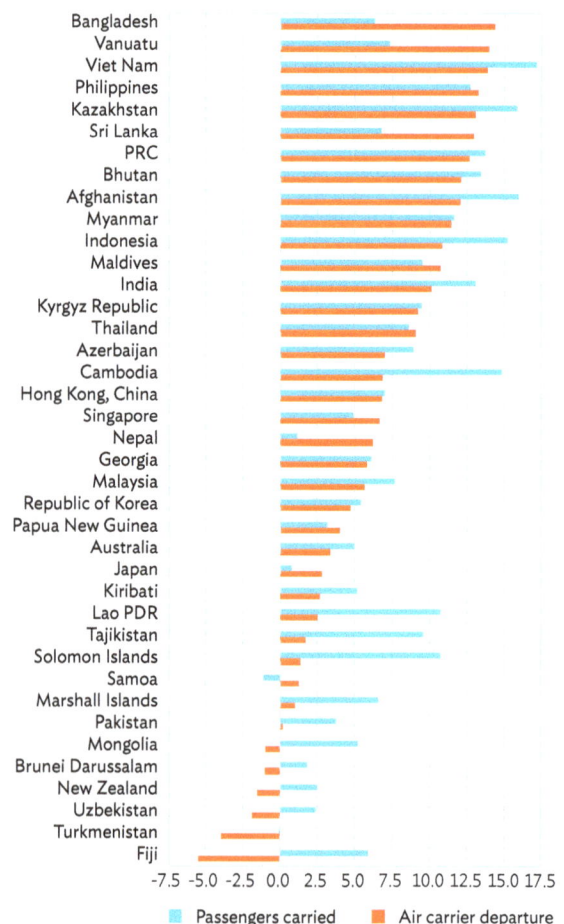

Lao PDR = Lao People's Democratic Republic, PRC = People's Republic of China.
Source: Table 2.5.6, Key Indicators for Asia and the Pacific 2018.

Figure 2.5.2: World's Highest Number of Mobile Phone Subscriptions, 2016
(million)

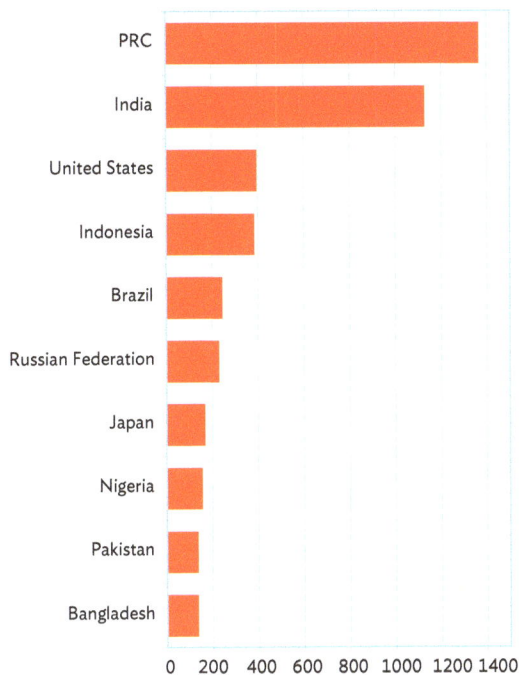

PRC = People's Republic of China.
Source: International Telecommunication Union.

economies in Asia and the Pacific with more than 100 million mobile phone subscriptions in 2016 included Japan (166.8 million), Pakistan (136.5 million), and Bangladesh (135.9 million).

In terms of mobile phone subscriptions per 100 people, Hong Kong, China (240.8); Maldives (189.9); and Thailand (173.8) led all economies in the region in 2016. The Federated States of Micronesia (22.3), Kiribati (45.5), and Papua New Guinea (46.8) had the lowest subscription rates (Table 2.5.9).

Data Issues and Comparability

Issues with the data organization, collection, compilation, and dissemination affect the availability, quality, and timeliness of road statistics. Some regions, especially the Pacific, have incomplete or no data. The most recent road data are usually 2–3 years old at the time of review.

Most data on telephone and internet subscriptions come from questionnaires sent by the International Telecommunication Union to participating economies. Other information and reports are sourced from national ministries in charge of telecommunications, and staff estimates.

Transport

Table 2.5.1:   Road Indicators—Network[a]
(km)

ADB Regional Member	Primary	Class I	Class II	Class III	Below III	Other	Total[b]	Year[c]
Developing ADB Member Economies								
Central and West Asia								
Afghanistan	...	10	2,549	...	1,461	...	4,020	2015
Armenia	...	147	721	58	40	...	966	2013
Azerbaijan	...	544	905	...	...	...	1,449	2017
Georgia	...	90	1,058	...	...	...	1,148	2017
Kazakhstan	...	557	5,407	6,389	475	...	12,828	2010
Kyrgyz Republic	...	...	303	1,324	136	...	1,763	2013
Pakistan	357	1,116	275	2,442	1,138	...	5,328	2015
Tajikistan	...	20	978	...	914	...	1,912	2015
Turkmenistan	...	60	...	2,120	24	...	2,204	2008
Uzbekistan	...	1,195	1,101	670	...	...	2,966	2008
East Asia								
China, People's Republic of[d]	8,437	230	1,855	321	5	...	10,847	2015
Hong Kong, China	...	...	...	...	...	...	...	
Korea, Republic of	457	423	40	...	...	...	920	2017
Mongolia	...	8	2,593	233	1,480	...	4,313	2017
Taipei,China	...						...	
South Asia								
Bangladesh	...	321	1,680	44	5	...	2,050	2017
Bhutan	...	7	116	...	47	...	170	2017
India	90	7,067	1,071	3,556	117	...	11,901	2015
Maldives	...	...	...	...	...	...	...	
Nepal	...	...	218	1,082	13	...	1,313	2013
Sri Lanka	...	60	545	45	...	...	650	2017
Southeast Asia								
Brunei Darussalam	...	...	...	...	...	...	...	
Cambodia	...	...	633	1,321	...	...	1,954	2017
Indonesia	409	603	3,045	...	...	34	4,091	2010
Lao People's Democratic Republic	...	...	244	2,307	306	...	2,857	2010
Malaysia	795	61	817	...	...	...	1,673	2010
Myanmar	...	320	575	1,702	1,928	...	4,525	2015
Philippines	...	665	2,048	687	...	...	3,400	2017
Singapore	13	6	...	...	...	...	19	2015
Thailand	572	4,075	848	26	...	...	5,523	2017
Viet Nam	...	1,202	1,915	...	...	...	3,117	2017
The Pacific								
Cook Islands	...	...	...	...	...	...	...	
Fiji	...	...	...	...	...	...	...	
Kiribati	...	...	...	...	...	...	...	
Marshall Islands	...	...	...	...	...	...	...	
Micronesia, Federated States of	...	...	...	...	...	...	...	
Nauru	...	...	...	...	...	...	...	
Palau	...	...	...	...	...	...	...	
Papua New Guinea	...	...	...	...	...	...	...	
Samoa	...	...	...	...	...	...	...	
Solomon Islands	...	...	...	...	...	...	...	
Timor-Leste	...	...	...	...	...	...	...	
Tonga	...	...	...	...	...	...	...	
Tuvalu	...	...	...	...	...	...	...	
Vanuatu	...	...	...	...	...	...	...	
Developed ADB Member Economies								
Australia	...	...	...	...	...	...	...	
Japan	1,138	...	...	...	...	...	1,138	2015
New Zealand	...	...	...	...	...	...	...	

... = data not available, ADB = Asian Development Bank, km = kilometer.

a The road network refers to the Asian Highway that consists of highway routes of international importance within Asia, including highway routes substantially crossing more than one subregion; highway routes within subregions that connected neighboring subregions; and highway routes located within member states that provide access to (a) capital cities; (b) main industrial and agricultural centers; (c) major air, sea, and river ports; (d) major container terminals and depots; and (e) major tourist attractions.
   "Primary" class in the classification refers to access-controlled motorways. Access-controlled motorways are used exclusively by automobiles. Motorcycles, bicycles, and pedestrians will not be allowed to enter the motorway to ensure traffic safety and the high running speed of automobiles.
   Class I refers to asphalt, cement, or concrete roads with four or more lanes.
   Class II refers to double bituminous treated roads with two lanes.
   Class III is also regarded as the minimum desirable standard usually described as a two-lane (narrow) road.
   Roads classified below class III are road sections below the minimum desirable standard.
b Sum of reported available data.
c The year data was received by the Secretariat of the United Nations Economic and Social Commission for Asia and the Pacific.
d Estimates for 2015 do not include approximately 15,400 km of potential Asian Highway routes.

Source: United Nations Economic and Social Commission for Asia and the Pacific. ESCAP Online Statistical Database. http://data.unescap.org/escap_stat/ (accessed 9 July 2018).

Table 2.5.2: Road Indicators—Vehicles

| ADB Regional Member | Number of Registered Vehicles, 2013 | | | | | | |
	Total	(per 1000 people)[b]	Four-Wheeled Vehicles	Two- and Three-Wheeled Vehicles	Heavy Trucks	Buses	Others
Developing ADB Member Economies							
Central and West Asia							
Afghanistan	655,357	23.8	407,608	68,090	81,416	20,589	77,654
Armenia	300,091 (2010)	98.6	247,723	28	40,924	11,396	20
Azerbaijan	1,135,936 (2012)	122.3	958,594	2,067	130,019	29,647	15,609
Georgia	951,649	212.2	774,453	4,830	151,057	21,309	–
Kazakhstan	3,926,487	230.5	3,190,057	74,762	398,753	94,417	168,498
Kyrgyz Republic	958,187	169.2	777,847	21,696	114,853	34,561	9,230
Pakistan	9,080,437 (2011)	51.3	3,095,900	5,560,218	223,152	201,167	–
Tajikistan	411,548	50.4	353,919	4,925	36,942	15,762	–
Turkmenistan	847,874 (2014)	159.8	676,622	37,275	114,004	19,973	–
Uzbekistan	...	...	...	...	...	...	...
East Asia							
China, People's Republic of[c]	250,138,212	183.8	137,406,846	95,326,138	5,069,292	...	12,335,936
Hong Kong, China	...	...	...	...	...	...	...
Korea, Republic of	23,150,619	459.1	15,078,354	2,117,035	970,805	4,984,425	–
Mongolia	675,064	232.9	491,771	25,771	151,530	5,992	–
Taipei,China[d]	21,510,650 (2016)	914.7	6,666,006	13,668,227	1,078,467	34,531	63,419
South Asia							
Bangladesh	2,088,566 (2014)	13.3	547,423	1,336,339	141,850	59,500	3,454
Bhutan	68,173 (2014)	91.5	46,575	9,758	9,397	475	1,968
India	159,490,578 (2012)	129.1	38,338,015	115,419,175	4,056,885	1,676,503	–
Maldives	61,412	141.3	10,256	50,775	145	140	96
Nepal	1,178,911 (2011)	44.5	133,992	891,018	47,930	35,100	70,871
Sri Lanka	5,203,678	252.9	832,840	3,566,184	329,648	93,428	381,578
Southeast Asia							
Brunei Darussalam	349,279 (2010)	903.0	...	...	...	...	...
Cambodia	2,457,569	167.4	67,645	2,068,937	45,625	4,473	270,889
Indonesia	104,211,132	418.8	10,838,592	86,253,257	5,156,362	1,962,921	–
Lao People's Democratic Republic	1,439,481	...	276,493	1,120,673	38,454	3,861	–
Malaysia	23,819,256	796.2	10,689,450	11,087,878	1,116,167	62,784	862,977
Myanmar	4,310,112 (2014)	82.9	386,049	3,712,220	127,947	22,253	61,643
Philippines	7,690,038	78.3	3,009,116	4,250,667	358,445	31,665	40,145
Singapore	974,170	180.4	763,008	144,934	48,719	17,065	444
Thailand	32,476,977 (2012)	488.4	11,829,221	19,169,418	901,014	137,609	439,715
Viet Nam	40,790,841	454.4	798,592	38,643,091	696,316	111,030	541,812
The Pacific							
Cook Islands	12,453	669.5	5,085	6,846	491	31	–
Fiji	86,535	100.4	...	...	...	...	...
Kiribati	3,452	32.2	1,926	701	536	289	–
Marshall Islands	2,116	39.5	1,917	52	26	63	58
Micronesia, Federated States of	8,337 (2010)	81.1	7,356	96	747	138	–
Nauru	...	...	...	...	...	...	...
Palau	7,102	405.7	...	...	...	...	...
Papua New Guinea	94,297 (2014)	11.8	61,255	1,155	21,075	10,812	–
Samoa	17,449	92.1	16,243	97	873	236	–
Solomon Islands	45,000	79.5	...	...	...	...	...
Timor-Leste[e]	63,553	56.0	14,621	48,143	651	138	...
Tonga	8,154	78.8	6,039	184	1,882	49	–
Tuvalu	...	...	...	...	...	...	...
Vanuatu	14,000	52.9	...	...	...	...	...
Developed ADB Member Economies							
Australia	17,180,596	743.2	15,871,827	744,732	416,902	93,034	54,101
Japan	91,377,312	717.6	76,137,715	11,948,432	...	...	3,291,072
New Zealand	3,250,066 (2012)	737.3	2,643,624	114,930	112,856	8,286	370,370

... = data not available, – = magnitude equals zero, ADB = Asian Development Bank.

a Figures refer to the same year indicated in the column for "Total" unless otherwise specified.
b Calculated by dividing the total number of registered vehicles by the midyear population in thousands.
c The "per 1,000 people" calculation used end-of-year population data instead of midyear data.
d The "Heavy Trucks" category includes a combination of heavy and light trucks.
e There is no renewal process for vehicles in Timor-Leste; hence, 2013 data refer to the total number of vehicles from 2006 to 2013.

Sources: World Health Organization. 2015. *Global Status Report on Road Safety 2015*. Geneva; For Armenia and Brunei Darussalam: Global Status Report on Road Safety 2013. For Taipei,China: Government of Taipei,China, Directorate-General of Budget, Accounting and Statistics. 2017. *Statistical Yearbook 2016*. Nantou City.

Table 2.5.3:   Road Indicators—Safety

ADB Regional Member	Estimated Road Traffic Deaths, 2013		Road User Deaths, 2013 (%)				
	Total	Death Rate (per 100,000 population)	Four-Wheeled Vehicles	Two- and Three-Wheeled Vehicles	Cyclists	Pedestrians	Others
Developing ADB Member Economies							
Central and West Asia							
Afghanistan	4,734	16	...	...	...	...	...
Armenia	546	18	54.7	–	0.3	35.8	9.2
Azerbaijan	943	10	62.1	0.5	0.3	30.5	6.7
Georgia	514	12	44.7	3.1	0.6	24.3	27.2
Kazakhstan	3,983	24	60.5	2.3	1.1	22.5	13.5
Kyrgyz Republic	1,220	22	67.3	–	1.1	31.6	0.1
Pakistan	25,781	14	...	...	...	...	...
Tajikistan	1,543	19	62.5	–	4.2	33.3	–
Turkmenistan	914	17	74.7	–	1.9	23.4	–
Uzbekistan	3,240	11	...	...	...	...	...
East Asia							
China, People's Republic of	261,367	19	19.2	26.8	8.1	26.1	19.8
Hong Kong, China	...	...	...	...	...	...	...
Korea, Republic of	5,931	12	33.2	16.3	5.5	38.9	6.1
Mongolia	597	21	47.0	19.3	0.2	30.6	2.9
Taipei,China	...	...	...	...	...	...	...
South Asia							
Bangladesh	21,316	14	41.5	10.8	1.8	32.2	13.7
Bhutan	114	15	94.9	1.7	–	3.4	–
India	207,551	17	17.2	33.9	3.5	9.1	36.2
Maldives	12	4	16.7	16.7	16.7	33.3	16.7
Nepal	4,713	17	...	...	...	...	...
Sri Lanka	3,691	17	5.7	40.8	11.0	29.8	12.7
Southeast Asia							
Brunei Darussalam	...	...	...	...	...	...	...
Cambodia	2,635	17	8.5	70.4	2.3	12.7	6.1
Indonesia	38,279	15	6.0	36.0	2.0	21.0	35.0
Lao People's Democratic Republic	971	14	18.7	66.9	2.7	9.6	2.1
Malaysia	7,129	24	23.7	62.1	2.2	6.6	5.5
Myanmar	10,809	20	26.0	23.0	9.0	26.0	16.0
Philippines	10,379	11	25.3	52.5	2.0	19.0	1.1
Singapore	197	4	17.5	45.6	9.4	26.9	0.6
Thailand	24,237	36	13.0	72.8	2.3	8.1	3.8
Viet Nam	22,419	25	...	...	...	...	...
The Pacific							
Cook Islands	5	24	40.0	60.0	–	–	–
Fiji	51	6	39.0	–	2.4	58.5	–
Kiribati	3	3	–	–	33.3	66.7	–
Marshall Islands	3	6	33.3	66.7	–	–	–
Micronesia, Federated States of	2	2	...	...	...	...	...
Nauru	...	...	...	...	...	...	...
Palau	1	5	–	–	–	100.0	–
Papua New Guinea	1,232	17	48.4	–	–	29.0	22.6
Samoa	30	16	–	–	–	76.5	23.5
Solomon Islands	108	19	...	...	...	...	...
Timor–Leste	188	17	...	...	...	...	...
Tonga	8	8	62.5	–	–	37.5	–
Tuvalu	...	...	...	...	...	...	...
Vanuatu	42	17	44.4	–	–	55.6	–
Developed ADB Member Economies							
Australia	1,252	5	64.2	17.9	4.2	13.2	0.6
Japan	5,971	5	32.4	17.4	13.7	36.2	0.3
New Zealand	272	6	65.7	15.4	3.1	11.8	3.9

... = data not available, – = magnitude equals zero, ADB = Asian Development Bank.

Source: World Health Organization. 2015. *Global Status Report on Road Safety 2015.* Geneva.

Table 2.5.4:   Rail Indicators

ADB Regional Member	Rail Lines, Total Route (km)				Rail Network, Length per Land Area (km per km² '000)			
	2000	2005	2010	2016	2000	2005	2010	2016
Developing ADB Member Economies								
Central and West Asia								
Afghanistan	...	...	...	...	...	...	...	...
Armenia	842.0	732.0	826.0	679.4	29.6	25.7	29.0	23.9
Azerbaijan	2,116.0	2,122.0	2,079.0	2,074.0	25.6	25.7	25.2	25.1
Georgia	1,562.0	1,513.0 (2007)	1,566.0	1,415.0	22.5	21.8 (2007)	22.5	20.4
Kazakhstan	13,545.0	14,204.0	14,202.0	15,529.8	5.0	5.3	5.3	5.8
Kyrgyz Republic	...	417.0 (2007)	417.0	424.0	...	2.2 (2007)	2.2	2.2
Pakistan	7,791.0	7,791.0	7,791.0	9,255.0 (2015)	10.1	10.1	10.1	12.0 (2015)
Tajikistan	...	616.0	621.0	597.0	...	4.4	4.4	4.3
Turkmenistan	...	2,529.0	3,115.0	3,115.0	...	5.4	6.6	6.6
Uzbekistan	3,645.0	4,014.0	4,227.0	4,304.0	8.6	9.4	9.9	10.1
East Asia								
China, People's Republic of	58,656.0	62,200.0	66,239.0	67,092.0	6.2	6.6	7.1	7.1
Hong Kong, China	...	...	...	...	...	...	...	...
Korea, Republic of	3,123.0	3,392.0	3,379.0	4,071.0	32.4	35.0	34.8	41.8
Mongolia	1,810.0	1,810.0	1,814.0	1,810.0	1.2	1.2	1.2	1.2
Taipei,China[a]	1,125.0	1,118.0	1,460.0	1,468.0	75.6	72.8	88.8	88.3 (2015)
South Asia								
Bangladesh	2,768.0	2,855.0	2,835.0	2,835.0 (2014)	21.3	21.9	21.8	21.8 (2014)
Bhutan	...	...	...	...	...	...	...	...
India	62,759.0	63,465.0	63,974.0	66,030.0 (2015)	21.1	21.3	21.5	22.2 (2015)
Maldives	...	...	...	...	...	...	...	...
Nepal	...	...	...	...	...	...	...	...
Sri Lanka	...	1,449.0 (2004)	1,463.0 (2008)	...	...	23.1 (2004)	23.3 (2008)	...
Southeast Asia								
Brunei Darussalam	...	...	...	...	...	...	...	...
Cambodia	601.0	650.0	...	...	3.4	3.7	...	...
Indonesia	...	...	4,684.0 (2012)	4,684.0 (2014)	...	...	2.6 (2012)	2.6 (2014)
Lao People's Democratic Republic	...	...	...	...	...	...	...	...
Malaysia	1,622.0	1,657.0	1,665.0	2,250.0 (2014)	4.9	5.0	5.1	6.8 (2014)
Myanmar	...	...	...	...	...	...	...	...
Philippines	491.0	491.0 (2004)	479.0 (2008)	...	1.6	1.6 (2004)	1.6 (2008)	...
Singapore	...	...	...	...	...	...	...	...
Thailand	4,103.0	4,044.0 (2004)	4,429.0	5,327.0 (2014)	8.0	7.9 (2004)	8.7	10.4 (2014)
Viet Nam	2,545.0 (2002)	2,671.0	2,347.0	2,347.0	8.2 (2002)	8.6	7.6	7.6
The Pacific								
Cook Islands	...	...	...	...	...	...	...	...
Fiji	...	...	...	...	...	...	...	...
Kiribati	...	...	...	...	...	...	...	...
Marshall Islands	...	...	...	...	...	...	...	...
Micronesia, Federated States of	...	...	...	...	...	...	...	...
Nauru	...	...	...	...	...	...	...	...
Palau	...	...	...	...	...	...	...	...
Papua New Guinea	...	...	...	...	...	...	...	...
Samoa	...	...	...	...	...	...	...	...
Solomon Islands	...	...	...	...	...	...	...	...
Timor-Leste	...	...	...	...	...	...	...	...
Tonga	...	...	...	...	...	...	...	...
Tuvalu	...	...	...	...	...	...	...	...
Vanuatu	...	...	...	...	...	...	...	...
Developed ADB Member Economies								
Australia	9,499.0	9,528.0	9,674.0 (2009)	...	1.2	1.2	1.3 (2009)	...
Japan	20,165.0	20,096.0	20,035.0	15,108.4	55.3	55.1	55.0	41.4
New Zealand	...	...	...	...	...	...	...	...

... = data not available, ADB = Asian Development Bank, km = kilometer, km² = square kilometer.

a   Taipei Metro and Kaohsiung Metro are not included.

Sources: World Bank. World Development Indicators. http://data.worldbank.org/indicator (accessed 12 July 2018); and Asian Development Bank estimates.
For Taipei,China: Government of Taipei,China, National Development Council. 2017. *Statistical Data Book*. Taipei City.

Table 2.5.5:   Railways—Passengers Carried and Goods Transported

ADB Regional Member	Passengers Carried (passenger-km million)				Goods Transported (t-km million)			
	2000	2005	2010	2016	2000	2005	2010	2016
Developing ADB Member Economies								
Central and West Asia								
Afghanistan	...	...	...	...	...	...	...	...
Armenia	47	30	50	50	354	654	346	640 (2015)
Azerbaijan	493	789	917	519	5,770	10,374 (2007)	8,250	6,211 (2015)
Georgia	453	720	655	465 (2015)	3,912	6,127	6,228	4,261 (2015)
Kazakhstan	10,215	12,129	15,448	18,165	124,983	171,855	213,174	188,159
Kyrgyz Republic	...	60 (2007)	99	41	...	752 (2007)	738	807
Pakistan	18,495	23,045	24,731	20,288 (2015)	3,754	4,796	6,187	3,301 (2015)
Tajikistan	...	50	33	18	1,326	1,274 (2007)	808	228
Turkmenistan	...	1,286	1,811	2,336	...	8,670	11,992	13,327
Uzbekistan	2,163	2,012	2,905	3,934	15,441	18,007	22,282	22,937
East Asia								
China, People's Republic of	441,468	583,320	791,158	695,955	1,333,606	1,934,612	2,451,185	1,920,285
Hong Kong, China	...	...	...	...	...	...	...	...
Korea, Republic of	28,097	31,004	33,027	23,747	10,803	10,108	9,452	9,479 (2015)
Mongolia	1,070	1,228	1,220	956	4,293	8,361 (2007)	10,287	12,371
Taipei,China[a]	10,037 (2001)	12,458 (2007)	16,489	21,456	1,179	982	873	564
South Asia								
Bangladesh	3,941	4,340	7,305	7,305 (2014)	777	896	710	710 (2014)
Bhutan	...	...	...	...	...	...	...	...
India	430,666	575,702	903,465	1,147,190 (2015)	305,201	407,398	600,548	681,696 (2015)
Maldives	...	...	...	...	...	...	...	...
Nepal	...	...	...	...	...	...	...	...
Sri Lanka	...	4,682	4,767 (2008)	...	88	138	135 (2008)	...
Southeast Asia								
Brunei Darussalam	...	...	...	...	...	...	...	...
Cambodia	45	45	...	...	92	92	...	...
Indonesia	...	25,535	20,283 (2012)	20,283 (2014)	...	4,698	7,166 (2012)	7,166 (2014)
Lao People's Democratic Republic	...	...	...	...	...	...	...	...
Malaysia	1,312	1,181	1,527	3,293 (2014)	907	1,178	1,384	3,071 (2014)
Myanmar	...	4,163 (2006)	...	...	...	885 (2006)	...	...
Philippines	171	83 (2006)	...	...	...	1 (2004)	...	...
Singapore	...	...	...	...	...	...	...	...
Thailand	9,935	9,195	8,037	7,504 (2014)	3,384	4,037	3,161	2,455 (2014)
Viet Nam	3,200	4,558	4,378	3,416	1,902	2,928	3,901	3,190
The Pacific								
Cook Islands	...	...	...	...	...	...	...	...
Fiji	...	...	...	...	...	...	...	...
Kiribati	...	...	...	...	...	...	...	...
Marshall Islands	...	...	...	...	...	...	...	...
Micronesia, Federated States of	...	...	...	...	...	...	...	...
Nauru	...	...	...	...	...	...	...	...
Palau	...	...	...	...	...	...	...	...
Papua New Guinea	...	...	...	...	...	...	...	...
Samoa	...	...	...	...	...	...	...	...
Solomon Islands	...	...	...	...	...	...	...	...
Timor-Leste	...	...	...	...	...	...	...	...
Tonga	...	...	...	...	...	...	...	...
Tuvalu	...	...	...	...	...	...	...	...
Vanuatu	...	...	...	...	...	...	...	...
Developed ADB Member Economies								
Australia	1,265	1,290	1,500	...	34,050	46,164	64,172	59,649 (2014)
Japan	240,793	239,246	244,235	206,722 (2015)	22,313	21,900	20,432	20,255 (2014)
New Zealand	...	...	...	...	4,078	...	...	...

... = data not available, ADB = Asian Development Bank, km = kilometer, t = metric ton.

a   Taipei Metro and Kaohsiung Metro are not included.

Sources: World Bank. World Development Indicators. http://data.worldbank.org/indicator (accessed 12 July 2018). For Taipei,China: Government of Taipei,China, Directorate-General of Budget, Accounting and Statistics. 2017. *Statistical Yearbook 2016*. Nantou City.

Table 2.5.6: Air Transport

ADB Regional Member	Carrier Departures Worldwide (takeoffs)				Freight (t-km million)				Passenger Carried ('000)			
	2000	2005	2010	2017	2000	2005	2010	2017	2000	2005	2010	2017
Developing ADB Member Economies												
Central and West Asia												
Afghanistan	3,409	...	21,677	23,682	7.8	...	108.0	25.1	150	...	1,999	1,859
Armenia	4,406	5,939	8,761	852 (2013)	8.8	7.0	6.0	1.0 (2013)	298	556	705	45 (2013)
Azerbaijan	8,012	12,470	9,885	25,365	47.2	11.9	7.8	751.1	546	1,134	797	2,331
Georgia	1,906	4,673	2,803	4,985	2.0	2.8	0.9	0.3	118	249	164	323
Kazakhstan	8,041	17,302	33,483	65,009	11.8	15.8	42.4	49.3	461	1,160	3,098	5,653
Kyrgyz Republic	6,051	5,228	7,371	27,097	3.7	2.0	1.3	0.0	241	226	376	1,127
Pakistan	63,956	48,905	64,932	66,346	340.3	407.9	333.0	249.9	5,294	5,364	6,588	9,920
Tajikistan	3,953	6,987	5,710	5,283	2.0	3.7	1.0	4.0	168	479	617	796
Turkmenistan	21,858	14,094	3,221	11,068	11.9	10.1	6.2	6.0	1,284	1,654	301	1,280
Uzbekistan	30,075	22,183	22,924	21,730	79.6	71.6	153.7	126.8	1,745	1,639	2,114	2,582
East Asia												
China, People's Republic of	572,921	1,349,269	2,377,789	4,359,033	3,900.1	7,579.4	17,193.9	23,323.6	61,892	136,722	266,293	551,235
Hong Kong, China	79,182	122,705	158,255	243,518	5,111.5	7,763.9	10,373.4	12,415.2	14,378	20,230	28,348	45,580
Korea, Republic of	226,910	221,424	280,427	496,326	7,651.3	7,432.6	12,942.7	11,002.2	34,331	33,888	36,988	84,045
Mongolia	6,200	5,332	6,528	5,277	8.4	6.1	3.9	8.4	254	295	391	603
Taipei,China[a]	586,560	479,499	360,409	527,025 (2016)	1.3	1.8	2.3	2.2 (2016)	48,407	44,268	41,091	63,253 (2016)
South Asia												
Bangladesh	6,313	7,399	19,300	61,902	193.9	183.5	164.4	61.7	1,331	1,634	1,819	3,786
Bhutan[b]	1,138	2,467	3,053	7,927	0.2	0.3	0.4	0.8	34	49	182	293
India	198,426	330,484	623,197	1,029,961	547.7	774.0	1,631.0	2,407.3	17,299	27,879	64,374	139,822
Maldives[c]	5,970	4,520	4,971	33,904	13.2	0.0	0.0	7.7	315	82	85	1,486
Nepal	12,130	6,255	45,990	33,767	17.0	6.9	6.5	6.0	643	480	918	780
Sri Lanka	5,206	19,712	20,921	41,272	255.7	310.4	339.0	398.6	1,756	2,818	3,008	5,342
Southeast Asia												
Brunei Darussalam	12,739	11,808	12,333	10,743	140.2	134.1	148.5	132.6	864	978	1,263	1,172
Cambodia[b]	4,648	3,207	5,105	14,372	4.1	1.2	0.0	0.9	125	169	278	1,305
Indonesia	159,027	320,724	520,932	916,471	408.5	439.8	665.7	1,056.0	9,916	26,836	59,384	110,253
Lao People's Democratic Republic	6,411	9,002	11,374	9,731	1.7	2.5	0.1	1.5	211	293	444	1,196
Malaysia	169,263	176,152	302,185	432,454	1,863.8	2,577.6	2,564.7	1,261.6	16,561	20,369	34,239	58,189
Myanmar	10,329	26,460	20,485	65,028	0.8	2.7	2.1	5.5	438	1,504	924	2,854
Philippines	44,547	58,944	205,318	369,158	289.9	322.7	460.2	756.9	5,756	8,057	22,575	44,087
Singapore	71,042	77,119	131,722	213,198	6,004.9	7,571.3	7,121.4	7,006.9	16,704	17,744	24,860	37,680
Thailand	101,591	124,347	201,306	445,736	1,712.9	2,002.4	2,938.7	2,393.3	17,392	18,903	28,781	71,192
Viet Nam	28,999	54,415	109,176	264,548	117.3	230.2	426.9	453.3	2,878	5,454	14,378	42,593
The Pacific												
Cook Islands	...	...	...	...	...	...	...	...	...	...	...	...
Fiji	57,776	41,886	26,127	22,075	90.8	92.1	77.1	102.6	586	871	1,259	1,558
Kiribati[d]	3,200	...	...	5,005	0.8	...	...	...	28	...	...	67
Marshall Islands[c]	2,324	3,083	3,480	2,756	0.2	0.3	0.3	0.7	16	26	28	47
Micronesia, Federated States of	...	...	...	...	...	...	...	...	...	...	...	...
Nauru	...	...	...	...	...	...	...	...	...	...	...	...
Palau	...	...	...	...	...	...	...	...	...	...	...	...
Papua New Guinea	27,512	19,606	32,741	53,696	22.3	21.1	28.5	29.2	1,100	819	1,405	1,865
Samoa[c]	10,877	11,439	12,492	13,433	2.2	1.8	1.6	0.0	164	267	271	135
Solomon Islands	11,481	12,318	7,388	14,365	1.0	0.8	2.5	3.8	75	91	143	428
Timor-Leste	...	...	...	...	...	...	...	...	...	...	...	...
Tonga[e]	3,814	5,255	...	...	0.0	0.0	...	...	52	75	...	...
Tuvalu	...	...	...	...	...	...	...	...	...	...	...	...
Vanuatu	1,402	1,580	17,212	12,920	1.8	1.8	0.2	2.3	102	112	248	339
Developed ADB Member Economies												
Australia	382,514	342,509	572,906	672,349	1,730.7	2,444.6	2,938.3	1,982.6	32,578	44,657	60,641	74,257
Japan	645,087	651,858	934,487	1,035,522	8,672.0	8,549.2	7,698.8	10,684.6	109,123	102,279	109,617	123,898
New Zealand	240,046	209,469	207,872	184,762	817.1	781.5	468.6	1,336.0	10,781	11,952	13,295	16,272

... = data not available, 0.0 = magnitude is less than half of unit employed, ADB = Asian Development Bank, km = kilometer, t = metric ton.

a Carrier departures worldwide for Taipei,China are based on the number of aircraft movements, both domestic and international. Freight is based on million ton.
b For the freight indicator, data for 2000 refer to 2002.
c For all indicators, data for 2010 refer to 2009.
d For all indicators, data for 2000 refer to 1998.
e For all indicators, data for 2005 refer to 2004.

Sources: World Bank. World Development Indicators. http://databank.worldbank.org/data/reports.aspx?source=world-development-indicators (accessed 12 July 2018).
For Taipei,China: Government of Taipei,China, Directorate-General of Budget, Accounting and Statistics. 2017. *Statistical Yearbook 2016*. Nantou City.

Table 2.5.7:   Container Port Traffic
(teu '000)

ADB Regional Member	2000	2005	2006	2007	2008	2009	2010	2011	2012	2013	2014	2015	2016
Developing ADB Member Economies													
Central and West Asia													
Afghanistan	...	...	...	...	...	...	...	...	...	...	...	...	...
Armenia	...	...	...	...	...	...	...	...	...	...	...	...	...
Azerbaijan	...	...	...	...	...	...	...	...	...	...	...	...	...
Georgia	...	...	...	185	254	182	242	284	358	403	385	222	304
Kazakhstan	...	...	...	...	...	...	...	...	...	...	...	...	...
Kyrgyz Republic	...	...	...	...	...	...	...	...	...	...	...	...	...
Pakistan	...	1,686	1,777	1,936	1,938	2,058	2,149	2,132	2,244	2,445	2,535	2,756	2,645
Tajikistan	...	...	...	...	...	...	...	...	...	...	...	...	...
Turkmenistan	...	...	...	...	...	...	...	...	...	...	...	...	...
Uzbekistan	...	...	...	...	...	...	...	...	...	...	...	...	...
East Asia													
China, People's Republic of	41,000	67,245	84,811	103,823	115,942	108,800	139,358	152,476	163,372	175,805	186,853	194,756	199,566
Hong Kong, China	...	22,602	23,539	23,998	24,494	21,040	23,600	24,404	23,100	22,290	22,300	20,114	19,580
Korea, Republic of	9,030	15,113	15,514	17,086	17,418	15,700	18,517	20,591	21,535	22,523	24,814	25,477	26,373
Mongolia	...	...	...	...	...	...	...	...	...	...	...	...	...
Taipei,China	...	12,791	13,102	13,720	12,971	11,352	12,937	14,518	13,878	14,047	15,050	14,492	14,865
South Asia													
Bangladesh	456	809	902	978	1,091	1,182	1,469	1,343	1,469	1,626	1,643	2,045	2,367
Bhutan	...	...	...	...	...	...	...	...	...	...	...	...	...
India	2,451	4,982	6,141	7,398	7,672	8,014	9,112	9,557	9,577	9,685	11,319	11,883	12,083
Maldives	...	...	...	48	54	56	50	53	55	80	84	84	82
Nepal	...	...	...	...	...	...	...	...	...	...	...	...	...
Sri Lanka	1,733	2,455	3,079	3,687	3,687	3,464	4,080	4,263	4,187	4,306	4,908	5,185	5,550
Southeast Asia													
Brunei Darussalam	...	...	...	...	90	86	93	105	109	122	128	128	125
Cambodia	...	...	...	253	259	208	224	238	255	286	424	474	482
Indonesia	3,798	5,503	4,316	6,583	7,405	7,255	8,089	9,674	10,428	10,811	11,637	12,032	12,432
Lao People's Democratic Republic	...	...	...	...	...	...	...	...	...	...	...	...	...
Malaysia	4,642	12,198	13,419	14,829	16,094	15,923	18,204	20,011	20,588	20,910	22,368	24,013	24,570
Myanmar	...	...	...	170	180	164	335	381	474	567	717	827	1,026
Philippines	3,032	3,634	3,676	4,351	4,471	4,307	5,087	5,315	5,642	5,826	6,176	7,210	7,421
Singapore	17,100	23,192	24,792	28,768	30,891	26,593	29,179	29,938	31,649	32,579	34,688	31,710	31,688
Thailand	3,179	5,115	5,574	6,339	6,726	5,898	6,521	7,036	7,324	7,547	8,119	8,359	8,239
Viet Nam	1,190	2,537	3,000	4,009	4,394	4,937	5,886	6,924	7,372	8,254	8,150	8,842	8,496
The Pacific													
Cook Islands	...	...	...	...	...	...	...	...	...	...	...	...	...
Fiji	...	...	...	...	...	...	87	102	82	88	260	89	89
Kiribati	...	...	...	...	...	...	...	...	...	...	...	...	...
Marshall Islands	...	...	...	...	...	...	...	...	...	...	...	...	...
Micronesia, Federated States of	...	...	...	...	...	...	...	...	...	...	...	...	...
Nauru	...	...	...	...	...	...	...	...	...	...	...	...	...
Palau	...	...	...	...	...	...	...	...	...	...	...	...	...
Papua New Guinea	...	...	...	282	255	262	230	250	274	364	382	276	329
Samoa	...	...	...	...	...	...	22	21	23	24	27	28	28
Solomon Islands	...	...	...	...	...	...	...	...	...	...	...	...	...
Timor-Leste	...	...	...	...	...	...	...	...	...	...	...	...	...
Tonga	...	...	...	...	...	...	...	...	...	...	...	...	...
Tuvalu	...	...	...	...	...	...	...	...	...	...	...	...	...
Vanuatu	...	...	...	...	...	...	...	...	...	...	...	...	...
Developed ADB Member Economies													
Australia	3,543	5,191	5,742	6,290	6,102	6,200	6,551	6,039	6,975	7,082	7,405	7,627	7,636
Japan	13,100	17,055	18,470	19,165	18,944	16,286	18,115	16,624	17,075	19,108	20,675	20,076	20,257
New Zealand	1,067	1,603	1,807	2,312	2,318	2,325	2,112	2,165	2,327	2,420	2,943	3,119	3,031

... = data not available, ADB = Asian Development Bank, teu = twenty-foot equivalent unit.

Sources: World Bank. World Development Indicators. http://data.worldbank.org/indicator (accessed 12 July 2018). For Taipei,China for 2005–2007: United Nations Conference on Trade and Development (UNCTAD). 2008 and 2010. *Review of Maritime Transport.* New York, NY: United Nations Publications. For Taipei,China for 2008–2016: UNCTAD. UNCTADstat. http://unctadstat.unctad.org/EN/Index.html (accessed 12 July 2018).

Table 2.5.8:   Access to Fixed Telephone, Mobile Phones, and Internet
('000)

ADB Regional Member	Telephone Subscribers		Mobile Phone Subscribers		Fixed Broadband Subscribers	
	2000	2016	2000	2016	2000	2016
Developing ADB Member Economies						
Central and West Asia						
Afghanistan	29.0	114.2	25.0 (2002)	21,603.0	0.2 (2004)	8.8
Armenia	533.4	531.6	17.5	3,434.6	0.0 (2001)	299.2
Azerbaijan	801.2	1,700.2	420.4	10,189.0	1.0 (2002)	1,803.7
Georgia	508.8	833.9	194.7	5,532.7	0.4 (2001)	689.6
Kazakhstan	1,834.2	3,931.1	197.3	25534.8	1.0 (2003)	2,349.9
Kyrgyz Republic	376.1	382.1	9.0	7,613.5	0.0 (2002)	240.9
Pakistan	3,053.5	3,104.4	306.5	136,489.0	14.6 (2005)	1,642.8
Tajikistan	218.5	468.0	1.2	9,400.0	0.0 (2003)	6.0
Turkmenistan	364.4	665.0	7.5	8,575.0	...	4.0
Uzbekistan	1,655.0	3,412.9	53.1	23,265.4	2.8 (2003)	2,746.4
East Asia						
China, People's Republic of	144,829.0	206,624.0	85,260.0	1,364,934.0	22.7	322,597.0
Hong Kong, China	3,925.8	4,318.3	5,447.3	17,585.0	444.5	2,626.0
Korea, Republic of	25,863.0	28,035.6	26,816.4	61,295.5	3,870.0	20,555.7
Mongolia	117.5	225.3	154.6	3,367.6	0.05 (2001)	226.1
Taipei,China	12,642.2	13,771.0	17,873.8	29,244.3	229.0	5,686.0
South Asia						
Bangladesh	491.3	766.2	279.0	135,981.8	43.7 (2007)	6,592.4
Bhutan	14.1	21.1	–	698.4	...	16.5
India	32,436.1	24,404.0	3,577.1	1,127,809.0	50.0 (2001)	18,653.3
Maldives	24.4	21.1	7.6	812.1	0.2 (2002)	29.3
Nepal	266.9	858.2	10.2	32,120.3	1.0 (2006)	224.2
Sri Lanka	767.4	2,479.8	430.2	25,797.2	0.3 (2001)	892.2
Southeast Asia						
Brunei Darussalam	80.5	74.2	95.0	523.5	1.9 (2001)	36.1
Cambodia	30.9	227.3	130.5	19,915.5	0.1 (2002)	96.7
Indonesia	6,662.6	10,752.9	3,669.3	385,573.4	4.0	5,227.4
Lao People's Democratic Republic	40.9	1,266.6	12.7	3,958.5	0.0 (2003)	24.4
Malaysia	4,628.0	4,837.2	5,121.7	43,912.6	4.0 (2001)	2,718.8
Myanmar	271.4	514.4	13.4	50,586.4	0.2 (2005)	89.7
Philippines	3,061.4	3,835.9	6,454.4	113,000.0	10.0 (2001)	5,649.4
Singapore	1,946.0	1,998.4	2,747.4	8,460.7	69.0	1,461.1
Thailand	5,591.1	4,706.0	3,056.0	119,669.0	1.6 (2001)	7,219.0
Viet Nam	2,542.7	5,598.0	788.6	120,600.2	1.1 (2002)	9,089.3
The Pacific						
Cook Islands	5.7	7.8 (2013)	0.6	11.5 (2013)	0.0 (2003)	2.7 (2013)
Fiji	86.4	74.2	55.1	1,044.7	7.0 (2005)	12.3
Kiribati	3.4	0.7	0.3	52.0	0.3 (2005)	0.1
Marshall Islands	4.0	2.4 (2014)	0.4	15.5 (2015)	...	1.0
Micronesia, Federated States of	9.6	6.9	–	23.4	0.0 (2003)	3.2
Nauru	1.8	1.9 (2009)	1.2	9.9	...	0.95 (2010)
Palau	...	...	...	...	...	...
Papua New Guinea	64.8	154.0	8.6	3,782.0	...	17.0
Samoa	8.5	9.7	2.5	151.0	0.0 (2004)	2.2
Solomon Islands	7.7	7.4	1.2	416.6	0.2 (2004)	1.6
Timor-Leste	2.0 (2003)	2.7	20.1 (2003)	1,492.1	0.0 (2003)	1.0
Tonga	9.7	11.0	0.2	80.0	0.0 (2002)	3.0
Tuvalu	0.7	2.0	0.5 (2004)	7.6	0.1 (2004)	1.0
Vanuatu	6.6	4.6	0.4	218.6	0.0 (2003)	4.5
Developed ADB Member Economies						
Australia	10,050.0	8,180.0	8,562.0	26,551.0	122.8 (2001)	7,374.0
Japan	61,957.1	64,099.2	66,784.4	166,852.8	854.7	39,805.6
New Zealand	1,831.0	1,760.0	1,542.0	5,800.0	4.7	1,530.5

... = data not available, 0.0 = magnitude is less than half of unit employed, – = magnitude equals zero, ADB = Asian Development Bank.

Source: International Telecommunication Union. World Telecommunication/ICT Indicators Database. http://www.itu.int/en/ITU-D/Statistics/Pages/stat/default. aspx (accessed 18 July 2018).

Communications

Table 2.5.9:   Access to Fixed Telephone, Mobile Phones, and Internet
(per 100 people)

ADB Regional Member	Fixed Telephone				Mobile Cellular				Fixed Broadband				Internet Users[a]			
	2000	2005	2010	2016	2000	2005	2010	2016	2000	2005	2010	2016	2000	2005	2010	2016
Developing ADB Member Economies																
Central and West Asia																
Afghanistan	0.1	...	0.1	0.3	–	4.8	35.5	62.3	...	0.0	0.0	0.0	...	1.2	4.0	10.6
Armenia	17.4	19.9	20.6	18.2	0.6	10.7	134.3	117.4	...	0.1	3.3	10.2	1.3	5.3	25.0	67.0
Azerbaijan	9.9	12.8	16.7	17.5	5.2	26.3	100.7	104.8	...	0.0	5.3	18.5	0.1	8.0	46.0	78.2
Georgia	10.8	12.7	26.3	21.2	4.1	26.2	94.0	140.9	...	0.1	4.3	17.6	0.5	6.1	26.9	58.0
Kazakhstan	12.2	17.4	24.7	21.9	1.3	34.7	118.3	142.0	...	0.0	5.3	13.1	0.7	3.0	31.6	74.6
Kyrgyz Republic	7.6	8.7	9.0	6.4	0.2	10.7	97.3	127.8	...	0.0	0.4	4.0	1.0	10.5	16.3	34.5
Pakistan	2.2	3.4	3.6	1.6	0.2	8.3	58.2	70.6	...	0.0	0.5	0.9	...	6.3	8.0	15.5
Tajikistan	3.5	4.1	4.8	5.4	0.0	3.9	77.7	107.6	...	...	0.1	0.1	0.0	0.3	11.6	20.5
Turkmenistan	8.1	8.4	10.2	11.7	0.2	2.2	62.9	151.4	...	...	0.0	0.1	0.1	1.0	3.0	18.0
Uzbekistan	6.7	6.8	6.6	10.9	0.2	2.7	73.2	74.0	...	0.0	0.4	8.7	0.5	3.3	15.9	46.8
East Asia																
China, People's Republic of	11.3	26.5	21.6	14.7	6.6	29.8	63.2	97.3	0.0	2.8	9.3	23.0	1.8	8.5	34.3	53.2
Hong Kong, China	58.9	55.6	62.1	59.1	81.7	125.1	196.3	240.8	6.7	24.3	30.9	36.0	27.8	56.9	72.0	87.5
Korea, Republic of	54.6	49.1	57.6	55.2	56.6	78.7	102.5	120.7	8.2	25.0	34.7	40.5	44.7	73.5	83.7	92.8
Mongolia	4.9	6.2	7.1	7.4	6.4	22.1	92.5	111.2	...	0.1	2.8	7.5	1.3	...	10.2	22.3
Taipei,China	57.9	64.1	71.1	58.5	81.8	98.1	120.5	124.1	1.0	19.2	23.0	24.1	28.1	58.0	71.5	79.7
South Asia																
Bangladesh	0.4	0.7	0.8	0.5	0.2	6.3	44.6	83.4	...	...	0.3	4.0	0.1	0.2	3.7	18.2
Bhutan	2.5	5.0	3.6	2.6	–	5.5	54.2	87.5	...	...	1.2	2.1	0.4	3.8	13.6	41.8
India	3.1	4.4	2.9	1.8	0.3	7.9	61.1	85.2	...	0.1	0.9	1.4	0.5	2.4	7.5	29.5
Maldives	8.7	10.1	7.8	4.9	2.7	63.9	135.6	189.9	...	1.0	4.3	6.9	2.2	6.9	26.5	59.1
Nepal	1.1	1.9	3.1	3.0	0.0	0.9	34.0	110.8	...	...	0.2	0.8	0.2	0.8	7.9	19.7
Sri Lanka	4.1	6.4	17.7	11.9	2.3	17.2	85.9	124.0	...	0.1	1.1	4.3	0.6	1.8	12.0	32.1
Southeast Asia																
Brunei Darussalam	24.2	23.0	20.6	17.5	28.5	63.8	111.9	123.7	...	2.2	5.6	8.5	9.0	36.5	53.0	90.0
Cambodia	0.3	0.2	2.5	1.4	1.1	8.0	57.0	126.3	...	0.0	0.2	0.6	0.0	0.3	1.3	32.4
Indonesia	3.1	6.0	16.9	4.1	1.7	20.7	87.1	147.7	0.0	0.0	0.9	2.0	0.9	3.6	10.9	25.4
Lao People's Democratic Republic	0.8	1.6	1.7	18.7	0.2	11.4	64.1	58.6	...	0.0	0.1	0.4	0.1	0.9	7.0	21.9
Malaysia	20.0	17.0	16.4	15.5	22.1	76.2	120.4	140.8	...	1.9	7.5	8.7	21.4	48.6	56.3	78.8
Myanmar	0.6	1.0	1.0	1.0	0.0	0.3	1.2	95.7	...	0.0	0.0	0.2	...	0.1	0.3	25.1
Philippines	3.9	3.9	3.6	3.7	8.3	40.3	88.7	109.4	...	0.1	...	5.5	2.0	5.4	25.0	55.5
Singapore	49.7	41.1	39.3	35.5	70.2	97.6	145.5	150.5	1.8	14.6	26.4	26.0	36.0	61.0	71.0	81.0
Thailand	8.9	10.8	10.2	6.8	4.9	46.6	106.7	173.8	...	0.8	4.8	10.5	3.7	15.0	22.4	47.5
Viet Nam	3.2	...	16.2	5.9	1.0	...	...	...	...	0.2	4.1	9.6	0.3	12.7	30.7	46.5
The Pacific																
Cook Islands	31.3	33.7	39.0	...	3.0	20.3	42.1	...	...	0.3	9.0	...	15.7	26.2	35.7	54.0
Fiji	10.7	13.7	15.1	8.3	6.8	24.9	81.2	116.2	...	0.9	2.7	1.4	1.5	8.5	20.0	46.5
Kiribati	4.0	4.5	8.2	0.6	0.4	0.7	10.3	45.5	...	0.3	0.8	0.1	1.8	4.0	9.1	13.7
Marshall Islands	7.7	...	...	...	0.9	1.3	...	...	...	...	...	1.9	1.5	3.9	7.0	29.8
Micronesia, Federated States of	9.0	11.7	8.2	6.6	–	13.3	26.6	22.3	...	0.0	1.0	3.0	3.7	11.9	20.0	33.4
Nauru	17.9	17.8	–	...	12.0	...	61.8	87.2	...	...	9.5	...	...	...	...	...
Palau	...	...	...	...	...	...	...	...	...	...	...	...	...	...	...	...
Papua New Guinea	1.2	1.0	1.7	1.9	0.2	1.2	26.9	46.8	...	...	0.1	0.2	0.8	1.7	1.3	9.6
Samoa	4.9	10.8	4.3	5.0	1.4	13.3	48.3	77.4	...	0.0	0.1	1.1	0.6	3.4	7.0	29.4
Solomon Islands	1.9	1.6	1.6	1.2	0.3	1.3	21.9	69.5	...	0.1	0.5	0.3	0.5	0.8	5.0	11.0
Timor-Leste	...	0.2	0.3	0.2	...	3.2	42.6	117.6	...	0.0	0.0	0.1	...	0.1	3.0	25.2
Tonga	9.9	13.6	29.8	10.3	0.2	29.6	52.1	74.7	...	0.6	1.1	2.8	2.4	4.9	16.0	40.0
Tuvalu	7.0	8.9	11.4	18.0	–	13.0	15.2	68.5	...	1.5	2.3	9.0	5.2	...	25.0	46.0
Vanuatu	3.6	3.3	3.0	1.7	0.2	6.1	71.9	80.8	...	0.0	0.2	1.7	2.1	5.1	8.0	24.0
Developed ADB Member Economies																
Australia	52.7	50.0	48.0	33.9	44.9	91.0	101.7	110.1	...	10.0	24.9	30.6	46.8	63.0	76.0	88.2
Japan	48.6	45.2	51.0	50.2	52.4	75.2	95.9	130.6	0.7	18.2	26.5	31.2	30.0	66.9	78.2	93.2
New Zealand	47.4	41.8	43.0	37.8	40.0	85.4	107.8	124.4	0.1	7.8	25.0	32.8	47.4	62.7	80.5	88.5

... = data not available, 0.0 = magnitude is less than half of unit employed, – = magnitude equals zero, ADB = Asian Development Bank.

a   The reference population differs across countries. For example, some countries refer to a population of people aged 6 years and older, some refer to 7 years and older, and others refer to ages from 16 to 74 years. Details are provided in the documentation of the International Telecommunication Union.

Source: International Telecommunication Union. World Telecommunication/ICT Indicators Database. http://www.itu.int/en/ITU-D/Statistics/Pages/stat/default.aspx (accessed 19 July 2018).

VI.   Energy and Electricity

Snapshot

- In 2015, Asia and the Pacific led the world by a wide margin in energy use, comprising 42.2% of the global total, compared to 29.4% in 2000.

- From 2000 to 2015, energy efficiency gains measured as the GDP per unit of energy used, were realized in 35 of 44 regional ADB member economies, while 9 economies experienced a decline.

- Energy production in Asia and the Pacific comprised 34.4% of the global total in 2015, up from 23.9% in 2000.

- As a share of domestic energy use, Timor-Leste (1,737.5%), Brunei Darussalam (490.4%), and Azerbaijan (310.0%) led all economies in energy exports in 2015.

In 2015, Asia and the Pacific accounted for 42.2% of the global energy use, compared to 29.4% in 2000 (Table 2.6.3). The Peoples' Republic of China (PRC) accounted for more than half the energy use in Asia and the Pacific in 2015, up from 36.1% in 2000, and is the region's leading energy consumer. India, at 15.7%, accounted for the next largest share of energy use in Asia and the Pacific in 2015, up from 13.7% in 2000. Japan was next at 7.7% in 2015, down from 18.4% in 2000.

From 2000 to 2015, energy efficiency gains were realized in 35 of 44 regional ADB member economies. The average level of energy efficiency—measured as the amount of GDP per unit use of energy—in Asia and the Pacific rose from $151.6 million per petajoule in 2000 to $187.2 million per petajoule in 2015, compared with global averages of $158.0 million and $197.0 million, respectively (Figure 2.6.1). South America led all regions in terms of energy efficiency in 2015, with an average of $263.9 million per petajoule use of energy, up from $228.7 million in 2000. Africa trailed all regions in energy efficiency in both 2000 and 2015 at $132.3 million per petajoule and $174.2 million per petajoule, respectively.

Figure 2.6.1: Gross Domestic Product per Unit of Energy Use
(constant 2011 $ million PPP per PJ)

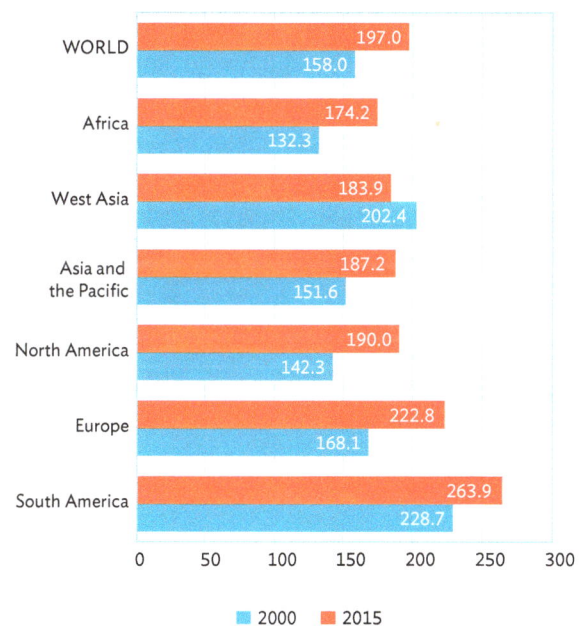

Region	2015	2000
WORLD	197.0	158.0
Africa	174.2	132.3
West Asia	183.9	202.4
Asia and the Pacific	187.2	151.6
North America	190.0	142.3
Europe	222.8	168.1
South America	263.9	228.7

$ = United States dollars, PPP = purchasing power parity, PJ = petajoule.
Sources: Table 2.6.3, Key Indicators for Asia and the Pacific 2018; and United Nations Statistics Division.

Among the 44 economies of Asia and the Pacific for which data were available, 35 increased their energy efficiency from 2000 to 2015, while 9 experienced a decline (Table 2.6.3). In the Pacific, 5 out of 11 ecomonies recorded lower output per unit use of energy in 2015 than in 2000. Most Pacific economies are highly dependent on imported petroleum for their energy requirements, making them vulnerable to price fluctuations in the international oil market (ADB 2011). In contrast with the economies in the Pacific, an overwhelming number of economies in Asia achieved energy efficiency gains during the review period: 9 of 10 in Central and West Asia, 3 of 4 (for which data were available) in East Asia, 5 of 6 in South Asia, and 9 of 10 in Southeast Asia. All three developed ADB member economies also achieved energy efficiency gains.

The region's energy production comprised 34.4% of the global total in 2015, up from 23.9% in 2000. In 2015, Asia and the Pacific accounted for 34.4% of global energy production, up slightly from 33.9% in 2010, but a significant increase from 23.9% in 2000 (Figure 2.6.2, Table 2.6.4). The region's growing share of global energy production during the review period was due almost entirely to expanded production in the PRC, whose share of global energy production increased from 10.0% in 2000 to 17.6% in 2015.

As the largest energy producer in Asia and the Pacific, with a 51.2% share of regional production, the PRC remains dependent on combustible fuels as its main source of electricity generation, accounting for 73.7% in 2015 (the latest year for which data were available), though this is down from 82.4% in 2000 (Table 2.6.1).

The next largest energy producers in Asia and the Pacific, and their respective regional production shares in 2015, were India (12.0%), Indonesia (9.1%), and Australia (8.1%). Combustible fuels also comprised a majority share of electricity production in 2015 (the latest year for which data were available) in all three of these economies: India (85.5%), Indonesia (91.5%), and Australia (87.8%).

As a share of domestic energy use, Timor-Leste (1,737.5%), Brunei Darussalam (490.4%), and Azerbaijan (310.0%) led all economies in energy exports in 2015. The oil- and gas-rich economies of Timor-Leste, Brunei Darussalam, and Azerbaijan led the region in terms of energy exports as a share of domestic energy use in 2015 (Figure 2.6.3). Conversely, a number of Pacific island economies (the

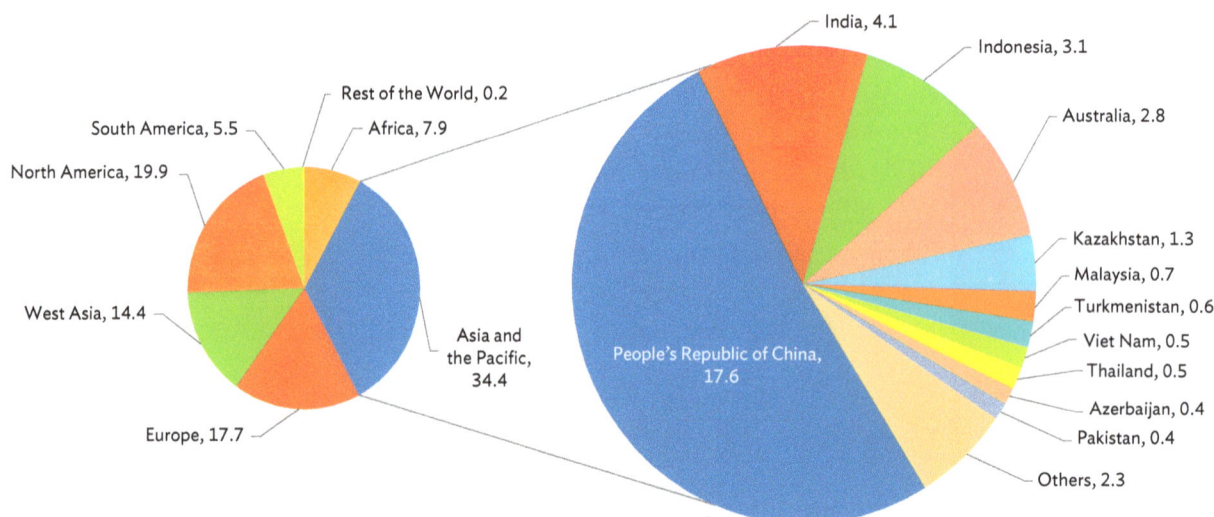

Figure 2.6.2: Energy Production by Global Region and by Economy in Asia and the Pacific, 2015 (petajoules, %)

Figure 2.6.3: Net Energy Imports as Share of Energy Use, 2000 and 2015
(%)

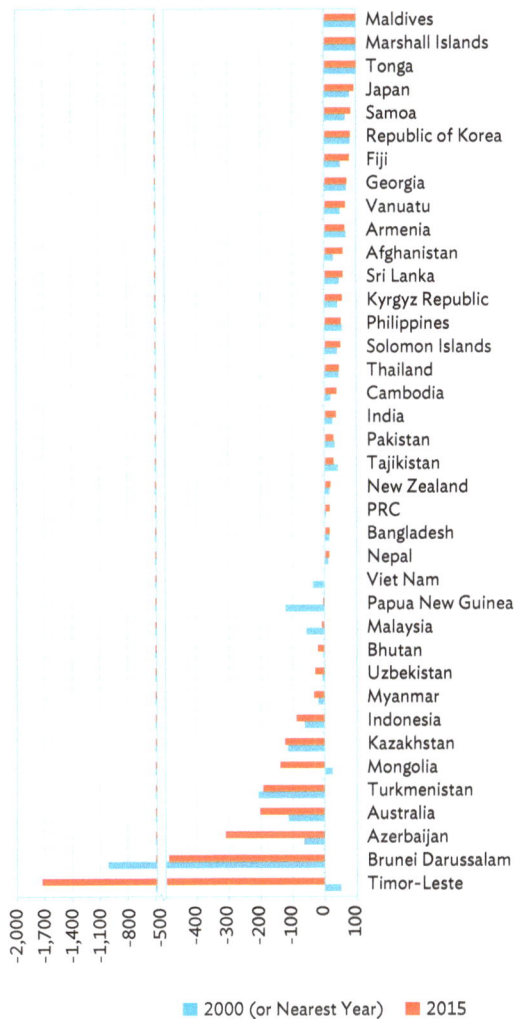

■ 2000 (or Nearest Year)   ■ 2015

PRC = People's Republic of China.
For Timor-Leste, data for earlier year is 2002 instead of 2000.
Source: Table 2.6.4, Key Indicators for Asia and the Pacific 2018.

Cook Islands, the Federated States of Micronesia, Kiribati, the Marshall Islands, Nauru, and Tonga) and Maldives were almost entirely dependent upon energy imports.

Data Issues and Comparability

Energy data are compiled by the United Nations Statistics Division (UNSD) using standard procedures that follow the definitions of the United Nations International Recommendations for Energy Statistics.[5] The UNSD Annual Questionnaire on Energy Statistics to the UN member economies is the primary source of information. Additional sources of information for the UNSD energy database include national, regional, and international statistical publications. These include, but are not limited to, publications from the International Energy Agency, the Statistical Office of the European Communities (Eurostat), the International Atomic Energy Agency, the Organization of the Petroleum Exporting Countries, and the Organización Latinoamericana de Energía. The UNSD prepares estimates where official data are incomplete or inconsistent. For the indicator on GDP per unit use of energy, the energy statistics adopt the territory principle, while national accounts are being compiled on the residency principle, which could be a potential source of inconsistency, although in practice differences are not huge (UN 2016).

Data for the household electrification indicator are lacking. Data are posted over a varied range of years (i.e., different starting and ending years) depending on data availability. These data may therefore not be comparable, limiting possibilities for analysis.

[5]   The full definitions can be found at https://unstats.un.org/UNSD/energy/ires/default.htm.

Table 2.6.1: Electricity Production and Sources

ADB Regional Member	Total Electricity Production (kWh billion)		Sources of Electricity (% of total)							
			Combustible fuels[a]		Hydropower		Solar		Others[b]	
	2000	2015	2000	2015	2000	2015	2000	2015	2000	2015
Developing ADB Member Economies										
Central and West Asia										
Afghanistan	0.7	1.1 (2016)	25.0	13.9 (2016)	75.0	86.1 (2016)	–	– (2016)	–	– (2016)
Armenia	6.0	7.3 (2016)	45.2	35.3 (2016)	21.2	32.1 (2016)	–	– (2016)	33.7	32.6 (2016)
Azerbaijan	18.7	24.7	91.8	93.3	8.2	6.6	–	0.0	–	0.0
Georgia	7.4	10.8	21.1	22.0	78.9	78.0	–	–	–	–
Kazakhstan	51.6	106.4	85.4	91.2	14.6	8.7	–	0.0	–	0.1
Kyrgyz Republic	16.0	13.0	14.4	14.8	85.6	85.2	–	–	–	–
Pakistan	65.8	115.1	70.1	65.2	29.3	29.5	–	–	0.6	5.3
Tajikistan	14.2	17.2	2.3	1.5	97.7	98.5	–	–	–	–
Turkmenistan	9.8	22.5	100.0	100.0	–	–	–	–	–	–
Uzbekistan	46.9	57.3	87.5	79.3	12.5	20.7	–	–	–	–
East Asia										
China, People's Republic of	1,355.6	5,814.6	82.4	73.7	16.4	19.4	–	0.7	1.2	6.2
Hong Kong, China	31.3	37.9	100.0	100.0	–	–	–	–	–	–
Korea, Republic of	290.1	552.9	60.5	67.8	1.9	1.0	0.0	0.7	37.6	30.4
Mongolia	2.9	5.7 (2016)	100.0	100.0 (2016)	–	– (2016)	–	– (2016)	–	– (2016)
Taipei,China	184.8	270.3 (2017)	...	...	...	...	...	...	...	...
South Asia										
Bangladesh	15.8	59.0	94.0	98.8	6.0	1.0	–	0.3	–	0.0
Bhutan	1.8	7.7	0.0	0.0	100.0	100.0	–	–	–	–
India	560.8	1,354.4	83.4	85.5	13.3	9.0	–	0.5	3.3	5.0
Maldives	0.1	0.4	100.0	98.7	–	–	–	1.3	–	–
Nepal	1.7	3.5	1.6	0.0	98.4	99.8	–	0.0	–	0.2
Sri Lanka	7.0	13.2	54.0	51.8	46.0	45.1	0.0	0.4	0.0	2.6
Southeast Asia										
Brunei Darussalam	2.8	4.2	100.0	100.0	–	–	–	0.0	–	–
Cambodia	0.3	4.4	85.9	54.4	14.1	45.5	–	0.1	–	–
Indonesia	99.5	263.1	83.5	91.5	13.8	6.7	–	0.0	2.7	1.8
Lao People's Democratic Republic	4.0	16.5	9.1	13.6	90.9	86.4	–	–	–	–
Malaysia	69.2	150.1	89.3	90.0	10.7	9.3	–	0.2	–	0.5
Myanmar	5.1	16.0	63.0	40.5	37.0	59.5	–	–	–	–
Philippines	45.3	90.8 (2016)	57.1	76.6 (2016)	17.2	8.9 (2016)	–	1.2 (2016)	25.6	13.3 (2016)
Singapore	31.7	50.3	100.0	100.0	–	–	–	–	–	–
Thailand	106.1	177.8	94.3	95.8	5.7	2.7	–	1.3	0.0	0.2
Viet Nam	26.6	174.9 (2016)	45.2	62.3 (2016)	54.8	37.6 (2016)	–	– (2016)	–	0.1 (2016)
The Pacific										
Cook Islands	0.0	0.0 (2016)	100.0	89.2 (2016)	–	– (2016)	–	10.8 (2016)	–	– (2016)
Fiji	0.7	0.9 (2016)	39.8	46.6 (2016)	60.2	53.0 (2016)	–	– (2016)	–	0.4 (2016)
Kiribati	0.0	0.0	100.0	92.7	–	–	–	7.3	–	–
Marshall Islands	0.1	0.1	100.0	99.8	–	–	–	0.2	–	–
Micronesia, Federated States of	0.1	0.1	99.8	98.4	–	0.1	0.2	1.5	–	–
Nauru	0.0	0.0	100.0	99.6	–	–	–	0.4	–	–
Palau	0.1	0.1	100.0	100.0	–	–	–	–	–	–
Papua New Guinea	2.4	4.2	52.9	65.5	39.2	24.4	–	–	7.8	10.1
Samoa	0.1	0.1	50.4	69.6	49.6	24.2	–	6.0	–	0.1
Solomon Islands	0.1	0.1 (2016)	100.0	97.9 (2016)	–	– (2016)	–	2.1 (2016)	–	– (2016)
Timor-Leste	0.1 (2002)	0.4	100.0 (2002)	100.0	– (2002)	–	– (2002)	–	– (2002)	–
Tonga	0.0	0.1 (2016)	100.0	92.1 (2016)	–	– (2016)	–	7.8 (2016)	–	0.0 (2016)
Tuvalu	0.0	0.0	100.0	71.8	–	–	–	28.2	–	–
Vanuatu	0.0	0.1 (2016)	100.0	79.5 (2016)	–	9.9 (2016)	–	2.8 (2016)	–	7.8 (2016)
Developed ADB Member Economies										
Australia	210.2	252.4	92.0	87.8	8.0	5.3	0.0	2.4	0.0	4.5
Japan	1,099.7	1,041.3	61.6	86.1	8.8	8.8	0.0	3.4	29.6	1.6
New Zealand	39.2	44.2	29.8	21.2	62.3	55.5	–	0.1	7.9	23.2

... = data not available, – = magnitude equals zero, 0.0 = magnitude is less than half of unit employed, ADB = Asian Development Bank, kWh = kilowatt-hour.

a Electricity from combustible fuels refers to the production of electricity from the combustion of fuels that are capable of igniting or burning, which would include coal, natural gas, oil, and other combustible fuels.

b Includes chemical heat, geothermal, nuclear, tide, other marine electricity, wind, wave, and other sources of energy.

Sources: United Nations. Energy Statistics Database. http://data.un.org/Explorer.aspx?d=EDATA (accessed 19 July 2018). For Taipei,China: Government of Taipei,China; Directorate-General of Budget, Accounting and Statistics; Official communication, 7 June 2018.

Table 2.6.2: **Electric Power Consumption and Electrification**

ADB Regional Member	Electric Power Consumption (kWh per capita)		Household Electrification Rate (% of households)	
	2000	2015	2000	2016
Developing ADB Member Economies				
Central and West Asia				
Afghanistan	31	126 (2016)	...	71.5 (2015)
Armenia	1,170	1,840	98.9	100.0
Azerbaijan	1,914	2,132	99.5 (2006)	...
Georgia	1,423	2,669	...	...
Kazakhstan	2,773	4,221	...	...
Kyrgyz Republic	1,891	1,790	...	99.8 (2012)
Pakistan	329	489	89.2 (2006)	93.6 (2012)
Tajikistan	2,146	1,464	...	99.1 (2012)
Turkmenistan	1,526	2,648	99.6	...
Uzbekistan	1,669	1,536	99.7 (2002)	...
East Asia				
China, People's Republic of	993	3,689	...	...
Hong Kong, China	5,446	6,023	...	...
Korea, Republic of	5,597	9,931	...	...
Mongolia	970	1,799 (2016)	67.3	...
Taipei,China	7,956	11,096 (2017)	...	...
South Asia				
Bangladesh	95	301	32.0	62.4 (2014)
Bhutan	696	2,613	41.1 (2003)	...
India	301	790	67.9 (2006)	88.2 (2015)
Maldives	325	835	...	99.8 (2009)
Nepal	55	136	24.6 (2001)	76.3 (2011)
Sri Lanka	290	560	...	...
Southeast Asia				
Brunei Darussalam	7,559	8,950	...	...
Cambodia	29	321	16.6	56.1 (2014)
Indonesia	374	827 (2016)	90.7 (2003)	96.0 (2012)
Lao People's Democratic Republic	120	636	46.3 (2002)	...
Malaysia	2,638	4,303	...	...
Myanmar	71	256	...	55.6
Philippines	469	718 (2016)	76.6 (2003)	87.5 (2013)
Singapore	7,233	8,584	...	...
Thailand	1,558	2,547	...	...
Viet Nam	283	1,690 (2016)	89.1 (2002)	...
The Pacific				
Cook Islands	1,389	1,703 (2016)	97.0 (2006)	99.5
Fiji	749	937 (2016)	...	84.0 (2009)
Kiribati	169	174	...	92.6 (2015)
Marshall Islands	1,476	1,415	...	90.0 (2011)
Micronesia, Federated States of	705	494	46.0	65.0 (2010)
Nauru	2,989	1,844	100.0 (2002)	100.0 (2011)
Palau	4,464	3,476	99.0 (2005)	98.3 (2015)
Papua New Guinea	409	463	...	19.5 (2010)
Samoa	515	600	98.0 (2006)	96.4
Solomon Islands	139	149 (2016)	14.0 (2005)	21.0 (2013)
Timor-Leste	52 (2002)	205	...	38.0 (2009)
Tonga	369	498 (2016)	89.0 (2006)	92.0 (2011)
Tuvalu	308	645	94.0 (2005)	97.3
Vanuatu	224	241 (2016)	...	57.8
Developed ADB Member Economies				
Australia	9,390	9,436	...	...
Japan	7,735	7,573	...	...
New Zealand	9,016	8,669	...	...

... = data not available, ADB = Asian Development Bank, kWh = kilowatt-hour.

Sources: For electric power consumption: United Nation's Energy Statistics Database. http://data.un.org/Explorer.aspx?d=EDATA (accessed 24 July 2018). For Taipei,China: Asian Development Bank estimates using economy source. For household electrification rate: International Development Association. Results Measurement System Online. http://data.worldbank.org/data-catalog/IDA-results-measurement (accessed 12 June 2018); United States Agency for International Development, Demographic and Health Surveys Program. The DHS Program STAT compiler. http://www.statcompiler.com/ (accessed 12 June 2018); and Secretariat of the Pacific Community, Pacific Regional Information System. National Minimum Development Indicators. http://www.spc.int/nmdi/MdiHome.aspx (accessed 12 June 2018).

Table 2.6.3:   **Use of Energy**

ADB Regional Member	Energy Use (PJ)				GDP per Unit Use of Energy (constant 2011 $ million PPP per PJ)			
	2000	2005	2010	2015	2000	2005	2010	2015
Developing ADB Member Economies								
Central and West Asia								
Afghanistan	32 a	36	137	145	730.6 a	791.2	339.4	420.9
Armenia	84	105	119	129	106.9	152.1	162.1	185.3
Azerbaijan	485	573	486	603	74.0	117.9	297.2	267.2
Georgia	93	135	140	197	155.1	152.1	188.8	170.3
Kazakhstan	1,560	2,352	3,363	3,258	94.9	103.1	97.5	126.7
Kyrgyz Republic	101	114	115	167	100.6	107.3	132.2	115.5
Pakistan	2,082	2,642	3,095	3,360	232.5	233.8	236.1	264.7
Tajikistan	91	99	94	114	80.6	118.2	171.2	198.0
Turkmenistan	625	805	951	1,160	38.5	38.4	53.2	71.9
Uzbekistan	2,130	2,050	1,809	1,783	29.0	39.2	66.9	100.1
East Asia								
China, People's Republic of	42,461	68,833	101,618	119,926	110.0	108.3	125.4	155.2
Hong Kong, China	570	579	550	583	397.8	481.5	614.4	670.3
Korea, Republic of	7,854	8,764	10,441	11,364	124.2	140.3	144.1	153.4
Mongolia	87	104	164	272	128.3	146.9	127.5	124.9
Taipei,China	...	...	...	...	...	...	...	...
South Asia								
Bangladesh	1,001	1,189	1,489	1,789	215.8	232.8	249.6	282.3
Bhutan	44	48	59	63	46.1	61.9	79.2	96.8
India	16,135	22,809	28,903	36,697	162.8	159.5	187.6	205.3
Maldives	7 b	9	13	19	379.8 b	328.5	336.6	301.8
Nepal	349	388	446	505	104.7	111.3	120.3	131.3
Sri Lanka	296	324	360	433	351.6	390.3	478.6	535.6
Southeast Asia								
Brunei Darussalam	73	76	136	114	374.6	398.6	230.2	273.2
Cambodia	142	144	223	295	117.8	181.5	161.9	173.1
Indonesia	4,970	7,087	8,330	9,452	247.1	218.3	245.5	283.2
Lao People's Democratic Republic	70	76	119	187	189.2	235.8	221.4	205.1
Malaysia	1,958	2,717	2,965	3,424	193.1	175.4	200.1	224.3
Myanmar	538	619	663	846	111.9	178.2	281.5	313.2
Philippines	1,551	1,469	1,631	2,050	212.4	280.7	321.6	341.1
Singapore	756	805	1,109	1,233	275.4	328.4	330.1	363.1
Thailand	3,075	4,067	4,945	5,412	188.1	185.4	183.3	193.3
Viet Nam	1,262	1,756	2,319	2,994	163.0	163.5	168.2	173.6
The Pacific								
Cook Islands	1	1	1	1	...	...	...	...
Fiji	22	24	22	38	246.1	254.3	287.4	199.0
Kiribati	1 a	1	1	1	173.2 a	182.4	177.7	221.1
Marshall Islands	2	2	2	2	75.5	84.2	91.2	97.1
Micronesia, Federated States of	2	2	2	2	167.5	172.8	170.8	170.8
Nauru	1	1 c	1	1	...	39.8 c	66.1	153.1
Palau	3	3	3	3	87.3	98.7	84.7	106.3
Papua New Guinea	99	126	141	159	154.5	135.1	160.9	192.6
Samoa	3	4	5	6	251.8	240.0	201.1	179.5
Solomon Islands	5	6	6	6	142.7	125.3	156.8	201.1
Timor-Leste	4 a	4	4	8	277.5	294.5	379.5	274.7
Tonga	1	2	2	2	451.3	249.9	259.5	276.0
Tuvalu	0	0	0	0	...	...	...	...
Vanuatu	2	2	3	3	261.2	273.2	232.2	247.6
Developed ADB Member Economies	**26,958**	**27,283**	**27,126**	**24,191**	**188.5**	**200.9**	**207.6**	**248.8**
Australia	4,540	4,762	5,431	5,261	148.8	166.4	167.9	198.2
Japan	21,671	21,774	20,862	17,984	198.3	209.2	219.5	267.8
New Zealand	747	747	833	946	146.0	177.4	168.5	168.3
DEVELOPING ADB MEMBER ECONOMIES d	**90,584**	**130,951**	**176,985**	**208,806**	**140.6**	**138.6**	**154.1**	**180.1**
ADB REGIONAL MEMBER ECONOMIES d	**117,542**	**158,234**	**204,111**	**232,997**	**151.6**	**149.4**	**161.2**	**187.2**
WORLD	**400,355**	**463,007**	**517,219**	**551,616**	**158.0**	**164.7**	**176.6**	**197.0**

... = data not available, 0 = magnitude is less than half of unit employed, $ = United States dollars, ADB = Asian Development Bank, GDP = gross domestic product, PPP = purchasing power parity, PJ = petajoule.

a   For 2000, data are for 2002.
b   For 2000, data are for 2001.
c   For 2005, data are for 2007.
d   Only for reporting economies with data corresponding to the year heading.

Sources: For energy use: United Nations Statistics Division. Official communication, 25 July 2018. For GDP per unit use of energy: Asian Development Bank estimates.

Table 2.6.4: Energy Production and Imports

ADB Regional Member	Energy Production (PJ)				Energy Imports, Net (% of energy use)			
	2000	2005	2010	2015	2000	2005	2010	2015
Developing ADB Member Economies								
Central and West Asia								
Afghanistan	18	23	41	60	28.0	36.1	70.1	58.6
Armenia	27	36	52	46	67.9	65.7	56.3	64.3
Azerbaijan	803	1,155	2,759	2,472	-65.6	-101.6	-467.7	-310.0
Georgia	28	53	58	58	69.9	60.7	58.6	70.6
Kazakhstan	3,367	5,131	6,770	7,338	-115.8	-118.2	-101.3	-125.2
Kyrgyz Republic	60	61	53	75	40.6	46.5	53.9	55.1
Pakistan	1,403	2,020	2,255	2,415	32.6	23.5	27.1	28.1
Tajikistan	53	66	65	82	41.8	33.3	30.9	28.1
Turkmenistan	1,928	2,584	1,982	3,407	-208.5	-221.0	-108.4	-193.7
Uzbekistan	2,307	2,446	2,309	2,344	-8.3	-19.3	-27.6	-31.5
East Asia								
China, People's Republic of	40,783	63,831	88,642	100,864	4.0	7.3	12.8	15.9
Hong Kong, China	...	...	...	...	...	...	...	...
Korea, Republic of	1,420	1,776	1,855	2,116	81.9	79.7	82.2	81.4
Mongolia	66	138	655	654	24.1	-32.7	-299.4	-140.4
Taipei,China	...	...	...	...	...	...	...	...
South Asia								
Bangladesh	857	1,027	1,304	1,509	14.4	13.6	12.4	15.7
Bhutan	46	53	73	77	-4.5	-10.4	-23.7	-22.2
India	12,090	18,315	22,598	23,538	25.1	19.7	21.8	35.9
Maldives	0	0	0	0	100.0	100.0	100.0	100.0
Nepal	310	349	384	430	11.2	10.1	13.9	14.9
Sri Lanka	156	163	184	181	47.3	49.7	48.9	58.2
Southeast Asia								
Brunei Darussalam	813	848	775	673	-1,013.7	-1,015.8	-469.9	-490.4
Cambodia	114	105	152	184	19.7	27.1	31.8	37.6
Indonesia	8,129	11,351	16,854	17,926	-63.6	-60.2	-102.3	-89.7
Lao People's Democratic Republic	70	73	117	185	0.0	3.9	1.7	1.1
Malaysia	3,082	3,770	3,450	3,748	-57.4	-38.8	-16.4	-9.5
Myanmar	648	927	969	1,141	-20.4	-49.8	-46.2	-34.9
Philippines	695	762	924	999	55.2	48.1	43.3	51.3
Singapore	...	...	25	28	...	...	97.7	97.7
Thailand	1,700	2,144	2,952	2,929	44.7	47.3	40.3	45.9
Viet Nam	1,733	2,612	2,747	3,043	-37.3	-48.7	-18.5	-1.6
The Pacific								
Cook Islands	...	...	...	0	...	...	...	100.0
Fiji	11	9	6	8	50.0	62.5	72.7	78.9
Kiribati	0	0	0	0	...	100.0	100.0	100.0
Marshall Islands	0	0	0	0	100.0	100.0	100.0	100.0
Micronesia, Federated States of	0	0	0	0	100.0	100.0	100.0	100.0
Nauru	...	...	0	0	...	...	100.0	100.0
Palau	...	...	...	...	...	...	...	...
Papua New Guinea	220	174	95	168	-122.2	-38.1	32.6	-5.7
Samoa	1	2	2	1	66.7	50.0	60.0	83.3
Solomon Islands	3	3	3	3	40.0	50.0	50.0	50.0
Timor-Leste	2 [a]	201	186	147	50.0 [a]	-4,925.0	-4,550.0	-1,737.5
Tonga	0	0	0	0	100.0	100.0	100.0	100.0
Tuvalu	...	...	...	0	...	...	...	...
Vanuatu	1	1	1	1	50.0	50.0	66.7	66.7
Developed ADB Member Economies	**14,743**	**16,198**	**18,508**	**17,982**				
Australia	9,731	11,451	13,620	15,938	-114.3	-140.5	-150.8	-202.9
Japan	4,384	4,175	4,118	1,269	79.8	80.8	80.3	92.9
New Zealand	628	572	770	775	15.9	23.4	7.6	18.1
DEVELOPING ADB MEMBER ECONOMIES [b]	**82,944**	**122,209**	**161,297**	**178,850**				
ALL ADB REGIONAL MEMBERS [b]	**97,685**	**138,407**	**179,805**	**196,832**				
WORLD	**408,238**	**476,469**	**530,321**	**572,353**				

... = data not available, 0 = magnitude is less than half of unit employed, ADB = Asian Development Bank, PJ = petajoule.

a For 2000, data are for 2002.
b Only for reporting economies with data corresponding to year heading.

Sources: For energy production: United Nations Statistics Division. Official communication, 25 July 2018. For net energy imports: Asian Development Bank estimates.

Table 2.6.5:   Retail Prices of Fuel Energy
($/L)

ADB Regional Member	Gasoline (Premium)				Diesel			
	2000	2005	2010	2017	2000	2005	2010	2017
Developing ADB Member Economies								
Central and West Asia								
Afghanistan	...	...	...	...	...	...	...	...
Armenia	0.51	0.73	1.01	0.78 (2016)	0.34	0.60	0.92	0.72 (2016)
Azerbaijan	...	...	...	...	...	...	...	...
Georgia	...	...	...	...	...	...	...	...
Kazakhstan	0.35	0.47	0.58	0.49	0.30	0.39	0.53	0.49
Kyrgyz Republic	...	...	...	...	...	...	...	...
Pakistan	0.48	0.82	0.80	0.73 (2016)	0.22	0.54	0.83	0.77 (2016)
Tajikistan	...	...	...	...	...	...	...	...
Turkmenistan	...	...	...	...	...	...	...	...
Uzbekistan	0.44	0.33 (2004)	...	...	...	...	...	...
East Asia								
China, People's Republic of	...	...	...	...	...	...	...	...
Hong Kong, China	1.32	1.60	1.75	1.80	0.80	1.00	1.25	1.53
Korea, Republic of	1.10	1.40	1.48	1.32	0.54	1.05	1.30	1.13
Mongolia	0.33	0.56	1.01	0.61	0.38	0.81 (2006)	0.96	0.98
Taipei,China	0.57	0.73	0.94	0.80	0.41	0.59	0.82	0.73
South Asia								
Bangladesh	...	...	...	...	...	...	...	...
Bhutan	...	...	...	...	...	...	...	...
India	0.58	0.86	1.05	...	0.32	0.64	0.83	...
Maldives	...	...	...	...	...	...	...	...
Nepal	0.58	0.87	1.22	...	0.33	0.58	0.95	...
Sri Lanka	0.65	0.80	1.02	0.77	0.32	0.50	0.65	0.62
Southeast Asia								
Brunei Darussalam	...	...	...	...	...	...	...	...
Cambodia	...	...	...	...	...	...	...	...
Indonesia	0.14	0.30	0.50	0.60 (2016)	0.07	0.27	0.50	...
Lao People's Democratic Republic	...	...	...	...	...	...	...	...
Malaysia	0.29	0.40	0.67	0.55 (2016)	0.18	0.29	0.57	0.45 (2016)
Myanmar	...	1.84 (2007)	1.41	0.76 (2015)	...	1.62 (2007)	1.37	0.80 (2015)
Philippines	0.37	0.57	0.96	0.91	0.28	0.51	0.76	0.63
Singapore	0.81	0.83 (2004)	...	...	0.33	0.56	0.89	0.97
Thailand	0.39	0.59	1.12 (2009)	...	0.32	0.50	0.90	0.76
Viet Nam	...	...	0.99 (2011)	0.85 (2015)	...	...	0.93 (2011)	0.68 (2015)
The Pacific								
Cook Islands	...	...	...	...	...	...	...	...
Fiji	...	...	...	...	...	...	...	...
Kiribati	...	...	...	...	...	...	...	...
Marshall Islands	...	...	...	...	...	...	...	...
Micronesia, Federated States of	...	...	...	...	...	...	...	...
Nauru	...	...	...	...	...	...	...	...
Palau	...	...	...	...	...	...	...	...
Papua New Guinea	...	...	...	...	...	...	...	...
Samoa	...	...	...	...	...	...	...	...
Solomon Islands	...	...	...	...	...	...	...	...
Timor-Leste	...	...	...	...	...	...	...	...
Tonga	...	...	...	...	...	...	...	...
Tuvalu	...	...	...	...	...	...	...	...
Vanuatu	0.78	1.23	1.50	...	...	...	...	...
Developed ADB Member Economies								
Australia	0.49	0.82	1.09	0.89	...	0.87	1.09	0.88
Japan	1.05	1.23	1.64	1.29	0.76	0.91	1.28	1.00
New Zealand	0.51	0.97	1.34	1.45	0.33	0.64	0.85	0.84

... = data not available, $ = United States dollars, ADB = Asian Development Bank, L = liter.

Source: Economy sources.

VII. Environment

Snapshot

- More than a third of the ADB member economies in Asia and the Pacific increased their total area of forested land in 2015, compared to the previous year. Since 2000, the total forested area in developing member economies has increased by 4.8%.

- As Asia and the Pacific's share of global GDP expands, so does its contribution to the global carbon dioxide (CO_2) emissions.

Key Trends

More than half of the ADB member economies in Asia and the Pacific increased their total area of forested land in 2015, compared to the previous year. From 2000 to 2015, the total forested area increased by 4.8% in developing ADB member economies and decreased by 2.4% in developed ADB member economies (Table 2.7.2). In 2015, 16 of 46 regional economies for which data were available expanded their forest land; and in 16 economies, the forest land remained unchanged. (Figure 2.7.1). Significant gains in reforestation were observed in Taipei,China (4.5%); the Philippines (3.1%); and Azerbaijan (2.4%). The biggest losses in the amount of forested land in 2015 occurred in Pakistan (2.8%), Myanmar (1.9%), and Timor-Leste (1.6%).

As Asia and the Pacific's share of global GDP expands, so does its contribution to the global CO_2 emissions. In 2014, Asia and the Pacific was responsible for nearly half (47.7%) of total global carbon dioxide emissions, while the region's top five emitters—the People's Republic of China (PRC), India, Japan, the Republic of Korea, and Indonesia contributed more than 85% of the region's total emissions (Figure 2.7.2).

Figure 2.7.1: Deforestation Rates, 2015
(%)

FSM = Federated States of Micronesia, Lao PDR = Lao People's Democratic Republic, PRC = People's Republic of China.
Note: Deforestation rates for Afghanistan, Brunei Darussalam, the Cook Islands, Georgia, Kazakhstan, Kiribati, Maldives, the Marshall Islands, Nepal, Palau, Samoa, Singapore, Tonga, Turkmenistan, Tuvalu, and Vanuatu are zero.
Source: Table 2.7.2, Key Indicators for Asia and the Pacific 2018.

Figure 2.7.2: Emissions of Carbon Dioxide Accounted for by Asia and the Pacific, 2014
(% of global carbon dioxide emissions)

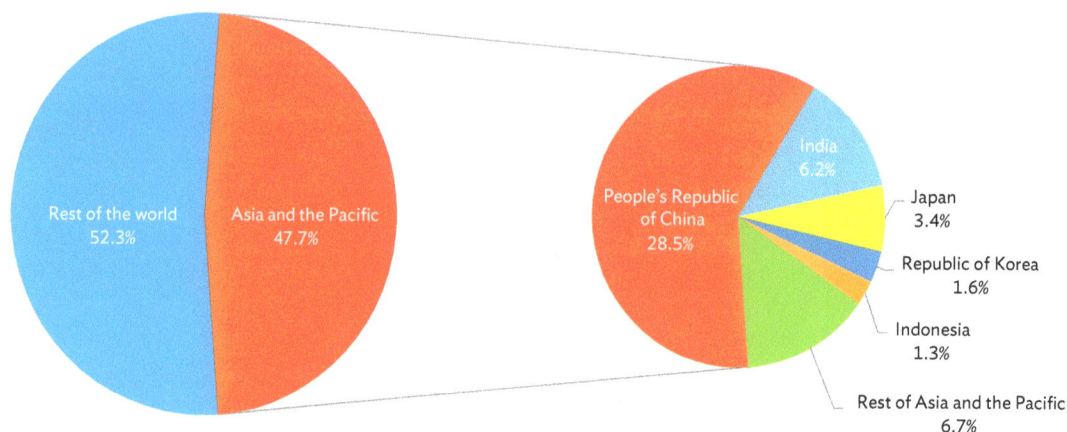

Rest of the world
52.3%

Asia and the Pacific
47.7%

People's Republic
of China
28.5%

India
6.2%

Japan
3.4%

Republic of Korea
1.6%

Indonesia
1.3%

Rest of Asia and the Pacific
6.7%

Sources: Table 2.7.2, Key Indicators for Asia and the Pacific 2018; and World Bank. World Development Indicators Online. http://data.worldbank.org/indicator (accessed 14 June 2018).

Data Issues and Comparability

Data on greenhouse gases (GHGs) have been compiled from the Emissions Database for Global Atmospheric Research, a joint project of the European Commission Joint Research Centre and the Netherlands Environmental Assessment Agency. This database applies a technology-based emissions factor approach consistently for all economies. It utilizes a consistent set of activity data for calculating various substances, GHGs, and air pollutants; and relies on the spatial allocation of emissions on a 0.1 degree by 0.1 degree grid.

There may be substantial uncertainty in economy-level data—especially for methane, nitrous oxide, and other GHGs—due to the limited accuracy of international activity data and the emission factors selected for calculating emissions on an economy level. However, since Intergovernmental Panel on Climate Change methodologies are consistently used, and data are based on international information sources, there is sound basis for comparability.[6]

The Food and Agricultural Organization of the UN monitors land use and forestry data using its own expert sources, country reports, satellite imagery, and official data reported on through questionnaires conducted by the organization.

---

6   More information on the methodologies can be found at http://edgar.jrc.ec.europa.eu/methodology.php.

Table 2.7.1: Agriculture Land Use
(% of total land area)

ADB Regional Member	Agricultural Land				Arable Land				Permanent Cropland			
	2000	2005	2010	2015	2000	2005	2010	2015	2000	2005	2010	2015
Developing ADB Member Economies												
Central and West Asia												
Afghanistan	57.8	58.1	58.1	58.1	11.8	12.0	11.9	11.9	0.1	0.2	0.2	0.2
Armenia	46.5	56.4	60.9	58.9	15.8	16.0	15.8	15.7	1.3	1.8	1.9	2.0
Azerbaijan	57.4	57.6	57.7	57.7	22.1	22.3	22.8	23.4	2.9	2.7	2.8	2.9
Georgia	43.2	36.3	35.7	36.7	11.4	6.8	6.0	6.4	3.9	1.6	1.8	2.3
Kazakhstan	79.8	78.6	80.4	80.4	11.2	10.6	10.6	10.9	0.1	0.0	0.0	0.0
Kyrgyz Republic	55.9	56.0	55.3	55.0	7.1	6.7	6.7	6.7	0.3	0.4	0.4	0.4
Pakistan	47.6	46.7	45.7	47.0	40.3	39.1	38.1	39.5	0.9	1.0	1.1	1.1
Tajikistan	32.7	33.4	34.0	34.2	5.6	5.4	5.4	5.3	0.7	0.8	0.9	1.0
Turkmenistan	75.5	74.2	72.4	72.0	4.1	4.3	4.1	4.1	0.1	0.1	0.1	0.1
Uzbekistan	64.2	62.9	62.7	62.9	10.5	10.3	10.2	10.3	0.8	0.8	0.8	0.9
East Asia												
China, People's Republic of	55.6	55.1	54.8	56.2	12.6	12.0	11.4	12.7	1.2	1.3	1.5	1.7
Hong Kong, China	6.7	6.7	5.2	4.9	4.8	4.8	3.3	3.0	1.0	1.0	1.0	1.0
Korea, Republic of	20.5	19.4	18.2	17.8	17.8	17.0	15.5	15.0	2.1	1.9	2.1	2.2
Mongolia	84.0	73.0	73.1	72.7	0.8	0.4	0.4	0.4	0.0	0.0	0.0	0.0
Taipei,China	24.0	23.5	23.0	22.5	17.5	17.0	16.9	16.7	6.5	6.5	6.1	5.8
South Asia												
Bangladesh	72.2	71.5	71.0	70.6	64.1	60.8	59.9	59.6	3.5	6.1	6.5	6.4
Bhutan	13.3	15.6	13.6	13.8	2.7	4.4	2.6	2.6	0.5	0.5	0.3	0.3
India	60.9	60.6	60.4	60.4	54.1	53.6	52.8	52.6	3.1	3.4	4.1	4.4
Maldives	30.0	30.0	26.3	26.3	10.0	10.0	13.0	13.0	16.7	16.7	10.0	10.0
Nepal	29.6	29.3	28.8	28.7	16.4	15.9	15.2	14.7	0.8	0.9	1.1	1.5
Sri Lanka	37.5	40.0	41.8	43.7	14.6	17.5	19.1	20.7	15.9	15.5	15.6	15.9
Southeast Asia												
Brunei Darussalam	1.9	2.1	2.5	2.7	0.4	0.4	0.8	0.9	0.8	0.9	1.1	1.1
Cambodia	27.0	30.3	30.9	30.9	21.0	21.0	21.5	21.5	0.8	0.9	0.9	0.9
Indonesia	26.0	28.6	30.7	31.5	11.3	12.7	13.0	13.0	8.6	9.9	11.6	12.4
Lao People's Democratic Republic	7.8	8.6	9.6	10.3	4.0	5.0	6.1	6.6	0.4	0.4	0.6	0.7
Malaysia	21.4	21.7	22.7	23.9	2.9	2.9	2.8	2.9	17.6	18.0	19.0	20.1
Myanmar	16.5	17.2	19.2	19.5	15.2	15.4	16.5	16.7	0.9	1.4	2.2	2.4
Philippines	37.7	38.1	40.6	41.7	16.9	16.8	17.8	18.7	15.8	16.3	17.8	17.9
Singapore	1.8	1.1	1.1	0.9	1.5	1.0	0.9	0.8	0.3	0.1	0.1	0.1
Thailand	38.8	38.4	41.2	43.3	30.6	29.8	30.8	32.9	6.6	7.1	8.8	8.8
Viet Nam	28.2	32.4	34.7	37.8	19.9	20.5	20.8	22.6	6.2	9.8	11.9	13.1
The Pacific												
Cook Islands	20.0	11.4	5.6	6.3	7.5	5.2	2.9	4.2	12.5	6.2	2.7	2.1
Fiji	23.4	23.4	23.3	23.3	9.3	9.3	9.0	9.0	4.5	4.5	4.7	4.7
Kiribati	42.0	42.0	42.0	42.0	2.5	2.5	2.5	2.5	39.5	39.5	39.5	39.5
Marshall Islands	66.7	72.2	72.2	63.9	5.6	11.1	11.1	11.1	44.4	44.4	44.4	36.1
Micronesia, Federated States of	32.1	32.1	31.4	31.4	3.6	3.6	2.9	2.9	24.3	24.3	24.3	24.3
Nauru	20.0	20.0	20.0	20.0	–	–	–	–	20.0	20.0	20.0	20.0
Palau	10.9	10.9	10.9	10.9	2.2	2.2	2.2	2.2	4.3	4.3	4.3	4.3
Papua New Guinea	2.2	2.3	2.6	2.6	0.5	0.5	0.7	0.7	1.4	1.3	1.5	1.5
Samoa	17.0	14.8	12.4	12.4	4.9	3.9	2.8	2.8	11.0	9.5	7.8	7.8
Solomon Islands	2.7	3.2	3.8	3.9	0.5	0.6	0.7	0.7	2.0	2.3	2.9	2.9
Timor-Leste	22.7	25.9	25.0	25.6	8.1	11.4	10.1	10.4	4.5	4.4	4.8	5.0
Tonga	41.7	41.7	44.4	45.8	20.8	20.8	23.6	25.0	15.3	15.3	15.3	15.3
Tuvalu	66.7	56.7	60.0	60.0	–	–	–	–	66.7	56.7	60.0	60.0
Vanuatu	14.4	15.0	15.3	15.3	1.6	1.6	1.6	1.6	9.3	9.9	10.3	10.3
Developed ADB Member Economies												
Australia	59.3	57.9	51.9	47.6	6.2	6.4	5.5	6.0	0.0	0.0	0.1	0.0
Japan	14.4	12.9	12.6	12.3	12.3	12.0	11.7	11.5	1.0	0.9	0.9	0.8
New Zealand	58.5	44.5	43.3	42.2	5.7	1.6	1.9	2.2	0.2	0.2	0.3	0.3

– = magnitude equals zero, 0.0 = magnitude is less than half of unit employed, ADB = Asian Development Bank.

Source: Food and Agriculture Organization of the United Nations. FAOSTAT Database. http://www.fao.org/faostat/en/#data/RL (accessed 4 June 2018).

Pollution

Table 2.7.2:   Deforestation and Pollution

ADB Regional Member	Deforestation Rate[a] (% change)		Carbon Dioxide Emissions[b] (t '000)		Nitrous Oxide Emissions (t '000 CO$_2$ equivalent)	
	2000	2015	2000	2014	2000	2012
Developing ADB Member Economies						
Central and West Asia						
Afghanistan	–	–	774	9,809	3,317	3,424
Armenia	0.06	-0.06	3,465	5,530	462	1,023
Azerbaijan	-0.23	-2.36	29,508	37,488	2,030	2,673
Georgia	-0.03	–	4,536	8,988	2,437	2,352
Kazakhstan	0.17	–	118,099	248,315	14,865	17,822
Kyrgyz Republic	-0.26	1.24	4,635	9,608	1,452	1,567
Pakistan	1.91	2.84	106,449	166,298	26,350	30,651
Tajikistan	-0.05	-0.10	2,237	5,189	1,110	1,848
Turkmenistan	–	–	37,539	68,423	3,046	4,924
Uzbekistan	-0.52	0.34	121,829	105,214	9,610	13,192
East Asia						
China, People's Republic of	-1.13	-0.75	3,405,180	10,291,927	414,138	587,166
Hong Kong, China	...	...	40,440	46,223	513	476
Korea, Republic of	0.13	0.12	447,561	587,156	18,576	14,979
Mongolia	0.69	0.77	7,506	20,840	5,058	3,548
Taipei,China	–	-4.54	229,840 (2001)	268,515	3,930 (2001)	4,503 (2014)
South Asia						
Bangladesh	0.18	0.18	27,869	73,190	20,770	26,683
Bhutan	-0.38	-0.36	396	1,001	281	555
India	-0.22	-0.25	1,031,853	2,238,377	207,700	239,755
Maldives	–	–	451	1,335	12	27
Nepal	2.30	–	3,069	8,031	4,232	4,598
Sri Lanka	0.42	0.32	10,238	18,394	2,044	2,174
Southeast Asia						
Brunei Darussalam	0.40	–	4,712	9,109	395	342
Cambodia	1.20	1.33	1,977	6,685	3,295	16,685
Indonesia	1.89	0.75	263,419	464,176	94,933	93,139
Lao People's Democratic Republic	0.67	-1.02	939	1,955	3,265	8,987
Malaysia	0.36	-0.06	125,734	242,821	13,822	15,310
Myanmar	1.23	1.85	10,088	21,632	31,300	26,783
Philippines	-0.68	-3.08	73,307	105,654	12,365	12,762
Singapore	–	–	49,006	56,373	6,635	1,909
Thailand	-1.80	-0.18	181,271	316,213	18,677	30,833
Viet Nam	-2.06	-0.88	53,645	166,911	19,746	34,494
The Pacific						
Cook Islands	-0.47	–	...	...	...	...
Fiji	-0.28	-0.48	843	1,170	343	344
Kiribati	–	–	29	62	3	4
Marshall Islands	–	–	77	103	0	0
Micronesia, Federated States of	-0.05	-0.05	125	150	11	11
Nauru	...	...	84	48	0	0
Palau	-0.38	–	249	260	0	0
Papua New Guinea	0.01	0.01	2,666	6,318	1,613	1,234
Samoa	-2.46	–	143	198	37	40
Solomon Islands	0.25	0.26	150	202	2,425	2,656
Timor-Leste	1.29	1.61	...	469	164	226
Tonga	–	–	95	121	22	22
Tuvalu	–	–	7	11	1	1
Vanuatu	–	–	84	154	118	109
Developed ADB Member Economies						
Australia	-0.02	-0.25	329,443	361,262	75,581	54,247
Japan	0.03	0.01	1,220,528	1,214,048	30,411	24,911
New Zealand	-0.48	-0.00	32,981	34,664	11,549	11,880

continued on next page

Table 2.7.2: Deforestation and Pollution (*continued*)

ADB Regional Member	Methane Emissions (t '000 CO$_2$ equivalent)		Other Greenhouse Gases[c] (t '000 CO$_2$ equivalent)	
	2000	**2012**	**2000**	**2012**
Developing ADB Member Economies				
Central and West Asia				
Afghanistan	9,384	13,763	126	349
Armenia	2,565	3,426	112	710
Azerbaijan	9,955	19,955	464	1,142
Georgia	4,137	5,019	3	227
Kazakhstan	38,779	71,350	14,065	30,363
Kyrgyz Republic	3,486	4,291	93	68
Pakistan	117,125	158,337	757	1,159
Tajikistan	3,304	5,408	798	367
Turkmenistan	21,241	22,009	124	595
Uzbekistan	37,233	47,333	298	989
East Asia				
China, People's Republic of	1,043,400	1,752,290	104,677	251,254
Hong Kong, China	2,695	3,147	155	150
Korea, Republic of	30,916	32,625	14,934	8,968
Mongolia	9,218	6,257	26,233	2,216
Taipei,China	12,646 (2001)	5,636 (2014)	6,304 (2001)	3,663 (2014)
South Asia				
Bangladesh	89,247	105,142	686	1,329
Bhutan	1,032	1,770	644	488
India	561,733	636,396	56,626	153,658
Maldives	34	52	0	–0
Nepal	21,206	23,982	2,443	7,995
Sri Lanka	9,606	11,864	441	91
Southeast Asia				
Brunei Darussalam	3,882	4,539	101	427
Cambodia	14,985	35,915	23,021	73,300
Indonesia	170,032	223,316	63,048	2,556
Lao People's Democratic Republic	7,219	15,011	13,588	136,841
Malaysia	29,309	34,271	5,144	3,866
Myanmar	66,942	80,637	78,176	406,274
Philippines	49,911	57,170	12,487	3,891
Singapore	1,684	2,386	1,410	3,299
Thailand	83,564	106,499	8,756	45,556
Viet Nam	75,430	113,564	5,782	25,707
The Pacific				
Cook Islands	...	...	...	...
Fiji	705	715	9	52
Kiribati	13	16	–	–0
Marshall Islands	6	8	...	...
Micronesia, Federated States of	28	30	...	...
Nauru	3	3	–0	–0
Palau	1	1	...	...
Papua New Guinea	2,001	2,143	1,949	2,188
Samoa	116	133	–0	0
Solomon Islands	1,394	1,449	0	0
Timor-Leste	450	732	–	–0
Tonga	58	61	–0	0
Tuvalu	3	3	–0	0
Vanuatu	267	254	0	–0
Developed ADB Member Economies				
Australia	128,133	125,588	520,911	174,653
Japan	47,496	38,957	51,527	71,746
New Zealand	26,584	28,658	1,506	1,764

... = data not available, – = magnitude equals zero, –0 or 0 = magnitude is less than half of unit employed, ADB = Asian Development Bank, CO$_2$ = carbon dioxide, t = metric ton.

a   Rate refers to percentage change over previous year. A negative value indicates that the deforestation rate is decreasing (i.e., reforestation).

b   Data from the World Bank are expressed in kilotons (kt), while data provided in the table are expressed in thousands of metric tons (t), using a conversion factor of 1 kt = 1000 t.

c   Other greenhouse gas emissions refer to hydrofluorocarbons, perfluorocarbons, and sulphur hexafluoride.

Sources: Food and Agriculture Organization. FAOSTAT Database. http://www.fao.org/faostat/en/#data/RL (accessed 6 June 2018); and World Bank. World Development Indicators Online. http://data.worldbank.org/indicator (accessed 7 June 2018). For Taipei,China: Government of Taipei,China, Directorate-General of Budget, Accounting and Statistics; and Statistical Yearbook 2016. http://eng.dgbas.gov.tw/lp.asp?CtNode=2351&CtUnit=1072&BaseDSD=36&mp=2 (accessed 7 June 2018).

Freshwater

Table 2.7.3:   Freshwater Resources

ADB Regional Member	Internal Renewable Freshwater Resources				Annual Freshwater Withdrawals	Water Productivity[a]
	(m³ billion per year)		(m³ per inhabitant per year)		(m³ billion)	(constant 2010 $ per m³)
	2002	2014	2002	2014		
Developing ADB Member Economies						
Central and West Asia	**370**	**370**	**1,554**	**1,210**		
Afghanistan	47	47	2,194	1,450	20 (2000)	...
Armenia	7	7	2,251	2,273	3 (2015)	3.5 (2015)
Azerbaijan	8	8	980	832	12 (2012)	4.5 (2012)
Georgia	58	58	12,555	14,532	2 (2008)	6.2 (2008)
Kazakhstan	64	64	4,287	3,651	20 (2010)	7.4 (2010)
Kyrgyz Republic	49	49	9,732	8,237	8 (2006)	0.5 (2006)
Pakistan	55	55	381	291	184 (2008)	0.9 (2008)
Tajikistan	63	63	9,905	7,482	11 (2006)	0.4 (2006)
Turkmenistan	1	1	305	261	28 (2004)	0.4 (2004)
Uzbekistan	16	16	651	547	49 (2005)	0.5 (2005)
East Asia[b]	**2,913**	**2,913**	**2,137**	**1,994**		
China, People's Republic of	2,813	2,813	2,141	1,999	594 (2015)	15.0 (2015)
Hong Kong, China	...	...	...	...	...	...
Korea, Republic of	65	65	1,387	1,289	29 (2005)	30.8 (2005)
Mongolia	35	35	14,239	11,761	1 (2009)	12.3 (2009)
Taipei,China	...	...	...	...	...	...
South Asia	**1,883**	**1,880**	**1,482**	**1,235**		
Bangladesh	105	105	771	652	36 (2008)	2.9 (2008)
Bhutan	81	78	135,361	100,671	0 (2008)	3.9 (2008)
India	1,446	1,446	1,326	1,103	648 (2010)	2.6 (2010)
Maldives	0	0	103	82	...	...
Nepal	198	198	8,084	6,951	9 (2006)	1.4 (2006)
Sri Lanka	53	53	2,770	2,549	13 (2005)	3.2 (2005)
Southeast Asia	**4,985**	**4,985**	**9,223**	**7,884**		
Brunei Darussalam	9	9	24,752	20,085	...	...
Cambodia	121	121	9,510	7,742	2 (2006)	4.1 (2006)
Indonesia	2,019	2,019	9,288	7,839	113 (2000)	4.0 (2000)
Lao People's Democratic Republic	190	190	34,606	27,992	3 (2005)	1.4 (2005)
Malaysia	580	580	23,769	19,122	11 (2005)	18.3 (2005)
Myanmar	1,003	1,003	20,600	18,610	33 (2000)	0.5 (2000)
Philippines	479	479	5,892	4,757	82 (2009)	2.3 (2009)
Singapore	1	1	145	107	...	...
Thailand	225	225	3,500	3,303	57 (2007)	5.5 (2007)
Viet Nam	359	359	4,387	3,846	82 (2005)	1.0 (2005)
The Pacific[b]	**892**	**892**	**111,664**	**84,640**		
Cook Islands	...	...	...	...	...	...
Fiji	29	29	35,001	32,003	0 (2005)	35.7 (2005)
Kiribati	...	...	...	...	...	...
Marshall Islands	...	...	...	...	...	...
Micronesia, Federated States of	...	...	...	...	...	...
Nauru	...	...	...	...	...	...
Palau	...	...	...	...	...	...
Papua New Guinea	801	801	141,695	105,132	0 (2005)	27.3 (2005)
Samoa	...	...	...	...	...	...
Solomon Islands	45	45	102,782	76,594	...	...
Timor-Leste	8	8	9,181	6,932	1 (2004)	0.5 (2004)
Tonga	...	...	...	...	...	...
Tuvalu	...	...	...	...	...	...
Vanuatu	10	10	51,546	37,793	...	...
Developed ADB Member Economies	**1,249**	**1,249**	**8,342**	**8,054**		
Australia	492	492	25,213	20,527	17 (2015)	78.0 (2015)
Japan	430	430	3,406	3,397	81 (2009)	67.4 (2009)
New Zealand	327	327	82,534	72,201	5 (2010)	28.2 (2010)
DEVELOPING ADB MEMBER ECONOMIES[b]	**11,043**	**11,040**	**3,229**	**2,808**		
ALL ADB REGIONAL MEMBERS[b]	**12,292**	**12,289**	**3,443**	**3,007**		

... = data not available, 0 = magnitude is less than half of unit employed, $ = United States dollars, ADB = Asian Development Bank, m³ = cubic meter.

a   Gross domestic product in constant 2010 United States dollars per cubic meter of total freshwater withdrawal.
b   For reporting economies only.

Sources: Food and Agriculture Organization. AQUASTAT Database. http://www.fao.org/nr/water/aquastat/data/query/index.html (accessed 11 June 2018); and World Bank. World Development Indicators Online. http://data.worldbank.org/indicator (accessed 11 June 2018).

VIII. Government and Governance

Snapshot

- 28 of 36 economies in Asia and the Pacific with available data for 2017 incurred a fiscal deficit.

- From 2000 to 2017, government expenditure as a share of GDP rose in 27 of 48 ADB member economies in the region.

- Since 2005, starting a business has become much easier—as measured by the number of days required to do so—in most developing ADB member economies. Reforms that lowered regulatory costs and simplified compliance procedures had the most impact on reducing the time needed to start a business.

Key Trends

28 of 36 economies in Asia and the Pacific with available data for 2017 incurred a fiscal deficit. As a percentage of GDP in 2017, the largest fiscal deficits—the excess of current expenditures over government revenue and current grants received—were in Brunei Darussalam (9.9%), Mongolia (6.2%), Pakistan (5.8%), and Myanmar (5.7%) as shown in Figure 2.8.1. Eight economies ran a fiscal surplus in 2017, with the top three being the Federated States of Micronesia (7.0%); Hong Kong, China (5.2%); and Palau (4.5%).

In 2017, deficits were present in all economies in South Asia and Southeast Asia, six of seven economies in Central and West Asia, five of nine economies in the Pacific, and two of four economies in East Asia.

From 2000 to 2017, government expenditure as a share of GDP rose in 27 of 48 ADB member economies in the region. In 2017, the highest shares of government expenditure as a percentage of GDP were observed in Nauru (99.9%), the Marshall Islands (65.1%), Tonga (50.4%), and Solomon Islands (49.9%) as shown in Figure 2.8.2. In terms of absolute change, the largest increases in government expenditure, as a share of GDP for countries with

Figure 2.8.1: Fiscal Balance as a Percentage of Gross Domestic Product, 2017
(%)

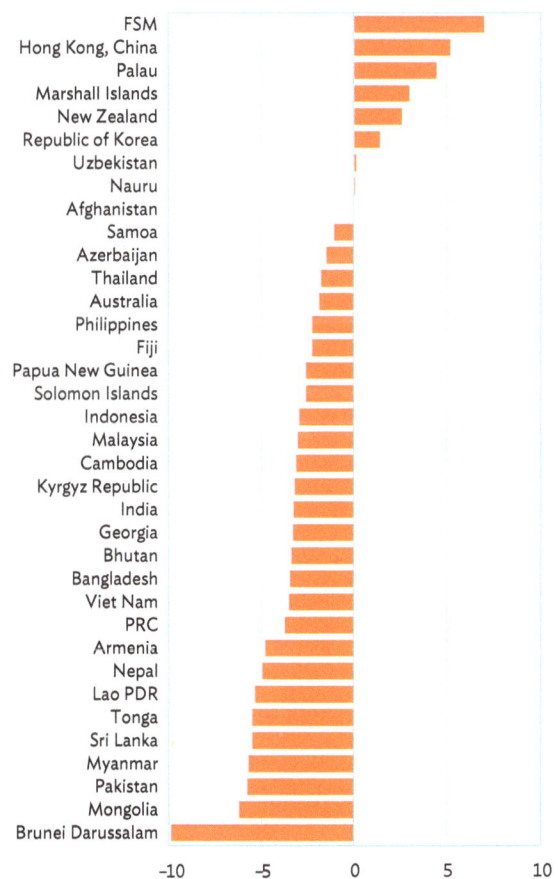

FSM = Federated States of Micronesia, Lao PDR = Lao People's Democractic Republic, PRC = People's Republic of China.
Source: Table 2.8.1, Key Indicators for Asia and the Pacific 2018.

available data from 2000 to 2017, were in Nauru (71.4 percentage points) and Tonga (28.2 percentage points) as illustrated by Table 2.8.4. The largest declines occurred in Palau (21.5 percentage points), and Papua New Guinea (13.9 percentage points); and Bhutan (10.9 percentage points).

Since 2005, starting a business has become much easier—as measured by the number of days required to do so—in most developing ADB member economies. Reforms that lowered regulatory costs and simplified compliance procedures had the most impact on reducing the time needed to start a business. From 2005 to 2017, the number of days required to start a business fell in 34 of 40 developing member economies for which data were available (Figure 2.8.3). During the review period, Timor-Leste led the way in terms of reducing the time required to start a business (from 167 days to 9 days), followed by Indonesia (from 164 days to 23 days), and Brunei Darussalam (from 122 days to 13 days). On the other hand, the number of days required to start a business increased in Cambodia (from 87 days to 99 days), Palau (from 24 days to 28 days), and Maldives (from 9 to 12 days), while it remained the same in Kiribati (31 days), the Marshall Islands (17 days), and the Federated States of Micronesia (16 days).

Online business registration, having a one-stop shop for business startup permits, and reduced minimum capital requirements are among the reforms that can expedite the business startup process. From 2016 to 2017, the most common types of business startup reforms were those that reduced the complexity and cost of regulatory processes and accessing credit (World Bank 2017a).

One of the largest declines in the time required to start a business occurred in Thailand, where the average number of days required fell from 28 days in 2016 to 5 days in 2017. This improvement was a result of the government abolishing the requirement for the country's labor department to obtain a company's seal and approve its work regulations (World Bank 2017b).

Figure 2.8.2: Total Government Expenditure as a Proportion of Gross Domestic Product, 2017
(%)

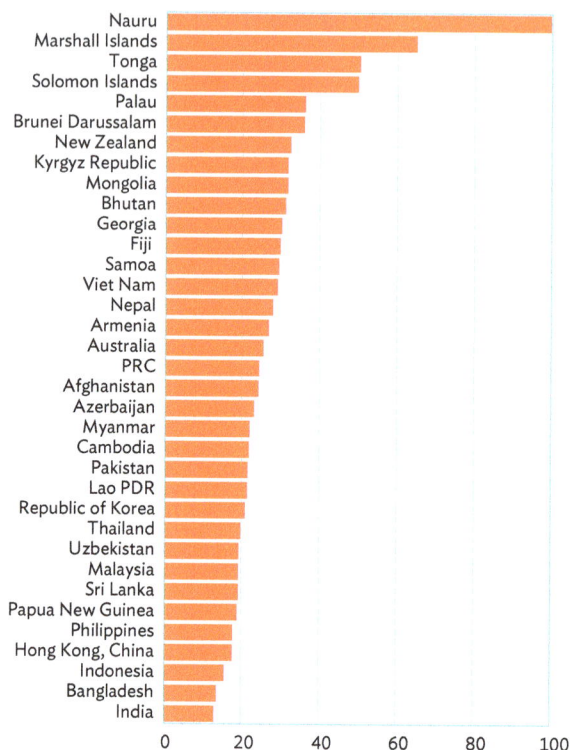

Lao PDR = Lao People's Democractic Republic, PRC = People's Republic of China.
Source: Table 2.8.4, Key Indicators for Asia and the Pacific 2018.

In 2017, Central and West Asia had the lowest (arithmetic) average number of days required to start a business (7.9 days), followed by East Asia (9.7 days), South Asia (16.5 days), the Pacific (21.3 days), and Southeast Asia (29.1 days) as shown in Table 2.8.6. For comparison, the (arithmetic) average among developed ADB member economies in 2017 was 5.1 days.

Data Issues and Comparability

Data on government expenditures and revenue are derived from economy sources and are therefore not standard throughout Asia and the Pacific. Data refer only to the central government, except for Bangladesh, Georgia, the Federated States of Micronesia, Kiribati, the Kyrgyz Republic, Mongolia, Pakistan,

Figure 2.8.3: Time Required to Start Business
(days)

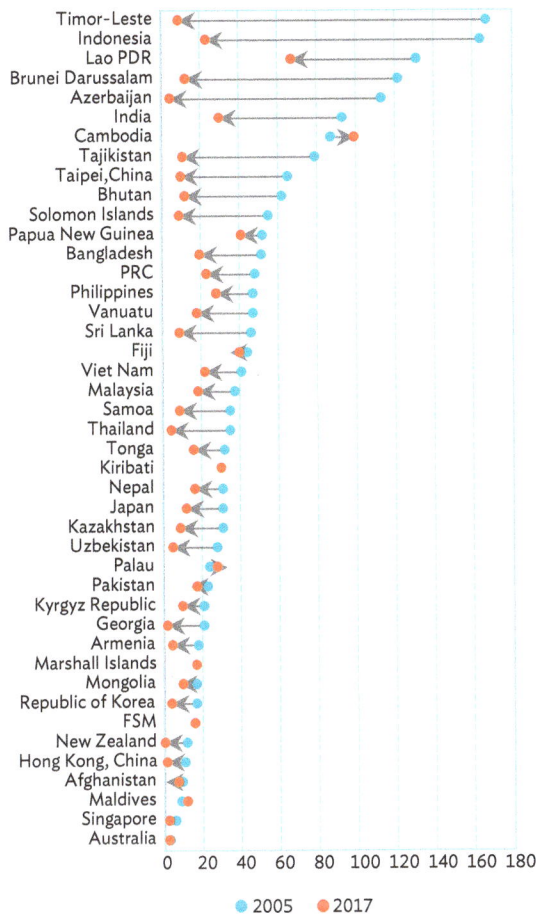

FSM = Federated States of Micronesia, Lao PDR = Lao People's Democratic Republic, PRC = People's Republic of China.
Source: Table 2.8.6, Key Indicators for Asia and the Pacific 2018.

Statistics on the time and cost for registering new businesses, and on perceived corruption, are taken from nonofficial sources. Common procedures are used in all economies and the researchers producing these data have refined their procedures over several surveys. However, because of the subjective nature of many of the data, they can only be used to give a broad idea of trends, levels, and rankings and small changes from one year to the next should be interpreted with caution.

and Tajikistan, where data refer to consolidated government or general government. For the People's Republic of China, data refer to consolidated central and local governments. For Australia, data refer to the Commonwealth Government.

Most economies generally follow the IMF's Government Finance Statistics guidelines, with some economies still using the 1986 version, while others have switched to the 2001 or 2014 guidelines. There is no single framework for an extended time series available in most economies that are using the 2014 guidelines. Furthermore, most economies record their transactions on a cash basis; a few, on an accrual basis.

Government Finance

Table 2.8.1:   **Fiscal Balance[a]**
(% of GDP)

ADB Regional Member	2000	2005	2010	2012	2013	2014	2015	2016	2017
Developing ADB Member Economies									
Central and West Asia									
Afghanistan[b]	-1.2 (2002)	-4.5	2.5	-0.5	2.3	-1.7	1.6	-0.1	-0.0
Armenia	-4.9	-1.9	-5.0	-1.5	-1.6	-1.9	-4.8	-5.5	-4.8
Azerbaijan	-1.0	-0.7	-0.9	-0.2	0.6	-0.5	-0.5	-0.4	-1.5
Georgia	-1.3	1.2	-5.6	-1.7	-2.1	-2.8	-2.6	-2.9	-3.3
Kazakhstan	-0.1	0.6	-2.4	-2.9	-1.9	-2.7	-2.2	-1.6	...
Kyrgyz Republic	-2.0	0.2	-4.9	-6.5	-0.7	-0.5	-1.4	-4.4	-3.2
Pakistan[c]	-4.9	-2.8	-6.0	-8.6	-8.1	-4.7	-5.2	-4.5	-5.8
Tajikistan	-0.6	0.2	-7.1	-3.4	-5.4	-3.8	-7.8	-10.4	...
Turkmenistan	-0.3	0.8	2.0	6.4	1.5	0.9	-0.7	...	...
Uzbekistan	-1.0	0.1	0.3	0.4	0.3	1.3	0.1	0.1	0.1
East Asia									
China, People's Republic of	-2.8	-1.2	-1.6	-1.6	-1.8	-1.8	-3.4	-3.8	-3.7
Hong Kong, China[d]	-0.6	1.0	4.2	3.2	1.0	3.6	0.6	4.5	5.2
Korea, Republic of	1.0	0.4	1.3	1.3	1.0	0.6	-0.0	1.0	1.4
Mongolia	-5.4	2.4	0.4	-6.4	-1.2	-3.8	-4.5	-15.3	-6.2
Taipei,China	-4.5	-0.3	-2.6	-2.8	-1.0	-0.8	0.2	-0.3	...
South Asia									
Bangladesh[c]	-4.5	-3.7	-2.8	-3.2	-3.8	-3.6	-3.9	-3.8	-3.4
Bhutan[c]	-3.9	-6.6	1.5	-1.1	-4.0	3.6	1.4	-1.1	-3.3
India[d]	-5.5	-4.0	-4.8	-4.9	-4.5	-4.1	-3.9	-3.5	-3.2
Maldives	-4.4	-7.0	-12.9	-6.7	-3.5	-2.4	-6.7	-10.4	...
Nepal[f]	-4.7	-2.4	-1.9	-2.2	0.5	0.6	-1.0	-0.5	-5.0
Sri Lanka	-9.3	-7.0	-7.0	-5.6	-5.4	-5.7	-7.6	-5.4	-5.5
Southeast Asia									
Brunei Darussalam[g]	10.9	21.1	15.6	15.7	10.1	-0.7	-14.5	-21.7	-9.9
Cambodia	-2.1	-0.7	-8.8	-6.8	-6.9	-3.8	-2.6	-2.7	-3.1
Indonesia[h]	-1.1	-0.5	-0.7	-1.8	-2.2	-2.1	-2.6	-2.5	-2.9
Lao People's Democratic Republic[i]	-4.6	-4.5	-2.2	-1.0	-5.2	-3.2	-3.8	-4.4	-5.4
Malaysia	-5.5	-3.4	-5.3	-4.3	-3.8	-3.4	-3.2	-3.1	-3.0
Myanmar[d,e]	0.7	-4.3 (2006)	-4.6	1.6	-1.4	-1.1	-4.3	-2.6	-5.7
Philippines	-3.7	-2.6	-3.5	-2.3	-1.4	-0.6	-0.9	-2.4	-2.2
Singapore[d]	9.7	6.4	7.6	8.6	8.1	7.2	4.3	5.2	...
Thailand[i,j]	-2.8	0.1	-2.9	-2.2	-0.6	-1.8	-1.2	-0.7	-1.7
Viet Nam[k]	-4.3	-1.0	-2.1	-3.4	-5.0	-4.4	-4.3	-4.2	-3.5
The Pacific									
Cook Islands[c]	-1.5	2.1	6.4	4.1	2.6	...	...	...	...
Fiji[l]	-3.1	-3.4	-2.2	-1.1	-0.5	-4.0	-3.2	-4.1	-2.2
Kiribati[m]	42.3	7.0	16.7 (2008)	...	...	...	...	...	...
Marshall Islands[i]	8.0	-21.9	3.4	-0.7	-0.2	3.2	2.8	4.0	3.0
Micronesia, Federated States of[i]	-3.5	-5.6	0.5	0.9	2.9	11.2	10.4	7.3	7.0
Nauru[c]	...	4.3	0.1	–	–	0.1	–	-0.1	0.1
Palau[i]	-13.1	1.6	-1.0	1.0	0.7	3.6	4.9	3.5	4.5
Papua New Guinea	-2.0	0.1	0.5	-3.1	-5.6	-5.3	-4.0	-4.6	-2.6
Samoa[c]	-0.7	2.0	-5.6	-7.2	-3.7	-5.1	-3.8	-0.4	-1.0
Solomon Islands	-0.6	-0.9	8.3	6.6	5.0	2.9	1.1	-4.6	-2.6
Timor-Leste	...	4.0	3.7	-31.6	-29.4	-54.8	-76.0	-115.6	...
Tonga[c]	-0.3	3.0	-2.7	-7.1	-0.8	1.9	-0.1	–	-5.5
Tuvalu[c]	-2.0	-7.8	-0.1	9.4	26.6	36.9	7.3	...	...
Vanuatu	-6.2	2.9	4.9	1.6	0.9	0.7	1.3	7.7	...
Developed ADB Member Economies									
Australia[c]	1.8	1.5	-3.5	-2.7	-1.4	-1.9	-2.3	-2.1	-1.8
Japan[d]	-6.1	-3.9	-7.5	-7.4	-6.8	-5.2	-4.5	-4.6	...
New Zealand[n]	1.8	5.8	-2.0	-1.9	-0.6	0.2	1.1	1.8	2.6

... = data not available, – = magnitude equals zero, -0.0 = magnitude is less than half of unit employed, ADB = Asian Development Bank, GDP = gross domestic product.

a   Data refer to fiscal balance (% of GDP) of central government, except for Bangladesh, Georgia, the Federated States of Micronesia, Kiribati, the Kyrgyz Republic, Mongolia, Pakistan, and Tajikistan, where data refer to fiscal balance of consolidated government or general government. For the People's Republic of China, data refer to fiscal balance of consolidated central and local governments. For Australia, data refer to the fiscal balance of the Commonwealth Government.

b   For 2012, government finance covers 9 months only (21 March to 20 December) due to the change of fiscal year (FY) effective in 2012 (FY1391). For 2013 onward, the fiscal year begins on 21 December and ends on 20 December.

c   Data are based on fiscal year ending 30 June.

d   Data are based on fiscal year beginning 1 April.

e   For 2012 onward, data were compiled based on International Monetary Fund's Government Finance Statistics Manual 2014 and are mapped to the current government finance structure followed in the Key Indicators publication. The data on 'disposal of nonfinancial assets' is treated as capital receipts, the 'acquisition of nonfinancial assets' as capital expenditure, and the 'net acquisition of nonfinancial assets' as capital account surplus/deficit.

f   Data are based on fiscal year ending 15 July.

g   For 2005 onward, data are based on fiscal year beginning 1 April. Data are derived as excess of revenue over expenditure (ordinary plus charged) less the sum of contribution to a development fund, contribution to a government trust fund, and capital and currency adjustments.

h   For 2000, data cover 9 months, from 1 April to 31 December.

i   Data are based on fiscal year ending 30 September.

j   For 2013 onward, data were compiled based on International Monetary Fund's Government Finance Statistics Manual 2014 and are mapped to the current government finance structure followed in the Key Indicators publication.

k   Tax revenue includes local government taxes.

l   For 2015 onward, data are based on fiscal year ending 31 July.

m   For 2000–2013, data are based on calendar year. For 2014 onward, data are based on fiscal year ending 30 June and are compiled following the International Monetary Fund's Government Finance Statistics Manual 2014.

n   For 2000–2008, data are based on fiscal year beginning 1 April. For 2009–2017, data are based on fiscal year ending 30 June. For 2009 onward, the fiscal balance refers to net operating balance which is also equal to the sum of net lending and acquisition of nonfinancial assets.

Source: Economy sources.

Table 2.8.2: Tax Revenue[a]
(% of GDP)

ADB Regional Member	2000	2005	2010	2012	2013	2014	2015	2016	2017
Developing ADB Member Economies									
Central and West Asia									
Afghanistan[b]	...	3.8	8.9	5.5	6.7	6.4	7.1	5.0	7.6
Armenia	14.8	14.3	20.2	22.0	22.0	22.0	21.2	21.3	20.8
Azerbaijan	12.2	14.0	12.4	12.7	13.2	14.2	16.2	14.9	13.3
Georgia	14.6	20.8	23.5	25.5	24.8	24.8	25.2	25.8	25.7
Kazakhstan	20.2	26.3	13.4	13.2	13.3	12.9	11.9	13.0	...
Kyrgyz Republic	11.7	16.2	17.9	20.6	20.5	20.6	19.7	19.7	19.8
Pakistan[c]	9.6	9.3	10.0	10.2	9.8	10.2	11.0	12.4	12.5
Tajikistan	13.1	16.5	18.0	19.6	20.8	22.7	21.9	20.6	...
Turkmenistan	23.0	20.9 (2004)	...	20.2	17.7	17.0	15.6	...	...
Uzbekistan	23.4 (2001)	20.6	20.0	19.6	19.6	19.6	19.1	18.1	17.3
East Asia									
China, People's Republic of	12.5	15.4	17.7	18.6	18.6	18.5	18.1	17.5	17.5
Hong Kong, China[d]	9.7	12.3	13.6	13.7	13.5	15.7	14.4	14.0	14.1
Korea, Republic of	17.0	13.9	14.0	14.7	14.1	13.8	14.0	14.8	15.3
Mongolia	21.2	22.8	27.6	25.2	26.5	23.2	22.1	20.7	23.2
Taipei,China	13.1	8.8	7.6	8.4	8.0	8.4	8.7	8.9	...
South Asia									
Bangladesh[c]	6.8	8.6	7.8	9.0	10.4	9.8	8.5	8.8	9.1
Bhutan[c]	10.0	9.4	13.3	15.1	14.6	13.5	13.9	13.4	13.6
India[d]	6.3	7.3	7.3	7.5	7.3	7.3	6.9	7.2	7.3
Maldives	13.8	11.6	8.8	15.5	17.5	19.1	19.9	20.5	...
Nepal[f]	8.7	9.2	13.4	13.9	15.3	15.9	16.7	18.7	20.3
Sri Lanka	14.2	13.7	11.3	10.4	10.5	10.1	12.4	12.3	12.6
Southeast Asia									
Brunei Darussalam[g]	23.4	33.1	24.0 (2009)	...	...	...	...	...	...
Cambodia	7.3	7.7	10.1	11.4	11.9	13.8	14.7	15.0	16.2
Indonesia[h]	8.3	12.5	10.5	11.4	11.3	10.9	10.8	10.4	10.8
Lao People's Democratic Republic[i]	10.6	9.7	13.5	13.4	13.5	13.6	13.5	12.7	12.0
Malaysia	13.2	14.8	13.3	15.6	15.3	14.8	14.3	13.8	13.1
Myanmar[d,e]	2.0	4.3 (2006)	3.2	4.5	5.5	5.9	6.1	6.5	6.1
Philippines	12.8	12.4	12.1	12.9	13.3	13.6	13.6	13.7	14.2
Singapore[d]	14.9	11.6	13.0	13.8	13.4	13.7	13.3	13.7	...
Thailand[i,j]	12.8	15.2	14.6	15.1	17.1	15.9	16.3	15.6	15.1
Viet Nam[k]	18.0	21.0	22.4	19.0	19.1	18.2	18.0	17.9	18.6
The Pacific									
Cook Islands[c]	22.3	25.3	25.5	23.6	25.5	...	...	...	...
Fiji[l]	20.0	21.1	21.6	24.2	24.3	24.8	24.6	25.5	25.1
Kiribati[m]	21.5	20.8	16.8	17.4	17.5	...	...	...	...
Marshall Islands[i]	15.2	18.0	16.8	15.7	15.8	15.7	17.3	17.6	18.3
Micronesia, Federated States of[l]	11.9	11.7	12.0	11.6	12.1	19.0	12.4	13.0	...
Nauru[c]	...	...	...	8.0	15.3	14.9	18.8	22.5	18.8
Palau[i]	16.4	17.3	17.1	18.2	18.4	19.3	19.4	19.7	19.5
Papua New Guinea	23.8	24.8	16.6	18.4	18.0	16.9	13.9	12.5	13.0
Samoa[c]	20.6	20.6	20.9	19.7	21.8	22.4	22.3	23.6	...
Solomon Islands	19.1	24.3	34.0	37.3	37.2	35.0	34.2	30.8	30.6
Timor-Leste	...	1.5	1.3	3.5	4.7	7.5	8.0	13.1	...
Tonga[c]	15.8	19.2	16.1	15.9	17.0	17.0	19.0	20.7	21.3
Tuvalu[c]	21.5	21.5	16.4	15.2	19.2	18.2	19.7	...	...
Vanuatu	15.7	16.4	16.3	16.5	17.2	17.2	16.0	16.3	...
Developed ADB Member Economies									
Australia[c]	23.2	24.9	20.6	21.2	22.1	22.1	22.0	22.3	22.2
Japan[d]	10.0	9.8	8.6	9.4	10.0	11.1	11.0	10.7	...
New Zealand[n]	32.7	35.9	26.9	27.1	28.3	27.4	28.5	28.7	28.9

... = data not available, ADB= Asian Development Bank, GDP = gross domestic product.

a   Data refer to tax revenues (% of GDP) of central government, except for Bangladesh, Georgia, the Federated States of Micronesia, Kiribati, the Kyrgyz Republic, Mongolia, Pakistan, and Tajikistan, where data refer to tax revenues of consolidated government or general government. For the People's Republic of China, data refer to tax revenues of consolidated central and local governments. For Australia, data refer to the tax revenues of the Commonwealth Government.

b   For 2012, government finance covers 9 months only (21 March to 20 December) due to the change of fiscal year (FY) effective in 2012 (FY1391). For 2013 onward, the fiscal year begins on 21 December and ends on 20 December.

c   Data are based on fiscal year ending 30 June.

d   Data are based on fiscal year beginning 1 April.

e   For 2012 onward, data were compiled based on the International Monetary Fund's Government Finance Statistics Manual 2014 and are mapped to the current government finance structure followed in the Key Indicators publication. Data on "disposal of nonfinancial assets" are treated as capital receipts, the "acquisition of nonfinancial assets" as capital expenditure, and the "net acquisition of nonfinancial assets" as capital account surplus/deficit.

f   Data are based on fiscal year ending 15 July.

g   For 2005 onward, data are based on fiscal year beginning 1 April. Data include duties, taxes, and licenses.

h   For 2000, data cover 9 months, from 1 April to 31 December.

i   Data are based on fiscal year ending 30 September.

j   For 2013 onward, data were compiled based on the International Monetary Fund's Government Financial Statistics Manual 2014 and are mapped to the current government finance structure followed in the Key Indicators publication.

k   Tax revenue includes local government taxes.

l   For 2015 onward, data are based on fiscal year ending 31 July.

m   For 2000–2013, data are based on calendar year.

n   For 2000–2008, data are based on fiscal year beginning 1 April. For 2009–2017, data are based on fiscal year ending 30 June.

Source: Economy sources.

Government Finance

Table 2.8.3: Total Government Revenue[a]
(% of GDP)

ADB Regional Member	2000	2005	2010	2012	2013	2014	2015	2016	2017
Developing ADB Member Economies									
Central and West Asia									
Afghanistan[b]	2.9 (2002)	6.9	10.8	7.5	9.2	8.2	9.7	10.4	11.5
Armenia	15.9	16.2	21.7	23.3	23.3	23.4	22.6	22.6	22.0
Azerbaijan	14.7	16.3	26.8	31.6	33.5	31.2	32.2	29.0	23.5
Georgia	15.5	27.1	27.1	28.9	27.3	27.3	28.3	28.6	28.4
Kazakhstan	22.9	27.6	14.2	14.3	13.8	13.5	12.7	14.0	...
Kyrgyz Republic	14.2	19.8	23.1	26.2	26.1	27.3	27.7	25.3	25.7
Pakistan[c]	12.1	12.6	14.2	12.8	13.3	14.5	14.4	15.0	15.5
Tajikistan	14.1	19.2	19.3	21.5	22.7	25.1	25.0	23.4	...
Turkmenistan	23.5	20.5	15.8	21.0	18.4	17.9	16.6	...	...
Uzbekistan	28.0	21.6	21.8	21.7	21.7	21.8	21.2	20.5	19.6
East Asia									
China, People's Republic of	13.4	16.9	20.1	21.7	21.7	21.8	22.1	21.5	20.9
Hong Kong, China[d]	16.8	17.5	21.2	21.7	21.3	21.2	18.8	23.0	23.0
Korea, Republic of	21.4	20.8	21.4	22.6	22.0	21.6	21.8	22.7	23.3
Mongolia	28.1	27.4	31.6	29.4	31.0	28.4	26.1	24.0	26.6
Taipei,China	17.7	14.3	10.7	11.0	11.5	10.9	11.6	11.1	...
South Asia									
Bangladesh[c]	8.5	10.6	9.5	10.9	12.4	11.9	9.7	10.0	10.3
Bhutan[c]	23.2	17.0	27.4	20.7	20.0	19.7	19.9	18.3	18.6
India[d]	9.5	9.7	10.6	9.3	9.4	9.3	9.2	9.8	9.0
Maldives	30.0	25.4	19.3	22.0	23.3	26.4	27.1	28.2	...
Nepal[f]	11.3	11.9	14.9	16.0	17.5	18.5	19.1	21.4	22.4
Sri Lanka	16.4	15.5	12.7	12.0	11.9	11.5	13.3	14.2	13.8
Southeast Asia									
Brunei Darussalam[g]	49.1	53.2	49.0	46.8	37.9	31.1	24.2	17.7	26.1
Cambodia	10.0	10.6	12.6	14.4	14.3	17.1	16.8	17.7	18.9
Indonesia[h]	14.7	17.8	14.5	15.5	15.1	14.7	13.1	12.5	12.8
Lao People's Democratic Republic[i]	13.1	11.7	15.3	15.2	15.6	16.1	15.8	15.0	14.5
Malaysia	17.4	19.6	19.4	21.4	20.9	19.9	18.9	17.3	16.3
Myanmar[d,e]	4.2	17.6 (2006)	14.2	20.8	20.5	22.5	19.2	18.4	16.4
Philippines	14.3	14.4	13.4	14.5	14.9	15.1	15.8	15.2	15.7
Singapore[d]	29.3	20.9	22.1	22.8	22.0	22.0	21.9	21.9	...
Thailand[i,j]	14.7	17.3	16.8	17.1	19.6	18.6	19.2	18.8	18.2
Viet Nam[k]	20.1	25.7	26.7	22.3	22.8	22.0	23.5	24.3	25.6
The Pacific									
Cook Islands[c]	27.0	29.3	34.1	33.4	35.3	...	...	...	...
Fiji[l]	25.5	24.2	25.4	27.0	27.0	27.6	27.4	30.5	27.6
Kiribati[m]	94.4	65.2	51.6 (2009)	86.9	85.5	...	...	...	...
Marshall Islands[i]	21.7	21.7	19.5	19.1	21.2	23.6	27.5	32.2	38.4
Micronesia, Federated States of[i]	22.6	19.7	21.4	22.9	26.7	36.9	37.1	36.1	...
Nauru[c]	...	33.1	39.2	31.9	39.1	60.0	64.7	94.1	92.6
Palau[i]	22.9	19.8	19.7	21.8	22.2	24.2	24.3	24.9	26.4
Papua New Guinea	25.7	26.8	17.8	19.5	18.8	18.8	16.0	13.5	14.4
Samoa[c]	25.6	24.1	23.6	22.7	23.8	24.6	24.9	26.1	26.7
Solomon Islands	21.6	26.7	37.0	43.0	51.4	47.2	46.6	40.3	40.8
Timor-Leste	...	9.7	22.7	5.4	6.5	10.1	12.0	18.3	...
Tonga[c]	21.1	22.8	20.1	18.1	19.7	20.1	22.3	24.1	25.4
Tuvalu[c]	215.6	55.7	52.6	57.2	83.8	75.2	106.9	...	...
Vanuatu	18.7	18.5	18.1	18.8	19.2	19.1	20.0	21.7	...
Developed ADB Member Economies									
Australia[c]	25.3	26.3	22.5	22.6	23.6	23.5	23.6	23.8	23.8
Japan[d]	11.7	11.5	9.9	10.8	11.6	12.5	12.6	12.2	...
New Zealand[n]	37.6	41.9	33.5	33.5	34.5	33.4	34.1	34.2	34.2

... = data not available, ADB = Asian Development Bank, GDP = gross domestic product.

a   Data refer to total government revenue (% of GDP) of central government, except for Bangladesh, Georgia, the Federated States of Micronesia, Kiribati, the Kyrgyz Republic, Mongolia, Pakistan, and Tajikistan, where data refer to the total revenue of consolidated government or general government. For the People's Republic of China, data refer to total revenue of consolidated central and local governments. For Australia, data refer to total revenue of the Commonwealth Government.

b   For 2012, government finance covers 9 months only (21 March to 20 December) due to the change of fiscal year (FY) effective in 2012 (FY1391). For 2013 onward, the fiscal year begins on 21 December and ends on 20 December.

c   Data are based on fiscal year ending 30 June.

d   Data are based on fiscal year beginning 1 April.

e   For 2012 onward, data were compiled based on the International Monetary Fund's Government Finance Statistics Manual 2014 and are mapped to the current government finance structure followed in the Key Indicators publication. Data on "disposal of nonfinancial assets" are treated as capital receipts, the "acquisition of nonfinancial assets" as capital expenditure, and the "net acquisition of nonfinancial assets" as capital account surplus/deficit.

f   Data are based on fiscal year ending 15 July.

g   For 2005 onward, data are based on fiscal year beginning 1 April. Data include duties, taxes, and licenses.

h   For 2000, data cover 9 months, from 1 April to 31 December.

i   Data are based on fiscal year ending 30 September.

j   For 2013 onward, data were compiled based on International Monetary Fund's Government Finance Statistics Manual 2014 and are mapped to the current government finance structure followed in the Key Indicators publication.

k   Tax revenue includes local government taxes.

l   For 2015 onward, data are based on fiscal year ending 31 July.

m   Data on total government revenue for 2000–2009 are not directly comparable with data for 2010 onward due to significant improvements in methodology and use of improved data starting 2010. For 2000–2013, data are based on calendar year.

n   For 2000–2008, data are based on fiscal year beginning 1 April. For 2009–2017, data are based on fiscal year ending 30 June.

Source: Economy sources.

Table 2.8.4: Total Government Expenditure[a]
(% of GDP)

ADB Regional Member	2000	2005	2010	2012	2013	2014	2015	2016	2017
Developing ADB Member Economies									
Central and West Asia									
Afghanistan[b]	7.7 (2002)	16.5	20.6	17.4	23.2	24.6	25.5	25.7	24.4
Armenia	20.1	18.0	27.6	25.2	25.1	25.6	28.0	28.8	27.0
Azerbaijan	16.2	16.8	27.6	31.6	31.4	31.1	31.7	26.9	23.3
Georgia	16.3	26.6	34.0	30.6	29.4	30.3	30.5	31.0	30.3
Kazakhstan	22.2	25.6	22.0	21.5	19.6	21.1	20.7	21.2	...
Kyrgyz Republic	18.0	20.4	31.2	34.5	29.3	30.3	31.3	31.8	31.8
Pakistan[c]	17.0	16.4	20.4	21.2	19.8	20.4	20.2	20.3	21.6
Tajikistan	14.7	19.4	25.1	25.1	28.5	28.8	33.6	33.8	...
Turkmenistan	23.9	19.7	13.8	14.7	16.9	17.0	17.3	...	...
Uzbekistan	28.9	21.5	21.5	21.3	21.4	20.4	21.1	20.5	19.4
East Asia									
China, People's Republic of	16.1	18.1	21.8	23.3	23.6	23.6	25.5	25.2	24.6
Hong Kong, China[d]	17.4	16.5	17.0	18.5	20.3	17.5	18.2	18.6	17.8
Korea, Republic of	17.2	20.1	19.8	20.8	21.1	21.0	21.2	20.9	21.0
Mongolia	28.6	22.7	29.2	35.5	31.5	31.8	30.7	37.5	31.8
Taipei,China	22.2	14.6	13.3	13.7	12.5	11.7	11.4	11.4	...
South Asia									
Bangladesh[c]	14.5	15.0	12.7	13.0	15.3	15.4	13.2	13.8	13.6
Bhutan[c]	42.2	35.4	35.6	35.8	34.7	29.0	27.6	30.1	31.3
India[d]	15.0	13.7	15.4	14.2	13.9	13.4	13.1	13.4	13.1
Maldives	37.3	38.8	33.2	29.8	27.0	29.1	34.8	39.0	...
Nepal[f]	17.5	15.3	19.0	19.3	17.8	18.8	20.1	22.0	28.0
Sri Lanka	25.0	23.8	19.3	17.5	17.3	17.2	20.9	19.6	19.3
Southeast Asia									
Brunei Darussalam[g]	40.6	32.1	33.3	31.0	27.8	31.8	38.7	39.4	36.0
Cambodia	14.8	13.2	21.4	21.2	21.1	20.9	19.4	20.4	22.0
Indonesia[h]	15.8	18.4	15.2	17.3	17.3	16.8	15.7	15.0	15.7
Lao People's Democratic Republic[i]	20.8	18.4	24.2	22.1	26.3	24.8	24.8	21.5	21.6
Malaysia	22.9	23.0	24.7	25.7	24.7	23.3	22.1	20.4	19.3
Myanmar[d,e]	3.5	19.2	18.9	19.2	22.0	23.5	23.5	21.0	22.1
Philippines	18.1	16.9	16.8	16.6	16.1	15.6	16.7	17.5	17.9
Singapore[d]	18.2	14.5	14.5	14.2	13.9	14.8	17.7	16.8	...
Thailand[i,j]	16.8	17.2	19.7	19.4	20.1	20.4	20.4	19.6	19.9
Viet Nam[k]	22.6	25.1	27.2	28.2	28.8	26.4	28.2	28.7	29.2
The Pacific									
Cook Islands[c]	31.0	33.3	33.0	36.5	41.2	...	...	...	...
Fiji[l]	28.6	27.6	27.7	28.3	27.6	31.3	30.6	34.6	29.8
Kiribati[m]	87.4	100.2	85.3	102.3	96.2	...	...	...	...
Marshall Islands[i]	57.8	83.9	56.7	51.5	53.3	49.4	57.0	58.4	65.1
Micronesia, Federated States of[f]	67.3	59.2	67.1	65.1	59.2	53.6	55.6	61.4	...
Nauru[c]	...	28.5	83.6	44.7	57.4	51.8	72.4	91.7	99.9
Palau[i]	57.7	40.3	47.9	43.3	40.1	39.8	34.3	37.7	36.2
Papua New Guinea	32.9	35.2	20.9	24.7	26.2	25.6	21.2	20.2	19.0
Samoa[c]	31.2	32.7	30.0	32.6	30.1	34.0	30.8	28.6	29.6
Solomon Islands	31.6	34.6	39.7	41.9	58.4	54.5	55.0	51.3	49.9
Timor-Leste	...	5.7	19.0	36.9	35.9	65.0	88.0	133.9	...
Tonga[c]	22.2	21.2	28.0	29.5	25.5	26.7	35.8	39.0	50.4
Tuvalu[c]	186.3	78.6	105.5	75.9	82.1	88.0	117.8	...	...
Vanuatu	26.0	18.4	22.2	21.8	20.6	21.4	22.8	24.3	...
Developed ADB Member Economies									
Australia[c]	23.5	24.8	26.1	25.3	25.0	25.4	25.8	26.0	25.6
Japan[d]	17.8	15.4	17.3	18.3	18.4	17.8	17.1	16.8	...
New Zealand[n]	35.7	35.8	36.2	35.8	35.7	34.0	33.9	33.5	32.5

... = data not available, ADB= Asian Development Bank, GDP = gross domestic product.

a Data refer to total expenditure (% of GDP) of central government, except for Bangladesh, Georgia, the Federated States of Micronesia, Kiribati, the Kyrgyz Republic, Mongolia, Pakistan, and Tajikistan, where data refer to total expenditure of consolidated government or general government. For the People's Republic of China, data refer to total expenditure of consolidated central and local governments. For Australia, data refer to total expenditure of the Commonwealth Government.

b For 2012, government finance covers 9 months only (21 March to 20 December) due to the change of fiscal year (FY) effective in 2012 (FY1391). For 2013 onward, the fiscal year begins on 21 December and ends on 20 December.

c Data are based on fiscal year ending 30 June.

d Data are based on fiscal year beginning 1 April.

e For 2012 onward, data were compiled based on International Monetary Fund's Government Finance Statistics Manual 2014 and are mapped to the current government finance structure followed in the Key Indicators publication. The data on 'disposal of nonfinancial assets' is treated as capital receipts, the 'acquisition of nonfinancial assets' as capital expenditure, and the 'net acquisition of nonfinancial assets' as capital account surplus/deficit.

f Data are based on fiscal year ending 15 July.

g For 2005 onward, data are based on fiscal year beginning 1 April. Data are derived as excess of revenue over expenditure (ordinary plus charged) less the sum of contribution to a development fund, contribution to a government trust fund, and capital and currency adjustments.

h For 2000, data cover 9 months, from 1 April to 31 December.

i Data are based on fiscal year ending 30 September.

j For 2013 onward, data were compiled based on International Monetary Fund's Government Financial Statistics Manual 2014 and are mapped to the current government finance structure followed in the Key Indicators publication.

k Tax revenue includes local government taxes.

l For 2015 onward, data are based on fiscal year ending 31 July.

m For 2000–2013, data are based on calendar year.

n For 2000–2008, data are based on fiscal year beginning 1 April. For 2009–2017, data are based on fiscal year ending 30 June.

Source: Economy sources.

Government Finance

Table 2.8.5: Government Expenditure by Economic Activity[a]
(% of GDP)

ADB Regional Member	Health			Education			Social Security and Welfare		
	2000	2010	2017	2000	2010	2017	2000	2010	2017
Developing ADB Member Economies									
Central and West Asia									
Afghanistan	...	...	...	...	...	...	...	...	...
Armenia	1.0	1.6	1.5	2.8	2.8	2.2	2.1	7.1	7.3
Azerbaijan	0.9	1.0	1.0	3.9	2.8	2.5	3.0	2.6	3.4
Georgia	0.6	2.2	3.0	2.2	2.9	3.8	4.3	6.9	7.3
Kazakhstan	...	...	...	...	...	...	...	...	...
Kyrgyz Republic	2.0	2.9	3.1	3.5	5.4	6.2	1.7	5.0	5.1
Pakistan	...	...	...	...	...	...	...	...	...
Tajikistan[b]	0.9	1.4	2.1 (2016)	2.3	4.0	5.8 (2016)	1.8	3.5	5.0 (2016)
Turkmenistan	...	...	...	...	...	...	...	...	...
Uzbekistan	...	2.8	2.8	...	7.2	6.3	...	2.2	0.9
East Asia									
China, People's Republic of[c]	...	1.2	1.8	3.3 (2002)	3.0	3.7	0.7	2.2	3.0
Hong Kong, China[d]	2.4	2.2	2.7	3.9	3.4	3.3	2.1	2.3	2.7
Korea, Republic of	0.1	0.2	0.3 (2016)	3.1	3.0	3.3 (2016)	3.0	4.5	5.6 (2016)
Mongolia	3.8	2.5	2.7	6.7	5.1	2.9	6.2	11.1	7.7
Taipei,China	0.2	0.2	0.1 (2016)	2.3	1.7	1.4 (2016)	5.6	3.1	3.4 (2016)
South Asia									
Bangladesh[e]	1.0	0.8	0.3	2.0	2.0	2.5	0.1	0.9	0.8
Bhutan[e]	...	3.0	2.7	...	6.7	6.7	...	3.1	3.3
India[d,f]	0.7	0.7	1.3 (2016)	3.2	1.9	4.6 (2016)	0.8	0.4	1.8 (2016)
Maldives	4.1	3.0	3.6 (2015)	7.4	5.0	4.8 (2015)	1.0	1.7	5.4 (2015)
Nepal[g]	0.9	1.5	1.7	2.4	3.9	4.2	0.9	0.8	1.5
Sri Lanka	1.6	1.2	1.5	2.4	1.6	1.9	2.8	1.7	2.0
Southeast Asia									
Brunei Darussalam[h]	2.1	1.8	...	4.2	3.6	...	1.2	0.8	...
Cambodia	0.9	1.3	1.2	1.3	1.6	2.3	0.2	0.5	0.8
Indonesia	...	...	...	...	...	...	...	...	...
Lao People's Democratic Republic[i]	1.0	...	...	1.0	...	...	...	...	...
Malaysia	1.5	2.0	1.9	5.6	6.1	4.5	0.9	1.2	0.9
Myanmar	...	...	...	...	...	...	...	...	...
Philippines	0.4	0.3	1.0	3.3	2.5	4.4	0.7	0.5	1.8
Singapore[d]	0.9	1.2	2.3 (2016)	3.8	3.0	3.0 (2016)	0.6	1.1	1.5 (2016)
Thailand[i]	1.3	1.9	1.2 (2016)	3.9	4.1	3.7 (2016)	0.9	1.7	2.4 (2016)
Viet Nam[j]	...	...	...	...	...	...	...	...	...
The Pacific									
Cook Islands[e]	3.1	3.3	...	3.2	4.9	...	...	...	...
Fiji[k]	2.3	2.1	1.9 (2016)	4.3	3.5	3.3 (2016)	0.1	0.1	0.1 (2016)
Kiribati	7.6	8.4	8.9 (2016)	11.0	9.9	8.8 (2016)	0.9	1.6	1.3 (2016)
Marshall Islands	...	...	...	...	...	...	...	...	...
Micronesia, Federated States of	...	...	...	...	...	...	...	...	...
Nauru	...	...	...	...	...	...	...	...	...
Palau	...	...	...	...	...	...	...	...	...
Papua New Guinea	1.6	...	...	5.1	...	...	...	...	...
Samoa[e]	4.0	3.7	4.1	4.9	4.3	4.1	1.1	1.2	1.5
Solomon Islands	...	...	...	...	...	...	...	...	...
Timor-Leste	...	0.9	4.4 (2016)	...	1.7	9.5 (2016)	...	3.5	11.1 (2016)
Tonga[e]	4.8	...	...	4.4	...	...	...	...	...
Tuvalu	...	...	...	...	...	...	...	...	...
Vanuatu	2.4	...	...	4.9	...	...	0.0	...	...
Developed ADB Member Economies									
Australia[e]	3.9	4.0	4.2	1.6	2.7	1.9	8.6	8.4	8.8
Japan[d]	6.1	7.1	7.5 (2016)	3.7	2.9	2.7 (2016)	10.2	15.8	16.0 (2016)
New Zealand[l]	5.3	7.0	6.5	4.9	6.8	5.9	11.7	12.5	10.8

... = data not available, 0.0 = magnitude is less than half of unit employed, ADB = Asian Development Bank, GDP = gross domestic product.

a Data refer to expenditure of the central government, except for Bangladesh, Georgia, Kiribati, the Kyrgyz Republic, Mongolia, and Tajikistan, where data refer to the consolidated expenditure of central and local governments. For Australia, data refer to the expenditure of the Commonwealth government.
b Expenditure on social security and welfare includes expenditure on defense.
c For 2000–2005, expenditure on education includes health expenditure.
d Data are based on fiscal year beginning 1 April.
e Data are based on fiscal year ending 30 June.
f Data for the central government refer to current and capital expenditure of administrative departments, excluding that of local bodies.
g Data are based on fiscal year ending 15 July.
h For 2005 onward, data are based on fiscal year beginning 1 April.
i Data are based on fiscal year ending 30 September.
j Total expenditure includes local government expenditure.
k For 2015 onward, data are based on fiscal year ending 31 July.
l For 2000–2008, data refer to fiscal year ending 31 March. For 2009–2017, data refer to fiscal year ending 30 June.

Source: Economy sources.

Table 2.8.6:   Indicators for Business Startups

ADB Regional Member	Cost of Business Startup Procedure (% of GNI per capita)			Time Required to Start Business (days)		
	2005	2010	2017	2005	2010	2017
Developing ADB Member Economies						
Central and West Asia[a]	**27.8**	**12.0**	**13.3**	**38.2**	**13.5**	**7.9**
Afghanistan	75.2	26.7	82.3	9.5	7.5	7.5
Armenia	6.1	3.1	0.9	18.0	14.0	4.5
Azerbaijan	12.3	3.1	1.8	113.0	8.0	4.5
Georgia	13.7	5.0	2.5	21.0	3.0	2.0
Kazakhstan	9.9	1.0	0.3	31.0	25.0	9.0
Kyrgyz Republic	10.4	3.7	2.1	21.0	14.0	10.0
Pakistan	25.6	17.8	7.6	23.0	20.0	17.5
Tajikistan	85.1	36.9	19.3	79.0	16.0	11.0
Turkmenistan	...	...	...	...	...	...
Uzbekistan	11.5	10.8	3.1	28.0	14.0	5.0
East Asia[a]	**9.3**	**5.7**	**3.9**	**31.6**	**18.0**	**9.7**
China, People's Republic of	13.6	4.5	0.6	48.0	38.0	22.9
Hong Kong, China	3.4	2.0	1.1	11.0	6.0	1.5
Korea, Republic of	15.7	14.7	14.6	17.0	14.0	4.0
Mongolia	9.6	3.2	1.4	17.0	17.0	10.0
Taipei,China	4.4	4.0	2.0	65.0	15.0	10.0
South Asia[a]	**44.8**	**28.0**	**13.5**	**48.8**	**30.6**	**16.5**
Bangladesh	56.1	21.2	22.3	51.5	26.5	19.5
Bhutan	16.9	6.1	3.9	62.0	46.0	12.0
India	62.0	50.5	14.8	93.0	30.0	29.8
Maldives	14.0	9.4	4.7	9.0	12.0	12.0
Nepal	69.9	46.6	24.9	31.0	31.0	16.5
Sri Lanka	50.0	33.9	10.4	46.0	38.0	9.0
Southeast Asia[a]	**55.6**	**39.4**	**14.1**	**74.4**	**54.9**	**29.1**
Brunei Darussalam	8.9 (2006)	13.6	1.1	121.5 (2006)	108.5	12.5
Cambodia	276.1	127.5	51.3	87.0	102.0	99.0
Indonesia	101.7	25.8	10.9	164.0	49.0	23.1
Lao People's Democratic Republic	17.4	8.9	3.5	131.0	85.0	67.0
Malaysia	26.6	17.5	5.4	37.5	17.5	18.5
Myanmar	...	157.7 (2012)	40.1	...	77.0 (2012)	14.0
Philippines	23.9	22.1	15.8	47.0	37.0	28.0
Singapore	0.9	0.7	0.5	6.0	2.5	2.5
Thailand	17.3	7.7	6.2	35.0	34.0	4.5
Viet Nam	27.6	12.1	6.5	41.0	36.0	22.0
The Pacific[a]	**59.4**	**37.1**	**28.5**	**47.3**	**39.5**	**21.3**
Cook Islands	...	...	...	...	...	...
Fiji	28.4	23.8	16.9	44.0	44.0	40.0
Kiribati	40.3	47.1	40.2	31.0	31.0	31.0
Marshall Islands	22.4	17.6	11.9	17.0	17.0	17.0
Micronesia, Federated States of	127.6	137.8	141.7	16.0	16.0	16.0
Nauru	...	...	...	...	...	...
Palau	4.7	5.7	2.9	24.0	28.0	28.0
Papua New Guinea	27.7	27.0	11.5	52.0	52.0	41.0
Samoa	46.4	9.8	7.2	35.0	9.0	8.9
Solomon Islands	135.5	78.5	29.0	55.0	55.0	9.0
Timor-Leste	125.4	5.7	0.5	167.0	110.0	9.0
Tonga	11.7	7.0	7.1	32.0	25.0	16.0
Tuvalu	...	...	...	...	...	...
Vanuatu	83.5	48.2	44.4	47.0	47.0	18.0
Developed ADB Member Economies[a]	**4.3**	**2.9**	**2.8**	**15.3**	**8.7**	**5.1**
Australia	1.9	0.7	0.7	3.0	2.5	2.5
Japan	10.7	7.5	7.5	31.0	23.0	12.2
New Zealand	0.2	0.4	0.3	12.0	0.5	0.5
DEVELOPING ADB MEMBER ECONOMIES[a]	**43.0**	**27.0**	**16.5**	**49.6**	**33.6**	**18.1**
ALL ADB REGIONAL MEMBERS[a]	**40.3**	**25.3**	**15.5**	**47.2**	**31.9**	**17.2**
WORLD	**84.4**	**44.7**	**25.3**	**50.1**	**34.9**	**19.8**

... = data not available, ADB = Asian Development Bank, GNI = gross national income.

a   Arithmetic average of reporting economies only.

Source: World Bank. Doing Business Online. http://data.worldbank.org/indicator (accessed 11 June 2018).

Governance

Table 2.8.7:   Corruption Perceptions Index[a]

ADB Regional Member	2000		2005		2010	2011	2012	2013	2014	2015	2016	2017	Rank in 2016[b]	Rank in 2017[b]
Developing ADB Member Economies														
Central and West Asia														
Afghanistan	...		2.5		1.4	1.5 |	8	8	12	11	15	15	169	177
Armenia	2.5		2.9		2.6	2.6 |	34	36	37	35	33	35	113	107
Azerbaijan	1.5		2.2		2.4	2.4 |	27	28	29	29	30	31	123	122
Georgia	2.4	(2002)	2.3		3.8	4.1 |	52	49	52	52	57	56	44	46
Kazakhstan	3.0		2.6		2.9	2.7 |	28	26	29	28	29	31	131	122
Kyrgyz Republic	...		2.3		2.0	2.1 |	24	24	27	28	28	29	136	135
Pakistan	2.3	(2001)	2.1		2.3	2.5 |	27	28	29	30	32	32	116	117
Tajikistan	...		2.1		2.1	2.3 |	22	22	23	26	25	21	151	161
Turkmenistan	...		1.8		1.6	1.6 |	17	17	17	18	22	19	154	167
Uzbekistan	2.4		2.2		1.6	1.6 |	17	17	18	19	21	22	156	157
East Asia														
China, People's Republic of	3.1		3.2		3.5	3.6 |	39	40	36	37	40	41	79	77
Hong Kong, China	7.7		8.3		8.4	8.4 |	77	75	74	75	77	77	15	13
Korea, Republic of	4.0		5.0		5.4	5.4 |	56	55	55	56	53	54	52	51
Mongolia	...		3.0		2.7	2.7 |	36	38	39	39	38	36	87	103
Taipei,China	5.5		5.9		5.8	6.1 |	61	61	61	62	61	63	31	29
South Asia														
Bangladesh	0.4	(2001)	1.7		2.4	2.7 |	26	27	25	25	26	28	145	143
Bhutan	...		6.0	(2006)	5.7	5.7 |	63	63	65	65	65	67	27	26
India	2.8		2.9		3.3	3.1 |	36	36	38	38	40	40	79	81
Maldives	...		3.3	(2007)	2.3	2.5 |	...	...	...	...	36	33	95	112
Nepal	...		2.5		2.2	2.2 |	27	31	29	27	29	31	131	122
Sri Lanka	3.7	(2002)	3.2		3.2	3.3 |	40	37	38	37	36	38	95	91
Southeast Asia														
Brunei Darussalam	...		...		5.5	5.2 |	55	60	...	...	58	62	41	32
Cambodia	...		2.3		2.1	2.1 |	22	20	21	21	21	21	156	161
Indonesia	1.7		2.2		2.8	3.0 |	32	32	34	36	37	37	90	96
Lao People's Democratic Republic	...		3.3		2.1	2.2 |	21	26	25	25	30	29	123	135
Malaysia	4.8		5.1		4.4	4.3 |	49	50	52	50	49	47	55	62
Myanmar	...		1.8		1.4	1.5 |	15	21	21	22	28	30	136	130
Philippines	2.8		2.5		2.4	2.6 |	34	36	38	35	35	34	101	111
Singapore	9.1		9.4		9.3	9.2 |	87	86	84	85	84	84	7	6
Thailand	3.2		3.8		3.5	3.4 |	37	35	38	38	35	37	101	96
Viet Nam	2.5		2.6		2.7	2.9 |	31	31	31	31	33	35	113	107
The Pacific														
Cook Islands	...		...		...	...	...	...	...	...	...	...	...	...
Fiji	...		4.0		...	...	...	...	...	...	...	...	...	...
Kiribati	...		3.3	(2007)	3.2	3.1 |	...	...	...	...	...	...	...	...
Marshall Islands	...		...		...	...	...	...	...	...	...	...	...	...
Micronesia, Federated States of	...		...		...	...	...	...	...	...	...	...	...	...
Nauru	...		...		...	...	...	...	...	...	...	...	...	...
Palau	...		...		...	...	...	...	...	...	...	...	...	...
Papua New Guinea	...		2.3		2.1	2.2 |	25	25	25	25	28	29	136	135
Samoa	...		4.5	(2007)	4.1	3.9 |	...	...	52	...	...	...	...	...
Solomon Islands	...		2.8	(2007)	2.8	2.7 |	...	...	...	...	42	39	72	85
Timor-Leste	...		2.6	(2006)	2.5	2.4 |	33	30	28	28	35	38	101	91
Tonga	...		1.7	(2007)	3.0	3.1 |	...	...	...	...	...	...	...	...
Tuvalu	...		...		...	...	...	...	...	...	...	...	...	...
Vanuatu	...		3.1	(2007)	3.6	3.5 |	...	...	...	...	...	43	...	71
Developed ADB Member Economies														
Australia	8.3		8.8		8.7	8.8 |	85	81	80	79	79	77	13	13
Japan	6.4		7.3		7.8	8.0 |	74	74	76	75	72	73	20	20
New Zealand	9.4		9.6		9.3	9.5 |	90	91	91	88	90	89	1	1

... = data not available, | = marks break in the series, ADB = Asian Development Bank.

a For 2000–2011, scores relate to perceptions of the degree of corruption as seen by business people and country analysts, and are not comparable over time; scores range from 10 (highly clean) to 0 (highly corrupt). From 2012 onward, an updated methodology was used to calculate scores, and these are presented on a scale of 100 (very clean) to 0 (highly corrupt). Due to the differences in methodology, scores prior to 2012 should not be compared with scores from 2012 onward.

b Based on the Transparency International index, an economy's rank indicates its position relative to other economies of the world; 2016 rankings compare 176 economies, while 2017 rankings compare 180 economies.

Source: Transparency International. https://www.transparency.org/news/feature/corruption_perceptions_index_2017 (accessed 15 June 2018).

References

ADB. 2011. *Promoting Energy Efficiency in the Pacific*. Consultant's report. Manila (TA 6485-REG).

ADB. 2017a. Population Aging in Asia and the Pacific: From Demographic Dividend to Demographic Tax. *Key Indicators in Asia and the Pacific 2017*. Manila.

ADB. 2017b. *Meeting Asia's Infrastructure Needs*. Manila. https://www.adb.org/sites/default/files/publication/227496/special-reportinfrastructure.pdf.

ADB. 2018a. *Asian Development Outlook 2018*. Manila.

ADB. 2018b. *Asian Development Outlook 2018 Supplement*. Manila.

C. Constantinescu et. al. 2018. *Global Trade Watch: Trade Developments in 2017*. Washington, DC: World Bank.

IMF. 2016. *Monetary and Financial Statistics Manual and Compilation Guide*. Washington, DC.

Knoema. World Data Atlas. Brunei Darussalam. National Accounts. https://knoema.com/atlas/Brunei-Darussalam/topics/Economy/National-Accounts-GDP-by-Expenditure-at-current-prices-US-Dollars/Gross-fixed-capital-formation (accessed 25 July 2018).

W. McMahon. 1998. Education and Growth in East Asia. Economics of Education Review. 17 (2). pp. 159-172.

J. P. Smith and M. Majmundar, eds. 2012. *Aging in Asia: Findings from New and Emerging Data Initiatives*. Washington, DC: National Academies Press.

UN. 2016. *Energy Statistics Compilers Manual*. New York.

UN. 2017. Department of Economic and Social Affairs, Population Division. *World Population Prospects, 2017 Revision*. https://esa.un.org/unpd/wpp/.

UN. 2018. United Nations Conference on Trade and Development. *World Investment Report 2018*. Geneva: United Nations.

World Bank. 2017a. *Doing Business 2018: Reforming to Create Jobs*. http://www.doingbusiness.org/reports/global-reports/doing-business-2018.

World Bank. 2017b. *Thailand Moves up in Global Doing Business Ranks*. 1 November. https://www.worldbank.org/en/news/press-release/2017/11/01/thailand-moves-up-in-global-doing-business-ranks.

World Bank. 2018. Global Knowledge Partnership on Migration and Development. *Migration and Remittances: Recent Developments and Outlook*. Washington, DC: World Bank.

PART III
Global Value Chains

Global Value Chain Participation in Asia and the Pacific: Variations Across Economies, Across Sectors, and Over Time

Snapshot

- Variations in global value chain (GVC) participation across economies in Asia and the Pacific reflect economies' relative positions in global production networks, which in turn reflect economies' endowments and comparative advantage. Economies where high-technology products comprise a large part of exports tend to have relatively high backward and low forward participation ratios, while economies whose exports are largely composed of natural resource-based products tend to show the opposite.

- Economies in the region generally participate more through the supply side of GVCs (forward participation), rather than through the demand side (backward participation), highlighting the importance for the region of trade in intermediate goods.

- Economy-level participation ratios mask substantial variations in GVC participation across sectors within economies, with more diversified economies showing more cross-sectoral variation in participation.

- Significant changes in participation ratios are possible over time, which economies accomplished via inter-sectoral shifts in the composition of exports, or intra-sectoral changes in GVC participation.

Since 2015, statistics on the participation of economies and sectors in global value chains (GVCs) have been published as part of *Key Indicators for Asia and the Pacific* (*Key Indicators*). The 2015 edition of *Key Indicators* covered 11 Asian economies for 2000, 2005, and 2011, and documented the exponential growth in trade in intermediates in these economies. The 2016 edition of the publication expanded its coverage to 13 Asian economies and added the years 2008 and 2015. It found a strong tendency for economies in Asia to localize production in response to the uncertainty brought about by the 2008 global financial crisis as well as growing domestic demand. Finally, last year's edition of *Key Indicators* focused on 2014–2016 and expanded its coverage to 23 economies from Asia and the Pacific. It found that an increase in the domestic content of exports helped mitigate the impact of the global trade slowdown on incomes in the region.

The GVC statistics in this publication cover 25 economies from Asia and the Pacific for the years 2010 and 2017. The GVC statistical methodologies are defined in Tables 3.1.1 and 3.1.2. The statistics themselves are presented in Tables 3.2.1 to 3.2.4. This accompanying analysis, which covers a longer period from 2000–2017, takes a closer look at how participation in GVCs varies in Asia and the Pacific—across economies, across sectors, and over time.[1]

Economies can participate in GVCs in two ways. They can use imported intermediate products in their exports, and they can export intermediate goods and services that other economies use in production. These two means of GVC participation for economies across Asia and the Pacific are

---

[1] The data presented in this Part III are not official statistics. Production and trade data from various sources were integrated into the input-output economic analysis framework and adjusted as required to conform to specific macroeconomic concepts. As such, data and statistics presented here could differ from relevant official statistics.

measured by constructing backward and forward participation ratios, following the approaches of Koopman et al. (2014) and Wang, Wei, and Zhu (2018). Specifically, the *backward participation ratio* denotes the foreign value-added contribution to an economy's (or economy-sector's) exports. The *forward participation ratio* shows how much of an economy's (or economy-sector's) locally generated value-added is embedded in the production of other economies. The methodology for constructing the backward and forward participation ratios are described in Box 3.1.1.

Variation Across Economies

Results based on the method described in Box 3.1.1 show that GVC participation varies widely across economies in Asia and the Pacific (Figure 3.1.1). Singapore leads in terms of its use of foreign inputs

---

Box 3.1.1: Constructing Backward and Forward Participation Ratios

Data on intermediate and final exports by economy-sector are extracted from the multiregional input-output tables (MRIOTs) database of the Asian Development Bank (ADB), and decomposed into 16 value-added terms following the methodology espoused by Wang, Wei, and Zhu (2018) and described in *Key Indicators* 2015. Backward and forward participation ratios are then estimated for each economy (and economy-sector) for each year by applying the following four equations to the 16 value-added terms of the decomposition.

For each economy i with sectors k exporting to all other economies j, the backward participation ratio (BPR_i) is given by:

$$BPR_i = \frac{\sum_k \sum_j DDC_{ij}^k + FVA\_FIN_{ij}^k + FVA\_INT_{ij}^k + FDC_{ij}^k}{\sum_k \sum_j EXP_{ij}^k} \qquad (1)$$

while for sector k in economy i, the backward participation ratio (BPR_i^k) is given by:

$$BPR_i^k = \frac{\sum_j DDC_{ij}^k + FVA\_FIN_{ij}^k + FVA\_INT_{ij}^k + FDC_{ij}^k}{\sum_j EXP_{ij}^k} \qquad (2)$$

where *BPR* is backward participation ratio, *DDC* is domestic double counted in total exports, *FVA_FIN* is foreign value-added in final goods exports, *FVA_INT* is foreign value-added in intermediate goods exports, *FDC* is foreign double counted in total exports, and *EXP* is total exports.[a] The index i stands for exporting economy, k stands for exporting sector, and j stands for importing economy.

The forward participation ratio of economy i (FPR_i) is given by:

$$FPR_i = \frac{\sum_k \sum_j DVA\_INT_{ij}^k + DVA\_INTrex_{ij}^k + RDV\_B_{ij}^k}{\sum_k \sum_j EXP_{ij}^k} \qquad (3)$$

while for sector k in economy i, the forward participation ratio (FPR_i^k) can be calculated as:

$$FPR_i^k = \frac{\sum_j DVA\_INT_{ij}^k + DVA\_INTrex_{ij}^k + RDV\_B_{ij}^k}{\sum_j EXP_{ij}^k} \qquad (4)$$

where *DVA_INT* stands for intermediates exports absorbed by direct importers, *DVA_INTrex* stands for intermediates sent to first importer and then re-exported to a third economy, and *RDV_B* stands for domestic value-added first exported then returned home.

---

[a] See *Key Indicators 2015* for a detailed description of these statistics and their intrepretation.

Sources:
R. Koopman, Z. Wang, and S.J. Wei. 2014. "Tracing Value-Added and Double-Counting in Gross Exports," *American Economic Review*, Vol. 104, No. 2 (February), pp. 459-94.

Z. Wang, S.J. Wei, and K. Zhu. 2018. Quantifying international production sharing at the bilateral and sector levels (No. w19677). National Bureau of Economic Research.

Figure 3.1.1: Global Value Chain Participation in Asia and the Pacific, 2017

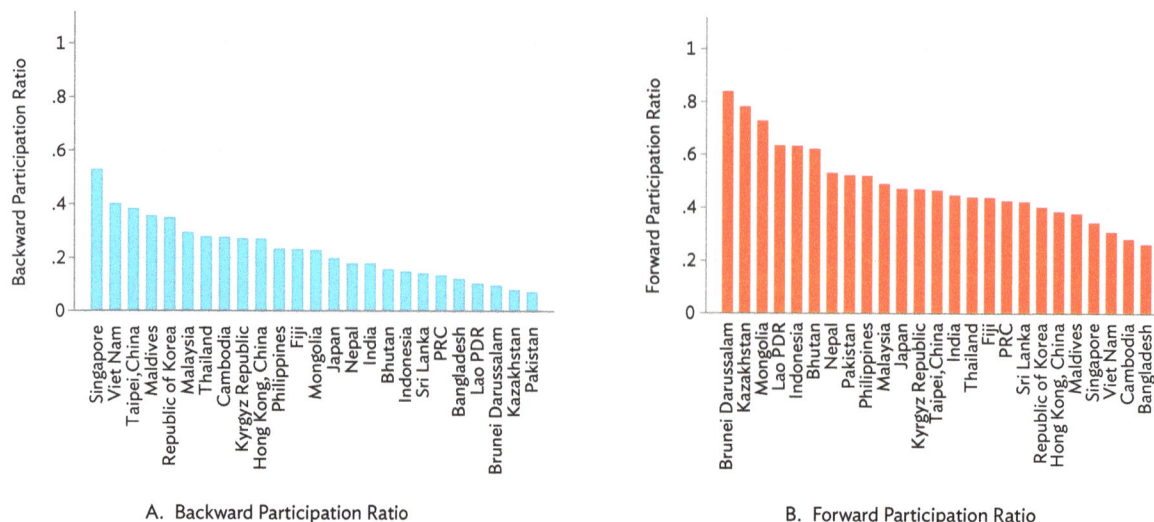

A. Backward Participation Ratio

B. Forward Participation Ratio

Lao PDR = Lao People's Democratic Republic, PRC = People's Republic of China.
Sources: Authors' calculations; and Asian Development Bank Multiregional Input–Output Tables 2017.

in the production of its exports, as evidenced by its backward participation ratio of close to 60%. It mainly imports intermediate inputs of coke, refined petroleum, and nuclear fuel; renting of machinery and equipment and other business activities; electrical and optical equipment; and water transport. The result is intuitive, given Singapore's pivotal position as a major transit point and oil-refining and trading hub, and its well-developed electronics-processing ecosystem.

Economies such as Viet Nam; Taipei,China; the Republic of Korea; and Malaysia, which are also leading exporters of electrical and optical equipment in the region, show similarly high backward participation ratios. This is primarily because the production processes in the high-technology manufacturing sector are highly fragmented and widely distributed geographically. Data show that Viet Nam is fast emerging as an assembly hub in the industry, while the other three economies host leading manufacturers of high-technology components such as electronic chips, the production

of which relies heavily on specific primary products and technical know-how imported from economies across the world.

At the other end of the spectrum, Pakistan lags in terms of its use of foreign inputs, with a backward participation ratio of close to 5%. Pakistan's main exports are textiles and textile products, whose inputs are mainly sourced domestically. Kazakhstan also exhibits notably lower backward participation rates. The country's main exports are in the sectors of mining and quarrying; basic metals and fabricated metal; and coke, refined petroleum, and nuclear fuel, and these are either primary goods or processed primary goods, which need few imported intermediate inputs to produce.

The forward participation of economies across Asia and the Pacific also vary substantially, but tell a somewhat different story. Panel B of Figure 3.1.1 shows that economies such as Brunei Darussalam, Kazakhstan, and Mongolia, whose exports are largely composed of natural resource-based products, are at the upstream segments of value chains. As a

Global Value Chains GVC Focus 207

result, these economies have the highest forward participation ratios, with 70%–80% of their exports going into the production of other economies.

Economies with the lowest forward participation are Bangladesh and Cambodia, whose main exports are in textiles and textile products. Although Bangladesh's textile sector is well integrated into global garment supply chains, the economy shows low forward participation since it produces largely final or near-end products. Cambodia also displays low participation due to the large contribution of textiles to its exports, but there is a distinction between the two economies. Specifically, data show that while foreign value-added is rather significant in Cambodia's textile exports (indicating high backward participation) the relevant numbers are low for Bangladesh. This is largely attributable to the fact that Cambodia specializes in assembly processes, whereas Bangladesh has localized assembly as well as upstream processes related to the sector.

A comparison of the magnitudes in panel A of Figures 3.1.1. against those in panel B illustrates that, except for Singapore and Viet Nam, economies in Asia and the Pacific seem to participate more through the supply side of GVCs, rather than through the demand side. Further analysis also indicates that most economy-sectors participate in relatively low value-adding segments of GVCs, signifying the need for policies aimed at developing and fostering conditions that enable local sectors to move up the value chain.

Given the frequent characterization of the People's Republic of China (PRC) as "the factory of the world," the economy's backward and forward participation ratios may strike many as being low. The reason for this is that, in many sectors and products, the PRC economy has well-developed

local supply chains and, hence, a relatively large share of the value-added in its exports originates domestically. However, it is also noteworthy that most of the domestic value-added exported by the PRC is through final products, which are not accounted for in this analysis.

Figure 3.1.2 further illustrates that when talking about GVC participation, it matters what kind of participation you are referring to. The correlation between backward and forward participation ratios is negative (-0.54), so economies which have high backward participation tend to have low forward participation, and vice versa. This reflects economies' positions along global production networks, and this in turn reflects their relative endowments and comparative advantage. For example, resource-rich Brunei Darussalam tends to export primary inputs and has a higher forward participation ratio than backward participation ratio. By contrast, Singapore is a small economy with few natural resources, and must use many foreign inputs in producing its exports, resulting in a high backward participation ratio and a low forward participation ratio.

Figure 3.1.2: Backward versus Forward Participation Ratios, 2017

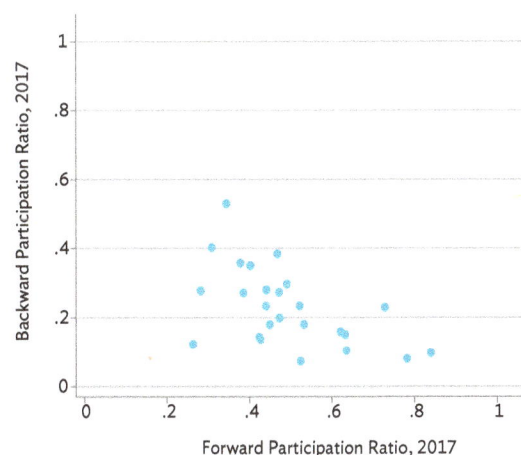

Sources: Authors' calculations; and Asian Development Bank Multiregional Input-Output Tables 2017.

These economy-level backward and forward participation ratios mask substantial variations in GVC participation across sectors within economies. The modified box-and-whisker plots in Figure 3.1.3—with the upper fence representing the 90th percentile and the lower fence representing the 10th percentile—show that GVC participation varies widely across sectors for almost all economies. Plots in Figure 3.1.3 show that economies can simultaneously participate extensively in GVCs in some sectors, while having almost zero participation in others.

For Hong Kong, China, exports are dominated by service sectors with low backward participation, such as wholesale trade and commission trade, financial intermediation, retail trade, air transport, and inland transport. This leads to a modest backward participation ratio for the aggregate economy. At the same time, the economy is also engaged in sectors with high backward participation, such as chemicals and chemical products, transport equipment, electrical and optical equipment, rubber and plastics, and general machinery. Thus, the presence of sectors with low backward participation and high backward participation ratios leads to the wide variation in Hong Kong, China.

Variations Across Sectors

For any given sector, variations in participation ratios across economies could be attributed to the nature of the sector categories in the MRIOTs (Figure 3.1.4). Each sector is made up of several subsectors, whose products and processes could be quite dissimilar to each other at a more granular level. Thus, those sectors whose products have dissimilar production processes will tend to show wider variation in participation ratios. For example, the mean backward participation ratio in the coke, refined petroleum, and nuclear fuel sector is high for the 25 economies in Asia and the Pacific covered by the MRIOTs. This is to be expected as many

Figure 3.1.3: Variations in Global Value Chain Participation within Economies of Asia and the Pacific, 2017

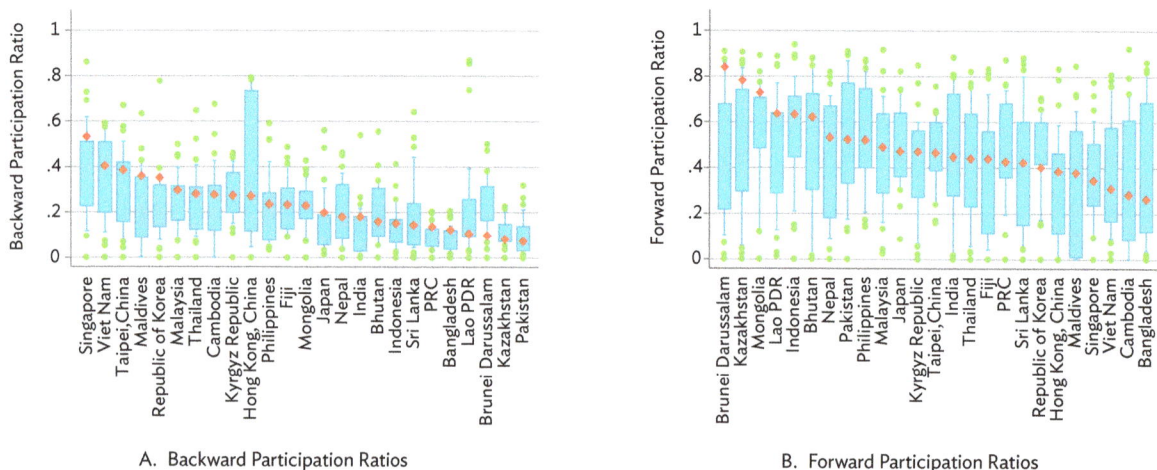

A. Backward Participation Ratios

B. Forward Participation Ratios

◆ Aggregate economy participation ratio
● Sector participation ratios above the 90th percentile and below the 10th percentile

Lao PDR = Lao People's Democratic Republic, PRC = People's Republic of China.
Note: Bars represent interquartile regions, with the upper quartile representing the 75th percentile and the lower quartile representing the 25th percentile. Upper and lower fences represent the 90th and 10th percentiles, respectively.
Sources: Authors' calculations; and Asian Development Bank Multiregional Input–Output Tables 2017.

Figure 3.1.4: Variations in Global Value Chain Participation within Sectors in Asia and the Pacific, 2017

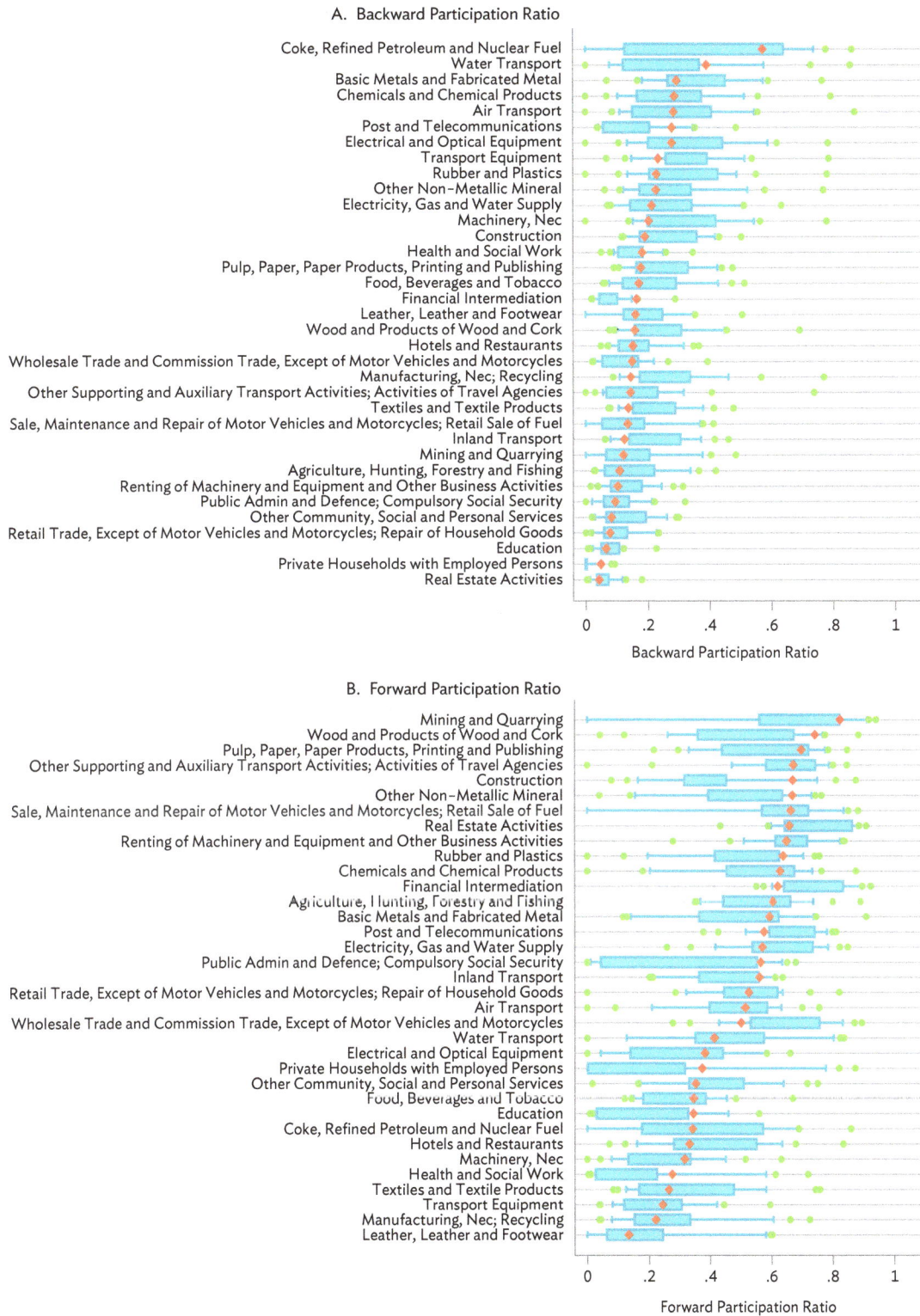

A. Backward Participation Ratio

B. Forward Participation Ratio

◆ Sector participation ratio
● Economy-sector participation ratios above the 90th percentile and below the 10th percentile

Sources: Authors' calculations; and Asian Development Bank Multiregional Input-Output Tables 2017.

economies import these products and use them in export production. However, the variation within the sector is quite high, with some economies (those which both extract and refine fuels) having little backward participation in this sector.

Compared to backward participation, forward participation ratios display a greater range (Figure 3.1.4). It may come as a surprise that sectors such as construction; real estate activities; financial intermediation; postage and telecommunications; and electricity, gas, and water supply show high mean forward participation ratios across all economies. After all, these sectors do not normally engage in direct exports in the traditional sense. However, these sectors provide the goods and services that enable other sectors to successfully engage in production processes and supply their products to domestic and foreign markets. The indirect contributions of these support sectors are counted in the domestic value-added portion of the exported product. Hence, the forward participation indices of such sectors tend to be relatively high even with little or no direct

exports attributable to them. Conversely, direct exporting sectors such as textiles, leather products, and appliance manufacturing show average lower forward participation rates due the final or near-complete nature of their exports.

Variations Over Time

Figure 3.1.5 shows how GVC participation has changed dramatically in Asian economies over time. For instance, the backward participation ratios of Viet Nam and Japan have increased by more than 10 percentage points from 2000 levels, while the forward participation ratios of these two economies have fallen. The opposite is true for economies such as Mongolia, Malaysia, and Indonesia, where backward participation fell, while forward participation increased. As was the case in levels documented in Figure 3.1.2, the changes in backward and forward participation ratios for the regional economies tend to have a negative relationship.

Figure 3.1.5: Changes in Participation Ratios over Time, 2000–2017

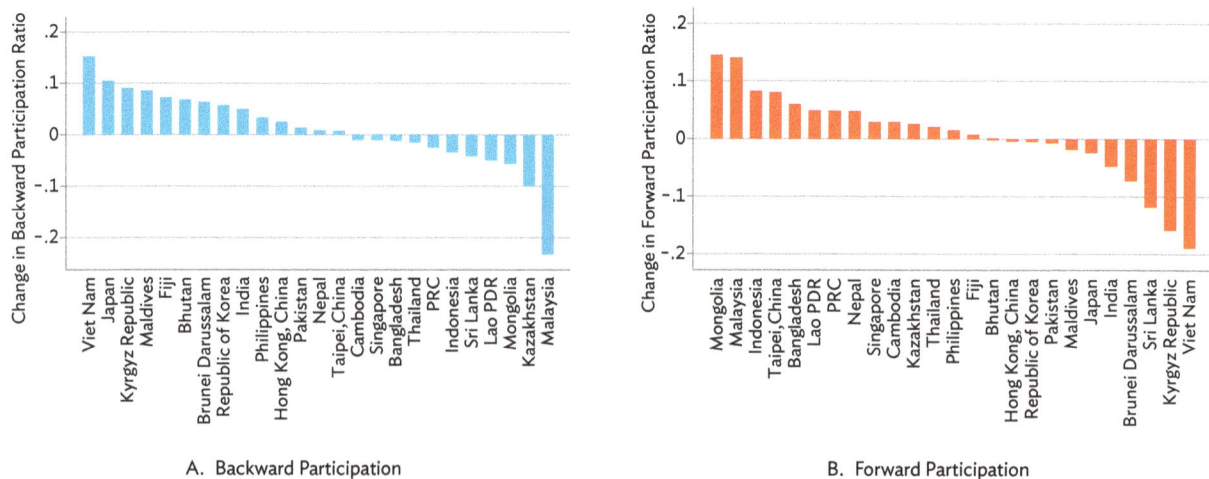

A. Backward Participation

B. Forward Participation

Lao PDR = Lao People's Democratic Republic, PRC = People's Republic of China.
Sources: Authors' calculations; and Asian Development Bank Multiregional Input-Output Tables 2000 and 2017.

These changes can be driven by shifts in each economy's main exports. In 2000, Viet Nam's main exports came from mining and quarrying, followed by agriculture, hunting, forestry, and fishing. The primary sectors are typically expected to have high forward participation ratios, given that their products are mainly extracted from natural resources within the economy. In 2017, Viet Nam's main exports had shifted to food, beverages, and tobacco; electrical and optical equipment; textile and textile products; and leather, leather products, and footwear in terms of total exports. In electrical and optical equipment especially, backward participation ratios are relatively high compared to industries in the primary sector.

The greatest decrease in backward participation is seen in Malaysia, which shows the second highest increase in its forward participation ratio. However, unlike in Viet Nam, the shift is partly driven by the increase in the domestic value-added in the intermediates used in the high-technology industry. While Malaysia's exports are still led by firms producing electrical and optical equipment, the sector's backward participation ratio declined from 0.70 in 2000 to 0.44 in 2017, as a greater share of intermediates were sourced domestically. Meanwhile, forward participation increased from 0.19 in 2000 to 0.35 in 2017. Thus, it appears that, in this sector, the economy has not only progressively localized upstream segments of the relevant GVCs already passing through it, but has also expanded its intermediate supplies to the global market. Given the sector's critical and increasing contribution to the Malaysian economy, further studies are needed to clarify this phenomenon and determine the extent to which it could be attributed to the "ecosystem" effect, i.e., whether already having the essential infrastructure, policies, and related businesses is helping Malaysia to attract more value chain segments and more businesses in the high-tech sector.

Conclusion

Analysis of the MRIOTs and GVC participation indices show that, although economies across Asia and the Pacific tend to participate in GVCs through both backward and forward linkages to varying degrees, forward participation is generally more pronounced and significant than backward participation. However, data also reveal that there is substantial variation in GVC participation across economies and sectors, and importantly, over time. For policymakers aiming to raise their economies' level of trade integration, this demonstrates that it is possible for economies to raise GVC participation substantially over a decade or two. Given these stylized facts, and the importance of global production networks as an avenue for economies to participate in the global economy, more comprehensive and in-depth exploration of various factors that determine GVC participation is required. Future editions of *Key Indicators* will delve more deeply into this issue.

References

Asian Development Bank. *Key Indicators for Asia and the Pacific*. Manila (3 years: 2015–2017).

Asian Development Bank. 2000, 2010—2017. Multiregion Input-Output Tables.

R. Koopman, Z. Wang, and S.J. Wei. 2014. "Tracing Value-Added and Double-Counting in Gross Exports," *American Economic Review*, Vol. 104, No. 2 (February), pp. 459-94.

Z. Wang, S.J. Wei, and K. Zhu. 2018. *Quantifying international production sharing at the bilateral and sector levels* (No. w19677). National Bureau of Economic Research.

Table 3.1.1: Definitions of Global Value Chains Terms and Indicators

Indicator	Definition
Domestic Value Added (DVA)	Domestic inputs of goods and services in the overall exports of an economy.
Domestic Value Added Absorbed Abroad (VAX_G)	All domestic value added embodied in the gross exports and ultimately absorbed abroad.
Domestic Value Added First Exported then Returned Home (RDV_B)	Domestic value added that are exported first, but then return to the home economy for domestic consumption. This would happen, for example, when the Philippines export electronic parts to the PRC for final assembly of laptops, which then return to the Philippines for final consumption.
Foreign Value Added (FVA)	Imported inputs of goods and services in the overall exports of an economy.
Global Value Chains (GVCs)	A network of interlinked stages of production for goods and services that straddles international borders. Typically, a GVC involves combining imported and domestically produced goods and services into products that are then exported for use as intermediates in the subsequent stage of production or as final consumption products.
GVC participation	There are various ways to measure economies' participation in GVCs. A simple metric is the share of foreign value added in total exports. It reflects the extent to which an economy uses foreign inputs in producing for exports. A more rigorous measure is Vertical Specialization (VS), which is the share of foreign value added and pure double counted terms in total exports.
Pure Double-Counted Terms (PDC)	In a GVC, some goods or services may cross the same national border for three or more times.
Revealed Comparative Advantage (RCA)	It is an index, introduced by Bela Balassa, to calculate the relative advantage an economy has in the export of any given good or service. An economy is said to have an RCA in a product if it exports more than its "fair share", or a share that is equal to or greater than the share of total world trade that the product represents.
Value Added Exports by Forward Industrial Linkages (VAX_F)	Domestic value added that is originated from a particular sector and ultimately absorbed abroad via the exports of all sectors in the source economy. For example, besides direct export, the value added of German business services sector may be exported as an input to German automobiles. This indicator is useful in understanding the contribution of a given sector to the economy's aggregate exports.
Value Added Exports by Backward Industrial Linkages (VAX_B)	Value added that is originated from all domestic sectors and ultimately absorbed abroad via the export of a particular sector in the source economy. For example, the domestic value added of German automobile exports includes that of all German sectors (e.g., business service, computers) used as inputs.

Source: Asian Development Bank. 2015. *Key Indicators for Asia and the Pacific 2015.* https://www.adb.org/publications/key-indicators-asia-and-pacific-2015

Table 3.1.2: Sector Aggregation

Aggregate Economic Sectors	Industry Sectors used by the World Input-Output Database
Primary Sector	Consists of the sectors Agriculture, Hunting, Forestry, and Fishing; Mining and Quarrying.
Low-Technology Sector	Consists of the sectors Food, Beverages, and Tobacco; Textiles and Textile Products; Leather, Leather Products, and Footwear; Wood and Products of Wood and Cork; Pulp, Paper, Paper Products, Printing, and Publishing; Rubber and Plastics; Manufacturing, NEC; Recycling; Electricity, Gas, and Water Supply; Construction.
High- and Medium-Technology Sector	Consists of the sectors Coke, Refined Petroleum, and Nuclear Fuel; Chemicals and Chemical Products; Other Non-Metallic Mineral; Basic Metals and Fabricated Metals; Machinery, NEC; Electrical and Optical Equipment; Transport Equipment.
Business Services Sector	Consists of the sectors Sale, Maintenance, and Repair of Motor Vehicles and Motorcycles; Retail Trade, Except of Motor Vehicles and Motorcycles; Repair of Household Goods; Hotels and Restaurants; Inland Transport; Water Transport; Air Transport; Other Supporting and Auxiliary Transport Activities; Activities of Travel Agencies; Post and Telecommunications; Financial Intermediation; Real Estate Activities; Renting of Machinery and Equipment; Other Business Activities.
Personal Services Sector	Consists of the sectors Public Administration and Defense; Compulsory Social Security; Education; Health and Social Work; Other Community, Social, and Personal Services; Private Households with Employed persons.

Source: Asian Development Bank. 2015. *Key Indicators for Asia and the Pacific 2015.* https://www.adb.org/publications/key-indicators-asia-and-pacific-2015

ADB Regional Member	Exports ($ million)	VAX_G	RDV_B	FVA	PDC
		(% share in exports)			
Bangladesh					
2010	331	94.02	0.06	4.83	1.09
2017	464	94.07	0.06	4.91	0.96
Bhutan					
2010	74	93.74	0.02	5.67	0.58
2017	104	91.82	0.02	7.41	0.75
Brunei Darussalam					
2010	4,845	93.03	0.00	4.74	2.23
2017	3,012	91.58	0.01	5.39	3.02
Cambodia					
2010	221	89.90	0.18	6.98	2.94
2017	1,002	88.87	0.21	7.32	3.60
China, People's Republic of					
2010	22,609	87.39	2.61	6.86	3.14
2017	24,181	89.58	3.29	4.67	2.45
Fiji					
2010	86	72.61	0.01	24.06	3.33
2017	168	74.96	0.01	21.84	3.19
Hong Kong, China					
2010	88	49.14	0.16	37.79	12.91
2017	125	63.20	0.26	28.26	8.29
India					
2010	24,905	94.34	0.75	3.51	1.40
2017	23,371	93.40	0.88	3.96	1.76
Indonesia					
2010	48,635	92.21	1.12	3.73	2.94
2017	48,489	92.96	1.27	3.18	2.59
Japan					
2010	2,588	66.03	1.59	20.94	11.44
2017	3,601	61.42	1.43	24.49	12.67
Kazakhstan					
2010	35,319	89.36	0.12	6.52	4.00
2017	20,223	91.43	0.09	5.13	3.34
Korea, Republic of					
2010	776	83.03	0.30	14.59	2.08
2017	933	83.42	0.70	12.34	3.53
Kyrgyz Republic					
2010	718	69.47	0.02	22.85	7.66
2017	406	77.43	0.10	17.66	4.82
Lao People's Democratic Republic					
2010	909	84.21	0.01	10.92	4.86
2017	2,471	91.81	0.05	6.16	1.99
Malaysia					
2010	13,156	91.40	0.33	5.57	2.70
2017	13,995	89.43	0.35	7.31	2.92

Table 3.2.1a: Value-Added Decomposition of Exports—Primary Sector

continued on next page

Table 3.2.1a: continued

ADB Regional Member	Exports ($ million)	VAX_G	RDV_B	FVA	PDC
Table 3.2.1a: Value-Added Decomposition of Exports—Primary Sector					
		(% share in exports)			
Maldives					
2010	20	54.95	0.00	38.75	6.30
2017	32	58.10	0.00	35.22	6.68
Mongolia					
2010	2,098	75.06	0.01	17.95	6.98
2017	4,524	76.41	0.01	17.52	6.05
Nepal					
2010	79	92.00	0.05	7.61	0.34
2017	60	91.37	0.06	8.14	0.42
Pakistan					
2010	1,534	96.58	0.08	2.75	0.59
2017	2,213	96.92	0.10	2.44	0.54
Philippines					
2010	1,265	91.61	0.23	6.16	2.00
2017	1,618	91.05	0.27	6.46	2.22
Singapore					
2010	60	67.28	0.15	24.97	7.59
2017	46	66.76	0.09	26.36	6.78
Sri Lanka					
2010	379	88.25	0.04	8.92	2.78
2017	840	89.52	0.04	8.78	1.66
Taipei,China					
2010	1,652	74.33	0.12	22.35	3.20
2017	1,895	75.89	0.14	19.80	4.17
Thailand					
2010	4,914	86.61	0.30	9.79	3.30
2017	10,886	88.22	0.24	8.91	2.63
Viet Nam					
2010	10,056	66.04	0.20	25.39	8.38
2017	19,987	63.81	0.19	27.37	8.63

0.00 = magnitude is less than half of unit employed, $ = United States dollars, FVA = foreign value-added, PDC = pure double counted terms, RDV_B = domestic value-added first exported then returned home, VAX_G = domestic value-added absorbed abroad.

Source: ADB Multi Region Input–Output Tables Database.

Table 3.2.1b: Value-Added Decomposition of Exports—Low-Technology Manufacturing Sector					
ADB Regional Member	**Exports**	**VAX_G**	**RDV_B**	**FVA**	**PDC**
	($ million)	(% share in exports)			
Bangladesh					
2010	13,022	85.18	0.01	13.36	1.45
2017	25,614	86.07	0.02	12.39	1.52
Bhutan					
2010	210	88.14	0.00	8.44	3.42
2017	281	88.93	0.00	8.28	2.79
Brunei Darussalam					
2010	28	61.04	0.01	35.58	3.38
2017	104	62.47	0.01	30.79	6.73
Cambodia					
2010	2,124	63.97	0.00	33.30	2.72
2017	5,287	64.67	0.01	33.24	2.09
China, People's Republic of					
2010	373,984	85.93	0.75	11.55	1.77
2017	538,939	89.85	1.16	7.58	1.40
Fiji					
2010	208	76.19	0.01	20.76	3.05
2017	347	77.57	0.00	19.32	3.11
Hong Kong, China					
2010	7,004	51.21	0.08	40.45	8.26
2017	7,591	51.69	0.09	40.72	7.51
India					
2010	50,210	81.07	0.43	15.52	2.99
2017	81,506	87.14	0.32	10.43	2.11
Indonesia					
2010	61,583	83.73	0.27	12.96	3.04
2017	96,989	83.90	0.23	12.87	3.00
Japan					
2010	48,927	85.06	1.62	8.84	4.48
2017	53,835	82.31	1.30	11.18	5.22
Kazakhstan					
2010	1,221	85.37	0.18	11.47	2.98
2017	1,072	86.90	0.35	10.58	2.17
Korea, Republic of					
2010	36,177	70.96	0.39	20.84	7.80
2017	49,251	70.50	0.57	20.10	8.83
Kyrgyz Republic					
2010	127	55.88	0.01	37.11	6.99
2017	329	61.78	0.08	31.62	6.53
Lao People's Democratic Republic					
2010	420	88.02	0.00	9.60	2.38
2017	2,719	88.60	0.02	8.87	2.51
Malaysia					
2010	39,595	71.25	0.12	22.22	6.41
2017	46,435	70.37	0.12	23.20	6.31

continued on next page

Table 3.2.1b: continued

Table 3.2.1b: Value-Added Decomposition of Exports—Low-Technology Manufacturing Sector					
ADB Regional Member	Exports	VAX_G	RDV_B	FVA	PDC
	($ million)	(% share in exports)			
Maldives					
2010	30	55.93	0.00	34.39	9.68
2017	158	58.24	0.00	37.40	4.36
Mongolia					
2010	126	76.77	0.01	18.64	4.58
2017	194	72.28	0.01	20.94	6.77
Nepal					
2010	222	75.09	0.02	22.98	1.91
2017	224	73.42	0.03	24.09	2.46
Pakistan					
2010	13,348	91.74	0.06	6.29	1.91
2017	14,582	92.53	0.10	5.76	1.61
Philippines					
2010	10,611	85.90	0.07	12.05	1.98
2017	14,420	85.32	0.11	12.44	2.13
Singapore					
2010	8,486	50.17	0.09	40.50	9.24
2017	9,851	55.43	0.08	36.72	7.77
Sri Lanka					
2010	5,783	78.47	0.01	18.84	2.67
2017	7,316	84.07	0.01	14.21	1.70
Taipei,China					
2010	22,044	57.30	0.14	30.65	11.91
2017	25,488	61.55	0.14	28.04	10.27
Thailand					
2010	32,266	73.88	0.14	21.40	4.57
2017	48,692	78.23	0.14	17.25	4.39
Viet Nam					
2010	30,398	64.91	0.03	31.15	3.91
2017	82,026	60.54	0.05	34.25	5.16

0.00 = magnitude is less than half of unit employed, $ = United States dollars, FVA = foreign value-added, PDC = pure double counted terms, RDV_B = domestic value-added first exported then returned home, VAX_G = domestic value-added absorbed abroad.

Source: ADB Multi Region Input–Output Tables Database.

ADB Regional Member	Exports ($ million)	VAX_G	RDV_B	FVA	PDC
		(% share in exports)			
Bangladesh					
2010	268	88.11	0.05	10.84	1.00
2017	600	89.18	0.04	10.19	0.60
Bhutan					
2010	104	78.82	0.02	19.64	1.52
2017	99	77.88	0.02	20.52	1.58
Brunei Darussalam					
2010	3,483	94.12	0.01	3.94	1.93
2017	2,395	92.86	0.01	4.85	2.29
Cambodia					
2010	26	63.79	0.01	32.74	3.46
2017	94	68.83	0.06	25.42	5.68
China, People's Republic of					
2010	1,012,325	73.05	2.28	18.72	5.96
2017	1,395,964	79.66	2.97	12.77	4.61
Fiji					
2010	24	62.79	0.01	32.28	4.92
2017	44	64.27	0.00	31.51	4.22
Hong Kong, China					
2010	9,308	21.00	0.03	57.74	21.23
2017	10,775	22.00	0.03	58.85	19.12
India					
2010	100,794	64.84	0.57	23.72	10.88
2017	159,752	67.23	0.49	22.12	10.15
Indonesia					
2010	58,388	77.47	0.46	15.84	6.23
2017	75,721	78.41	0.46	14.96	6.17
Japan					
2010	591,966	80.66	1.21	12.68	5.45
2017	644,100	76.03	0.98	16.36	6.63
Kazakhstan					
2010	12,533	89.22	0.19	6.69	3.90
2017	8,072	92.31	0.22	4.26	3.21
Korea, Republic of					
2010	427,863	61.37	0.33	28.55	9.74
2017	558,619	60.67	0.38	28.39	10.56
Kyrgyz Republic					
2010	654	75.81	0.01	15.90	8.29
2017	1,022	73.16	0.02	19.36	7.46
Lao People's Democratic Republic					
2010	15	46.10	0.01	48.61	5.28
2017	30	75.14	0.08	16.44	8.34
Malaysia					
2010	71,360	60.25	0.22	26.87	12.66
2017	71,743	61.34	0.33	24.27	14.07

Table 3.2.1c: Value-Added Decomposition of Exports—Medium- and High-Technology Manufacturing Sector

continued on next page

Table 3.2.1c: continued

Table 3.2.1c: Value-Added Decomposition of Exports—Medium- and High-Technology Manufacturing Sector					
ADB Regional Member	**Exports**	**VAX_G**	**RDV_B**	**FVA**	**PDC**
	($ million)	(% share in exports)			
Maldives					
2010	1	61.24	0.01	31.01	7.75
2017	4	68.11	0.00	27.98	3.91
Mongolia					
2010	58	65.36	0.01	25.04	9.59
2017	122	74.92	0.01	18.93	6.15
Nepal					
2010	83	60.26	0.09	34.75	4.91
2017	90	59.02	0.11	36.58	4.28
Pakistan					
2010	1,352	78.34	0.07	17.99	3.60
2017	1,658	80.31	0.12	16.13	3.45
Philippines					
2010	21,598	62.82	0.19	22.34	14.64
2017	25,201	51.88	0.20	29.81	18.10
Singapore					
2010	139,236	34.38	0.12	45.07	20.43
2017	163,847	35.55	0.11	46.64	17.70
Sri Lanka					
2010	899	58.87	0.02	32.85	8.25
2017	509	54.21	0.03	37.82	7.94
Taipei,China					
2010	240,938	51.31	0.22	31.57	16.89
2017	267,892	55.93	0.23	28.31	15.54
Thailand					
2010	79,186	55.47	0.26	31.88	12.39
2017	110,470	55.58	0.24	31.96	12.22
Viet Nam					
2010	11,609	49.06	0.08	35.35	15.50
2017	35,976	44.35	0.12	36.48	19.05

0.00 = magnitude is less than half of unit employed, $ = United States dollars, FVA = foreign value-added, PDC = pure double counted terms, RDV_B = domestic value-added first exported then returned home, VAX_G = domestic value-added absorbed abroad.

Source: ADB Multi Region Input–Output Tables Database.

Table 3.2.1d: Value-Added Decomposition of Exports—Business Services Sector					
ADB Regional Member	**Exports**	**VAX_G**	**RDV_B**	**FVA**	**PDC**
	($ million)	(% share in exports)			
Bangladesh					
2010	1,577	96.99	0.05	2.13	0.82
2017	2,012	97.30	0.10	1.87	0.73
Bhutan					
2010	123	74.94	0.00	20.31	4.75
2017	225	77.46	0.01	17.40	5.13
Brunei Darussalam					
2010	613	77.94	0.01	16.44	5.61
2017	446	74.63	0.01	18.46	6.89
Cambodia					
2010	1,598	81.76	0.01	14.35	3.88
2017	2,927	80.27	0.01	15.55	4.17
China, People's Republic of					
2010	276,698	86.97	2.65	7.11	3.26
2017	362,212	90.37	3.19	4.37	2.07
Fiji					
2010	824	70.29	0.01	25.01	4.69
2017	1,269	76.96	0.01	18.78	4.25
Hong Kong, China					
2010	125,939	74.94	0.17	20.14	4.75
2017	172,005	76.78	0.18	19.31	3.73
India					
2010	128,581	88.18	0.94	8.01	2.87
2017	107,667	94.50	0.63	3.75	1.12
Indonesia					
2010	12,906	88.56	0.32	8.32	2.80
2017	12,573	91.08	0.31	6.60	2.01
Japan					
2010	188,197	90.10	1.24	6.18	2.49
2017	155,946	91.51	0.90	5.32	2.26
Kazakhstan					
2010	13,190	91.43	0.32	6.46	1.80
2017	12,611	92.12	0.37	5.85	1.66
Korea, Republic of					
2010	50,285	79.58	0.46	14.68	5.27
2017	95,041	83.61	0.51	11.74	4.15
Kyrgyz Republic					
2010	217	70.74	0.01	22.37	6.87
2017	622	69.13	0.02	23.03	7.82
Lao People's Democratic Republic					
2010	191	80.65	0.01	13.81	5.52
2017	759	85.81	0.02	10.46	3.72
Malaysia					
2010	35,348	82.77	0.13	13.20	3.89
2017	32,674	80.50	0.17	14.39	4.95

continued on next page

Table 3.2.1d: continued

ADB Regional Member	Table 3.2.1d: Value-Added Decomposition of Exports—Business Services Sector				
	Exports	VAX_G	RDV_B	FVA	PDC
	($ million)	(% share in exports)			
Maldives					
2010	1,709	69.51	0.00	24.75	5.74
2017	3,012	64.19	0.00	28.29	7.52
Mongolia					
2010	668	78.67	0.01	16.03	5.29
2017	1,012	81.11	0.03	14.28	4.58
Nepal					
2010	355	82.94	0.03	13.95	3.09
2017	415	78.94	0.04	17.08	3.94
Pakistan					
2010	3,963	93.49	0.07	5.21	1.23
2017	5,377	94.08	0.12	4.62	1.18
Philippines					
2010	18,373	92.21	0.11	5.95	1.72
2017	31,645	90.95	0.15	6.79	2.11
Singapore					
2010	135,393	58.82	0.11	29.05	12.02
2017	200,924	55.45	0.13	33.23	11.19
Sri Lanka					
2010	3,182	85.62	0.03	11.58	2.77
2017	6,521	89.24	0.03	8.58	2.15
Taipei,China					
2010	49,626	77.90	0.29	15.51	6.30
2017	76,514	79.88	0.27	14.38	5.47
Thailand					
2010	31,850	80.21	0.20	15.42	4.16
2017	88,998	85.31	0.15	11.79	2.76
Viet Nam					
2010	10,332	73.59	0.06	22.13	4.22
2017	26,671	74.20	0.09	21.12	4.59

0.00 = magnitude is less than half of unit employed, $ = United States dollars, FVA = foreign value-added, PDC = pure double counted terms, RDV_B = domestic value-added first exported then returned home, VAX_G = domestic value-added absorbed abroad.

Source: ADB Multi Region Input–Output Tables Database.

Table 3.2.1e: Value-Added Decomposition of Exports—Personal Services Sector					
ADB Regional Member	**Exports**	**VAX_G**	**RDV_B**	**FVA**	**PDC**
	($ million)	(% share in exports)			
Bangladesh					
2010	393	97.88	0.03	1.69	0.39
2017	2,045	97.80	0.05	1.66	0.49
Bhutan					
2010	9	87.14	0.00	11.19	1.67
2017	28	83.43	0.00	14.55	2.02
Brunei Darussalam					
2010	31	82.04	0.01	13.82	4.14
2017	56	83.92	0.00	15.09	0.99
Cambodia					
2010	71	80.12	0.01	14.63	5.24
2017	109	80.33	0.02	15.67	3.98
China, People's Republic of					
2010	12,136	88.48	0.86	8.95	1.71
2017	14,606	92.61	1.11	5.18	1.11
Fiji					
2010	18	85.63	0.01	12.06	2.30
2017	39	88.15	0.00	11.49	0.36
Hong Kong, China					
2010	1,094	85.96	0.13	10.87	3.03
2017	1,200	87.89	0.16	9.31	2.63
India					
2010	10,837	94.06	0.01	5.90	0.03
2017	11,295	97.00	0.01	2.96	0.03
Indonesia					
2010	2,009	90.25	0.20	8.12	1.44
2017	2,047	92.88	0.17	6.09	0.86
Japan					
2010	3,677	94.24	0.66	4.18	0.92
2017	3,453	93.75	0.47	4.98	0.80
Kazakhstan					
2010	360	88.15	0.02	10.94	0.90
2017	251	94.01	0.04	5.47	0.48
Korea, Republic of					
2010	3,802	84.51	0.48	11.74	3.26
2017	4,578	82.82	0.39	13.77	3.02
Kyrgyz Republic					
2010	59	79.10	0.00	16.68	4.21
2017	335	83.32	0.00	13.73	2.94
Lao People's Democratic Republic					
2010	13	85.88	0.00	13.75	0.36
2017	168	90.89	0.01	7.50	1.60
Malaysia					
2010	2,468	83.13	0.08	14.67	2.12
2017	2,437	84.68	0.08	13.48	1.76

continued on next page

Table 3.2.1e: continued

Table 3.2.1e: Value-Added Decomposition of Exports—Personal Services Sector					
ADB Regional Member	Exports ($ million)	VAX_G	RDV_B	FVA	PDC
		(% share in exports)			
Maldives					
2010	31	73.44	0.00	19.23	7.32
2017	105	76.38	0.00	17.92	5.70
Mongolia					
2010	6	84.83	0.00	13.30	1.87
2017	42	82.12	0.01	15.74	2.14
Nepal					
2010	328	90.93	0.04	7.01	2.03
2017	474	91.77	0.05	6.70	1.47
Pakistan					
2010	902	95.38	0.03	4.24	0.35
2017	1,311	95.56	0.04	4.06	0.33
Philippines					
2010	695	90.83	0.06	6.98	2.12
2017	1,418	89.11	0.12	8.00	2.77
Singapore					
2010	1,003	79.89	0.15	13.59	6.37
2017	1,634	80.54	0.16	13.54	5.77
Sri Lanka					
2010	2	90.13	0.04	7.99	1.83
2017	560	88.82	0.01	9.71	1.46
Taipei,China					
2010	1,314	84.28	0.07	14.90	0.75
2017	1,784	79.82	0.08	18.61	1.48
Thailand					
2010	4,016	84.38	0.11	13.88	1.62
2017	8,275	88.12	0.10	10.65	1.14
Viet Nam					
2010	580	78.05	0.02	21.03	0.90
2017	1,840	76.38	0.03	22.53	1.06

0.00 = magnitude is less than half of unit employed, $ = United States dollars, FVA = foreign value-added, PDC = pure double counted terms, RDV_B = domestic value-added first exported then returned home, VAX_G = domestic value-added absorbed abroad.

Source: ADB Multi Region Input–Output Tables Database.

ADB Regional Member	Exports ($ million)	VAX_G	RDV_B	FVA	PDC
		(% share in exports)			
Bangladesh					
2010	15,590	86.93	0.02	11.71	1.34
2017	30,734	87.77	0.03	10.83	1.37
Bhutan					
2010	521	83.92	0.01	13.15	2.92
2017	736	84.14	0.01	12.83	3.02
Brunei Darussalam					
2010	9,000	92.28	0.01	5.36	2.35
2017	6,012	90.25	0.01	6.68	3.06
Cambodia					
2010	4,041	72.71	0.01	24.03	3.24
2017	9,419	72.31	0.03	24.70	2.95
China, People's Republic of					
2010	1,697,752	78.46	2.00	15.02	4.53
2017	2,335,901	83.85	2.58	10.14	3.43
Fiji					
2010	1,160	71.60	0.01	24.13	4.27
2017	1,866	76.83	0.01	19.30	3.86
Hong Kong, China					
2010	143,434	70.35	0.16	23.52	5.98
2017	191,697	72.77	0.17	22.32	4.74
India					
2010	315,328	80.28	0.69	13.80	5.23
2017	383,592	81.59	0.50	12.81	5.10
Indonesia					
2010	183,521	84.40	0.56	11.05	4.00
2017	235,820	84.46	0.52	11.15	3.86
Japan					
2010	835,356	83.06	1.24	10.98	4.72
2017	860,935	79.24	0.98	14.02	5.76
Kazakhstan					
2010	62,624	89.68	0.18	6.66	3.48
2017	42,229	91.71	0.21	5.32	2.77
Korea, Republic of					
2010	518,902	64.01	0.35	26.53	9.11
2017	708,423	64.61	0.41	25.46	9.52
Kyrgyz Republic					
2010	1,774	71.31	0.01	21.05	7.63
2017	2,713	72.75	0.04	20.74	6.48
Lao People's Democratic Republic					
2010	1,548	84.45	0.01	11.30	4.24
2017	6,146	89.54	0.03	7.97	2.45
Malaysia					
2010	161,928	70.74	0.18	20.83	8.25
2017	167,285	70.28	0.24	20.47	9.02

Table 3.2.1f: Value-Added Decomposition of Exports—All Sectors

continued on next page

Table 3.2.1f: continued

Table 3.2.1f: Value-Added Decomposition of Exports—All Sectors					
ADB Regional Member	**Exports**	**VAX_G**	**RDV_B**	**FVA**	**PDC**
	($ million)	(% share in exports)			
Maldives					
2010	1,790	69.19	0.00	24.97	5.84
2017	3,310	64.24	0.00	28.46	7.30
Mongolia					
2010	2,955	75.77	0.01	17.68	6.54
2017	5,894	77.09	0.02	17.10	5.79
Nepal					
2010	1,067	82.66	0.03	14.85	2.46
2017	1,263	81.96	0.05	15.38	2.61
Pakistan					
2010	21,099	91.72	0.06	6.49	1.73
2017	25,141	92.60	0.10	5.82	1.48
Philippines					
2010	52,542	78.82	0.14	13.94	7.10
2017	74,301	76.57	0.16	15.71	7.55
Singapore					
2010	284,178	46.66	0.11	37.18	16.04
2017	376,303	46.90	0.12	39.07	13.91
Sri Lanka					
2010	10,245	79.34	0.02	17.45	3.20
2017	15,747	85.71	0.02	12.19	2.08
Taipei,China					
2010	315,574	56.17	0.23	28.86	14.74
2017	373,573	61.43	0.23	25.35	12.99
Thailand					
2010	152,231	66.32	0.22	25.03	8.44
2017	267,321	71.94	0.19	20.97	6.91
Viet Nam					
2010	62,975	63.72	0.07	29.43	6.78
2017	166,500	59.80	0.09	31.67	8.44

0.00 = magnitude is less than half of unit employed, $ = United States dollars, FVA = foreign value-added, PDC = pure double counted terms, RDV_B = domestic value-added first exported then returned home, VAX_G = domestic value-added absorbed abroad.

Source: ADB Multi Region Input–Output Tables Database.

ADB Regional Member	VAX_G	DVA_B	DVA_F	VAX_B	VAX_F
			Value-Added Export Measure to Gross Exports Ratio (%)		
Bangladesh					
2010	94.02	94.10	513.18	94.02	513.06
2017	94.07	94.15	584.52	94.07	584.33
Bhutan					
2010	93.74	93.75	99.96	93.74	99.94
2017	91.82	91.84	100.65	91.82	100.63
Brunei Darussalam					
2010	93.03	93.03	122.00	93.03	121.99
2017	91.58	91.58	122.38	91.58	122.37
Cambodia					
2010	89.90	90.09	234.25	89.90	234.07
2017	88.87	89.10	129.53	88.87	129.32
China, People's Republic of					
2010	87.39	90.36	827.30	87.39	808.62
2017	89.58	93.13	1,042.87	89.58	1,012.96
Fiji					
2010	72.61	72.61	116.91	72.61	116.90
2017	74.96	74.97	98.72	74.96	98.71
Hong Kong, China					
2010	49.14	49.29	39.26	49.14	39.14
2017	63.20	63.46	58.94	63.20	58.71
India					
2010	94.34	95.13	157.06	94.34	155.86
2017	93.40	94.33	178.28	93.40	177.02
Indonesia					
2010	92.21	93.38	132.18	92.21	130.96
2017	92.96	94.29	149.65	92.96	148.25
Japan					
2010	66.03	67.69	238.89	66.03	234.63
2017	61.42	62.90	185.95	61.42	182.89
Kazakhstan					
2010	89.36	89.48	79.59	89.36	79.47
2017	91.43	91.53	79.91	91.43	79.81
Korea, Republic of					
2010	83.03	83.35	610.00	83.03	607.09
2017	83.42	84.23	679.62	83.42	675.57
Kyrgyz Republic					
2010	69.47	69.48	63.26	69.47	63.24
2017	77.43	77.52	63.13	77.43	63.06
Lao People's Democratic Republic					
2010	84.21	84.21	80.91	84.21	80.90
2017	91.81	91.85	96.80	91.81	96.75
Malaysia					
2010	91.40	91.81	244.66	91.40	243.97
2017	89.43	89.83	230.37	89.43	229.65

Table 3.2.2a: Value-Added Exports by Various Measures—Primary Sector

continued on next page

Table 3.2.2a: continued

Table 3.2.2a: Value-Added Exports by Various Measures—Primary Sector					
ADB Regional Member	**VAX_G**	**DVA_B**	**DVA_F**	**VAX_B**	**VAX_F**
	Value-Added Export Measure to Gross Exports Ratio (%)				
Maldives					
2010	54.95	54.95	465.29	54.95	465.27
2017	58.10	58.11	279.09	58.10	279.09
Mongolia					
2010	75.06	75.07	63.74	75.06	63.73
2017	76.41	76.43	55.94	76.41	55.93
Nepal					
2010	92.00	92.05	166.10	92.00	166.03
2017	91.37	91.44	207.99	91.37	207.87
Pakistan					
2010	96.58	96.66	470.91	96.58	470.58
2017	96.92	97.02	380.44	96.92	380.03
Philippines					
2010	91.61	91.85	393.88	91.61	393.36
2017	91.05	91.33	365.94	91.05	365.33
Singapore					
2010	67.28	67.49	86.65	67.28	86.47
2017	66.76	66.87	73.40	66.76	73.29
Sri Lanka					
2010	88.25	88.30	220.22	88.25	220.15
2017	89.52	89.56	147.19	89.52	147.14
Taipei,China					
2010	74.33	74.42	112.77	74.33	112.52
2017	75.89	76.01	126.06	75.89	125.80
Thailand					
2010	86.61	86.93	202.69	86.61	202.16
2017	88.22	88.49	179.13	88.22	178.77
Viet Nam					
2010	66.04	66.29	102.68	66.04	102.49
2017	63.81	64.10	102.02	63.81	101.81

DVA_B = domestic value-added exports by backward industrial linkages, DVA_F = domestic value-added exports by forward industrial linkages, VAX_B = value-added exports by backward industrial linkages, VAX_F = value-added exports by forward industrial linkages, VAX_G = domestic value-added absorbed abroad.

Source: ADB Multi Region Input–Output Tables Database.

Table 3.2.2b: Value-Added Exports by Various Measures—Low-Technology Manufacturing Sector

ADB Regional Member	VAX_G	DVA_B	DVA_F	VAX_B	VAX_F
	Value-Added Export Measure to Gross Exports Ratio (%)				
Bangladesh					
2010	85.18	85.19	45.64	85.18	45.63
2017	86.07	86.09	48.36	86.07	48.35
Bhutan					
2010	88.14	88.14	98.35	88.14	98.34
2017	88.93	88.93	94.31	88.93	94.31
Brunei Darussalam					
2010	61.04	61.04	173.85	61.04	173.84
2017	62.47	62.48	58.44	62.47	58.43
Cambodia					
2010	63.97	63.97	54.16	63.97	54.16
2017	64.67	64.67	49.98	64.67	49.97
China, People's Republic of					
2010	85.93	86.59	64.11	85.93	63.11
2017	89.85	90.96	65.70	89.85	64.37
Fiji					
2010	76.19	76.19	62.15	76.19	62.15
2017	77.57	77.57	60.26	77.57	60.26
Hong Kong, China					
2010	51.21	51.25	52.14	51.21	52.04
2017	51.69	51.73	49.63	51.69	49.53
India					
2010	81.07	81.43	48.65	81.07	48.31
2017	87.14	87.44	45.29	87.14	45.06
Indonesia					
2010	83.73	83.97	48.78	83.73	48.62
2017	83.90	84.11	48.65	83.90	48.51
Japan					
2010	85.06	86.77	142.30	85.06	139.96
2017	82.31	83.68	122.16	82.31	120.48
Kazakhstan					
2010	85.37	85.54	126.99	85.37	126.73
2017	86.90	87.23	114.70	86.90	114.35
Korea, Republic of					
2010	70.96	71.40	81.58	70.96	81.12
2017	70.50	71.11	81.25	70.50	80.67
Kyrgyz Republic					
2010	55.88	55.90	50.72	55.88	50.71
2017	61.78	61.86	53.27	61.78	53.21
Lao People's Democratic Republic					
2010	88.02	88.02	72.05	88.02	72.05
2017	88.60	88.62	74.05	88.60	74.03
Malaysia					
2010	71.25	71.36	32.45	71.25	32.38
2017	70.37	70.47	33.38	70.37	33.31

continued on next page

Table 3.2.2b: continued

Table 3.2.2b: Value-Added Exports by Various Measures—Low-Technology Manufacturing Sector					
ADB Regional Member	**VAX_G**	**DVA_B**	**DVA_F**	**VAX_B**	**VAX_F**
	Value-Added Export Measure to Gross Exports Ratio (%)				
Maldives					
2010	55.93	55.93	267.37	55.93	267.36
2017	58.24	58.24	211.97	58.24	211.97
Mongolia					
2010	76.77	76.77	92.83	76.77	92.82
2017	72.28	72.29	153.07	72.28	153.04
Nepal					
2010	75.09	75.11	52.48	75.09	52.46
2017	73.42	73.45	50.63	73.42	50.60
Pakistan					
2010	91.74	91.80	33.05	91.74	33.03
2017	92.53	92.63	33.74	92.53	33.70
Philippines					
2010	85.90	85.96	67.06	85.90	66.99
2017	85.32	85.42	67.61	85.32	67.52
Singapore					
2010	50.17	50.24	69.95	50.17	69.78
2017	55.43	55.47	67.71	55.43	67.58
Sri Lanka					
2010	78.47	78.49	55.63	78.47	55.62
2017	84.07	84.08	65.62	84.07	65.61
Taipei,China					
2010	57.30	57.44	60.27	57.30	60.09
2017	61.55	61.67	65.67	61.55	65.49
Thailand					
2010	73.88	74.00	58.76	73.88	58.61
2017	78.23	78.35	63.27	78.23	63.13
Viet Nam					
2010	64.91	64.93	42.17	64.91	42.15
2017	60.54	60.56	40.32	60.54	40.29

DVA_B = domestic value-added exports by backward industrial linkages, DVA_F = domestic value-added exports by forward industrial linkages, VAX_B = value-added exports by backward industrial linkages, VAX_F = value-added exports by forward industrial linkages, VAX_G = domestic value-added absorbed abroad.

Source: ADB Multi Region Input–Output Tables Database.

ADB Regional Member	VAX_G	DVA_B	DVA_F	VAX_B	VAX_F
	Value-Added Export Measure to Gross Exports Ratio (%)				
Bangladesh					
2010	88.11	88.16	139.26	88.11	139.21
2017	89.18	89.22	134.48	89.18	134.43
Bhutan					
2010	78.82	78.84	34.37	78.82	34.37
2017	77.88	77.91	42.73	77.88	42.72
Brunei Darussalam					
2010	94.12	94.13	48.82	94.12	48.81
2017	92.86	92.87	47.83	92.86	47.82
Cambodia					
2010	63.79	63.80	106.83	63.79	106.81
2017	68.83	68.90	94.74	68.83	94.67
China, People's Republic of					
2010	73.05	75.21	47.59	73.05	46.24
2017	79.66	82.56	45.47	79.66	43.93
Fiji					
2010	62.79	62.79	84.17	62.79	84.16
2017	64.27	64.27	83.49	64.27	83.49
Hong Kong, China					
2010	21.00	20.97	5.77	21.00	5.76
2017	22.00	21.97	4.66	22.00	4.65
India					
2010	64.84	65.39	41.82	64.84	41.46
2017	67.23	67.71	37.59	67.23	37.33
Indonesia					
2010	77.47	77.91	50.84	77.47	50.55
2017	78.41	78.86	48.45	78.41	48.19
Japan					
2010	80.66	81.84	53.75	80.66	52.98
2017	76.03	76.99	48.66	76.03	48.05
Kazakhstan					
2010	89.22	89.40	63.65	89.22	63.52
2017	92.31	92.53	61.49	92.31	61.36
Korea, Republic of					
2010	61.37	61.69	44.85	61.37	44.60
2017	60.67	61.03	44.46	60.67	44.18
Kyrgyz Republic					
2010	75.81	75.82	70.69	75.81	70.68
2017	73.16	73.18	67.24	73.16	67.22
Lao People's Democratic Republic					
2010	46.10	46.10	117.26	46.10	117.25
2017	75.14	75.22	246.04	75.14	245.93
Malaysia					
2010	60.25	60.46	38.90	60.25	38.76
2017	61.34	61.66	39.63	61.34	39.42

Table 3.2.2c: Value-Added Exports by Various Measures—Medium- and High-Technology Manufacturing Sector

continued on next page

Table 3.2.2c: continued

Table 3.2.2c: Value-Added Exports by Various Measures—Medium- and High-Technology Manufacturing Sector					
ADB Regional Member	**VAX_G**	**DVA_B**	**DVA_F**	**VAX_B**	**VAX_F**
	Value-Added Export Measure to Gross Exports Ratio (%)				
Maldives					
2010	61.24	61.25	481.84	61.24	481.82
2017	68.11	68.12	244.28	68.11	244.27
Mongolia					
2010	65.36	65.37	78.50	65.36	78.49
2017	74.92	74.93	90.08	74.92	90.07
Nepal					
2010	60.26	60.35	48.40	60.26	48.34
2017	59.02	59.13	50.85	59.02	50.77
Pakistan					
2010	78.34	78.41	68.13	78.34	68.08
2017	80.31	80.42	69.42	80.31	69.34
Philippines					
2010	62.82	63.01	37.63	62.82	37.52
2017	51.88	52.08	35.58	51.88	35.46
Singapore					
2010	34.38	34.45	27.42	34.38	27.33
2017	35.55	35.61	25.87	35.55	25.79
Sri Lanka					
2010	58.87	58.89	61.21	58.87	61.19
2017	54.21	54.24	86.72	54.21	86.70
Taipei,China					
2010	51.31	51.52	42.93	51.31	42.74
2017	55.93	56.15	49.53	55.93	49.32
Thailand					
2010	55.47	55.73	35.56	55.47	35.40
2017	55.58	55.82	35.07	55.58	34.93
Viet Nam					
2010	49.06	49.14	48.35	49.06	48.27
2017	44.35	44.47	44.13	44.35	44.03

DVA_B = domestic value-added exports by backward industrial linkages, DVA_F = domestic value-added exports by forward industrial linkages, VAX_B = value-added exports by backward industrial linkages, VAX_F = value-added exports by forward industrial linkages, VAX_G = domestic value-added absorbed abroad.

Source: ADB Multi Region Input–Output Tables Database.

ADB Regional Member	VAX_G	DVA_B	DVA_F	VAX_B	VAX_F
	Value-Added Export Measure to Gross Exports Ratio (%)				
Bangladesh					
2010	96.99	97.05	269.69	96.99	269.61
2017	97.30	97.41	373.13	97.30	372.96
Bhutan					
2010	74.94	74.94	90.23	74.94	90.23
2017	77.46	77.47	83.77	77.46	83.76
Brunei Darussalam					
2010	77.94	77.94	96.35	77.94	96.34
2017	74.63	74.64	104.44	74.63	104.43
Cambodia					
2010	81.76	81.77	73.44	81.76	73.43
2017	80.27	80.28	90.74	80.27	90.72
China, People's Republic of					
2010	86.97	90.13	155.69	86.97	151.48
2017	90.37	93.87	200.00	90.37	193.69
Fiji					
2010	70.29	70.30	67.76	70.29	67.76
2017	76.96	76.97	77.43	76.96	77.42
Hong Kong, China					
2010	74.94	75.12	74.07	74.94	73.90
2017	76.78	76.97	75.65	76.78	75.47
India					
2010	88.18	89.16	105.49	88.18	104.47
2017	94.50	95.16	148.73	94.50	147.81
Indonesia					
2010	88.56	88.88	226.59	88.56	225.47
2017	91.08	91.40	323.22	91.08	321.67
Japan					
2010	90.10	91.41	155.75	90.10	153.48
2017	91.51	92.47	183.64	91.51	181.52
Kazakhstan					
2010	91.43	91.75	139.86	91.43	139.48
2017	92.12	92.50	128.71	92.12	128.29
Korea, Republic of					
2010	79.58	80.17	193.78	79.58	192.72
2017	83.61	84.23	160.78	83.61	159.78
Kyrgyz Republic					
2010	70.74	70.76	114.64	70.74	114.62
2017	69.13	69.14	100.00	69.13	99.95
Lao People's Democratic Republic					
2010	80.65	80.66	127.36	80.65	127.35
2017	85.81	85.82	119.13	85.81	119.10
Malaysia					
2010	82.77	82.91	110.70	82.77	110.48
2017	80.50	80.67	119.66	80.50	119.33

Table 3.2.2d: Value-Added Exports by Various Measures—Business Services Sector

continued on next page

Table 3.2.2d: continued

Table 3.2.2d: Value-Added Exports by Various Measures—Business Services Sector					
ADB Regional Member	**VAX_G**	**DVA_B**	**DVA_F**	**VAX_B**	**VAX_F**
	Value-Added Export Measure to Gross Exports Ratio (%)				
Maldives					
2010	69.51	69.51	60.56	69.51	60.56
2017	64.19	64.19	51.65	64.19	51.65
Mongolia					
2010	78.67	78.68	105.77	78.67	105.75
2017	81.11	81.15	150.70	81.11	150.66
Nepal					
2010	82.94	82.96	101.79	82.94	101.75
2017	78.94	78.98	95.84	78.94	95.79
Pakistan					
2010	93.49	93.56	151.07	93.49	150.96
2017	94.08	94.20	142.00	94.08	141.82
Philippines					
2010	92.21	92.33	111.30	92.21	111.11
2017	90.95	91.11	97.44	90.95	97.24
Singapore					
2010	58.82	58.98	64.64	58.82	64.50
2017	55.45	55.62	62.64	55.45	62.49
Sri Lanka					
2010	85.62	85.65	106.68	85.62	106.65
2017	89.24	89.27	98.24	89.24	98.22
Taipei,China					
2010	77.90	78.25	112.14	77.90	111.72
2017	79.88	80.18	97.24	79.88	96.92
Thailand					
2010	80.21	80.42	128.16	80.21	127.77
2017	85.31	85.46	108.50	85.31	108.26
Viet Nam					
2010	73.59	73.65	105.64	73.59	105.55
2017	74.20	74.30	108.39	74.20	108.25

DVA_B = domestic value-added exports by backward industrial linkages, DVA_F = domestic value-added exports by forward industrial linkages, VAX_B = value-added exports by backward industrial linkages, VAX_F = value-added exports by forward industrial linkages, VAX_G = domestic value-added absorbed abroad.

Source: ADB Multi Region Input–Output Tables Database.

ADB Regional Member	VAX_G	DVA_B	DVA_F	VAX_B	VAX_F
Table 3.2.2e: Value-Added Exports by Various Measures—Personal Services Sector					
	Value-Added Export Measure to Gross Exports Ratio (%)				
Bangladesh					
2010	97.88	97.92	328.60	97.88	328.52
2017	97.80	97.85	174.83	97.80	174.76
Bhutan					
2010	87.14	87.14	103.45	87.14	103.44
2017	83.43	83.43	70.56	83.43	70.55
Brunei Darussalam					
2010	82.04	82.04	178.38	82.04	178.37
2017	83.92	83.92	123.82	83.92	123.81
Cambodia					
2010	80.12	80.13	96.19	80.12	96.18
2017	80.33	80.35	118.31	80.33	118.28
China, People's Republic of					
2010	88.48	89.32	218.04	88.48	213.17
2017	92.61	93.69	366.55	92.61	356.14
Fiji					
2010	85.63	85.64	123.08	85.63	123.07
2017	88.15	88.15	103.41	88.15	103.41
Hong Kong, China					
2010	85.96	86.12	330.89	85.96	330.23
2017	87.89	88.08	447.44	87.89	446.43
India					
2010	94.06	94.01	128.99	94.06	128.62
2017	97.00	96.99	142.78	97.00	142.43
Indonesia					
2010	90.25	90.43	131.78	90.25	131.28
2017	92.88	93.04	162.51	92.88	161.91
Japan					
2010	94.24	94.92	465.21	94.24	458.47
2017	93.75	94.23	532.08	93.75	525.65
Kazakhstan					
2010	88.15	88.14	51.73	88.15	51.71
2017	94.01	94.03	91.46	94.01	91.40
Korea, Republic of					
2010	84.51	85.10	273.41	84.51	271.85
2017	82.82	83.25	285.82	82.82	284.08
Kyrgyz Republic					
2010	79.10	79.10	61.38	79.10	61.38
2017	83.32	83.32	70.00	83.32	70.00
Lao People's Democratic Republic					
2010	85.88	85.88	65.70	85.88	65.70
2017	90.89	90.90	73.24	90.89	73.23
Malaysia					
2010	83.13	83.19	118.18	83.13	117.97
2017	84.68	84.74	110.36	84.68	110.11

continued on next page

Table 3.2.2e: continued

Table 3.2.2e: Value-Added Exports by Various Measures—Personal Services Sector					
ADB Regional Member	**VAX_G**	**DVA_B**	**DVA_F**	**VAX_B**	**VAX_F**
	Value-Added Export Measure to Gross Exports Ratio (%)				
Maldives					
2010	73.44	73.45	93.62	73.44	93.62
2017	76.38	76.38	131.05	76.38	131.04
Mongolia					
2010	84.83	84.84	596.36	84.83	596.29
2017	82.12	82.12	194.90	82.12	194.86
Nepal					
2010	90.93	90.96	71.12	90.93	71.09
2017	91.77	91.82	74.56	91.77	74.52
Pakistan					
2010	95.38	95.41	91.07	95.38	91.04
2017	95.56	95.60	90.17	95.56	90.12
Philippines					
2010	90.83	90.90	116.99	90.83	116.86
2017	89.11	89.24	108.74	89.11	108.57
Singapore					
2010	79.89	80.13	124.51	79.89	124.25
2017	80.54	80.76	120.82	80.54	120.56
Sri Lanka					
2010	90.13	90.17	5,570.73	90.13	5,569.25
2017	88.82	88.83	109.53	88.82	109.51
Taipei,China					
2010	84.28	84.30	284.11	84.28	283.25
2017	79.82	79.82	232.25	79.82	231.61
Thailand					
2010	84.38	84.48	84.47	84.38	84.31
2017	88.12	88.21	86.78	88.12	86.65
Viet Nam					
2010	78.05	78.06	85.86	78.05	85.81
2017	76.38	76.39	79.28	76.38	79.22

DVA_B = domestic value-added exports by backward industrial linkages, DVA_F = domestic value-added exports by forward industrial linkages, VAX_B = value-added exports by backward industrial linkages, VAX_F = value-added exports by forward industrial linkages, VAX_G = domestic value-added absorbed abroad.

Source: ADB Multi Region Input–Output Tables Database.

ADB Regional Member	VAX_G	DVA_B	DVA_F	VAX_B	VAX_F
Table 3.2.2f: Value-Added Exports by Various Measures—All Sectors					
	Value-Added Export Measure to Gross Exports Ratio (%)				
Bangladesh					
2010	86.93	86.95	86.95	86.93	86.93
2017	87.77	87.80	87.80	87.77	87.77
Bhutan					
2010	83.92	83.93	83.93	83.92	83.92
2017	84.14	84.15	84.15	84.14	84.14
Brunei Darussalam					
2010	92.28	92.29	92.29	92.28	92.28
2017	90.25	90.26	90.26	90.25	90.25
Cambodia					
2010	72.71	72.72	72.72	72.71	72.71
2017	72.31	72.34	72.34	72.31	72.31
China, People's Republic of					
2010	78.46	80.45	80.45	78.46	78.46
2017	83.85	86.43	86.43	83.85	83.85
Fiji					
2010	71.60	71.60	71.60	71.60	71.60
2017	76.83	76.83	76.83	76.83	76.83
Hong Kong, China					
2010	70.35	70.50	70.50	70.35	70.35
2017	72.77	72.94	72.94	72.77	72.77
India					
2010	80.28	80.97	80.97	80.28	80.28
2017	81.59	82.09	82.09	81.59	81.59
Indonesia					
2010	84.40	84.95	84.95	84.40	84.40
2017	84.46	84.98	84.98	84.46	84.46
Japan					
2010	83.06	84.30	84.30	83.06	83.06
2017	79.24	80.22	80.22	79.24	79.24
Kazakhstan					
2010	89.68	89.86	89.86	89.68	89.68
2017	91.71	91.91	91.91	91.71	91.71
Korea, Republic of					
2010	64.01	64.36	64.36	64.01	64.01
2017	64.61	65.02	65.02	64.61	64.61
Kyrgyz Republic					
2010	71.31	71.32	71.32	71.31	71.31
2017	72.75	72.79	72.79	72.75	72.75
Lao People's Democratic Republic					
2010	84.45	84.46	84.46	84.45	84.45
2017	89.54	89.57	89.57	89.54	89.54
Malaysia					
2010	70.74	70.92	70.92	70.74	70.74
2017	70.28	70.51	70.51	70.28	70.28

continued on next page

Table 3.2.2f: continued

Table 3.2.2f: Value-Added Exports by Various Measures—All Sectors					
ADB Regional Member	VAX_G	DVA_B	DVA_F	VAX_B	VAX_F
	Value-Added Export Measure to Gross Exports Ratio (%)				
Maldives					
2010	69.19	69.19	69.19	69.19	69.19
2017	64.24	64.24	64.24	64.24	64.24
Mongolia					
2010	75.77	75.79	75.79	75.77	75.77
2017	77.09	77.11	77.11	77.09	77.09
Nepal					
2010	82.66	82.70	82.70	82.66	82.66
2017	81.96	82.01	82.01	81.96	81.96
Pakistan					
2010	91.72	91.78	91.78	91.72	91.72
2017	92.60	92.70	92.70	92.60	92.60
Philippines					
2010	78.82	78.96	78.96	78.82	78.82
2017	76.57	76.74	76.74	76.57	76.57
Singapore					
2010	46.66	46.78	46.78	46.66	46.66
2017	46.90	47.01	47.01	46.90	46.90
Sri Lanka					
2010	79.34	79.36	79.36	79.34	79.34
2017	85.71	85.73	85.73	85.71	85.71
Taipei,China					
2010	56.17	56.39	56.39	56.17	56.17
2017	61.43	61.66	61.66	61.43	61.43
Thailand					
2010	66.32	66.53	66.53	66.32	66.32
2017	71.94	72.12	72.12	71.94	71.94
Viet Nam					
2010	63.72	63.79	63.79	63.72	63.72
2017	59.80	59.88	59.88	59.80	59.80

DVA_B = domestic value-added exports by backward industrial linkages, DVA_F = domestic value-added exports by forward industrial linkages, VAX_B = value-added exports by backward industrial linkages, VAX_F = value-added exports by forward industrial linkages, VAX_G = domestic value-added absorbed abroad.

Source: ADB Multi Region Input–Output Tables Database.

Table 3.2.3a: Revealed Comparative Advantage by Aggregate Sector (Traditional Method)		
ADB Regional Member	**2010**	**2017**
	(ratio)	
Bangladesh		
Business Services Sector	0.40	0.25
Low-Technology Manufacturing Sector	5.47	5.21
Medium- and High-Technology Manufacturing Sector	0.04	0.04
Personal Services Sector	1.32	3.46
Primary Sector	0.20	0.15
Bhutan		
Business Services Sector	0.94	1.17
Low-Technology Manufacturing Sector	2.65	2.38
Medium- and High-Technology Manufacturing Sector	0.43	0.29
Personal Services Sector	0.88	1.96
Primary Sector	1.30	1.43
Brunei Darussalam		
Business Services Sector	0.27	0.28
Low-Technology Manufacturing Sector	0.02	0.11
Medium- and High-Technology Manufacturing Sector	0.83	0.87
Personal Services Sector	0.18	0.48
Primary Sector	4.95	5.08
Cambodia		
Business Services Sector	1.57	1.19
Low-Technology Manufacturing Sector	3.44	3.51
Medium- and High-Technology Manufacturing Sector	0.01	0.02
Personal Services Sector	0.92	0.60
Primary Sector	0.50	1.08
China, People's Republic of		
Business Services Sector	0.65	0.59
Low-Technology Manufacturing Sector	1.44	1.44
Medium- and High-Technology Manufacturing Sector	1.27	1.30
Personal Services Sector	0.37	0.32
Primary Sector	0.12	0.10
Fiji		
Business Services Sector	2.83	2.59
Low-Technology Manufacturing Sector	1.17	1.16
Medium- and High-Technology Manufacturing Sector	0.04	0.05
Personal Services Sector	0.81	1.08
Primary Sector	0.68	0.91
Hong Kong, China		
Business Services Sector	3.49	3.42
Low-Technology Manufacturing Sector	0.32	0.25
Medium- and High-Technology Manufacturing Sector	0.14	0.12
Personal Services Sector	0.40	0.33
Primary Sector	0.01	0.01
India		
Business Services Sector	1.62	1.07
Low-Technology Manufacturing Sector	1.04	1.33
Medium- and High-Technology Manufacturing Sector	0.68	0.91
Personal Services Sector	1.80	1.53
Primary Sector	0.73	0.62
Indonesia		
Business Services Sector	0.28	0.20
Low-Technology Manufacturing Sector	2.20	2.57
Medium- and High-Technology Manufacturing Sector	0.68	0.70
Personal Services Sector	0.57	0.45
Primary Sector	2.44	2.08

continued on next page

Table 3.2.3a: continued

Table 3.2.3a: Revealed Comparative Advantage by Aggregate Sector (Traditional Method)		
ADB Regional Member	**2010**	**2017**
	(ratio)	
Japan		
Business Services Sector	0.90	0.69
Low-Technology Manufacturing Sector	0.38	0.39
Medium- and High-Technology Manufacturing Sector	1.51	1.63
Personal Services Sector	0.23	0.21
Primary Sector	0.03	0.04
Kazakhstan		
Business Services Sector	0.84	1.14
Low-Technology Manufacturing Sector	0.13	0.16
Medium- and High-Technology Manufacturing Sector	0.43	0.42
Personal Services Sector	0.30	0.31
Primary Sector	5.19	4.85
Korea, Republic of		
Business Services Sector	0.39	0.51
Low-Technology Manufacturing Sector	0.46	0.43
Medium- and High-Technology Manufacturing Sector	1.76	1.71
Personal Services Sector	0.38	0.34
Primary Sector	0.01	0.01
Kyrgyz Republic		
Business Services Sector	0.49	0.87
Low-Technology Manufacturing Sector	0.47	0.76
Medium- and High-Technology Manufacturing Sector	0.79	0.82
Personal Services Sector	1.73	6.41
Primary Sector	3.72	1.51
Lao People's Democratic Republic		
Business Services Sector	0.49	0.47
Low-Technology Manufacturing Sector	1.78	2.76
Medium- and High-Technology Manufacturing Sector	0.02	0.01
Personal Services Sector	0.45	1.42
Primary Sector	5.40	4.07
Malaysia		
Business Services Sector	0.87	0.74
Low-Technology Manufacturing Sector	1.60	1.73
Medium- and High-Technology Manufacturing Sector	0.94	0.93
Personal Services Sector	0.80	0.76
Primary Sector	0.75	0.85
Maldives		
Business Services Sector	3.80	3.47
Low-Technology Manufacturing Sector	0.11	0.30
Medium- and High-Technology Manufacturing Sector	0.00	0.00
Personal Services Sector	0.91	1.65
Primary Sector	0.10	0.10
Mongolia		
Business Services Sector	0.90	0.65
Low-Technology Manufacturing Sector	0.28	0.21
Medium- and High-Technology Manufacturing Sector	0.04	0.04
Personal Services Sector	0.10	0.37
Primary Sector	6.53	7.78
Nepal		
Business Services Sector	1.32	1.25
Low-Technology Manufacturing Sector	1.36	1.11
Medium- and High-Technology Manufacturing Sector	0.17	0.15
Personal Services Sector	16.09	19.50
Primary Sector	0.68	0.49

continued on next page

Table 3.2.3a: continued

Table 3.2.3a: Revealed Comparative Advantage by Aggregate Sector (Traditional Method)		
ADB Regional Member	**2010**	**2017**
	(ratio)	
Pakistan		
Business Services Sector	0.75	0.82
Low-Technology Manufacturing Sector	4.14	3.62
Medium- and High-Technology Manufacturing Sector	0.14	0.14
Personal Services Sector	2.24	2.71
Primary Sector	0.67	0.89
Philippines		
Business Services Sector	1.39	1.62
Low-Technology Manufacturing Sector	1.32	1.21
Medium- and High-Technology Manufacturing Sector	0.88	0.74
Personal Services Sector	0.69	0.99
Primary Sector	0.22	0.22
Singapore		
Business Services Sector	1.90	2.04
Low-Technology Manufacturing Sector	0.20	0.16
Medium- and High-Technology Manufacturing Sector	1.05	0.95
Personal Services Sector	0.18	0.23
Primary Sector	0.00	0.00
Sri Lanka		
Business Services Sector	1.24	1.58
Low-Technology Manufacturing Sector	3.70	2.90
Medium- and High-Technology Manufacturing Sector	0.19	0.07
Personal Services Sector	0.01	1.85
Primary Sector	0.34	0.54
Taipei,China		
Business Services Sector	0.63	0.78
Low-Technology Manufacturing Sector	0.46	0.43
Medium- and High-Technology Manufacturing Sector	1.63	1.56
Personal Services Sector	0.22	0.25
Primary Sector	0.05	0.05
Thailand		
Business Services Sector	0.83	1.27
Low-Technology Manufacturing Sector	1.39	1.14
Medium- and High-Technology Manufacturing Sector	1.11	0.90
Personal Services Sector	1.38	1.61
Primary Sector	0.30	0.41
Viet Nam		
Business Services Sector	0.65	0.61
Low-Technology Manufacturing Sector	3.16	3.08
Medium- and High-Technology Manufacturing Sector	0.39	0.47
Personal Services Sector	0.48	0.57
Primary Sector	1.47	1.22

Source: ADB Multi Region Input–Output Tables Database.

Table 3.2.3b: Revealed Comparative Advantage by Aggregate Sector (Value-Added Method)		
ADB Regional Member	**2010**	**2017**
	(ratio)	
Bangladesh		
Business Services Sector	0.77	0.65
Low-Technology Manufacturing Sector	3.44	3.46
Medium- and High-Technology Manufacturing Sector	0.10	0.11
Personal Services Sector	2.61	3.50
Primary Sector	0.80	0.72
Bhutan		
Business Services Sector	0.63	0.71
Low-Technology Manufacturing Sector	3.71	3.22
Medium- and High-Technology Manufacturing Sector	0.30	0.26
Personal Services Sector	0.57	0.83
Primary Sector	1.08	1.21
Brunei Darussalam		
Business Services Sector	0.17	0.20
Low-Technology Manufacturing Sector	0.05	0.08
Medium- and High-Technology Manufacturing Sector	0.75	0.81
Personal Services Sector	0.18	0.34
Primary Sector	4.57	4.87
Cambodia		
Business Services Sector	0.98	0.91
Low-Technology Manufacturing Sector	3.07	2.92
Medium- and High-Technology Manufacturing Sector	0.03	0.05
Personal Services Sector	0.64	0.50
Primary Sector	1.13	1.36
China, People's Republic of		
Business Services Sector	0.78	0.84
Low-Technology Manufacturing Sector	1.38	1.32
Medium- and High-Technology Manufacturing Sector	1.29	1.21
Personal Services Sector	0.53	0.70
Primary Sector	0.88	0.89
Fiji		
Business Services Sector	1.65	1.60
Low-Technology Manufacturing Sector	1.22	1.10
Medium- and High-Technology Manufacturing Sector	0.09	0.10
Personal Services Sector	0.73	0.74
Primary Sector	0.78	0.83
Hong Kong, China		
Business Services Sector	2.27	2.17
Low-Technology Manufacturing Sector	0.28	0.20
Medium- and High-Technology Manufacturing Sector	0.02	0.01
Personal Services Sector	0.98	1.01
Primary Sector	0.00	0.00
India		
Business Services Sector	1.31	1.18
Low-Technology Manufacturing Sector	0.75	0.88
Medium- and High-Technology Manufacturing Sector	0.60	0.73
Personal Services Sector	1.50	1.35
Primary Sector	0.98	0.95
Indonesia		
Business Services Sector	0.46	0.47
Low-Technology Manufacturing Sector	1.51	1.77
Medium- and High-Technology Manufacturing Sector	0.70	0.70
Personal Services Sector	0.46	0.44
Primary Sector	2.65	2.59

continued on next page

Table 3.2.3b: continued

Table 3.2.3b: Revealed Comparative Advantage by Aggregate Sector (Value-Added Method)		
ADB Regional Member	**2010**	**2017**
	(ratio)	
Japan		
Business Services Sector	1.02	0.97
Low-Technology Manufacturing Sector	0.78	0.72
Medium- and High-Technology Manufacturing Sector	1.65	1.74
Personal Services Sector	0.66	0.70
Primary Sector	0.06	0.07
Kazakhstan		
Business Services Sector	0.81	0.97
Low-Technology Manufacturing Sector	0.22	0.24
Medium- and High-Technology Manufacturing Sector	0.52	0.49
Personal Services Sector	0.09	0.16
Primary Sector	3.21	2.98
Korea, Republic of		
Business Services Sector	0.72	0.77
Low-Technology Manufacturing Sector	0.69	0.65
Medium- and High-Technology Manufacturing Sector	2.10	2.07
Personal Services Sector	0.85	0.75
Primary Sector	0.09	0.10
Kyrgyz Republic		
Business Services Sector	0.48	0.73
Low-Technology Manufacturing Sector	0.40	0.67
Medium- and High-Technology Manufacturing Sector	1.34	1.34
Personal Services Sector	0.78	3.13
Primary Sector	2.30	0.93
Lao People's Democratic Republic		
Business Services Sector	0.46	0.38
Low-Technology Manufacturing Sector	1.81	2.76
Medium- and High-Technology Manufacturing Sector	0.05	0.05
Personal Services Sector	0.18	0.59
Primary Sector	3.61	3.11
Malaysia		
Business Services Sector	0.84	0.77
Low-Technology Manufacturing Sector	0.88	0.99
Medium- and High-Technology Manufacturing Sector	0.88	0.93
Personal Services Sector	0.69	0.60
Primary Sector	1.80	1.96
Maldives		
Business Services Sector	2.05	1.70
Low-Technology Manufacturing Sector	0.50	1.18
Medium- and High-Technology Manufacturing Sector	0.01	0.02
Personal Services Sector	0.64	1.71
Primary Sector	0.47	0.30
Mongolia		
Business Services Sector	0.78	0.78
Low-Technology Manufacturing Sector	0.41	0.49
Medium- and High-Technology Manufacturing Sector	0.07	0.09
Personal Services Sector	0.41	0.48
Primary Sector	3.83	3.99
Nepal		
Business Services Sector	1.01	0.89
Low-Technology Manufacturing Sector	1.04	0.83
Medium- and High-Technology Manufacturing Sector	0.17	0.17
Personal Services Sector	7.23	9.01
Primary Sector	0.95	0.87

continued on next page

Table 3.2.3b: continued

Table 3.2.3b: Revealed Comparative Advantage by Aggregate Sector (Value-Added Method)		
ADB Regional Member	**2010**	**2017**
	(ratio)	
Pakistan		
Business Services Sector	0.76	0.76
Low-Technology Manufacturing Sector	1.79	1.59
Medium- and High-Technology Manufacturing Sector	0.17	0.19
Personal Services Sector	1.16	1.34
Primary Sector	2.39	2.59
Philippines		
Business Services Sector	1.21	1.26
Low-Technology Manufacturing Sector	1.34	1.29
Medium- and High-Technology Manufacturing Sector	0.72	0.60
Personal Services Sector	0.54	0.71
Primary Sector	0.77	0.74
Singapore		
Business Services Sector	1.62	1.66
Low-Technology Manufacturing Sector	0.35	0.28
Medium- and High-Technology Manufacturing Sector	1.05	0.92
Personal Services Sector	0.26	0.29
Primary Sector	0.00	0.00
Sri Lanka		
Business Services Sector	1.03	1.11
Low-Technology Manufacturing Sector	3.10	2.68
Medium- and High-Technology Manufacturing Sector	0.25	0.13
Personal Services Sector	0.45	1.20
Primary Sector	0.66	0.66
Taipei,China		
Business Services Sector	0.77	0.75
Low-Technology Manufacturing Sector	0.59	0.55
Medium- and High-Technology Manufacturing Sector	2.13	2.21
Personal Services Sector	0.57	0.47
Primary Sector	0.07	0.07
Thailand		
Business Services Sector	0.99	1.17
Low-Technology Manufacturing Sector	1.47	1.20
Medium- and High-Technology Manufacturing Sector	1.02	0.77
Personal Services Sector	0.92	0.98
Primary Sector	0.63	0.72
Viet Nam		
Business Services Sector	0.67	0.68
Low-Technology Manufacturing Sector	2.50	2.50
Medium- and High-Technology Manufacturing Sector	0.51	0.61
Personal Services Sector	0.34	0.39
Primary Sector	1.65	1.46

Source: ADB Multi Region Input–Output Tables Database.

Table 3.2.4a: Vertical Specialization, Disaggregated—Bangladesh

	Exports	VS	FVA_FIN	FVA_INT	DDC	FDC
	($ million)	(% of gross exports)	(% of VS)			
Agriculture, Hunting, Forestry, and Fishing						
2010	329	5.94	26.73	54.85	0.25	18.17
2017	458	5.91	27.43	56.28	0.29	16.00
Leather, Leather Products, and Footwear						
2010	280	9.32	78.97	12.77	0.01	8.24
2017	950	8.92	80.50	11.33	0.02	8.15
Textiles and Textile Products						
2010	12,647	14.95	78.71	11.52	0.06	9.70
2017	24,516	14.11	76.87	12.15	0.08	10.90

$ = United States dollars, DDC = domestic value-added double counted in exports, FDC = foreign value-added double counted in exports, FVA_FIN = foreign value-added in exports for final consumption, FVA_INT = foreign value-added in intermediate exports, VS = vertical specialization.

Source: ADB Multi Region Input–Output Tables Database.

Table 3.2.4b: Vertical Specialization, Disaggregated—Bhutan

	Exports	VS	FVA_FIN	FVA_INT	DDC	FDC
	($ million)	(% of gross exports)	(% of VS)			
Agriculture, Hunting, Forestry, and Fishing						
2010	49	4.36	46.64	42.08	0.01	11.26
2017	52	5.35	38.58	49.17	0.01	12.24
Basic Metals and Fabricated Metal						
2010	34	31.18	22.86	65.69	0.01	11.44
2017	50	31.37	39.25	52.46	0.01	8.28
Electricity, Gas, and Water Supply						
2010	196	10.86	7.89	59.64	0.01	32.47
2017	245	8.28	7.60	59.20	0.01	33.19

$ = United States dollars, DDC = domestic value-added double counted in exports, FDC = foreign value-added double counted in exports, FVA_FIN = foreign value-added in exports for final consumption, FVA_INT = foreign value-added in intermediate exports, VS = vertical specialization.

Source: ADB Multi Region Input–Output Tables Database.

Table 3.2.4c: Vertical Specialization, Disaggregated—Brunei Darussalam

	Exports	VS	FVA_FIN	FVA_INT	DDC	FDC
	($ million)	(% of gross exports)	(% of VS)			
Air Transport						
2010	224	24.48	38.34	41.92	0.02	19.72
2017	22	26.11	35.51	33.84	0.01	30.64
Coke, Refined Petroleum, and Nuclear Fuel						
2010	3,396	5.73	9.96	57.08	0.02	32.93
2017	2,331	6.81	7.59	59.90	0.02	32.49
Mining and Quarrying						
2010	4,843	6.96	1.77	66.23	0.02	31.98
2017	2,990	8.28	0.78	63.53	0.02	35.67

$ = United States dollars, DDC = domestic value-added double counted in exports, FDC = foreign value-added double counted in exports, FVA_FIN = foreign value-added in exports for final consumption, FVA_INT = foreign value-added in intermediate exports, VS = vertical specialization.

Source: ADB Multi Region Input–Output Tables Database.

Table 3.2.4d: Vertical Specialization, Disaggregated—Cambodia

	Exports	VS	FVA_FIN	FVA_INT	DDC	FDC
	($ million)	(% of gross exports)	(% of VS)			
Agriculture, Hunting, Forestry, and Fishing						
2010	221	9.91	30.00	40.40	0.08	29.51
2017	990	10.88	31.31	35.77	0.21	32.71
Hotels and Restaurants						
2010	880	15.13	58.29	27.26	0.01	14.44
2017	1,260	17.54	59.34	25.91	0.02	14.74
Textiles and Textile Products						
2010	1,950	36.50	84.74	8.59	0.01	6.66
2017	4,777	35.88	86.82	8.07	0.01	5.11

$ = United States dollars, DDC = domestic value-added double counted in exports, FDC = foreign value-added double counted in exports, FVA_FIN = foreign value-added in exports for final consumption, FVA_INT = foreign value-added in intermediate exports, VS = vertical specialization.

Source: ADB Multi Region Input–Output Tables Database.

Table 3.2.4e: Vertical Specialization, Disaggregated—China, People's Republic of

	Exports	VS	FVA_FIN	FVA_INT	DDC	FDC
	($ million)	(% of gross exports)		(% of VS)		
Basic Metals and Fabricated Metal						
2010	103,206	21.94	21.49	45.70	4.66	28.15
2017	166,177	16.70	21.67	44.25	5.56	28.52
Electrical and Optical Equipment						
2010	561,086	28.14	58.81	17.48	4.37	19.34
2017	749,449	19.74	54.19	20.37	5.42	20.02
Textiles and Textile Products						
2010	177,812	12.12	77.07	12.34	1.45	9.15
2017	232,261	7.94	73.99	13.61	2.03	10.36

$ = United States dollars, DDC = domestic value-added double counted in exports, FDC = foreign value-added double counted in exports, FVA_FIN = foreign value-added in exports for final consumption, FVA_INT = foreign value-added in intermediate exports, VS = vertical specialization.

Source: ADB Multi Region Input–Output Tables Database.

Table 3.2.4f: Vertical Specialization, Disaggregated—Fiji

	Exports	VS	FVA_FIN	FVA_INT	DDC	FDC
	($ million)	(% of gross exports)		(% of VS)		
Air Transport						
2010	217	51.59	21.15	63.25	0.00	15.60
2017	265	43.94	22.32	61.09	0.00	16.58
Food, Beverages, and Tobacco						
2010	153	25.05	48.42	38.45	0.01	13.12
2017	242	23.59	49.51	36.98	0.01	13.50
Hotels and Restaurants						
2010	345	21.11	57.75	30.00	0.01	12.24
2017	485	19.01	54.47	30.85	0.01	14.66

0.0 = magnitude is less than half of unit employed, $ = United States dollars, DDC = domestic value-added double counted in exports, FDC = foreign value-added double counted in exports, FVA_FIN = foreign value-added in exports for final consumption, FVA_INT = foreign value-added in intermediate exports, VS = vertical specialization.

Source: ADB Multi Region Input–Output Tables Database.

Table 3.2.4g: Vertical Specialization, Disaggregated—Hong Kong, China

	Exports	VS	FVA_FIN	FVA_INT	DDC	FDC
	($ million)	(% of gross exports)		(% of VS)		
Financial Intermediation						
2010	12,960	10.30	25.17	50.15	1.11	23.57
2017	21,662	8.66	25.63	52.99	1.04	20.34
Retail Trade, except of Motor Vehicles and Motorcycles; Repair of Household Goods						
2010	14,206	10.01	64.77	25.77	0.74	8.72
2017	19,224	8.51	68.37	23.92	0.45	7.26
Wholesale Trade and Commission Trade, except of Motor Vehicles and Motorcycles						
2010	71,290	27.88	55.02	32.02	0.49	12.47
2017	98,185	26.59	54.23	33.98	0.31	11.48

$ = United States dollars, DDC = domestic value-added double counted in exports, FDC = foreign value-added double counted in exports, FVA_FIN = foreign value-added in exports for final consumption, FVA_INT = foreign value-added in intermediate exports, VS = vertical specialization.

Source: ADB Multi Region Input–Output Tables Database.

Table 3.2.4h: Vertical Specialization, Disaggregated—India

	Exports	VS	FVA_FIN	FVA_INT	DDC	FDC
	($ million)	(% of gross exports)		(% of VS)		
Coke, Refined Petroleum, and Nuclear Fuel						
2010	27,678	50.65	21.18	42.22	0.52	36.08
2017	48,926	53.79	21.13	42.65	0.51	35.71
Renting of Machinery and Equipment, and Other Business Activities						
2010	81,864	11.58	24.90	49.75	0.99	24.36
2017	71,270	4.20	51.03	30.47	1.22	17.27
Transport Equipment						
2010	16,052	28.53	65.78	20.07	0.27	13.88
2017	33,876	21.73	70.28	17.71	0.26	11.74

$ = United States dollars, DDC = domestic value-added double counted in exports, FDC = foreign value-added double counted in exports, FVA_FIN = foreign value-added in exports for final consumption, FVA_INT = foreign value-added in intermediate exports, VS = vertical specialization.

Source: ADB Multi Region Input–Output Tables Database.

Table 3.2.4i: Vertical Specialization, Disaggregated—Indonesia						
	Exports	VS	FVA_FIN	FVA_INT	DDC	FDC
	($ million)	(% of gross exports)	(% of VS)			
Coke, Refined Petroleum, and Nuclear Fuel						
2010	15,422	10.10	22.52	48.38	0.85	28.25
2017	16,670	12.38	21.00	45.23	0.81	32.96
Electrical and Optical Equipment						
2010	14,883	35.94	59.10	19.03	0.34	21.53
2017	17,919	31.64	57.81	20.14	0.32	21.73
Food, Beverages, and Tobacco						
2010	21,957	8.42	21.74	57.96	0.73	19.57
2017	39,531	8.12	26.99	55.19	0.70	17.12

$ = United States dollars, DDC = domestic value-added double counted in exports, FDC = foreign value-added double counted in exports, FVA_FIN = foreign value-added in exports for final consumption, FVA_INT = foreign value-added in intermediate exports, VS = vertical specialization.

Source: ADB Multi Region Input–Output Tables Database.

Table 3.2.4j: Vertical Specialization, Disaggregated—Japan						
	Exports	VS	FVA_FIN	FVA_INT	DDC	FDC
	($ million)	(% of gross exports)	(% of VS)			
Basic Metals and Fabricated Metal						
2010	99,376	25.29	7.63	52.99	2.37	37.01
2017	110,891	30.76	9.26	53.42	1.80	35.53
Electrical and Optical Equipment						
2010	170,482	16.42	34.83	29.32	3.26	32.59
2017	170,863	19.90	34.22	33.11	2.49	30.18
Transport Equipment						
2010	173,959	14.18	72.83	16.73	0.91	9.53
2017	190,032	18.83	70.69	19.25	0.74	9.32

$ = United States dollars, DDC = domestic value-added double counted in exports, FDC = foreign value-added double counted in exports, FVA_FIN = foreign value-added in exports for final consumption, FVA_INT = foreign value-added in intermediate exports, VS = vertical specialization.

Source: ADB Multi Region Input–Output Tables Database.

Table 3.2.4k: Vertical Specialization, Disaggregated—Kazakhstan						
	Exports	VS	FVA_FIN	FVA_INT	DDC	FDC
	($ million)	(% of gross exports)	(% of VS)			
Basic Metals and Fabricated Metal						
2010	9,479	8.45	3.06	49.07	0.55	47.31
2017	6,112	6.97	2.49	42.51	0.40	54.60
Coke, Refined Petroleum, and Nuclear Fuel						
2010	2,201	15.63	24.29	47.46	0.30	27.96
2017	1,056	6.06	27.67	50.98	0.51	20.83
Mining and Quarrying						
2010	34,362	10.58	4.70	56.65	0.45	38.20
2017	19,406	8.45	6.69	52.62	0.44	40.25

$ = United States dollars, DDC = domestic value-added double counted in exports, FDC = foreign value-added double counted in exports, FVA_FIN = foreign value-added in exports for final consumption, FVA_INT = foreign value-added in intermediate exports, VS = vertical specialization.

Source: ADB Multi Region Input–Output Tables Database.

Table 3.2.4l: Vertical Specialization, Disaggregated—Korea, Republic of						
	Exports	VS	FVA_FIN	FVA_INT	DDC	FDC
	($ million)	(% of gross exports)	(% of VS)			
Chemicals and Chemical Products						
2010	49,484	39.88	4.83	59.04	0.94	35.18
2017	64,148	39.29	5.14	59.23	1.02	34.60
Electrical and Optical Equipment						
2010	164,945	35.01	44.60	24.45	1.23	29.72
2017	233,163	34.71	35.31	34.01	1.58	29.09
Transport Equipment						
2010	102,407	31.42	82.49	11.29	0.20	6.02
2017	112,959	31.89	76.60	14.74	0.28	8.37

$ = United States dollars, DDC = domestic value-added double counted in exports, FDC = foreign value-added double counted in exports, FVA_FIN = foreign value-added in exports for final consumption, FVA_INT = foreign value-added in intermediate exports, VS = vertical specialization.

Source: ADB Multi Region Input–Output Tables Database.

Table 3.2.4m: Vertical Specialization, Disaggregated—Kyrgyz Republic

	Exports	VS	FVA_FIN	FVA_INT	DDC	FDC
	($ million)	(% of gross exports)		(% of VS)		
Agriculture, Hunting, Forestry, and Fishing						
2010	714	30.51	31.60	43.43	0.01	24.96
2017	380	22.11	43.64	35.77	0.04	20.54
Basic Metals and Fabricated Metal						
2010	626	22.89	12.08	52.85	0.01	35.06
2017	961	26.24	35.40	35.74	0.01	28.84
Inland Transport						
2010	34	40.58	23.86	51.73	0.01	24.40
2017	179	41.61	25.60	51.16	0.02	23.23

$ = United States dollars, DDC = domestic value-added double counted in exports, FDC = foreign value-added double counted in exports, FVA_FIN = foreign value-added in exports for final consumption, FVA_INT = foreign value-added in intermediate exports, VS = vertical specialization.

Source: ADB Multi Region Input–Output Tables Database.

Table 3.2.4n: Vertical Specialization, Disaggregated—Lao People's Democratic Republic

	Exports	VS	FVA_FIN	FVA_INT	DDC	FDC
	($ million)	(% of gross exports)		(% of VS)		
Agriculture, Hunting, Forestry, and Fishing						
2010	102	4.06	12.19	63.89	0.02	23.91
2017	581	3.24	8.11	51.06	0.08	40.74
Electricity, Gas, and Water Supply						
2010	175	9.29	12.02	56.20	0.01	31.77
2017	1,663	7.15	16.97	54.88	0.02	28.13
Mining and Quarrying						
2010	807	17.26	13.24	55.75	0.01	31.00
2017	1,890	9.66	29.13	48.13	0.02	22.72

$ = United States dollars, DDC = domestic value-added double counted in exports, FDC = foreign value-added double counted in exports, FVA_FIN = foreign value-added in exports for final consumption, FVA_INT = foreign value-added in intermediate exports, VS = vertical specialization.

Source: ADB Multi Region Input–Output Tables Database.

Table 3.2.4o: Vertical Specialization, Disaggregated—Malaysia

	Exports	VS	FVA_FIN	FVA_INT	DDC	FDC
	($ million)	(% of gross exports)		(% of VS)		
Coke, Refined Petroleum, and Nuclear Fuel						
2010	14,158	19.91	11.51	45.74	0.68	42.08
2017	17,338	23.73	8.47	47.30	0.47	43.76
Electrical and Optical Equipment						
2010	26,071	44.60	34.50	26.36	0.65	38.49
2017	37,007	44.33	36.94	26.78	0.73	35.55
Food, Beverages, and Tobacco						
2010	19,583	26.08	47.51	37.51	0.23	14.75
2017	21,630	26.14	51.15	34.75	0.19	13.91

$ = United States dollars, DDC = domestic value-added double counted in exports, FDC = foreign value-added double counted in exports, FVA_FIN = foreign value-added in exports for final consumption, FVA_INT = foreign value-added in intermediate exports, VS = vertical specialization.

Source: ADB Multi Region Input–Output Tables Database.

Table 3.2.4p: Vertical Specialization, Disaggregated—Maldives

	Exports	VS	FVA_FIN	FVA_INT	DDC	FDC
	($ million)	(% of gross exports)		(% of VS)		
Air Transport						
2010	36	41.95	28.55	54.57	0.01	16.88
2017	124	38.79	35.38	55.58	0.01	9.03
Food, Beverages, and Tobacco						
2010	12	35.41	72.10	22.12	0.00	5.78
2017	92	42.67	71.12	23.02	0.00	5.86
Hotels and Restaurants						
2010	1,399	26.83	40.76	38.18	0.00	21.06
2017	2,603	36.58	43.49	35.77	0.00	20.74

0.00 = magnitude is less than half of unit employed, $ = United States dollars, DDC = domestic value-added double counted in exports, FDC = foreign value-added double counted in exports, FVA_FIN = foreign value-added in exports for final consumption, FVA_INT = foreign value-added in intermediate exports, VS = vertical specialization.

Source: ADB Multi Region Input–Output Tables Database.

Table 3.2.4q: Vertical Specialization, Disaggregated—Mongolia					
	Exports	VS	FVA_FIN	FVA_INT	DDC	FDC
	($ million)	(% of gross exports)	(% of VS)			
Agriculture, Hunting, Forestry, and Fishing						
2010	104	13.27	24.28	55.01	0.01	20.71
2017	246	11.10	17.27	61.41	0.02	21.31
Inland Transport						
2010	79	29.19	23.96	54.61	0.01	21.42
2017	162	33.79	19.38	62.78	0.03	17.82
Mining and Quarrying						
2010	1,994	25.54	8.61	63.19	0.01	28.18
2017	4,278	24.29	0.36	73.86	0.02	25.75

$ = United States dollars, DDC = domestic value-added double counted in exports, FDC = foreign value-added double counted in exports, FVA_FIN = foreign value-added in exports for final consumption, FVA_INT = foreign value-added in intermediate exports, VS = vertical specialization.

Source: ADB Multi Region Input–Output Tables Database.

Table 3.2.4r: Vertical Specialization, Disaggregated—Nepal					
	Exports	VS	FVA_FIN	FVA_INT	DDC	FDC
	($ million)	(% of gross exports)	(% of VS)			
Inland Transport						
2010	80	29.92	43.55	44.32	0.00	12.12
2017	103	37.23	35.99	49.74	0.00	14.27
Other Community, Social, and Personal Services						
2010	228	7.81	20.90	61.40	0.01	17.69
2017	350	9.01	21.27	62.08	0.01	16.64
Other Supporting and Auxiliary Transport Activities; Activities of Travel Agencies						
2010	108	18.48	35.56	44.90	0.01	19.53
2017	115	23.22	23.84	55.70	0.01	20.44

0.00 = magnitude is less than half of unit employed, $ = United States dollars, DDC = domestic value-added double counted in exports, FDC = foreign value-added double counted in exports, FVA_FIN = foreign value-added in exports for final consumption, FVA_INT = foreign value-added in intermediate exports, VS = vertical specialization.

Source: ADB Multi Region Input–Output Tables Database.

Table 3.2.4s: Vertical Specialization, Disaggregated—Pakistan					
	Exports	VS	FVA_FIN	FVA_INT	DDC	FDC
	($ million)	(% of gross exports)	(% of VS)			
Agriculture, Hunting, Forestry, and Fishing						
2010	1,450	3.44	38.02	44.34	0.06	17.58
2017	2,014	3.11	31.13	50.74	0.06	18.07
Food, Beverages, and Tobacco						
2010	2,355	6.33	47.79	35.97	0.03	16.21
2017	2,612	5.80	48.85	36.17	0.03	14.94
Textiles and Textile Products						
2010	9,915	8.19	48.01	26.26	0.03	25.70
2017	10,858	7.41	48.73	27.77	0.03	23.47

$ = United States dollars, DDC = domestic value-added double counted in exports, FDC = foreign value-added double counted in exports, FVA_FIN = foreign value-added in exports for final consumption, FVA_INT = foreign value-added in intermediate exports, VS = vertical specialization.

Source: ADB Multi Region Input–Output Tables Database.

Table 3.2.4t: Vertical Specialization, Disaggregated—Philippines					
	Exports	VS	FVA_FIN	FVA_INT	DDC	FDC
	($ million)	(% of gross exports)	(% of VS)			
Electrical and Optical Equipment						
2010	15,773	38.24	28.13	27.31	0.48	44.08
2017	16,417	52.09	30.97	26.48	0.28	42.27
Food, Beverages, and Tobacco						
2010	7,957	10.18	51.14	33.79	0.08	14.99
2017	11,467	12.06	48.44	38.39	0.09	13.08
Renting of Machinery and Equipment, and Other Business Activities						
2010	10,815	6.16	9.28	60.70	0.36	29.66
2017	19,120	6.83	10.14	59.52	0.33	30.00

$ = United States dollars, DDC = domestic value-added double counted in exports, FDC = foreign value-added double counted in exports, FVA_FIN = foreign value-added in exports for final consumption, FVA_INT = foreign value-added in intermediate exports, VS = vertical specialization.

Source: ADB Multi Region Input–Output Tables Database.

Table 3.2.4u: Vertical Specialization, Disaggregated—Singapore

	Exports	VS	FVA_FIN	FVA_INT	DDC	FDC
	($ million)	(% of gross exports)		(% of VS)		
Electrical and Optical Equipment						
2010	62,507	62.35	37.94	28.43	0.56	33.07
2017	62,848	61.82	37.89	29.70	0.57	31.83
Water Transport						
2010	26,594	71.58	0.50	58.61	1.17	39.72
2017	40,737	72.77	1.42	67.57	1.43	29.59
Wholesale Trade and Commission Trade, except of Motor Vehicles and Motorcycles						
2010	57,602	33.21	17.62	58.63	0.75	23.00
2017	73,653	39.33	18.72	59.93	1.08	20.27

$ = United States dollars, DDC = domestic value-added double counted in exports, FDC = foreign value-added double counted in exports, FVA_FIN = foreign value-added in exports for final consumption, FVA_INT = foreign value-added in intermediate exports, VS = vertical specialization.

Source: ADB Multi Region Input–Output Tables Database.

Table 3.2.4v: Vertical Specialization, Disaggregated—Sri Lanka

	Exports	VS	FVA_FIN	FVA_INT	DDC	FDC
	($ million)	(% of gross exports)		(% of VS)		
Agriculture, Hunting, Forestry, and Fishing						
2010	336	12.28	38.25	37.48	0.03	24.24
2017	655	11.59	59.79	25.35	0.02	14.84
Food, Beverages, and Tobacco						
2010	1,527	13.41	65.59	23.40	0.01	11.01
2017	2,527	11.40	66.62	22.84	0.01	10.52
Textiles and Textile Products						
2010	2,978	28.21	76.95	13.05	0.03	9.97
2017	3,756	17.85	76.05	15.22	0.02	8.71

$ = United States dollars, DDC = domestic value-added double counted in exports, FDC = foreign value-added double counted in exports, FVA_FIN = foreign value-added in exports for final consumption, FVA_INT = foreign value-added in intermediate exports, VS = vertical specialization.

Source: ADB Multi Region Input–Output Tables Database.

Table 3.2.4w: Vertical Specialization, Disaggregated—Taipei,China

	Exports	VS	FVA_FIN	FVA_INT	DDC	FDC
	($ million)	(% of gross exports)		(% of VS)		
Chemicals and Chemical Products						
2010	34,858	58.97	2.98	62.19	0.44	34.38
2017	33,010	55.58	3.88	64.18	0.42	31.51
Electrical and Optical Equipment						
2010	134,799	44.07	28.49	33.73	1.23	36.55
2017	157,158	39.14	18.50	43.02	1.49	36.99
Wholesale Trade and Commission Trade, except of Motor Vehicles and Motorcycles						
2010	26,495	12.32	27.24	44.97	1.12	26.67
2017	41,832	12.21	30.27	44.42	0.89	24.42

$ = United States dollars, DDC = domestic value-added double counted in exports, FDC = foreign value-added double counted in exports, FVA_FIN = foreign value-added in exports for final consumption, FVA_INT = foreign value-added in intermediate exports, VS = vertical specialization.

Source: ADB Multi Region Input–Output Tables Database.

Table 3.2.4x: Vertical Specialization, Disaggregated—Thailand

	Exports	VS	FVA_FIN	FVA_INT	DDC	FDC
	($ million)	(% of gross exports)		(% of VS)		
Basic Metals and Fabricated Metal						
2010	41,816	48.04	13.00	55.68	0.38	30.94
2017	50,566	43.01	14.21	55.89	0.51	29.39
Food, Beverages, and Tobacco						
2010	15,291	26.90	58.30	30.51	0.16	11.03
2017	24,479	20.06	58.01	30.36	0.25	11.38
Transport Equipment						
2010	16,465	39.40	52.46	24.86	0.23	22.44
2017	20,684	29.72	64.85	21.50	0.25	13.40

$ = United States dollars, DDC = domestic value-added double counted in exports, FDC = foreign value-added double counted in exports, FVA_FIN = foreign value-added in exports for final consumption, FVA_INT = foreign value-added in intermediate exports, VS = vertical specialization.

Source: ADB Multi Region Input–Output Tables Database.

Table 3.2.4y: Vertical Specialization, Disaggregated—Viet Nam						
	Exports	VS	FVA_FIN	FVA_INT	DDC	FDC
	($ million)	(% of gross exports)	(% of VS)			
Electrical and Optical Equipment						
2010	6,994	53.75	39.97	26.79	0.08	33.16
2017	21,571	58.74	23.45	36.33	0.23	39.98
Food, Beverages, and Tobacco						
2010	12,422	34.59	66.69	25.74	0.05	7.53
2017	31,432	37.94	60.36	30.01	0.10	9.54
Textiles and Textile Products						
2010	7,283	35.32	82.19	9.50	0.09	8.22
2017	20,710	41.31	76.86	12.13	0.15	10.86

$ = United States dollars, DDC = domestic value-added double counted in exports, FDC = foreign value-added double counted in exports, FVA_FIN = foreign value-added in exports for final consumption, FVA_INT = foreign value-added in intermediate exports, VS = vertical specialization.

Source: ADB Multi Region Input–Output Tables Database.

Definitions

This section contains the definitions of statistical indicators that are covered in Part I – Sustainable Development Goals (SDGs) and Part II – Regional Trends and Tables. The definitions are taken mostly from the Asian Development Bank's Development Indicators Reference Manual, including websites and publications of international and private organizations such as the Food and Agriculture Organization of the United Nations (FAO); International Labour Organization (ILO); International Monetary Fund (IMF); International Telecommunication Union (ITU); Organisation for Economic Co-operation and Development (OECD); Transparency International; United Nations Children's Fund (UNICEF); United Nations Educational, Scientific and Cultural Organization (UNESCO); United Nations Population Division (UNPD); United Nations Statistics Division (UNSD); World Bank; World Health Organization (WHO); and United Nations World Tourism Organization (UNWTO). The SDG indicators are arranged according to their respective goals and targets before they are defined, while the indicators for the Regional Trends and Tables are grouped according to their themes and subtopics before they are defined. In many instances, the indicators themselves, rather than their growth rates or ratios to another indicator, are defined.

Sustainable Development Goals

Goals and Targets	Statistical Indicators	Definition
Goal 1. End poverty in all its forms everywhere		
Target 1.1: By 2030, eradicate extreme poverty (currently measured as people living on less than $1.90 a day) for all people everywhere.	1.1.1a: Proportion of population living below the international poverty line, by sex, age, employment status, and geographical location (urban or rural)	Proportion of the population living on less than $1.90 a day, measured at 2011 international prices, adjusted for purchasing power parity (PPP). Note: The PPP conversion factor for private consumption is the number of units of a country's currency required to buy the same amount of goods and/or services in the domestic market as a United States (US) dollar would buy in the US.
	1.1.1b: Proportion of employed population living below the international poverty line, by sex	Proportion of the employed population living in households with per capita consumption or income below the international poverty line of $1.90. Note: The proportion of working poor in total employment (also known as the working poverty rate) combines data on household income or consumption with labor force framework variables measured at the individual level, and sheds light on the relationship between household poverty and employment. The numbers are International Labour Organization modeled estimates. Employed persons refer to all persons of working age who, during a short reference period such as a day or a week, performed work for others in exchange for pay or profit.
Target 1.2: By 2030, reduce at least by half the proportion of men, women, and children of all ages living in poverty in all its dimensions, according to national definitions.	1.2.1: Proportion of population living below the national poverty line, by sex, age, and geographical location (urban or rural)	Percentage of the total population living below the national poverty line. Note: National poverty rates are defined at country-specific poverty lines in local currencies, which are different in real terms across countries and different from the international poverty line of $1.90 a day. Thus, national poverty rates cannot be compared across countries or with the poverty rate of $1.90 a day.
Goal 2. End hunger, achieve food security and improved nutrition, and promote sustainable agriculture		
Target 2.1: By 2030, end hunger and ensure access by all people, in particular the poor and people in vulnerable situations, including infants, to safe, nutritious, and sufficient food all year round.	2.1.1: Prevalence of undernourishment	Proportion of the population whose habitual food consumption is insufficient to provide the dietary energy levels that are required to maintain a normal active and healthy life. Note: Undernourishment is defined as the condition by which a person has access, on a regular basis, to amounts of food that are insufficient to provide the energy required for conducting a normal, healthy, and active life, given his or her own dietary energy requirements.

(continued on next page)

Goals and Targets	Statistical Indicators	Definition
Target 2.2: By 2030, end all forms of malnutrition, including achieving, by 2025, the internationally agreed targets on stunting and wasting in children under 5 years of age, and address the nutritional needs of adolescent girls, pregnant and lactating women, and older persons.	2.2.1: Prevalence of stunting (height for age <-2 standard deviation from the median of World Health Organization (WHO) Child Growth Standards) among children under 5 years of age	Prevalence of stunting—height-for-age <-2 standard deviation from the median of WHO Child Growth Standards—among children under 5 years of age. Note: Stunting refers to the impaired growth and development that children experience from poor nutrition, repeated infection, and inadequate psychosocial stimulation.
	2.2.2.a: Prevalence of malnutrition (weight for height <-2 standard deviation from the median of WHO Child Growth Standards) among children under 5 years of age (wasting)	Prevalence of wasting—weight for height <-2 standard deviation from the median of WHO Child Growth Standards—among children under 5 years of age.
	2.2.2.b: Prevalence of malnutrition (weight for height >+2 standard deviation from the median of WHO Child Growth Standards) among children under 5 years of age (overweight)	Prevalence of overweight—weight for height >+2 standard deviation from the median of WHO Child Growth Standards—among children under 5 years of age.
Target 2.a: Increase investment, including through enhanced international cooperation, in rural infrastructure, agricultural research and extension services, technology development, and plant and livestock gene banks in order to enhance agricultural productive capacity in developing countries, in particular least developed countries.	2.a.1: The agriculture orientation index for government expenditures	The Agriculture Orientation Index for Government Expenditures is defined as the agriculture share of government expenditures divided by the agriculture share of gross domestic product (GDP), where agriculture refers to the agriculture, forestry, fishing, and hunting sector. The measure is a currency-free index, calculated as the ratio of these two shares. National governments are requested to compile government expenditures according to the international Classification of Functions of Government, and agriculture share of GDP according to the System of National Accounts.
	2.a.2: Total official flows (official development assistance (ODA) plus other official flows) to the agriculture sector	Gross disbursements of total ODA and other official flows from all donors to the agriculture sector.
Goal 3. Ensure healthy lives and promote well-being for all at all ages		
Target 3.1: By 2030, reduce the global maternal mortality ratio to less than 70 per 100,000 live births.	3.1.1: Maternal mortality ratio	Number of maternal deaths during a given time period per 100,000 live births during the same time period. Note: The term maternal deaths refers to the annual number of female deaths from any cause related to, or aggravated by, pregnancy or its management (excluding accidental or incidental causes) during pregnancy and childbirth or within 42 days of termination of pregnancy, irrespective of the duration and site of the pregnancy, expressed per 100,000 live births, for a specified time period.

(continued on next page)

Goals and Targets	Statistical Indicators	Definition
	3.1.2: Proportion of births attended by skilled health personnel	Percentage of deliveries attended by health personnel trained in providing lifesaving obstetric care, including giving the necessary supervision, care, and advice to women during pregnancy, labor, and the post-partum period; conducting deliveries on their own; and caring for newborns. Traditional birth attendants, even if they receive a short training course, are not included. Note: Having a skilled attendant at the time of delivery is an important lifesaving intervention for both mothers and babies. Not having access to this key assistance is detrimental to women's health and gender empowerment because it could cause the death of the mother or long-lasting disability, especially in marginalized settings.
Target 3.2: By 2030, end preventable deaths of newborns and children under 5 years of age, with all countries aiming to reduce neonatal mortality to at least as low as 12 per 1,000 live births and under-5 mortality to at least as low as 25 per 1,000 live births.	3.2.1: Under-5 mortality rate	The probability of a child born in a specific year or period dying before reaching the age of 5 years, if subject to age specific mortality rates of that period, expressed per 1,000 live births. Note: The under-5 mortality rate as defined here is, strictly speaking, not a rate (i.e., the number of deaths divided by the number of population at risk during a certain period of time) but a probability of death derived from a life table and expressed as a rate per 1000 live births.
	3.2.2: Neonatal mortality rate	Probability that a child born in a specific year or period will die during the first 28 completed days of life, if subject to age-specific mortality rates of that period, expressed per 1,000 live births. Note: Neonatal deaths (deaths among live births during the first 28 completed days of life) may be subdivided into early neonatal deaths, occurring during the first 7 days of life, and late neonatal deaths, occurring after the seventh day but before the 28th completed day of life.
Target 3.3: By 2030, end the epidemics of AIDS, tuberculosis, malaria, and neglected tropical diseases; and combat hepatitis, water-borne diseases, and other communicable diseases.	3.3.1: Number of new HIV infections per 1,000 uninfected population, by sex, age, and key populations	Number of new HIV infections per 1,000 person-years among the uninfected population.
	3.3.2: Tuberculosis incidence per 100,000 population	Estimated number of new and relapse tuberculosis cases (all forms of tuberculosis, including cases in people living with HIV) arising in a given year, expressed as a rate per 100,000 population.
	3.3.3: Malaria incidence per 1,000 population	The number of new cases of malaria per 1,000 people at risk each year.
Target 3.4: By 2030, reduce by one third premature mortality from noncommunicable diseases through prevention and treatment, and promote mental health and well-being.	3.4.1: Mortality rate attributed to cardiovascular disease, cancer, diabetes, or chronic respiratory disease	Probability of dying between the ages of 30 and 70 years from cardiovascular diseases, cancer, diabetes, or chronic respiratory diseases, defined as the percentage of 30-year-old people who would die before their 70th birthday from cardiovascular disease, cancer, diabetes, or chronic respiratory disease, assuming that a person would experience current mortality rates at every age and he or she would not die from any other cause of death (e.g., injuries or HIV/AIDS).
	3.4.2: Suicide mortality rate	The number of suicide deaths in a year, divided by the population and multiplied by 100,000. Note: The number of suicide deaths refers to crude suicide rates (per 100,000 population).
Target 3.6: By 2020, halve the number of global deaths and injuries from road traffic accidents.	3.6.1: Death rate due to road traffic injuries	Number of road traffic fatal injury deaths per 100,000 population.

(continued on next page)

Goals and Targets	Statistical Indicators	Definition
Target 3.7: By 2030, ensure universal access to sexual and reproductive health care services, including for family planning, information, and education, and the integration of reproductive health into national strategies and programs	3.7.1: Proportion of women of reproductive age (15-49 years) who have their need for family planning satisfied by modern methods	The percentage of women of reproductive age (15-49 years) who desire either to have no (additional) children or to postpone the next child, and who are currently using a modern contraceptive method.
	3.7.2: Adolescent birth rate (aged 15-19 years) per 1,000 women in that age group	Annual number of births to females aged 15-19 years per 1,000 females in the respective age group.
Target 3.9: By 2030, substantially reduce the number of deaths and illnesses from hazardous chemicals and air, water, and soil pollution and contamination.	3.9.1: Mortality rate attributed to household and ambient air pollution	Expressed as the number of deaths and death rate. Death rates are calculated by dividing the number of deaths by the total population (or indicated if a different population group is used, e.g., children under 5 years). Note: Evidence from epidemiological studies has shown that exposure to air pollution is linked to, among others, the important diseases taken into account in this estimate: - acute respiratory infections in young children (estimated under 5 years of age); - cerebrovascular diseases (stroke) in adults (estimated above 25 years of age); - ischemic heart diseases in adults (estimated above 25 years of age); - chronic obstructive pulmonary disease in adults (estimated above 25 years of age); and - lung cancer in adults (estimated above 25 years of age).
	3.9.2: Mortality rate attributed to unsafe water, unsafe sanitation, and lack of hygiene—exposure to unsafe water, sanitation, and hygiene for all (WASH) services	Number of deaths from unsafe water, unsafe sanitation, and lack of hygiene —exposure to unsafe water, sanitation and hygiene for all (WASH) services—in a year, divided by the population, and multiplied by 100,000.
Goal 4. Ensure inclusive and equitable quality education and promote lifelong learning opportunities for all		
Target 4.2: By 2030, ensure that all girls and boys have access to quality early childhood development, care, and preprimary education, so that they are ready for primary education.	4.2.2: Participation rate in organized learning (1 year before the official primary entry age), by sex	Percentage of children in the given age range who participate in one or more organized learning programs, including programs which offer a combination of education and care. Note: An organized learning program is one that consists of a coherent set or sequence of educational activities designed with the intention of achieving predetermined learning outcomes or the accomplishment of a specific set of educational tasks. Early childhood and primary education programs are examples of organized learning programs. The official primary entry age is the age at which children are obliged to start primary education, according to national legislation or policies.

(continued on next page)

Goals and Targets	Statistical Indicators	Definition
Target 4.c: By 2030, substantially increase the supply of qualified teachers, including through international cooperation for teacher training in developing countries, especially least developed countries and small island developing states.	4.c.1.a: Proportion of teachers in pre-primary education who have received at least the minimum organized teacher training	Percentage of teachers by level of education taught (pre-primary, primary, lower secondary, and upper secondary education) who have received at least the minimum organized pedagogical teacher training pre-service and in-service required for teaching at the relevant level in a given country.

Note:
Number of teachers in a given level of education who are trained is expressed as a percentage of all teachers in that level of education. |
	4.c.1.b: Proportion of teachers in primary education who have received at least the minimum organized teacher training	
	4.c.1.c: Proportion of teachers in lower secondary education who have received at least the minimum organized teacher training	
	4.c.1.d: Proportion of teachers in upper secondary education who have received at least the minimum organized teacher training	
Goal 5. Achieve gender equality and empower all women and girls		
Target 5.3: Eliminate all harmful practices, such as child, early, and forced marriage, and female genital mutilation.	5.3.1: Proportion of women aged 20-24 years who were married or in a union before age 15 and before age 18	Proportion of women aged 20-24 years who were married or in a union before age 15 and before age 18.

Note:
Both formal (i.e., marriages) and informal unions are covered under this indicator. Informal unions are generally defined as those in which a couple lives together (i.e., cohabits) for some time, intends to have a lasting relationship, but for which there has been no formal civil or religious ceremony. |
| **Target 5.5:** Ensure women's full and effective participation in, and equal opportunities for leadership at, all levels of decision-making in political, economic, and public life. | 5.5.1: Proportion of seats held by women (a) in national parliaments and (b) local governments | The proportion of seats held by women in national parliaments, as of 1 February of reporting year, is currently measured as the number of seats held by women members in single or lower chambers of national parliaments, expressed as a percentage of all occupied seats.

Note:
National parliaments can be bicameral or unicameral. This indicator covers the single chamber in unicameral parliaments and the lower chamber in bicameral parliaments. It does not cover the upper chamber of bicameral parliaments. Seats are usually won by members in general parliamentary elections. Seats may also be filled by nomination, appointment, indirect election, rotation of members, and by-election.

Seats refer to the number of parliamentary mandates, or the number of members of parliament. |
| | 5.5.2: Proportion of women in managerial positions | Proportion of females in the total number of persons employed in senior and middle management. Senior and middle management correspond to major group 1 in International Standard Classification of Occupations (ISCO)-08 and ISCO-88, minus category 14 in ISCO-08 (hospitality, retail, and other services managers) and minus category 13 in ISCO-88 (general managers), since these comprise mainly managers of small enterprises.

Note:
The indicator provides information on the proportion of women who are employed in decision-making and managerial roles in government, large enterprises, and institutions, thus providing some insight into women's power in decision-making and in the economy (especially compared to men's power in those areas). |

(continued on next page)

Goals and Targets	Statistical Indicators	Definition
Goal 6. Ensure availability and sustainable management of water and sanitation for all		
Target 6.1: By 2030, achieve universal and equitable access to safe and affordable drinking water for all.	6.1.1: Proportion of population using safely managed drinking water services	Proportion of population using an improved basic drinking water source that is located on premises, available when needed, and free of fecal (and priority chemical) contamination. Note: Improved drinking water sources include the following: piped water into a dwelling, yard, or plot; public taps or standpipes; boreholes or tubewells; protected dug wells; protected springs; packaged water; delivered water and rainwater. A water source is considered to be 'located on premises' if the point of collection is within the dwelling, yard, or plot. 'Available when needed': households are able to access sufficient quantities of water when needed. 'Free from faecal and priority chemical contamination': water complies with relevant national or local standards. In the absence of such standards, reference is made to the WHO Guidelines for Drinking Water Quality (http://www.who.int/water_sanitation_health/dwq/guidelines/en/). E. coli or thermotolerant coliforms are the preferred indicator for microbiological quality, and arsenic and fluoride are the priority chemicals for global reporting. The WHO/UNICEF Joint Monitoring Programme (JMP) for Water Supply, Sanitation, and Hygiene estimates access to basic services for each country, separately in urban and rural areas, by fitting a regression line to a series of data points from household surveys and censuses. This approach was used to report on use of 'improved water' sources for Millennium Development Goal monitoring. The JMP is evaluating the use of alternative statistical estimation methods as more data become available. The JMP 2017 update and SDG baselines report describes in more detail how data on availability and quality from different sources, can be combined with data on use of different types of supplies, as recorded in the current JMP database to compute the safely managed drinking water services indicator. https://washdata.org/report/jmp-2017-report-final.
Target 6.2: By 2030, achieve access to adequate and equitable sanitation and hygiene for all, and end open defecation, paying special attention to the needs of women and girls and those in vulnerable situations.	6.2.1a: Proportion of population using safely managed sanitation services	The proportion of population using safely managed sanitation services, including a hand-washing facility with soap and water, is currently being measured by the proportion of the population using a basic sanitation facility that is not shared with other households and where excreta is safely disposed in situ or treated off-site. Note: Improved sanitation facilities include flush or pour-flush toilets to sewer systems, septic tanks or pit latrines, ventilated improved pit latrines, pit latrines with a slab, and composting toilets. Safely disposed in situ; when pit latrines and septic tanks are not emptied, the excreta may still remain isolated from human contact and can be considered safely managed. For example, with the new SDG indicator, households that use twin pit latrines or safely abandon full pit latrines and dig new facilities, a common practice in rural areas, would be counted as using safely managed sanitation services. Treated off-site; not all excreta from toilet facilities conveyed in sewers (as wastewater) or emptied from pit latrines and septic tanks (as faecal sludge) reaches a treatment site. For instance, a portion may leak from the sewer itself or, due to broken pumping installations, be discharged directly to the environment. Similarly, a portion of the faecal sludge emptied from containers may be discharged into open drains, to open ground or water bodies, rather than being transported to a treatment plant. And finally, even once the excreta reaches a treatment plant a portion may remain untreated, due to dysfunctional treatment equipment or inadequate treatment capacity, and be discharged to the environment. For the purposes of SDG monitoring, adequacy of treatment will initially be assessed based on the reported level of treatment.

(continued on next page)

Goals and Targets	Statistical Indicators	Definition
Target 6.4: By 2030, substantially increase water-use efficiency across all sectors and ensure sustainable withdrawals and supply of freshwater to address water scarcity and substantially reduce the number of people suffering from water scarcity.	6.4.2: Level of water stress; freshwater withdrawal as a proportion of available freshwater resources	Ratio of total freshwater withdrawn by all major sectors to total renewable freshwater resources, after taking into account environmental water requirements. Note: Total freshwater withdrawal is the volume of freshwater extracted from its source (rivers, lakes, aquifers) for agriculture, industries, and municipalities. Freshwater withdrawal includes primary freshwater (not withdrawn before), secondary freshwater (previously withdrawn and returned to rivers and groundwater, such as discharged wastewater and agricultural drainage water) and fossil groundwater. Main sectors, as defined by International Standard Industrial Classification standards, include agriculture, forestry and fishing, manufacturing, electricity industry, and services. Environmental water requirements are the quantities of water required to sustain freshwater and estuarine ecosystems. This indicator is also known as water withdrawal intensity. Total renewable freshwater resources are expressed as the sum of internal and external renewable water resources. Internal renewable water resources are defined as the long-term average annual flow of rivers and recharge of groundwater, generated from endogenous precipitation, for a given country. External renewable water resources refer to the flows of water entering the country, taking into consideration the quantity of flows reserved to upstream and downstream countries through agreements or treaties.
Target 6.a: By 2030, expand international cooperation and capacity-building support to developing countries in water- and sanitation-related activities and programs, including water harvesting, desalination, water efficiency, wastewater treatment, recycling, and reuse technologies.	6.a.1: Amount of water- and sanitation-related ODA that is part of a government-coordinated spending plan	Proportion of total water- and sanitation-related ODA disbursements that are included in a government's budget. Note: The amount of water- and sanitation-related ODA is a quantifiable measurement as a proxy for "international cooperation and capacity development support" in financial terms. A low value of this indicator (near 0%) would suggest that international donors are investing in water- and sanitation-related activities and programs in the country, outside the purview of the national government. A high value (near 100%) would indicate that donors are aligned with the national government and national policies and plans for water and sanitation.
Goal 7. Ensure access to affordable, reliable, sustainable, and modern energy for all		
Target 7.1: By 2030, ensure universal access to affordable, reliable, and modern energy services.	7.1.1: Proportion of population with access to electricity	Percentage of the population with access to electricity. Note: Access to electricity addresses major critical issues in all the dimensions of sustainable development. The target has a wide range of social and economic impacts, including facilitating development of household-based income-generating activities and lightening the burden of household tasks.
	7.1.2: Proportion of population with primary reliance on clean fuels and technology	Number of people using clean fuels and technologies for cooking, heating and lighting divided by total population reporting that any cooking, heating or lighting, expressed as percentage. "Clean" is defined by the emission rate targets and specific fuel recommendations (i.e. against unprocessed coal and kerosene) included in the normative guidance WHO guidelines for indoor air quality: household fuel combustion.

(continued on next page)

Goals and Targets	Statistical Indicators	Definition
Target 7.2: By 2030, increase substantially the share of renewable energy in the global energy mix.	7.2.1: Renewable energy share in total final energy consumption	Percentage of final consumption of energy that is derived from renewable resources. Note: Renewable energy consumption includes consumption of energy derived from hydro, solid biofuels, wind, solar, liquid biofuels, biogas, geothermal, marine sources, and waste. Total final energy consumption is calculated from national balances and statistics as total final consumption minus nonenergy use.
Target 7.3: By 2030, double the global rate of improvement in energy efficiency.	7.3.1: Energy intensity measured in terms of primary energy and GDP	Energy supplied to the economy per unit value of economic output. Note: Total energy supply, as defined by the International Recommendations for Energy Statistics, is made up of production, plus net imports, minus international marine and aviation bunkers plus-stock changes. GDP is the measure of economic output. For international comparison purposes, GDP is measured in constant terms at PPP.
Goal 8. Promote sustained, inclusive, and sustainable economic growth, full and productive employment, and decent work for all		
Target 8.1: Sustain per-capita economic growth in accordance with national circumstances and, in particular, at least 7% GDP growth per annum in the least developed countries.	8.1.1: Annual growth rate of real GDP per capita	Percentage change in the real GDP per capita between 2 consecutive years. Note: Real GDP per capita is calculated by dividing GDP at constant prices by the population of a country or area. The data for real GDP are measured in constant US dollars to facilitate the calculation of country growth rates and aggregation of the country data.
Target 8.2: Achieve higher levels of economic productivity through diversification, technological upgrading, and innovation, including through a focus on high-value-added and labor-intensive sectors.	8.2.1: Annual growth rate of real GDP per employed person	Annual percentage change in real GDP per employed person.
Target 8.5: By 2030, achieve full and productive employment and decent work for all women and men, including for young people and persons with disabilities, and equal pay for work of equal value.	8.5.2: Unemployment rate, by sex and age	Percentage of persons in the labor force who are unemployed. Note: Unemployed persons are defined as all those of working age (usually persons aged 15 and above) who were not in employment, carried out activities to seek employment during a specified recent period, and were currently available to take up employment given a job opportunity, where: (i) "not in employment" is assessed with respect to the short reference period for the measurement of employment; (ii) to "seek employment" refers to any activity when carried out, during a specified recent period comprising the past 4 weeks or 1 month, for the purpose of finding a job or setting up a business or agricultural undertaking; (iii) the point when the enterprise starts to exist should be used to distinguish between search activities aimed at setting up a business and the work activity itself, as evidenced by the enterprise's registration to operate or by when financial resources become available, the necessary infrastructure or materials are in place, or the first client or order is received, depending on the context; and (iv) "currently available" serves as a test of readiness to start a job in the present, assessed with respect to a short reference period comprising that used to measure employment (depending on national circumstances, the reference period may be extended to include a short subsequent period not exceeding 2 weeks in total, so as to ensure adequate coverage of unemployment situations among different population groups).
Target 8.6: By 2020, substantially reduce the proportion of youth not in employment, education, or training.	8.6.1: Proportion of youth (aged 15-24 years) not in education, employment, or training	Proportion of youth (aged 15-24 years) who are not in education, employment, or training, also known as "the NEET rate." It conveys the number of young persons not in education, employment, or training as a percentage of the total youth population.

(continued on next page)

Goals and Targets	Statistical Indicators	Definition
Target 8.7: Take immediate and effective measures to eradicate forced labor, end modern slavery and human trafficking, and secure the prohibition and elimination of the worst forms of child labor, including recruitment and use of child soldiers, and, by 2025, end child labor in all its forms.	8.7.1: Proportion of children aged 5-17 years engaged in child labor	The number of children aged 5-17 years reported to be in child labor during the reference period (usually the week prior to the survey). The proportion of children in child labor is calculated as the number of children in child labor, divided by the total number of children in the population.
Target 8.10: Strengthen the capacity of domestic financial institutions to encourage and expand access to banking, insurance, and financial services for all.	8.10.1: Number of commercial bank branches and ATMs per 100,000 adults	The number of commercial bank branches per 100,000 adults refers to the number of commercial banks branches reported by the central bank or the main financial regulator of the country every year. To make it comparable, this number is presented as a reference per 100,000 adults in the respective country. The number of ATMs per 100,000 adults, refers to the number of ATMs in the country for all types of institutions, such as commercial banks, non-deposit-taking microfinance institutions, deposit-taking micro finance institutions, credit unions, financial cooperatives, and others. This information is reported every year by the central bank or the main financial regulator of the country. To make it comparable, this number is presented as a reference per 100,000 adults in the respective country.
	8.10.2: Proportion of adults (aged 15 years and older) with an account at a bank or other financial institution or with a mobile-money service provider	Percentage of adults (aged 15+) who report having an account (of their own or held with someone else) at a bank or another type of financial institution, or have personally used a mobile-money service in the past 12 months.
Goal 9. Build resilient infrastructure, promote inclusive and sustainable industrialization, and foster innovation		
Target 9.1: Develop quality, reliable, sustainable, and resilient infrastructure, including regional and transborder infrastructure, to support economic development and human well-being, with a focus on affordable and equitable access for all.	9.1.2: Passenger volume by road transport, measured in millions of passenger-kilometers	Passenger and freight volumes are the sums of the passenger and freight volumes reported for the road and air carriers in terms of number of people and metric tons of cargo, respectively. The International Transport Forum collects data on transport (rail and road) statistics on annual basis from all its member countries. Data are collected from transport ministries, statistical offices, and other institutions designated as official data sources. Although there are clear definitions for all the terms used in this survey, countries might have different methodologies to calculate passenger-kilometers and ton-kilometers. Methods could be based on traffic or mobility surveys, using very different sampling methods and estimating techniques, which could affect the comparability of the statistics.
	9.1.2: Freight volume by road transport, measured in millions of ton-kilometers	
	9.1.2: Passenger volume by air transport, measured in millions of passenger-kilometers	
	9.1.2: Freight volume by air transport, measured in thousands of ton-kilometers	
Target 9.2: Promote inclusive and sustainable industrialization and, by 2030, significantly raise industry's share of employment and GDP, in line with national circumstances, and double its share in least developed countries.	9.2.1: Manufacturing value added as a proportion of GDP and per capita	Manufacturing value added (MVA) as a proportion of GDP is a ratio between MVA and GDP, both reported in constant 2010 US dollars. MVA per capita is calculated by dividing MVA in constant 2010 US dollars by the population of a country or area.
	9.2.2: Manufacturing employment as a proportion of total employment	Share of manufacturing employment in total employment.

(continued on next page)

Goals and Targets	Statistical Indicators	Definition
Target 9.4: By 2030, upgrade infrastructure and retrofit industries to make them sustainable, with increased resource-use efficiency and greater adoption of clean and environmentally sound technologies and industrial processes, with all countries taking action in accordance with their respective capabilities.	9.4.1: Carbon dioxide (CO_2) emissions per unit of value added	CO_2 emissions per unit value added is an indicator calculated as ratio between CO_2 emissions from fuel combustion and the value added of associated economic activities. The indicator can be calculated for the whole economy (total CO_2 emissions to GDP) or for specific sectors, notably the manufacturing sector (CO_2 emissions from manufacturing industries per MVA). CO_2 emissions per unit of GDP are expressed in kilograms of CO_2 per constant 2010 US dollar PPP GDP. CO_2 emissions from manufacturing industries per unit of MVA are measured in kilograms of CO_2 equivalent per unit of MVA in constant 2010 US dollars.
Target 9.5: Enhance scientific research and upgrade the technological capabilities of industrial sectors in all countries, in particular developing countries, including, by 2030, encouraging innovation and substantially increasing the number of research and development workers per 1 million people and public and private research and development spending.	9.5.1: Research and development expenditure as a proportion of GDP	Amount of research and development expenditure divided by the total output of the economy.
	9.5.2: Researchers (full-time equivalent) per million inhabitants	Number of research and development workers per 1 million people.
Target 9.a: Facilitate sustainable and resilient infrastructure development in developing countries through enhanced financial, technological, and technical support to African countries, least developed countries, landlocked developing countries, and small island developing states.	9.a.1: Total official international support (ODA plus other official flows) to infrastructure	Gross disbursements of total ODA and other official flows from all donors in support of infrastructure.
Target 9.b: Support domestic technology development, research, and innovation in developing countries, including by ensuring a conducive policy environment for, among other things, industrial diversification and value addition to commodities.	9.b.1: Proportion of medium- and high-tech industry value added in total value added	Ratio of the value added by medium- and high-tech (MHT) industry to total MVA. Note: Industrial development generally entails a structural transition from resource-based and low-tech activities to MHT activities. A modern, highly complex production structure offers better opportunities for skills development and technological innovation. MHT activities are also the high-value addition industries of manufacturing with higher technological intensity and labor productivity. Increasing the share of MHT sectors also reflects the impact of innovation.

(continued on next page)

Goals and Targets	Statistical Indicators	Definition
Target 9.c: Significantly increase access to information and communications technology, and strive to provide universal and affordable access to the Internet in least developed countries by 2020.	9.c.1.a: Proportion of the population covered by narrowband (2G) mobile networks	Proportion of the population covered by a mobile network, broken down by technology, refers to the percentage of inhabitants living within range of a mobile-cellular signal, irrespective of whether or not they are mobile-phone subscribers or users. This is calculated by dividing the number of inhabitants within range of a mobile-cellular signal by the total population and multiplying by 100. Note: Coverage refers to Long-Term Evolution (LTE), broadband (3G), and narrowband (2G) mobile-cellular technologies: 2G mobile population coverage refers to the percentage of inhabitants within range of a mobile networks with access to data communications (e.g. Internet) at downstream speeds below 256 Kbit/s. This includes mobile-cellular technologies such as general packet radio service (GPRS), code division multiple access (CDMA) 2000 1x and most enhanced data for GSM (global system for mobile communications) evolution (EDGE) implementations. 3G population coverage refers to the percentage of inhabitants that are within range of at least a 3G mobile-cellular signal, irrespective of whether or not they are subscribers. Long-term evolution (LTE) population coverage refers to the percentage of inhabitants that live within range of LTE/LTE-Advanced, mobile WiMAX/WirelessMAN or other more advanced mobile-cellular networks, irrespective of whether or not they are subscribers.
	9.c.1.b: Proportion of the population covered by 3G mobile networks	
	9.c.1.c: Proportion of the population covered by LTE mobile networks	
Goal 10. Reduce inequality within and among countries		
Target 10.1: By 2030, progressively achieve and sustain income growth of the bottom 40% of the population at a rate higher than the national average.	10.1.1.a: Growth rates of household expenditure or income per capita among the bottom 40% of the population	The growth rate in the welfare aggregate of the bottom 40% of the population is calculated as the annualized average growth rate in per capita real consumption or income of the bottom 40% of the income distribution in a country from household surveys over a period of approximately 5 years.
	10.1.1.b: Growth rates of household expenditure or income per capita	The national average growth rate in the welfare aggregate is calculated as the annualized average growth rate in per capita real consumption or income of the total population in a country from household surveys over a period of approximately 5years.
Goal 11. Make cities and human settlements inclusive, safe, resilient, and sustainable		
Target 11.1: By 2030, ensure access for all to adequate, safe, and affordable housing and basic services, and upgrade slums.	11.1.1: Proportion of the urban population living in slums, informal settlements, or inadequate housing	The proportion of the urban population living in slums, informal settlements, or inadequate housing is currently being measured by the proportion of the urban population living in slums. This indicator integrates the component of the slums and informal settlements that has been monitored for the past 15 years by United Nations (UN)-Habitat in mostly developing countries with a new component—inadequate housing— that applies largely to the developed countries. By integrating these two components, the indicator is now universal and can be monitored in both developing and developed regions. The inadequate housing component allows capturing housing informality in more developed countries and wealthier urban contexts.

(continued on next page)

Goals and Targets	Statistical Indicators	Definition
Target 11.5: By 2030, significantly reduce the number of deaths and the number of people affected, and substantially decrease the direct economic losses relative to global GDP caused by disasters, including water-related disasters, with a focus on protecting the poor and people in vulnerable situations	11.5.2: Direct economic loss in relation to global GDP, damage to critical infrastructure, and number of disruptions to basic services, attributed to disasters	Direct economic loss is the monetary value of total or partial destruction of physical assets existing in the affected area. Direct economic loss is nearly equivalent to physical damage. Note: The original national disaster loss databases usually register physical damage value (housing unit loss, infrastructure loss, etc.), which needs conversion to a monetary value according to the United Nations International Strategy for Disaster Reduction methodology*. The converted global value is divided by global GDP (inflation adjusted, constant US dollars) calculated from the World Bank Development Indicators.
Target 11.6: By 2030, reduce the adverse per capita environmental impact of cities, including by paying special attention to air quality and municipal and other waste management.	11.6.2: Annual mean levels of fine particulate matter (PM), e.g., PM2.5 and PM10 in cities, measured in total (population weighted) micrograms per cubic meter	The mean annual concentration of fine suspended particles of less than 2.5 microns in diameters (PM2.5) is a common measure of air pollution. Note: The mean is a population-weighted average for urban population in a country and is expressed in micrograms per cubic meter.
Goal 12. Ensure sustainable consumption and production patterns		
Target 12.2: By 2030, achieve the sustainable management and efficient use of natural resources	12.2.1: Material footprint, material footprint per capita, and material footprint per GDP	Material footprint is the attribution of global material extraction to domestic final demand of a country. The total material footprint is the sum of the material footprint for biomass, fossil fuels, metal ores, and nonmetal ores.
	12.2.2: Domestic material consumption, domestic material consumption per capita, and domestic material consumption per GDP	Domestic material consumption is a standard material flow accounting indicator and reports the apparent consumption of materials in a national economy.
Goal 13. Take urgent action to combat climate change and its impacts		
Target 13.1: Strengthen resilience and adaptive capacity to climate-related hazards and natural disasters in all countries.	13.1.1.a: Number of persons affected by disasters	Number of people who died, went missing, or were directly affected by disasters per 100,000 population. Directly affected means people who have suffered injury, illness, or other health effects; who were evacuated, displaced, or relocated; or have suffered direct damage to their livelihoods, economic, physical, social, cultural, and/or environmental assets.
	13.1.1.b: Number of deaths due to disasters	The number of people who died during, or directly after, a disaster, as a direct result of the hazardous event.
	13.1.2: Number of countries that adopt and implement national disaster risk reduction strategies in line the Sendai Framework for Disaster Risk Reduction 2015–2030	Proportion of local governments that adopt and implement local disaster risk reduction strategies in line with national disaster risk reduction strategies. Note: An open-ended intergovernmental expert working group on indicators and terminology relating to disaster risk reduction established by the UN General Assembly (resolution 69/284) is developing a set of indicators to measure global progress in the implementation of the Sendai Framework. These indicators will eventually reflect the agreements on the Sendai Framework indicators.

(continued on next page)

Goals and Targets	Statistical Indicators	Definition
Goal 14. Conserve and sustainably use the oceans, seas, and marine resources for sustainable development		
Target 14.5: By 2020, conserve at least 10% of coastal and marine areas, consistent with national and international law and based on the best available scientific information.	14.5.1: Coverage of protected areas in relation to marine areas	The indicator measures the coverage of protected areas in relation to marine areas and shows temporal trends in the mean percentage of important sites for marine biodiversity (i.e., those that contribute significantly to the global persistence of biodiversity or key biodiversity areas) that are wholly covered by designated protected areas. Note: The International Union for Conservation of Nature (IUCN) defines a protected area as "a clearly defined geographical space, recognized, dedicated and managed, through legal or other effective means, to achieve the long-term conservation of nature with associated ecosystem services and cultural values."
Goal 15. Protect, restore, and promote sustainable use of terrestrial ecosystems, sustainably manage forests, combat desertification, halt and reverse land degradation, and halt biodiversity loss		
Target 15.1: By 2020, ensure the conservation, restoration, and sustainable use of terrestrial and inland freshwater ecosystems and their services, in particular forests, wetlands, mountains, and drylands, in line with obligations under international agreements.	15.1.1: Forest area as a proportion of total land area	Size of forest cover in relation to total land area.
	15.1.2: Proportion of important sites for terrestrial and freshwater biodiversity that are covered by protected areas, by ecosystem type	Proportion of important sites for terrestrial and freshwater biodiversity that are covered by protected areas shows temporal trends in the mean percentage of each important site for terrestrial and freshwater biodiversity (i.e., those that contribute significantly to the global persistence of biodiversity) that is covered by designated protected areas.
Target 15.4: By 2030, ensure the conservation of mountain ecosystems, including their biodiversity, in order to enhance their capacity to provide benefits that are essential for sustainable development	15.4.1: Coverage by protected areas of important sites for mountain biodiversity	Coverage by protected areas of important sites for mountain biodiversity shows temporal trends in the mean percentage of each important site for mountain biodiversity (i.e., those that contribute significantly to the global persistence of biodiversity) that is covered by designated protected areas. Note: Protected areas, as defined by the IUCN (IUCN; Dudley 2008), are clearly defined geographical spaces, recognized, dedicated, and managed, through legal or other effective means, to achieve the long-term conservation of nature with associated ecosystem services and cultural values. Importantly, a variety of specific management objectives are recognized within this definition, spanning conservation, restoration, and sustainable use: "(i) Category Ia: Strict nature reserve; (ii) Category Ib: Wilderness area; (iii) Category II: National park; (iv) Category III: Natural monument or feature; (v) Category IV: Habitat/species management area; (vi) Category V: Protected landscape/seascape; (vii) Category VI: Protected area with sustainable use of natural resources."
Target 15.5: Take urgent and significant action to reduce the degradation of natural habitats, halt the loss of biodiversity and, by 2020, protect and prevent the extinction of threatened species.	15.5.1: Red List Index	The Red List Index measures changes in aggregate extinction risk across groups of species. It is based on genuine changes in the number of species in each category of extinction risk on the IUCN Red List of Threatened Species (IUCN 2015), which is expressed as changes in an index ranging from 0 to 1. Note: The Red List Index value ranges from 1 (all species are categorized as "Least Concern") to 0 (all species are categorized as "Extinct"), indicating how far the set of species has moved overall toward extinction.

(continued on next page)

Goals and Targets	Statistical Indicators	Definition
Goal 16. Promote peaceful and inclusive societies for sustainable development; provide access to justice for all; and build effective, accountable, and inclusive institutions at all levels		
Target 16.1: Significantly reduce all forms of violence and related death rates everywhere.	16.1.1: Number of victims of intentional homicide per 100,000 population, by sex and age	Total count of victims of intentional homicide divided by the total population, expressed per 100,000 population. Intentional homicide is defined as the unlawful death inflicted upon a person with the intent to cause death or serious injury (International Classification of Crime for Statistical Purposes, ICCS 2015). Population refers to total resident population in a given country in a given year. Note: This indicator is widely used at national and international levels to measure the most extreme form of violent crime, providing a direct indication of lack of security.
Target 16.3: Promote the rule of law at the national and international levels, and ensure equal access to justice for all.	16.3.2: Unsentenced detainees as a proportion of the overall prison population	Total number of persons held in detention who have not yet been sentenced, as a percentage of the total number of persons held in detention, on a specified date.
Target 16.5: Substantially reduce corruption and bribery in all their forms.	16.5.2: Proportion of businesses that had at least one contact with a public official and that paid a bribe to a public official, or were asked for a bribe by those public officials during the previous 12 months	Proportion of firms that were asked for a gift or informal payment when meeting with tax officials. Note: This indicator aims to ascertain whether or not firms have been solicited for gifts or informal payments (i.e., bribes) when meeting with tax officials. Paying taxes are required of formal forms in most countries, and the rationale for this indicator is to measure the incidence of corruption during this routine interaction.
Target 16.9: By 2030, provide legal identity, including birth registration, for all.	16.9.1: Proportion of children under 5 years of age whose births have been registered with a civil authority, by age	Proportion of children under 5 years of age whose births have been registered with a civil authority.
Goal 17. Strengthen the means of implementation and revitalize the Global Partnership for Sustainable Development		
Target 17.4: Assist developing countries in attaining long-term debt sustainability through coordinated policies aimed at fostering debt financing, debt relief, and debt restructuring, as appropriate, and address the external debt of highly indebted poor countries to reduce debt distress	17.4.1: Debt service as a proportion of exports of goods and services	Percentage of debt services (principle and interest payments) to the exports of goods and services. Debt services covered in this indicator refer only to public and publicly guaranteed debt.

Goals and Targets	Statistical Indicators	Definition
Target 17.9: Enhance international support for implementing effective and targeted capacity-building in developing countries to support national plans to implement all the Sustainable Development Goals, including through North-South, South-South, and triangular cooperation.	17.9.1: Dollar value of financial and technical assistance (including through North-South, South-South, and triangular cooperation) committed to developing countries	Gross disbursements of total ODA and other official flows from all donors for capacity-building and national planning.

Note:
ODA refers to "those flows to countries and territories on the Development Assistance Committee List of ODA Recipients and to multilateral institutions which are (i) provided by official agencies, including state and local governments, or by their executive agencies; and (ii) each transaction is administered with the promotion of the economic development and welfare of developing countries as its main objective; and is concessional in character and conveys a grant element of at least 25% (calculated at a rate of discount of 10%).

Other official flows (excluding officially supported export credits) are defined as transactions by the official sector that do not meet the conditions for eligibility as ODA, either because they are not primarily aimed at development or because they are not sufficiently concessional. |
| **Target 17.18:** By 2020, enhance capacity-building support to developing countries, including for least developed countries and small island developing states, to increase significantly the availability of high-quality, timely, and reliable data disaggregated by income, gender, age, race, ethnicity, migratory status, disability, geographic location, and other characteristics relevant in national contexts. | 17.18.3: Number of countries with a national statistical plan that is fully funded and under implementation, by source of funding | Count of countries that are either (i) implementing a strategy, (ii) designing a strategy, or (iii) awaiting adoption of a strategy in the current year.

Note:
The indicator is based on the annual Status Report on National Strategies for the Development of Statistics. In collaboration with its partners, PARIS21 reports on country progress in designing and implementing national statistical plans.

This indicator can be disaggregated by geographical area. Regional-level aggregates are based on the total count of national strategies. |
| **Target 17.19:** By 2030, build on existing initiatives to develop measurements of progress on sustainable development that complement GDP, and support statistical capacity-building in developing countries. | 17.19.1: Dollar value of all resources made available to strengthen statistical capacity in developing countries | US dollar value of ongoing statistical support in developing countries.

Note:
The indictor is based on the Partner Report on Support to Statistics, which is designed and administered by PARIS21 to provide a snapshot of the US dollar value of ongoing statistical support in developing countries. |
| | 17.19.2: Number of countries that have conducted at least one population and housing census in the last 10 years | Countries that have conducted at least one population and housing census in the last 10 years. This includes countries that compile their detailed population and housing statistics from population registers, administrative records, sample surveys, other sources, or a combination of those sources. |

Regional Trends and Tables

Indicator	Definition
PEOPLE	
Population	
Midyear Population	Estimates of the midyear de facto population. De facto population includes all persons physically present in the country during the census day, including foreign, military, and diplomatic personnel and their accompanying household members; and transient foreign visitors in the country or in harbors.
Growth Rates in Population	Number of people added to (or subtracted from) a population over a given period of time because of natural increase and net migration, expressed as a percentage of the population at the given period of time.
Net International Migration Rate	Number of immigrants minus the number of emigrants over a period, divided by the person-years lived by the population of the receiving country over that period. It is expressed as net number of migrants per 1,000 population.
Urban Population (as % of total population)	Population living in urban areas, defined in accordance with the national definition or as used in the most recent population census. Because of national differences in the characteristics that distinguish urban from rural areas, the distinction between urban and rural populations is not amenable to a single definition that would be applicable to all countries. National definitions are most commonly based on size of locality. Population that is not urban is considered rural. The estimated population living in urban areas at midyear as a percentage of the total midyear population in a country.
Age Dependency Ratio	Ratio of the nonworking-age population to the working-age population. Since countries define working age differently, a straightforward application of the definition will lead to noncomparable data. The Asian Development Bank therefore uses the following United Nations definition that can be calculated directly from an age distribution: $$\frac{\text{Population aged (0–14) + (65 and over) years}}{\text{Population aged (15–64) years}} \times 100$$
Labor Force and Employment	
Labor Force Participation Rate	Percentage of the labor force to the working-age population. The labor force is the sum of those employed and unemployed but seeking work. The labor force participation rate measures the extent of the economically active working-age population in an economy. It provides an indication of the relative size of the supply of labor available for the production of goods and services in the economy. It must be noted that the definition of working-age population varies across countries.
Employment in Agriculture	Employment in agriculture, including forestry and fishing, that corresponds to division 1 (International Standard of Industrial Classification [ISIC] revision 2), tabulation categories A and B (ISIC revision 3), and category A of ISIC revision 4.
Employment in Industry	Employment in industry includes mining and quarrying; manufacturing; electricity, gas, steam, and air-conditioning supply; water supply; sewage, waste management, and remediation activities; and construction.
Employment in Mining and Quarrying	Employment in mining and quarrying that corresponds to division 2 (ISIC revision 2), tabulation category C (ISIC revision 3), and category B of ISIC revision 4.
Employment in Manufacturing	Employment in manufacturing that corresponds to division 3 (ISIC revision 2), tabulation category D (ISIC revision 3), and category C of ISIC revision 4.
Employment in Electricity, Gas, Steam, and Air-Conditioning Supply; Water Supply; Sewerage, Waste Management and Remediation Activities	Employment in electricity, gas, steam, and air-conditioning supply; water supply; sewerage, waste management, and remediation activities that corresponds to division 4 (ISIC revision 2), tabulation category E (ISIC revision 3), and categories D and E of ISIC revision 4.
Employment in Construction	Employment in construction that corresponds to division 5 (ISIC revision 2), tabulation category F (ISIC revisions 3), and category F of ISIC revision 4.

(continued on next page)

Indicator	Definition
Employment in Service	Employment in service includes wholesale and retail trade; repair of motor vehicles and motorcycles; accommodation and food service activities; transportation and storage; information and communication; financial and insurance activities; real estate activities; and other services.
Employment in Wholesale and Retail Trade; Repair of Motor Vehicles and Motorcycles	Employment in wholesale and retail trade; repair of motor vehicles and motorcycles that corresponds to division 6 (subdivisions 61 and 62, ISIC revision 2); tabulation category G (ISIC revision 3); and category G of ISIC revision 4.
Employment in Accommodation and Food Service Activities	Employment in accommodation and food service activities that corresponds to division 6 (subdivision 63, ISIC revision 2); tabulation category H (ISIC revision 3); and category I of ISIC revision 4.
Employment in Transportation and Storage	Employment in transport and storage that corresponds to division 7 (subdivision 71, ISIC revision 2); tabulation category I (sub-categories 60–63, ISIC revision 3); and category H of ISIC revision 4.
Employment in Information and Communication	Employment in information and communication that corresponds to division 7 (subdivision 72, ISIC revision 2); tabulation category I (subcategory 64, ISIC revision 3); and category J of ISIC revision 4.
Employment in Financial and Insurance Activities	Employment in financial and insurance activities that corresponds to division 8 (subdivisions 81–82, ISIC revision 2), tabulation category J (ISIC revision 3), and category K of ISIC revision 4.
Employment in Real Estate Activities	Employment in real estate activities that corresponds to division 8 (subdivision 83, ISIC revision 2); tabulation category K (subcategory 70, ISIC revision 3); and category L of ISIC revision 4.
Employment in Other Services	Employment in other services that corresponds to divisions 9 and 0 (ISIC revision 2), tabulation categories L to Q (ISIC revision 3), and categories M to U of ISIC revision 4.
Poverty Indicators	
Proportion of Population below $1.90 a Day (2011 PPP)	Percentage of the population living on less than $1.90 a day at 2011 purchasing power parity (PPP).
Proportion of Population below $3.20 a Day (2011 PPP)	Percentage of the population living on less than $3.20 a day at 2011 PPP.
Income Ratio of Highest 20% to Lowest 20%	Income or consumption share that accrues to the richest 20% of the population, divided by the income or consumption share of the lowest 20% of the population.
Gini Coefficient or Index	Measure of the degree to which an economy's income distribution diverges from perfect equal distribution. A value of zero (0) implies perfect equality while a value of one (1) implies perfect inequality.
Human Development Index	Composite index of long and healthy life (measured by life expectancy at birth), knowledge (measured by expected years of schooling and mean years of schooling), and decent standard of living (measured by gross national income per capita in United States [US] PPP dollars).
Social Indicators	
Life Expectancy at Birth	Number of years that a newborn is expected to live if prevailing patterns of mortality at the time of his or her birth are to stay the same throughout his or her life.
Crude Birth Rate	Ratio of the total number of live births in a given period to the midyear total population of the same period, expressed per 1,000 people.
Crude Death Rate	Ratio of the number of deaths occurring within a given period to the midyear total population of the same period, expressed per 1,000 people.
Total Fertility Rate	Number of children that would be born to a woman if she were to live to the end of her childbearing years and bear children in accordance with current age-specific fertility rates.
Primary Education Completion Rate	Total number of new entrants in the last grade of primary education, regardless of age, expressed as a percentage of the total population at the theoretical entrance age to the last grade of primary education. This indicator is also known as "gross intake rate to the last grade of primary." The ratio can exceed 100% due to overaged and underaged children who enter primary school late, early, and/or repeat grades.

(continued on next page)

Indicator	Definition
Adult Literacy Rate	The percentage of the population aged 15 years and over who can both read and write (with understanding) a short simple statement on his or her everyday life. Generally, literacy also encompasses numeracy, i.e., the ability to make simple arithmetic calculations.
Primary Pupil–Teacher Ratio	Average number of pupils (students) per teacher at the primary level of education in a given school year. This indicator is used to measure the level of human resources input in terms of number of teachers in relation to the size of the primary pupil population.
Secondary Pupil–Teacher Ratio	Average number of pupils (students) per teacher at the secondary level of education in a given school year. This indicator is used to measure the level of human resources input in terms of number of teachers in relation to the size of the secondary pupil population.
Physicians	Physicians, including general and specialist medical practitioners, expressed in terms of the number per 1,000 people.
Hospital Beds	In-patient beds for both acute and chronic care available in public, private, general, and specialized hospitals and rehabilitation centers expressed in terms of the number per 1,000 people.
Number of Adults Living with HIV	All adults, defined as men and women aged 15 years and over years, with HIV infection, whether or not they have developed symptoms of AIDS, estimated to be alive at the end of a specific year.

ECONOMY AND OUTPUT

National Accounts

Indicator	Definition
Gross Domestic Product	Unduplicated market value of the total production activity of all resident producer units within the economic territory of a country during a given period. It is calculated without making deductions for depreciation of fabricated assets or for depletion and degradation of natural resources. Transfer payments are excluded from the calculation of gross domestic product (GDP). GDP can be calculated using the production, expenditure, and income approaches.

Production-based GDP is the sum of the gross value added by all resident producers in the economy, plus any taxes and minus any subsidies not included in the value of the products. Gross value added is the net output of an industry after adding up all outputs and subtracting intermediate inputs.

Income-based GDP is the sum of the compensation of employees, mixed income, operating surplus, consumption of fixed capital, and taxes, less subsidies on production and imports.

Expenditure-based GDP is the sum of final consumption expenditure of households, nonprofit institutions serving households, and the government; gross capital formation; and exports minus imports of goods and services.

GDP can be measured at current prices (the prices of the current reporting period), and constant prices (obtained by expressing values in terms of a base period and chain volume measure). |
GDP at PPP	Measures obtained by using PPP to convert the GDP into a common currency, and by valuing them at a uniform price level. They are the spatial equivalent of a time series of GDP for a single country expressed at constant prices. At the level of GDP, they are used to compare the economic size of countries.
GDP at Current US Dollar	GDP at local currency units are obtained from the economy sources and are converted to US dollars using the official exchange rates from the International Monetary Fund (IMF). The exchange rates used are expressed as the average rate for a period of time (average of period), calculated as annual averages based on the monthly averages (local currency units relative to the US dollar).
GDP per Capita at PPP	GDP at PPP, divided by the midyear population.

(continued on next page)

Indicator	Definition
GNI per Capita, Atlas Method	The gross national income (GNI) converted to US dollars using the World Bank Atlas method, divided by the midyear population. GNI is the sum of value added by all resident producers, plus any product taxes (less subsidies) not included in the valuation of output, plus net receipts of primary income (compensation of employees and property income) from abroad. GNI, calculated in national currency, is usually converted to US dollars at official exchange rates for comparisons across economies, although an alternative rate is used when the official exchange rate is judged to diverge by an exceptionally large margin from the rate actually applied in international transactions. To smooth fluctuations in prices and exchange rates, a special Atlas method of conversion is used by the World Bank. This applies a conversion factor that averages the exchange rate for a given year and the 2 preceding years, adjusted for differences in rates of inflation between the country, and through 2000, the G-5 countries (France, Germany, Japan, the United Kingdom, and the US). From 2001, these countries include the Euro area, Japan, the United Kingdom, and the US.
GDP per Capita at Current US Dollar	GDP at current US dollar value, divided by the midyear population.
Agriculture Value Added	The gross output of agriculture, less the corresponding value of intermediate consumption. The industrial origin of value added is determined by ISIC revision 4, where agriculture corresponds to ISIC Section A and includes agriculture, forestry, and fishing.
Industry Value Added	The gross output of industry sectors, less the corresponding value of intermediate consumption. The industrial origin of value added is determined by ISIC revision 4, where industry corresponds to ISIC Sections B-F and includes mining and quarrying (B); manufacturing (C); electricity, gas, steam, and air-conditioning supply (D); water supply; sewage waste management, and remediation activities (E); and construction (F).
Services Value Added	The gross output of services sectors, less the corresponding value of intermediate consumption. The industrial origin of value added is determined by ISIC revision 4. Services corresponds to ISIC Sections G-U and includes wholesale and retail trade; repair of motor vehicles and motorcycles (G); transport and storage (H); accommodation and food service activities (I); information and communication (J); financial and insurance activities (K); real estate activities (L); professional, scientific, and technical activities (M); administrative and support service activities (N); public administration and defense; compulsory social security (O); education (P); human health and social work activities (Q); arts, entertainment, and recreation (R); other service activities (S); activities of households as employers; undifferentiated goods- and services-producing activities of households for own use (T); and activities of extraterritorial organizations and bodies (U).
Household Consumption Expenditure	Market value of all goods and services, including durable products (such as cars, washing machines, and home computers), purchased or received as income in kind by households. It excludes purchases of dwellings, but includes imputed rent for owner-occupied dwellings. It also includes payments and fees to governments to obtain permits and licenses. The expenditure of nonprofit institutions serving households is generally recorded as the consumption of households for most economies.
Government Consumption Expenditure	Includes all current outlays on purchases of goods and services (including wages and salaries). It also includes most expenditure on national defense and security, but excludes government military expenditures that are part of public investment.
Gross Capital Formation	Total value of gross fixed capital formation, changes in inventories, and acquisitions less disposals of valuables. Gross fixed capital formation is the value of acquisitions less disposals of tangible goods (such as buildings) and intangible goods (such as computer software) that are intended for use in production during several accounting periods. Changes in inventories are changes in stocks of produced goods and goods for intermediate consumption, and the net increase in the value of work in progress. Valuables are goods (such as precious metals and works of art) that are acquired in the expectation that they will retain or increase their value over time.
Exports of Goods and Services	Consist of sales, bartering, or gifts or grants of goods and services from residents to nonresidents. The treatment of exports in the System of National Accounts is generally identical with that in the balance of payments accounts as described in the IMF's Balance of Payments Manual.

(continued on next page)

Indicator	Definition
Imports of Goods and Services	Consist of purchases, bartering, or receipts of gifts or grants of goods and services by residents from nonresidents. The treatment of imports in the System of National Accounts is generally identical with that in the balance of payments accounts as described in the IMF's Balance of Payments Manual.
Gross Domestic Saving	Difference between GDP and final consumption expenditure, where final consumption expenditure is the sum of the final consumption of household, nonprofit institutions serving households, and the government.
Production	
Agriculture Production Index	Relative level of the aggregate volume of agricultural production for each year in comparison with the base period. It is based on the sum of price-weighted quantities of different agricultural commodities produced after deductions of quantities used as seed and feed weighted in a similar manner. The resulting aggregate therefore represents disposable production for any use, except as seed and feed.
Manufacturing Production Index	An index covering production in manufacturing. The exact coverage, the weighting system, and the methods of calculation vary from country to country, but the divergences are less important than, for example, in the case of price and wage indexes.
MONEY, FINANCE, AND PRICES	
Prices	
Consumer Price Index	An index that measures changes in prices against a reference period of a basket of goods and services purchased by households. Based on the purpose of the consumer price index, different baskets of goods and services can be selected. For macroeconomic purposes, a broad-based basket is used to represent the relative price movement of household final consumption expenditure.
Food Consumer Price Index	An index that measures the change over time in the general level of prices of food and nonalcoholic beverage items that households acquire, pay for, or use for consumption. This is done by measuring the cost of purchasing a fixed basket of consumer food and beverages of constant quality and similar characteristics, with the products in the basket being selected to be representative of households' expenditure during a specified period.
Nonfood Consumer Price Index	An index that measures the change over time, in general level, of the prices of nonfood items that household acquire, pay for, or use for consumption. The nonfood index includes items such as clothing, housing and repairs, water, electricity, fuel, services, and miscellaneous goods, or all items in the basket of goods and services other than food and nonalcoholic beverages.
Food and Nonalcoholic Beverages Price Index	An index that covers food and nonalcoholic beverages purchased by the household mainly for consumption or preparation at home including services for food processing for own-consumption. The index corresponds to Classification of Individual Consumption by Purpose (COICOP) Version 1999 division 01. Excluded are food and nonalcoholic beverages that are provided as part of a food-serving service under hotels and restaurants (COICOP division 11).
Alcoholic Beverages, Tobacco, and Narcotics Price Index	An index that covers the purchase of alcoholic beverages, tobacco, and narcotics, regardless of where these are consumed, but not provided as part of a food-and-beverage-serving service under hotels and restaurants. Services for the production of alcohol for own-consumption are also included. The index corresponds to COICOP division 02. Excluded are alcoholic beverages purchased for immediate consumption in hotels, restaurants, cafes, bars, kiosks, street vendors, automatic vending machines, etc. classified under restaurants, cafes, and the like (COICOP Group 11.1.1).
Clothing and Footwear Price Index	An index that covers all clothing materials, garments, articles and accessories, footwear and related services, including cleaning, repair, and hire of clothing and footwear, and the purchase of secondhand clothing and footwear. The index corresponds to COICOP division 03.
Housing, Water, Electricity, Gas, and Other Fuels Price Index	An index that covers goods and services for the use of the house or dwelling and its maintenance and repair; the supply of water and miscellaneous services related to the dwelling; and energy used for heating or cooling. The index corresponds to COICOP division 04.

(continued on next page)

Indicator	Definition
Furnishings, Household Equipment, and Routine Household Maintenance Price Index	An index that covers a wide range of products to equip the house or dwelling and the household durables, semidurables, and nondurables as well as some household services. Includes all kinds of furniture (including lightning equipment, household textiles, glassware, tableware and household utensils), major and smaller electric household appliances, tools and equipment for house and garden, and goods for routine household maintenance. The index also includes the repair, installation, and rental services of the goods. Domestic services by paid staff in private service, supplied by enterprises or self-employed persons, window-cleaning and disinfecting services, as well as dry-cleaning and laundering of household textiles and carpets, are also included. The index corresponds to COICOP division 05.
Health Price Index	An index that covers health services provided during an overnight stay, services that do not require an overnight stay, diagnostic imaging services, medical laboratory services, patient emergency transportation, and emergency rescue services. The index also includes medicines and health products, covering all products that are separately invoiced from health services, except when administered under the direct supervision of a health care professional during an overnight stay. The index corresponds to COICOP division 06.
Transport Price Index	An index that covers four main categories of goods and services for transportation: (i) purchase of vehicles covers motor cars, motor cycles, bicycles, and animal-drawn vehicles; (ii) goods and services for the operation of the personal transport equipment cover parts and accessories for personal transport equipment, fuels and lubricants, and the repair and maintenance of personal transport equipment including expenditures for parking spaces in garages or in public places, expenditures for tolls, and expenditures to acquire a driving certificate; (iii) transport services provided by the market, structured by the mode of transport; and (iv) transport services of goods covers postal and courier services, removal and storage services, and the delivery of any kinds of goods when charged separately. The index corresponds to COICOP division 07. It excludes purchases of recreational vehicles such as camper vans, caravans, trailers, aeroplanes, and boats that are classified under the Recreation and Culture Price Index.
Communication Price Index	An index that covers three main groups of goods and services: (i) information and communication equipment, including equipment for the capture, recording, and reproduction of sound and vision; software; and information and communication services; (ii) information and communication services including telephones and other communication services, internet access services, television and radio licenses, fee and subscription services including streaming services of films and music; and (iii) repair, maintenance, and rental of information and communication equipment. The index corresponds to COICOP division 08.
Recreation and Culture Price Index	An index that covers a wide range of goods and services for recreation, sport, and culture and is structured into eight groups: (i) recreation durables such as photographic equipment, other major durables for recreation, such as camper vans, boats, yachts, aeroplanes, and the like; (ii) nonmajor durable recreational goods such as games and toys, including video game computers, celebration articles, equipment for sport, camping, and open-air recreation; (iii) garden products and plants and flowers and purchases of pets and expenditures for pets, excluding veterinary services; (iv) recreational services cover rental, maintenance, and repair of goods, veterinary and other services for pets, recreational and leisure services, such as amusement parks, games of chance and expenditures for sporting services, both expenditures for practicing sports as well as expenditures for attendance of sport events; (v) cultural goods such as musical instruments and audio-visual media; (vi) cultural services such as cinemas, theatres, concerts, museums, and other cultural sites, and photographic services; (vii) newspapers, all kinds of books, stationery and drawing materials; and (viii) package holidays that include transportation, accommodation, food provision, or tour guide. The index corresponds to COICOP division 09.
Education Price Index	An index that covers educational services only. It includes: (i) education by radio or television broadcasting as well as e-learning and correspondence courses; (ii) admission and registration fees as well as tuition fees; and (iii) other education-related fees such as camps and/or field trips, course fees, diploma fees, examination fees, graduation fees, laboratory fees, physical education fees, etc. The index corresponds to COICOP division 10. It excludes expenditures on other education-related goods and services such as school uniforms, education support services, such as health-care services, transport services (except in the case of excursions that are part of the normal school program), text books and academic journals, stationery, catering services, and accommodation services.

(continued on next page)

Indicator	Definition
Restaurants and Hotels Price Index	An index that covers services provided by restaurants, cafes, and similar facilities, either with full or limited- or self-service, or by canteens, cafeterias, or refectories at work or at school and other educational establishment's premises. It also includes catering services and accommodation services. The index corresponds to COICOP division 11.
Miscellaneous Goods and Services Price Index	An index that covers insurance and financial services. It also includes personal care, prostitution, personal effects not elsewhere classified, social protection, financial services not elsewhere classified, and other services not elsewhere classified. The index corresponds to COICOP division 12.
Wholesale Price Index	A measure that reflects changes in the prices paid for goods at various stages of distribution up to the point of retail. It can include prices of raw materials for intermediate and final consumption, prices of intermediate or unfinished goods, and prices of finished goods. The goods are usually valued at purchasers' prices.
Producer Price Index	A measure of the change in the prices of goods and services, either as they leave their place of production or as they enter the production process. A measure of the change in the prices received by domestic producers for their outputs or of the change in the prices paid by domestic producers for their intermediate inputs.
GDP Deflator	A measure of the annual rate of price change in the economy as a whole for the period shown, obtained by dividing GDP at current prices by GDP at constant prices.
Money and Finance	
Money Supply	Refers to the total amount of money in circulation in a specific country. Money supply can be measured in different ways: M1 (Narrow Money) is a measure of money supply that includes all coins and notes (M0) as well as personal money in current accounts. M2 (Intermediate Money) is the sum of M1 and personal money in deposit accounts. M3 (Broad Money) is the sum of M2 and government and other deposits. According to the Organization for Economic Co-operation and Development, M3 includes currency, deposits with an agreed maturity of up to 2 years, deposits redeemable at notice of up to 3 months and repurchase agreements, money market fund shares or units, and debt securities up to 2 years. Not all countries publish the same types of aggregates, and even when aggregates are the same name (e.g., M1, M2, M3, etc.), their asset composition often differs significantly. Cross-country differences in national definitions of lowered-ordered aggregates also arise from differences in the maturity categories of nontransferable deposits included in a particular money aggregate. For example, the definition of M2 in one country may include time deposits with maturities of 1 year or less, whereas another country's M2 definition may include time deposits with maturities of 2 years or less. When the monetary policy strategy consists of monetary aggregate targeting, the choice of the definition of the targeted aggregate is guided mainly by two considerations. The aggregate should be sufficiently sensitive to interest rate changes for the central bank to be able to control it and display a stable relationship over time to the movement of the overall price level.
Interest Rate on Savings Deposits	Rate paid by commercial and similar banks for savings deposits.
Interest Rate on Time Deposits	Rate paid by commercial and similar banks for time deposits.
Lending Interest Rate	Bank rate that usually meets the short- and medium-term financing needs of the private sector. This rate is normally differentiated according to creditworthiness of borrowers and objectives of financing.
Yield on Short-Term Treasury Bills	Rate at which short-term securities are issued or traded in the market.
Domestic Credit Provided by Banking Sector	Includes all credits to various sectors on a gross basis, except credit to the central government, which is net. The banking sector includes monetary authorities, deposit money banks, and other banking institutions for which data are available (including institutions that do not accept transferable deposits, but do incur such liabilities as time and savings deposits). Examples of other banking institutions are savings and mortgage loan institutions and building and loan associations.

(continued on next page)

Indicator	Definition
Ratio of Bank Nonperforming Loans to Total Gross Loans	Value of nonperforming loans, divided by the total value of the loan portfolio (including nonperforming loans before the deduction of loan loss provisions). The amount recorded as nonperforming should be the gross value of the loan as recorded in the balance sheet, not just the amount that is overdue.
Stock Market Price Index	Index that measures changes in the prices of stocks traded in the stock exchange. The price changes of the stocks are usually weighted by their market capitalization.
Stock Market Capitalization	The share price multiplied by the number of shares outstanding (also known as market value).
Exchange Rates	
Official Exchange Rate	The exchange rate determined by national authorities or the rate determined in the legally sanctioned exchange market. It is calculated as an annual average based on the monthly averages (local currency units relative to the US dollar).
Purchasing Power Parity Conversion Factor	Number of units of country B's currency that are needed in country B to purchase the same quantity of an individual good or service, which one unit of country A's currency can purchase in country A.
Price Level Index	Ratio of the relevant PPP to the exchange rate. It is expressed as an index on a base of 100. A price level index (PLI) greater than 100 means that, when the national average prices are converted at exchange rates, the resulting prices tend to be higher on average than prices in the base country (or countries) of the region (and vice versa). At the level of GDP, PLIs provide a measure of the differences in the general price levels of countries. PLIs are also referred to as comparative price levels.
GLOBALIZATION	
Balance of Payments	
Trade in Goods Balance	Difference between exports and imports of goods.
Trade in Services Balance	Difference between exports and imports of services.
Current Account Balance	Sum of net exports of goods, services, net income, and net current transfers.
Workers' Remittances and Compensation of Employees, Receipts	Consist of (i) Current transfers from migrant workers who are residents of the host country to recipients in their country of origin. To count as a resident, the worker must have been living in the host country for more than 1 year. (ii) Compensation of employees of migrants who have lived in the host country for less than 1 year. (iii) Migrants' transfers, defined as the net worth of migrants who are expected to remain in the host country for more than 1 year, which are transferred from one country to another at the time of migration.
Foreign Direct Investment	Refers to net inflows of investment to acquire a lasting management interest (10% or more of voting stock) in an enterprise operating in an economy other than that of the investor. It is the sum of equity capital, reinvestment of earnings, other long-term capital, and short-term capital as shown in the balance of payments.
External Trade	
Merchandise Exports or Imports	Covering all movable goods, with a few specified exceptions, the ownership of which changes between a resident and a foreigner. For merchandise exports, it represents the value of the goods and related distributive services at the customs frontier of the exporting economy, i.e., the free on board (FOB) value. Merchandise imports, on the other hand, are reported in cost, insurance, and freight (CIF) values.
Trade in Goods	Sum of merchandise exports and merchandise imports.
Direction of Trade	
Direction of Trade: Merchandise Exports and Imports	The direction of trade represents the value of merchandise exports and imports disaggregated according to a country's primary trading partners. Imports are reported on a CIF basis and exports are reported on an FOB basis, with the exception of a few countries for which imports are also available FOB. Time series data includes estimates derived from reports of partner countries for nonreporting and slow-reporting countries.

(continued on next page)

Indicator	Definition
International Reserves	
International Reserves	External assets that are readily available to, and controlled by, monetary authorities for meeting balance-of-payments financing needs, for intervention in exchange markets to affect the currency exchange rate, and for other related purposes (such as maintaining confidence in the currency and the economy, and serving as a basis for foreign borrowing).
	Consist of monetary gold, special drawing rights holdings, reserve position in the IMF, currency and deposits, securities (including debt and equity securities), financial derivatives, and other claims (loans and other financial instruments).
Ratio of International Reserves to Imports	International reserves outstanding at the end of the year as a proportion of imports of goods from the balance of payments during the year, where imports of goods are expressed in terms of a monthly average. It is a useful measure for reserve needs of countries with limited access to capital markets.
Capital Flows	
Net Official Development Assistance	Concessional flows to developing economies and multilateral institutions provided by official agencies, including state and local governments, or by their executing agencies, administered with the objective of promoting the economic development and welfare of developing economies, and containing a grant element of at least 25%. Net flow takes into account principal repayments for loans, offsetting entries for forgiven debt, and recoveries made on grants.
Net Other Official Flows	Official sector transactions with countries on the Development Assistance Committee List of Official Development Assistance Recipients, which do not meet the conditions for eligibility as official development assistance, either because they are not primarily aimed at development, or because they have a grant element of less than 25%. The Development Assistance Committee list of recipients of official development assistance is available at http://www.oecd.org/dac/financing-sustainable-development/development-finance-standards/daclist.htm. Net flow takes into account principal repayments for loans, offsetting entries for forgiven debt, and recoveries made on grants.
Net Private Flows	Sum of direct investment and portfolio investment.
	Direct investment is a category of international investment made by a resident entity in one economy (direct investor) with the objective of establishing a lasting interest in an enterprise that is resident in an economy other than that of the investor (direct investment enterprise). "Lasting interest" implies the existence of a long-term relationship between the direct investor and the enterprise and a significant degree of influence by the direct investor on the management of the direct investment enterprise. Direct investment involves both the initial transaction between the two entities and all subsequent capital transactions between them and among affiliated enterprises, both incorporated and unincorporated.
	Portfolio investment is the category of international investment that covers investment in equity and debt securities, excluding any such instruments that are classified as direct investment or reserve assets.
Aggregate Net Resource Flows	Sum of net official development assistance, net other official flows, and net private flows.
External Indebtedness	
Total External Debt	Debt owed to nonresidents repayable in currency, goods, or services. It is the sum of public, publicly guaranteed, and private nonguaranteed long-term debt, use of IMF credit, and short-term debt. Short-term debt includes all debt having an original maturity of 1 year or less and interest in arrears on long-term debt.
Public and Publicly Guaranteed Debt	Comprises long-term external obligations of public debtors, including the national government, political subdivisions (or an agency of either), and autonomous public bodies, and external obligations of private debtors that are guaranteed for repayment by a public entity.

(continued on next page)

Indicator	Definition
External Debt as a Percentage of GNI	Total external debt as a percentage of GNI. GNI is the sum of value added by all resident producers plus any product taxes (less subsidies) not included in the valuation of output, plus net receipts of primary income (compensation of employees and property income) from abroad.
External Debt as a Percentage of Exports of Goods and Services and Primary Income	Total external debt as a percentage of exports of goods, services, and income. Exports of goods, services, and primary income constitute the total value of exports of goods and services, receipts of compensation of nonresident workers, and investment income from abroad.
Total Debt Service Paid	The sum of principal repayments and interest actually paid in currency, goods, or services on long-term debt, interest paid on short-term debt, and repayments (repurchases and charges) to the IMF.
Total Debt Service Paid as a Percentage of Exports of Goods and Services and Primary Income	Total debt service as a percentage of exports of goods, services, and primary income.
Tourism	
International Tourist Arrivals	The number of tourists (overnight visitors) who travel to a country other than that in which they usually reside, and outside their usual environment, for a period not exceeding 12 months, and whose main purpose of visit is other than the activity remunerated from within the country visited. In some cases, data may also include same-day visitors when data on overnight visitors are not available separately. Data refer to the number of arrivals and not to the number of people.
International Tourism, Receipts	The receipts earned by a destination country from inbound tourism and covering all tourism receipts resulting from expenditures made by visitors from abroad. These include lodging, food and drinks, fuel, transport in the country, entertainment, shopping, etc. This concept includes receipts generated by overnight visits as well as by same-day trips. It does, however, exclude the receipts related to international transport by contracted residents of the other countries (for instance ticket receipts from foreigners travelling with a national company).
TRANSPORT AND COMMUNICATIONS	
Transport	
Road Traffic Deaths	Death caused by a road traffic crash and occurring within 24 hours (Azerbaijan, the Federated States of Micronesia, Solomon Islands, Timor-Leste, Vanuatu); 7 days (Afghanistan, the People's Republic of China, Kiribati, Tajikistan, Viet Nam); 30 days (Australia, Bhutan, Brunei Darussalam, Cambodia, Georgia, Indonesia, Kazakhstan, the Republic of Korea, Malaysia, the Maldives, the Marshall Islands, Myanmar, New Zealand, Pakistan, Singapore, Sri Lanka); 35 days in Nepal; 1 year (Japan, the Kyrgyz Republic, the Lao People's Democratic Republic, Mongolia, Tonga); unlimited time period (Armenia, Bangladesh, the Cook Islands, India, Palau, the Philippines, Thailand); no definition for other countries.
Road Network	Refers to the Asian Highway that consists of highway routes of international importance within Asia, including highway routes substantially crossing more than one subregion; highway routes within subregions that connect neighboring subregions; and highway routes located within member states that provide access to: (a) capital cities; (b) main industrial and agricultural centers; (c) major air, sea, and river ports; (d) major container terminals and depots; and (e) major tourist attractions.
Motor Vehicles	Include cars, buses, freight vehicles, and two- and three-wheeled vehicles.
Container Port Traffic	Measures the flow of containers from land to sea transport modes, and vice versa, in 20-foot equivalent units, a standard-size container. Data refer to coastal shipping as well as international journeys. Transshipment traffic is counted as two lifts at the intermediate port (once to offload and again as an outbound lift) and includes empty units.
Air Transport, Passengers Carried	Air passengers carried include both domestic and international aircraft passengers of air carriers registered in the country.
Air Transport, Carrier Departures Worldwide	Registered carrier departures worldwide are domestic takeoffs and takeoffs abroad of air carriers registered in the country.

(continued on next page)

Indicator	Definition
Air Transport, Freight	Air freight is the volume of freight, express, and diplomatic bags carried on each flight stage (operation of an aircraft from takeoff to its next landing), measured in metric tons multiplied by kilometers traveled.
Rail Lines	Rail lines are the length of railway route available for train service, irrespective of the number of parallel tracks.
Rail Network	Length of rail lines divided by the land area.
Railways, Passengers Carried	Passengers carried by railway are the number of passengers transported by rail multiplied by kilometers traveled.
Railways, Goods Transported	Goods transported by railway are the volume of goods transported by railway, measured in metric tons multiplied by kilometers traveled.
Communications	
Telephone Subscribers	Fixed-telephone subscriptions refer to the sum of active number of analogue fixed telephone lines, voice-over-IP subscriptions, fixed wireless local loop subscriptions, ISDN voice-channel equivalents, and fixed public payphones.
Mobile Phone Subscribers	The proportion of individuals who used a mobile telephone in the 3 months prior to data collection. A mobile (cellular) telephone refers to a portable telephone subscribing to a public mobile telephone service using cellular technology, which provides access to the PSTN. This includes analogue and digital cellular systems and technologies such as IMT-2000 (3G) and IMT- Advanced. Users of both postpaid subscriptions and prepaid accounts are included.
Fixed-Broadband Subscribers	Fixed-broadband subscriptions refer to fixed subscriptions to high-speed access to the public internet (a TCP/IP connection), at downstream speeds equal to, or greater than, 256 kilobits per second. This includes cable modem, DSL, fiber-to-the-home/building, other fixed (wired)- broadband subscriptions, satellite broadband and terrestrial fixed wireless broadband. This total is measured irrespective of the method of payment. It excludes subscriptions that have access to data communications (including the Internet) via mobile-cellular networks. It should include fixed WiMAX and any other fixed wireless technologies. It includes both residential subscriptions and subscriptions for organizations.
Internet Users	The frequency of internet use by individuals who used the internet from any location in the 3 months prior to data collection. The internet is a worldwide public computer network. It provides access to a number of communication services, including the web, and carries e-mail, news, entertainment, and data files, irrespective of the device used (not assumed to be only via a computer—it may also be by mobile telephone, tablet, personal digital assistant, games machine, digital television, etc.). Access can be via a fixed or mobile network.
ENERGY AND ELECTRICITY	
Energy	
GDP per Unit of Energy Use	The ratio of GDP to total energy use (measured per petajoule) with GDP converted to 2011 constant international dollars using PPP rates. An international dollar has the same purchasing power over GDP as a US dollar has in the US.
Energy Production	Primary energy production that is the capture or extraction of fuels or energy from natural energy flows, the biosphere, and natural reserves of fossil fuels within the national territory in a form suitable for use. Inert matter removed from the extracted fuels and quantities reinjected, flared, or vented are not included. The resulting products are referred to as primary products.
Energy Use	Energy production plus imports minus exports, minus international marine bunkers, minus international aviation bunkers, minus stock changes. Also referred to as energy supply.
Energy Imports, Net	Energy imports, net estimated as energy use less production, both measured in petajoules.

(continued on next page)

Indicator	Definition
Electricity	
Electricity Production	Gross production, which is the sum of the electrical energy production by all the generating units and/or installations concerned (including pumped storage), measured at the output terminals of the main generators. Also referred to as electricity generation.
Sources of Electricity	Refers to the different types of technology and/or processes for the generation or production of electricity, including: (i) electricity from combustible fuels, which refers to the production of electricity from the combustion of fuels that are capable of igniting or burning, i.e., reacting with oxygen to produce a significant rise in temperature; (ii) hydro electricity, which refers to electricity produced from devices driven by fresh, flowing, or falling water; (iii) nuclear electricity, which refers to electricity generated by nuclear plants; and (iv) other electricity, which includes solar, wind, wave, tidal, other marine electricity, geothermal, electricity generated from chemical heat, and electricity from other sources not elsewhere specified.
Electric Power Consumption Per Capita	Total electricity consumption divided by midyear population, where consumption refers to energy-industries-own-use and final consumption. Energy-industries-own-use refers to the consumption of electricity for the direct support of the production and preparation for use of fuels and energy. Final consumption refers to the consumption of electricity by manufacturing, construction and nonfuel mining, transport, and households and other consumers (nonenergy use being irrelevant for electricity).
Household Electrification Rate	Percentage of households with an electricity connection.
ENVIRONMENT	
Land	
Agricultural Land or Area	Land area that is arable, under permanent crops, and/or under permanent meadows and pastures.
Arable Land	Land under temporary agricultural crops (multiple-cropped areas are counted only once), temporary meadows for mowing or pasture, land under market, and kitchen gardens and land temporarily fallow (less than 5 years). The abandoned land resulting from shifting cultivation is not included. Data for arable land are not meant to indicate the amount of land that are potentially cultivable.
Permanent Cropland	Land cultivated with long-term crops that do not have to be replanted for several years (such as cocoa and coffee); land under trees and shrubs producing flowers, such as roses and jasmine; and nurseries (except those for forest trees, which should be classified under "forest"). Permanent meadows and pastures are excluded from land under permanent crops.
Deforestation Rate	Rate of permanent conversion of natural forest area into other uses, including shifting cultivation, permanent agriculture, ranching, settlements, and infrastructure development. Deforested areas do not include areas logged but intended for regeneration or areas degraded by fuel-wood gathering, acid precipitation, or forest fires. A negative rate indicates reforestation or increase in forest area.
Pollution	
Carbon Dioxide Emissions	Carbon dioxide emissions, largely by-products of energy production and use, account for the largest share of greenhouse gases, which are associated with global warming. Anthropogenic carbon dioxide emissions result primarily from fossil fuel combustion and cement manufacturing. In combustion, different fossil fuels release different amounts of carbon dioxide for the same level of energy used: oil releases about 50% more carbon dioxide than natural gas, while coal releases about twice as much. Cement manufacturing releases about half a metric ton of carbon dioxide for each metric ton of cement produced. Data for carbon dioxide emissions include gases from the burning of fossil fuels and cement manufacture, but excludes emissions from land use such as deforestation.
Nitrous Oxide Emissions	Nitrous oxide emissions are mainly from fossil fuel combustion, fertilizers, rainforest fires, and animal waste. Nitrous oxide is a powerful greenhouse gas, with an estimated atmospheric lifetime of 114 years, compared with 12 years for methane. The per-kilogram global warming potential of nitrous oxide is nearly 310 times that of carbon dioxide within 100 years.

(continued on next page)

Indicator	Definition
Methane Emissions	Methane emissions are those stemming from human activities such as agriculture and from industrial methane production. A kilogram of methane is 21 times as effective at trapping heat in the earth's atmosphere as a kilogram of carbon dioxide within 100 years.
Other Greenhouse Gases	By-product emissions of hydrofluorocarbons, perfluorocarbons, and sulfur hexafluoride.
Freshwater	
Internal Renewable Water Resources	Internal renewable water resources (IRWR) refer to the long-term average annual flow of rivers and recharge of aquifers generated from endogenous precipitation. Double-counting of surface water and groundwater resources is avoided by deducting the overlap from the sum of the surface water and groundwater resources. IRWR in billion cubic meters per year refers to surface water produced internally, plus groundwater produced internally deducted by the overlap between surface water and groundwater. IRWR in cubic meters per inhabitant per year is calculated as total annual IRWR divided by total population.
Annual Freshwater Withdrawals	Sum of surface water withdrawal and groundwater withdrawal. Total water withdrawal summed by sector deducted by: desalinated water produced, direct use of treated wastewater, and direct use of agricultural drainage water.
Water Productivity	Water productivity is the ratio of the net benefits from crop, forestry, fishery, livestock, and mixed agricultural systems to the amount of water used to produce those benefits. It is calculated as GDP in constant US dollar prices, divided by annual total water withdrawal.
GOVERNMENT AND GOVERNANCE	
Government Finance	
Fiscal Balance	Difference between total revenue (including grants) and total expenditure (including net lending). This provides a picture of the overall financial position of the government. When the difference is positive, then the fiscal position is in surplus; otherwise, it is in deficit.
Tax Revenue	Compulsory transfers to the central government for public purposes. Certain compulsory transfers such as fines, penalties, and most social security contributions are excluded. Refunds and corrections of erroneously collected tax revenue are treated as negative revenue.
Total Government Revenue	Includes current and capital revenues. Current revenue is the revenue accruing from taxes as well as all current nontax revenues, except transfers received from foreign governments and international institutions. Major items of nontax revenue include receipts from government enterprises, rents and royalties, fees and fines, forfeits, private donations, and repayments of loans properly defined as components of net lending. Capital revenue constitutes the proceeds from the sale of nonfinancial capital assets.
Total Government Expenditure	The sum of current and capital expenditures. Current expenditure comprises purchases of goods and services by the central government, transfers to noncentral government units and to households, subsidies to producers, and interest on public debt. Capital expenditure covers outlays for the acquisition or construction of capital assets and for the purchase of intangible assets, as well as capital transfers to domestic and foreign recipients. Loans and advances for capital purposes are also included.
Government Expenditure on Education	Consists of expenditure by government to provide education services at all levels.
Government Expenditure on Health	Consists of expenditure by government to provide medical products, appliances, and equipment; outpatient services; hospital services; public health services; among others.
Government Expenditure on Social Security and Welfare	Consists of expenditure by government to provide benefits in cash or in kind to persons who are sick, fully or partially disabled, of old age, survivors, or unemployed, among others.

(continued on next page)

Indicator	Definition
Governance	
Cost of Business Startup Procedure	Cost to register a business normalized by presenting it as a percentage of GNI per capita. It includes all official fees and fees for legal or professional services if such services are required by law or commonly used in practice. Fees for purchasing and legalizing company books are included if these transactions are required by law. Although value-added tax registration can be counted as a separate procedure, value-added tax is not part of the incorporation cost. Company law, commercial codes, and specific regulations and fee schedules are used as sources for calculating costs. In the absence of fee schedules, a government officer's estimate is taken as an official source. In the absence of a government officer's estimate, estimates by incorporation experts are used. If several incorporation experts provide different estimates, the median reported value is applied. In all cases, the cost excludes bribes.
Time Required to Start a Business	Number of calendar days needed to complete the procedures to legally operate a business. If a procedure can be accelerated at additional cost, the fastest procedure, independent of cost, is chosen.
Corruption Perceptions Index	Ranks countries and territories based on how corrupt or otherwise their public sector is perceived to be. It is a composite index—a combination of polls—drawing on corruption-related data collected by a variety of reputable institutions. The index reflects the views of observers from around the world, including experts living and working in the countries and territories evaluated. From 2000 to 2011, scores ranged from 10 (highly clean) to 0 (highly corrupt). From 2012 onwards, calculation of the score has used an updated methodology and is now presented on a 100 (very clean) to 0 (highly corrupt) scale. Due to this difference in methodology, scores from years prior to and including 2011 should not be compared with scores from 2012 onward. A country's rank indicates its position relative to the other countries or territories included in the index. It is important to keep in mind that a country's rank can change simply because new countries enter the index or others drop out.

www.ingramcontent.com/pod-product-compliance
Lightning Source LLC
Chambersburg PA
CBHW061234270326
41929CB00031B/3484